THE AMERICAN ALMANAC OF JOBS AND SALARIES

THE AMERICAN ALMANAC OF JOBS AND SALARIES

Newly Revised and Updated
1997-1998 Edition

JOHN W. WRIGHT

AVON BOOKS NEW YORK

THE AMERICAN ALMANAC OF JOBS AND SALARIES (1997–1998 Edition) is an original publication of Avon Books. This edition has never before appeared in book form.

AVON BOOKS
A division of
The Hearst Corporation
1350 Avenue of the Americas
New York, New York 10019

Published by arrangement with the author
ISBN: 0-380-78361-4

Sixth Avon Books Trade Edition, First Printing: October 1996

Printed in the U.S.A.

QM 10 9 8 7 6 5 4 3 2 1

This book is gratefully dedicated to my mother,
Elizabeth Wright,
who taught me about the dignity of work.

Acknowledgments

The two people most responsible for the digging, searching, and revising that produced this new edition are John Rosenthal and Susan Konig; their superb work speaks for itself. In addition, I have continued to use categories as well as text from my co-author on the previous edition, Edward J. Dwyer. As with previous editions, I have utilized extensively the services of specialists in several fields: Robert L. Spring (Science and Engineering), Christopher D. Stack (Computers), Jennifer Wright (Health Care), and Mary Quigley (Newspapers and Magazines). Other contributors included Greg Dimitriadis, Bill Konig, and David Camella.

It is a pleasure once again to acknowledge the contribution of Doug Dietrich, founder of Dietrich Associates in Phoenixville, Pennsylvania, whose salary surveys in several important areas will prove very beneficial to all our readers.

At Avon Books, Tom Colgan has been an ideal editor for this book, keeping us all on track with his good sense and easygoing manner.

J.W.W.

Preface to the Sixth Edition

The last edition of this book appeared at the end of the Bush recession when unemployment hovered around 8.5 percent and jobs were being eliminated at an alarming rate. Today the economy appears strong, almost robust, with unemployment below 6 percent and inflation holding at 3 percent or less for several years. So why are so many Americans telling pollsters and the media how bad things are and how nervous they feel abut their future and the future of their children?

The answers can be found in the labor history of the past 15 years. When this book first appeared in 1982, the American workforce was confronting the realities of the worst recession in over 40 years. Not only did unemployment reach Depression-like double-digit figures but inflation stubbornly remained at historically high levels. At the same time tens of thousands of employees lost their jobs (and benefits) as already huge corporations merged to produce larger ones, but with fewer workers. Not surprisingly the stockholders and managers all made so much money that many, like T. Boone Pickens, became media stars who trumpeted the glories of market capitalism far and wide. But in this atmosphere was born the cynicism that pervades the American workforce today.

No matter how often politicians or public relation flaks trumpet the glories of the "Reagan Revolution," the hard, harsh facts for working people are incontrovertible: real wages have been falling for almost a decade and could sink to the 1970 level in a year or two, and the whole idea of job security based on faithful service has been relegated to a distant, almost mythical past. According to a *New York Times* estimate, 43 million jobs were lost between 1979 and 1995. Of course tens of millions of new jobs were also created during that time—27 million more than were lost—but many if not most of these paid less, provided fewer benefits, and held little promise of lasting for many years. During this time, too, so many manufacturing and assembling jobs were sent overseas that the solid high-wage base of the working class was substantially eroded.

The word "downsizing" entered the American Heritage Dictionary in 1982 and since then millions of people have experienced its meaning firsthand. But downsizing took on a wholly new meaning when the media began to report that the stock prices of major corporations that eliminated jobs quickly surged thereby bringing rewards to their stockholders, most notably the highest members of the management team whose compensation was directly tied to the corporation's performance on the stock market.

So for those at the top, rewards have never been greater. In 1995 while everyone else was happy to have a 3 or 4 percent raise, compensation for CEOs rose 15 percent as their *median* salary and bonus reached $2 million a year. Over a 20-year period this represents such a dramatic increase that it can only be a manifestation of a new relationship of top management to the ordinary worker. In 1975 the average CEO's salary at a large corporation was about 41 times higher than the company's average salary, today that figure is 225 times and according to compensation expert, Graef Crystal, far greater than the ratio in any other industrialized country.

Some of the resentment and ill will caused by the growing gap between the top wage earners and those in the middle as well as at the bottom surfaced briefly during the Republican primary campaign of Pat Buchanan. While it is doubtful that either major party could or would present a coherent plan for reversing the trends of the last decade, the year 2000 might be the ideal presidential election for new and forward thinking. In the meantime welcome to the once lost world of unbridled capitalism. And good luck in your search for a meaningful job.

J.W.W.
New York City, June 1996

> Labor is prior to, and independent of, capital. Capital is only the fruit of labor, and could never have existed if labor had not first existed. Labor is the superior of capital, and deserves much the higher consideration.
>
> Abraham Lincoln, First Annual
> Message to Congress, 1861

Table of Contents

Introduction

This book is about work and its rewards in contemporary America. As the success of the previous editions has demonstrated, such a book is bound to be of interest to students of American life, and to students just beginning life in the world of work. It is also a book for career changers seeking guidelines and for women seeking equal pay for equal work.

With such audiences in mind, the *Almanac* has deliberately been given a white-collar service sector orientation. The largest entries are all aimed at the career-minded. They will find detailed information on accountants, doctors, engineers, lawyers, scientists, and health-care workers as well as the most up-to-date information on jobs in computer technology. Whether readers are interested in a specialized field such as human resources, public relations, or purchasing, or in a particular kind of business such as advertising, banking, or insurance, they will find complete job descriptions and an evaluation of future job opportunites as well as a full range of salaries for most levels and positions. Special entries on the starting salaries of new college graduates and newly minted M.B.A.s will prove invaluable to younger members of the workforce. This emphasis on white-collar careers is, however, not based simply on some biased point of view, nor is it a cynical attempt to boost sales. In fact, it reflects the very real and extraordinary changes in the character and shpe of the American workforce that have occurred over the last four decades.

Between 1950 and 1990, for example, while the population was growing by just over 60 percent, the labor force doubled in size. The single most dramatic change was the growth in the number of women workers, from 18 million to 56 million. In 1950, about 30 percent of the total workforce were women, but by 1991, women made up nearly half of all working people. Other important changes, such as the growth in the white-collar workforce from less than 40 percent to more than half, and the rise in education levels of all workers—close to 80 percent have finished high school, compared to less than half in the 1950s—are indications of a society significantly rearranging its daily worklife.

The kind of work being done by Americans has changed just as drastically. For example, the number of workers employed in the production of goods (including manufacturing, mining, and construction, but not agriculture), grew from 20 million to 23 million between 1960 and 1991. But as a percentage of the workforce, these workers declined from 37 percent to 17 percent. Moreover, the number of production workers in relation to nonproduction workers declined from five-to-one in 1950 to less than two-to-one today, while the precentage of blue collar workers declined from 40 percent of the workforce in 1950 to under 25 percent in 1991. These trends have continued through the decade.

In many industries, the number of production workers has been declining steadily for many reasons, including, but not limited to automation, increased competition from abroad, and the aging of particular segments of American industries. Between 1960 and 1985, the steel and auto industries each lost half a million jobs; textiles lost 600,000, and manufacturing lost over 1.1 million. Although manufacturing rallied in the late 1980s, jobs in this industry resumed their decline in the 1990s, and 1991 levels were lower than they were at any point in the 1980s. Meanwhile, agriculture, which accounted for 11 percent of the workforce in 1950, employed less than 2 percent in 1991.

While America's production industries were waning, the so-called service industries were booming. Over the past four decades the service sector has grown from 27 million employees to over 85 million, and from 55 percent of the workforce to over 78 percent. Today more than 75 percent of working Americans are employed in areas such as accounting, banking, engineering, consumer services, education, health care, legal work, transportation, wholesale and retail trade. Moreover, there are millions employed in the public sector. In 1950, just over 6 million civilian employees—about 10 percent of all workers— were employed by federal, state, and local governments; by 1992 almost 19 million civilians—17 percent of the labor force—were on public payrolls.

This last point should help to explain why so much space in the *Almanac* is given to the section "On the Public Payroll." This is the first book to present an in-depth look at the jobs and salary levels of the enormous federal bureaucracy, from typists and secretaries to members of the senior Executive Service. Of course, the salaries and perks of the president, his cabinet, and his advisors are all included, along with those of federal judges and members of Congress. But the large entry on the highest paying jobs in almost every federal agency is what reveals more about levels of pay in Washington than a mere cataloguing of the top officials.

On the state and local government level, the *Almanac* contains information on high-ranking officials in every state and many major cities. Public employees ranging from city managers and police chiefs to bus drivers, sanitation workers and social workers are all included. Wherever possible, examples of salary scales in the states, selected cities, and in institutions are provided. Under "Univeristy and College Professors," for example, the salaries of full professors, associate professors, assistant professors, and instructors are listed for almost 100 public and private institutions nationwide.

Despite the *Almanac's* obvious emphases, it is designed to provide data for a wide variety of occupations. So, in addition to professional careers, high-paying white-collar occupations, and bureaucratic sine-cures, the Almanac also gives all kinds of information on ordinary jobs in the workaday world. Office workers, construction workers, and maintenance workers are all included.

Finally, a word about the section called "In the Public Eye and Behind the Scenes." Although some of the entries contain valuable career information for people interested in modeling or working in film or television, the major attraction here is bound to be the high-salaried public personalities so familiar to millions of Americans. Included, among other, are movies stars, musicians, singers, and professional athletes. Readers will discover that in the world of television, movies, and sports many stars and personalities surpass the magical sum of $10 million a year. (They will also discover elsewhere in the book that many corporate executives, Wall Street financiers, and Hollywood producers among other executives have also reached that exalted plateau.)

The point of this section goes beyond a mere inventory of hightly compensated celebrities. When people can be paid so much money for their acting skills or their athletic ability, or for simply reading the news on television, the effects can be as interesting as they are various. First, this practice drives up the salaries of the hightest-paid people in other industries. Why should the heads of major corporations , large law firms, or accounting firms make less than Madonna, Barry Bonds, Oprah Winfrey, or David Letterman? Second, such high payments help to point out just how inequitable the distribution of income is: Since only 5 percent of all workers earn over $75,000 while total family income is about $35,000 for half of America's families, these celebrities have attained extraordinary wealth.

Most Americans have only hazy notions about how earnings are distributed in this country. Only 12.3 percent of the 66 million familes earned more thant $75,000 in 1990, while over 70 percent made less than $50,000 (the median was $35,353). If this trend continues—and there's no indication it can be stopped—the number of families earning $75,000 or more will increase but they will be an increasingly smaller percentage. People's responses to these figures usually vary on the basis of their own economic status. Those individuals making about $75,000 are almost always incredulous when told that they are among the top 5 percent of all wage earners; and people earning $40,000 find it hard to believe they make more than most families.

One could argue that by its very nature this *Almanac* also raises serious questions about the kinds of work America values most. Just about everyone who did research on this book was struck at some time by the glaring inconsistencies and obvious inequities that exist in our pay structure. Here are a few random examples:

- Why do most "creative" directors in advertising agencies earn more thant most doctors?
- Why do successful traders and brokers on Wall Street earn more than the most highly regarded scientists?
- Why do senior engineers always earn less than their companies' controllers?
- Why do architects almost always earn significantly less thant accountants?
- Why do directors of nursing make so much less then hospital administrators?
- Why do most laborers earn less thant most truck drivers?
- Why do most college football coaches earn more thant most full professors?
- Why do librarians and flight attendants earn about the same amount?

While the notion of comparing job worth is not new, only in recent years has it become a way of fighting for higher pay. Women, particularly, have used this argument in their struggle to establish economic equality. The surge of women into the workforce over the last twenty years is one of the most important developments in American labor history. The insistence of many women that pay levels are influenced more by gender than by the marketplace is bringing about a radical shift in women's wage rates, especially in the public employment sector.

By providing a wide range of information—as well as opinion—we hope we won't be accused of playing the careerist's game, in which good job possibilities and large compensation potential are seen as the only vital factors in a career path. It is not unusual today to hear young people entering college say they intend to study computer science even though their math grades are below average; or others express an interest in signing on for a six-year program leading to a law degree when they have no idea about the everyday demands of the profession or the protential future difficulties caused by the sudden surege in the number of lawyers all around the country. Such premature or unrealistice career choices often make for very disgruntled thirty-year-olds.

We know we can't stop the trend toward that kind of thinking but believe it's important to take a stand against it. Our goal remains the presentation of an overview of the American workforce that will help people understand its present character and its future shape. We can only hope that readers will use this information wisely and that they will fine it valuable in planning their future forays into the world of work.

THE AMERICAN WORKFORCE TODAY

In 1994 about 127 million people were employed in the U.S. More than 10 percent of the workforce (12.9 million) occupied executive, managerial, and administrative positions. The largest single grouping in this category was the 4 million elementary and secondary school teachers. About 3.2 million worked in health-related occupations, and just over 3 million were employed in engineering and science-related jobs. In a society that is growing increasingly litigious, the number of lawyers and judges topped 800,000 in 1994. About 25 million Americans were engaged in trade, mainly retail selling, while another 20 million worked in service-providing industries. The standard manufacturing and construction sectors employed just over 28 million people, or 22 percent of the total workforce.

THE GROWTH INDUSTRIES OF THE 1990s

	Number Employed (in thousands)			
Industry	**1989**	**1995**	**Change in Number 1989–95**	**Percentage Change 1989–95**
Agriculture	2,934	3,440	506	17.2%
Mining	679	627	−52	−7.7
Construction	7,232	7,666	434	6.0
Manufacturing	21,569	20,493	−1,076	−5.0
Transportation, Communications, and other utilities	8,049	8,709	660	8.2
Wholesale trade	4,492	4,986	494	11.0
Retail trade	19,138	21,086	1,948	10.2
Finance, Insurance, and Real Estate	7,968	7,983	15	0.2
Services	38,329	43,953	5,624	14.7
Public Administration	5,456	5,957	501	9.2
TOTAL EMPLOYED	115,846	124,900	9,054	7.8

SOURCE: Bureau of Labor Statistics, *Employment and Earnings,* Jan. 1996 monthly.

During the 1980s, three sectors of the American economy experienced an overall decline in the number of jobs, even though the total number of jobs in the economy grew by 16.7 percent overall. Mining (−30.6 percent), agriculture (−12.8 percent), and manufacturing (−1.7 percent) were the losers. Public administration jobs grew by only 2.1 percent during the same time period. Finance and services were the biggest growth sectors with each gaining 33 percent in the number of jobs. Other sectors experiencing above-average growth were transportation, communication and utilities (+23.4 percent), and retail trade (+17.6 percent). Construction (+16.4 percent) and wholesale trade (+14.6 percent) grew at a slightly less than average pace. In times of recession, of course, construction jobs decline significantly except in those rapidly developing areas of the country, most notably Florida. In 1992 construction employed 4 percent of all workers down from 5 percent in 1990.

The recession of the early 1990s helped to heighten public awareness about these shifts in the character of work available to Americans. The continuous decline of the manufacturing sector, while not unexpected, looked even more threatening under the media microscope. In 1992 The Conference Board reported a significant decline in the number of manufacturing jobs nationwide between 1988 and 1991, a trend that has continued unabated with over a million jobs lost between 1989–95.

One significant result of this changing character of the workforce is the continuous decline of labor unions over the last 20 years. And clearly they will continue to decline. Today the American labor movement stands at its lowest point in decades. In 1955, 35 percent of the workforce belonged to unions, but, in 1995, only 15 percent held membership cards. Moreover, union membership declined by over 5 million members. This decrease has been fed not only by the declining fortunes of traditional manufacturing industries and the unions' failures to realize widespread penetration into the white-collar ranks, but also by a concerted effort on management's part to weaken the role of unions. Outside of some traditional bastions of union solidarity like the Teamsters, labor unions appear to be a weak shell of their former power. Since the 1980s, labor unions have by and large been willing to grant concessions on wages in return for staving off cuts in benefits and gaining improved job security protections.

In the early 1990s, the labor movement seized some opportunities to halt its decline. In the health-care area, for instance, where pay and working conditions have declined relatively in the past decade, opportunities to organize workers have been successfully pursued. Also, the unions have shown a new sophistication in the use of public relations. In their strike against Eastern Airlines, the unions have successfully raised the specter of a pivotal struggle betwen good, honest workers and demon management. But in the long term, the shift to a white-collar-dominated service economy has probably fated labor unions to a relatively small role in the working world of the 1990s.

U.S. MEMBERSHIP IN AFL-CIO AFFILIATED UNIONS, BY SELECTED UNION, 1979–93

Labor organization	(Numbers in thousands) 1979	1985	1993
Total[1]	13,621	13,109	13,229
Actors and Artistes	75	100	93
Automobile, Aerospace and Agriculture (UAW)	NA	974	771
Bakery, Confectionery and Tobacco	131	115	99
Boiler Makers, Iron Shipbuilders[2,3]	129	110	58
Bricklayers	106	95	84
Carpenters[2]	626	609	408
Clothing and Textile Workers (ACTWU)[2]	308	228	143
Communications Workers (CWA)	485	524	472
Electrical Workers (IBEW)	825	791	710
Electronic, Electrical, and Salaried[2,4]	243	198	143
Operating Engineers	313	330	305
Firefighters	150	142	151
Food and Commercial Workers (UFCW)[2]	1,123	989	997
Garment Workers (ILGWU)	314	210	133
Glass, Molders, Pottery, and Plastics[2]	50	72	73
Government, American Federation (AFGE)	236	199	149
Graphic Communications[2]	171	141	95
Hotel Employees and Restaurant Employees	373	327	258
Ironworkers	146	140	91
Laborers	475	383	408
Letter Carriers (NALC)	151	186	210
Longshoremans Association	63	65	58
Machinists and Aerospace (IAM)[2]	688	520	474
Marine Engineers Beneficial Assn.	23	22	52
Mine Workers	NA	NA	75
Office and Professional Employees	83	90	89
Oil, Chemical, Atomic Workers (OCAW)	146	108	86
Painters	160	133	106
Paperworkers International	262	232	188
Plumbing and Pipefitting	228	226	220
Postal Workers	245	232	249
Retail, Wholesale, Department Store	122	106	80
Rubber, Cork, Linoleum, Plastic	158	106	81
Seafarers	84	80	80
Service Employees (SEIU)[2,5]	537	688	919
Sheet Metal Workers	120	108	108
Stage Employees, Moving Picture Machine Operators	50	50	51
State, County, Municipal (AFSCME)[5]	899	997	1,167
Steelworkers	964	572	421

U.S. MEMBERSHIP IN AFL-CIO AFFILIATED UNIONS, BY SELECTED UNION, 1979–93

	(Numbers in thousands)		
Labor organization	**1979**	**1985**	**1993**
Teachers (AFT)	423	470	574
Teamsters[6]	NA	NA	1,316
Transit Union	94	94	94
Transport Workers	85	85	78
Transportation Union, United	121	52	60

NOTE: NA = Not applicable.
Figures represent the labor organizations as constituted in 1989 and reflect past merger activity. Membership figures based on average per capita paid membership to the AFL-CIO for the 2-year period ending in June of the year shown and reflect only actively-employed members. Labor unions shown had a membership of 70,000 or more in 1989.
[1]Includes other AFL-CIO affiliated unions, not shown separately.
[2]Figures reflect mergers with one or more unions since 1979.
[3]Includes Blacksmiths, Forgers and Helpers.
[4]Includes Machine and Furniture Workers.
[5]Excludes Hospital and Health Care Employees which merged into both unions on June 1, 1989 (membership of 23,000 in 1985, and 58,000 in 1989).
[6]Includes Chauffeurs, Warehousemen and Helpers.
SOURCE: American Federation of Labor and Congress of Industrial Organizations, *Report of the AFL-CIO Executive Council* (annual).

This continuing decline in high-paying goods-producing jobs is the most worrisome aspect for the future of the workforce. Automation and cheap foreign labor are the two most obvious causes and neither factor will disappear. If anything such government action and the North American Free Trade Agreement will both hasten the decline in the number of available jobs and continue to lower the wage rates of American workers.

JOB GROWTH IN THE NEAR FUTURE

Barring any sudden and dramatic action by the federal government to stimulate a return to manufacturing, the long-term occupational trends will continue into the next century. White-collar service-oriented work, especially in health care and business services, will be the major growth area. The competition for jobs will continue to be more intense than in previous years in part because of the sluggish economy, but also because of the enormous numbers in the workforce. This demographic glitch has caused more havoc in the job market than is generally recognized. Even engineers and computer scientists have felt the pinch in recent years, although it must be noted that these occupations and others in the science and technology areas still have unemployment rates of less than 3 percent. Of course demographics can also have a positive influence. The so-called baby-boomlet of the late 1980s, for example, will create tens of thousands of new teaching positions over the next decade, aided in turn by increasing retirements.

The government's prevailing social policies have also influenced the job market. Without government funding, for example, there could never have been the dramatic increase in health care services that has fueled the enormous job-growth in this sector (of the 12 fastest growing jobs in the U.S., eight are health care related). The same applies to the criminal justice system where governments at all levels decided to build more prisons and to contain crime through arrests rather than prevention. The result has been an enormous growth in the number of judges, lawyers, police, and corrections officers and although the crime trends continue upward, the rate of growth has declined dramatically.

The accompanying tables provide a good overview of the short-term projections the Department of Labor is making for occupations that will grow and those on the decline. More details can be found in specific entries.

OCCUPATIONS WITH THE LARGEST NUMBER OF NEW JOBS, 1994–2005
(Numbers in thousands)

	Employment		Change in Employment	
Occupation	**1994**	**2005**	**Number**	**Percent**
Cashiers	3,005	3,567	562	19%
Janitors and cleaners, including maids and housekeeping cleaners	3,043	3,602	559	18
Salespersons, retail	3,842	4,374	532	14
Waiters and waitresses	1,847	2,326	479	26
Registered nurses	1,906	2,379	473	25
General managers and top executives	3,046	3,512	466	15
Systems analysts	483	928	445	92
Home health aides	420	848	428	102
Guards	867	1,282	415	48
Nursing aides, orderlies, and attendants	1,265	1,652	387	31
Teachers, secondary school	1,340	1,726	386	29
Marketing and sales worker supervisors	2,293	2,673	380	17
Teacher aides and educational assistants	932	1,296	364	39
Receptionists and information clerks	1,019	1,337	318	31
Truckdrivers light and heavy	2,565	2,837	271	11
Secretaries, except legal and medical	2,842	3,109	267	9
Clerical supervisors and managers	1,340	1,600	261	19

OCCUPATIONS WITH THE LARGEST NUMBER OF NEW JOBS, 1994–2005
(Numbers in thousands)

Occupation	Employment		Change in Employment	
	1994	2005	Number	Percent
Child care workers	757	1,005	248	33%
Maintenance repairers, general utility	1,273	1,505	231	18
Teachers, elementary	1,419	1,639	220	16
Personal and home care aides	179	391	212	119
Teachers, special education	388	593	206	53
Licensed practical nurses	702	899	197	28
Food service and lodging managers	579	771	192	33
Food preparation workers	1,190	1,378	187	16
Social workers	557	744	187	34
Lawyers	656	839	183	28
Financial managers	768	950	182	24
Computer engineers	195	372	177	90
Hand packers and packagers	942	1,102	160	17

SOURCE: Bureau of Labor Statistics, *Monthly Labor Review,* November 1995

FASTEST GROWING OCCUPATIONS, 1994–2005
(Numbers in thousands)

Occupation	Employment		Change in Employment	
	1994	2005	Number	Percent
Personal and home care aides	179	391	212	119%
Home health aides	420	848	428	102
Systems analysts	483	928	445	92
Computer engineers	195	372	177	90
Physical and corrective therapy assistants and aides	78	142	64	83
Electronic pagination systems workers	18	33	15	83
Occupational therapy assistants and aides	16	29	13	82
Physical therapists	102	183	81	80
Residential counselors	165	290	126	76
Human services workers	168	293	125	75
Occupational therapists	54	93	39	72
Manicurists	38	64	26	69
Medical assistants	206	327	121	59

FASTEST GROWING OCCUPATIONS, 1994–2005
(Numbers in thousands)

Occupation	Employment 1994	Employment 2005	Change in Employment Number	Change in Employment Percent
Paralegals	110	175	64	58%
Medical records technicians	81	126	45	56
Teachers, special education	338	593	206	53
Amusement and recreation attendants	267	406	139	52
Corrections officers	310	468	158	51
Operations research analysts	44	67	22	50
Guards	867	1,282	415	48
Speech-language pathologists and audiologists	85	125	39	46
Detectives, except public	55	79	24	44
Surgical technologists	46	65	19	43
Dental hygienists	127	180	53	42
Dental assistants	190	269	79	42
Adjustment clerks	373	521	148	40
Teacher aides and educational assistants	932	1,296	364	39
Data processing and equipment repairers	75	104	29	38
Nursery and greenhouse managers	19	26	7	37
Securities and financial sales workers	246	335	90	37

SOURCE: Bureau of Labor Statistics, *Monthly Labor Review*, November 1995.

OCCUPATIONS WITH THE LARGEST JOB DECLINES, 1994–2005
(Numbers in thousands)

Occupation	Employment 1994	Employment 2005	Change in Employment Number	Change in Employment Percent
Farmers	1,276	1,003	−273	−21%
Typists and word processors	646	434	−212	−33
Bookkeeping, accounting, and auditing clerks	2,181	2,003	−178	−8
Bank tellers	559	407	−152	−27
Sewing machine operators, garment	531	391	−140	−26
Cleaners and servants, private household	496	387	−108	−22

OCCUPATIONS WITH THE LARGEST JOB DECLINES, 1994–2005
(Numbers in thousands)

Occupation	Employment		Change in Employment	
	1994	2005	Number	Percent
Computer operators, except peripheral equipment	259	162	−98	−38%
Billing, posting, and calculating machine operators	96	32	−64	−67
Duplicating, mail, and other office machine operators	222	166	−56	−25
Textile draw-out and winding machine operators and tenders	190	143	−47	−25
File clerks	278	236	−42	−15
Freight, stock, and material movers, hand	765	728	−36	−5
Farm workers	906	870	−36	−4
Machine tool cutting operators and tenders, metal and plastic	119	85	−34	−29
Central office operators	48	14	−34	−70
Central office and PBX installers and repairers	84	51	−33	−39
Electrical and electronic assemblers	212	182	−30	−14
Station installers and repairers, telephone	37	11	−26	−70
Personnel clerks, except payroll and timekeeping	123	98	−26	−21
Data entry keyers, except composing	395	370	−25	−6
Bartenders	373	347	−25	−7
Inspectors, testers, and graders, precision	654	629	−25	−4
Directory assistance operators	33	10	−24	−70
Lathe and turning machine tool setters and set-up operators, metal and plastic	71	50	−22	−31
Custom tailors and sewers	84	63	−21	−25
Machine feeders and offbearers	262	242	−20	−8
Machinists	369	349	−20	−5
Service station attendants	167	148	−20	−12
Machine forming operators and tenders, metal and plastic	171	151	−19	−11
Communication, transportation, and utilities operations managers	154	135	−19	−12

SOURCE: Bureau of Labor Statistics, *Monthly Labor Review,* November 1995.

JOB GROWTH BY REGION

In a country as vast and economically diverse as the United States, regional employment levels can be as different as winters in Maine and Arizona, and as volatile as the value of pork bellies. In 1995, for example, the unemployment rates in many parts of New England topped 10 percent while the rates in almost all of the western states and many upper midwestern states were below 6 percent.

Employment in the United States is expected to grow by more than 58 million new jobs by the year 2025, according to the National Planning Association, a Washington economic research organization. Almost half of that growth is projected for 30 metropolitan statistical areas, primarily in the southern and western U.S. Each of the top 30 metropolitan areas are projected to grow by a minimum of 470,000 jobs. Ten areas will have growth of a million or more; 12 more will have growth of 600,000 or more. Seven of the top 30 areas are in California, five are in Florida, and four in Texas.

Not surprisingly the areas projected to have the slowest job growth—or even a loss of jobs—are all in the Northeast and the Midwest. New York City will be hit the hardest according to the National Planning Association as businesses search for lower taxes and wages. Whether the talent will follow is all speculation, of course.

Charting regional and metropolitan area job growth is chancy at best and all the projections included in the accompanying tables are based on population growth and the age of the area's workforce. But this gives an incomplete picture of the job market. For although many large cities have high unemployment rates and little if any new job growth, they often have many more jobs available because of the large number of retirements, firings, job changes, deaths, and other so-called separations.

10 METROPOLITAN AREAS WITH FASTEST JOB GROWTH, 1995–2025

Rank	Metropolitan Statistical Area	Number of Jobs (in thousands) 1995	2025	Change in Employment 1995–2025
1.	Punta Gorda, FL	44	106	140.9%
2.	Orlando, FL	880	1,880	113.6
3.	Bryan-College Station, TX	78	164	110.3
4.	Naples, FL	106	220	107.5
5.	Fort Pierce-Port St. Lucie, FL	121	249	105.8
6.	Austin-San Marcos, TX	667	1,360	103.9

10 METROPOLITAN AREAS WITH FASTEST JOB GROWTH, 1995–2025

Rank	Metropolitan Statistical Area	Number of Jobs (in thousands) 1995	2025	Change in Employment 1995–2025
7.	Olympia, WA	98	199	103.1%
8.	Las Vegas, NV	631	1,278	102.5
9.	Laredo, TX	68	136	100.0
10.	McAllen-Edinburg Mission, TX	165	329	99.4

SOURCE: NPA Data Services, Inc., Washington, D.C., 1996.

30 METROPOLITAN AREAS WITH HIGHEST JOB-GROWTH, 1995–2025
(Numbers in thousands)

Rank	Metropolitan Statistical Area	Number of Jobs 1995	2025	Change in Employment 1995–2025
1.	Atlanta, GA	2,252	4,057	1,805
2.	Houston, TX	2,171	3,785	1,614
3.	Phoenix, AZ	1,470	2,913	1,443
4.	Washington, D.C.-MD-VA	3,035	4,443	1,407
5.	Dallas, TX	1,994	3,372	1,378
6.	Los Angeles-Long Beach, CA	4,823	6,162	1,339
7.	Seattle, WA	1,503	2,704	1,201
8.	San Diego, CA	1,393	2,583	1,190
9.	Orange County, CA	1,502	2,622	1,120
10.	Tampa-St. Petersburg-Clearwater, FL	1,190	2,236	1,047
11.	Orlando, FL	880	1,880	1,000
12.	Denver, CO	1,222	2,167	945
13.	Minneapolis-St. Paul, MN	1,833	2,713	880
14.	Chicago, IL	4,546	5,330	784
15.	Riverside-San Bernardino, CA	1,074	1,808	734
16.	Sacramento, CA	769	1,495	726
17.	Austin-San Marcos, TX	667	1,360	693
18.	Boston-Worcester-Lawrence-Lowell-Brockton, MA-NH	3,419	4,066	646
19.	Las Vegas, NV-AZ	631	1,278	646
20.	Salt Lake City-Ogden, UT	756	1,397	641

30 METROPOLITAN AREAS WITH HIGHEST JOB-GROWTH, 1995–2025
(Numbers in thousands)

Rank	Metropolitan Statistical Area	Number of Jobs 1995	Number of Jobs 2025	Change in Employment 1995–2025
21.	Portland-Vancouver, OR-WA	1,036	1,637	602
22.	Fort Worth-Arlington, TX	818	1,420	602
23.	Fort Lauderdale, FL	739	1,321	582
24.	Miami, FL	1,150	1,727	577
25.	San Jose, CA	1,008	1,537	528
26.	San Antonio, TX	808	1,335	527
27.	Raleigh-Durham-Chapel Hill, NC	671	1,175	504
28.	Oakland, CA	1,169	1,666	497
29.	Baltimore, MD	1,373	1,846	473
30.	West Palm Beach-Boca Raton, FL	523	995	472

SOURCE: NPA Data Services, Inc., Washington, D.C., 1996.

SALARIES AND WAGES

According to the Conference Board, average annual salary increases in all industries, which had ranged as high as 10.6 percent in 1981, then leveled off to 5 percent in 1987, but dropped to 4% in 1996. Since 1981, the average annual salary increase has exceeded the increase in the Consumer Price Index every year except one, 1990, when the CPI increase was 5.4 percent, compared to a 5 percent increase in salaries.

In the 1950s, average hourly earnings of nonfarm workers increased by 2.5 percent (with inflation factored in), then increased again by 1.7 percent in the 1960s. In the 1970s, there was a small increase of 0.2 percent, but in the 1980s, they declined 0.3 percent. Average weekly earnings in manufacturing have in fact declined by 14 percent since 1973; median household income for manufacturing workers has dropped about 6 percent.

With the annual growth rate of the labor supply expected to be 1.5 percent a year through the 1990s, and the economy expanding at 3 percent there is bound to be more intense competition for experienced workers. While this will put upward pressure on wages, for the best jobs it will also compel American businesses to hire more minorities, more women, and more older workers. Unfortunately it will also keep their wages low.

In 1995 the Labor Department reported that real wages in the U.S. had declined in 1994 by an astonishing 2.3 percent. This helped to highlight the trend in declining wages since 1973. Only the wages of college graduates have risen (5 percent) during these years.

Education will continue to play a major role in what workers earn. For young people who do not attend college, there is a high likelihood that they will encounter unemployment or a worklife of jobs with poverty-level income and little chance of advancement. Low-paying service jobs are one of the fastest growing sectors of the labor force and should be responsible for a large percentage of the job growth for non-college graduates. Unemployment rates for high school graduates are double that of college graduates, and median monthly incomes are half of what a college graduate earns. (See in Part IX "The New College Graduate.")

For the college-educated and technically trained, the prospects are obviously brighter, though even this group won't find it easy to get a good-paying job. The glut of college graduates that began in the 1970s is expected to continue through the 1990s and will worsen as the 21st century approaches: The number of graduates will increase while the number of jobs requiring a college degree will decrease. The labor force simply is not able to find college level jobs for the increasing percentage of the population—25 percent today, up from 10 percent in 1960—with a college education. The effect of a global workforce of scientists, engineers, and computer specialists will be to worsen the problem for Americans.

A Note About the Salary Data

About 125 million people hold jobs in the United States today, while another 6 million are listed as unemployed. This book was the first serious attempt to chart the salary ranges and wage rates for a significant portion of the workforce and it has remained the most complete report on the subject for over a decade. The figures we provide are almost all taken from published sources and, with only one or two exceptions, they are all from 1994 or 1995. In all cases the source and date are provided, usually in the form of a footnote.

The size and scope of that task required us to eliminate several factors that we know to be important when measuring compensation levels. Unfortunately, the reader will not find any seriuos discussion of fringe benefits, pension plans, or cost of living adjustments (COLA). In large companies the cost of employee benefits has increased from 24 percent of pay in 1957 to just over 50 percent by 1992.

The kind of salary data available varied widely from occupation to occupation. As a rule we found that the salaries of people earning under $75,000 a year are fairly easy to discover through the Bureau of Labor Statistics, and even from want ads and employment agencies. Salaries over $75,000, however, are usually regarded as a sacred matter of privacy, even by the people paid from public payrolls. Virtually all of the occupations at this salary level are white-collar jobs requiring a college education. Contrary to popular opinion the salary rates for these jobs are firmly established in the same way that the wages of blue-collar workers or office workers are. These rates are usually published in the form of salary surveys conducted by professional organizations or publications directly involved in the field. Whenever posible we have used data from both of these groups as well as from a few private compensation firms.

Because the sources are disparate the figures provided are sometimes listed as "average" (the total sum of all the salaries in the survey divided by the number of respondents); sometimes as "median" (the salary figure that falls exactly in the middle of the survey: one-half of the respondents earn less than that, one-half earn more); occasionally a survey provided salaries for the first, second, third, or fourth "quartiles" (generally speaking these figures are the average salaries for all respondents within the bottom 25 percent, the first quartile, to the top 25 percent, or fourth quartile).

Finally, the designation NA has two functions. Usually it means "not available"; although we do not specify the reason, in most cases it indicates a weakness in the survey data; for those on public payrolls, however, NA in a chart signifies "not applicable."

MEDIAN WEEKLY SALARIES FOR SELECTED JOBS, 1991–1995

Job	Median Salary 1991	Median Salary 1995	Percent Change
Architects	$ 623	$ 724	16.2%
Automobile mechanics	385	466	21.0
Bank tellers	281	300	6.8
Bartenders	249	293	17.1
Bookkeeping/accounting/auditing clerks	645	386	−40.2
Carpenters	425	466	9.6
Cashiers	218	237	8.7
Chemists	687	680	− 1.0
Child care workers	132	180	36.4
Clergy	459	498	8.5
Clinical laboratory technologists/ technicians	461	524	13.7
Computer programmers	662	743	12.2
Economists	732	752	2.7
Editors/reporters	593	617	4.0
Frm workers	239	258	7.9
Financial managers	743	758	2.0
Hairdressers/cosmetologists	263	286	8.7
Insurance salespeople	513	602	17.3
Janitors/cleaners	292	293	0.3
Lawyers	1,008	1,125	11.6
Librarians	521	596	14.4
Machinists	476	368	−22.7
Mail carriers	580	648	11.7
Marketing/advertising/public relations managers	784	900	14.8
Mechanical engineers	836	925	10.6
Nurses	634	695	9.6
Office machine repairers	468	561	19.9
Operations and systems researchers/ analysts	755	758	0.4

MEDIAN WEEKLY SALARIES FOR SELECTED JOBS, 1991–1995

Job	Median Salary 1991	Median Salary 1995	Percent Change
Personnel/labor relations managers	$752	$ 696	− 7.4%
Physicians	984	1,140	15.9
Police officers/detectives	595	738	24.0
Professors/college teachers	756	843	11.5
Real estate salespeople	517	589	13.9
Salespeople, apparel	246	264	7.3
Secretaries	359	396	10.3
Sewing machine operators	326	251	−23.0
Social workers	466	515	10.5
Taxicab drivers/chauffeurs	339	352	3.8
Teachers, elementary school	537	640	19.1
Travel agents	408	413	1.2
Truck drivers (heavy trucks)	429	481	12.1
Waiters/waitresses	218	271	24.3

SOURCE: Bureau of Labor Statistics.

25 METROPOLITAN AREAS WITH HIGHEST AVERAGE ANNUAL PAY, 1994

Rank	Metropolitan Area	Average Annual Pay
1.	New York	$39,933
2.	San Jose (CA)	39,127
3.	Middlesex-Somerset-Hunterdon (NJ)	36,690
4.	San Francisco	36,510
5.	Newark	35,910
6.	New Haven-Bridgeport-Stamford-Danbury-Waterbury	35,535
7.	Trenton	35,345
8.	Bergen-Passaic (NJ)	34,675
9.	Anchorage	34,098
10.	Washington, D.C.	33,949
11.	Kokomo (IN)	33,231
12.	Flint (MI)	33,219
13.	Detroit	33,203
14.	Hartford	33,172
15.	Jersey City	33,012
16.	Oakland	32,157

25 METROPOLITAN AREAS WITH HIGHEST AVERAGE ANNUAL PAY, 1994

Rank	Metropolitan Area	Average Annual Pay
17.	Los Angeles-Long Beach	$31,831
18.	Boston-Worcester-Lawrence-Lowell-Brockton	31,403
19.	Chicago	31,339
20.	Nassau-Suffolk (NY)	30,765
21.	Philadelphia	30,519
22.	Huntsville (AL)	30,389
23.	Houston	30,349
24.	Orange County (CA)	30,315
25.	Seattle-Bellevue-Everett	30,181

SOURCE: Bureau of Labor Statistics, *Average Annual Pay Levels in Metropolitan Areas, 1994,* October 27, 1995.

25 METROPOLITAN AREAS WITH LOWEST AVERAGE ANNUAL PAY, 1994

Rank	Metropolitan Area	Average Annual Pay
1.	Jacksonville (NC)	$16,334
2.	Myrtle Beach (SC)	17,498
3.	McAllen-Edinburg-Mission (TX)	17,683
4.	Brownsville-Harlingen-San Benito (TX)	17,952
5.	Yuma (AZ)	17,996
6.	Yakima (WA)	18,398
7.	Laredo (TX)	18,730
8.	Visalia-Tulare-Porterville (CA)	18,807
9.	Bryan-College Station (TX)	19,255
10.	Fort Walton Beach (FL)	19,333
11.	Sumter (SC)	19,334
12.	Grand Forks (ND-MN)	19,418
13.	Goldsboro (NC)	19,445
14.	Las Cruces (NM)	19,451
15.	Rapid City (SD)	19,584
16.	Enid (OK)	19,601
17.	Panama City (FL)	19,865
18.	Clarksville-Hopkinsville (TN-KY)	19,893
19.	Daytona Beach (FL)	19,910

25 METROPOLITAN AREAS WITH LOWEST AVERAGE ANNUAL PAY, 1994

Rank	Metropolitan Area	Average Annual Pay
20.	Great Falls (MT)	$19,985
21.	Merced (CA)	20,007
22.	Punta Gorda (FL)	20,049
23.	El Paso (TX)	20,221
24.	Lawton (OK)	20,268
25.	Lawrence (KS)	20,287

SOURCE: Bureau of Labor Statistics, *Average Annual Pay Levels in Metropolitan Areas, 1994*, October 27, 1995.

THE AMERICAN ALMANAC OF JOBS AND SALARIES

I

On the Public Payroll

In 1992, the latest year for which data is available, more than 20 million men and women—or one in six working Americans—were on the public payroll:

3.0 million civilians worked for the federal government
1.9 million were in the military
4.6 million worked for state governments
2.7 million worked for municipalities
2.3 million worked for counties
6.2 million worked for towns, villages, and school districts

Despite attempts by politicians everywhere to create a smaller, leaner government, the number of people on the public payroll continues to grow steadily. As the accompanying table shows, public sector employment has more than doubled since 1957. The biggest culprit has not been the federal government—federal employment has remained fairly constant since the end of World War II and is required by law to decline by 27,000 jobs (12 percent) by 1999—but rather state and local governments, which have nearly tripled in size since 1957.

Such statistics have made the subject of public employment—its uses and abuses, accomplishments and wastefulness—a political issue of central importance, and it will remain so throughout the 1990s. By presenting as much information about salaries of public employees as is possible within the limits of this book, we hope to add something of value to the ongoing debate. That discussion is bound to include such items as wide regional discrepancies for people doing the same job; the issue of "work comparability" (who decides what a job is worth and how that decision is made); the paradoxical situation of governors, mayors, and legislators voting themselves large salary increases while opposing the wage demands of other public employees.

This section is the largest in the book. It is divided into three parts: the federal government, including leading government officials and an analysis of the salary scales in the infamous federal bureaucracy; the salaries of state and local government officials—the most important management jobs in government; and, finally, some examples of salaries and wages for common, everyday jobs on the state and local level.

CIVILIAN GOVERNMENT EMPLOYMENT AND PAYROLLS, OCTOBER 1992

Level of Government	Number of Employees[1]	Salaries/Wages (millions)
All Government	18,745,000	$43,119.7
Federal (Civilian)	3,047,000	9,936.6
State	4,595,000	9,828.2
Local (Total)	11,103,000	23,354.8
County	2,253,000	4,698.3
Municipal	2,665,000	6,207.2
Township	424,000	685.3
School District	5,134,000	10,394.2
Special District	627,000	1,369.9

[1]Numbers may not add up due to independent rounding.
SOURCE: U.S. Dept. of Commerce, *Public Employment 1992* (1994).

Jobs and Salaries in the Federal Government

At the end of the eighteenth century the influential French philosopher and statesman Saint-Simon noted with considerable dismay that before the Revolution the royal bureaucracy had grown so all-pervasive that 80,000 men were needed just to administer the salt tax. In our own day, Jack Anderson, a somewhat less than philosophical observer of the political scene, has calculated that America's 3 million civilian employees and 1.8 million military personnel drain the taxpayers of over $100 billion a year. Unlike the case in monarchies or dictatorships, the cost of ruling is always a major element in the administration of democracies and republics. In contemporary times the salaries and perquisites of politicians and bureaucrats have taken on a new importance in representative forms of government.

Every republic such as ours eventually faces the dilemma of just how much money its citizens should pay government officials, especially those in the highest ranks. Giving too much may raise the specter of elitism, but paying too little makes officials vulnerable to bribery and corruption, a vulnerability all too frequently proven in American history. In any event, no systematic method for determining equitable pay scales in government service has ever been established. Instead, every few years Congress and the president seem to take a rather casual look at the economy and at salary ranges in the private sector and arrive at a set of figures somewhere in the upper-middle range. For the top levels today that's over $100,000 a year.

Over the last 30 years or so the inflationary spiral has added a new dimension to the question of how much government officials should be paid. Since 1965 the salary for just about every important federal job (except the president and vice-president) has at least doubled. These increases took place despite the fact that in 1978 President Carter froze the salaries of many upper-level bureaucrats at $51,000; in 1982 President Reagan raised the limit to $57,500. Today, those freezes seem a long way in the past, as most senior level bureaucrats earn over $100,000.

The vast size of the federal government and the complex nature of its operations preclude any simple responses to the issues involved in pay cuts for politicians and federal employees. It is our hope that the long list of facts and figures that follow will help our readers to make informed judgments in the future.

UNDERSTANDING THE FEDERAL PAY SYSTEM

If you only browse through the listings in this section, you'll get the impression that this is an unwieldy, amorphous mass of information, reflecting perhaps what we all believe to be the chaotic state of the federal bureaucracy itself. But in fact the federal salary system has, relatively speaking, a logical structure that can be easily understood, keeping two things in mind. First, *never* divide the nearly 5.0 million federal employees according to branch of government, since just about everybody works for the Executive Branch (the Legislative Branch employs only 38,000 people; the Judicial, only 22,000). Included in the Executive Branch are the military, the independent agencies, and the executive departments (State, Defense, etc.).

Second, always think in terms of four basic categories: civilian and military employees, blue-collar and white-collar workers. All federal employees are paid under salary schedules formulated on these rather obvious distinctions. Since most people know that the military has a separate pay scale, let's look at civilian workers first.

White-Collar Workers

More than 75 percent of the more than 30 million federal civilian employees are classified as white-collar workers. Most work under the so-called General Schedule or the Executive Schedule, while some top officials are under the new Senior Executive Service. In 1994, the average annual salary of white-collar workers in the federal government was $39,070.

THE GENERAL SCHEDULE

Because almost 1.5 million people work under this salary scale, it is by far the most important in the federal government. It consists of 15 grades (GS-1 to GS-15), each with a salary range of ten steps, each defined according to level of responsibility, type of work, and required qualifications. Theoretically, employees are promoted through steps 1, 2, and 3 on a yearly basis—i.e., they move one step each year—while in steps 4, 5, and 6 they move one step every two years; and in steps 7, 8, and 9 they move one step every three years. How this works in practice is another matter. Frequently, when people are promoted to a higher GS level, they begin at a step higher than 1 so that their salaries will surpass what they were making at the lower GS level but at an advanced step. For example, someone at GS-5, step 7 ($22,006) who was promoted to GS-6 would have to start at least at step 4 or else suffer a cut in pay.

GENERAL SCHEDULE EMPLOYEES AND MEAN SALARY BY GRADE

Grade	Employees	Mean Salary
GS-1	370	$13,038
GS-2	2,443	14,880
GS-3	25,764	17,003
GS-4	97,627	19,597
GS-5	166,176	22,133
GS-6	108,556	24,804
GS-7	140,609	27,274
GS-8	41,034	30,892
GS-9	145,110	32,973
GS-10	16,090	37,700
GS-11	210,657	39,952
GS-12	239,332	48,051
GS-13	159,427	58,230
GS-14	85,490	69,539
GS-15	40,325	83,925
Total	1,479,010	39,070

SOURCE: Office of Personnel Management, *Pay Structure of the Federal Civil Service* (1994).

THE GENERAL SCHEDULE

	1	2	3	4	5	6	7	8	9	10
GS-1	$11,903	$12,300	$12,695	$13,090	$13,487	$13,720	$14,109	$14,503	$14,521	$14,891
2	13,382	13,701	14,145	14,521	14,683	15,115	15,547	15,979	16,411	16,843
3	14,603	15,090	15,577	16,064	16,551	17,038	17,525	18,012	18,499	18,986
4	16,393	16,939	17,485	18,031	18,577	19,123	19,669	20,215	20,761	21,307
5	18,340	18,951	19,562	20,173	20,784	21,395	22,006	22,617	23,228	23,839
6	20,443	21,124	21,805	22,486	23,167	23,848	24,529	25,210	25,891	26,572
7	22,717	23,474	24,231	24,988	25,745	26,502	27,259	28,016	28,773	29,530
8	25,159	25,998	26,837	27,676	28,515	29,354	30,193	31,032	31,871	32,710
9	27,789	28,715	29,641	30,567	31,493	32,419	33,345	34,271	35,197	36,123
10	30,603	31,623	32,643	33,663	34,683	35,703	36,723	37,743	38,763	39,783
11	33,623	34,744	35,865	36,986	38,107	39,228	40,349	41,470	42,591	43,712
12	40,298	41,641	42,984	44,327	45,670	47,013	48,356	49,699	51,042	52,385
13	47,920	49,517	51,114	52,711	54,308	55,905	57,502	59,099	60,696	62,293
14	56,627	58,515	60,403	62,291	64,179	66,067	67,955	69,843	71,731	73,619
15	66,609	68,829	71,049	73,269	75,489	77,709	79,929	82,149	84,369	86,589

SOURCE: U.S. Office of Personnel Management, *Pay Structure of the Federal Civil Service, 1994* (1995).

FOREIGN SERVICE STAFF AND OFFICERS SCHEDULE[1]

Step	Class 1	Class 2	Class 3	Class 4	Class 5	Class 6	Class 7	Class 8	Class 9
1	$66,609	$53,973	$43,734	$35,438	$28,715	$25,670	$22,948	$20,515	$18,340
2	68,607	55,592	45,046	36,501	29,576	26,440	23,636	21,130	18,890
3	70,665	57,260	46,397	37,596	30,464	27,233	24,346	21,764	19,457
4	72,785	58,978	47,789	38,724	31,378	28,050	25,076	22,417	20,041
5	74,969	60,747	49,223	39,886	32,319	28,892	25,828	23,090	20,642
6	77,218	62,569	50,700	41,082	33,289	29,759	26,603	23,783	21,261
7	79,535	64,447	52,221	42,315	34,287	30,651	27,401	24,496	21,899
8	81,921	66,380	53,787	43,584	35,316	31,571	28,223	25,231	22,556
9	84,378	68,371	55,401	44,892	36,375	32,518	29,070	25,988	23,233
10	86,589	70,423	57,063	46,239	37,467	33,494	29,942	26,767	23,930
11	86,589	72,535	58,775	47,626	38,591	34,498	30,840	27,570	24,647
12	86,589	74,711	60,538	49,054	39,748	35,533	31,765	28,398	25,387
13	86,589	76,953	62,354	50,526	40,941	36,599	32,718	29,249	26,148
14	86,589	79,261	64,225	52,042	42,169	37,697	33,700	30,127	26,933

[1]As of January 1, 1993.
SOURCE: U.S. Department of State.

50 WHITE-COLLAR FEDERAL GOVERNMENT OCCUPATIONS: NUMBER EMPLOYED AND AVERAGE ANNUAL SALARIES

Occupation	Total Number Employed	Average Annual Salary
Air Traffic Controller	25,468	$54,363
Architect	2,156	50,436
Border Patrol	3,965	36,915
Cartographer	4,517	44,405
Chaplain	612	48,296
Chemist	7,395	52,691
Clerk-typist	10,868	19,531
Computer Operator	7,417	27,651
Computer Specialist	56,577	46,444
Criminal Investigator	32,638	53,233
Dentist	893	79,126
Doctor	10,689	81,505
Economist	5,796	58,419
Engineer, Aerospace	410	55,751
Engineer, Chemical	24,699	68,271
Engineer, Civil	14,815	52,779
Engineer, Electrical	9,168	58,455
Engineer, General	21,616	62,575
Engineer, Mechanical	12,636	51,533
Engineer, Nuclear	3,534	58,172
Engineer, Petroleum	1,422	53,639
Engineering Technician	24,635	37,301
Hospital Administrator	630	71,326
Inspector, Aviation Safety	2,947	59,912
Inspector, Customs	6,470	36,136
Inspector, Food	6,652	29,614
Internal Revenue Agent	15,730	48,304
Lawyer, General	4,877	37,363
Librarian	3,171	45,497
Library Technician	3,297	23,837
Management and Program Analyst	40,397	47,969
Mathematician	2,074	54,560
Medical Technologist	5,604	36,423
Messenger	148	18,477
Museum Curator	389	49,878
Nurse	43,285	43,181
Nurses' Assistant	15,159	20,814
Paralegal	4,877	37,363
Pharmacist	4,309	48,916
Photographer	1,725	35,985

50 WHITE-COLLAR FEDERAL GOVERNMENT OCCUPATIONS: NUMBER EMPLOYED AND AVERAGE ANNUAL SALARIES

Occupation	Total Number Employed	Average Annual Salary
Physicist	3,508	$63,755
Psychologist	3,941	54,485
Secretary	93,205	24,247
Security Guard	5,463	22,220
Social Insurance Claims Examiner	7,293	37,078
Social Worker	5,154	41,463
Statistician	2,797	52,587
Telephone Operator	1,889	19,150
Veterinarian	2,100	51,104
Writer and Editor	1,940	40,081

SOURCE: U.S. Office of Personnel Management, *Occupations of Federal White-Collar and Blue-Collar Workers,* September 1993.

THE EXECUTIVE SCHEDULE

The Executive Schedule covers senior-level employees only in the Executive Branch. It was established in 1964 as a way of attracting first-rate managers to Washington by paying salaries that went beyond the maximums of the General Schedule. It also enabled a newly elected president to hand-pick top officials across the whole spectrum of government, theoretically freeing the administration from the stranglehold of a bureaucracy not politically committed to the executive's programs. On the other hand, it greatly increased the power of presidential patronage.

Most of the jobs that fall under the Executive Schedule can be found in the listings of executive departments and independent agencies. But first, here's a quick look at how the system is structured.

Level I—All cabinet members.

Level II—Some special presidential assistants, deputy secretaries of major departments (e.g., State, Defense), secretaries of Army, Navy, and Air Force; a few chief administrators, including the heads of the Agency for International Development and the Federal Aviation Administration; the U.S. representatives to the United Nations and to NATO.

Level III—Most presidential advisors; chief administrators of large, independent agencies; most under secretaries in executive departments.

Level IV—Most assistant secretaries, deputy under secretaries, and general counsels in executive departments; many directors such as those at Civil Defense, National Cancer Institute, and National Institutes of Health.

Level V—Many deputy assistant secretaries, most administrators, commissioners, and directors.

THE EXECUTIVE SCHEDULE

Level	Employees	1994 Salary
I	25	$148,400
II	252	133,600
III	84	123,100
IV	32	115,700
V	17	108,200
Total Employees	410	(average salary) $119,561

SOURCE: U.S. Office of Personnel Management, *Pay Structure of the Federal Civil Service, 1994* (1995).

THE SENIOR EXECUTIVE SERVICE

In 1979, fifteen years after the establishment of the Executive Schedule, Congress approved yet another form of compensation for top-level government bureaucrats. This time, however, double-digit inflation and pervasive public skepticism about the size and efficiency of the federal bureaucracy required that strong justification be made for any increase in government salaries. According to the director of the Office of Personnel Management, the purpose of this new system was "to create a cadre of extraordinarily competent and dedicated people who will be accountable for the execution of government programs. Its members will be eligible for additional compensation and benefits based on their performance."

Linking compensation to performance in a government job struck most observers as such a novel idea that few took notice of the relevant details. The Senior Executive Service is limited temporarily to 8,500 members, almost all drawn from Senior Level management and from the Executive Levels IV and V. By law, 90 percent of Senior Executive Service members must be on career assignment and not subject to removal by a change in presidential administrations, and not in jobs requiring Senate confirmation. Moreover, the law also stipulates that 70 percent of all SES members must have held not less than five current, continuous years of federal civilian service. In other words, the upper echelon of the existing structure would remain protected from any presidential promise to revamp the bureaucracy or threat to introduce modern management techniques into government. And, in addition, they would be better paid.

The Senior Executive Service currently has six salary rates, the lowest equaling the first step of GS-16, the highest not to exceed the rate for Level IV of the Executive Schedule. There are no grades for the SES, and each member negotiates his or her salary individually with the particular agency. Unlike the General Schedule and Executive Schedule, pay rates in the Senior Executive Service are not subject to automatic annual cost-of-living increases. Therefore, the 1994 salaries were determined by Executive Order after Bill Clinton took office.

THE SENIOR EXECUTIVE SCHEDULE

Level	Employees	1994 Salary
ES-1	561	$92,900
ES-2	638	97,400
ES-3	1,061	101,800
ES-4	3,673	107,300
ES-5	1,309	111,800
ES-6	580	115,700
Total Employees	7,822	(average salary) $110,668

SOURCE: U.S. Office of Personnel Management, *Pay Structure of the Federal Civil Service, 1994* (1995).

The true financial rewards of the SES, however, are to be found in its bonus system. So-called "Performance Awards" are given to the best managers within an agency as judged by a Performance Review Board and approved by an agency head or an agency Executive Review Board. Lump-sum payments of up to 20 percent of the recipient's base salary will be made every year. According to the government's official booklet, "If you are a top performer, you may receive a bonus every year."

"Presidential Ranks" are another way of rewarding exceptional SES employees with cash bonuses. The first of these, "Meritorious Executive," carries with it a lump-sum payment of $10,000, while "Distinguished Executive" adds $20,000 to the recipient's income. These awards, given for exceptional performance over an extended period of time, are limited each year to 5 percent (about 425) of SES membership for the Meritorious and 1 percent (about 85) for the Distinguished.

The designers of this system realized that a few executives would stand out immediately and might receive several different awards. For this reason, total compensation for members of the Senior Executive Service is not to exceed the salary of cabinet-level appointees at Level I of the Executive Schedule, which in 1994 was $148,400.

Blue-Collar Workers

THE FEDERAL WAGE SYSTEM

About 325,000 blue-collar workers throughout the country are paid under this system, which is based on locally prevailing wage rates for trade, craft, and labor occupations. The Defense Department employs three quarters of these workers (238,692) at installations here and abroad. Another 10 percent (32,438) work for the Veterans Administration, 3.6 percent (11,615) for the Department of the Interior, and 2 percent (6,471) for the Tennessee Valley Authority. In 1993, the average annual salary for blue-collar workers in the federal government was $30,623, an 8.7 percent increase since 1991. Salaries averaged $31,144 for men and $25,696 for women. Below are average salary figures for the most common blue-collar jobs. Although these salaries appear to be in line with private sector wages, critics of federal pay policies claim that given the extremely good benefits all federal employees receive, these basic salary rates are much too high. Of course, most of these critics earn two to three times what blue collar workers make.

50 BLUE-COLLAR OCCUPATIONS IN THE FEDERAL GOVERNMENT: EMPLOYEES AND AVERAGE ANNUAL SALARIES

Title	Total Number Employed	Average Salary
Air-Conditioning Mechanic	3,732	$32,208
Aircraft Mechanic	14,174	33,422
Automotive Mechanic	6,802	31,584
Banknote Engraver	18	76,857
Boiler Plant Operator	3,046	33,259
Boilermaker	1,122	34,423
Bowling Equipment Repairer	15	26,015
Carpenter	3,624	31,499
Cook	3,877	29,743
Crane Operator	1,414	33,582
Custodian	15,494	20,982
Electric Power Controller	2,545	40,300
Electrician	8,478	33,394
Electronics Mechanic	11,938	33,360
Elevator Operator	38	19,749
Engineering Equipment Operator	3,756	32,470
Explosives Operator	1,302	27,934
Food Service Worker	9,328	21,096
Forklift Operator	1,208	26,346

50 BLUE-COLLAR OCCUPATIONS IN THE FEDERAL GOVERNMENT: EMPLOYEES AND AVERAGE ANNUAL SALARIES

Title	Total Number Employed	Average Salary
Gardener	1,319	$26,928
Heavy Mobile Equipment Mechanic	11,516	31,620
Instrument Mechanic	2,075	34,149
Insulator	1,224	32,372
Laborer	7,827	20,867
Laundry Worker	1,517	20,834
Lock and Dam Operator	1,391	31,072
Machinist	7,247	34,216
Maintenance Mechanic	12,918	31,277
Maintenance, Miscellaneous	3,758	41,518
Marine Machinery Mechanic	3,947	35,005
Materials Handler	20,769	26,630
Meat Cutter	1,906	28,622
Motor Vehicle Operator	9,468	27,835
Offset Press Operator	1,329	34,049
Packer	2,987	26,473
Painter	6,304	30,209
Pipefitter	7,138	34,354
Plasterer	114	30,388
Plumber	1,588	30,513
Rigger	2,728	32,551
Roofer	198	29,375
Sewing Machine Operator	278	23,755
Sheet Metal Mechanic	10,039	31,683
Shipfitter	2,379	34,500
Telephone Mechanic	654	34,157
Toolmaker	830	36,667
Tractor Operator	1,364	26,069
Warehouse Worker	924	28,977
Welder	4,620	33,016
Woodworker	1,161	29,348

SOURCE: U.S. Office of Personnel Management, *Occupations of Federal White-Collar and Blue-Collar Workers*, September 1993.

The Postal Service

If the Watergate scandal exposed Richard Nixon's profound contempt for our laws and political traditions, his reorganization of the federal postal structure revealed his passionate, if somewhat naive, belief in the American system of free enterprise. According to one aspect of this theory, any operation can be made efficient if it is run for profit. So first the Post Office was made an independent agency, not part of the executive branch, not subject to the whims of presidential patronage. Next, high-powered executives were brought in to administer this enormous operation. In order to attract the right personnel, the Postal Service was given a separate salary schedule that, at least in the upper-echelon and in the middle-management positions, was competitive with the outside world. (See entry on the Postal Service in the section called "Plum Jobs.")

But despite employing more highly paid executives than any other agency except possibly, NASA, the Postal Service has turned a profit only twice (in 1982 and 1989) since the reorganization. In 1993, the Postal Service lost more than $2.2 billion, although half this deficit was due to a one-time payment to restructure the organization's long-term debt. The Postal Service will likely turn a profit in 1995, primarily on the strength of a three-cent increase in the price of first class stamps. Despite the increase, the first in four years and the longest interval between increases, postal rates in the United States are among the lowest in the world. Moreover, despite legendary complaints about incompetence and slow mail service (or in the case of one Chicago zip code, no service whatsoever), most customers report satisfaction with the Postal Service. An April 1990 Roper poll found that 70 percent of those interviewed indicated they were satisfied with the Postal Service.

During the late 1980s and early 1990s, automation allowed the Postal Service to reduce its workforce from almost 800,000 in 1989 to 682,000 in 1992. Since then, however, the number of employees has crept back up to 719,000, as of July 1994. Almost half (314,344) of these employees were clerks, maintenance employees, motor vehicle operators, or special delivery messengers represented by the American Postal Workers' Union (APWU). Another 223,012 were city delivery letter carriers represented by the National Association of Letter Carriers (NALC). The other two major bargaining units, the National Postal Mail Handlers' Union (NPMHU) and the National Rural Letter Carriers' Association (NRLCA), represented close to 100,000 employees between them.

In 1995, an arbitrator settled acrimonious contract disputes between the Postal Service and three major unions. Under the terms of the new contract, the average postal employee will earn about $27,000 plus benefits valued at nearly $7,000. The contract includes automatic increases each year on top of a Cost of Living Adjustment. As this book went to press, the Postal Service was still negotiating with the Mail Handlers' Union. According to a Census Bureau survey, Postal Service workers are better paid than comparably skilled employees in the private sector.

SALARIES OF POSTAL EMPLOYEES[1] 1994

Position	Starting Salary	Maximum Salary
Clerk/Carrier (Grade 5)	$25,240	$35,604
Mail Handler	21,286	33,689

[1]Salaries include cost-of-living adjustments ranging from $1,789 for starting mail handlers to $4,514 for experienced carriers and clerks.
SOURCE: U.S. Postal Service, *Contract Negotiations Background Information.*

MAXIMUM POSTAL CLERK AND CARRIER SALARIES, 1980–94

Fiscal Year	Maximum Salary	Fiscal Year	Maximum Salary	Fiscal Year	Maximum Salary
1980	$20,320	1985	$25,874	1990	$31,516
1981	21,930	1986	26,923	1991	32,147
1982	22,792	1987	27,949	1992	33,476
1983	23,653	1988	28,615	1993	34,243
1984	24,826	1989	30,038	1994	35,604

SOURCE: U.S. Postal Service, *Contract Negotiations Background Information.*

Pay Rates in the Military

For the majority of positions in the armed forces, the educational requirements are low, and with the end of the cold war, so is the likelihood of ever seeing combat duty, making a career in the military an attractive option for poor people. Average pay rates in the military nearly doubled during Ronald Reagan's presidency alone. Soldiers also receive free room and board, albeit a barracks bunk and military mess hall, so their paychecks go a lot further than those of people who pay monthly rent and grocery bills. The lowliest private earns over $10,000 per year in what amounts to spending money, while a Navy lieutenant with ten years of service brings in more than $37,000 annually. Salaries for enlisted personnel average more than $25,000, while the average officer's total compensation package tops $50,000.

MONTHLY BASE PAY OF MILITARY PERSONNEL[1]

Pay Grade	Army Rank	Navy Rank	2 years of service	10 years of service	26 years of service
Commissioned Officers					
O-10	General	Admiral	$7,223.70	$7,501.20	$9,614.70
O-9	Lt. General	Vice-Admiral	6,346.50	6,646.50	8,482.80
O-8	Maj. General	Rear Admiral	5,769.60	6,346.50	7,686.00
O-7	Brig. General	Commodore	4,971.00	5,495.80	6,783.00
O-6	Colonel	Captain	3,790.20	4,038.60	5,959.50
O-5	Lt. Colonel	Commander	3,239.70	3,463.80	4,862.70
O-4	Major	Lt. Commander	2,832.00	3,212.70	4,065.60
O-3	Captain	Lieutenant	2,416.50	3,102.30	3,516.30
O-2	1st Lieutenant	Lieutenant (J.G.)	2,058.00	2,608.80	2,608.80
O-1	2nd Lieutenant	Ensign	1,703.10	2,058.00	2,058.00
Warrant Officers					
W-5	Chief Warrant Officer	Chief Warrant Officer	NA[2]	NA	$4,182.00
W-4	Chief Warrant Officer	Chief Warrant Officer	2,362.50	2,748.30	3,760.80
W-3	Chief Warrant Officer	Chief Warrant Officer	2,170.80	2,526.30	3,185.10
W-2	Chief Warrant Officer	Chief Warrant Officer	1,896.30	2,253.30	2,772.00
W-1	Warrant Officer	Warrant Officer	1,674.30	2,058.00	2,472.90
Enlisted Personnel					
E-9	Sgt. Major	Master C.P.O.	NA	$2,561.70	$3,297.90
E-8	Master Sgt.	Senior C.P.O.	NA	2,209.80	2,945.10
E-7	Sergeant First Class	Chief Petty Officer	1,619.10	1,913.70	2,649.90
E-6	Staff Sergeant	Petty Officer, 1st Class	1,406.40	1,701.90	1,934.10
E-5	Sergeant	Petty Officer, 2nd Class	1,232.40	1,554.90	1,641.60
E-4	Corporal	Petty Officer, 3rd Class	1,115.40	1,322.40	1,322.40
E-3	Pvt. 1st Class	Seaman	1,049.70	1,134.60	1,134.60
E-2	Private	Seaman Apprentice	957.60	957.60	957.60
E-1	Recruit	Seaman Recruit	854.40	854.40	854.40

[1]Effective January 1, 1995. [2]N.A.: Not Applicable. SOURCE: U.S. Department of Defense.

BASIC ALLOWANCES

In addition to their salaries, military personnel not living on a base receive supplementary allowances for quarters and subsistence.

MONTHLY BASIC ALLOWANCE FOR QUARTERS

Pay Grade	Single Rate	Married Rate
Officers		
O-7 through O-10	$749.40	$922.50
O-6	687.60	830.70
O-5	662.10	800.70
O-4	613.80	705.90
O-3	492.00	584.10
O-2	390.00	498.90
O-1	328.50	445.80
Warrant Officers		
W-5	$623.40	$681.30
W-4	553.80	624.60
W-3	465.30	572.40
W-2	413.10	526.50
W-1	345.90	455.40
Enlisted Personnel		
E-9	$454.80	$599.40
E-8	417.60	552.60
E-7	356.40	513.00
E-6	322.80	474.30
E-5	297.60	426.30
E-4	258.90	370.80
E-3	254.10	345.00
E-2	206.40	328.50
E-1	183.90	328.50

SOURCE: U.S. Department of Defense.

BASIC ALLOWANCE FOR SUBSISTENCE

Officers: $146.16 per month ($1,753.92 per year)

Enlisted Members:

	E-1, LESS THAN FOUR MONTHS	ALL OTHER ENLISTED
When on leave, or authorized to mess separately:	$6.44/day	$ 6.98/day
When rations in-kind are not available:	7.26/day	7.87/day
When assigned to duty under emergency conditions where no messing facilities of the United States are available:	9.63/day	10.42/day

PLUM JOBS: HIGH-PAYING POSITIONS IN THE FEDERAL GOVERNMENT

In recent years, every time a new president is elected, Congress issues a large book called *U.S. Government Policy and Supporting Positions.* Known popularly as *The Plum Book,* it lists several thousand key jobs in all the executive departments and independent agencies.

In the pages that follow the upper echelon of the federal bureaucracy can be found. Keep in mind that many of these jobs are presidential appointments so they represent the heart of the executive's power of patronage. The data reflects plum jobs (and salaries) at the end of the Bush Administration, since the Clinton *Plum Book* will not be published until 1997 at the earliest.

Executive Departments

DEPARTMENT OF AGRICULTURE

Secretary	Level I
Deputy Secretary	Level II
2 Under Secretaries	Level III
7 Assistant Secretaries	Level IV
Inspector General	Level IV
General Counsel	Level IV

13 Associate and Assistant General Counsels	Senior Executive Service
4 Administrators	Level V
10 Associate Administrators	Senior Executive Service
23 Deputy Administrators	Senior Executive Service
49 State Directors	GS-15
State Director	GS-14
3 Speech Writers	GS-15
12 Special Assistants	Senior Executive Service
5 Executive Assistants	Senior Executive Service
54 Confidential Assistants	GS 12–15

DEPARTMENT OF COMMERCE

Secretary	Level I
Deputy Secretary	Level II
5 Under Secretaries	Level III
14 Assistant Secretaries	Level IV
General Counsel	Level IV
Inspector General	Level IV
2 Directors	Level IV
Deputy Assistant Secretary	Level V
Chief Scientist	Level V
2 Assistant Commissioners	Level V
3 Deputy Under Secretaries	Senior Executive Service
38 Deputy Assistant Secretaries	Senior Executive Service
79 Directors	Senior Executive Service
8 Deputy Directors	Senior Executive Service

DEPARTMENT OF DEFENSE

Note: The listing of jobs for this department runs to thirty-eight pages in the *Plum Book* compared to six for Treasury, nine for Health and Human Services, and eighteen for State.

Office of the Secretary

Secretary	Level I
Deputy Secretary	Level II
2 Deputy Under Secretaries	Level III
Deputy Under Secretary	Level IV
11 Assistant Secretaries	Level IV

Comptroller	Level IV
Director, Research	Level IV
General Counsel	Level IV
Inspector General	Level IV
Assistant Secretary	Level V
21 Deputy Assistant Secretaries	Senior Executive Service
116 Directors	Senior Executive Service
26 Deputy Directors	Senior Executive Service

Department of the Air Force

Secretary	Level II
Under Secretary	Level IV
3 Assistant Secretaries	Level IV
General Counsel	Level IV
3 Principal Deputy Assistant Secretaries	Senior Executive Service
7 Deputy Assistant Secretaries	Senior Executive Service
6 Assistant General Counsels	Senior Executive Service

Department of the Army

Secretary	Level II
Under Secretary	Level IV
4 Assistant Secretaries	Level IV
General Counsel	Level V
4 Principal Deputies	Senior Executive Service
8 Deputies	Senior Executive Service
26 Directors	Senior Executive Service
17 Technical Directors	Senior Executive Service

Department of the Navy

Secretary	Level II
Under Secretary	Level IV
4 Assistant Secretaries	Level IV
General Counsel	Level V
2 Principal Deputy Assistant Secretaries	Senior Executive Service
10 Deputy Assistant Secretaries	Senior Executive Service

HEALTH AND HUMAN SERVICES

Secretary	Level I
Deputy Secretary	Level II
6 Assistant Secretaries	Level IV
2 Commissioners	Level IV

2 Administrators	Level IV
General Counsel	Level IV
Inspector General	Level IV
Director	Level IV
Commissioner	Level V
20 Deputy Assistant Secretaries	Senior Executive Service
2 Deputies to Deputy Assistant Secretaries	Senior Executive Service
9 Associate General Counsels	Senior Executive Service
10 Regional Chief Counsels	Senior Executive Service
10 Regional Directors	Senior Executive Service

DEPARTMENT OF HOUSING AND URBAN DEVELOPMENT

Secretary	Level I
Deputy Secretary	Level II
8 Assistant Secretaries	Level IV
General Counsel	Level IV
Inspector General	Level IV
17 Deputy Assistant Secretaries	Senior Executive Service

DEPARTMENT OF THE INTERIOR

Secretary	Level I
Deputy Secretary	Level II
6 Assistant Secretaries	Level IV
8 Deputy Assistant Secretaries	Senior Executive Service
Solicitor	Level IV
Deputy Solicitor	Senior Executive Service
6 Associate Solicitors	Senior Executive Service
8 Regional Solicitors	Senior Executive Service
3 Directors	Level V
3 Commissioners	Level V
24 Directors	Senior Executive Service
16 Deputy Directors	Senior Executive Service
10 Associate Directors	Senior Executive Service
21 Assistant Directors	Senior Executive Service
12 Area Directors	Senior Executive Service
23 Regional Directors	Senior Executive Service
12 State Directors	Senior Executive Service

DEPARTMENT OF JUSTICE

Attorney General	Level I
Director, FBI	Level II
Deputy Attorney General	Level II
Associate Attorney General	Level III
Solicitor General	Level III
Administrator, Drug Enforcement	Level III
Deputy Administrator, Drug Enforcement	Level IV
10 Assistant Attorneys General	Level IV
Inspector General	Level IV
Commissioner, Immigration and Naturalization	Level IV
4 Directors	Level IV
Special Counsel	Level V
10 Associate Deputy Attorneys General	Senior Executive Service
28 Deputy Assistant Attorneys General	Senior Executive Service
4 Deputy Solicitors General	Senior Executive Service
92 U.S. Attorneys	$110,100

DEPARTMENT OF LABOR

Secretary	Level I
Deputy Secretary	Level II
10 Assistant Secretaries	Level IV
Inspector General	Level IV
Solicitor of Labor	Level IV
Commissioner of Labor Statistics	Level V
Wage and Hour Administrator	Level V
Deputy Under Secretary	Senior Executive Service
16 Deputy Assistant Secretaries	Senior Executive Service
2 Associate Assistant Secretaries	Senior Executive Service
2 Associate Solicitors	Senior Executive Service
21 Directors	Senior Executive Service
3 Deputy Directors	Senior Executive Service
6 Administrators	Senior Executive Service
4 Deputy Administrators	Senior Executive Service
24 Regional Administrators	Senior Executive Service

DEPARTMENT OF STATE (Domestic only)

Secretary	Level I
Deputy Secretary	Level II
Ambassador-at-Large	Level II
4 Under Secretaries	Level III
Counselor	Level III
3 Ambassadors-at-Large	Level IV
16 Assistant Secretaries	Level IV
Chief Financial Officer	Level IV
Chief of Protocol	Level IV
Inspector General	Level IV
Legal Advisor	Level IV
5 Deputy Legal Advisors	Senior Executive Service
19 Assistant Legal Advisors	Senior Executive Service
61 Deputy Assistant Secretaries	Senior Executive Service or Senior Foreign Service
42 Directors	Senior Executive Service or Senior Foreign Service
54 Office Directors	Senior Foreign Service
23 Country Directors	Senior Foreign Service

DEPARTMENT OF TRANSPORTATION

Secretary	Level I
Deputy Secretary	Level II
2 Administrators	Level II
2 Administrators	Level III
4 Administrators	Level IV
4 Assistant Secretaries	Level IV
Inspector General	Level IV
General Counsel	Level IV
Associate Deputy Secretary	Level V
9 Deputy Assistant Secretaries	Senior Executive Service
25 Deputy Directors	Senior Executive Service
31 Associate Administrators	Senior Executive Service
18 Deputy Associate Administrators	Senior Executive Service
20 Regional Administrators	Senior Executive Service

DEPARTMENT OF THE TREASURY

Secretary	Level I
Deputy Secretary	Level II
Under Secretary for International Affairs	Level III
Commissioner of IRS	Level III
Comptroller of the Currency	Level III
Director, Office of Thrift Supervision	Level III
9 Assistant Secretaries	Level IV
Inspector General	Level IV
General Counsel	Level IV
Chief Counsel, IRS	Level V
22 Deputy Assistant Secretaries	Senior Executive Service
55 Directors	Senior Executive Service

DEPARTMENT OF VETERANS AFFAIRS

Secretary	Level I
Deputy Secretary	Level II
Chief Benefits Director	Level III
Chief Medical Director, VHA	Level III
6 Assistant Secretaries	Level IV
General Counsel	Level IV
Inspector General	Level IV
Chairman, Board of Veterans' Appeals	Level IV
Director, National Cemetery System	Level IV
11 Deputy Assistant Secretaries	Senior Executive Service
9 Assistant General Counsels	Senior Executive Service
167 Directors of VA Medical Centers	Senior Executive Service
6 Associate Chief Medical Directors	Senior Executive Service
7 Directors, VA Benefits	Senior Executive Service
4 Area Directors, VA Benefits	Senior Executive Service
40 Regional Office Directors	Senior Executive Service

Independent Agencies—Selected

ACTION

Director	Level III
Deputy Director	Level IV
Associate Director, Anti-Poverty	Level V

ADMINISTRATIVE CONFERENCE OF UNITED STATES

Chairman	Level II

APPALACHIAN REGIONAL COMMISSION

Federal Chairman	Level III
Alternate Chairman	Level V

CENTRAL INTELLIGENCE AGENCY

Director	Level II
Deputy Director	Level III

COMMODITY FUTURES TRADING COMMISSION

Chairman	Level III
4 Commissioners	Level IV

CONSUMER PRODUCT SAFETY COMMISSION

Chairman	Level III
4 Commissioners	Level IV

DEFENSE NUCLEAR FACILITIES SAFETY BOARD

Chairman	Level III
Vice-Chairman	Level III
3 Members	Level III

ENVIRONMENTAL PROTECTION AGENCY

Administrator	Level II
Deputy Administrator	Level III
9 Assistant Administrators	Level IV
General Counsel	Level IV
7 Associate General Counsels	Senior Executive Service

3 Associate Administrators	Senior Executive Service
10 Regional Administrators	Senior Executive Service
10 Deputy Regional Administrators	Senior Executive Service

EQUAL EMPLOYMENT OPPORTUNITY COMMISSION

Chairman	Level III
Vice-Chairman	Level IV
3 Members	Level IV
12 Directors	Senior Executive Service

EXPORT-IMPORT BANK OF THE UNITED STATES

President	Level III
First Vice-President	Level IV
3 Board Members	Level IV

FARM CREDIT ADMINISTRATION

Chairman	Level III
2 Members	Level IV

FEDERAL COMMUNICATIONS COMMISSION

Chairman	Level III
4 Commissioners	Level IV

FEDERAL DEPOSIT INSURANCE CORPORATION

Chairman	Level III
CEO, Resolution Trust Corp.	Level III
Vice-Chairman	Level IV
Member	Level IV

FEDERAL ELECTION COMMISSION

Chairman	Level IV
Vice-Chairman	Level IV
4 Members	Level IV
Staff Director	Level IV
General Counsel	Level V

FEDERAL EMERGENCY MANAGEMENT AGENCY

Director	Level II
Deputy Director	Level IV
3 Associate Directors	Level IV
3 Administrators	Level IV
3 Assistant Administrators	Senior Executive Service
2 Deputy Associate Directors	Senior Executive Service
2 Deputy Assistant Associate Directors	Senior Executive Service
10 Regional Directors	Senior Executive Service

FEDERAL ENERGY REGULATORY COMMISSION

Chairman	Level III
4 Members	Level IV
Executive Director	Senior Executive Service
Deputy Executive Director	Senior Executive Service
3 Associate Executive Directors	Senior Executive Service
General Counsel	Senior Executive Service
4 Associate General Counsels	Senior Executive Service
7 Assistant General Counsels	Senior Executive Service
19 Directors	Senior Executive Service

FEDERAL LABOR RELATIONS AUTHORITY

Chairman	Level IV
3 Members	Level V

FEDERAL MARITIME COMMISSION

Chairman	Level III
4 Members	Level IV

FEDERAL MEDIATION AND CONCILIATION SERVICE

Director	Level III

FEDERAL MINE SAFETY AND HEALTH REVIEW COMMISSION

Chairman	Level III
4 Members	Level IV

FEDERAL RESERVE SYSTEM

Chairman	Level II
Vice-Chairman	Level III
5 Governors	Level III

FEDERAL TRADE COMMISSION

Chairman	Level III
4 Members	Level IV
5 Directors	Senior Executive Service
4 Deputy Directors	Senior Executive Service
6 Associate Directors	Senior Executive Service
3 Assistant Directors	Senior Executive Service

GENERAL SERVICES ADMINISTRATION

Administrator	Level III
Inspector General	Level IV
6 Associate Administrators	Senior Executive Service
10 Regional Administrators	Senior Executive Service
8 Deputy Regional Administrators	Senior Executive Service
4 Commissioners	Senior Executive Service
3 Deputy Commissioners	Senior Executive Service

INTER-AMERICAN FOUNDATION

President	Level IV

INTERNATIONAL DEVELOPMENT COOPERATION AGENCY

Director	Level II
Deputy Director	Level III
Administrator, AID	Level II
Deputy Administrator, AID	Level III
President Overseas Private Investment Corp.	Level III
Exec. Vice-President	Level III
Director, Trade and Development	Level III
Associate Administrator, AID	Level IV
9 Assistant Administrators	Level IV

INTERSTATE COMMERCE COMMISSION

Chairman	Level III
4 Commissioners	Level IV
5 Directors	Senior Executive Service

MERIT SYSTEMS PROTECTION BOARD

Chairman	Level III
Vice-Chairman	Level IV
Member	Level IV
Legal Counsel to the Member	Senior Executive Service
General Counsel	Senior Executive Service
Director, Office of Appeals	Senior Executive Service

NATIONAL AERONAUTICS AND SPACE ADMINISTRATION

Administrator	Level II
Deputy Administrator	Level III
Inspector General	Level IV
52 Directors	Senior Executive Service
12 Deputy Directors	Senior Executive Service
9 Associate Administrators	Senior Executive Service
3 Assistant Administrators	Senior Executive Service

NATIONAL ARCHIVES AND RECORDS ADMINISTRATION

Archivist of United States	Level III
Assistant Archivist	Senior Executive Service
Deputy Assistant Archivist	Senior Executive Service

NATIONAL CREDIT UNION ADMINISTRATION

Chairman	Level III
Vice-Chairman	Level IV
Member	Level IV

NATIONAL FOUNDATION ON THE ARTS AND HUMANITIES

Chairman, Humanities	Level III
Director, Museum Services	Level IV
3 Deputy Chairmen	Senior Executive Service
9 Directors	Senior Executive Service

NATIONAL LABOR RELATIONS BOARD

Chairman	Level III
4 Members	Level IV
General Counsel	Level IV

NATIONAL MEDIATION BOARD

Chairman	Level III
2 Members	Level IV

NATIONAL SCIENCE FOUNDATION

Director	Level II
Deputy Director	Level III
4 Assistant Directors	Senior Executive Service
32 Directors (various programs)	Senior Executive Service

NATIONAL TRANSPORTATION SAFETY BOARD

Chairman	Level III
Vice-Chairman	Level IV
3 Members	Level IV

NUCLEAR REGULATORY COMMISSION

Chairman	Level II
4 Commissioners	Level III
Inspector General	Level IV
34 Directors (various offices)	Senior Executive Service
19 Deputy Directors	Senior Executive Service
5 Regional Administrators	Senior Executive Service

OCCUPATIONAL SAFETY AND HEALTH REVIEW COMMISSION

Chairman	Level III
2 Commissioners	Level IV

OFFICE OF GOVERNMENT ETHICS

Director	Level III

OFFICE OF NAVAJO AND HOPI RELOCATION

Commissioner	Level IV

OFFICE OF PERSONNEL MANAGEMENT

Director	Level II
Deputy Director	Level III
Inspector General	Level IV
8 Directors	Senior Executive Service
5 Associate Directors	Senior Executive Service
5 Regional Directors	Senior Executive Service
3 Deputy Directors	Senior Executive Service

5 Deputy Associate Directors	Senior Executive Service
14 Assistant Directors	Senior Executive Service

OFFICE OF SPECIAL COUNSEL

Special Counsel	Level IV

PANAMA CANAL COMMISSION

Administrator	Level IV
Deputy Administrator	Level IV

PEACE CORPS

Director	Level III
Deputy Director	Level IV

POSTAL RATE COMMISSION

Chairman	Level III
4 Commissioners	Level IV

SECURITIES AND EXCHANGE COMMISSION

Chairman	Level III
4 Commissioners	Level IV

SELECTIVE SERVICE SYSTEM

Director	Level IV

SMALL BUSINESS ADMINISTRATION

Administrator	Level III
Deputy Administrator	Level IV

4 Associate Deputy Administrators	Senior Executive Service
11 Regional Administrators	Senior Executive Service

TENNESSEE VALLEY AUTHORITY

Chairman	Level III
2 Members of Board	Level IV

U.S. ARMS CONTROL AND DISARMAMENT AGENCY

Director	Level II
Deputy Director	Level III
Chief Science Advisor	Level IV
4 Assistant Directors	Level IV
5 Deputy Assistant Directors	Senior Executive Service

U.S. COMMISSION ON CIVIL RIGHTS

Chairman	Level IV
Vice-Chairman	Level IV
4 Commissioners	Level IV

U.S. INFORMATION AGENCY

Director	Level II
Deputy Director	Level III
4 Associate Directors	Level IV
Inspector General	Level IV

EXECUTIVE OFFICE OF THE PRESIDENT

The growth in the power of the presidency can be seen very clearly in both the size and the nature of the executive staff. There are about 400 full-time civilian employees in the White House. This includes everyone from gardeners, domestics, and telephone operators to press secretaries, deputy secretaries, and special assistants to deputy secretaries. All of the lower level jobs are paid under the General Schedule. By law the president's staff may not have more than 25 people at Level II, 25 people at Level III, and 50 at the GS-18 level. (See previous section, "Plum Jobs" for some specific jobs).

Perks of the Presidency

The president receives an annual salary of $200,000 from which all private living costs must be paid. But the perks of office insure that the president rarely has to open his wallet. Indeed, George Bush occasionally forgot to carry cash during his tenure and had to have aides pay for his personal purchases, reimbursing them later. A staff of about 100 attends to the first family's every need. In addition to the usual assortment of butlers, maids, painters, carpenters, electricians, and plumbers, the president's staff includes five chefs, a phalanx of secret service agents, and a military nurse to give him a rubdown each night. The president receives free health care at Bethesda Naval Hospital, while members of his staff may utilize the free clinic at the White House for emergencies and minor ailments. When the president travels, he has at his disposal a total of 23 aircraft including Marine helicopters and two Boeing 747s; local transportation is provided by two armored limousines costing $600,000 each. And of course the nation's highest office comes with two palatial residences: the White House in Washington (which has an annual operating budget of $7.2 million), and the Camp David retreat in Maryland's Catoctin Mountains (just a free helicopter ride away).

In recent years, the most enriching aspect of the presidency has become the memoirs that are nearly de rigueur. Ronald Reagan, for example, negotiated a deal for an estimated $6 million for two books on his presidency. Reagan earned an additional $2 million simply by delivering two 20-minute speeches to a Japanese media company after his presidency.

The office of the vice-president, though much derided, is not without its own set of perks. The second-in-command receives $94,000 annually and is allowed to reside rent-free at the 16-room Admiral's House on grounds adjacent to the Naval Observatory. The budget for the house is $285,000, including $75,000 for entertainment. In addition, the vice-president has a staff of 70 with an annual budget of $2.1 million. In early 1993, former vice-president Dan Quayle signed a book contract for his memoirs estimated at a minimum of $1 million.

EXECUTIVE OFFICE OF THE PRESIDENT

President	$200,000
Expense Allowance	50,000
Travel Allowance	100,000
Vice-President	94,000
Expense Allowance	10,000

OFFICE OF MANAGEMENT AND BUDGET

Director	Level I
Deputy Director	Level II
Deputy Director	Level III
2 Administrators	Level III

COUNCIL OF ECONOMIC ADVISORS

Chairman	Level II
2 Members	Level IV

COUNCIL ON ENVIRONMENTAL QUALITY

Chairman	Level II
2 Members	Level IV

NATIONAL SECURITY COUNCIL

Executive Secretary	Level IV

OFFICE OF U.S. TRADE REPRESENTATIVE

U.S. Trade Representative	Level I
3 Deputies	Level III
4 Senior Advisors	Senior Executive Service
11 Assistant Trade Representatives	Senior Executive Service
5 Deputy Assistant Trade Representatives	Senior Executive Service

OFFICE OF SCIENCE AND TECHNOLOGY POLICY

Director	Level II
4 Associate Directors	Level III

NATIONAL SPACE COUNCIL

Executive Secretary	Level III

OFFICE OF NATIONAL DRUG CONTROL POLICY

Director	Level I
2 Deputy Directors	Level III
1 Associate Director	Level IV

MEMBERS OF CONGRESS AND THEIR STAFFS

Senate	
President pro tempore, majority and minority leaders	$148,400
Expense allowance	10,000
Senators	133,600
Expense allowance for majority and minority whips	5,000
Expense allowance for chairmen of majority and minority conference committees	3,000
House of Representatives	
Speaker of the House	$171,500
Expense allowance	25,000
Minority and majority leaders	148,400
Expense allowance	10,000
432 Representatives	133,600
Expense allowance for majority and minority whips	5,000

In addition to these direct salaries, for years members of Congress earned many times their salaries in honoraria for speaking engagements, often before political action committees (PACs) that sought to influence national policy. But faced with mounting opposition to these honoraria, the House in 1991 voted to ban its members from accepting speaking fees (in exchange for a substantial pay raise); the Senate followed suit a year later. In addition, since 1976, members of Congress have been subject to a 15 percent limit on earnings over and above their salaries. This limit does not, however, apply to unearned income from stocks and bonds.

The 1991–92 check-floating scandal at the House bank attracted unprecedented media and public attention to the perks of elected office. Some perks, such as the sergeant-at-arms who routinely fixed parking tickets for members of Congress, were abolished in the wake of the check scandal, as were the House bank and post office. But many others, like $5 haircuts, taxpayer-subsidized meals, and free airport parking remain. An abbreviated list of the job-related and not-so-related benefits includes the following:

Pension: 401-K plan, optional civil service retirement.

Medical: Staff of doctors available for members at the Capitol.

Franking: free mailing to constituents (this privilege is especially abused around reelection time, when incumbents flood their constituents' mailboxes with information to fend off political challengers).

Parking: special tags allow parking at any curb space in Washington except fire hydrants, fire stations, and loading docks.

Decorations: Plants supplied by the U.S. Botanical Garden; two framed reproductions available from the National Gallery of Art on request.

Phone: Free long-distance calls via two WATS lines per member.

Exercise: Gym in Rayburn House Office Building; exercise rooms in Russell and Dirksen Senate office buildings.

Members of Congress also receive free office space with furnishings in Washington and at home, free printing service, and generous stationery allowances. Large amounts of money are allocated for keeping members in touch with their constituents. Members of the House make 26 trips to their home areas; senators make an average of 40. House members also receive an average expense allowance of $176,000 for maintaining contact with their home districts (the actual amount depends on each member's travel distance to and from Washington and the cost of office space in their home district). Senators' expense allowances range from $44,000 to $200,000. Special allowances also exist for travel abroad on government business, a chore some lame duck members have found especially necessary in the months after they were defeated for reelection.

The most important benefit of all, finally, is the allowance every member of Congress receives to hire and maintain a personal staff to assist with everything from filing, typing, and speechwriting to hosting parties, dealing with the media, and shaping legislation. Each member of the House of Representatives may employ a maximum of 22 people at a total cost not to exceed $515,760. Senators may employ as many people as they wish, but also under strictly controlled limitations based on state populations. For example, senators representing California receive $1,764,000, while senators from the least populous states receive $814,000. Senators also receive an allowance of $280,000 for three employees to work on committees.

Despite this impressive array of pay and perquisites, congressional salaries and benefits have been long regarded as short-term rewards. Many of the rewards of congressional service are realized, as they are with the presidency, after the congressman or senator leaves office. The power and prestige of national office almost always enables members to build lucrative law practices, to serve as officers of corporations, and to earn large fees for speaking engagements.

THE FEDERAL JUDICIARY

Judges

	Salary 1992	Salary 1995
Chief Justice of the United States	$166,200	$171,500
Associate Justices of the Supreme Court	159,000	164,100
United States Circuit Judges	137,300	141,700
United States District Judges	129,500	133,600
Judges, Court of International Trade	129,500	133,600
Judges, United States Claims Court	129,500	133,600
United States Bankruptcy Judges	119,140	123,000
United States Magistrates (Full-time)	119,140	123,000

All federal judges are also allowed a personal staff consisting of secretaries and law clerks. These people are paid under the Judicial Salary Plan, which is roughly equivalent to the General Schedule. The salary range for career law clerks is $26,798 to $70,987. Most one-year law clerks are hired at a grade of GS 11-1, or $33,623 in 1994. All 24 law clerks working for Supreme Court justices earn $31,619.

Judicial Offices: Administrative Office of U.S. Courts

Director	$129,500	$133,600
Deputy Director	119,140	123,000

Federal Judicial Center

Director	$129,500	$133,600
Deputy Director	119,140	123,000

ARE FEDERAL EMPLOYEES OVERPAID?

Every November, a favorite theme of most political speeches is the need to control the federal bureaucracy. Some politicians stress the difficulty of making it more responsive to the people, others, the importance of reducing its size. Rarely, however, does anyone mention the delicate topic of rapidly rising pay rates in the federal civil service. One reason is that very few politicians want to be on record as opposing raises for 3 million voters; another is that, like most of us, politicians can't believe that bureaucrats could actually be overpaid.

Comparisons with salaries in private industry have been the crucial element in determining federal pay rates since 1970, when Congress passed a law guaranteeing government employees salaries comparable to those of private industry workers doing similar jobs. This was simple enough to implement for blue-collar workers because union contracts spell out, often in great detail, wage rates and job responsibilities. Establishing comparability standards for white-collar employees, however, has proved extremely difficult despite an elaborate monitoring system set up by the Bureau of Labor Statistics. Moreover, in recent years several economists have challenged the bureau's methods of evaluating federal pay and have determined that federal workers are in fact more generously rewarded than private-industry workers, especially if the excellent benefits given to federal workers are considered. Still, every two years or so the Bureau of Labor Statistics provides a survey comparing private and federal salaries.

Comparison of Annual Salaries in Private Industry and the Federal Government, 1990

The following table is based on a report published by the Bureau of Labor Statistics called *White Collar Pay: Private Goods-Producing Industries* (March 1990). All government salaries are based on the General Schedule: minimum and maximum salaries are steps 1 and 10, respectively, of each grade. Many descriptions of job-level designations can be found in appropriate entries throughout this book.

Occupation	Average in Private Industry	Salary Rates in the Federal Government			
		GS Level	Average	Minimum (Step 1)	Maximum (Step 10)
Accountants					
I	$ 23,842	GS-5	$18,699	$16,305	$21,201
II	28,200	GS-7	23,005	20,195	26,252
III	35,489	GS-9	27,793	24,705	32,121
IV	45,095	GS-11	33,812	29,891	38,855
V	56,871	GS-12	40,801	35,825	46,571
VI	72,440	GS-13	49,003	42,601	55,381
Accounting Clerks					
I	$ 13,984	GS-2	$12,564	$11,897	$14,973
II	16,929	GS-3	14,284	12,982	16,879
III	20,213	GS-4	16,453	14,573	18,947
IV	24,279	GS-5	18,699	16,305	21,201
Attorneys					
I	$ 38,587	GS-9	$27,793	$24,705	$32,121
II	46,053	GS-11	33,812	29,891	38,855
III	59,087	GS-12	40,801	35,825	46,571
IV	78,561	GS-13	49,003	42,601	55,381
V	96,178	GS-14	58,363	50,342	65,444
VI	120,967	GS-15	70,316	59,216	76,982
Auditors					
I	$ 25,393	GS-5	$18,699	$16,305	$21,201
II	30,135	GS-7	23,005	20,195	26,252
III	37,589	GS-9	27,793	24,705	32,121
IV	46,344	GS-11	33,812	29,891	38,855
Buyers					
I	$ 24,022	GS-5	$18,699	$16,305	$21,201
II	29,854	GS-7	23,005	20,195	26,252
III	38,854	GS-9	27,793	24,705	32,121
IV	46,209	GS-11	33,812	29,891	38,855
Chemists					
I	$ 26,109	GS-5	$18,699	$16,305	$21,201
II	32,168	GS-7	23,005	20,195	26,252
III	40,385	GS-9	27,793	24,705	32,121
IV	49,065	GS-11	33,812	29,891	38,855
V	59,518	GS-12	40,801	35,825	46,571
VI	72,835	GS-13	49,003	42,601	55,381
VII	85,395	GS-14	58,363	50,342	65,444

Occupation	Average in Private Industry	Salary Rates in the Federal Government			
		GS Level	Average	Minimum (Step 1)	Maximum (Step 10)
Computer Operators					
I	$ 15,677	GS-4	$16,453	$14,573	$18,947
II	19,839	GS-5	18,699	16,305	21,201
III	24,727	GS-6	21,075	18,174	23,628
IV	29,029	GS-7	23,005	20,195	26,252
V	33,390	GS-8	26,160	22,367	29,081
Drafters					
I	$ 14,397	GS-2	$12,564	$11,897	$14,973
II	19,152	GS-3	14,284	12,982	16,879
III	22,859	GS-4	16,453	14,573	18,947
IV	28,835	GS-5	18,699	16,305	21,201
V	34,900	GS-7	23,005	20,195	26,252
Engineers					
I	$ 31,224	GS-5	$18,699	$16,305	$21,201
II	35,398	GS-7	23,005	20,195	26,252
III	41,287	GS-9	27,793	24,705	32,121
IV	49,365	GS-11	33,812	29,891	38,855
V	59,444	GS-12	40,801	35,825	46,571
VI	70,332	GS-13	49,003	42,601	55,381
VII	80,998	GS-14	58,363	50,342	65,444
VIII	91,392	GS-15	70,316	59,216	76,982
File Clerks					
I	$ 12,372	GS-1	$10,947	$10,581	$13,232
II	14,652	GS-2	12,564	11,897	14,973
III	18,052	GS-3	14,284	12,982	16,879
Key Entry Operators					
I	$ 14,945	GS-2	$12,564	$11,897	$14,973
II	18,756	GS-3	14,284	12,982	16,879
Personnel Clerks/Assistants					
I	$ 15,153	GS-3	$14,284	$12,982	$16,879
II	18,579	GS-4	16,453	14,573	18,947
III	22,119	GS-5	18,699	16,305	21,201
IV	26,643	GS-6	21,075	18,174	23,628

Occupation	Average in Private Industry	Salary Rates in the Federal Government			
		GS Level	Average	Minimum (Step 1)	Maximum (Step 10)
Personnel Supervisors/Managers					
I	$ 46,504	GS-11	$33,812	$29,891	$38,855
II	58,658	GS-12	40,801	35,825	46,571
III	75,600	GS-13	49,003	42,601	55,381
IV	93,324	GS-14	58,363	50,342	65,444
Secretaries					
I	$ 18,810	GS-4	$16,453	$14,573	$18,947
II	21,175	GS-5	18,699	16,305	21,201
III	23,893	GS-6	21,075	18,174	23,628
IV	27,542	GS-7	23,005	20,195	26,252
V	32,317	GS-8	26,160	22,367	29,081
Typists					
I	$ 14,921	GS-2	$12,564	$11,897	$14,973
II	18,974	GS-3	14,284	12,982	16,879

SOURCE: U.S. Bureau of Labor Statistics, *White Collar Pay: Private Goods-Producing Industries,* March 1990.

While it appears that federal employees have not kept up with their civilian counterparts over the past decade, no one knows for sure. Furthermore, the issue of executive- and managerial-level salaries in the federal government has recently arisen, as an apparent talent drain has raised major concern about recruiting highly capable people to run government agencies and departments.

Salaries for these high-level jobs in the private sector tend to be set by market conditions. In this context, government service has always paid less, and it was assumed that incumbents would be willing to sacrifice a portion of their private earning power for the public good. In the 1980s, however, either the willingness to make that sacrifice diminished or the amount of the sacrifice became prohibitive. Therefore, the Commission on Executive, Legislative, and Judicial Salaries was asked to study the situation. Late in 1988 the commission, citing a 35 percent erosion in the purchasing power of high-level officials over the past two decades, recommended increasing the top salaries (including those of legislators) by 50 percent.

The commission proposed raising the salaries of the top 2,498 federal officials to over $100,000 each. The recommendation was based on making federal officials' pay comparable to the not-for-profit private sector. For instance, the executive director of the Port Authority of New York and New Jersey is reported to earn $170,000, while the public health director for the city of Milwaukee earns $118,000. As a point of comparison, the commission's proposal would raise cabinet-level officers to $155,000; deputy and under secretaries to $135,000; and division heads, agency heads, and assistant secretaries to between $115,000 and $125,000. The president's salary would increase to $350,000, legislators to $135,000 each, and the justices of the Supreme Court to $165,000 each.

Many of these recommendations have been put into effect despite the spiraling deficit and the general public skepticism about the size and usefulness of the federal bureaucracy. Congress remains silent because of the public's outcry about the enormous raise it gave itself, and meanwhile the costs grow and grow.

How to Find a Job in the Federal Government

The government of the United States employs slightly more than 3 million civilians, so it should not be surprising that there are literally thousands of job openings all the time and in many parts of the country as well as overseas. In 1994 more than 500,000 people found jobs in the federal government, jobs spanning the entire employment spectrum from professional (the government employs over 25,000 lawyers, and more than 40,000 accountants), technical (there are over 100,000 engineers and 49,000 computer specialists), and clerical (there are over 100,000 secretaries) to almost every kind of blue-collar occupation (over 15,000 aircraft mechanics, 10,000 pipefitters, and 23,000 warehouse workers are among those employed as of 1992).

So, yes, federal jobs are plentiful, but finding one can require arduous searching so it's important to overcome some common prejudices. The prospect of a "government job" has rather negative connotations for some people who conjure up images of an insurmountable bureaucracy and employees lost under stacks of paper. Opportunities in the federal government can, however, far exceed these expectations. Salaries are not quite commensurate with similar positions in private corporations, but job security and excellent benefits are also strong incentives. The government continues to be an important employer of minorities, offering and enforcing equal opportunity programs which are often sidestepped in the private sector.

A trip to one of the 44 Offices of Personnel Management Federal Job Information Centers (FJIC) can be daunting for any prospective federal employee. Posted in these offices are the semimonthly Federal Job Opportunities Listings. Published on the first and sixteenth of every month, these are long lists of current federal job vacancies, although they are by no means complete.

The first list, *GPA 001,* contains the jobs in the region where the Federal Job Information Center is located; the second list, *Nationwide,* gives federal job opportunities anywhere in the nation or the world. These lists can also be requested through the mail by writing to the FJIC in a particular location. The positions available can range from unskilled worker to nuclear physicist and run the gamut on the General Salary Schedule.

As a guide through the application procedure, the code and control numbers for each position are included on the Opportunities Listings. Each position also has a Qualifications Information Statement (QIS) which gives the required skills, education, and experience necessary for each opening. Applications and QIS statements can be obtained at the FJIC window or by written request. These job centers may also have federal personnel manuals and other reference books on hand.

As incongruous as it may seem, the federal government does not keep a list of *all* federal jobs currently available. Many agencies of the federal government have direct-hire authority and will fill positions rapidly instead of going through the FJIC. To be aware of agency openings you must keep in contact with those agencies which are of interest to you. In recent years, for example, the Central Intelligence Agency has been actively recruiting economists, among other specialists, on many college campuses.

There are two privately run publications that can be very helpful. *Federal Jobs Digest,* a bi-weekly newspaper, tracks federal job vacancies, lists U.S. Postal Exams, and has articles about job fairs, a "College Corner," and veterans' information. Each issue contains an average of approximately 3,000 jobs (Phone: 1-800-824-5000). *Federal Career Opportunities* is a similar publication concentrating on the G-5 level and above. It also catalogs federal job openings in a systematic manner (Phone: 703-281-0200). Both publications are also available at most major libraries.

JOBS FOR COLLEGE GRADUATES

In November 1990, the federal government began a new program to attract college graduates into civil service jobs. The Administrative Careers with America (ACWA) program encompasses 100 types of entry-level jobs which are on the GS-5 to GS-7 levels of the General Schedule (salaries range from $16,973 to $27,332 per annum). The positions are divided into six occupational groups:

1. Benefits Review, Tax, and Legal
2. Business, Finance, and Management
3. Law Enforcement and Investigation
4. Personnel, Administration, and Computers
5. Health, Safety, and Environmental Occupations
6. Writing and Public Information

To be eligible for this program, the applicant must have a bachelor's degree (or expect to receive one within eight months) or a minimum of three years of work experience. A combination of education and experience is also acceptable. There is a written test for each of the six occupational groups. Each test is administered periodically across the nation. After passing the test, the candidate's name is placed on a list from which agencies with vacancies select. A series of interviews is then conducted by the specific agency.

To apply for Administrative Careers with America, first obtain a copy of the Qualifications Information Statement (QIS) for one of the six occupational groups. These can be obtained from any Federal Job Information Center located across the country and can be requested by mail.

Jobs and Salaries in State and Local Government

In the first part of this section will be found the salaries for thousands of leading state and local government leaders—the management team, so to speak, of the political system. Included are governors, mayors, district attorneys, state judges, police and fire chiefs, and commissioners of everything from aviation and sanitation to budgets and zoos. There is a listing for every state and for an array of major cities and counties, and even a sprinkling of data from small towns and villages.

Whether the reader peruses this information or merely skims over each part, he or she will be struck by the incredible diversity of salary levels throughout the country. Some patterns can be seen. For instance, large states and cities usually pay their officials better than small ones do, and the salaries of officials in large cities are usually comparable to those in their state government. But to explain why salaries of officials in Texas are so high when their public employees are paid so poorly, or why Tennessee and South Carolina have such well-paid officials when they rank near the bottom among all states in per capita income is beyond the scope of this book.

Readers should keep in mind, however, that just as the pressure for higher executive salaries in the private sector comes from within, so it is with politicians. If the voters express concern, the reason most often cited for a pay raise is that other officials in the same job elsewhere are getting more money. Another tactic is for the governor or mayor to take the lead in a propaganda campaign aimed at convincing the voters that pay raises are needed at the executive level in order to attract highly talented people into government. Sometimes the question never becomes an issue. On the state level, for example, pay raises for executives are frequently tied to increases for legislators, so bipartisan support is easily achieved.

None of the above is meant to imply that most government officials are currently overpaid, nor does it mean they shouldn't receive salary adjustments for inflation. There is, of course, the age-old argument that government service should be just that, service—not a means to a substantial income. After all, anyone in government paid $65,000 a year or more is earning double the median family income for the entire nation. And, finally, it is imperative for the people to remember that most elected officials are only politicians, not experts in finance, technology, or administration, and their earnings should reflect this.

WHERE THE JOBS ARE STATE BY STATE:
GOVERNMENT EMPLOYMENT AND PAYROLLS BY STATE, OCTOBER 1992[1]

State	Employment (in Thousands)				October Payroll (in Millions)	
	Total	Federal	State	Local	State	Local
U.S. Total	18,686	2,988[2]	4,595	11,103	$9,828	$23,355
Alabama	323	58	95	170	177	280
Alaska	70	16	27	26	77	75
Arizona	268	40	65	163	122	351
Arkansas	170	20	53	96	99	138
California	2,024	312	386	1,326	1,062	3,448
Colorado	288	57	72	159	165	311
Connecticut	198	25	64	110	175	295
Delaware	49	5	24	19	49	45
District of Columbia	279	223	NA	56	NA	171
Florida	879	114	188	577	355	1,129
Georgia	530	93	127	310	234	549
Hawaii	102	25	62	15	131	41
Idaho	87	11	26	50	43	75
Illinois	796	106	164	525	347	1,102
Indiana	397	43	116	238	228	426
Iowa	220	20	60	140	136	224
Kansas	221	26	56	139	101	225
Kentucky	256	38	86	133	166	233
Louisiana	317	35	103	179	190	287
Maine	97	16	27	54	52	88
Maryland	413	137	98	180	223	439
Massachusetts	382	62	102	218	223	517
Michigan	639	59	173	408	402	875
Minnesota	344	34	84	227	191	436
Mississippi	203	26	55	121	94	170
Missouri	363	66	90	206	153	359
Montana	83	12	24	47	38	71
Nebraska	138	16	35	88	60	149
Nevada	85	12	21	52	50	126
New Hampshire	73	8	21	43	38	83
New Jersey	544	74	132	338	352	897
New Mexico	148	28	53	67	88	111
New York	1,428	149	290	989	833	2,689
North Carolina	480	51	127	302	258	531
North Dakota	64	8	22	34	34	45
Ohio	755	95	177	485	353	926
Oklahoma	266	46	79	141	133	225
Oregon	226	31	63	132	130	261

WHERE THE JOBS ARE STATE BY STATE:
GOVERNMENT EMPLOYMENT AND PAYROLLS BY STATE, OCTOBER 1992[1]

	Employment (in Thousands)				October Payroll (in Millions)	
State	**Total**	**Federal**	**State**	**Local**	**State**	**Local**
Pennsylvania	728	132	173	422	$ 401	$ 922
Rhode Island	65	10	24	31	55	76
South Carolina	261	33	91	138	158	238
South Dakota	67	10	18	40	29	45
Tennessee	341	54	91	197	160	352
Texas	1,278	179	278	821	553	1,549
Utah	152	35	46	70	81	111
Vermont	43	5	14	23	31	38
Virginia	569	168	142	259	253	516
Washington	390	69	120	201	249	471
West Virginia	123	17	40	65	65	116
Wisconsin	369	30	97	242	211	464
Wyoming	51	7	13	31	22	53

[1]Employment data are for December 31, 1992. Excludes seasonal and on-call employees, employees outside the 50 states, the Public Health Service's Commissioned Corps, the CIA, the National Security Agency, and the Defense Intelligence Agency.
[2]Includes 41,601 employees of the Federal Courts and the FBI not allocated by state.
SOURCE: U.S. Department of Commerce, *Public Employment: 1991* (1992); U.S. Office of Personnel Management.

THE 50 STATES AND DISTRICT OF COLUMBIA

In the following pages can be found the 1994–1995 salaries for almost every elected and many appointed officials in every state of the union, including all judges who fall under state jurisdiction. Expense allowances are noted whenever they are a significant part of the remuneration, but not every perquisite has been included. All governors, for example, have cars, most have private planes, and about half have private helicopters. In addition, governors of all but five states (Arkansas, Idaho, Massachusetts, Rhode Island, and Vermont) have fully staffed private residences. (The governor of California's residence is paid for by a private nonprofit foundation). The reader should assume that all government officials receive some kind of travel and food benefits.

Most browsers in this section will notice right away that the highest salaries are, quite predictably, paid in the largest, wealthiest states (California, New York, Texas) or heavily industrialized ones (Michigan, Ohio), while small states (Delaware, Rhode Island), or sparsely settled ones (the Dakotas) and impoverished areas (Maine, Mississippi) pay substantially less. Of course, the state of Alaska has special requirements, so just about everyone there earns at least $70,000.

Note that the salaries of some important state administrators (Corrections, Education, Personnel, etc.) also appear in other sections of the book. Check the index for references. The major source of all state figures is *The Book of the States, 1994–95,* published by the Council on State Governments.

ALABAMA

Governor	$81,151	*Judges*	
Lieutenant Governor	49,740	Supreme Court	$107,125
Secretary of State	57,204	Court of Criminal Appeals	106,125
Attorney General	90,475	Court of Civil Appeals	106,125
Treasurer	57,204	Circuit Courts	72,500

The Legislature: 140 members each receive $10 a day for 105 days plus $2,280. They also receive $50 three times a week for committee meetings. The Speaker of the House receives an additional $2 per legislative day.

Selected Administrative Officials

Agriculture	$ 56,806	Highways	$61,073
Banking	61,073	Historic Preservation	64,500
Budget	72,514	Insurance	61,073
Commerce	91,340	Labor	61,073
Community Affairs	61,073	Natural Resources	61,073
Consumer Affairs	51,220	Parks and Recreation	46,358
Corrections	78,000	Personnel	98,525
Education	148,035	Planning	55,008
Elections	29,068	Public Utility Regulation	51,482
Employment Services	46,358	Purchasing	49,972
Energy	55,088	Solid Waste Management	46,358
Environmental Protection	71,000	Tourism	61,073
General Services	43,004	Transportation	33,618
Health	135,000		

ALASKA

Governor	$81,648	*Judges*	
Lieutenant Governor	76,188	Supreme Court	$105,876
Attorney General	86,760	Court of Appeals	98,688
		Superior Courts	96,000

The Legislature: 60 members receive $24,012 each plus $151 for expenses; legislators in Juneau receive $113. The President of the Senate and the Speaker of the House each receives an additional $500 a year.

Selected Administrative Officials

Administration	$83,844	Health	$89,820
Agriculture	70,092	Historic Preservation	65,508
Banking	86,740	Insurance	77,964
Civil Rights	80,772	Labor	83,844
Commerce	83,844	Licensing	70,092
Community Affairs	83,844	Natural Resources	83,844
Consumer Affairs	77,964	Parks and Recreation	86,940
Corrections	83,844	Personnel	72,468
Education	83,844	Public Utility Regulation	72,468
Elections	75,144	Social Services	83,844
Employment Services	75,144	Solid Waste Management	60,864
Environmental Protection	83,844	Tourism	67,800
General Services	80,772	Transportation	83,844

ARIZONA

Governor	$75,000	*Judges*	
Secretary of State	47,735	Supreme Court	$91,728
Attorney General	76,400	Court of Appeals	89,544
Treasurer	54,600	Superior Courts	87,360

The Legislature: 90 members receive $15,000 each plus $35 for expenses ($60 for those living outside Maricopa County).

Selected Administrative Officials

Administration	$ 86,844	Health	$105,000
Agriculture	82,240	Historic Preservation	46,000
Banking	73,706	Insurance	82,091
Budget	86,000	Labor	80,772
Civil Rights	85,430	Natural Resources	54,524
Commerce	80,000	Parks and Recreation	81,772
Consumer Affairs	83,000	Personnel	76,000
Corrections	103,140	Public Utility Regulation	79,000
Education	54,600	Purchasing	66,313
Employment Services	71,000	Social Services	98,000
Energy	62,000	Solid Waste Management	62,000
Environmental Protection	96,000	Tourism	74,485
General Services	75,000	Transportation	100,000

ARKANSAS

Governor	$60,000	*Judges*	
Lieutenant Governor	29,000	Supreme Court	$93,349
Secretary of State	37,500	Court of Appeals	90,379
Attorney General	50,000	Chancery Courts	87,439
Treasurer	37,500	Circuit Courts	87,439

The Legislature: 135 members receive $12,000 each biennial session plus $82 for those living more than 50 miles from the capital. The president pro tem of the Senate and the Speaker of the House each receive an additional $1,500 per year.

Selected Administrative Officials

Administration	$ 91,000
Agriculture	59,675
Banking	79,001
Budget	62,466
Corrections	84,776
Education	87,380
Employment Services	83,703
Energy	67,682
Environmental Protection	69,831
General Services	72,795
Health	126,353

Highways	$95,720
Historic Preservation	48,611
Insurance	68,410
Labor	72,961
Natural Resources	51,000
Parks and Recreation	67,610
Personnel	62,466
Public Utility Regulation	68,745
Purchasing	62,466
Social Services	91,817
Solid Waste Management	69,831
Tourism	49,284

CALIFORNIA

Governor	$114,286	*Judges*	
Lieutenant Governor	90,000	Supreme Court	$127,267
Secretary of State	90,000	Courts of Appeal	119,314
Attorney General	102,000	Superior Courts	104,262
Treasurer	85,714		

The Legislature: 120 members receive $52,500 each plus $101 per day for expenses. The president pro tem of the Senate and the Speaker of the Assembly each receive an additional $10,500 per year. The majority and minority leaders in both houses receive an additional $5,250 per year.

Selected Administrative Officials

Agriculture	$101,343	Highways	$ 67,788
Banking	95,052	Historic Preservation	64,896
Civil Rights	83,869	Insurance	90,526
Commerce	106,410	Labor	101,343
Community Affairs	82,164	Natural Resources	101,343
Consumer Affairs	95,052	Parks and Recreation	95,052
Corrections	95,052	Personnel	95,052
Education	99,804	Planning	95,052
Elections	78,233	Public Utility Regulation	100,173
Employment Services	95,052	Purchasing	82,164
Energy	95,403	Social Services	95,052
Environmental Protection	101,343	Tourism	86,196
General Services	95,052	Transportation	95,052
Health	99,805		

COLORADO

Governor	$60,000	*Judges*	
Lieutenant Governor	48,500	Supreme Court	$84,000
Secretary of State	48,500	Court of Appeals	79,500
Attorney General	60,000	District Court	75,000
Treasurer	48,500		

The Legislature: 100 members receive $17,500 each plus $99 per day for expenses ($45 for Denver area legislators).

Selected Administrative Officials

Agriculture	$77,800	Historic Preservation	$59,500
Banking	69,528	Labor	77,800
Budget	77,800	Licensing	77,800
Civil Rights	69,528	Natural Resources	77,800
Community Affairs	69,528	Parks and Recreation	66,216
Consumer Affairs	67,000	Personnel	77,800
Corrections	77,800	Public Utility Regulation	58,400
Education	94,478	Purchasing	69,528
Elections	77,000	Social Services	77,800
Employment Services	77,800	Solid Waste Management	66,216
Energy	65,000	Tourism	69,528
Environmental Protection	66,216	Transportation	86,300
Health	90,000		

CONNECTICUT

Governor	$78,000	*Judges*	
Lieutenant Governor	55,000	Supreme Court	$106,533
Secretary of State	49,999	Apellate Court	99,087
Attorney General	60,000	Superior Courts	94,647
Treasurer	50,000		

The Legislature: 187 members receive $16,760 each. The president pro tem of the Senate and the Speaker of the House each receive an additional $6,400 a year; the majority and minority leaders of the both the House and Senate receive $5,290 a year. Assistant leaders in both houses earn additional amounts ranging from $2,540 to $4,914.

Selected Administrative Officials

Administration	$77,848	General Services	$71,169
Agriculture	67,639	Health	78,732
Banking	67,639	Highways	72,681
Budget	83,098	Historic Preservation	44,426
Civil Rights	67,639	Insurance	67,639
Community Affairs	67,639	Labor	72,681
Consumer Affairs	67,639	Natural Resources	63,238
Corrections	78,732	Parks and Recreation	68,396
Education	78,732	Personnel	72,681
Elections	54,054	Public Utility Regulation	80,015
Employment Services	67,639	Solid Waste Management	48,317
Energy	67,639	Tourism	56,217
Environmental Protection	72,681	Transportation	78,732

DELAWARE

Governor	$95,000	*Judges*	
Lieutenant Governor	38,400	Supreme Court	$105,100
Secretary of State	80,700	Superior Courts	99,900
Attorney General	88,900		
Treasurer	71,600		

The Legislature: 62 members receive $24,900 each plus $5,000 a year for expenses. The president pro tem of the Senate and the Speaker of the House each receive an additional $9,828 a year; the majority and minority leaders of both the House and Senate receive $7,644 a year.

Selected Administrative Officials

Administration	$ 78,732	Historic Preservation	$58,800
Agriculture	69,300	Insurance	66,000
Banking	74,600	Labor	75,200
Budget	86,400	Licensing	52,300
Civil Rights	6,700	Parks and Recreation	63,400
Consumer Affairs	48,100	Personnel	80,700
Corrections	80,700	Planning	75,200
Education	101,900	Public Utility Regulation	50,600
Elections	43,200	Purchasing	53,000
Energy	28,100	Solid Waste Management	73,100
Environmental Protection	80,700	Tourism	45,900
Health	106,500	Transportation	80,700
Highways	73,600		

FLORIDA

Governor	$97,850	*Judges*	
Lieutenant Governor	93,728	Supreme Court	$103,457
Secretary of State	96,861	District Court of Appeals	98,284
Attorney General	96,490	Circuit Courts	93,111
Treasurer	96,861		

The Legislature: 160 members receive $22,560 each plus $75 a day for 60 days. The president of the Senate and the Speaker of the House each receive an additional $8,772 a year.

Selected Administrative Officials

Administration	$ 75,200	Health	$161,877
Agriculture	96,490	Highways	91,670
Budget	91,155	Historic Preservation	64,502
Civil Rights	31,200	Labor	69,907
Commerce	91,670	Parks and Recreation	76,583
Community Affairs	91,670	Personnel	68,116
Consumer Affairs	67,980	Planning	74,160
Corrections	91,470	Public Utility Regulation	90,097
Education	96,861	Purchasing	70,145
Elections	63,744	Social Services	52,020
Employment Services	77,250	Solid Waste Management	61,800
Energy	75,000	Tourism	65,405
Environmental Protection	91,670	Transportation	90,177
General Services	91,670		

GEORGIA

Governor	$94,390	*Judges*	
Lieutenant Governor	61,647	Supreme Court	$96,118
Secretary of State	75,811	Court of Appeals	95,509
Attorney General	77,536	Superior Courts	73,344
Treasurer	81,500		

The Legislature: 236 members receive $10,641 each plus $59 per day and $4,800 a year expense allowance. The president pro tem of the Senate and the Speaker pro tem in the House each receive $4,800 a year. The Speaker of the House receives $63,582.

Selected Administrative Officials

Administration	$69,850	Energy	$66,816
Agriculture	75,815	Environmental Protection	82,403
Banking	73,521	General Services	71,586
Budget	86,070	Historic Preservation	55,122
Civil Rights	60,456	Insurance	73,950
Commerce	84,852	Labor	75,810
Community Affairs	84,834	Licensing	61,218
Consumer Affairs	66,816	Natural Resources	81,333
Corrections	73,512	Parks and Recreation	81,512
Education	77,536	Personnel	84,870
Elections	68,136	Public Utility Regulation	79,972
Employment Services	65,610	Purchasing	60,744

Social Services	$70,000	Tourism	$80,472
Solid Waste Management	58,512	Transportation	105,000

HAWAII

Governor	$94,780	*Judges*	
Lieutenant Governor	90,041	Supreme Court	$93,780
Attorney General	85,302	Intermediate Court	89,780
		Circuit Courts	86,780

The Legislature: 76 members receive $32,000 each plus a $5,000 a year expense allowance. Legislators not from Oahu receive an additional $80 a day. The president of the Senate and the Speaker of the House each receive an additional $5,000 a year.

Selected Administrative Officials

Agriculture	$85,302	Highways	$83,580
Banking	74,652	Insurance	74,655
Budget	85,032	Labor	85,302
Civil Rights	68,412	Natural Resources	85,302
Commerce	85,302	Parks and Recreation	58,932
Community Affairs	74,880	Personnel	85,302
Consumer Affairs	74,655	Planning	85,302
Corrections	85,302	Public Utility Regulation	77,964
Education	90,041	Purchasing	50,364
Employment Services	74,028	Social Services	85,302
Energy	85,116	Solid Waste Management	61,572
Environmental Protection	76,404	Transportation	85,302
Health	85,302		

IDAHO

Governor	$75,000	*Judges*	
Lieutenant Governor	20,000	Supreme Court	$79,183
Secretary of State	62,500	Court of Appeals	78,183
Attorney General	67,500	District Courts	74,214
Treasurer	62,500		

The Legislature: 105 members receive $12,000 each plus $70 per day for expenses (legislators who don't establish a second residence receive $40 per day plus $25 for round-trip travel) in addition to $500 a year expense allowance. The president pro tem of the Senate and the Speaker of the House each receive an additional $3,000 a year.

Selected Administrative Officials

Administration	$65,125	Historic Preservation	$51,022
Agriculture	66,747	Insurance	63,565
Banking	68,390	Labor	59,093
Civil Rights	48,610	Licensing	40,955
Commerce	63,565	Parks and Recreation	68,390
Community Affairs	39,998	Personnel	65,125
Corrections	71,843	Public Utility Regulation	59,987
Education	62,500	Purchasing	46,301
Elections	57,637	Social Services	71,843
Employment Services	65,125	Solid Waste Management	49,795
Energy	53,602	Tourism	46,301
Environmental Protection	70,075	Transportation	85,176
Health	85,176		

ILLINOIS

Governor	$103,097	*Judges*	
Lieutenant Governor	72,775	Supreme Court	$103,097
Secretary of State	90,968	Appellate Court	97,032
Attorney General	90,968	Circuit Courts	82,977
Treasurer	78,839		

The Legislature: 177 members receive $38,420 each plus $81 per day for expenses. The Speaker of the House receives an additional $16,000 a year; the president pro tem of the Senate (who also serves as the majority leader) and the minority leaders of both the House and Senate each receive $16,000; the majority leader of the House receives an additional $13,500. Assistant leaders in the Senate earn an additional $12,000, while in the House, supplements range from $6,000 to $11,500 for assistant leaders.

Selected Administrative Officials

Administration	$ 75,806	Commerce	$72,775
Agriculture	72,775	Corrections	85,000
Banking	75,444	Education	133,076
Budget	82,000	Elections	73,500
Civil Rights	63,071	Employment Service	78,839

Energy	$63,071	Natural Resources	$72,775
Environmental Protection	72,775	Personnel	52,752
Health	78,839	Planning	76,875
Highways	84,876	Public Utility Regulation	72,881
Historic Preservation	61,320	Purchasing	55,656
Insurance	66,710	Social Services	76,991
Labor	66,710	Solid Waste Management	59,964
Licensing	66,710	Transportation	78,839

INDIANA

Governor	$77,200	*Judges*	
Lieutenant Governor	64,000	Supreme Court	$81,000
Secretary of State	46,000	Court of Appeals	76,500
Attorney General	59,200	Circuit Courts	61,740
Treasurer	46,000	Superior Courts	61,740

The Legislature: 150 members receive $11,600 each plus $105 per day for expenses. The president pro tem of the Senate and the Speaker of the House each receive an additional $6,500 a year. The speaker pro tem in the House and the majority and minority leaders in both houses earn an additional $5,000 per year. Other Senate leaders receive supplements ranging from $1,500 to $5,000 per year.

Selected Administrative Officials

Administration	$71,804	Historic Preservation	$38,142
Agriculture	47,814	Insurance	54,106
Banking	66,196	Labor	55,718
Budget	81,120	Natural Resources	73,190
Civil Rights	53,560	Parks and Recreation	51,948
Community Affairs	64,402	Personnel	66,950
Consumer Affairs	61,802	Planning	70,096
Corrections	73,086	Public Utility Regulation	56,212
Education	63,100	Purchasing	55,510
Elections	41,236	Social Services	73,450
Employment Services	38,558	Solid Waste Management	45,292
Energy	42,484	Tourism	59,566
Environmental Protection	75,218	Transportation	75,218
Health	89,856		

IOWA

Governor	$76,700	*Judges*	
Lieutenant Governor	60,000	Supreme Court	$90,300
Secretary of State	60,000	Court of Appeals	86,800
Attorney General	73,600	District Courts	82,500
Treasurer	60,000		

The Legislature: 150 members receive $18,100 each plus $50 per day for expenses ($35 for Polk County legislators). The president pro tem of the Senate receives an additional $1,000 a year, and the Speaker of the House, and the majority and minority leaders of both the House and Senate each receive $9,800.

Selected Administrative Officials

Agriculture	$60,000	Highways	$72,030
Banking	57,750	Historic Preservation	65,062
Budget	73,273	Insurance	61,505
Civil Rights	50,586	Labor	58,422
Commerce	59,850	Licensing	42,866
Community Affairs	63,440	Natural Resources	72,429
Consumer Affairs	70,096	Parks and Recreation	60,778
Corrections	70,500	Personnel	68,250
Education	99,900	Public Utility Regulation	68,194
Employment Services	71,703	Purchasing	50,482
Energy	69,971	Social Services	76,856
Environmental Protection	69,971	Solid Waste Management	60,778
General Services	68,000	Tourism	64,293
Health	68,250	Transportation	82,206

KANSAS

Governor	$74,476	*Judges*	
Lieutenant Governor	71,642	Supreme Court	$84,465
Secretary of State	59,112	Court of Appeals	81,451
Attorney General	68,328	District Courts	73,430
Treasurer	59,400	District Magistrate Judge	34,670

The Legislature: 165 members receive $62 a day in salary each plus $73 for expenses. The president pro tem of the Senate (whose official title is vice-president) and the Speaker pro tem of the House each receive an additional

$4,999. The Speaker of the House earns an additional $9,415. The majority and minority leaders of both the House and Senate each receive an additional $8,836 a year. Supplements for assistant leaders range from $15 per day to $4,999 per year.

Selected Administrative Officials

Administration	$ 76,920	Health	$ 78,000
Agriculture	65,880	Historic Preservation	41,892
Banking	57,000	Insurance	63,000
Budget	72,180	Labor	70,000
Civil Rights	42,720	Licensing	46,371
Commerce	76,200	Parks and Recreation	60,600
Community Affairs	49,440	Personnel	70,000
Consumer Affairs	47,112	Public Utility Regulation	70,500
Corrections	79,200	Social Services	63,425
Education	102,125	Solid Waste Management	29,856
Elections	35,688	Tourism	70,000
Employment Services	73,200	Transportation	70,000
Energy	29,988		

KENTUCKY

Governor	$81,647	*Judges*	
Lieutenant Governor	69,412	Supreme Court	$78,273
Secretary of State	67,378	Court of Appeals	75,078
Attorney General	69,412	Circuit Courts	71,883
Treasurer	69,412		

The Legislature: 138 members each receive $100 a day plus $75 for expenses. The president of the Senate and the Speaker of the House each receive an additional $25 per legislative day. The president pro tem of the Senate and the Speaker of the House pro tem each receive an additional $15 per legislative day, while the majority and minority leaders in both houses receive an additional $20 per legislative day.

Selected Administrative Officials

Administration	$ 59,370	Education	$135,000
Agriculture	69,412	Elections	59,177
Banking	61,383	Employment Service	59,177
Civil Rights	63,000	Energy	52,839
Community Affairs	60,600	Environmental Protection	60,600
Corrections	62,620	Health	112,000

Highways	$70,708	Personnel	$70,000
Historic Preservation	46,000	Public Utility Regulation	70,500
Insurance	63,000	Social Services	63,425
Labor	70,000	Solid Waste Management	29,856
Licensing	46,371	Tourism	70,000
Parks and Recreation	60,600	Transportation	70,000

LOUISIANA

Governor	$73,440	*Judges*	
Lieutenant Governor	63,367	Supreme Court	$94,000
Secretary of State	60,169	Court of Appeals	89,000
Attorney General	66,566	District Courts	84,000
Treasurer	60,169		

The Legislature: 144 members receive $16,800 each plus $75 per day for expenses. The president of the Senate and the Speaker of the House each receive an additional $32,000 a year.

Selected Administrative Officials

Administration	$69,156	Historic Preservation	$45,600
Agriculture	60,169	Insurance	60,169
Banking	75,920	Labor	60,328
Budget	69,360	Licensing	61,380
Civil Rights	34,000	Natural Resources	58,451
Community Affairs	62,500	Parks and Recreation	45,600
Consumer Affairs	40,000	Personnel	86,616
Corrections	60,320	Planning	51,768
Education	95,000	Public Utility Regulation	64,008
Elections	60,169	Purchasing	61,692
Employment Services	47,413	Social Services	60,320
Energy	55,728	Solid Waste Management	60,000
Environmental Protection	68,000	Tourism	52,008
Health	75,000	Transportation	70,000

MAINE

Governor	$69,992	*Judges*	
Secretary of State	49,587	Supreme Judicial Court	$83,616
Attorney General	66,123	Superior Court	79,073
Treasurer	60,008		

The Legislature: 186 members receive $9,975 each plus $70 per day for expenses. The president of the Senate and the Speaker of the House each receive an additional $4,000 a year; the majority and minority leaders of both the House and Senate each receive an additional $2,250 a year.

Selected Administrative Officials

Administration	$77,896	Historic Preservation	$60,154
Agriculture	64,188	Insurance	63,461
Banking	69,846	Labor	70,658
Budget	62,462	Licensing	30,742
Civil Rights	52,666	Parks and Recreation	61,256
Consumer Affairs	54,995	Personnel	62,462
Corrections	70,658	Planning	68,557
Education	77,896	Public Utility Regulation	76,336
Elections	47,216	Purchasing	50,024
Employment Services	57,138	Social Services	74,110
Environmental Protection	64,188	Solid Waste Management	60,466
General Services	62,462	Tourism	54,226
Health	74,110	Transportation	77,896

MARYLAND

Governor	$120,000	*Judges*	
Lieutenant Governor	100,000	Court of Appeals	$99,000
Secretary of State	70,000	Court of Special Appeals	92,500
Attorney General	100,000	Circuit Courts	89,000
Treasurer	100,000		

The Legislature: 188 members receive $28,000 each plus $98 per day for expenses.

Selected Administrative Officials

Agriculture	$85,027	Employment Services	$57,868
Banking	62,497	Energy	62,497
Budget	99,175	Environmental Protection	85,027
Civil Rights	67,496	General Services	85,027
Commerce	62,497	Health	99,175
Community Affairs	62,497	Highways	93,500
Consumer Affairs	62,497	Historic Preservation	62,497
Corrections	72,896	Insurance	90,000
Education	91,828	Labor	62,497
Elections	62,497	Licensing	85,027

Natural Resources	$91,828	Purchasing	$40,959
Parks and Recreation	57,868	Social Services	67,496
Personnel	85,027	Solid Waste Management	40,959
Planning	67,496	Tourism	57,868
Public Utility Regulation	72,896	Transportation	99,175

MASSACHUSETTS

Governor	$75,000	*Judges*	
Lieutenant Governor	60,000	Supreme Judicial Court	$90,450
Secretary of State	85,000	Appeals Court	83,708
Attorney General	62,500	Trial Court	80,360
Treasurer	60,000		

The Legislature: 200 members receive $30,000 each plus $2,400 a year in expenses and $5 to $50 per day in travel expenses, depending on distance from the capital.

Selected Administrative Officials

Administration	$73,156	Highways	$73,156
Agriculture	53,570	Historic Preservation	63,273
Banking	69,015	Insurance	66,000
Budget	77,547	Labor	55,648
Civil Rights	50,117	Licensing	63,273
Community Affairs	69,015	Natural Resources	77,547
Consumer Affairs	64,482	Personnel	73,156
Corrections	58,912	Public Utility Regulation	69,075
Education	77,547	Purchasing	73,156
Elections	69,015	Social Services	77,547
Energy	63,272	Solid Waste Management	68,048
Environmental Protection	66,606	Tourism	50,117
Health	77,547	Transportation	70,666

MICHIGAN

Governor	$112,025	*Judges*	
Lieutenant Governor	84,315	Supreme Court	$111,941
Secretary of State	109,000	Court of Appeals	107,463
Attorney General	109,000	Circuit Courts	61,565
Treasurer	87,300	Recorder's Court (Detroit)	102,968

The Legislature: 148 members receive $47,723 each per year.

Selected Administrative Officials

Agriculture	$87,300	Historic Preservation	$74,980
Banking	75,000	Insurance	74,980
Budget	87,300	Labor	87,300
Civil Rights	87,300	Licensing	85,942
Commerce	87,300	Natural Resources	87,300
Community Affairs	74,980	Parks and Recreation	74,980
Consumer Affairs	68,131	Personnel	85,942
Corrections	87,300	Public Utility Regulation	75,000
Education	87,300	Purchasing	46,520
Employment Services	74,980	Social Services	90,285
Environmental Protection	87,300	Solid Waste Management	74,980
General Services	74,980	Tourism	74,980
Health	87,300	Transportation	87,300

MINNESOTA

Governor	$109,053	*Judges*	
Lieutenant Governor	59,981	Supreme Court	$94,395
Secretary of State	59,981	Court of Appeals	88,945
Attorney General	85,194	District Courts	83,494
Treasurer	59,981		

The Legislature: 201 members receive $27,929 each plus $50 per day for expenses and up to $450 a month housing for senators. Representatives living more than 50 miles from the capital receive $48 per day and up to $500 a month for housing. The Speaker of the House and the majority and minority leaders of both the House and Senate each receive an additional $11,191.60 a year.

Selected Administrative Officials

Administration	$67,500	Employment Services	$64,832
Agriculture	67,500	Energy	56,146
Banking	67,500	Environmental Protection	54,622
Civil Rights	60,000	Health	67,500
Commerce	67,500	Highways	78,300
Community Affairs	65,500	Labor	67,500
Consumer Affairs	74,300	Licensing	66,649
Corrections	67,500	Natural Resources	67,500
Education	78,500	Parks and Recreation	58,026

Personnel	$67,500	Social Services	$70,386
Planning	67,500	Solid Waste Management	63,496
Public Utility Regulation	54,497	Tourism	67,484
Purchasing	67,484	Transportation	78,500

MISSISSIPPI

Governor	$75,600	*Judges*	
Lieutenant Governor	40,800	Supreme Court	$90,800
Secretary of State	59,400	Chancery Courts	81,200
Attorney General	68,400	Circuit Courts	81,200
Treasurer	59,400		

The Legislature: 174 members receive $10,000 each plus $82 per day for expenses.

Selected Administrative Officials

Administration	$51,656	Highways	$80,125
Agriculture	59,400	Historic Preservation	58,000
Banking	59,200	Insurance	59,400
Community Affairs	47,461	Licensing	59,400
Corrections	68,572	Parks and Recreation	71,005
Education	97,344	Personnel	73,614
Elections	45,604	Planning	50,133
Employment Services	61,600	Public Utility Regulation	43,600
Energy	47,461	Purchasing	43,392
Environmental		Social Services	39,259
Protection	71,005	Solid Waste Management	34,667
Health	98,304	Tourism	47,462

MISSOURI

Governor	$91,615	*Judges*	
Lieutenant Governor	55,286	Supreme Court	$92,910
Secretary of State	73,450	Court of Appeals	86,755
Attorney General	79,505	Circuit Courts	
Treasurer	73,450	Municipal Division of	
		Circuit Courts	up to 70,810

The Legislature: 197 members receive $22,862.52 each plus $35 per day for expenses. The president pro tem of the Senate and the Speaker of the

House each receive an additional $2,500 a year. The majority and minority leaders of the Senate receive $1,500 a year on top of their salaries.

Selected Administrative Officials

Administration	$79,505	Highways	$82,596
Agriculture	70,422	Historic Preservation	36,408
Banking	60,105	Insurance	70,422
Budget	66,639	Labor	70,422
Civil Rights	52,056	Licensing	56,448
Community Affairs	66,612	Natural Resources	70,422
Corrections	70,422	Parks and Recreation	60,094
Education	80,280	Personnel	56,461
Elections	34,992	Planning	66,639
Employment Services	67,000	Public Utility Regulation	70,422
Energy	43,969	Purchasing	56,461
Environmental Protection	63,735	Social Services	73,450
General Services	56,461	Solid Waste Management	43,830
Health	86,244	Tourism	56,448

MONTANA

Governor	$55,850	*Judges*	
Lieutenant Governor	40,310	Supreme Court	$64,452
Secretary of State	37,525	District Courts	63,178
Attorney General	50,646		
Treasurer	54,305		

The Legislature: 150 members receive $57.07 for each day of the biennial session, plus $50 for expenses. The president of the Senate and the Speaker of the House each receive an additional $5 per legislative day.

Selected Administrative Officials

Administration	$61,265	Energy	$52,452
Agriculture	67,274	Environmental Protection	78,409
Banking	75,031	General Services	58,926
Budget	67,234	Health	93,045
Civil Rights	73,894	Historic Preservation	62,500
Community Affairs	44,148	Insurance	32,999
Consumer Affairs	46,992	Labor	54,305
Corrections	67,298	Licensing	40,845
Education	96,372	Natural Resources	41,099
Employment Services	57,372	Parks and Recreation	43,091

Personnel	$50,014	Solid Waste Management	$45,261
Public Utility Regulation	48,590	Tourism	43,780
Purchasing	35,996	Transportation	47,667
Social Services	54,305		

NEBRASKA

Governor	$65,000	*Judges*	
Lieutenant Governor	47,000	Supreme Court	$88,157
Secretary of State	52,000	Court of Appeals	83,749
Attorney General	64,500	District Courts	81,546
Treasurer	49,500		

The Legislature: 49 members receive $12,000 each plus $73 per day for expenses; legislators residing within 50 miles of the capital receive $26 per day.

Selected Administrative Officials

Administration	$61,265	Historic Preservation	$62,500
Agriculture	67,274	Insurance	65,106
Banking	75,031	Labor	55,967
Budget	67,234	Licensing	55,692
Civil Rights	73,894	Natural Resources	58,220
Community Affairs	44,148	Parks and Recreation	77,411
Consumer Affairs	46,992	Personnel	60,800
Corrections	67,298	Planning	54,421
Education	96,372	Public Utility Regulation	46,968
Employment Services	57,372	Social Services	62,778
Energy	52,452	Solid Waste Management	54,996
Environmental Protection	78,409	Tourism	44,952
General Services	58,926	Transportation	80,500
Health	93,045		

NEVADA

Governor	$90,000	*Judges*	
Lieutenant Governor	20,000	Supreme Court	$85,000
Secretary of State	62,000	District Courts	79,000
Attorney General	85,000		
Treasurer	62,000		

The Legislature: 63 members receive $30 for each day of the biennial session plus $66 for expenses. The president pro tem of the Senate and the Speaker of the House each receive an additional $2 per legislative day.

Selected Administrative Officials

Administration	$80,950	Historic Preservation	$34,177
Agriculture	60,000	Insurance	69,997
Banking	60,655	Labor	47,284
Civil Rights	53,290	Natural Resources	80,950
Commerce	80,950	Parks and Recreation	57,000
Consumer Affairs	46,100	Personnel	68,000
Corrections	80,950	Public Utility Regulation	69,997
Education	80,950	Purchasing	40,752
Elections	38,220	Social Services	81,294
Employment Services	63,991	Solid Waste Management	75,000
Environmental Protection	75,000	Tourism	66,393
Health	63,210	Transportation	80,950

NEW HAMPSHIRE

Governor	$82,325	*Judges*	
Secretary of State	50,955	Supreme Court	$95,623
Attorney General	73,492	Superior Court	89,628
Treasurer	50,955		

The Legislature: 424 members receive $100 each. The president of the Senate and the Speaker of the House each receive an additional $25 a year.

Selected Administrative Officials

Administration	$73,492	Health	$84,765
Agriculture	43,127	Historic Preservation	45,088
Banking	54,883	Insurance	73,492
Budget	50,955	Labor	73,492
Civil Rights	34,593	Parks and Recreation	43,127
Commerce	73,492	Personnel	50,955
Community Affairs	59,410	Public Utility Regulation	73,492
Corrections	56,842	Purchasing	36,134
Education	73,492	Social Services	73,492
Employment Services	50,955	Solid Waste Management	36,133
Energy	46,575	Tourism	36,133
Environmental Protection	56,842	Transportation	73,492

NEW JERSEY

Governor	$ 85,000	*Judges*	
Secretary of State	100,225	Supreme Court	$115,000
Attorney General	100,255	Appellate Division of the Superior Court	108,000
Treasurer	100,225	Superior Court	100,000

The Legislature: 120 members receive $35,000 each. The president of the Senate and the Speaker of the House each receive an additional $11,667 a year.

Selected Administrative Officials

Banking	$50,999	Insurance	100,225
Budget	59,991	Labor	83,667
Civil Rights	54,383	Licensing	78,000
Community Affairs	60,471	Natural Resources	74,500
Consumer Affairs	60,827	Parks and Recreation	71,199
Corrections	64,906	Personnel	100,225
Education	76,017	Planning	94,500
Elections	55,793	Public Utility Regulation	83,472
Energy	54,887	Purchasing	86,100
Environmental Protection	64,906	Social Services	100,225
General Services	64,906	Solid Waste Management	73,980
Health	67,300	Tourism	80,000
Highways	64,906	Transportation	100,225
Historic Preservation	49,085		

NEW MEXICO

Governor	$90,000	*Judges*	
Lieutenant Governor	65,500	Superior Court	77,250
Secretary of State	65,500	Court of Appeals	73,388
Attorney General	72,500	District Courts	69,719
Treasurer	65,500		

The Legislature: 112 members receive $75 a day each.

Selected Administrative Officials

Banking	$50,999	Civil Rights	$54,383
Budget	59,991	Community Affairs	60,471

Consumer Affairs	$60,827	Insurance	$64,563
Corrections	64,906	Labor	64,906
Education	76,017	Licensing	65,341
Elections	55,793	Natural Resources	43,163
Energy	54,887	Parks and Recreation	58,025
Environmental Protection	64,906	Personnel	59,277
General Services	64,906	Public Utility Regulation	61,940
Health	67,300	Purchasing	49,314
Highways	64,906	Social Services	57,208
Historic Preservation	49,085	Solid Waste Management	49,655
		Tourism	64,906

NEW YORK

Governor	$130,000	*Judges*	
Lieutenant Governor	110,000	Court of Appeals	$125,000
Secretary of State	90,832	Appellate divisions of Supreme Court	119,000
Attorney General	110,000	Supreme Court	113,000

The Legislature: 211 members receive $57,500 each plus $89 per day for legislators on in-state business or $130 per day for business out of the state or in the New York City metro area. The president pro tem of the Senate (also serves as majority leader) and the Speaker of the House each receive an additional $30,000 a year. The minority leader of the Senate and the majority and minority leaders of the House receive an additional $25,000 a year. Assistant leaders receive supplements ranging from $9,000 to $24,500 per year.

Selected Administrative Officials

Agriculture	$ 90,832	General Services	$ 95,635
Banking	90,832	Health	102,335
Budget	100,528	Insurance	90,832
Civil Rights	82,614	Labor	95,635
Consumer Affairs	76,421	Parks and Recreation	90,832
Corrections	102,335	Personnel	90,832
Education	136,500	Public Utility Regulation	95,635
Elections	82,614	Social Services	102,335
Energy	90,832	Transportation	102,335
Environmental Protection	95,635		

NORTH CAROLINA

Governor	$93,777	*Judges*	
Lieutenant Governor	77,289	Supreme Court	$91,855
Secretary of State	77,289	Court of Appeals	86,996
Attorney General	77,289	Superior Court	77,289
Treasurer	77,289		

The Legislature: 170 members receive $13,206 each plus $92 per day and $522 a month in expense allowances. The president pro tem of the Senate receives an additional $35,622 per year plus $1,320 a month expense allowance. The deputy president pro tem receives $20,298 per year plus $780 per month in expenses. Majority and minority leaders in the Senate receive an additional $15,918 per year plus a $622 per month in expenses. The Speaker of the House receives an additional $22,596. The speaker pro tem receives $7,272, and the majority and minority leaders in the House receive $2,892 a year.

Selected Administrative Officials

Administration	$77,289	Highways	$98,550
Agriculture	77,289	Historic Preservation	53,707
Banking	74,389	Insurance	77,289
Budget	94,070	Labor	77,289
Civil Rights	45,412	Natural Resources	77,289
Commerce	77,289	Parks and Recreation	60,495
Community Affairs	62,133	Personnel	77,289
Corrections	77,289	Planning	59,514
Education	77,289	Public Utility Regulation	78,289
Elections	41,871	Purchasing	67,701
Employment Services	74,389	Social Services	78,806
Energy	51,431	Solid Waste Management	44,169
Environmental Protection	69,938	Tourism	63,022
Health	94,372	Transportation	77,289

NORTH DAKOTA

Governor	$68,280	*Judges*	
Lieutenant Governor	56,112	Supreme Court	$71,555
Secretary of State	51,744	District Courts	65,970
Attorney General	58,416		
Treasurer	51,744		

The Legislature: 147 members receive $2,160 per year plus $90 for each day of the biennial session and $35 a day for expenses, not to exceed $600 a month. The president pro tem of the Senate, the Speaker of the House, and the majority and minority leaders of both houses each receive $10 for each calendar day of the session.

Selected Administrative Officials

Administration	$ 68,724	Health	$110,724
Agriculture	51,744	Historic Preservation	$35,880
Banking	52,992	Insurance	51,744
Community Affairs	44,604	Labor	51,744
Consumer Affairs	33,732	Natural Resources	40,176
Corrections	49,200	Parks and Recreation	53,124
Education	52,788	Personnel	47,316
Elections	26,880	Public Utility Regulation	51,744
Employment Services	59,016	Solid Waste Management	42,720
Energy	41,040	Tourism	41,412
Environmental Protection	60,864	Transportation	65,712

OHIO

Governor	$110,250	*Judges*	
Lieutenant Governor	57,011	Supreme Court	$101,150
Secretary of State	81,445	Court of Appeals	94,200
Attorney General	85,517	Courts of Common Pleas	72,650
Treasurer	85,517		

The Legislature: 132 members receive $42,426.90 each. The president of the Senate and the Speaker of the House each receive an additional $23,706.83 a year. The Senate president pro tem and minority leader each earn an additional $17,913 per year. Other Senate leaders earn additional amounts, ranging from $1,958.68 to $14,411.53 per year.

Selected Administrative Officials

Administration	$ 89,253	Corrections	$87,734
Agriculture	78,749	Education	119,621
Banking	68,099	Elections	64,896
Budget	93,896	Employment Services	89,971
Civil Rights	72,613	Energy	64,501
Commerce	60,590	Environmental Protection	84,011
Community Affairs	74,651	Health	97,698
Consumer Affairs	55,245	Historic Preservation	58,489

Insurance	$78,749	Purchasing	$65,686
Labor	78,749	Social Services	93,891
Natural Resources	85,051	Solid Waste Management	61,963
Personnel	67,766	Tourism	54,600
Public Utility Regulation	85,010	Transportation	91,998

OKLAHOMA

Governor	$70,000	*Judges*	
Lieutenant Governor	40,000	Supreme Court	$83,871
Secretary of State	42,500	Court of Appeals	78,660
Attorney General	55,000	District Courts and Judges	71,330
Treasurer	50,000		

The Legislature: 149 members receive $32,000 each plus $35 per day for expenses for members unable to live at home. The president pro tem of the Senate receives an additional $14,940 a year; the Senate majority and minority leaders each receive an additional $10,304 a year. The Speaker of the House receives an additional $46,944 per year; majority and minority leaders in the House receive an additional $42,303.96 per year.

Selected Administrative Officials

Administration	$69,320	Highways	$73,100
Agriculture	63,000	Historic Preservation	55,020
Banking	71,954	Insurance	62,000
Civil Rights	48,228	Labor	42,140
Commerce	93,450	Personnel	59,661
Consumer Affairs	47,920	Public Utility Regulation	52,000
Corrections	72,180	Purchasing	53,140
Education	55,000	Social Services	85,000
Elections	65,962	Solid Waste Management	45,150
Energy	64,493	Tourism	63,441
Environmental Protection	70,000	Transportation	72,934
Health	95,620		

OREGON

Governor	$80,000	*Judges*	
Secretary of State	61,500	Supreme Court	$83,700
Attorney General	66,000	Court of Appeals	81,700
Treasurer	61,500	Tax Court	78,600
		Circuit Courts	76,200

The Legislature: 90 members each receive $13,104 per year plus $73 per day for expenses. The president of the Senate and the Speaker of the House each receive an additional $11,868 a year.

Selected Administrative Officials

Administration	$88,296	Historic Preservation	$71,400
Agriculture	76,332	Insurance	76,332
Banking	69,180	Labor	61,500
Budget	76,332	Parks and Recreation	76,332
Civil Rights	62,784	Personnel	76,332
Community Affairs	78,600	Planning	69,180
Corrections	84,096	Public Utility Regulation	76,332
Education	61,500	Purchasing	62,784
Elections	69,180	Social Services	92,760
Employment Services	76,332	Solid Waste Management	56,904
Energy	56,904	Tourism	62,784
Environmental Protection	76,332	Transportation	84,096
Health	76,332		

PENNSYLVANIA

Governor	$105,000	*Judges*	
Lieutenant Governor	83,000	Supreme Court	$108,045
Secretary of State	72,000	Superior Court	104,444
Attorney General	84,000	Commonwealth Court	104,444
Treasurer	84,000	Courts of Common Pleas	92,610

The Legislature: 253 members each receive $47,000 per year. Per diem living expenses are $88 for Senators, $109 for House members. The president pro tem of the Senate and the Speaker of the House each receive an additional $26,370 a year. The majority and minority leaders of both the House and Senate each receive an additional $21,097 a year.

Selected Administrative Officials

Agriculture	$72,000	Elections	$49,174
Banking	72,000	Employment Services	74,900
Budget	80,000	Energy	71,531
Civil Rights	74,211	Environmental Protection	75,900
Commerce	76,000	General Services	76,000
Community Affairs	72,000	Health	80,000
Corrections	80,000	Highways	75,900
Education	80,000	Historic Preservation	66,993

Insurance	$72,000	Public Utility Regulation	$78,500
Labor	80,000	Purchasing	61,301
Natural Resources	80,000	Social Services	71,750
Parks and Recreation	68,440	Solid Waste Management	62,670
Personnel	75,900	Transportation	80,000
Planning	80,000		

RHODE ISLAND

Governor	$69,900	*Judges*	
Lieutenant Governor	52,000	Supreme Court	$99,431
Secretary of State	52,000	Superior Court	89,521
Attorney General	55,000		
Treasurer	52,000		

The Legislature: 150 members receive $5 a day each. The Speaker of the House receives an additional $5 a day.

Selected Administrative Officials

Administration	$ 83,763	Insurance	$ 63,676
Agriculture	51,139	Labor	70,922
Banking	58,294	Licensing	53,516
Budget	82,557	Parks and Recreation	59,343
Civil Rights	41,073	Personnel	72,283
Community Affairs	69,079	Planning	79,656
Corrections	83,763	Public Utility Regulation	77,156
Education	105,000	Purchasing	78,191
Elections	38,057	Social Services	105,383
Employment Services	80,954	Solid Waste Management	42,724
Environmental Protection	78,626	Tourism	52,189
Health	112,593	Transportation	99,159

SOUTH CAROLINA

Governor	$103,998	*Judges*	
Lieutenant Governor	44,737	Supreme Court	$92,986
Secretary of State	90,203	Court of Appeals	88,338
Attorney General	90,203	Circuit Courts	88,338
Treasurer	90,203		

The Legislature: 170 members receive $10,400 each plus $83 per day for expenses. The president of the Senate receives an additional $1,575 per year; the president pro tem receives an additional $7,500 a year; the Speaker of the House receives an additional $11,000 a year; and the speaker pro tem receives an additional $3,600 per year.

Selected Administrative Officials

Administration	$75,442	Historic Preservation	$ 33,552
Agriculture	90,203	Insurance	70,784
Budget	73,462	Labor	63,913
Civil Rights	70,784	Natural Resources	51,000
Commerce	85,107	Parks and Recreation	65,660
Consumer Affairs	70,784	Personnel	73,462
Corrections	99,314	Public Utility Regulation	58,438
Education	90,203	Purchasing	44,157
Elections	52,207	Social Services	87,087
Employment Services	95,137	Solid Waste Management	42,456
Energy	57,120	Tourism	44,157
Environmental Protection	71,004	Transportation	103,273
Health	99,314		

SOUTH DAKOTA

Governor	$72,475	*Judges*	
Lieutenant Governor	9,889	Supreme Court	$72,079
Secretary of State	49,244	Circuit Courts	67,314
Attorney General	61,556		
Treasurer	49,244		

The Legislature: 105 members receive $4,267 each in odd-numbered years and $3,733 in even-numbered years, plus $75 per day for expenses.

Selected Administrative Officials

Administration	$64,742	Education	$64,472
Agriculture	61,491	Elections	34,143
Banking	68,543	Employment Services	33,613
Civil Rights	24,170	Energy	67,742
Commerce	64,642	Environmental Protection	73,784
Consumer Affairs	52,000	Health	67,742
Corrections	66,486	Highways	56,634

Historic Preservation	$46,300	Public Utility Regulation	$50,315
Labor	58,329	Purchasing	55,307
Licensing	28,911	Social Services	77,278
Natural Resources	64,742	Solid Waste Management	48,500
Parks and Recreation	52,944	Tourism	61,384
Personnel	64,742	Transportation	74,507

TENNESSEE

Governor	$85,000	*Judges*	
Secretary of State	80,700	Supreme Court	$96,348
Attorney General	100,200	Court of Criminal Appeals	91,860
Treasurer	80,800	Chancery Courts	87,900
		Circuit Courts	87,900
		Criminal Courts	87,900

The Legislature: 132 members received $16,500 each plus $82 per day for expenses. The president of the Senate (who also serves as lieutenant governor) and the Speaker of the House each receive an additional $750 per session plus $5,700 in local office expenses.

Selected Administrative Officials

Agriculture	$68,892	Historic Preservation	$42,120
Banking	71,388	Insurance	71,388
Budget	70,740	Labor	68,892
Civil Rights	60,756	Natural Resources	75,732
Consumer Affairs	43,368	Parks and Recreation	59,028
Corrections	75,732	Personnel	71,388
Education	80,076	Planning	47,844
Elections	57,300	Public Utility Regulation	80,700
Employment Services	71,388	Purchasing	55,284
Energy	44,004	Social Services	50,916
Environmental Protection	70,836	Solid Waste Management	60,024
General Services	68,892	Tourism	71,388
Health	75,732	Transportation	75,732

TEXAS

Governor	$99,122	*Judges*	
Lieutenant Governor	99,122	Supreme Court	$94,865
Secretary of State	76,967	Court of Appeals	89,952
Attorney General	79,247	District Courts	85,217
Treasurer	79,247		

The Legislature: 181 members receive $7,200 a year each plus $90 per day for expenses.

Selected Administrative Officials

Agriculture	$79,247	Health	$148,681
Banking	97,066	Historic Preservation	53,362
Budget	79,567	Insurance	150,000
Civil Rights	54,768	Labor	53,515
Commerce	79,536	Licensing	62,494
Community Affairs	92,000	Natural Resources	85,288
Corrections	94,420	Parks and Recreation	80,204
Education	135,139	Personnel	48,552
Elections	71,767	Public Utility Regulation	72,101
Employment Services	82,432	Purchasing	56,238
Environmental Protection	82,027	Tourism	68,173
General Services	73,520	Transportation	93,558

UTAH

Governor	$77,250	*Judges*	
Lieutenant Governor	60,000	Supreme Court	$89,300
Attorney General	65,000	Court of Appeals	82,250
Treasurer	60,000	District Courts	81,200

The Legislature: 104 members receive $85 for each day the legislature is in session (up to 45 days) plus $35 per day living expenses. The president of the Senate and the Speaker of the House each receive an additional $1,000 a year. The majority and minority leaders in each house receive an additional $500 a year.

Selected Administrative Officials

Administration	$58,504	Banking	$53,633
Agriculture	49,650	Budget	53,633

Civil Rights	$33,659	Licensing	$35,538
Commerce	53,663	Natural Resources	58,506
Consumer Affairs	33,659	Parks and Recreation	41,823
Corrections	58,504	Personnel	58,504
Education	60,134	Public Utility Regulation	37,521
Employment Services	46,625	Purchasing	35,538
Energy	28,585	Social Services	58,056
Environmental Protection	58,506	Solid Waste Management	68,212
Historic Preservation	35,338	Tourism	58,443
Insurance	49,600	Transportation	58,506
Labor	49,650		

VERMONT

Governor	$80,724	*Judges*	
Lieutenant Governor	33,654	Supreme Court	$73,890
Secretary of State	50,793	Superior Courts	70,188
Attorney General	61,027	District Courts	70,188
Treasurer	50,793		

The Legislature: 180 members each receive $8,160 per year plus $50 a day for rent and $37.50 (or $32 for commuters) for meals. The Speaker of the House receives additional $8,200 per year.

Selected Administrative Officials

Administration	$63,003	Insurance	$56,659
Agriculture	58,406	Labor	53,268
Banking	56,649	Licensing	45,510
Consumer Affairs	61,027	Natural Resources	67,059
Corrections	60,590	Parks and Recreation	56,035
Education	70,304	Personnel	52,000
Elections	34,673	Public Utility Regulation	70,179
Employment Services	55,016	Purchasing	48,131
Energy	61,984	Social Services	66,227
Environmental Protection	55,494	Solid Waste Management	56,617
General Services	57,990	Tourism	52,104
Health	71,468	Transportation	67,995
Historic Preservation	47,486		

VIRGINIA

Governor	$110,000	*Judges*	
Lieutenant Governor	32,000	Supreme Court	$102,700
Secretary of State	73,023	Court of Appeals	97,565
Attorney General	97,500	Circuit Courts	95,340
Treasurer	82,330		

The Legislature: 140 members receive $18,000 each plus $93 per day for expenses. The Speaker of the House receives an additional $10,200 a year.

Selected Administrative Officials

Administration	$ 99,556	General Services	$ 78,829
Agriculture	80,246	Health	111,059
Banking	80,246	Highways	103,442
Budget	90,662	Historic Preservation	64,832
Civil Rights	49,635	Insurance	97,566
Commerce	99,566	Labor	71,074
Community Affairs	76,633	Natural Resources	99,566
Consumer Affairs	52,280	Parks and Recreation	64,832
Corrections	98,706	Public Utility Regulation	97,566
Education	111,059	Purchasing	83,459
Elections	53,581	Social Services	90,156
Employment Services	81,439	Tourism	76,345
Energy	90,900	Transportation	99,566
Environmental Protection	90,652		

WASHINGTON

Governor	$121,000	*Judges*	
Lieutenant Governor	62,700	Supreme Court	$107,200
Secretary of State	64,300	Court of Appeals	101,900
Attorney General	92,000	Superior Courts	96,600
Treasurer	79,500		

The Legislature: 147 members receive $25,900 each plus $66 per day for expenses. The Speaker of the House receives an additional $8,000 a year. The majority and minority leaders in the Senate and the minority leader in the House each receive an additional $4,000 a year.

Selected Administrative Officials

Administration	$87,000	Historic Preservation	$ 53,616
Agriculture	87,500	Insurance	77,200
Banking	90,057	Labor	87,500
Civil Rights	67,542	Licensing	87,500
Commerce	90,057	Natural Resources	86,600
Consumer Affairs	90,600	Parks and Recreation	83,629
Corrections	90,057	Personnel	90,057
Education	86,600	Public Utility Regulation	83,629
Elections	57,732	Purchasing	60,660
Employment Services	68,640	Social Services	104,064
Energy	72,120	Solid Waste Management	63,744
Environmental Protection	90,057	Tourism	63,744
Health	90,057	Transportation	105,065

WASHINGTON, D.C.

Judges

Court of Appeals	$141,700
Superior Court	133,600

WEST VIRGINIA

Governor	$72,000	*Judges*	
Secretary of State	43,200	Supreme Court of	
Attorney General	50,400	Appeals	72,000
Treasurer	50,400	Circuit Courts	65,000

The Legislature: 134 members receive $6,500 per month each plus $70 per day for expenses. The president of the Senate and the Speaker of the House each receive an additional $50 a legislative day plus $100 a day for 80 days each calendar year. The majority and minority leaders in the House and the Senate each receive an additional $25 a legislative day.

Selected Administrative Officials

Administration	$70,000	Community Affairs	$95,000
Agriculture	46,800	Consumer Affairs	39,900
Banking	38,300	Corrections	45,000
Budget	36,420	Education	70,000
Civil Rights	40,000	Employment Services	65,000
Commerce	70,000	Environmental Protection	70,000

General Services	$34,032	Public Utility Regulation	$50,000
Historic Preservation	29,712	Purchasing	38,976
Insurance	47,800	Social Services	70,000
Labor	35,700	Solid Waste Management	46,000
Natural Resources	65,000	Tourism	65,000
Parks and Recreation	65,000	Transportation	70,000
Personnel	38,976		

WISCONSIN

Governor	$92,283	*Judges*	
Lieutenant Governor	49,673	Supreme Court	$94,906
Secretary of State	45,088	Court of Appeals	89,358
Attorney General	82,706	Circuit Courts	83,773
Treasurer	45,088		

The Legislature: 132 members receive $35,070 each plus $75 per day for expenses. The Speaker of the Assembly receives an additional $300 per year.

Selected Administrative Officials

Administration	$92,281	Highways	$79,760
Agriculture	86,537	Historic Preservation	57,012
Banking	63,461	Insurance	81,203
Budget	70,495	Labor	91,120
Civil Rights	59,331	Licensing	64,325
Commerce	81,025	Natural Resources	92,281
Community Affairs	54,000	Parks and Recreation	65,346
Corrections	84,000	Personnel	77,160
Education	79,787	Public Utility Regulation	68,000
Elections	57,549	Purchasing	59,193
Employment Services	73,145	Social Services	92,281
Energy	58,884	Solid Waste Management	73,947
Environmental Protection	83,309	Tourism	58,965
Health	71,616	Transportation	89,318

WYOMING

Governor	$70,000	*Judges*	
Secretary of State	55,000	Supreme Court	$85,000
Attorney General	71,298	District Courts	77,000
Treasurer	55,000		

The Legislature: 90 members receive $75 a day each plus $60 for expenses. The president of the Senate and the Speaker of the House each receive an additional $78 per day. The majority and minority leaders in the House and Senate receive an additional $75 per day.

Selected Administrative Officials

Administration	$64,087	Insurance	$54,500
Agriculture	66,201	Labor	47,861
Banking	54,504	Licensing	55,383
Budget	63,036	Natural Resources	65,808
Civil Rights	37,358	Parks and Recreation	54,027
Commerce	65,662	Personnel	50,000
Consumer Affairs	35,414	Planning	52,849
Corrections	65,662	Public Utility Regulation	61,233
Education	55,000	Purchasing	47,500
Employment Services	53,604	Solid Waste Management	52,860
Energy	33,204	Tourism	59,301
Environmental Protection	59,884	Transportation	70,704
Health	65,662		

Large Cities

In this section we provide annual salaries of the leading officials in a range of major American cities. The data is primarily taken from publications of the International City/County Management Association. The section includes a table that shows the average annual salaries for municipal officials across the United States, and a table listing the salaries of individual officials in the largest cities.

AVERAGE SALARIES OF MUNICIPAL OFFICIALS, 1987–1994[1]

Title	Salary 1987	Salary 1989	Salary 1991	Salary 1993	Salary 1994
Mayor	$ 7,595	$ 8,472	$ 9,209	$ 9,963	$10,191
City Manager	49,241	54,666	60,803	65,221	67,274
Chief Appointed Administrator	38,756	44,054	49,467	53,999	56,074
Assistant City Manager/Assistant CAO	40,879	46,057	51,945	56,285	58,216
City Clerk	26,511	29,733	32,799	35,305	36,366
Chief Financial Officer	39,521	44,950	50,136	54,050	55,946
Treasurer	32,371	31,617	34,851	38,122	38,236
Director of Public Works	36,521	41,268	45,919	49,689	51,274

AVERAGE SALARIES OF MUNICIPAL OFFICIALS, 1987–1994[1]

Title	Salary 1987	Salary 1989	Salary 1991	Salary 1993	Salary 1994
Engineer	$42,755	$45,767	$51,278	$55,006	$56,798
Police Chief	36,342	40,129	44,563	48,412	50,104
Fire Chief	37,470	40,855	45,406	49,263	50,820
Planning Director	38,872	43,549	48,948	52,476	54,501
Personnel Director	36,934	40,911	46,310	50,276	52,183
Director of Parks/Recreation	39,088	41,167	45,948	49,650	51,453
Superintendent of Parks	28,756	33,747	37,743	40,707	42,042
Director of Recreation	29,400	32,300	36,627	39,432	40,975
Librarian	28,704	32,632	36,297	39,376	40,889
Director of Data Processing	37,679	43,266	48,495	52,262	54,088
Purchasing Director	30,816	33,767	37,562	40,760	42,367

[1]Average salaries are for cities that have consistently reported data over the past six years.
SOURCE: International City/County Management Association, *Municipal Yearbook, 1995.*

MUNICIPAL OFFICERS' SALARIES IN 65 LARGE CITIES, 1995[1]

City	Mayor	City Council President	City Council Member
Albuquerque, NM	$ 70,283	$ 14,056	$ 7,028
Anaheim, CA	12,000	NA[2]	12,000
Arlington, TX	3,000	NA	2,400
Atlanta	100,000	0	18,400
Austin, TX	35,000	NA	30,000
Baltimore	60,000	53,000	29,000
Baton Rouge, LA	85,516	0	3,600
Birmingham, AL	68,000	17,400	15,000
Boston	100,000	45,000	45,000
Buffalo	79,380	52,920	41,895
Charlotte, NC	20,000	NA	12,000
Chicago	80,000	0	27,600
Cincinnati	50,686	NA	46,879
Cleveland	82,500	46,287	35,683
Colorado Springs	0	NA	0
Columbus, OH	95,000	30,000	25,000
Corpus Christi, TX	9,000	0	6,000
Dallas	$50 per meeting	NA	$50 per meeting
Denver	93,000	38,402	38,402
Detroit	125,300	65,000	63,000

MUNICIPAL OFFICERS' SALARIES IN 65 LARGE CITIES, 1995[1]

City	Mayor	City Council President	City Council Member
El Paso, TX	$ 27,562	NA[2]	$16,537
Fort Worth, TX	$75 per meeting	0	$75 per meeting
Fresno, CA	57,270	NA	33,120
Houston	133,975	NA	34,900
Indianapolis	83,211	$ 9,985	9,985
Jacksonville, FL	100,745	34,127	25,595
Kansas City, MO	47,000	NA	19,500
Las Vegas	43,984	NA	33,480
Long Beach, CA	86,659	NA	21,664
Los Angeles	117,876	90,680	90,680
Louisville, KY	71,464	27,995	27,995
Memphis	100,000	0	6,000
Mesa, AZ	19,200	NA	96,000
Miami	5,000	NA	5,000
Milwaukee	102,544	50,563	45,146
Minneapolis	71,500	52,500	52,500
Nashville	75,000	8,652	5,562
New Orleans	85,880	42,500	42,500
New York	130,000	105,000	55,000
Newark, NJ	0	NA	0
Norfolk, VA	17,000	NA	15,000
Oakland	89,000	NA	33,000
Oklahoma City	2,000	NA	$20 per meeting
Omaha	71,930	23,402	19,502
Philadelphia	0	0	0
Phoenix	37,500	NA	18,000
Pittsburgh	69,007	39,287	39,347
Portland, OR	75,254	0	65,644
Sacramento, CA	$925 per month	NA	$925 per month
St. Louis	90,246	50,310	22,765
St. Paul	75,216	3,000	30,000
San Antonio, TX	$50 per meeting	NA	$20 per meeting
San Diego, CA	65,000	NA	49,000
San Francisco	130,083	23,924	23,924
San Jose, CA	80,000	NA	52,800
San Juan, Puerto Rico	0	NA	NA
Santa Ana, CA	2,400	NA	1,500
Seattle	95,398	63,892	63,892
Tampa	110,000	19,928	19,928
Toledo	75,000	4,500	18,500
Tucson, AZ	24,000	NA	12,000
Tulsa	70,000	12,000	12,000

MUNICIPAL OFFICERS' SALARIES IN 65 LARGE CITIES, 1995[1]

City	Mayor	City Council President	City Council Member
Virginia Beach, VA	$ 20,000	NA[2]	$18,000
Washington, D.C.	90,705	81,885	71,885
Wichita, KS	12,500	NA	7,500

[1]All salaries are annual unless otherwise noted.
[2]NA: Not available
SOURCE: National League of Cities, Data Base Report, March 14, 1995.

Average Salaries of County Officials, 1987–1994

Many functions of county government vary dramatically from one area of the country to another, and so, therefore do the salaries of county officials. Following are some averages for key positions in county government by region as compiled by the International City/County Management Association and *City and State* Government Manager.

AVERAGE SALARIES OF COUNTY OFFICIALS, 1987–94[1]

Title	Salary 1987	Salary 1989	Salary 1991	Salary 1993	Salary 1994
Governing Board Chair/ President	$15,834	$16,512	$18,016	$19,741	$19,947
County Manager	54,598	62,388	68,742	73,712	76,183
County Administrator	43,339	47,413	51,804	55,890	58,539
Clerk to the Governing Board	24,373	27,174	29,956	32,027	32,976
Chief Financial Officer	29,549	36,602	40,269	44,357	45,815
County Health Officer	43,926	46,036	50,514	55,100	58,037
Planning Director	34,962	39,635	44,229	47,140	49,064
County Engineer	46,968	49,268	54,182	57,764	59,581
Director of Welfare/Human Services	38,650	44,178	48,700	51,271	52,931
Chief Law Enforcement Officer	31,948	37,904	41,257	44,179	45,722
Purchasing Director	32,083	38,091	42,226	44,870	46,365
Personnel Director	37,710	42,986	47,976	51,932	53,888

[1]Average salaries are for counties that have consistently reported data over the past six years.
SOURCE: International City/County Management Association, *Municipal Yearbook, 1995.*

AVERAGE SALARIES OF COUNTY OFFICIALS BY GEOGRAPHIC REGION, 1994[1]

Position	Average Salaries				
	All Counties	Northeast	North Central	South	West
Governing Board Chair/ President/County Judge	$21,614	$30,259	$13,810	$24,317	$28,621
County Manager	75,113	67,856	71,667	73,663	83,333
County Administrator	49,066	49,147	48,426	48,058	52,516
Clerk to the Governing Board	32,501	33,933	30,341	33,659	34,391
Chief Financial Officer	41,396	45,220	36,381	41,547	48,415
County Health Officer	48,914	62,357	39,427	58,815	53,051
Planning Director	45,593	44,378	36,137	45,861	47,919
County Engineer	50,938	58,417	46,719	52,289	58,263
Director of Welfare/Human Services	48,126	49,726	45,580	47,098	53,450
Chief Law Enforcement Officer	41,744	42,491	36,916	44,688	45,505
Purchasing Director	38,915	37,680	39,917	36,542	47,785
Personnel Director	45,102	43,649	44,945	43,392	49,711

[1]Average salaries are for counties that have consistently reported data over the past six years.
SOURCE: International City/County Management Association, *Municipal Yearbook, 1995.*

TOP COUNTY SALARIES, 1992

County	Salary	County	Salary
Board Leader			
Orange, CA	$ 82,044	Allegheny, PA	$70,000
Orange, FL	80,900	Hennepin, MN	66,841
Santa Clara, CA	77,621	San Bernadino, CA	60,888
Cook, IL	74,000	Kern, CA	60,460
San Diego, CA	72,296	Riverside, CA	59,778
Budget Director			
Dade, FL	$100,200	Broward, FL	$88,900
Montgomery, MD	96,635	Suffolk, NY	88,477
Cook, IL	96,413	Harris, TX	87,966
Milwaukee, WI	91,352	Westchester, NY	87,570
Santa Clara, CA	89,563	Prince George's, MD	86,000
Finance Director/Treasurer			
Santa Clara, CA	$117,909	Montgomery, MD	$92,115
Nassau, NY	110,354	San Diego, CA	91,619
Westchester, NY	104,460	Pinellas, FL	89,286
Palm Beach, FL	95,054	Alameda, CA	88,848
Fairfax, VA	94,693	Dade, FL	87,500

SOURCE: *City and State Government Manager,* Sixth Annual Salary Survey, 1992.

Salaries and Wages of Public Employees

The jobs represented in this section are for state and local government employees only. Over the last two decades, these workers have become a potent force in the American economy; their numbers have grown from 6 million in 1960 to 9.8 million in 1970 and to 15.6 million in 1992. The importance of their work in maintaining the smooth and orderly functioning of society has increased just as steadily, especially in the key areas of education, public safety, transportation, and, most notably, health care. (See the separate section on that subject, Part VII, for salaries of public workers in hospitals.)

Ironically, it is precisely their increased power and influence that have made public employees the targets of politicians and citizens' groups who seek to blame them for high taxes, budget deficits, and the frequently mediocre quality of public service. This has led in turn to government resistance to pay increases for its employees and then, predictably, to strikes and slowdowns by workers. Finally, to complete the circle, when higher taxes are sought, the government can point to the necessity of giving higher salaries to its employees.

The combination of relatively low wages with continual governmental and public disapproval has helped to increase markedly the unionization of government employees. The American Federation of State, Municipal, and County Workers (AFSCME), for example, has achieved a membership of over a million in just the last few years. Millions of other workers belong to trade unions, or other AFL-CIO–related organizations. How this will affect the relationship of employer and employee in the future is difficult to predict exactly, but the possibility of more strikes by public employees would seem to be a fairly safe bet, state or city laws to the contrary notwithstanding.

One note of caution for the researcher and the careful reader: the figures given below are base salaries *only;* they do not include overtime, pension, or health benefits, items which in the past made public service attractive to many people. Today, of course, the benefits of public employees do not differ substantially from those of many working people in the private sector.

JOBS AND SALARIES OF KEY PUBLIC EMPLOYEES

Corrections Officers

The approximately 300,000 people who stand guard in our prison facilities are among the most underpaid members of the working community. The image of the prison guard, "the screw," planted in the minds of the American public by the gangster films of the '30s and '40s, has given the job a distasteful aura which the new euphemism "correction officer" cannot hide. In fact these men and women perform a vital function. This is especially true in maximum-security prisons where they must deal unarmed with the constant threat of violence while at the same time are restrained by rules no policeman need obey. Although they are frequently the victims of prisoner outbursts against the mythological "system," the guards are always cited as a real cause of prisoner upheavals. Policemen usually argue that because they constantly deal with life-and-death situations they are entitled to higher pay than other public employees, and most people accept that premise. But why then do prison guards almost always earn significantly less than police in the same geographic area?

Jobs for corrections officers should be plentiful through the end of the century, as legislation requiring mandatory minimum sentencing for convicted felons will mean more and longer prison terms and a correspondingly greater need for prison guards. The following table lists salary ranges for various correction department workers.

ANNUAL SALARIES OF CORRECTIONAL DEPARTMENT PERSONNEL, 1994

State	Director of Corrections	Entry-Level Officer[1]	State	Director of Corrections	Entry-Level Officer[1]
Alabama	$78,000	$16,502	Idaho	$71,843	$20,883
Alaska	83,844	30,684	Illinois	85,000	22,236
Arizona	103,140	17,755	Indiana	73,086	NA
Arkansas	84,776	16,822	Iowa	70,500	23,317
California	95,052	23,316	Kansas	79,200	17,424
Colorado	77,800	22,044	Kentucky	62,620	13,668
Connecticut	78,732	22,958	Louisiana	60,320	14,736
Delaware	80,700	18,598	Maine	70,658	17,721
District of Columbia	—	23,621	Maryland	72,896	20,772
			Massachusetts	58,912	28,114
Florida	91,470	16,181	Michigan	87,300	21,924
Georgia	73,512	17,646	Minnesota	67,500	23,615
Hawaii	85,302	NA[2]	Mississippi	68,572	15,299

ANNUAL SALARIES OF CORRECTIONAL DEPARTMENT PERSONNEL, 1994

State	Director of Corrections	Entry-Level Officer[1]
Missouri	$70,422	$17,436
Montana	54,304	16,064
Nebraska	67,298	18,599
Nevada	80,950	22,484
New Hampshire	56,842	20,249
New Jersey	100,225	29,125
New Mexico	64,906	15,103
New York	102,335	22,192
North Carolina	77,289	18,197
North Dakota	49,200	15,948
Ohio	87,734	21,258
Oklahoma	72,180	15,965
Oregon	84,096	21,864
Pennsylvania	80,000	19,362
Rhode Island	$83,763	$23,521
South Carolina	99,314	15,921
South Dakota	66,486	15,100
Tennessee	75,732	14,100
Texas	94,420	15,576
Utah	58,504	17,748
Vermont	60,590	18,200
Virginia	98,706	16,788
Washington	90,057	22,380
West Virginia	45,000	16,000
Wisconsin	84,000	18,781
Wyoming	65,662	15,700
Federal Bureau of Prisons	—	19,713[3]

[1]As of June 30, 1994.
[2]NA: Not Available.
[3]As of October, 1992.
SOURCE: Council of State Governments, *The Book of States, 1994–95;* American Correctional Association, *Vital Statistics in Corrections 1994* (1995).

Fire Fighters

More than 90 percent of America's 305,000 paid fire fighters work for municipalities. Some county governments, especially in the South and West, provide fire protection through paid personnel. No matter what the jurisdiction, however, salaries of fire fighters are always discussed in relation to police pay. The struggle is always for parity, something the police usually resist on the familiar grounds that their work is more dangerous. The injury and death statistics, however, reveal at the very least that fire fighting is frequently a hazardous occupation and, given various circumstances, at times more dangerous than police work. The whole question of compensation based on danger becomes even more complicated when we realize that taxpayers are forced to pay the same salaries to police officers who perform office work, or to fire fighters who rarely have to leave the firehouse, as to those in obviously high-risk situations.

Resolving the issue of hazardous-duty pay will not be easy, but surely some kind of bonus or merit system could be established. As the salaries of public employees continue to lag further and further behind the Consumer Price Index, some way of rewarding excellence must be found or the grim prospect of continual strikes and sick-outs will become a reality.

The Department of Labor projects average growth in the number of fire fighters, with paid fire fighters gradually supplanting volunteers as smaller communities see their populations expand. Low educational requirements and high job security insure that the supply of qualified fire fighters almost always exceeds the demand, so competition for jobs is always high.

Median weekly earnings for firefighters were $636 in 1995. Lieutenants and fire captains earned considerably more. Benefits paid to fire fighters include liberal pension plans (which often allow retirement at half pay at age 50 after 25 years of service) as well as medical and liability insurance, vacation, sick leave, and several paid holidays.

SALARY RANGES OF FIREFIGHTERS IN SELECTED CITIES WITH POPULATIONS OVER 250,000

City	Total Personnel	Starting Salary	Maximum Salary
Albuquerque, NM	496	$16,647	$31,683
Anaheim, CA	243	29,906	44,204
Arlington, TX	393	26,688	34,056
Austin, TX	850	22,266	43,347
Buffalo	885	27,427	37,078
Chicago	4,931	29,496	45,366
Cincinnati	751	32,835	36,560
Corpus Christi, TX	325	22,236	29,592
Dallas	1,664	23,901	32,025
Fort Worth, TX	681	25,632	30,859
Fresno, CA	247	39,438	46,692
Honolulu, HI	1,031	25,184	33,120
Houston	3,262	27,154	35,532
Jacksonville, FL	980	26,196	35,724
Las Vegas	376	29,328	42,172
Los Angeles	3,365	31,529	47,522
Louisville, KY	541	21,569	24,762
Mesa, AZ	301	24,479	36,569
Milwaukee	1,631	21,447	36,500
Minneapolis	477	26,728	41,262
Nashville	1,089	24,021	32,745
Norfolk, VA	479	22,162	36,991
Oklahoma City	994	24,211	33,259
Omaha	538	28,609	37,190
Phoenix, AZ	1,375	26,936	38,904
Pittsburgh	904	22,647	36,660

SALARY RANGES OF FIREFIGHTERS IN SELECTED CITIES WITH POPULATIONS OVER 250,000

City	Total Personnel	Starting Salary	Maximum Salary
Sacramento, CA	468	$31,615	$46,627
San Diego, CA	951	32,790	41,616
St. Paul	441	32,745	43,124
Toledo	534	26,822	38,611
Tucson, AZ	461	27,192	36,444
Virginia Beach, VA	363	23,237	33,693
Wichita, KS	381	22,281	30,371

SOURCE: International City/County Management Association, *Municipal Yearbook 1995*.

Librarians

The vast majority of the nation's 141,000 librarians work for a federal, state, or municipal institution or system. Nearly 85 percent of those librarians are women, which may account for a salary level that must be considered low. Yet even among librarians, men earn more than women—an average of $323 more in 1993. This disparity is emphasized when seen in relation to the training required, as well as the increasing need for specialization and updating of knowledge. Anyone who has used a good library lately knows that the "information explosion" has destroyed the image of the librarian as a bespectacled spinster whose main tasks were collecting pennies for overdue books and shushing high-spirited children. More often than not, a librarian today has at least one advanced degree, as well as a full understanding of computer-based storage. As our need to have access to information grows, so too will the salaries of librarians (if in fact we still call them that).

Job prospects for librarians are actually much stronger than one might expect given that public libraries are often the first government institution to have their budgets slashed during financial hard times. Indeed, cutbacks for libraries have been a regular part of state and local budgeting politics ever since Richard Nixon was president. But because of the cutbacks, the prospect of fewer jobs dissuaded people from entering the field. So after more than doubling in the 1960s, the number of librarians has remained constant ever since. Today, as many of the older librarians are beginning to retire, there are openings in many areas of the country for well-trained librarians, especially for children's librarians and academic librarians. Several states across the country have actually reported shortages of children's librarians. Many large corporations are also hiring experienced, highly trained librarians to help them organize their own information and to tell them what outside sources they should utilize.

In numerical terms, the number of 1993 library school graduates who found jobs by the spring of 1994 was up considerably over their 1991 counterparts. But because the number of 1993 graduates was much higher than the number of 1991 graduates, the percentage of graduates finding employment was not significantly different this year than it was two years ago. And more disturbing is the fact that nearly 11 percent of 1993 graduates were able to find only part-time or nonprofessional work, compared with 6.6 percent two years earlier.

The following tables give a representative sample of librarians' salaries throughout the country and point out the gender-based differences in librarians' salaries on all levels and geographical regions. Since most school systems pay their librarians on the same scale as their teachers, figures for school librarians (92 percent of whom were women in 1993) are not included here. It should be noted too that the Department of Labor estimates that 71,000 people are employed in various capacities under the job title *library technician.* Pay rates for library technicians vary widely by employer, geographical region, number of hours, and the type of worked performed; full-time library technicians in the federal government average $23,900 annually.

AVERAGE STARTING SALARIES OF LIBRARIANS, 1985–1993

Year	Average Starting Salary
1985[1]	$19,753
1986	20,874
1987	22,247
1988	23,491
1989	24,581
1990	25,306
1991	25,583
1992	26,666
1993	27,116

[1]Average beginning salary for 1982–1984 figured at $17,693.

SOURCE: *Library Journal,* October 15, 1994. Reprinted by permission.

SALARIES OF LIBRARIANS BY REGION AND TYPE OF LIBRARY, 1993

	Low Salary		Median Salary		High Salary	
Library Type/Region	**Women**	**Men**	**Women**	**Men**	**Women**	**Men**
Public Libraries						
Northeast	$13,000	$14,100	$26,300	$26,800	$44,000	$44,500
Southeast	13,700	16,500	23,750	22,800	34,000	36,000
Midwest	13,000	14,000	24,900	24,000	39,400	42,000
Southwest	18,000	18,000	24,000	23,560	33,000	27,000
West	15,000	26,200	28,000	29,250	72,000	37,000
All Public Libraries	13,000	14,000	25,000	26,000	72,000	44,500
School Libraries						
Northeast	$16,000	$25,000	$29,500	$27,000	$56,455	$44,500
Southeast	13,000	21,000	24,000	24,000	39,000	30,000
Midwest	14,500	20,650	27,550	25,750	64,132	42,000
Southwest	15,000	24,000	26,000	33,500	43,000	29,000
West	16,500	14,000	30,578	31,000	45,000	50,000
All School Libraries	13,000	14,000	27,000	25,000	64,132	50,000
College/University						
Northeast	$13,440	$19,000	$26,000	$28,000	$46,000	$50,100
Southeast	14,000	16,800	24,000	25,000	35,000	36,000
Midwest	13,000	17,000	25,000	27,000	45,000	42,000
Southwest	13,000	13,000	24,400	24,750	33,500	40,000
West	14,784	20,000	27,500	27,000	47,000	38,000
All College Libraries	13,000	13,000	25,000	26,000	47,000	50,100
Special Libraries						
Northeast	$13,000	$16,305	$28,900	$29,000	$65,000	$53,000
Southeast	15,000	33,600	26,000	26,500	36,000	30,000
Midwest	13,200	20,000	26,500	29,936	40,000	39,800
Southwest	14,800	33,000	27,000	26,000	36,500	48,000
West	15,000	33,090	28,000	30,000	54,000	35,000
All Special Libraries	13,000	16,305	28,000	28,000	65,000	53,000

SOURCE: *Library Journal,* October 15, 1994. Reprinted by permission.

JOB PLACEMENTS AND AVERAGE SALARIES OF LIBRARY SCHOOL GRADUATES, 1991–1993

	Class of 1991	Class of 1993
Total Graduates	3,907	4,754
Number (percent) finding full-time work	1,786 (45.7)	2,034 (42.8)
Number (percent) finding part-time or nonprofessional work	257 (6.6)	502 (10.6)
Total Number (percent) Finding Library Work	2,043 (52.3)	2,536 (53.3)
Average Salary	$25,583	$27,116

SOURCE: *Library Journal,* October 15, 1994. Reprinted by permission.

Police

Local police agencies, sheriff's agencies, and state police agencies collectively employed 793,020 persons (including 595,869 sworn officers) during fiscal 1990 and had operating and capital expenses totaling more than $41 billion. Although the representation of women and minorities continues to grow, law enforcement agencies remain overwhelmingly white male bastions. In 1990, women made up 8.1 percent of local police department officers (up from 7.6 percent in 1987) and 15.4 percent of sheriff's department officers (up from 12.6 percent in 1987). Blacks comprised 10.5 percent of local police departments (up from 9.3 percent) and 9.8 percent of sheriff's department officers (compared with 8.3 percent in 1987). Meanwhile, Hispanic officers increased their numbers from 4.5 percent to 5.2 percent in local police departments and from 4.3 percent to 4.7 percent in sheriff's departments.

AVERAGE BASE STARTING SALARIES FOR STATE POLICE AGENCIES, 1990

Position	Average Salary
Entry-Level Officer	$22,780
Sergeant	30,100
Director or Equivalent	56,900

SOURCE: U.S. Department of Justice, *Sourcebook of Criminal Justice Statistics, 1990,* (1991).

SALARY RANGES OF POLICE OFFICERS IN SELECTED CITIES WITH POPULATIONS OVER 250,000

City	Total Personnel	Starting Salary	Maximum Salary
Albuquerque, NM	769	$16,640	$33,322
Anaheim, CA	527	34,736	46,550
Arlington, TX	393	28,632	35,640
Austin, TX	1,270	24,086	44,633
Buffalo	1,080	28,814	38,956
Chicago	13,067	34,884	50,544
Cincinnati	986	34,625	38,552
Corpus Christi, TX	554	23,076	32,736
Dallas	4,931	29,496	45,366
Fort Worth, TX	1,374	26,760	32,217
Fresno, CA	455	41,520	49,656
Honolulu, HI	2,329	27,240	40,608
Houston	6,778	27,154	35,532
Jacksonville, FL	2,303	29,364	43,236
Los Angeles	10,070	33,157	47,001
Louisville, KY	235	19,781	25,334
Mesa, AZ	708	28,470	40,443
Milwaukee	2,545	26,954	36,500
Minneapolis	1,034	27,875	43,065
Nashville	1,480	25,247	32,745
Norfolk, VA	772	23,270	38,841
Oklahoma City	1,214	36,851	30,004
Omaha	761	30,217	39,525
Phoenix, AZ	3,073	27,040	40,893
Pittsburgh	1,365	36,645	38,065
Sacramento, CA	930	32,463	49,435
San Diego, CA	2,476	31,609	44,922
St. Paul	719	32,745	43,124
Toledo	710	30,278	38,606
Tucson, AZ	1,010	28,548	38,268
Virginia Beach, VA	965	23,237	33,693
Wichita, KS	657	22,688	30,140

SOURCE: International City/County Management Association, *Municipal Yearbook, 1995.*

AVERAGE BASE STARTING SALARY FOR SELECTED POSITIONS IN LOCAL POLICE DEPARTMENTS, 1990

	Average Base Starting Salary, 1990[1]		
Population Served	Entry-Level Officer	Sergeant	Chief of Police
All Sizes	$18,910	$25,420	$30,240
1,000,000 or More	$26,560	$40,420	$85,320
500,000–999,999	25,110	33,900	67,300
250,000–499,999	25,370	35,120	62,770
100,000–249,999	24,960	34,330	59,190
50,000–99,999	23,300	32,140	51,600
25,000–49,999	23,150	31,200	46,400
10,000–24,999	21,630	28,950	40,930
2,500–9,999	18,710	24,110	29,960
Under 2,500	15,870	19,960	20,610

[1]Average salaries are based on the minimum starting salary offered by a department and have been rounded to the nearest 10 dollars. Computation of average salary excludes departments with no full-time employee in that position.
SOURCE: U.S. Department of Justice, *Sourcebook of Criminal Justice Statistics, 1990* (1991).

AVERAGE BASE STARTING SALARY FOR SELECTED POSITIONS IN SHERIFFS' DEPARTMENTS, 1990

	Average Base Starting Salary[1]		
Population Served	Entry-Level Deputy	Sergeant	Sheriff
All Sizes	$17,420	$21,870	$33,530
1,000,000 or More	$26,180	$35,530	$80,350
500,000–999,999	22,950	32,100	61,490
250,000–499,999	20,130	26,860	53,710
100,000–249,999	19,530	24,830	44,900
50,000–99,999	18,300	23,100	38,460
25,000–49,999	16,950	21,510	33,050
10,000–24,999	16,940	20,840	30,320
Under 10,000	15,860	18,560	24,530

[1]Average salaries are based on the minimum starting salary offered by a department and have been rounded to the nearest 10 dollars. Computation of average salary excludes departments with no full-time employee in that position.
SOURCE: U.S. Department of Justice, *Sourcebook of Criminal Justice Statistics, 1990* (1991).

Sanitation Workers

The Census Bureau lists 120,000 sanitation employees on state and local government payrolls, but how many of these are actually involved in garbage collection seems impossible to ascertain. One reason is the very low status this job has in our society. (The Bureau of Labor Statistics, for example, does not even list it in a gigantic 700-page vocational handbook published for high school students every year.) Most garbage men work for municipal governments.

Following is a list of salaries for workers in major American cities which reveals extraordinary regional differences, a trend that seems to be dying out for other kinds of publicly funded jobs. Some major cities—notably Boston, San Francisco, and Seattle—hire private firms for all trash collection, as do most counties and smaller municipalities.

SALARY RANGES OF SANITATION WORKERS IN SELECTED CITIES WITH POPULATIONS OVER 500,000[1]

City	Total Personnel	Starting Salary	Maximum Salary[2]
Baltimore	854	$17,347	$19,843
Chicago	2,156	28,295	28,295
Cleveland	374	18,346	23,156
Columbus, OH	296	18,969	22,875
Dallas	590	17,292	21,012
Denver	172	16,824	24,552
Honolulu, HI	510	20,652	NA
Indianapolis	149	11,960	19,156
Jacksonville, FL	321	14,016	19,428
Memphis	691	14,550	17,867
Milwaukee	365	22,468	24,632
Philadelphia	1,930	17,884	21,560
Phoenix, AZ	340	21,504	27,772
San Antonio, TX	423	13,260	17,904
San Diego, CA	353	23,664	29,724

[1]Based on 1987 U.S. Census Bureau population estimates.
[2]Includes longevity pay where paid.
SOURCE: International City Management Association, *Municipal Yearbook, 1992.*

Social Workers

Virtually all of the nearly 438,000 social workers in America are employed by a government agency, usually a city, county, or state welfare agency or hospital facility. About 70 percent are engaged as caseworkers in public assistance functions, particularly the determination of whether or not a person or family is eligible for welfare funds. Other social workers deal with orphaned or abandoned children, pregnant teenagers, battered wives, and more frequently today with lonely and poor old people who are without care.

An important branch of this occupation is psychiatric social work, which usually requires graduate school training. Acting as a liaison between the psychiatrist, the patient, and his family, as well as between the family and the hospital, the psychiatric social worker prepares family histories, conducts interviews with all parties, and explains treatments and their purpose.

Since all social workers must possess a college diploma and many supervisory personnel often have master's degrees, this must be regarded as a low-paying position. Compared to teachers, whose certification requirements are similar but who work many fewer hours, social workers are paid significantly less.

AVERAGE ANNUAL SALARIES OF SOCIAL SERVICE CASEWORKERS

Region	Average Minimum	Average Maximum	Median
East	$19,073	$32,560	$25,817
Midwest	17,358	29,500	24,305
South	16,453	30,573	23,513
West	17,756	31,319	24,538

SOURCE: American Public Welfare Association, 1990. Reprinted by permission.

AVERAGE ANNUAL SALARIES OF CASEWORK SUPERVISORS

Region	Average Minimum	Average Maximum	Median
East	$25,493	$37,301	$31,397
Midwest	23,709	35,099	29,404
South	23,382	37,992	30,687
West	25,488	36,608	31,048

SOURCE: American Public Welfare Association, 1990. Reprinted by permission.

AVERAGE ANNUAL SALARIES OF CASEWORK MANAGERS

Region	Average Minimum	Average Maximum	Median
East	$34,453	$49,730	$42,091
Midwest	24,430	42,681	33,555
South	25,435	48,365	36,900
West	27,991	46,590	37,291

SOURCE: American Public Welfare Association, 1990. Reprinted by permission.

AVERAGE ANNUAL SALARIES OF STATE DIRECTORS OF SOCIAL SERVICES

State	Salary	State	Salary
Alabama	NA	Montana	$ 54,305
Alaska	$83,844	Nebraska	62,778
Arizona	98,000	Nevada	81,294
Arkansas	91,817	New Hampshire	73,492
California	95,052	New Jersey	100,225
Colorado	77,800	New Mexico	57,208
Connecticut	NA	New York	102,335
Delaware	86,400	North Carolina	78,806
Florida	52,020	North Dakota	70,044
Georgia	70,000	Ohio	93,891
Hawaii	85,302	Oklahoma	58,000
Idaho	71,843	Oregon	92,760
Illinois	76,991	Pennsylvania	71,750
Indiana	73,450	Rhode Island	105,383
Iowa	76,856	South Carolina	87,087
Kansas	78,000	South Dakota	77,278
Kentucky	63,425	Tennessee	50,916
Louisiana	60,320	Texas	89,116
Maine	74,110	Utah	58,506
Maryland	67,496	Vermont	66,227
Massachusetts	77,547	Virginia	90,156
Michigan	90,285	Washington	104,064
Minnesota	70,386	West Virginia	70,000
Mississippi	39,259	Wisconsin	92,281
Missouri	73,450	Wyoming	70,380

SOURCE: Council of State Governments, *The Book of the States, 1994–95* (1995).

Teachers and Administrators, Grades K–12

By far the largest number of public employees work in the educational system. Over 50 percent of all state and local government workers are paid under education budgets, and about 20 percent of all municipal employees work in schools or universities.

More than 1.6 million persons are employed as kindergarten and elementary school teachers. Another 1.3 million-plus serve as secondary school teachers. And an additional 358,000 work in special education. Over 80 percent of the primary school teachers and 90 percent of secondary school teachers work in public schools.

In general, the number of teachers tends to parallel the number of school-age children. Thus, in the 1960s and 1970s, when children of the postwar baby boom generation filled the schools, teaching positions were at an all-time high. By the 1980s, however, as the number of school-age children declined, so did the number of teachers. According to the American Federation of Teachers, a total of 100,000 teachers were laid off between 1981 and 1982 alone. The decline in the growth rate of teachers also flattened out wage rates, causing teacher salaries to grow at less than the rate of inflation.

In the 1990s, however, as baby boomers' children begin their educational experiences, the number of teachers is expanding again, even during recessionary periods. And with the population of school-age children expected to keep increasing until the year 2002, according to the Census Bureau, teacher openings should continue to grow faster than the rate of growth for all jobs. But because teachers are paid by taxpayer money, their salaries are unlikely to equal those in private sector jobs with similar educational and training requirements. On the other hand, teachers usually enjoy good job benefits and work only nine to ten months of the year.

The average teacher salary was $36,933 in 1994–95, a 3.1 percent increase over the previous year. That is also a 56.7 percent increase since 1984–85—in current dollars. When inflation is taken into account, teacher salaries have gone up only 11.6 percent in 20 years. Of course, when taxpayers are footing the bill, it's not inappropriate to ask why teachers' salaries should increase at a faster rate than the rest of the economy.

The national average also reflects a wide disparity in salary by state. Teachers in Alaska, Connecticut, Michigan, New York, and New Jersey, for example all averaged over $46,000, while the average teacher salary in Mississippi, Louisiana, and North and South Dakota was less than $27,000. The state averages themselves also fail to reflect vast differences in salaries from one end of the state to the other—school payrolls are under local control—as well as cost-of-living indexes that make some salaries worth more than others. Salaries are higher for public school teachers than for private school teachers.

The principal reason why teachers (not to mention nurses, librarians, and social workers) earn less than other white-collar workers has to do in large part with gender discrimination. These occupations have traditionally been occupied by women, who earn considerably less than men for the same or similar work. To this day, 70 percent of public school teachers and 78 percent of private school teachers are women, with the percentages even more pronounced on the elementary level than on the secondary level. So while teachers' unions may be standardizing pay rates within the profession, the monetary rewards of the job remain a severe handicap to attracting and retaining the most talented people. So too do the often rigid teacher licensing requirements that force prospective teachers to take courses most deem irrelevant and boring.

In an attempt to make it easier for teachers to move from state to state without having to be recertified, the National Board for Professional Teaching Standards in 1993 created a national teacher certification program. Many states have already agreed to drop state licensing requirements for nationally certified teachers who relocate there; North Carolina has promised to repay the $975 exam fee and grant a 4 percent raise to any teacher who completes the program. The board graduated its first 81 teachers in January 1995.

The greatest demand for teachers in the 1990s should be in those states with the fastest expanding populations and where the school enrollment rates will be increasing: Florida, Arizona, Georgia, California, Tennessee, and Texas, among others. For information about job opportunities in teaching, a group called Recruiting New Teachers, Inc., provides a toll-free number (1-800-45-TEACH) that offers guidance on how to become a teacher and sends the names of prospective teachers to a network of school districts and teachers' colleges.

AVERAGE ANNUAL SALARIES OF PUBLIC SCHOOL TEACHERS, 1994–1995

State	Average Salary	Rank	State	Average Salary	Rank
Alabama	$31,144	37	Delaware	$39,076	12
Alaska	47,951	2	Florida	32,588	27
Arizona	32,090[1]	29	Georgia	32,828	26
Arkansas	28,409	45	Hawaii	38,518	14
California	40,667[1]	10	Idaho	29,783	41
Colorado	34,571	24	Illinois	41,041	8
Connecticut	51,300	1	Indiana	36,516[1]	18

AVERAGE ANNUAL SALARIES OF PUBLIC SCHOOL TEACHERS, 1994–1995

State	Average Salary	Rank	State	Average Salary	Rank
Iowa	$31,511	32	North Dakota	$26,327	49
Kansas	34,936	27	Ohio	36,685	17
Kentucky	32,257	28	Oklahoma	27,971	46
Louisiana	26,574	48	Oregon	38,700	13
Maine	31,856	31	Pennsylvania	44,489	6
Maryland	40,636	11	Rhode Island	40,729	9
Massachusetts	42,078[1]	7	South Carolina	30,341	40
Michigan	47,412[1]	3	South Dakota	26,017[1]	50
Minnesota	37,412	15	Tennessee	31,270	35
Mississippi	26,910	47	Texas	31,310	33
Missouri	31,217	36	Utah	28,676	44
Montana	28,785	43	Vermont	36,311[1]	19
Nebraska	30,822	39	Virginia	33,753	25
Nevada	34,836	23	Washington	36,120	20
New Hampshire	34,974[1]	21	Washington, D.C.	42,959	NA
New Jersey	46,801	5	West Virginia	31,923	30
New Mexico	28,865	42	Wisconsin	37,349[1]	16
New York	47,250	4	Wyoming	31,300	34
North Carolina	31,079	38			
			U.S. average	$36,933	

[1]Estimate.
SOURCE: National Education Association.

STATE DIRECTORS OF EDUCATION

Most states have two entirely separate administrative offices for education: one sets policy for elementary, secondary, and special education; the other for the university, college, and community college systems.

SALARIES OF STATE DIRECTORS OF EDUCATION

State	Education	Higher Education	State	Education	Higher Education
Alabama	$148,035	$106,500	Arkansas	$ 87,380	$ 89,833
Alaska	83,844	NA	California	99,804	111,750
Arizona	54,600	115,700	Colorado	94,478	66,200

SALARIES OF STATE DIRECTORS OF EDUCATION

State	Education	Higher Education	State	Education	Higher Education
Connecticut	78,732	NA	New Hampshire	$ 73,492	$ 35,285
Delaware	101,900	$ 54,600	New Jersey	100,225	100,225
Florida	96,861	174,900	New Mexico	76,017	698,732
Georgia	77,536	134,000	New York	136,500	136,500
Hawaii	90,041	150,000	North Carolina	77,289	145,370
Idaho	62,500	90,334	North Dakota	52,788	126,192
Illinois	133,076	132,000	Ohio	119,621	126,194
Indiana	63,100	113,728	Oklahoma	55,000	155,000
Iowa	99,900	99,900	Oregon	61,500	133,668
Kansas	102,125	132,000	Pennsylvania	80,000	74,900
Kentucky	135,000	91,692	Rhode Island	105,000	112,289
Louisiana	95,000	104,000	South Carolina	90,203	82,429
Maine	77,896	NA	South Dakota	64,472	104,210
Maryland	91,828	91,828	Tennessee	80,076	127,800
Massachusetts	77,547	80,067	Texas	135,139	NA
Michigan	87,300	69,342	Utah	60,134	NA
Minnesota	78,500	93,350	Vermont	70,304	NA
Mississippi	97,344	NA	Virginia	111,059	108,847
Missouri	80,280	85,000	Washington	86,600	95,004
Montana	44,009	87,499	West Virginia	70,000	105,000
Nebraska	96,372	68,598	Wisconsin	79,787	141,298
Nevada	80,950	129,950	Wyoming	55,000	64,260

SOURCE: Council of State Governments, *The Book of the States, 1994–95.*

School Superintendents

In response to complaints about the state of primary education in our nation's cities, many communities are beginning to hold school superintendents responsible. Houston, Philadelphia, Minneapolis, and Cincinnati are just a few of the cities that have indexed school superintendents' salaries to the test scores of the students they oversee. The Philadelphia superintendents' contracts are structured so that they get a bonus of up to 16 percent if student achievement improves over their five-year term, but take a 5 percent pay cut if it doesn't. In Houston, a superintendent can be fired if students' scores on a state-wide test don't rise.

Of course, such innovations are not without pitfalls. Educators experimented with similar pay-for-performance agreements during the 1970s, but abandoned them after learning that many superintendents were raising test scores by giving students the answers to the standardized tests in advance.

Teacher Aides and School Bus Drivers

Most of the nation's 885,000 teacher aides work in elementary schools in large cities; an increasing number are being hired to help in bilingual programs. Most school districts pay aides by the hour, but in areas where aides are considered essential, salaries are calculated on a monthly basis and a distinction is drawn between teaching and nonteaching personnel. The average hourly rate for teachers' aides involved in teaching was $8.31 an hour in 1992–93; for those involved in nonteaching it was $7.82.

According to the Educational Research Service, school bus drivers employed by public schools averaged $10.04 per hour during the 1991–92 school year and, given recent trends, have not risen greatly since. Since driving a school bus is a part-time job, most school bus drivers probably earn less than $20,000 per year. As school enrollments continue to grow, however, the number of jobs for school bus drivers is expected to increase. And because of high turnover, these jobs should be easy to get.

School Counselors

Counselors use a variety of methods to enable students to understand their abilities better, advising them on personal, special, educational, and career problems and concerns. High school counselors advise on college admissions requirements and financial aid, noncollege career options, and social, behavioral and other problems. About 154,000 people are employed as counselors, mostly in secondary schools. Jobs as counselors are expected to grow faster than the overall rate of job growth between now and the year 2005. The average salary of school counselors in 1992 was about $40,400.

University and College Professors

The number of students enrolled as undergraduates and graduate students in America's 3,638 accredited colleges and universities continues to increase each year. Although the growth has not been as high as the 41 percent recorded between 1970 and 1980, enrollment at institutions of higher education jumped about 20 percent between 1980 and 1992. It stands to reason, therefore, that the number of teachers required to instruct this army of would-be scholars is also increasing. In fact, the number of instructors is growing even faster than the number of students. According to the U.S. Department of Education, in 1980 there were 686,000 teachers at public, private, and religious institutions of higher education charged with instructing 10.5 million undergraduates and 1.5 million graduate students. That's 17.49 students per instructor. By 1992, the number of undergrads had jumped to 12.5 million, while the number of graduate students skyrocketed to 2.1 million. Instructors, meanwhile, increased to 880,000, a ratio of 16.54 students per instructor. Wages for teachers are ordinarily determined by the salary scale at each institution. There are usually four levels in each scale, with promotion coming from recommendations by senior faculty members:

Instructor—An entry-level position for persons who have not quite completed the requirement for the Ph.D. degree (usually they are in the midst of writing a dissertation). For the most part, instructors teach 9 to 12 hours a week, all in the basic courses: English composition, surveys of history, general chemistry, etc. Salaries for the 56,000 instructors in the United States averaged $29,680 in 1994–95. Average total compensation (including health insurance, disability protection, retirement contributions, and, in some cases, room and board) was $37,870.

Assistant Professor—This is also an entry-level job, but usually the Ph.D. is required. These people also teach 9 to 12 hours a week, and frequently supervise the running of the large undergraduate courses. At the same time, they must write scholarly articles or books if they wish to become permanent, tenured members of the faculty. To be granted tenure by the department means that you have been accepted as a competent scholar and teacher, that you are eligible for promotion, and that you can be dismissed from your job only for the gravest of reasons (ineptitude or failure to live up to your potential are *not* included). Salaries for the 111,000 assistant professors averaged $39,050 in 1994–95; total compensation averaged $49,350.

Associate Professor—Almost always a tenured position, this rank has become increasingly difficult to obtain. These people teach an average of 6 to 9 hours a week, usually most of the upper-division courses, a few graduate courses; and they occasionally supervise doctoral dissertations. The 116,000 associate professors in the United States averaged $47,040 in salary; their total compensation averaged $59,350.

Full Professor—Promotion to the highest level is based exclusively on one's publications and intellectual standing within the academic community; only rarely does teaching ability enter into the decision. At most universities, full professors teach 3 to 6 hours a week and supervise doctoral dissertations. Salaries for the 162,000 full professors averaged $63,450 in 1994–95; average total compensation was $78,890.

STUDENTS AND INSTRUCTORS IN HIGHER EDUCATION, 1980–1992

Category	1980	1985	1992
Undergraduate Students	10,475,000	10,597,000	12,485,000
Graduate Students	1,521,000	1,650,000	2,073,000
All Students	11,996,000	12,247,000	14,558,000
Instructors	686,000	715,000	880,000
Students per Instructor	17.49	17.12	16.54

SOURCE: U.S. Department of Education, *Digest of Education Statistics,* 1993.

Since 1980, there have been two developments that reflect important changes in the wage and salary practices in the colleges and universities. The first is the need to pay sciences, computer science, engineering, and business teachers more money than professors in other disciplines to prevent them from seeking careers in private industry. While the results of this practice won't be known for several years, it is probably safe to predict that the complaints from professors in the humanities and social sciences will be long, loud, and probably of a legal nature.

The second change worth noting centers on the role played by the so-called *adjunct professor,* a part-time employee in just about every institution of higher learning. About 40 percent of all college teaching jobs are held by adjuncts, up from 22 percent in 1970. Adjuncts are usually young and always untenured, and they work without fringe benefits, job security, or a guarantee of advancement. The going rate across the country is $1,200 to $1,500 per semester course, so the possibility of earning even $15,000 a year is fairly remote. Many universities hire adjuncts to teach, lessening the need to hire full-time, tenure-track professors.

The following tables list average salaries for all four ranks, arranged according to type of institution. Although many of the schools included are private institutions, they all receive so much public funding in the form of federal grants, state aid, etc., that it is not inappropriate to include their facilities under the rubric of the public payroll. The source for all of these figures is the 1994–95 salary survey conducted by the American Association of University Professors.

THE IVY LEAGUE

University, Location	Professor	Associate	Assistant	Instructor
Brown University, Providence, RI	$ 77,000	$53,000	$44,900	NA
Columbia University, New York City	91,800	58,500	41,800	NA
Cornell University, Ithaca, NY	80,500	57,600	49,100	NA
Dartmouth College, Hanover, NH	80,500	54,800	45,000	NA
Harvard University, Cambridge, MA	104,200	60,000	52,700	$41,600
University of Pennsylvania, Philadelphia	93,200	64,000	54,700	NA
Princeton University, Princeton, NJ	98,200	58,200	45,100	41,400
Yale University, New Haven, CT	96,500	54,500	46,200	40,000

NA: Not Available.
SOURCE: American Association of University Professors, *Annual Report on the Economic Status of the Profession, 1994–95*. Reprinted by permission.

MAJOR PRIVATE UNIVERSITIES

University, Location	Professor	Associate	Assistant	Instructor
Baylor University, Waco, TX	$63,600	$49,200	$40,100	NA
Brandeis University, Waltham, MA	70,600	50,900	41,700	NA
Brigham Young University, Provo, UT	61,100	45,500	38,100	$33,100
Case Western Reserve University, Cleveland	78,000	54,800	48,100	38,700
Clark University, Worcester, MA	66,800	47,600	43,000	NA
Clemson University, Clemson, SC	62,000	46,100	40,000	22,800
Colgate University, Hamilton, NY	71,100	53,400	41,800	NA
Duke University, Durham, NC	89,000	60,900	47,800	NA
Emory University, Atlanta	84,000	56,000	47,100	NA
Howard University, Washington, D.C.	65,900	48,100	41,100	34,300
Johns Hopkins University, Baltimore	81,900	55,000	45,100	39,400
Lehigh University, Bethlehem, PA	76,600	54,800	45,100	NA
Marquette University, Milwaukee	71,100	52,600	43,800	NA

MAJOR PRIVATE UNIVERSITIES

University, Location	Professor	Associate	Assistant	Instructor
New York University, New York City	$93,000	$61,100	$52,200	$39,600
Northwestern University, Evanston, IL	89,500	61,700	51,800	NA
Old Dominion University, Norfolk, VA	62,600	46,100	39,200	30,300
Purdue University, West Lafayette, IN	73,600	49,100	43,300	27,500
Rice University, Houston, TX	84,200	55,800	49,000	37,400
Southern Methodist University, Dallas	76,400	51,100	45,500	NA
Stanford University, Palo Alto, CA	99,900	68,100	53,800	NA
Syracuse University, Syracuse, NY	66,000	49,200	40,500	32,100
Temple University, Philadelphia	78,100	61,200	47,200	34,700
Tufts University, Medford, MA	75,800	57,700	46,200	NA
Tulane University, New Orleans	73,500	52,000	43,300	NA
University of Chicago	92,900	61,000	53,400	36,800
Vanderbilt University, Nashville	83,100	54,500	43,600	38,600
Wake Forest University, Winston-Salem, NC	71,000	54,400	44,400	33,100
Washington and Lee University, Lexington, VA	71,400	50,600	40,300	NA
Washington University, St. Louis	81,300	54,600	47,300	NA
Wesleyan University, Middletown, CT	74,700	51,900	43,400	NA

NA: Not Available.

SOURCE: American Association of University Professors, *Annual Report on the Economic Status of the Profession, 1994–95.* Reprinted by permission.

MAJOR STATE UNIVERSITIES

University, Location	Professor	Associate	Assistant	Instructor
University of Alabama, Tuscaloosa	$63,800	$47,600	$40,600	$26,400
University of Alaska, Fairbanks	66,500	55,500	44,300	37,100
Arizona State University, Tempe	64,800	48,800	41,400	NA
University of Arizona, Tucson	67,700	47,400	43,00	NA
University of Arkansas, Fayetteville	57,600	44,500	38,900	25,600
University of California, Berkeley	80,100	53,700	45,700	NA
University of Californiaa, Los Angeles	78,000	52,900	44,300	NA
University of Colorado, Boulder	69,600	52,300	44,300	33,400
University of Connecticut, Storrs	78,300	58,900	46,700	40,000
University of Delaware, Newark	75,700	54,800	46,600	31,900
University of Florida, Gainesville	64,000	45,800	41,000	37,800
Florida State University, Tallahassee	59,600	43,300	40,500	18,300
University of Georgia, Athens	64,900	46,700	40,000	25,700
University of Hawaii, Manoa	73,800	55,700	47,400	36,200
University of Idaho, Moscow	53,100	42,400	38,600	30,000
University of Illinois, Urbana	71,800	51,200	44,300	NA
Indiana University, Bloomington	69,500	49,100	40,600	NA
University of Iowa, Iowa City	72,400	51,800	44,200	40,900
University of Kansas, Lawrence	61,100	44,700	38,500	NA
University of Kentucky, Lexington	65,700	48,700	42,200	47,900
Louisiana State University, Baton Rouge	59,300	43,700	37,900	26,300
University of Maine, Orono	56,700	43,400	36,100	27,200
University of Maryland, College Park	73,000	49,900	43,100	32,900
University of Masssachusetts, Amherst	70,700	53,400	43,900	43,800
Michigan State University, East Lansing	67,200	50,700	43,100	32,800
University of Michigan, Ann Arbor	81,400	60,100	48,100	42,000
University of Minnesota, Minneapolis-St. Paul	70,600	49,900	43,700	NA
University of Mississippi, University	59,800	46,100	40,100	27,000
University of Missouri, Columbia	64,000	48,800	42,500	30,400
University of Montana, Missoula	45,800	37,000	33,700	24,100
University of Nebraska, Lincoln	67,500	48,400	41,300	25,200
University of Nevada, Reno	66,300	48,800	39,700	NA
University of New Hampshire, Durham	64,800	49,600	40,700	NA
New Mexico State University, Las Cruces	55,000	45,100	37,600	24,000
State University of New York at Albany	75,400	53,700	42,000	NA
State University of New York at Buffalo	78,900	56,100	44,200	28,900
University of North Carolina, Chapel Hill	74,700	53,900	44,500	41,300
North Carolina State University, Raleigh	70,000	50,700	43,600	34,700

MAJOR STATE UNIVERSITIES

University, Location	Professor	Associate	Assistant	Instructor
University of North Dakota, Grand Forks	$47,400	$39,800	$35,100	$30,800
Ohio State University, Columbus	72,600	50,700	42,900	31,500
University of Oklahoma, Norman	61,000	44,500	36,300	22,800
University of Oregon, Eugene	59,400	44,400	37,900	28,400
Pennsylvania State University, University Park	74,700	52,600	42,600	29,000
University of Rhode Island, Kingston	66,500	49,600	43,900	NA
Rutgers State University, New Brunswick, NJ	93,000	67,100	51,900	33,400
University of South Carolina, Columbia	63,700	47,400	41,000	29,200
University of South Dakota, Vermillion	49,100	37,700	34,800	23,400
University of Tennessee, Knoxville	65,200	49,200	43,200	28,500
University of Texas, Austin	74,300	48,500	43,700	32,900
Texas A&M University, College Station	65,900	46,900	40,900	NA
University of Utah, Salt Lake City	64,800	45,500	39,700	29,100
University of Vermont, Burlington	61,300	46,700	37,300	NA
University of Virginia, Charlottesville	79,500	52,900	43,700	31,800
University of Washington, Seattle	67,800	48,200	42,200	31,200
West Virginia University, Morgantown	54,300	44,200	37,100	29,600
University of Wisconsin, Madison	70,100	52,300	46,200	34,600
University of Wyoming, Laramie	56,500	43,800	39,700	38,200

NA: Not Available.

SOURCE: American Association of University Professors, *Annual Report on the Economic Status of the Profession, 1994–95.* Reprinted by permission.

WELL-KNOWN PRIVATE COLLEGES

College	Professor	Associate	Assistant	Instructor
Amherst College, Amherst, MA	$74,900	$51,400	$44,000	NA
Barnard College, New York City[1]	74,300	53,600	40,500	NA
Bowdoin College, Brunswick, ME	74,200	53,100	41,500	NA
Bryn Mawr College, Bryn Mawr, PA	64,800	48,900	40,300	$31,300
Carleton College, Northfield, MN	65,100	50,200	41,000	NA
Colby College, Waterville, ME	77,500	55,200	41,000	NA
Colorado College, Colorado Springs	63,700	49,800	40,500	NA
Franklin and Marshall College, Lancaster, PA	69,400	48,900	39,100	NA

WELL-KNOWN PRIVATE COLLEGES

College	Professor	Associate	Assistant	Instructor
Haverford College, Haverford, PA	$68,200	$51,600	$40,800	NA
Lafayette College, Easton, PA	70,700	52,700	42,500	NA
Middlebury College, Middlebury, VT	73,500	52,200	42,300	$38,000
Mills College, Oakland, CA[1]	59,500	46,700	40,100	NA
Mount Holyoke College, South Hadley, MA[1]	71,500	52,800	42,700	NA
Skidmore College, Saratoga Springs, NY	66,000	50,700	40,200	NA
Smith College, Northampton, MA[1]	76,300	56,500	42,500	35,900
Swarthmore College, Swarthmore, PA	75,800	54,800	43,100	NA
Vassar College, Poughkeepsie, NY	69,700	53,800	41,200	36,500
Wellesley College, Wellesley, MA[1]	81,100	57,000	46,600	NA
William and Mary, Williamsburg, VA	69,300	51,700	38,200	29,100
Williams College, Williamstown, MA	73,400	51,500	43,300	NA

NA: Not Available.
[1]Women's college.
SOURCE: American Association of University Professors, *Annual Report on the Economic Status of the Profession, 1994–95.* Reprinted by permission.

MAJOR CATHOLIC COLLEGES AND UNIVERSITIES

Institution	Professor	Associate	Assistant	Instructor
Boston College, Chestnut Hill, MA	$83,800	$59,500	$54,800	$36,800
Catholic University of America, Washington, DC	61,500	46,600	38,900	NA
College of the Holy Cross, Worcester, MA	70,900	52,300	42,200	NA
De Paul University, Chicago	72,100	56,200	43,400	36,100
DePauw University, Greencastle, IN	55,600	44,800	36,200	NA
Duquesne University, Pittsburgh	62,500	49,300	41,100	39,900
Fordham University, New York City	76,100	59,600	44,700	40,600
Georgetown University, Washington, DC	88,500	56,600	43,600	36,100
Loyola University, Chicago	77,500	54,300	43,600	NA
University of Notre Dame, S. Bend, Ind.	82,700	58,300	48,200	45,800

NA: Not Available.
SOURCE: American Association of University Professors, *Annual Report on the Economic Status of the Profession, 1994–95.* Reprinted by permission.

INSTITUTES OF TECHNOLOGY

Institute	Professor	Associate	Assistant	Instructor
California Institute of Technology, Pasadena	$100,700	$75,600	$60,100	NA
Carnegie-Mellon University, Pittsburgh	85,500	57,700	50,300	NA
Georgia Institute of Technology, Atlanta	73,200	55,000	49,200	$25,500
Massachusetts Institute of Technology, Cambridge	93,100	66,000	52,500	34,800
Rensselaer Polytechnic Institute, Troy, NY	77,400	55,200	49,900	NA
Rochester Institute of Technology, Rochester, NY	57,100	47,400	41,100	32,700
Texas Tech University, Lubbock	62,900	44,100	36,900	25,200
Virginia Polytechnic Institute, Blacksburg	67,200	47,700	42,600	26,200

NA: Not Available.

SOURCE: American Association of University Professors, *Annual Report on the Economic Status of the Profession, 1994–95*. Reprinted by permission.

AVERAGE SALARIES OF COLLEGE PROFESSORS BY DISCIPLINE

Discipline	Professor	Associate	Assistant	Instructor
Agricultural Business and Production	$62,277	$47,028	$40,149	$31,515
Architecture	62,403	46,528	37,892	31,700
Biological Sciences/Life Sciences	66,078	47,074	40,397	28,125
Business Management	82,175	63,627	59,242	37,289
Communications	61,323	45,324	37,512	29,141
Computer and Information Sciences	79,070	59,290	50,838	31,714
Education	60,011	45,226	36,982	28,885
Engineering	77,793	57,238	49,488	32,628
English	60,594	42,721	35,380	24,606
Foreign Languages	60,373	43,010	35,095	25,724
Health Professions and Related Sciences	80,208	60,017	52,004	35,951
Home Economics	60,579	45,733	37,739	29,972
Law	93,772	67,259	62,515	38,035
Liberal Arts	59,658	43,356	36,602	31,037
Library Science	63,975	47,335	38,481	28,685
Mathematics	67,109	47,143	40,249	28,075
Philosophy and Religion	60,957	42,684	34,642	27,134
Physical Sciences	69,504	47,407	41,157	30,425
Psychology	65,664	45,322	37,904	32,657
Public Administration	65,380	48,144	38,582	35,117

AVERAGE SALARIES OF COLLEGE PROFESSORS BY DISCIPLINE

Discipline	Professor	Associate	Assistant	Instructor
Social Sciences and History	$65,974	$45,993	$38,290	$32,141
Visual and Performing Arts	55,131	41,291	33,450	27,755
Average for all Disciplines	$68,725	$49,738	$42,925	$30,513

SOURCE: Oklahoma State University, Office of Planning and Budget and Institutional Research, *1994–95 Faculty Salary Survey*. Reprinted by permission.

University and College Administrators

The growth of education has naturally led to an increase in the number of people needed to oversee the maintenance and development of individual institutions on a daily as well as a long-term basis. In most universities, the organizational structure established to carry out these tasks resembles those found in large corporations: chancellors and presidents—frequently referred to as CEOs—are advised by several vice presidents, each of whom is responsible for a particular university activity and for overseeing the work of the deans, who, in a sense, serve as plant or unit managers. Because administrators now function as a managerial class, their salaries, especially in relation to those of senior faculty members, have never been higher. Witness the salaries and benefits paid to some of the highest-paid university presidents:

Best-Paid University Presidents, 1993–94

President	Institution	Salary and Benefits
John R. Silber	Boston University	$564,020
Peter Diamondopoulos	Adelphi University	523,626
James Doughdrill, Jr.	Rhodes College	461,458
Joe B. Wyatt	Vanderbilt University	459,046

SOURCE: Chronicle of Higher Education.

At some universities, the careful reader will note, the salary of a dean in a nontechnical area will be $20,000 higher than that of the average full professor in the same school of study.

The general salary data, as well as the title and job descriptions given below, are taken from a survey administered by the College and University Personnel Association, (CUPA). More than 1,500 schools responded to its questionnaires, so we feel confident that the figures presented here are representative of national salary ranges. Overall, the median salaries of all college and university administrators rose by 4.4 percent for the 1994–95 academic year. The biggest increases came in academic (4.1 percent) and administrative (5.9 percent) positions. Salary increases were highest at two-year institutions, where median salaries jumped 5.4 percent over 1993–94 levels.

JOB TITLES AND RESPONSIBILITIES OF COLLEGE AND UNIVERSITY ADMINISTRATORS

Chief Executive Officer of a System—(multicampus operation)—Frequently called a chancellor, sometimes a president. He or she is the principal administrative official responsible for the direction of all operations for all units of the system. He or she reports to a governing board.

Chief Executive Officer of a Single Institution—Usually called a president, directs entire campus operation.

Executive Vice-President—The principal administrative official reporting directly to the CEO.

Chief Academic Officer—Often called the provost, he or she is responsible for the direction of the academic program. All matters concerning the faculty, research, curriculum, admissions, and library fall under this office's jurisdiction.

Chief Business Officer—Responsible for the direction of business and financial affairs, including supervision of purchasing, physical plant management, personnel services, accounting, and investments.

Chief Financial Officer—Responsible for investments, accounting, budgets, and related matters.

Chief Planning Officer—Responsible for long-range planning and allocation of resources, including budget planning, sponsoring institutional research, and building additional facilities; frequently implements state and federal regulations.

Chief Budgeting Officer—Responsible for current budgetary operations.

Chief Development Officer—Responsible for institutional development and fund-raising programs; frequently oversees alumni relations and public relations departments.

Chief Public Relations Officer—Responsible for all relations with the public, the media, alumni, and legislators.

Director of Alumni Affairs—Coordinates contacts and services to alumni; develops mailing lists and organizes alumni activities and events.

Chief Student Affairs Officer—Responsible for the direction of all student services and student life programs, including student counseling and testing, career development and placement, student activities, residence life, and minority support programs.

Chief Admissions Officer—Responsible for the admission of undergraduates and, in some institutions, graduate and professional students. May also oversee administration of scholarships.

Registrar—Responsible for student registrations and records. Schedules classes and classrooms, maintains grades for graduation clearance.

Director of Student Financial Aid—Directs the administration of all forms of student aid, including loans and scholarships. Administers all loan programs and awards fellowships.

Director of Career Development and Placement—Provides job placement and counseling services to undergraduates, graduates, and alumni.

Director of Student Counseling—Provides counseling and testing services for all students.

MEDIAN ANNUAL SALARIES OF ADMINISTRATORS IN HIGHER EDUCATION

Title	Large Public Universities	Large Private Universities	Private Religious Institutions	Two-Year Junior Colleges
Chancellor, System	$116,142	$120,000	$90,000	$98,789
President, Institution	103,000	140,000	97,987	91,203
Executive Vice-President	92,299	122,175	65,950	77,475
Chief Academic Officer	85,500	90,000	67,991	68,884
Chief Business Officer	78,900	89,439	66,528	66,437

MEDIAN ANNUAL SALARIES OF ADMINISTRATORS IN HIGHER EDUCATION

Title	Large Public Universities	Large Private Universities	Private Religious Institutions	Two-Year Junior Colleges
Chief Financial Officer	$71,901	$72,000	$60,600	$57,784
Chief Planning Officer	73,166	74,550	57,294	68,398
Chief Budgeting Officer	59,495	65,000	53,058	50,997
Chief Development Officer	72,500	82,800	62,543	51,327
Chief Public Relations Officer	53,334	57,601	39,160	40,400
Director of Alumni Affairs	44,714	41,700	34,802	30,048
Chief Student Affairs Officer	72,875	71,500	54,080	60,933
Chief Admissions Officer	51,169	55,639	41,988	44,348
Registrar	49,169	42,900	36,427	40,058
Director of Student Financial Aid	46,215	44,656	37,282	41,185
Director of Career Development and Placement	43,780	39,303	33,250	36,513
Director of Student Counseling	50,040	42,997	36,755	43,800

SOURCE: College and University Personnel Association, *Administrative Compensation Survey, 1994–95* (1995). Reprinted by permission.

MEDIAN ANNUAL SALARIES OF DEANS IN HIGHER EDUCATION

Discipline	Large Public Universities	Large Private Universities	Private Religious Institutions	Two-Year Junior Colleges
Arts and Sciences	$ 79,454	$ 85,143	$70,000	$56,930
Business	78,600	89,650	72,650	55,130
Continuing Education	65,369	65,850	53,360	56,987
Education	82,400	70,100	50,664	59,816
Engineering	101,498	109,000	74,400	58,600
Fine Arts	76,456	69,373	48,650	56,671
Graduate Programs	84,041	81,082	57,512	NA
Health-Related Professions	68,389	80,487	53,100	56,000
Humanities	64,792	54,545	44,000	56,032
Nursing	74,952	72,072	58,741	52,298
Occupational Studies/ Vocational Education	60,364	51,447	34,163	56,495
Sciences	74,449	65,521	47,741	58,099
Social Sciences	66,334	52,473	45,577	57,268
Dean of Students	58,700	56,984	41,767	54,995

SOURCE: College and University Personnel Association, *Administrative Compensation Survey, 1994–95* (1995). Reprinted by permission.

II

In the Public Eye and Behind the Scenes

This section is devoted to the world of entertainment, to the whole spectrum of public performance. Included here are famous actors, athletes, and television personalities, as well as highly acclaimed ballet dancers, classical musicians, and stars of the Metropolitan Opera. In each category we provide salary information for almost every level from union-established minimums to the highest echelon of what today is called "superstardom." In the section on television personalities, for example, you'll find nationally known names such as Tom Brokaw and Ted Koppel, but you'll also learn about anchorpersons in Des Moines and Green Bay. Another example is the section on models, in which Cindy Crawford and Claudia Schiffer are intermingled with unknowns who work in showrooms and at studios, or who appear in the pages of *Playboy.*

Of course, only a small number of people hold these jobs. Combining statistics from the Department of Labor with those from the major associations and unions representing athletes and performers, a generous estimate would be 160,000 all together. There are, however, more than twice that number working behind the scenes to assure the smooth functioning of the entertainment system. This includes television technicians, film directors, costume designers, stagehands, fashion photographers, athletic coaches, story analysts, choreographers, and many others. In order to show the occupational and economic relationships between the public performers and the support staff, we decided to keep them together in one integrated section. The juxtaposition resulted in a picture that resembles the basic structure of the American pay system, with the highest salaries being 10, 20, even 30 times higher than those of the overwhelming majority of employees.

Most of us are so dazzled by the vast sums paid to film stars, TV talkshow hosts, and professional athletes that we think of their salaries as aberrations having no relation whatsoever to the everyday world of work and pay. And as aberrations many people assume that these high salaries have no effect on pay levels outside the world of entertainment. Not only are both these assumptions false, they also preclude any exploration of just what the limits of pay in relation to work might be.

Whether any one person's work can actually be worth $14 million or more a year (David Letterman's new salary) is in itself an interesting and at least debatable question. But when the subjects are athletes, entertainers, talkshow hosts, and news commentators, the value of their work in relation to their pay simply cannot stand up under even the mildest forms of scrutiny. For no matter how much we admire the pitching prowess of a David Cone or the verbal skills of a Dan Rather, and no matter how many millions watch David Letterman, it is difficult, at best, to think of what they do as being worth 50 or 100 times more than the work of the best scientists, the best engineers, most doctors, and all justices of the Supreme Court.

No wonder high-salaried people who have great responsibilities (chief executives at large corporations, for example) or those who have mastered a large body of complicated knowledge (criminal lawyers or high-powered accountants) frequently justify their earnings by pointing to those of people in show business.

In fact, as shown by the tables on the following pages, the top-paid corporate executives did not earn as much as the top-earning entertainers in 1994; but, their earnings far outstripped those in professional sports. Whether it is more difficult to run a large corporation than it is to become heavyweight champion of the world or a world-famous rock star is, of course, subject to debate. So is the question of who might return greater value to society per dollar earned. Certainly when the figure in question is $20 million or more, attempts to justify such compensation strain credibility. But when one considers that NBC reportedly pays Tom Brokaw $3 million to read the news, the salaries of corporate executives seem perfectly reasonable.

Such comparisons have the value of highlighting the way large salaries of public performers can drive up those in the world of business. But the comparisons should not obscure the more interesting fact that the highest salaries in big business and show business come from the same source, America's largest corporations. Just a glance through the pages in this part will show that television is the most lucrative medium for any performer. Moreover, the economic power of the television industry is so pervasive that it affects salary levels in areas seemingly outside its perimeters. The astronomical sums guaranteed to movie stars, for example, are largely predicated on the sale of films to television, frequently before production has begun.

More often than not, in fact, the deal to make a film is based on guaranteed dollars from a television network.

THE HIGHEST PAID ENTERTAINERS, 1994

Name	Estimated Income, 1994
Oprah Winfrey	$66,000,000
Bill Cosby	58,000,000
Johnny Carson	42,000,000
Bryan Adams	37,000,000
Geraldo Rivera	32,000,000
Sylvester Stallone	20,000,000
Macaulay Culkin	16,000,000
Bruce Willis	15,000,000
David Letterman	14,000,000

SOURCE: *Premiere* magazine; magazine articles.

The escalating salaries of professional athletes over the last decade can also be traced to revenues generated from television. Sure, baseball owners have raised ticket prices, but certainly not enough to pay the average player a million dollars a year, not to mention the 17 players who receive more than $5 million a year. As long as the fees for broadcasting ball games can be raised, the owners can keep increasing players' pay and the smart ones can still make a profit themselves. Conversely, if TV money dries up, there is less to spend on player salaries without raising ticket prices. The proof of this was seen in 1994, when CBS realized it spent far too much for the rights to broadcast major league baseball games. Without this cash infusion, the owners attempted to impose a salary cap on the players in an attempt to fix the other side of the ledger sheet, which prompted the players to go out on strike for 234 days, the longest work stoppage in sports history.

But let's not belabor the point. If television provides the bulk of the money for the high salaries of public performers, advertising revenues are in turn the chief source of television's seemingly bottomless purse. Of the more than $138 billion spent on advertising in 1994, more than 20 percent went to television networks and local stations, most of it from large national advertisers like General Mills, McDonald's, and the three big auto makers. Ultimately, of course, the source of all advertising revenue is the American consumer, who pays the bill in increased prices for goods and services. The figure comes to over $300 per family, or more than twice what it was a decade ago.

Now, how much of this is actually allocated to paying the salaries of television stars and athletes has never been determined and probably shouldn't be. For to think only in financial terms misses the point. The essential question is whether these multimillion dollar salaries are creating a new kind of American aristocracy whose economic security is based not on an ancestral blood connection nor on the booty left by more talented or ruthless forbearers, but on the wealth acquired through being famous. And not famous for an achievement, an accomplishment, a discovery, a daring feat, or any other traditional reason, but simply because of what one does on television.

While most Americans do not begrudge these individuals these large sums of money, they are keenly aware of the inherent injustices in a system that allows celebrities to earn so much more than intelligent, productive members of society. Whether anything could ever be done about it remains, at least at this time in our history, a very academic question.

In the Public Eye

ACTORS

Acting is an enormously seductive occupation, and thousands of young people succumb to its magic and mystery every year. Most of them can be found in New York or Los Angeles working as typists, messengers, waitresses, clerks, or busboys, jobs that allow some flexibility in terms of hours. This enables them to take acting classes, go to auditions, and appear in nonpaying showcase productions, while still earning a living. The notion that some of America's most famous and accomplished actors started just this way, from the time of Henry Fonda and Jimmy Stewart to Tom Hanks and Susan Sarandon, keeps the dream of success alive.

From a pedestrian, career-minded point of view, of course, these people are simply wasting their time, since the odds of ever finding work as an actor are extremely small. Approximately 60,000 actors a year are paid for their efforts, but there are at least 140,000 professionals looking for jobs. According to all three major unions representing actors, the unemployment rate among their members is extremely high and likely to remain so.

For example, the Actor's Equity Association (AEA), which represents all stage actors, including Broadway, Off-Broadway, Off-Off Broadway, and regional theatrical stage actors all over the country, had 17,000 unemployed members during the 1993–94 season; that's 53 percent of the total. Those AEA members who did find work worked an average of 17.9 weeks and earned an average annual salary of $12,570. Of those working, 28 percent earned less than $2,500.

Of the 78,000 members of the Screen Actors Guild (SAG), nearly 80 percent earned less than $5,000 in 1994; only 5 percent earned over $50,000.

The American Federation of Television and Radio Artists (AFTRA) members number approximately 64,015, yet dramatic serials, including such major television shows as *Roseanne* and *ER,* employ only 2,000 principal actors, extras, and occasional players per year. Radio shows, television commercials, and other broadcasts using AFTRA performers employ even fewer persons.

There are many actors who belong to both SAG and AFTRA or to all three of the major performers' unions, so the number of the unemployed reported by each does not represent a total of nonworking actors. But still the situation is grim. Those who do finally get that break, be it big or small, will find that the unions do a good job of taking care of their own, and remuneration for actors is often rewarding, though the art of propelling oneself into high-paying jobs sometimes takes more practice and concentration than is actually required by the coveted role.

Stage Actors

On Broadway, actors are guaranteed weekly minimum salaries of $1,000. The average top salary is much higher—approximately $3,500 weekly—and stars receive even more.

In so-called Off-Broadway theaters, actors' wages are dependent on the size of the theater. Off-Broadway theaters are those New York City theaters which have the capability of seating between 100 and 499 persons. According to the 1995 Actors' Equity contract for Off-Broadway performers, salaries are graduated between $355 and $609 weekly, with stars always receiving more as negotiated in their own contracts.

Off-Off Broadway theaters are those with fewer than 100 seats. Salaries for actors in Off-Off Broadway theaters depend upon whether the theater is privately run or is publicly funded and run as a nonprofit organization. Actors performing in funded nonprofit theaters are guaranteed a Fairshare Minimum Reimbursement determined by the size of the theater and its gross revenues.

Theaters with productions of under $5,000 come under the Basic Showcase Code as nonfunded stage companies. Actors for these Off-Off Broadway theaters receive no salary, but they are paid a so-called "carfare expense" of $2.50 per day, and this is awarded for four weeks of rehearsal and twelve weeks of performance.

Regional theaters are the last category but certainly a growing and important element in the revitalized life of the American stage. Payment for actors in many regional theaters is regulated by Actors' Equity Association. Regional theaters are divided into categories A–D, according to each theater's gross. New stage companies without financial histories are assigned a category by AEA speculation based on their number of seats, their weekly gross, and their budget for the season. By way of example, an A theater would be the Tyrone Guthrie in Minneapolis or the American Conservatory Theater in San Francisco. All touring companies, such as the American Conservatory, must pay their actors on either an A or B level, depending upon the company's gross. The well-known Actors' Theatre of Louisville, Kentucky, where the plays of many of America's newest playwrights have premiered, is a B theater.

MINIMUM WEEKLY SALARIES FOR ACTORS IN REGIONAL THEATER	
A theaters	$592
B+ theaters	572
B theaters	552
C theaters	525
D theaters	441

SOURCE: Actor's Equity Association contract, 1995.

Television Actors

All actors appearing on television must be members of the Screen Actors' Guild or the American Federation of Radio and Television Artists. Most are members of both. The unions set rules governing basic working conditions, including the minimum pay rates. These rates vary depending on whether the program is a series shown during the day—i.e., a soap opera—or a series aired during the prime time hours of 8:00 p.m. to 11:00 p.m. (Eastern time). Minimum rates also depend on whether the actor has a series contract or works on a freelance basis. Freelance actors in prime time are paid on either a daily, three-day, or weekly rate; those in soap operas are paid per episode; all minimum rates go up after 18 months. Finally, there are also minimum rates for bit players, known officially as "five lines or less performers." The basic rates are shown in the accompanying tables.

Stars, of course, earn considerably more than scale. Although well-known television actors rarely come close to making what major film stars do, the pay is very good and the work far less demanding.

On the long-running soap operas, for example, the leading characters routinely make over $400,000 a year, and breakout stars earn double that. Susan Lucci—who is better known for not winning a daytime Emmy Award despite more than a dozen nominations than she is for her role as Erica Kane on *All My Children*—is the highest-paid TV soap star, according to *TV Guide,* with an annual salary of $1 million. And that doesn't include the money she receives for pitching Ford cars and trucks. Apparently, her lack of awards hasn't affected her financial rewards.

The highest TV salaries, however, are reserved for the programs that attract the largest audiences, so prime-time players do best of all, as the accompanying charts make clear. When a show runs for years, the actors' value increases proportionately.

The amounts paid to lead actors in hit TV series continue to escalate. In the early 1980s, Larry Hagman, received $85,000 per episode of *Dallas,* while Linda Evans and Joan Collins reportedly each received $75,000 per episode of *Dynasty.* Alan Alda was the first to break the $200,000 per episode barrier for his work on *M*A*S*H*. Today, Roseanne receives $600,000 for each episode of the show that bears her name, plus huge syndication fees. Fellow comic Jerry Seinfeld earns $250,000 per episode of his show, *Seinfeld.* That makes him underpaid by comparison; nevertheless, it's quite a sum for a show whose story lines proudly claim to deal with "nothing."

Still, the king of prime-time television, at least in terms of salary, is Bill Cosby. In the early 1990s, Cosby received a staggering $56 million per year as actor, writer, and producer on *The Cosby Show,* as well as for writing and producing its successful spin-off, *A Different World.* When these shows ended their long runs, Cosby embarked on an hour-long drama series, *The Cosby Mysteries,* of which he was star, writer, and producer. And though the show met with lukewarm critical reviews, his paycheck for it in 1994 was a cool $58 million.

Even actors in series that aren't top ten pull in anywhere from $15,000 to $75,000 per episode, and sometimes more. *Northern Exposure* star Rob Morrow made headlines when he refused to work unless the producers increased his weekly salary of $35,000. After frantic negotiations, the network managed to lure him back at an undisclosed price; soon thereafter, he was written out of the show.

MINIMUM DAILY RATES FOR TELEVISION ACTORS

Day Actor	
Actor	$ 504
Stuntperson	504
Airplane Pilot (Studio)	673
Airplane Pilot (Location)	877
3-Day Actor	
Actor (½ or 1 hr. show)	$1,276
Stuntperson (½ or 1 hr. show)	1,379
Actors & Stuntpersons (1½ hr. or 2 hr. show)	1,503
Weekly Actor	
Actor	$1,752
Stuntperson	1,880
Airplane Pilot	1,880
Airplane Pilot (Flying or taxiing—daily adjustment)	579

MINIMUM DAILY RATES FOR TELEVISION ACTORS	
Multiple Programs—Weekly	
Other than Stuntpersons or Pilots (1/2 & 1 hr. show)	$1,295
(1 1/2 hr. show)	1,523
(2 1/2 hr. show)	1,797
Pilots & Stuntpersons (1/2 & 1 hr. show)	2,070
(1 1/2 hr. show)	2,295
(2 1/2 hr. show)	2,548
Term Actors	
10 out of 13 weeks (per week)	$1,503
20 out of 26 weeks (per week)	1,250
Beginners: 0–6 months	673
6–12 months	754
Series	
1/2 hr. 13 out of 13	$1,752
Less than 13	2,002
1 hr. 13 out of 13	2,105
Less than 13	2,350
1 1/2 hr. 13 out of 13	2,805
Less than 13	3,178
2 hrs. 13 out of 13	3,506
Less than 13	4,064
2 or more series in combined format: 1 hr.	2,747
1 1/2 hr.	3,710
2 hr.	4,740
TV Trailers	
On or Off Camera	$ 504

Per Diem on Overnight Locations

All actors shall be entitled to a basic $53.00 per diem allowance for meals on overnight locations.

(The producer shall have the right to deduct from the per diem the appropriate amount for each such meal furnished—see schedule below; however, the first major meal served shall be deducted at the lunch rate.)

Breakfast	$10.50
Lunch	15.00
Dinner	27.50

SOURCE: SAG contract, 1994–95.

Since American television runs on a 24-hour-a-day schedule, programming must be found to fill up all this time. That's why so many of the same old shows keep cropping up at all hours of the day and night. For many actors this has proved to be a financial windfall. Since 1954, producers have had to pay actors a fee almost every time a program is rerun. By 1979 this was big business. In recent years the Screen Actors' Guild has issued checks worth an estimated $50 million to its members for reruns just in the United States.

Known in the business as "residuals," these payments are based on individual agreements between actors and producers. Of course, stars make the most, but there are minimums based on the number of times a series is rerun. The first time a series or an episode from a series is rebroadcast (usually in the spring or summer after the initial fall and winter airing), all actors receive exactly what they did the first time. Anytime the show is rerun in prime time (a rare occurrence after the first year), all actors are also paid exactly what they were paid the first time. After this, residuals become a complicated matter based on percentages of base salaries and union minimums, usually 50 percent on first reruns not shown in prime time, 40 percent on the second, descending to 5 percent on the thirteenth rerun.

Some famous programs such as *Bonanza* and *Gunsmoke* became so popular around the world that producers found it more economical to purchase the principal actors' residual rights for a lump sum. *Bonanza*'s Lorne Greene supposedly received several million dollars, while James Arness, Amanda Blake, and Milburn Stone of *Gunsmoke* each received $1 million. The cast of *Star Trek,* on the other hand, received residuals for only six reruns and only based on minimum rates. No one could have predicted the show's immense popularity in reruns in the 20 years since it went off the air: *Star Trek* has run in more than 100 markets and has inspired seven feature-length movies and almost as many sequel series. The actors in the original series received payment only for their participation in the movies.

Today, as entertainment technology expands and new devices for information storage and retrieval spring up year after year, actors find their faces on the front of videotape boxes and on the screens of airport pay TVs. Under an agreement worked out by the unions and the people who run pay television, the actors receive 4.5 percent of the distributor's worldwide gross if the program is played on each of the distributor's pay television systems for 10 days out of one year. The same 4.5 percent take on the worldwide gross applies if a videotape producer releases 100,000 cassettes of the actor's show or if a distributor sells his show to cable television. As the late actor Ted Knight, best known for his role as the anchorman on the *Mary Tyler Moore Show,* said, "Anytime they show an actor's face on the screen he should get paid for it."

Actors in Advertising

If it weren't for radio and television commercials, a great many more actors would be out of work. Over 45,000 TV commercials alone are made every year, and many actors maintain their livelihoods from the seemingly bottomless purse of advertising. All minimum pay rates are set by SAG or AFTRA, and the figures below are based on the 1994–95 contracts. The basic contracts are very long and at times exceedingly complex, so the tables printed here are only representative.

TELEVISION COMMERCIALS

Minimum pay rates depend on such obvious factors as whether the actors are on-camera and whether they speak or sing or just have their hands shown. The union contract also lists minimum payments for different kinds of commercials, including *dealer commercials,* which are made for local use only, and *program commercials,* which pay actors on the basis of how often they are shown.

MINIMUM RATES FOR TV COMMERCIAL SESSIONS[1]

On Camera	
Principal performers, Stunt performers, Solo/Duo Singers and Dancers	$443.25
Group Singers/Dancers 3–5	324.50
Group Speakers 3–5	324.50
Group Singers/Dancers/Speakers 6–8	287.25
Group Singers/Dancers/Speakers 9 or more	237.60
Off Camera	
Principal performers, Solo/Duo Singers and Dancers	$333.30
Group Singers/Speakers 3–5	189.95
Group Singers/Speakers 6–8	163.10
Group Singers/Speakers 9 or more	133.00

[1]At the end of the session, principal performers are advised of the number of commercials made and, in addition to session fee, receive the equivalent of a session fee in excess of one.
SOURCE: Screen Actor's Guild contract, 1994–95.

The most successful actors in commercials can make a great deal of money. What everyone hopes for, of course, is to become a spokesperson for a particular brand name. The name Bill Cosby, for example, has become synonymous with Jell-O after his years of touting the company's products in commercials that earned him over $1 million annually. Those ads proved so successful that Kodak also enlisted Cosby's services. Candice Bergen has similarly come to represent Sprint telephone services, while Jerry Seinfeld is now the face of the American Express Card. Officials at both companies are tight-lipped about what they pay for these endorsements, but it is safe to assume the rewards are substantial, given that both actors are major stars in top-rated sitcoms.

MINIMUM DAILY RATES FOR CABLE TV COMMERCIALS

The compensation to each principal performer for each 13-week cycle of cable use of a commercial shall be computed by multiplying the applicable unit price by the aggregate unit weight of all cable systems and networks on which the commercial is aired (see next page). Although the contract is complicated, what it means is that actors are well paid for commercials. However, in no event shall compensation be less than the session fee, nor, for the first 18 months of the contract term, more than the price for 160 units.

RADIO COMMERCIALS

Those reassuring voices on the radio offering promises of fast relief or urging you to run to the local supermarket are compensated in many different ways. There are prime-time contracts and commercial contracts, national contracts and local contracts, but in order to give some idea of the pay rates for this work, we have provided some of the basic minimum rates for radio actors and announcers set by AFTRA. These minimums are applicable whether the commercial is aired nationally, regionally, or to a single small town in the foothills of the Appalachians. Each performer's or announcer's rate of pay depends on how many times the commercial is aired; how many announcers, actors, singers, or dancers are employed in the commercial; and where and to how many places the advertisement is broadcast.

CABLE UNITS AND PRICES PER UNIT

	Principals		Groups					
			On Camera			Off Camera		
Cable	On Camera	Off Camera	3–5	6–8	9 +	3–5	6–8	9 +
Minimum	$443.25	$333.30	$324.60	$287.25	$237.60	$187.95	$163.10	$133.00
Units 1–50	4.57	3.43	3.35	2.96	2.45	1.94	1.68	1.37
Units 51–100	3.97	2.99	2.90	2.57	2.12	1.68	1.46	1.19
Units 101–150	3.37	2.53	2.47	2.18	1.71	1.43	1.24	1.01
Units 151–160	2.77	2.09	2.03	1.80	1.49	1.18	1.02	0.83
Maximum (160 Units)	$673.06	$506.02	$492.84	$435.90	$360.72	$285.54	$247.56	$201.74

SOURCE: AFTRA 1994 Television Commercials Memorandum of Agreement.

PROGRAM USE FEES FOR TV COMMERCIALS

	Principals		Groups					
			On Camera			Off Camera		
	On Camera	Off Camera	3–5	6–8	9 +	3–5	6–8	9 +
1st Use	$ 443.25	$ 333.30	$ 324.50	$ 287.25	$237.60	$187.95	$163.10	$133.00
2nd Use	122.70	96.00	113.70	97.35	79.65	61.70	53.65	44.00
3rd Use	97.35	76.35	89.00	80.65	65.95	57.65	49.35	40.30
4–13 Each Use	97.35	76.35	84.00	75.65	62.00	52.65	45.95	37.65
14+ Each Use	46.65	34.65	29.00	24.65	20.00	21.00	19.70	16.35
13 Use Guaranteed	1,410.05	1,093.00	1,175.95	1,050.70	862.85	715.54	623.80	510.45
14–18 Each Use	92.00	69.88	67.25	58.86	48.07	44.43	40.06	33.02

SOURCE: AFTRA contract, 1994.

MINIMUM FEES FOR RADIO NETWORK PROGRAM COMMERCIALS[1]

One week's use:	
Soloists, Duos, Actors, and Announcers	$371.85
Group Singers	279.00
Four weeks' use:	
Soloists, Duos, Actors, and Announcers	$603.35
Group Singers:	
3–5	463.95
6–8	414.90
9 or more	379.00
Eight weeks' use:	
Soloists, Duos, Actors, and Announcers	$961.10
Group Singers:	
3–5	739.45
6–8	660.85
9 or more	591.95
Thirteen weeks' use:	
Soloists, Duos, Actors, and Announcers	$1,192.55
Group Singers:	
3–5	917.25
6–8	820.15
9 or more	751.35

[1]Fees per person, per commercial.
SOURCE: AFTRA contract, 1994.

Celebrities in Advertising

The tradition of using famous names and faces in advertising dates back to the turn of the century. Stars of the first magnitude, including Sarah Bernhardt, Lillian Russell, and Enrico Caruso, were the start of a long line of well-known performers who took part in what is known as the *celebrity endorsement technique.* Legendary movie stars from Douglas Fairbanks, Mary Pickford, and Charlie Chaplin to Spencer Tracy, Clark Gable, and Gary Cooper all put their seal of approval on American brand names. So too have genuine heroes such as Amelia Earhart, Charles Lindbergh, and Neil Armstrong. Celebrities have always done endorsements because the money was good, while advertisers discovered that well-known people gave their ads a much stronger impact. The same is true today.

The use of celebrities in commercials has more than doubled since 1970. The reason for this astonishing increase is, in ad lingo, "clutter," the presence of so many ads for such a variety of products all lumped together between screaming program promotions. To get their message heard, to make it memorable in a medium devoted to the ephemeral, advertisers are willing to part with vast sums of money to persuade well-known people to appear in their commercials.

Most recipients of this wealth today are formerly first-rate actors who have passed their prime, such as Lauren Bacall or John Forsythe, or would-be actors who will most likely never reach stardom. Others are active or recently retired athletes trying to cash in on their inevitably short-lived fame. A sterling example is ex-pro baseball and football player Bo Jackson, whose "Bo Knows" campaign for Nike athletic shoes continued successfully even after an injury ended his phenomenal sports career. What all this means is that American consumers, by absorbing the costs of celebrity advertising through higher prices, are enabling some not extraordinarily talented people to live like Arab sheiks. As an old ad used to say, "There's gotta be a better way."

One problem plaguing celebrity endorsements, however, has been the unexpected fall from grace. Allegations of sexual misconduct ended Michael Jackson's long-term contract as creative consultant and performer in Pepsi-Cola commercials—a stint for which he'd been receiving $5 million every three years. And O. J. Simpson's role as defendant in a double murder trial obviously curtailed his other roles as celebrity spokesperson for Hertz Rent-A-Car and Tropicana orange juice.

Another phenomenon which has grown by leaps and bounds is the TV "infomercial." Program-length commercials featuring celebrities as hosts and guests have blossomed into a $750 million businesss. And though infomercials were once considered the "ugly stepchild of advertising," celebrities are now waiting in line to host them, said Steve Howard, president of Williams Television Time, an infomercial production company. "We used to have to beat down their doors to get them [to participate]; now, they're flocking to us."

The reason, no doubt, is money. A star can make up to $100,000 for shooting an infomercial, in addition to royalties which can go as high as 5 percent of gross sales, according to *Time.* After filming an infomercial for The Perfect Smile tooth whitener, Vanna White received roughly $1 million in royalties in the first four months alone (gross sales reached $20 million during that period). Which is probably why Ali MacGraw hawks beauty products, Victoria Principal promotes a skin care line, and Angela Lansbury sells children's videotapes in program-length commercials.

FEES FOR CELEBRITIES IN ADS AND COMMERCIALS

Cher: The reigning queen of the half-hour "informercial," Cher is reportedly paid $1 million annually to promote Lori Davis Hair Care Products. The stint was so successful, in fact, that the superstar decided to buy and promote her very own line of cosmetics.

Bill Cosby: One of Hollywood's wealthiest men, Cosby has worked for Jell-O, Ford, Del Monte, Coca-Cola, Texas Instruments, E.F. Hutton, Chrysler, and Kodak. His fees are said to be over $1 million per client annually—a very conservative estimate.

Kathie Lee Gifford: Regis Philbin's outspoken morning show co-host has literally been singing the praises of Carnival Cruise lines in TV ads for several years now, reportedly to the tune of $1 million annually.

"They wouldn't think of shilling products back home," reports *People* magazine, but in Japan where "yen for integrity is a steal," America's top box office draws peddle Japanese wares. For $1 million annually, *Eddie Murphy* can be seen kissing a Toyota on Japanese television. For the same price, *Arnold Schwarzenegger* sells soup, *Sylvester Stallone* hustles ham, and brat-packer *Charlie Sheen* plugs Tokyo Air Conditioners.

Not all celebrities, though, are willing to cash in on their fame, no matter how tempting the offer. Late night TV's hottest commodity *David Letterman*—who has never publicly endorsed a product, turned down a five-year, $25-million offer to do Purina Dog Food commercials.

Other stars have seen so much success in endorsements—not only for themselves but for the products they peddle, that they've developed their own products to sell in hopes of reaping *all* the benefits. *Elizabeth Taylor* has four fragrance lines—including Passion and White Diamonds, and *Mariel Hemingway* is the chief spokesperson for her perfume, appropriately called "Mariel."

Stuntmen and Extras

There are over 2,000 stuntmen in the Screen Actors Guild. The men and women who risk life and limb for film are well rewarded, and rightfully so. Take 32-year-old Dan Robinson, for example, who in the filming of *Highpoint* sky-dove in a business suit for 1,150 feet from Toronto's CN Tower before he opened a safety chute and floated 300 feet to the ground. Dan received $150,000 for the six-second fall.

For falling off horses, out of cars, and down stairwells and similar antics, stuntpersons command the same minimum price as principal performers ($250 for an eight-hour day). But most professional stuntpeople, especially stunt drivers, make up to $8,000 or $9,000 a day or from $100,000 to $150,000 a year, if the business at hand is particularly risky.

Even the hordes of nonacting persons who make up the corps of extras in movies and television are guaranteed minimum salaries, and the pay isn't at all bad for standing around in period costume all day and reading comics between takes. If they do something special, such as riding a horse or a motorcycle or just driving a car, they are placed on a higher scale. If they are employed to do special little silent bits, such as deal cards in a major casino scene or even play dead in a battle scene, they are paid a higher rate. Below are the basic minimum daily rates for extras through 1995 under the Screen Extras Guild contract; also included are additional daily allowances for particular kinds of work and skills.

MINIMUM DAILY RATES FOR EXTRAS IN TV AND FILM

General Extra	$ 99.00
Special Ability Extra	109.00
Silent Bit Extra	150.00
Choreographed Dancers	245.00
Stand-In	109.00
Photo Double	109.00

DAILY ADDITIONAL ALLOWANCES FOR EXTRAS DOING SPECIAL WORK

Wet, snow or smoke work	$14.00
Work requiring body makeup, skull cap, hairpiece	18.00
Formal attire (furs, uniforms, etc.) required	18.50
Wardrobe changes required, 1st change	9.25
each additional change	6.75
Carrying luggage	5.50/piece
Riding a motorcycle	35.00
Riding a bicycle	12.00

SOURCE: Screen Extras Guild, 1995.

The Actor as Conglomerate

TV and movie personalities have learned to cash in on their celebrity in a multitude of ways. Bill Cosby, for instance, has a TV show, does numerous commercials, has his own production company, and has appeared on the silver screen. From these multiple interests, Cosby has earned nearly $60 million over the past year. According to *Forbes,* Oprah Winfrey earned about $66 million in 1994 from all sources, which include the production company that owns the rights to Oprah's syndicated talk show. The key to such large earnings, in addition to a winning personality and a modicum of talent, seems to lie in diversification. Top TV stars inevitably try their hands in movies with mixed results. Six of the eleven top grossing actors of 1990–91 established themselves as hit TV personalities before moving to Hollywood. Many appear in commercials; some have their own production companies. It is a safe bet all have an entourage of accountants, lawyers, and managers to advise them. In its list of the 100 most powerful people in Hollywood, *Premiere* magazine printed several of the following fees for movie actors. Other figures are reprinted from newspapers and other industry publications, which are ever-fascinated by the spiralling salaries in this glamorous industry.

HIGHEST PAID MOVIE ACTORS

Name	*Movie*	*Fee*
Sylvester Stallone	*Three-picture deal*	$20 million per film
Jim Carrey	*Cable Guy*	20 million
Harrison Ford	*Devil's Own*	20 million
Arnold Schwarzenegger	*Junior*	15 million
Bruce Willis	*Die Hard III*	15 million
Tom Cruise	*Interview With the Vampire*	14 million
Demi Moore	*StripTease*	12 million
Sean Connery	*The Rock*	12 million
Jack Nicholson	*Wolf*	10 million
Kurt Russell	*Escape from L.A.*	10 million
Warren Beatty	*Love Affair*	9 million
Brad Pitt	*Devil's Own*	8 million
Sandra Bullock	*Kate & Leopold*	8 million
John Travolta	*Broken Arrow*	7 million
Sharon Stone	*The Last Dance*	6 million

SOURCE: *Premiere* magazine, May 1995 newspaper articles.

The power of Hollywood actors is undeniable. Those with a proven track record of box office power can command enormous fees, even before it is determined what their next movie will be. Sylvester Stallone, for example, was promised $20 million by Savoy Pictures to star in a movie that has yet to be determined. Some stars, like Al Pacino, have what is called a "pay-or-play" fee: Pacino won't even look at a script if the movie pays him less than $6 million; and while Keanu Reeves is newer to superstardom, he commands an $8 million pay-or-play fee.

Many of Hollywood's biggest names also get a percentage of the box office gross receipts, or "points," as they are known in the industry. This sweetens the deal, and it's safe to assume that most of the stars listed above have gotten such offers. Robert Redford's total of $24 million for starring in *Indecent Proposal* came from a combination of actors' fees and a draw on box office receipts. Jack Nicholson's deal for his participation in the first *Batman* movie was even sweeter. In addition to a seven figure acting salary, Nicholson received a percentage of the film's receipts as well as a portion of the licensing and merchandising revenue accrued through sales of Batman T-shirts, hats, posters, etc.

OTHER PERFORMERS

Dancers

In opera, ballet, musical comedy, or on television variety shows, dancing has been, in step with its tribal, ritualistic origins, a group activity. But it has also, especially in the twentieth century, supported the ego demands of solo performers. The flamboyantly ill-fated Nijinsky and Isadora Duncan come immediately to mind, but more recently relatively stable superstars in leotards, such as Mikhail Baryshnikov and the late Rudolf Nureyev, have added a new vitality to dance that has helped to increase its following.

But as in any of the performing arts, stars are stars and the rest are just so many hoofers, nameless legs in a Rockettes lineup or a Busby Berkeley fantasy. Broadway stage shows and various ballet troupes across the country always offer spots for a handful of dancers, but it is mainly a young person's vocation, and many drop out or become instructors or choreographers.

In all, only about 8,000 dancers are paid to perform on the stage, screen, and television. Considering the time, the practice, and the wear and tear on the body that go into perfecting a single routine, dancers are perhaps the most underpaid of all performing artists. For opera and other stage productions, excluding ballet, dancers receive a little over $400 a week, and even though television has been blamed for reducing the availability of these types of dancing forums, it has opened up an entirely new and certainly more lucrative source of revenue for dancers. Whether they appear on a regularly scheduled program or on a variety special, their salary usually depends upon the time they spend on camera, and they are a far cry from the salaries the old song-and-dance men made in vaudeville, even if the acts haven't changed all that much.

MINIMUM TELEVISION PAY FOR DANCERS

Program Length and Group Size	Pay
15 minutes or less	
3 or more persons	$354
Over 15 minutes to 30 minutes	
3 or more persons	548
Over 30 minutes to 60 minutes	
3 or more persons	681
Over 60 minutes to 90 minutes	
3 or more persons	782
Over 90 minutes to 120 minutes	
3 or more persons	907

SOURCE: AFTRA, 1995.

BALLET

The notion of an economically deprived, self-sacrificing artist is certainly not a foreign one to dancers, particularly those who have confined themselves to the ballet. Some would argue that the term "starving artist" best describes the plight of ballet dancers. But over the past ten or twenty years, the dance world has made a valiant and somewhat successful effort to change this image.

It's no secret that only a dozen or so ballet dancers have ever commanded six-figure incomes. And those such as Natalia Makarova, Mikhail Baryshnikov, and Rudolf Nureyev, whose annual incomes have, at one time or another, exceeded $1 million can be counted on the fingers of one hand.

While no one goes into ballet for the money, the economic forecast for dancers who have risen through the ranks of ballet companies is considerably brighter than it was just ten years ago. In the past, even those ballet dancers fortunate enough to be with a company were considered lucky if they could secure just forty performances a year. Today, dance companies operating under union contracts like the National Basic Dance Agreement of the AFL-CIO–affiliated American Guild of Musical Artists (AGMA) can guarantee their dancers as many as forty weeks of work a year.

Alexander Dubé, AGMA's administrator for dance, notes that the AGMA contracts provide seniority increases and, in many instances, benefits like supplemental disability insurance, dental insurance, and vacation pay. This is something quite new and unusual in the world of ballet.

Pay scales have also risen considerably. Under AGMA's 1993–1996 contract, a third-or-more-year corps de ballet dancer with the New York City Ballet will now earn a minimum of $1240 per week for a minimum of 38 weeks. This is more than the company's principal dancers earned just 10 or 12 years ago. And, Dubé notes, "Most of the shows run for forty-two weeks."

In contrast, *new* dancers in companies which operate under the AGMA Basic Dance Agreement will get a base salary this season of $492 a week. Under the same contract, corps de ballet dancers will draw a minimum of $628, soloists will earn $684, and principals will make $736.

Most estimates put the annual salaries of principal dancers with the leading ballet companies at $60,000 to $70,000. For long-time principals with the larger New York City companies, estimates are $80,000 to $100,000. Major modern dance companies, whose budgets are considerably smaller than those of ballet troupes, are said to pay closer to the minimums set forth in the AGMA National Basic Dance Agreement.

Additionally, the AGMA base salaries plus the many extras, note one manager, can add up to a very respectable living wage. Corps members who make $18,000 actually get several thousand dollars more each year when you add on the comprehensive health and pension plans, as well as the as-yet-untaxed unemployment benefits dancers are entitled to for the weeks they don't work, and still more with overtime and other extras. AGMA's newest unemployment benefit, noted Mr. Dubé, is career transition counseling and training for dancers who wish to retire and pursue other careers.

MINIMUM WEEKLY SALARY OF BALLET DANCERS UNDER THE AGMA NATIONAL BASIC DANCE AGREEMENT[1]

New Dancer in a Ballet Company	$492
Corps de Ballet Dancer	628
Solo Dancer	684
Principal Dancer	736

[1]Figures do not include standard AGMA benefits such as health coverage, pension, and severance/exit pay.

SOURCE: AGMA National Basic Dance Agreement contract, 1993–96.

Models

Many of today's best known faces come not from the worlds of politics, or even entertainment, but rather, the world of modeling. They beam at us from billboards and television screens, selling products from cosmetics to candy to Cadillacs.

Modeling can be an exciting and glamorous career for those few people who make it. But the field is extremely competitive, and once begun, the model's career is usually short-lived. "Women come in at seventeen and are usually out by twenty-three or twenty-five," said model Michael Taylor in *The New York Times.*

An estimated 60,000 people, including part-timers, work as models in the United States. Geographically, there are some jobs to be found in most urban areas, but New York, center of the American fashion industry, is the model's Mecca. Anyone who wants to try for the big time will sooner or later have to crack the Big Apple where the twelve largest agencies represent more than 1,000 women and 600 men.

It's difficult to determine exact salary figures since the vast majority of models work freelance through agencies. Earnings roller coaster with the number of assignments for which a model gets called in and also depend on the kind of modeling he or she does. The biggest money is in television work, where hourly rates are high and models, under union regulations, earn residuals when their commercials are rerun. In addition to doing television and magazine work, models also work on runways, in fashion shows, in designer showrooms, and in art classes. For a steadily working fashion model, $30,000 to $60,000 is a safe estimate for an average annual salary.

USA Today estimates that there are roughly 5,000 "professional models" working in the United States; but there are even fewer "supermodels," the few dozen fortunate ones who earn upwards of $1 million a year. The most successful usually become household names and become closely associated with a product or products that are marketed using the consumer's familiarity with the model: the celebrity personifies the product. Cindy Crawford, for example, has a multi-year contract with Revlon to pitch its entire line of products for $1.5 million a year (as well as a lucrative deal with Pepsi). Christie Brinkley represents several products, including Cover Girl cosmetics; Christy Turlington has renewed her contract with Calvin Klein, valued at $1.2 million a year, to promote its Eternity fragrance line. Other supermodels include Isabella Rossellini, Linda Evangelista, and Fashion Café owners Claudia Schiffer, Naomi Campbell, and Elle Macpherson. These models may receive as much as $15,000 to $25,000 a day, as compared to rates of $1,250 to $3,500 for other professional models. The remaining 4,500 people who identify themselves as models will likely never reach these lofty heights.

HIGHEST PAID MODELS OF 1994

Rank and Name	1994 Earnings
1. Cindy Crawford	$6.5 million
2. Claudia Schiffer	5.3 million
3. Christy Turlington	4.8 million
4. Linda Evangelista	3.0 million
5. Elle Macpherson	3.0 million
6. Niki Taylor	2.4 million
7. Isabella Rossellini	2.3 million
8. Kate Moss	2.2 million
9. Naomi Campbell	2.1 million
10. Bridget Hall	2.0 million

SOURCE: *Forbes* magazine.

FITTING (OR FIT) MODELS

There's nothing like the real thing—so when garment manufacturers have a nearly finished outfit, they call in a fitting model to see how it looks on a real woman or man. Often some final adjustments will have to be made. Fit models don't command the hourly rates that their runway colleagues might, but they tend to work more. And their career can last as long as their shape fills the manufacturer's requirements. One model, Margaret Rogers, known as the queen of the queen-sized models, works exclusively for Lane Bryant, a fashion chain for large-sized women.

Fit models get paid by the hour. Rates range from an average of $50 in Manhattan's garment district to about $100 for a top fit model working for one of the major designers. According to the Eileen Ford Agency, session rates of $250 to $450 are quite common.

SHOW MODELS

These tend to be the tall, lithe creatures of perfect proportions conjured up by the mere word "model." They work at fashion shows put on by designers and department stores, which can involve considerable travel around the country and even around the world. Runway models earn between $200 and $750 per hour, or instead sometimes arrange a flat fee for an entire fashion show. Some very experienced models command significantly more.

PHOTOGRAPHIC MODELS

These are the superstars. They're hired by magazines, advertising agencies, and freelance photographers. They're used to sell a variety of products, including but not exclusively fashion and beauty. All of them work through agencies. Being signed with one of New York's top five is probably as close to a guarantee of success as anyone can get in this field. (See the section on models' agents in "The Middlemen" in Part IX.)

Editorial Work—for fashion or beauty layouts inside a magazine—pays between $150 and $250 per day. Magazine covers sometimes pay even less than the inside pages. Models are often glad to get these assignments for the exposure they bring. Modeling for billboards yields $2,000 to $10,000 for a six-month period. Daily rates range between $1,500 and $7,500. Television is paid on union scale. According to a spokesman at the Eileen Ford Agency, models in a TV commercial can expect $2,000 to $3,000 per eight-hour-day photo session. Residuals add approximately $450 per 13 weeks.

According to representatives from both the Ford and Wilhelmina agencies, a beauty model can make $20,000 to $50,000 in the short run of a commercial. With an exclusive signing for a particular product where she becomes the spokesperson for the product, it could guarantee her $150,000 up front.

Pinning down annual salary figures for these models is almost impossible. A spokesman for the Ford Agency gave annual salary ranges of "$50,000 to $350,000 or more."

Hourly rates are the same for men and women models, but the field remains somewhat more lucrative for women. Things are, however, beginning to change. "Men are catching up to women, though women are still booked more," noted one Wilhelmina executive. "Some men here make over $300,000, and there are more men models around now than before." Fabio and Lucky Vanos (the Diet Coke man) illustrate that male models can become household names, a very new phenomenon.

Still, Ford represents 400 women compared with 150 men, and women stand to make $50,000 to $100,000 more than their male counterparts.

There are several reasons for this disparity. Two main ones are that catalog work, the bread and butter of business, requires far more women than men models; also, the biggest money comes from exclusive contracts, mostly with cosmetic companies, which leaves men out in the cold. However, due to different social standards for male and female beauty, male models can work longer. Men who can make the transition to the appealing "older, worldly-man look" can make their careers last twice as long as that of most women models.

Today, some female models have found a novel way to lengthen their careers—they start earlier. Some of today's most talked-about new faces are 16, 15, even as young as 12. Brooke Shields, once the reigning princess of the current pubescent model craze, began her career as a one-year-old Ivory Soap baby and has since become a sought-after (and very wealthy) international cover girl, pinup, and film presence.

Of course, the ultimate goal of most models is to become a celebrity like Cheryl Tiegs or Suzanne Somers, both of whom parlayed modeling careers into successful roles as actresses and advertising "spokespersons" for all kinds of products. In 1980, Tiegs reportedly received more than $1 million for allowing Sears, Roebuck to put her name on the rear end of a new line of jeans, while Somers is paid, according to *Advertising Age,* between $500,000 and $700,000 a year to help tout the merits of Ace Hardware stores. Oscar-winner Jessica Lange had a lucrative career promoting hair products via the Wilhelmina Agency before that agency helped her land her first acting role in *King Kong* in 1976.

A number of other former models have gone on to enjoy lucrative careers on the silver screen, including Michelle Pfeiffer, Kim Basinger, Renée Russo, and Cybill Shepherd.

THE CENTERFOLD

Occupational requirements have burgeoned in every field, it seems. Even models (or aspiring models) who pose nude for the *Playboy* or *Penthouse* centerfold must be more than just what meets the eye. In these inflationary times, the *Playboy* "Playmate" or *Penthouse* "Pet," as they are called, must have intangible qualities, too. Says one *Penthouse* magazine promotions executive, "A good body and face are not sufficient anymore to make a girl a *Penthouse* Pet." *Playboy*'s Playmate promotions director Louise Gilliam says much the same thing: "We look for a blend of the girl next door and something extra, something we perceive as the *Playboy* girl." Playmates do a great deal of promotional work, says Gilliam, "helping us to sell ourselves and our image."

Besides posing for an *au naturel* pictorial, a centerfold's work often includes travel all around the country to attend different events, to become a sort of magazine mascot at a wide variety of promotional functions. A centerfold may host store openings and attend auto and boat shows and almost any other convention or event which presents a good promotional opportunity for the sponsoring magazine.

Very often, her magazine debut becomes a springboard for a career in modeling, advertising, public relations, or entertainment. Perhaps the most famous playmate to go on to an acting career is *Baywatch* star Pamela Anderson, who was Miss February 1990. Other celebrities who first came to national attention through the pages of *Playboy* are actress and Guess jeans girl Anna Nicole Smith and actress/model Shannon Tweed, Miss November 1981 and 1982's Playmate of the Year.

Just who are these pinups and where are they discovered? "We receive pictures from photographers all over the world, girls or their husbands or boyfriends send in photos," says Gilliam. "The twelve Playmates of the Month are selected from thousands of photos we receive each year. And most of the girls we select *are* unknown, so, really, everyone has a chance to become a Playmate. Every once in a while, we take someone found through unsolicited material." Playmates of the Year are chosen by Playboy publisher Hugh Hefner himself, although reader response to the year's array of monthly Playmates is taken into account.

Life as a Playmate can go on for quite some time. "With the right personalities and the ability to handle crowds and life on the road—well, the good ones get booked all the time," says Gilliam. "The Playmate's life expectancy has no bounds."

THE WAGES OF SEX APPEAL

Activity	Fee
Playboy Playmate of the Month	$20,000 for pictorial spread in magazine and appearances on videotape; $750–$2,500 per day for personal appearances
Playboy Playmate of the Year	$100,000 plus a car; $800–$2,000 a day for promotional appearances

While the prospect of $20,000 for posing nude in a national magazine may seem enticing to many an undiscovered model, it takes a lot more money to convince a celebrity to disrobe for *Playboy*'s cameras. The list of already-established stars who have posed for *Playboy* ranges from swimsuit model Stephanie Seymour to actress Bo Derek to presidential daughter Patti Davis Reagan. Many intangible factors go into deciding how much such celebrities receive, but the general rule is the bigger the celebrity, the greater the payout. Even a minor celebrity earns more than the Playmate of the Year for a nude pictorial. According to *Playboy* spokeswoman Elizabeth Norris, the majority of celebrities who pose for *Playboy* earn "in the hundreds of thousands of dollars," but far less than the $1 million figure that is often rumored in news accounts.

Musicians

The incomes of musicians—like those of others independently employed and involved in any creative or artistic field—vary so widely from person to person that it is difficult to list any precise statistics. The variation is dependent not only on skill and fame but also on geographical location, age, instrument played, music performed or taught, and other less obvious factors. Even after determining these factors as accurately as possible, variation may still be great.

For example, many musicians actually earn their living through teaching rather than performing. The income of an experienced classical piano teacher in New York City who rarely performs but who possesses a fairly good reputation can be over $250 per hour. Other teachers charge $15–$60 an hour. The average, however, would not be $155 per hour, nor even $100. It probably is considerably less, but again any actual figure would be meaningless.

According to the Music Educators National Conference, music teachers in public schools earn between $18,000, and $50,000 a year; teachers in parochial schools can expect $16,000 to $35,000 annually; teachers in a college, university, or conservatory earn from $25,000 to $70,000 a year.

The following few statistics must be understood in this context. They are by no means intended to be comprehensive, but they should give some idea of the range and diversity of salaries and incomes for the estimated 235,000 performing musicians in America.

Three other points must also be borne in mind. The first applies to many fields as well as to music. The highest paid musicians—the highest paid teachers and those who can support themselves with ease entirely on fees from performing—are very few and earn considerably more than musicians in the next-highest income bracket. Moreover, the vast majority, who include many well-known and excellent musicians, fall into an even lower income bracket. It is not news, however, that musicians earn very little; they are usually underpaid in relation to their talents and their training, at least if one takes a glance at the salaries of others in this book. A closer look at the fees and salaries for musicians will clarify this point.

The fee a musician is paid for a performance may, in some instances, seem high. However, this fee frequently must cover expenses, travel, publicity, and manager's fees (if the artist has an agent). Thus, $1,000 to a solo artist for one concert may give the musician at most a couple of hundred dollars after all expenses are paid. Managers' fees alone are usually 20 percent of all concert fees. (Most managers also demand 20 percent of their clients' fees for concerts they did not even contract or handle themselves.)

It must also be remembered that $1,000 for a two-hour performance does not represent an income of $500 per hour. This fee is supposedly cov-

GUARANTEED ANNUAL SALARIES OF MUSICIANS IN SYMPHONY ORCHESTRAS

Orchestra	Guaranteed Salary[1] Entry	Guaranteed Salary[1] Career	Orchestra	Guaranteed Salary[1] Entry	Guaranteed Salary[1] Career
Atlanta Symphony	$52,780	$54,860	New Jersey Symphony	$23,870	$24,490
Baltimore Symphony	56,420	60,580	New York City Opera	29,000	30,160
Boston Symphony	71,500	75,920	New York Philharmonic	71,760	76,180
Chicago Lyric Opera	35,397	36,629	North Carolina Symphony	31,900	32,780
Chicago Symphony	72,800	79,805	Oregon Symphony Orchestra	31,498	31,498
Cincinnati Symphony	61,360	62,400	Philadelphia Orchestra	70,720	75,920
Cleveland Orchestra	67,600	73,840	Phoenix Symphony	19,006	20,751
Dallas Symphony	54,340	56,420	Pittsburgh Symphony	63,960	67,080
Detroit Symphony	60,584	62,344	Rochester Philharmonic	30,635	31,537
Florida Orchestra	22,500	23,940	San Antonio Symphony	24,570	25,740
Hawaii Symphony	30,000	31,260	San Diego Symphony Orchestra	28,440	30,600
Houston Symphony	53,820	55,120	San Francisco Ballet	24,575	25,719
Indianapolis Symphony	48,100	51,220	San Francisco Symphony	70,330	74,490
Los Angeles Philharmonic	70,200	74,360	San Francisco Opera	44,472	47,012
Louisville Orchestra	22,102	22,701	St. Louis Symphony	58,240	60,320
Metropolitan Opera	67,870	67,870	St. Paul Chamber Orchestra	43,535	44,685
Milwaukee Symphony	41,790	43,182	Syracuse Symphony Orchestra	21,317	21,722
Minnesota Orchestra	63,180	64,740	Utah Symphony	35,152	36,452
National Symphony	59,280	69,680			

[1]All figures are valid for 1994–1995. Benefits and seniority payments are not included.
SOURCE: The American Federation of Musicians.

ering all the hours of practicing and preparation for this concert during which the musician received no other income. A lawyer is often paid for each separate hour he works on a case. If the lawyer spends 100 hours at $100 per hour on a case, he can expect to earn $10,000. A musician, on the other hand, earns the same fee no matter how many hours he spends in preparation. This preparation may take weeks, months, or even years.

The final consideration is that many professional musicians will play for no money or even lose money merely for the experience and exposure. This is true even of very well-known artists, not merely young or unaccomplished performers. The Bosendorfer concert series in New York, for example, features many artists of international renown. Yet this series pays nothing to these artists; they perform for free. Most young musicians must rent a hall and pay for publicity and other expenses just to get the opportunity to perform and gain exposure. This is almost always a great financial *loss* to the musician. Very few musicians ever make even a small profit from performances.

Singers

About 20,000 Americans are employed as singers every year. This figure includes all kinds of performers—from those who sing advertising jingles on radio and television, or "The Star-Spangled Banner" in sports arenas to Metropolitan Opera divas and the current stars of popular music who appear in famous nightclubs and large concert halls across the country. As is true with most entertainers in this section, only a handful of singers achieve anything like fame or success. A few, such as Sinatra, Elvis, or more recently Michael Jackson, Bruce Springsteen, Madonna, and the artist formerly known as Prince become living legends as well as corporations worth tens of millions of dollars.

Singing stars at every level make most of their money through record sales, but almost all of them count on personal appearances to boost interest in their recordings. The strain of concert performing is said to be enormous, but the pay's not bad either. All well-known singers ask for a minimum guarantee before accepting a concert date; this figure is then measured against an agreed-upon percentage of the box-office receipts, and the performer takes the larger of the two. Some of the very top singers, such as Phil Collins, Whitney Houston, and Madonna take a minimum *plus* a percentage.

The largest fees for public appearances are paid by the people who run the casinos in Las Vegas and Atlantic City. Singers usually work on a weekly basis, doing two shows a night for seven nights. By now it is a hallowed show-business tradition for big-name performers to do a week in a casino, and for their agents to publicize the extraordinary fees.

Recent years have been very good for package record deals and for those lucky enough to have secured them. Madonna, for example, signed a $60 million deal with Warner Music in 1992. She and the entertainment giant formed a separate company—Maverick Entertainment—which includes record and music publishing units as well as TV, film, merchandising, and book divisions. She also got a jump in record advances from $3 million to $5 million per album, and an increase in royalties on their sales to 20 percent, which is among the highest rates in the industry.

However, the life span of a superstar can be unpredictable. An album with less than impressive sales, or an event or rumor that tarnishes the reputation of the artist can grind his megastardom to a halt. Which is why record companies express caution when making deals with even the largest of stars, often adding clauses that give them an "out," should the superstar's popularity suddenly wane.

And it does happen. Michael Jackson, for example, signed the highest entertainment deal ever—$1 billion with Sony—in 1992. This included $65 million for six albums and one film, as well as his own record label. It seemed a promising venture for Sony; the superstar's two releases in the 1980s—*Thriller* and *Bad*—achieved record-breaking sales; the former was the best-selling album of all time. However, sales on Jackson's *Dangerous* album were disappointing. His accompanying world tour was cut short by a drug addiction problem and allegations of sexual misconduct, and so, reportedly, was his deal with Sony.

Prince likewise made headlines in 1992 when he signed a $100 million deal with Warner Brother Records, was made a vice-president of the company and was given an office at its Los Angeles headquarters. However, there was a contingency clause: in what is known as a "mini-maxi" deal, he was granted a $10 million advance for his first album, with advances on subsequent albums to depend on the success of the previous release. It was a wise move by Warner Brothers because Prince has since changed his image, his name to an unpronouncable symbol (the artist formerly known as Prince), and his ability to sell albums to "lukewarm."

ROYALTIES FOR SINGERS

The money you plunk down on the music store counter has a long road to travel before any of it reaches the pocket of the man or woman who made the recording. Yes, recording artists earn royalties, a percentage of the income from each copy sold. But before there's any profit to be shared with the talent, a lot of money invested must first be recovered.

Probably about half the cover price stays with the distributor. What remains goes to the company, which passes on the artist's percentage after deducting the money it has laid out in production, advertising, and promotion costs—not just on the current release, but on all previous projects which may have flopped. Having received some money (which often takes several albums), the artist has still further deductions to make, to his or her producer, manager, and songwriter.

The royalty figure itself varies greatly from artist to artist and is an item of delicate negotiation at contract time. A rate might begin at 10 percent for an unrecorded, untried talent, rising to 12 percent for a well-known performer, or to as high as 25 percent for an acknowledged superstar such as Michael Jackson. As part of her agreement with Warner Music, Madonna receives 20 percent of the royalties on her albums. Arrangements are always subject to change. In the words of one major recording company's vice-president for Eastern operations, "Joe Unknown becomes a superstar, we renegotiate." Royalties depend, of course, on the number of CDs a company anticipates selling, and it's not unusual for contracts to provide escalating royalty scales that reward a larger than expected sales volume.

In the past, companies commonly offered new artists contracts which paid royalties on 90 percent, not 100 percent, of sales income. This was an added way to protect themselves against the financial risk posed by laying out production costs for unproven artists. This practice is changing today, however, probably in reflection of increased competition among companies in an era where a star's loyalty to one label is mere nostalgia.

OPERA

The hierarchy of American opera is very simple to define: there's the Metropolitan Opera and everyone else. Most opera singers' salaries are set by the American Guild of Musical Artists (AGMA). The 1995 weekly minimum for a singer in a lead or feature role is $650. Supplemental and solo bit singers receive minimum weekly pay of $541 plus a per diem, for a maximum of six weeks. At the Met, on the other hand, the chorus members' salaries are considerably higher; they range from $951 to well over $1,100 per week. Star performers at the Met receive $12,000 per performance, actually far less than they would in Europe. Less well-known singers at smaller houses can earn $2,000 to $4,000 per performance.

As in other areas of public performance, however, superstar economics keeps driving up the fees to attract singers who will in turn bring in customers. Unlike movies, television, or professional sports, however, opera is already a money-losing enterprise requiring outlandish ticket prices, heavy corporate subsidies, and occasional grants from publicly supported foundations such as the National Endowment for the Arts. Perhaps, as some observers have noted, the music will never die, but the elaborate spectacles may soon be only a memory. After all, the great singers are drawing better than ever for concerts requiring no costumes or sets costing hundreds of thousands of dollars.

TELEVISION AND RADIO

Many aspiring singers try to find work doing television or radio commercials and, if they're lucky, an occasional TV series. Payment for this work is regulated by AFTRA, so a singer is paid the same minimum rate as an actor if he or she sings alone or in a duo or is on- or off-camera. Since most singers get work singing in groups of three or more, the union has established pay scales for their benefit. More often than not the work involves making singing commercials, so we've included several examples of union rates for this field. The sources for all of these rates are the 1994–95 AFTRA and SAG contracts.

MINIMUM DAILY RATES FOR SINGERS ON TV PROGRAMS

	On Camera	Off Camera
Solo and Duo	$544	$544
Groups 3–8	478	288
Groups 9 plus	417	250
Mouthing 1–16	400	NA
Mouthing 17 plus	313	NA

SOURCE: SAG Contract, 1994–95

MINIMUM RATES FOR RADIO "SESSION" FEES[1]

Actor, Announcer, Solo, Duo	$185.00
Group Singers: 3–5	136.40
6–8	120.70
9 or more	107.15

[1]Producers employ performers on the basis of recording sessions. A recording session is no more than 90 minutes in duration.

SOURCE: AFTRA contract.

MINIMUM FEES FOR RADIO DEALER COMMERCIALS[1]

Rates are for a six-month period of use:	
Actor, Announcer	$606.20
Solo, Duo	480.85
Group Singers: 3–5	313.50
6–8	250.85
9 or more	156.75
Sound Effects Performers	158.55

[1]A dealer commercial is one made for a designated manufacturer or distributor for delivery to and use by its local dealers for which the dealer contracts station time and is limited to use as a Wild Spot or Local Program commercial.
SOURCE: AFTRA contract.

Television Personalities

Back in the early days of radio, some anonymous person must have been faced with the problem of what to call all those people who, while not actors or singers or comedians or musicians, were still an integral part of broadcasting. After all, Harlow Wilcox of the *Fibber McGee and Molly* program and Don Wilson of Jack Benny's show were not simply announcers; and Ted Mack was perceived as something more than the person who introduced aspiring amateur performers to the radio audience. These people became popular and famous in their own right and were very well paid, too. Somewhere along the line they were dubbed "radio personalities," and the term has stuck to their media descendants till today.

Pat Sajak and Alex Trebek are contemporary examples of the television personality. They are MCs of game shows varying in content from the inane to the offensive, and most Americans know their names and faces better than they do those of cabinet members. And, of course, game-show hosts earn much more money: Estimates range from $40,000 to $75,000 per program.

The air waves are filled with people like this; people who have no outstanding talents but do have a certain confidence and ease of manner and can make small talk readily and continuously. So also included under "television personalities" would be hosts of interview-type programs (Oprah Winfrey, Larry King, and Phil Donahue, for example) and the principals on the morning programs that combine news and chatter (*Today* and *Good Morning America*). Sports commentators, as opposed to play-by-play announcers, would also be listed here on the basis that it is essentially their persona, not their expertise, should they possess any, that makes them popular (Bob Costas and Dick Vitale are two examples). As the accompanying list makes plain, these personalities are among the highest salaried people in all America.

Some readers may be surprised to see well-known news broadcasters on a list of personalities, but in our opinion, they fit the basic description given above. Only rarely do network anchors write their own material, and even if they did, that feat would hardly qualify them for such astronomical salaries as they all receive. No, they are paid this kind of money because they are well-known TV personalities in the same way that Regis Philbin and Kathie Lee Gifford are. They read the news very well and present the appropriate image of Olympian detachment combined with an air of unspoken knowledge and suitable hints of sophistication.

The injection of entertainment values into news programs has not been confined to the networks. During the last decade, local stations learned that news programs, the basic staple of local broadcasting, could be profitable if the number of people watching could be increased. But this bottom-line approach meant that everyday news could not be dull, boring, or filled with unrelieved stories of gloom and doom. And so was born the "happy talk" news format in which predictions of imminent economic collapse and updates on the latest murder count are intermingled with stories about community spirit and uplifting episodes of brotherhood, humane treatment of animals, and harmony among the races. All of this is punctuated by lighthearted banter among the personalities who appear every night: the anchorperson(s), the news reporters, the sportscaster, and the weatherperson.

These news personalities are paid on the same basis as everyone else in broadcasting, in relation to the size of the viewing audience. So, stations in Des Moines or Green Bay (the 62nd and 67th largest markets respectively) pay anchorpersons about $60,000 a year and about the same to weatherpersons; sportcasters average between $30,000 to $40,000 while news reporters, always the lowest paid on news shows, make between $25,000 and $30,000, or less if they are just starting out. In the ten largest markets,[1] the salaries are significantly higher, averaging about $500,000 for anchorperson, and $100,000 to $200,000 for news reporters. (See also the figures in the section called "Behind the Scenes in Television.")

To insiders, especially in New York and Los Angeles, these figures will seem very low. But bear in mind that they are averages which include people at the smallest stations. The largest ones, those owned and operated by the networks, always pay the highest. In Chicago, for example, anchors earn several million a year, the same as Chuck Scarborough in New York and Jerry Dumphy in Los Angeles. In other major markets, salaries for anchors are usually $300,000 to $450,000 a year, or two to three times what

[1]In size order they are: New York, Los Angeles, Chicago, Philadelphia, San Francisco, Boston, Detroit, Washington, D.C., Cleveland, and Dallas.

news reporters make. In New York, for example, popular news reporters on affiliated stations frequently make $100,000 to $200,000 a year.

ESTIMATED SALARIES OF FAMOUS NETWORK TV PERSONALITIES

Oprah Winfrey	$66 million	Tom Brokaw	3 million
Johnny Carson	42 million	Chuck Scarborough	3 million
Geraldo Rivera	32 million	Connie Chung[1]	2 million +
Jay Leno	14 million	Bob Costas	2 million +
David Letterman	14 million	Joan Lunden	2 million
Barbara Walters	10 million	Terry Bradshaw	1.5 million
John Madden	7.5 million	Ted Koppel	1 million +
Peter Jennings	7 million	Sue Simmons	1 million
Diane Sawyer	7 million	Storm Field	600,000 +
Dan Rather	4 million		

[1]Chung continues to earn her contractual salary despite being fired from the *CBS Evening News*.
SOURCE: *TV Guide*, assorted magazine articles.

Individual contracts bristle with perks, personal fee systems, and deferred tax benefits. Dan Rather is not "just" CBS' premier anchor, he is also managing editor of the *CBS Evening News*. So great is his power that he has handpicked his own stable of correspondents from the CBS pool. People on Rather's "A-Team" appear much more frequently on the air. Some correspondents, who aren't "allowed" on at all, drop completely out of sight and eventually slide right off the network. In turn, those chosen benefit from the exposure next time their contracts come up. Those who languish but stay on complain bitterly.

A colleague from another network sympathizes. "Those guys have to be thinking, What are we? Chopped liver?"

Rather is one of the privileged few broadcast millionaires who are the leading men—as well as directors—in America's new national theater, television news. It is not as a figure of speech that agent Hookstratten calls the main men at the networks "the principal players." ABC correspondent Charles Gibson uses similar terms: "image makers" and "facemen." They are, he believes, "vitally important and they are worth their money. Whatever ABC pays Ted Koppel, he is worth it. *Nightline* makes a lot of profit. Ted is a hot property and that's Ted's show."

The proof is in the profits. When a ratings point on just one prime-time network news broadcast is worth $70 million, according to industry sources, the anchor who brings in those ratings may be said to be getting no more than his fair share.

"It's the free enterprise system," said a spokesperson for NBC news. "All is fair in the marketplace."

"We journalists exist in an entertainment medium," explains Bill Moyers. "Star quality attracts viewers in the same way marquees attract audiences to the theater." While the idea may "offend journalistic sensibility," Moyers says, "it is the principle of a hired servant getting his due the same way a stockholder does. I think Dan Rather deserves a proportionate share of what he brings to the bank."

Profit is the key word at local markets, too. "The profitability of local stations is a big, silent subject," says New York agent Alfred Gelter. "Owning a television station is like owning a license to steal." The newspeople who help bring in this money, Geller believes, "deserve every penny they get."

"I have no problem in local anchors trying to get as much as they can," says ABC legal correspondent Tim O'Brien, but he thinks "the role" is overrated. "The problem is with the stations who pay so much. They could find marketable anchors they don't have to pay $600,000 to a million."

In fact, many agents are reportedly fuming over their anchors' low salaries, noting that NBC is particularly tough. What they fail to mention, though, is that, like professional ball players, newsmen and their agents have been raking in big money for quite some time. Anchors receive $2 to $4 million a year, important senior correspondents make $500,000 to $750,000, and even the average, run-of-the-mill correspondent earns approximately $150,000.

In the art of judging who gets the big money in TV news, executives rely on an alchemy of numbers and gut feelings. A recent series of talent raids in St. Louis, one of the 20 largest markets, proved how much difference a popular anchor can make. The CBS affiliate KMOV was ranked a low second or third in the late 1980s and "sought to reach first or second place with a vengeance," says general manager Allan Cohen.

First, KMOV hired a news anchor, then a consumer reporter and another reporter who was made weekend anchor. "We became an extremely competitive second-place station by the end of 1987, challenging number one," Cohen says. In 1991, he hired Zip Rzeppa, a popular sportscaster.

"We've seen continued ratings growth and a strengthening in demographics," Mr. Cohen says. Arbitron reports that KMOV's 5 p.m. news broadcast rose from a 9 point rating to a 15, and the 10 p.m. broadcast rose from 13 to 17 rating points while competitor ABC's numbers plummeted.

In St. Louis, where anchors typically make $200,000 to $250,000, the jump in ratings was worth "several multiples of the anchors' salaries," said an industry source familiar with that market. How did Cohen know whom to pursue? "I just went with my instincts."

In Los Angeles, the high-paid anchor range is around $500,000 with the city's number one anchor, Jerry Dumphy of KABC, reportedly being paid over a million.

When anchor Patricia Toyota left KNBC for more money at KCBS—a rumored $450,000—a superior told Noyes, "Think of how much money you'll save."

Even salaries at PBS are relatively high for the few on-air news people. Jim Lehrer reportedly makes $350,000. Paul Duke probably makes close to $150,000. Duke was making $47,000 a year at NBC in 1973, the year he decided to go to PBS for $58,000, he says. "In those days that was a pretty good salary for a congressional correspondent for NBC."

At smaller markets, the story is radically different. According to Richard Herbst, vice-president and general manager of Quincy Broadcasting in Quincy, Illinois, the country's 153rd market, "reporters begin at $15,000 a year and can go up to $25,000 as an anchor." The station gets people with some but not much experience—usually they have worked at a station in the town where they were attending journalism school. But, "if they have the dynamics and personality to become an anchor," Herbst says, "in five years they'll be earning $150,000 in a larger market."

New York talent agent Sherlee Barish cautions against the optimism all these figures may induce in would-be television correspondents. "You can't talk about reporters in the same breath as anchors. Anchors can demand exorbitant salaries; that's the nature of the beast. But they're just a handful. In most of the country these poor kids are just struggling along at a living wage."

Women, especially, should not consider television the land of golden opportunity, though salaries for women on prime-time news magazine shows have grown substantially. Aside from Barbara Walters, only three women have reached the million-dollar bracket. When Phyllis George left *CBS Morning News,* it was revealed that her $800,000 salary was to increase by $100,000 for two successive years, bringing her to a total of a million by 1987. Diane Sawyer, a correspondent for ABC's *Prime-Time Live,* and several other ABC Shows, reportedly earns $7 million, and Connie Chung continued to earn $2 million a year from CBS, despite her celebrated firing from the *Evening News.*

The top beats pay the top money. With few exceptions, women do not have the top beats. Washington attorney Cynthia Riley, who has a large number of network and local clients of both sexes, believes that once a woman "carves out a niche, it doesn't make one bit of difference what sex she is. Your value is who you are and what you are," says Riley, whose clients include ABC's Brit Hume and Charlie Gibson.

Will salaries keep rising? Most sources feel that, except for top talent, they have "leveled off." "The bottom line has taken over the industry," says an inside source. Nearly everyone points nervously to Fred Graham, CBS legal correspondent, who reportedly was offered $255,000 in a new contract, turned it down and was out of a job. Says a top agent: "For the first time, there are pay cuts at local stations and the networks. Networks are offering to keep people on but at 10 percent pay reductions. Some will take them."

Many network correspondents say privately and in identical words: "There are people who would do it for less." They would do it for less themselves. "After a certain amount, how much money do I need? How much money does anybody need?" asks a star correspondent, rhetorically. At the same time, he says, he isn't turning down the money. There's no telling how long it will keep pouring in.

"Most contracts have a termination clause; they can be dumped in 13 weeks," says an agent. "It's like sports," says Brit Hume. "You get 20 years if you're lucky. By the time you're approaching 50, your salary is high and you may begin to look like a big expense. There comes a point where you're not going to be signed up again."

MINIMUM RATES FOR TV SPORTSCASTERS

	1995–96	1996–97
Sportscasters		
Per Event	$ 906	$ 938
Per Week	2,301	2,382
Assistant Sportscasters/Color Persons		
Per Event	$ 557	$ 576
Per Week	1,422	1,472
Championship Events		
Sportscaster	$ 970	$1,004
Assistant Sportscaster	605	626
Major League Baseball—Doubleheader		
Sportscaster	$ 970	$1,004
Assistant Sportscaster	605	626

SOURCE: AFTRA contracts, 1995.

Paul Duke adds, "By and large, television is a young man's game. Networks think nothing of turning out people in their 50s."

Only a few broadcasters grow old on the air, Walter Cronkite and Mike Wallace among them. "We're all looking for one thing," says Sam Donaldson, "to cross the golden line when your value depends on your showing up and age doesn't matter. David Brinkley is clearly paid to walk in the door. The viewers and the networks know he's a first-class broadcaster and appreciate his intrinsic worth."

For the rest, it's critical to stash the cash, says Donaldson. "You can get trapped by the money. We're all astounded by the figures. But any correspondent with sense ought to be prepared to live on a lot less."

THE WORLD OF SPORTS

THE PROS

The public's anxiety about salaries in professional sports dates at least as far back as 1930, when a sportswriter asked Babe Ruth how he could justify earning $5,000 more than President Hoover. ("I had a better year than he did," Ruth is reported to have said.) Since then, each salary increase in pro sports has brought with it renewed complaints about how professional athletes are overpaid. When Jim "Catfish" Hunter became the first free agent to strike it rich, earning $578,200 in 1975, many people predicted that such outlandish salaries and infectious greed would surely wreck the sport. These dour predictions returned in 1981 when Dave Winfield broke the $2 million mark, in 1989 when Kirby Puckett became the first $3 million-a-year player, in 1991 when Bobby Bonilla broke $5 million, and the year after that when Barry Bonds and Ryne Sandberg both broke the $7 million dollar mark before anybody else had even topped $6 million. Yet despite all the high salaries, Major League baseball continued to set attendance records year after year.

So if the people still come out to see them, why shouldn't the players earn what entertainers in other fields make? The top movie stars, like Arnold Schwarzenegger, Jack Nicholson, and two-time Oscar winner Tom Hanks routinely command more for a single picture than baseball players earn over an entire season. TV's David Letterman works more days than most baseball or basketball players, but he gets $14 million a year for a mere hour per night on the stage. And at prices approaching $300 per ticket for her most recent tour, Barbra Streisand certainly didn't have a salary cap on her earnings.

Moreover, despite claims by current owners that their franchises are unprofitable, that clearly can't be the case when cities are making extraordinary offers to land expansion teams. (Owners in most of the professional sports refuse to open their books to allow independent auditors to verify their claims of lost money.) In baseball's last expansion, investors in Miami and

Denver each shelled out $95 million for the privilege of owning a National League franchise, before paying a single player or coach's salary. In the previous expansion, which brought baseball to Seattle and Toronto in 1977, the franchise fees were a mere $6.5 and $7 million, respectively. Today, that wouldn't even pay Barry Bonds's salary.

Was it worth it? Six months before their initial season started, the two expansion teams had each sold out nearly half their stadiums to season-ticket holders. The Colorado Rockies lost 95 games in their inaugural (1993) season playing in a football stadium hastily reconfigured for baseball but nevertheless managed to attract four million fans to the ballpark. They were on schedule to break the four-million mark again in 1994 before the labor impasse between players and owners derailed the 1994 season.

The profits of owning a major league franchise are so alluring that the city of St. Petersburg, Florida, spent $110 million to build a domed stadium even though it had no baseball team. The city has come close to getting a team no fewer than eight times, the most recent being when investors there paid more than $100 million to move the San Francisco Giants to Florida. But the league voided the deal and forced Giants owner, Bob Lurie, to sell the team—for $15 million less—to a group that would keep the Giants in San Francisco. Finally, in 1995, the major league baseball owners rewarded St. Petersburg (as well as Phoenix, Arizona) with an expansion franchise due to start play in 1998, after the ownership groups in those two cities each fork over another $155 million for the privilege.

HIGHEST PAID SPORTS PERSONALITIES, 1995 (in millions)

Rank, Athlete	Sport	Salary or Winnings	Endorsements & other income	Total Earnings
1. Michael Jordan	Basketball	$ 3.9	$40.0	$43.9
2. Mike Tyson	Boxing	40.0	0.0	40.0
3. Deion Sanders	Football/Baseball	16.5	6.0	22.5
4. Riddick Bowe	Boxing	22.0	0.2	22.2
5. Shaquille O'Neal	Basketball	4.9	17.0	21.9
6. George Foreman	Boxing	10.0	8.0	18.0
7. Andre Agassi	Tennis	3.0	13.0	16.0
8. Jack Nicklaus	Golf	0.6	14.5	15.1
9. Michael Schumacher	Auto racing	10.0	5.0	15.0
10. Wayne Gretzky	Hockey	8.5	6.0	14.5
11. Arnold Palmer	Golf	0.1	14.0	14.1
12. Drew Bledsoe	Football	13.2	0.7	13.9
13. Gerhard Berger	Auto racing	12.0	1.5	13.5
14. Evander Holyfield	Boxing	11.0	2.0	13.0
15. Pete Sampras	Tennis	4.7	6.5	11.2

HIGHEST PAID SPORTS PERSONALITIES, 1995 (in millions)

Rank, Athlete	Sport	Salary or Winnings	Endorsements & other income	Total Earnings
16. Cal Ripken	Baseball	6.3	4.0	10.3
17. Greg Norman	Golf	1.7	8.0	9.7
18. David Robinson	Basketball	7.9	1.7	9.6
19. Patrick Ewing	Basketball	7.5	2.0	9.5
20. Dale Earnhardt	Auto racing	2.4	6.0	8.4
21. Ki-Jana Carter	Football	7.9	0.5	8.4
22. Jean Alesi	Auto racing	7.0	1.0	8.0
23. Ken Griffey, Jr.	Baseball	6.2	1.7	7.9
24. Grant Hill	Basketball	2.8	5.0	7.8
25. Frank Thomas	Baseball	6.3	1.5	7.8
26. Boris Becker	Tennis	3.3	4.5	7.8
27. Hakeem Olajuwon	Basketball	5.8	2.0	7.8
28. Michael Chang	Tennis	2.6	5.0	7.6
29. Barry Bonds	Baseball	6.8	0.7	7.5
30. Steffi Graf	Tennis	2.5	5.0	7.5
31. Greg Maddux	Baseball	6.8	0.4	7.2
32. Charles Barkley	Basketball	4.1	3.0	7.1
33. Pernell Whitaker	Boxing	7.0	0.0	7.0
34. Mark Messier	Hockey	6.0	1.0	7.0
35. Steve Young	Football	4.0	3.0	7.0
36. Joe Carter	Baseball	6.5	0.5	7.0
37. Jerry Rice	Football	6.0	1.0	7.0
38. Michael Irvin	Football	6.2	0.7	6.9
39. Cecil Fielder	Baseball	6.4	0.3	6.7
40. Dan Marino	Football	4.5	1.7	6.2

SOURCE: *Forbes* Magazine, December 18, 1995. Note: this table counts signing bonuses and other upfront moneys in the year in which they were given, rather than averaging them out over the life of a contract.

If television was the treasure chest of the 1970s and 1980s for professional sports, team merchandise sales may be the cash cow of the 1990s. Licensing the team names, colors, and logos to manufacturers of everything from hats, towels, shirts, and jackets to garbage cans, phones, and umbrellas has become a multibillion dollar business for the four professional leagues. The National Hockey League's recent expansion history offers an example of the importance of merchandising in today's sports landscape. The league expanded to San Jose in 1991 and Tampa Bay in 1992, two cities not known for their icy locales. Yet despite the second worst record in the NHL, the San Jose Sharks trailed only the NBA champion Chicago Bulls in team-merchandise sales. In 1994, teams were added in Anaheim and Miami, not because of a great base of hockey fans, but because the franchise's owners, Disney and Blockbuster Entertainment chairman H. Wayne Huizenga, have proven successful at merchandising apparel and souvenirs. The success of team merchandise sales has been so strong that the National Football League created the World League of American Football in 1990, primarily, cynics say, so that it could sell team merchandise in Europe.

The following lists were current as of March 1996. And, of course, the ever-continuing salary escalation in all sports insures that the rankings will be valid only until the next mega-contract is signed. Every salary in this section has been drawn from usually reputable sources: *The Sporting News, Sports Illustrated, The New York Times, Sport,* and various league officials. But because of the public outcry over the money being paid to professional athletes, players and their agents don't always reveal exact details of their contracts. Consequently, some salary information may be estimated. Note also that salary figures from some sources include upfront moneys and signing bonuses in a single year, while other sources average these amounts over the lifetime of a contract. Therefore, figures from different tables are not directly comparable.

MAJOR LEAGUE BASEBALL

Never have the minutiae of baseball players' salaries and club owners' profits come under such close scrutiny as they were in 1994 and 1995, when a 232-day-long impasse between players and owners caused the first-ever cancellation of the World Series and at press time, showed no signs of ending. Signs of discontent hovered around baseball for much of the 1994 season, as owners threatened unilaterally to implement a salary cap or similar measure (such as a luxury tax) to hold players' salaries down league-wide. In claiming that they needed to control costs, owners asserted that as many as 19 teams were losing money. They later revised this number to 12, and a few weeks later admitted that as few as six or eight teams were operating in the red. Their refusal to open their books, however, continues to cast doubts on these claims of unprofitability.

But the longest work stoppage in professional sports history didn't officially begin until August 12, 1994, when the players, in an attempt to prevent the imposition of a cap, went on strike before the end of the collective bargaining agreement. The players chose this date in hopes of resolving the dispute in time for the playoffs and the World Series. But on September 14, with no agreement in sight and negotiators for both sides rarely talking to each other, the owners canceled the remainder of the season, including all postseason games. The move also thrust the winter off season into turmoil, as it was unclear when contracts ended, who was eligible for arbitration and who was a free agent. Spring training camps opened in February 1995, not with major leaguers, but with replacement players—strikebreakers who had never played in the majors or whose experience was limited to a few innings.

As opening days at stadiums across the country loomed, the players won a vital battle that led to the end of the strike: a March 26 U.S. District Court injunction against the owners for unfair labor practices. The court order did nothing to bring either side to the bargaining table, but it did force the owners to play under the terms of the expired collective bargaining agreement (which had no salary cap). The players agreed to end the strike and return to work. And without enough votes to lock the players out, the owners reluctantly agreed to let the players back and to dismiss the replacements. Major leaguers quickly traveled to Florida and Arizona for another, abbreviated, spring training session before embarking on a 144-game regular season beginning on April 25.

The fallout from the return to the status quo was almost immediate. The Montreal Expos, a so-called small market team because they fail to attract large crowds to their stadium, dealt outfielder Marquis Grissom and closer John Wetteland to two big market teams—the Atlanta Braves and the New York Yankees, respectively—because both were soon to be eligible for arbitration. They also refused to re-sign outfielder Larry Walker, who signed with the Colorado Rockies as a free agent for $5.5 million. Those three teams all made the playoffs, while the Expos, owners of the best record in baseball in 1994, finished fourth in their division in 1995 with a 67–76 record.

The other anticipated effect of the strike and its "resolution" was the plummeting salaries of major league stars somewhat below the superstar level. A glut of free agents became available all at once on April 2, creating a buyer's market for owners seeking to fill gaps in their lineups. As a result, many players took huge pay cuts simply to latch on to a team. Nobody took a bigger pay cut than Andre Dawson, who signed on with the Florida Marlins for $500,000, a $3.9 million pay decrease from the $4.4 million the Red Sox paid him the year before. Tom Browning took a $3.2 million pay cut to sign on with the Kansas City Royals, while Teddy Higuera signed on with the San Diego Padres for $275,000, or $3.225 million less than the Brewers were paying him in 1994. The Oakland A's played hardball with several pitchers and succeeded in knocking several million dollars off their payroll. Dennis Eckersley took a $1.3 million pay cut, Bob Welch signed for $2.2 million less than his 1994 salary, and Dave Stewart returned to Oakland from Toronto for $1 million, or $3.25 million less than what the Blue Jays had paid him.

The $6 Million Club

The title of this section was "The million dollar a year ballplayer" when it first appeared in the 1987–88 edition. These days, that's an average salary, making even utility infielders and relief pitchers million-dollar-a-year ballplayers. As recently as 1992, a $6 million-per-year contract would have been a watershed. These days, it is the going rate for superstars of the highest caliber.

Player	Position	1996 Team	Average Salary (millions)
Ken Griffey Jr.	Outfield	Seattle Mariners	$8.50
Barry Bonds	Outfield	San Francisco Giants	7.29
Frank Thomas	First Base	Chicago White Sox	7.25
Cecil Fielder	First Base	Detroit Tigers	7.24
Ryne Sandberg	Second Base	Chicago Cubs	7.10
Jeff Bagwell	First Base	Houston Astros	6.88
Cal Ripken Jr.	Shortstop	Baltimore Orioles	6.50
Joe Carter	Outfield	Toronto Blue Jays	6.50
David Cone	Pitcher	New York Yankees	6.50
Lenny Dykstra	Outfield	Philadelphia Phillies	6.22
Mo Vaughn	First Base	Boston Red Sox	6.20
Kirby Puckett	Outfield	Minnesota Twins	6.00

Milestones in Salary History

Each of the following players was the best-paid player in baseball at the time he signed his contract. Adjusted for inflation, Babe Ruth's 1923 salary would be worth less than $400,000 today.

Year	Player	Team	Average Salary
1923	Babe Ruth	New York Yankees	$ 50,000
1947	Hank Greenberg	Pittsburgh Pirates	100,000
1959	Ted Williams	Boston Red Sox	125,000
1975	Jim "Catfish" Hunter	New York Yankees	578,000
1979	Nolan Ryan	Houston Astros	1,130,000
1981	Dave Winfield	New York Yankees	2,200,000
1989	Kirby Puckett	Minnesota Twins	3,000,000
1990	Jose Canseco	Oakland Athletics	4,700,000

Year	Player	Team	Average Salary
1991	Roger Clemens	Boston Red Sox	5,380,000
1991	Bobby Bonilla	New York Mets	5,800,000
1992	Ryne Sandberg	Chicago Cubs	7,100,000
1992	Barry Bonds	San Francisco Giants	7,290,000
1996	Ken Griffey, Jr.	Seattle Mariners	8,500,000

Salary Arbitration

In order to bring a semblance of order to the free agent market, the owners and players agreed in 1974 to a system of binding arbitration. Under this system, the player and the team each submit suggested salaries for the coming year to an impartial arbitrator who chooses between the two alternatives. For many years, the salaries players procured through arbitration were overshadowed by the gigantic dollar amounts landed by free agents. But during the "collusion" years, when owners collectively refused to sign the big free agents, the players turned more and more to arbitration as a way of augmenting their compensation. Until 1990, the top salary won by a player in an arbitration hearing was the $1.975 million first baseman Don Mattingly wrested from the New York Yankees in 1987. But after leading their team to its first divisional championship in 10 years, Pittsburgh pitcher Doug Drabek and slugger Bobby Bonilla took the Pirates to arbitration and shattered that record. Drabek won his arbitration hearing and walked away with $3.35 million; Bonilla lost his arbitration and was "forced" to accept the team's offer of $2.4 million.

Since then, arbitration awards have kept pace with the spiraling salaries obtained through free agency (the owners started spending for the big free agents again in 1991 after an arbitrator found them guilty of collusion). Texas Rangers' outfielder Ruben Sierra broke the $5 million barrier in 1992. By 1993, Seattle's Ken Griffey had broken the $6 million mark, and Detroit's Cecil Fielder had surpassed $7 million in arbitration awards.

HIGHEST PAID PLAYERS BY POSITION, 1994[1]

Position	National League Player, Team	Base Salary
Catcher	Benito Santiago, Florida Marlins	$3,800,000
First Base	Gregg Jefferies, St. Louis Cardinals	4,600,000
Second Base	Craig Biggio, Houston Astros	3,150,000
Third Base	Bobby Bonilla, New York Mets	6,000,000
Shortstop	Barry Larkin, Cincinnati Reds	4,000,000
Left Field	Barry Bonds, San Francisco Giants	4,750,000
Center Field	Marquis Grissom, Montreal Expos	3,560,000
Right Field	Gary Sheffield, Florida Marlins	4,625,000
Starting Pitcher	John Smiley, Cincinnati Reds	4,600,000
Relief Pitcher	John Franco, New York Mets	3,500,000

Position	American League Player, Team	Base Salary
Catcher	Mike Macfarlane, Kansas City Royals	$2,600,000
First Base	Wally Joyner, Kansas City Royals	4,600,000
Second Base	Roberto Alomar, Toronto Blue Jays	5,000,000
Third Base	Robin Ventura, Chicago White Sox	3,500,000
Shortstop	Cal Ripken, Baltimore Orioles	5,400,000
Left Field	Rickey Henderson, Oakland Athletics	4,300,000
Center Field	Ken Griffey, Seattle Mariners	4,500,000
Right Field	Joe Carter, Toronto Blue Jays	4,500,000
Designated Hitter	Jose Canseco, Texas Rangers	4,400,000
Starting Pitcher	Jack McDowell, Chicago White Sox	5,300,000
Relief Pitcher	Duane Ward, Toronto Blue Jays	3,500,000

[1]Salaries in this table are actual amounts players were scheduled to receive in 1994, so they may differ from the amounts in tables elsewhere in this chapter, which list average salaries over the life of each player's contract. In anticipation of a lengthy work stoppage, many players—shrewdly—scheduled their contracts to receive less in 1994 and more in other years. Each player lost 52 days of the normal 183-day season during 1994, so each player's actual take-home pay was decreased by 28 percent.

SOURCE: Major League Baseball Association.

AVERAGE BASEBALL PLAYER SALARIES BY TEAM, 1979–94

Team	1994	1988	1985	1979
Atlanta Braves	1,550,073	$373,448	$540,988	$ 90,366
Baltimore Orioles	1,463,971	411,891	438,256	101,266
Boston Red Sox	1,180,056	590,368	386,597	145,692
California Angels	661,267	399,322	433,818	155,564
Chicago Cubs	934,172	451,845	413,765	104,116
Chicago White Sox	1,204,109	204,979	348,488	74,673
Cincinnati Reds	1,270,789	297,458	336,786	165,144
Cleveland Indians	1,122,115	294,980	219,879	98,023
Colorado Rockies	850,463	NA	NA	NA
Detroit Tigers	1,327,750	589,791	406,755	63,377
Florida Marlins	647,104	NA	NA	NA
Houston Astros	1,163,340	509,323	352,004	73,660
Kansas City Royals	1,347,360	467,036	368,469	91,583
Los Angeles Dodgers	1,326,521	572,685	424,273	134,305
Milwaukee Brewers	733,073	361,740	430,843	137,309
Minnesota Twins	993,390	424,546	258,039	70,703
Montreal Expos	746,440	334,572	315,328	142,829
New York Mets	989,206	592,412	389,365	93,607
New York Yankees	1,634,577	676,820	546,364	199,236
Oakland Athletics	920,300	382,500	352,004	41,220
Philadelphia Phillies	1,060,286	481,407	399,728	197,926
Pittsburgh Pirates	688,083	305,100	392,271	174,439
San Diego Padres	456,036	407,423	400,497	103,819
San Francisco Giants	1,274,267	399,916	320,370	120,737
Seattle Mariners	940,536	223,850	169,694	61,830
St. Louis Cardinals	931,950	513,713	386,505	116,628
Texas Rangers	1,054,160	206,535	257,753	128,806
Toronto Blue Jays	1,437,058	465,949	385,995	67,044
Average Salary	1,068,159	438,729	371,157	113,558

SOURCE: Major League Baseball Players Association.

Details of a Few Big Contracts

Today's sports contracts are a far cry from a simple agreement to play for a set period of time for a set amount of dollars. Most contracts are packed with signing bonuses, incentive clauses, no-trade provisions, guaranteed and deferred payments, cost-of-living increases, and in some cases, postretirement offers. And, of course, the number of zeroes on the contracts is constantly increasing.

Barry Bonds—A month after sportswriters named Bonds the National League's Most Valuable Player for 1992, the San Francisco Giants made the outfielder baseball's richest player as well, giving him $43.75 million over six years. Bonds earned $4 million in 1993 and $4.75 million in 1994, but in 1995, his salary skyrocketed to $7.75 million. In the final year of his contract, 1998, Bonds will earn a minimum of $8.5 million. The deal also included a signing bonus of $2.5 million, a $200,000 payoff if he is traded (he can veto a trade to either of the two Canadian teams), and a guaranteed single hotel room whenever the team is on the road. Bonds received a $100,000 bonus for winning the Most Valuable Player Award in 1993. If he wins the award again, he gets $250,000; he gets $750,000 for a third MVP and $1 million for a fourth.

David Cone—By fueling the New York Yankees' 1995 drive for a wild card spot, Cone cemented his reputation as baseball's best mercenary pitcher. Thus he was assured of making at least $6 million when he signed a new contract for 1996 and beyond. In the end, though, he chose a deal from the Yankees that didn't pay him any more money than similar offers from the Baltimore Orioles or New York Mets ($6.2 million a year for three years), but gave him greater flexibility four and five years down the road.

Ryne Sandberg—In 1992, the Cubs signed Sandberg to a four-year, $28.4 million contract extension, making baseball's first $7-million player, skipping the $6-million plateau entirely. Before Sandberg's signing, Bobby Bonilla's $5.8-million salary was the league's highest. The contract included a $2.5 million signing bonus, a guaranteed salary of $5.1 million in 1993, 1994, and 1995, a $7.1 million salary in 1996, and $1.65 million in incentives. Curiously, Sandberg retired unexpectedly in the middle of the 1993 season and sat out the next two (cheapest) years of the contract before returning for the 1996 season.

Cal Ripken—The ironman shortstop for the Baltimore Orioles signed the second most lucrative contract in baseball history in 1992 when he inked a five-year, $30.5-million deal that gave him an average salary of $6.1 million per year. The contract includes a $3 million signing bonus and a front-office position worth $2 million after he retires. Judging from the national media attention that descended on Baltimore in August of 1995, when Ripken eclipsed Lou Gehrig's consecutive game streak, both Ripken and the Orioles got their money's worth.

NATIONAL FOOTBALL LEAGUE

Although they subject their bodies to far greater punishment than their counterparts in other sports (making their careers far shorter), professional football players continue to earn considerably less than today's high-priced baseball and basketball players. In fact, the average 1994 NFL salary of $659,000 was little more than half that of professional baseball or basketball players (when they weren't on strike or locked out).

The NFL in 1993 became the second professional league to adopt a salary cap (the NBA was the first). Under the terms of this collective bargaining agreement, players with five years experience whose contracts have expired may the sell their services to the highest bidder. Each team may protect one so-called "franchise player" from becoming a free agent, as long as it pays him at least as much as the average of the five top-paid players at his position. In addition, each team retains the right to match any offer made to a free agent by another team. Lastly, the 1993 accord set a salary cap that limits player salaries to 64 percent of gross revenues (and gradually reduces it to 62 percent over three years) and limits rookie salaries to a total of $2 million per team.

The cap was designed to limit the amount teams would be able to spend on players, and thus maintain competitive balance between the big market teams in New York and Los Angeles and the small market teams in Green Bay and New Orleans. But through clever accounting maneuvers, such as spreading out a signing bonus over several years, a team may spend what it wishes on players and then figure out how to manipulate the numbers so they fit under the cap. In 1994, for example, a total of 18 clubs spent more than the $34.6 million cap; two teams, the Washington Redskins and the Arizona Cardinals, went as much as $8 million over this figure. The cap amount is based on the total gross revenues taken in by the NFL each year divided by 28 (the number of teams in the league). The cap for 1995 was $37.1 million. It is scheduled to be removed in 1999, when the current collective bargaining agreement expires.

The Dallas Cowboys made the greatest mockery of the salary cap in September 1995, when they signed defensive back Deion Sanders to a $35 million deal. Critics, including the NFL, which sued Cowboys owner Jerry Jones over the contract, said America's team was able to fit Sanders under the cap simply by paying him most of the money in years after the cap expires.

Ironically, even with the salary cap, player expenditures had little to do with success on the field. Of the 10 teams whose player payrolls were under the salary cap, five made the playoffs. Meanwhile, only 7 of the 18 teams above the cap qualified for postseason play. The 1995 Super Bowl champion San Francisco 49ers had a team payroll of $34,644,000, just $42,000 over the cap.

Quarterbacks continue to dominate the NFL's salary pyramid, though not as much as they have in recent years. Signal callers averaged $1.15 million in 1994; starting quarterbacks averaged $2.58 million. But only five of the NFL's 10 best paid players were quarterbacks in 1994, compared with nine out of ten in 1992. Defensive ends or tackles (usually sack specialists) saw their incomes increase considerably, with six defensive linemen counted among the NFL's top 20 earners. Nevertheless, quarterbacks still averaged about twice as much as players at any other position.

Most of the top-paid players got their money in annual salaries, but a few cracked the top 20 by dint of a gigantic signing bonus. Witness the example of Detroit quarterback Scott Mitchell. Mitchell was so impressive in a stint as Dan Marino's backup in Miami during the 1993 season that the Lions offered him a deal that paid him more up front ($1.67 million) than it did in 1994 salary ($1.4 million). The Lions may regret the move, however: Mitchell played erratically through nine games before breaking his hand and being replaced by aging veteran Dave Krieg. Krieg went 5–2 in seven starts (compared with Mitchell's 4–5 record) and led the Lions to the playoffs, at the relatively bargain price of $825,000. Dan "Big Daddy" Wilkinson was another signing bonus beneficiary. As the NFL's number one overall draft choice, Wilkinson was able to hold out until the Cincinnati Bengals offered him a $2.5 million signing bonus. But the player landing the biggest upfront bonus was wide receiver Andre Rison, whose five-year $17-million deal with the Cleveland Browns paid him a $5 million signing bonus. But don't expect to see Rison's name among the highest paid players any time soon, however. For cap purposes, the signing bonus is spread over the life of the contract; his annual salary starts at $578,000 for 1995 and doesn't reach its highest level, $3.7 million, until 1998. By then, who knows what football players will be making.

In 1995, salaries continued to escalate. Michael Irvin of the Cowboys, generally regarded as the game's best wide receiver, inked a five-year, $15 million pact, with $5 million paid upfront. He was quickly eclipsed by two Penn State standouts who had never played a down in the NFL. Quarterback Kerry Collins wrested a $7 million signing bonus from the expansion Carolina Panthers to go along with salaries ranging from $757,000 in 1995 to $1.9 million in 2001. Not to be outdone, the Cincinnati Bengals gave the league's overall top draft pick, Ki-Jana Carter, a $7.1-million signing bonus as part of a seven-year $19.2-million deal. Weeks after he signed the contract, Carter injured himself and missed his entire rookie season.

AVERAGE NFL SALARY BY POSITION, 1994

Position	All Players	Starters
Quarterback	$1,147,200	$2,582,600
Defensive End	770,600	1,225,300
Offensive Lineman	688,800	1,061,900
Defensive Tackle	656,200	1,122,600
Linebacker	604,900	966,500
Cornerback	560,600	1,002,000
Wide Receiver	551,500	1,012,700
Running Back	540,600	985,800
Safety	510,000	776,300
Tight End	426,100	841,000
Kicker/Punter	419,000	419,000
Leaguewide average salary (1994)		$ 659,000

SOURCE: NFL Players Association.

NFL TEAM PAYROLLS, 1994

Team	Payroll	Team	Payroll
Washington Redskins	$42,597,000	San Francisco 49ers	$34,644,000
Arizona Cardinals	42,492,000	Philadelphia Eagles	34,630,000
Seattle Seahawks	40,562,000	Buffalo Bills	34,613,000
New England Patriots	39,811,000	**SALARY CAP[1]**	**$34,602,000**
Indianapolis Colts	38,955,000	New York Giants	34,325,000
Detroit Lions	38,415,000	Chicago Bears	34,150,000
San Diego Chargers	38,332,000	Minnesota Vikings	33,928,000
Houston Oilers	38,255,000	Los Angeles Rams	33,571,000
New Orleans Saints	38,248,000	Tampa Bay Buccaneers	32,132,000
Kansas City Chiefs	37,822,000	Cincinnati Bengals	31,855,000
Los Angeles Raiders	37,741,000	Dallas Cowboys	31,344,000
Atlanta Falcons	36,330,000	Miami Dolphins	31,276,000
New York Jets	35,658,000	Denver Broncos	31,196,000
Green Bay Packers	35,226,000	Pittsburgh Steelers	30,888,000
Cleveland Browns	34,859,000		

[1]The salary cap does not calculate actual dollars spent; signing bonuses and other incentives may be spread over a multiyear contract for cap purposes.
SOURCE: The National Football League.

TOP PAID PLAYERS IN THE NATIONAL FOOTBALL LEAGUE, 1994

Player, Position	Team	Base Salary	Bonuses	Cap Value
Steve Young, QB	San Francisco 49ers	$4,025,000	500,000	$4,525,000
John Elway, QB	Denver Broncos	3,000,000	1,665,000	4,383,000
Reggie White, DE	Green Bay Packers	3,150,000	1,125,000	4,275,000
Stan Humphries, QB	San Diego Chargers	3,000,000	601,800	3,601,800
Barry Sanders, RB	Detroit Lions	2,575,000	925,000	3,479,900
Dan Wilkinson, DT	Cincinnati Bengals	965,000	2,500,000	3,465,000
Rod Woodson, CB	Pittsburgh Steelers	2,000,000	1,400,400	3,400,400
Joe Montana, QB	Kansas City Chiefs	2,500,000	775,000	3,275,000
Jim Kelly, QB	Buffalo Bills	2,800,000	475,000	3,275,000
Emmitt Smith, RB	Dallas Cowboys	2,200,000	1,000,800	3,200,800
Scott Mitchell, QB	Detroit Lions	1,400,000	1,666,700	3,066,700
Troy Aikman, QB	Dallas Cowboys	1,750,000	1,377,200	3,027,900
Neil Smith, DE	Kansas City Chiefs	1,900,000	1,075,000	2,975,000
Jerry Rice, WR	San Francisco 49ers	2,000,000	963,300	2,963,300
Tony Bennett, DE	Indianapolis Colts	2,200,000	750,000	2,950,000
Randall Cunningham, QB	Philadelphia Eagles	2,500,000	428,600	2,928,600
Junior Seau, LB	San Diego Chargers	2,025,000	930,800	2,885,700
Boomer Esiason, QB	New York Jets	2,700,000	175,000	2,875,000
Michael Dean Perry, DT	Cleveland Browns	2,412,500	453,700	2,866,200
Bruce Smith, DT	Buffalo Bills	2,800,000	NA	2,800,000
Thurman Thomas, RB	Buffalo Bills	2,800,000	NA	2,800,000

SOURCE: NFL Players Association.

The biggest signing bonus was reserved for a more proven player. Drew Bledsoe, the New England Patriots' talented young quarterback, negotiated an $11.5-million signing bonus as part of an overall contract worth $42 million over seven years. The total package is second only to the eight-year $50-million deal signed by Troy Aikman of the Cowboys.

In 1996, the New York Jets made Neil O'Donnell the league's fourth-best paid player by inking the former Steelers quarterback to a five-year, $25-million contract.

NATIONAL BASKETBALL ASSOCIATION

When it was installed prior to the 1984 season, the NBA's salary cap was hailed as the move that would bring the league back from the brink of fiscal collapse. Enough teams were on the verge of bankruptcy to threaten the health of the entire league. But by limiting team salaries to an agreed-upon amount each year, all franchises could compete on an even plane, regardless of the size of their pocketbooks, markets, or local TV contracts. Owners in other sports leagues pointed to the NBA's cap as a sensible way to limit salaries while maintaining competitive balance by insuring that the best players didn't all flock to the richest teams in the major media cities.

In later years, as the NBA's health returned, players and even general managers began griping that the cap limited player movement (whether via free agency or trades) because players could only go to teams that could fit them under their salary cap. Finally, in 1993, Chris Dudley found the loophole in the cap that allowed him (and ultimately others) to move freely from team to team with hardly any consideration of the cap. Before the beginning of the 1993–94 season, Dudley signed a contract with the Portland Trail Blazers that would pay him $790,000—the exact amount Portland had left under its salary cap, but also an amount $400,000 less than Dudley earned the year before. Why would Dudley accept the lower amount? Because of the provision in the salary cap that says a team may go over the cap by any amount to re-sign its own free agents. Dudley structured the contract so that it allowed him to become a free agent after the first year, and then paid him $10.2 million over the next six years.

The NBA challenged the contract in U.S. District Court and lost, whereupon the practice became commonplace. Since then, the Chicago Bulls signed Croatian swingman Toni Kukoc to a similar contract as did the Atlanta Hawks with Craig Ehlo and the Phoenix Suns with Danny Manning. The league had to wait until 1995, when it negotiated its new labor agreement with the players, to close this loophole and bring salaries down. The new agreement, reached only after the players failed to decertify the union that negotiated the deal, allows teams to go over the cap only to re-sign free agents who have been with the team for three or more years.

Meanwhile, some have begun to question how well the salary cap has actually maintained competitive balance. During the 1970s, before the salary cap was implemented, small market teams like Milwaukee, Golden State, Portland, Washington, and Seattle won the NBA Championship. In the 11 years since the cap was implemented, a total of six teams have won the title—Boston, Chicago, Detroit, Houston, Philadelphia, and the Los Angeles Lakers—all perennial large NBA markets.

Some would argue that the cap has done little to control salaries either. Certainly no player ever earned eight- or nine-figure incomes before the cap.

Since the cap, these contracts seem commonplace. New York Knick center Patrick Ewing became the first $5-million a year man in 1992, when he negotiated a contract that paid him $33 million over six years. At the time, the $5.5-million average salary made him the highest-paid player in professional team sports. He was quickly eclipsed, however, not only by scores of baseball players, but also by an NBA center who had never played a single game. Shaquille O'Neal, the first pick in the 1992 draft, left college after his junior year to sign with the Orlando Magic for a record $40 million over seven years.

Since then, the earnings of these two 7-footers have been dwarfed by contracts signed by players both smaller and even less experienced than O'Neal. Charlotte Hornets forward Larry Johnson signed a 12-year deal in 1993 that will pay him $84 million, almost as much as the value of the franchise. New Jersey's Derrick Coleman, who plays the same position as Johnson, then decided he was worth at least that much and cornered the Nets into signing an eight-year, $75 million deal that would pay him close to $18 million in the final year.

Among the class of 1994, Jason Kidd signed with Dallas for $54 million over nine years, and Glenn Robinson, after abandoning a quest to become the first $100 million player, signed with Milwaukee for $68 million over ten years. Both players signed their contracts before playing a single NBA game.

The new labor agreement will put an end to contracts of this sort for untested rookies. A leaguewide scale will determine the approximate value of each pick in the college draft, with teams allowed to pay no more than 20 percent higher than the dollar amount specified in the scale. It's no wonder, then, that the first four picks in the NBA draft left college early to cash in on NBA contracts before the new agreement went into effect. And the fifth pick overall, Kevin Garnett, skipped college completely, going straight from high school to the NBA.

TOP PAID PLAYERS IN THE NBA

Player	Team	Average Salary
Derrick Coleman	New Jersey Nets	$9.4 million
Anfernee Hardaway	Orlando Magic	7.7 million
Glenn Robinson	Milwaukee Bucks	6.8 million
Jason Kidd	Dallas Mavericks	6.0 million
Shaquille O'Neal	Orlando Magic	5.7 million
Patrick Ewing	New York Knicks	5.5 million
Chris Webber	Washington Bullets	5.0 million

SOURCE: NBA Players Association.

Ironically, the NBA's best player, Michael Jordan, earns only about $4 million per year in basketball salary. And during his "sabbatical" from the beginning of the 1993 season to March 1995, when he attempted to become a major league baseball player, he earned even less. But Jordan's earnings from endorsements, ranging from Hanes underwear to Gatorade to his own line of Nike shoes, brings his Air-ness more than $35 million annually.

NATIONAL HOCKEY LEAGUE

In June 1994, the New York Rangers won the NHL's Stanley Cup, something that hadn't happened in 54 years. Then something even more improbable happened. Three months later, following one of the most financially successful seasons in league history, team owners locked the players out during training camp, claiming that they could no longer operate under the terms of the collective bargaining agreement that had expired the year before. This decision came just a year after the league signed a contract with ESPN to brodacast a national game of the week; after successful franchises caught on in warm-weather cities like Tampa Bay, Anaheim, and San Jose; after sales of NHL merchandise continued to skyrocket; and after a season in which the league's biggest market, New York, was attracting national media attention for an entire spring. Nevertheless, the owners continued to claim huge losses (as much as $37.6 million in 1993–1994 alone according to some sources), and kept the Zambonis off the ice for 103 days until they reached a new collective bargaining agreement with the players. Finally, on January 13 (Friday the 13th), owners and players reached an agreement that most observers say was a whitewash in favor of the owners' side.

HOCKEY'S HIGHEST PAID PLAYERS, 1994–1995

Player	Team	Average Annual Salary
Wayne Gretzky	Los Angeles Kings	$6.5 million
Mark Messier	New York Rangers	6.0 million
Scott Stevens	New Jersey Devils	5.8 million
Pavel Bure	Vancouver Canucks	4.5 million
Al MacInnis	St. Louis Blues	3.5 million
Bret Hull	St. Louis Blues	3.5 million
Mario Lemieux	Pittsburgh Penguins	3.5 million
Eric Lindros	Philadelphia Flyers	3.5 million
Pat La Fontaine	Buffalo Sabres	3.5 million
Patrick Roy	Montreal Canadiens	3.5 million[1]
Steve Yzerman	Detroit Red Wings	3.0 million
Bill Ranford	Edmonton Oilers	3.0 million

HOCKEY'S HIGHEST PAID PLAYERS, 1994–1995

Player	Team	Average Annual Salary
Doug Gilmour	Toronto Maple Leafs	$3.0 million[1]
Paul Kariya	Anaheim Mighty Ducks	2.8 million
Jaromir Jagr	Pittsburgh Penguins	2.8 million
Joe Sakic	Quebec Nordiques	2.8 million[1]
Peter Forsberg	Quebec Nordiques	2.8 million[1]
Sergei Fedorov	Detroit Red Wings	2.7 million
Chris Chelios	Chicago Blackhawks	2.6 million
Brendan Shanahan	St. Louis Blues	2.6 million

[1]Canadian dollars.
SOURCE: *The Hockey News,* March 24, 1995.

NHL TEAM PAYROLLS, 1995

Team	Payroll	Team	Payroll
Los Angeles Kings	$24,320,000	San Jose Sharks	$14,584,000
St. Louis Blues	23,131,000	Calgary Flames	14,340,000[1]
New York Rangers	22,032,000	Philadelphia Flyers	14,238,000
Pittsburgh Penguins	22,043,000	Montreal Canadiens	14,230,000[1]
Detroit Red Wings	20,530,000	Quebec Nordiques	13,978,000[1]
Buffalo Sabres	19,850,000	New York Islanders	13,419,500
New Jersey Devils	18,638,000	Anaheim Mighty Ducks	13,194,000
Vancouver Canucks	18,267,000[1]	Winnipeg Jets	13,047,000[1]
Chicago Blackhawks	18,160,000	Boston Bruins	12,035,000
Toronto Maple Leafs	16,521,000[1]	Florida Panthers	11,735,000
Dallas Stars	16,197,000	Tampa Bay Lightning	10,114,000
Hartford Whalers	15,635,000	Edmonton Oilers	9,669,000[1]
Washington Capitals	14,883,000	Ottawa Senators	9,365,000[1]
		Average Team Payroll	15,929,057

[1]Canadian payrolls are expressed in U.S. dollars based on a conversion rate of $0.71 per Canadian dollar.
SOURCE: *The Hockey News,* March 24, 1995.

Under the terms of the new agreement, players are eligible for unrestricted free agency, but not until they turn 32 years old, an age that few players reach while still on skates. Meanwhile, players between the ages of 18 and 24 are subject to to a salary cap that increases from $850,000 in

1995 to $1.075 million in 2000. Players under the age of 22 are subject to the salary cap for three years; 22- and 23-year-olds are limited for two years; and 24-year-olds for one year. Players between the ages of 24 and 32 are eligible to be come restricted free agents, meaning that the player's previous club has the right to match any free agent signing offer. Teams losing a free agent receive draft picks (depending on the value of the player lost) as compensation. Players 24 to 32 are also eligible for salary arbitration, but if they choose arbitration, they may not become free agents.

What all of this means, according to most experts, is much lower salaries than the 1993–1994 average of $653,000. This figure is nearly double the 1991–1992 amount of $368,603, but is misleading because it magnifies the eight-digit contracts signed by a handful of superstars like Mario Lemieux, Wayne Gretzky, Mark Messier, and Eric Lindros. The median salary—the midpoint at which half the salaries in the NHL are higher and half are lower, and thus more accurately reflects what the "average" player earns—is a lot lower than the average salary figure so often quoted by team owners.

SOME HIGHLY PAID COACHES AND MANAGERS

Salaries of coaches and managers have escalated at the same rate as those of the players in all sports. However, it is a rare coach who makes as much as his superstar players. Former Washington Redskins' coach Joe Gibbs was the exception rather than the rule when his 1990 salary of $1.2 million eclipsed that of Wilber Marshall, then the team's highest-paid player at $1.1 million. That same year, Steeler coach Chuck Noll, in his twenty-second season, earned $800,000, the same salary paid to quarterback Bubby Brister. Don Shula is the NFL's highest paid coach with an annual salary of $1.6 million, even though his Miami Dolphins haven't won a Super Bowl since 1974. Meanwhile, Jimmy Johnson earned $1 million (up from $550,000) the year after his Dallas Cowboys won Super Bowl XXVII. After Johnson won a second Super Bowl, Cowboys owner Jerry Jones rewarded him by firing him. San Francisco coach George Seifert, however, was more justly compensated after he directed the 49ers to their triumph over San Diego in Super Bowl XXIX. He signed a two-year contract extension worth an average of $1.4 million, making him the NFL's second highest-paid coach (behind Shula).

In professional football and hockey overall, the average coach's salary is about double the average player's salary. But in basketball and baseball, the highest-paid coaches or managers barely make what the average player earns. Former Knicks coach Pat Riley and former Nets coach Chuck Daly, both of whom won championships in other cities, were lured to the New York City area by contracts in excess of $1 million per year, making them the only coaches with salaries comparable to the average NBA salary of $1.1

million. In baseball, the highest-paid managers earn about $750,000, or a quarter of a million dollars less than the average player. The relatively low salaries earned by coaches and managers in these sports is another reason owners usually find it easier to fire the coach when things go badly instead of getting rid of the players responsible for a losing season.

PLAYERS' UNION LEADERS

Because players' associations in the four major sports represent all the players in their sports and negotiate collective bargaining agreements for them, it is tempting to think of them as unions. But the similarities end there; and the differences are great, especially when it comes to salaries earned by both the players and their leaders at the bargaining table. The disparity between salaries earned by professional athletes and members of other unions has been well documented—in this book as well as countless other sources. Therefore it should surprise no one that their negotiating representatives earn salaries closer to that of the people they represent than to other union leaders. In fact, where most union leaders earn a lot more than even the highest-paid person they represent, the leaders of the four major sports unions take home salaries that are closer to the average for their union. The following table shows salaries for players association leaders in baseball, basketball, and football—salaries for NHL Players' Association leader Bob Goodenow are unavailable—and for various union leaders.

SALARIES OF UNION LEADERS AND MEMBERS, 1993

Leader and Union	Leader's Salary, 1993	Average Member's Salary, 1993
Gene Upshaw, executive director, National Football League Players Association	$1,236,443	$ 750,000
Donald Fehr, executive director and general counsel, Major League Baseball Players Association	950,000	1,200,000
Charles Grantham, executive director, National Basketball Association Players Association[1]	550,307	1,500,000
J. Randolph Babbitt, president, Air Line Pilots Association	272,681	80,000
Lane Kirkland, president, AFL-CIO	204,672	30,784
Ronald Carey, president, Teamsters Association	191,033	NA
Owen F. Bieber, president, United Auto Workers	103,938	NA
Richard L. Trumka, president, United Mine Workers of America	80,656	NA

[1]Resigned April 14, 1995.
SOURCE: U.S. Department of Labor.

Of course, when you consider that these leaders are battling league commissioners like David Stern, who earns $6 million a year from the NBA, their salaries seem low.

BOXING

The relationship between television and boxing has changed considerably since the "Friday Night Fights" days of the 1950s, when boxing was such a regular part of the television landscape that three or four fights were shown two nights a week. The corruption and gangsterism of the 1960s, combined with a notable decline in talent, caused boxing to disappear almost completely from television. What revived it a decade later was the emergence of Muhammad Ali as boxing's official shill and its best showman. One of the greatest fighters of all time, Ali taught everyone, including television executives, how the tube could be used to rekindle interest in boxing.

In 1970, Ali was a full-fledged media celebrity, not only because of his fighting ability but for his refusal to serve in the military, his opposition to the Vietnam War, and the subsequent removal of his heavyweight crown. When he returned to boxing, he was a welcome guest on all the TV talk shows, and he made sure he stayed in the news by always making the slightly outrageous remark, usually something to do with race. As a result, tens of millions of people would learn of his upcoming bouts, and many would pay $20 to 25 to watch them on closed-circuit television. Later, when his boxing skills had declined, Ali continued to fight lesser opponents. But his popularity was such that advertisers felt he could attract enough viewers to warrant a prime-time audience on network television. The last hurrah came in 1980 when Ali, after a year of retirement, returned to fight the new champ, Larry Holmes. Although everyone in boxing knew that Holmes would win easily, Ali was able to command a purse of $8 million from the closed-circuit TV audience, while Holmes received only $2.5 million.

Since then, the advent of pay-per-view cable television (in which viewers pay a flat fee for a single event rather than for a month of programming) has vastly expanded boxing's closed-circuit audience to include private homes. And the paydays have increased correspondingly. Meanwhile, frequency and quality of title fights have decreased as each successive champion makes sure he lines up a tomato can or two for his initial defense (and for his first big payday) before fighting a boxer that could actually beat him.

The other big change in the boxing world in the past few years was the March 25, 1995, release from prison of former heavyweight champ Mike Tyson. In the five years since Buster Douglas stunningly knocked out Tyson to become the heavyweight champion of the sport's three major organizations—The World Boxing Association (WBA), the World Boxing Council

(WBC), and the International Boxing Federation (IBF)—boxing has been reeling. Six new boxing organizations cropped up, making a total of nine different sanctioning bodies, which between February 1990 and March 1995, awarded heavyweight title belts to no fewer than 21 different boxers. The last time all the belts were in the same hand was in November 1992, when Riddick Bowe won a decision over Evander Holyfield. It's no wonder, then, that most boxing experts felt that the entire heavyweight division was merely on hold until Tyson's return to the ring. Indeed, Tyson's return to boxing, less than a week after his release from prison, was accompanied by dollar signs with nine digits after them—that is, $100 million paydays for at least his first few fights.

Although not every payday is as rich as this one, the one-time payments involved in a major title bout are usually large enough to land the recipient near the top of the list of best-paid athletes. But their reign is usually short and the dropoff is usually precipitous. Moreover, the biggest rewards are shared only by a handful of fighters—usually the heavyweight champion, the leading two or three challengers, and occasionally a champion with a lot of charisma from a lower weight class, such as Julio Cesar Chavez (who earned $8 million in 1994), Sugar Ray Leonard, or Marvin Hagler.

EARNINGS OF TOP BOXERS, 1994

Boxer	Division	Earnings (Million)	Endorsements (Million)	Total (Million)
Michael Moorer	Heavyweight	$12.0	$0.1	$12.1
Evander Holyfield	Heavyweight	10.0	2.0	12.0
George Foreman	Heavyweight	3.5	5.0	8.5
Julio Cesar Chavez	Superlightweight	8.0	0.5	8.5
Lennox Lewis	Heavyweight	8.0	0.3	8.3
James Toney	Supermiddleweight	6.2	0	6.2
Pernell Whitaker	Welterweight	5.2	0	5.2

SOURCE: *Forbes* magazine, December 19, 1994.

TENNIS

Tennis players were one of the first groups of athletes to recognize the value of endorsement income. Simply by donning a clothier's shirt or shorts, using a manufacturer's racquet, or running around in a company's shoes, tennis players could create lots of free advertising for a sporting goods maker . . . and earn millions of dollars for doing it. Today, the top players earn much more for their endorsements than in winning tournaments. Of course, endorsements are a kind of two-edged sword. The richest contracts usually go to the best players, so if players want to keep their endorsement income high, they have to keep their games at a high level as well. There are exceptions, though. André Agassi's long-haired flashy style earned him huge endorsement contracts with Nike, Canon cameras, and several other manufacturers long before he became a top-ranked player (and long before he lost his hair). On the flip side, Sergei Bruguera ranked second in tournament winnings in 1994 with over $3 million, but because very few people know who he is, his endorsement deals are far more moderate.

EARNINGS OF TOP TENNIS PLAYERS, 1994[1]

Men	Earnings	Women	Earnings
Pete Sampras	$3,607,812	Arantxa Sanchez Vicario	$2,943,665
Sergei Bruguera	3,031,874	Conchita Martinez	1,540,167
Stefan Edberg	2,489,161	Steffi Graf	1,487,980
Goran Ivanisevic	2,060,278	Jana Novotna	876,119
Michael Stich	2,033,623	Natasha Zvereva	874,592
Boris Becker	2,029,756	Gabriela Sabatini	874,470
André Agassi	1,941,667	Martina Navratilova	851,082
Jim Courier	1,921,584	Mary Pierce	768,614
Michal Chang	1,789,495	Gigi Fernandez	742,650
Andrei Medvedev	1,211,134	Lindsay Davenport	600,745
Wayne Ferreira	1,063,341	Anke Huber	456,731
Jacco Eltingh	1,053,619	Meredith McGrath	381,942
Yevgeny Kafelnikov	1,011,563	Kimiko Date	376,904
Alberto Berasategui	939,651	Amanda Coetzer	361,791
Paul Haarhuis	930,961	Larisa Nieland	359,012
Todd Martin	888,342	Julie Halard	357,273
Mark Woodforde	885,924	Lori McNeil	337,046
Marc Rosset	768,004	Brenda Schultz	334,046
Jonas Bjorkman	756,552	Magdalena Maleeva	324,347
Jonathan Stark	689,379	Iva Majou	318,152

[1]Includes prize money from singles, doubles, and mixed doubles tournaments.
SOURCE: Association of Tennis Professionals, Women's Tennis Association

GOLF

It's still very much a man's world on the golf links—at least in terms of earnings. Male professional golfers continue to earn nearly twice as much as their female counterparts. This is due in no small part to the increased coverage the men's tour receives. Television ratings for women's golf have never risen anywhere near those of men's golf. In recent years, even the men's senior tour, featuring such old favorites as Arnold Palmer and Jack Nicklaus, has surpassed the women's tour in terms of viewer interest. It wasn't until 1989, when Betsy King earned $654,132, that the leading women's golfer topped the half-million-dollar mark. The top female money winner in 1994, Laura Davies, earned only slightly more than that. Moreover, her total of $687,201 would place her eighteenth on the men's list. Meanwhile, Nick Price earned more in 1994 alone ($1.5 million) than most women pro golfers have earned in their entire careers.

EARNINGS OF TOP GOLFERS, 1994

Men	Earnings	Women	Earnings
Nick Price	$1,499,927	Laura Davies	$687,201
Greg Norman	1,330,307	Beth Daniel	659,426
Mark McCumber	1,208,209	Liselotte Neumann	505,701
Tom Lehman	1,031,144	Dottie Mochrie	472,728
Fuzzy Zoeller	1,016,804	Donna Andrews	429,015
Loren Roberts	1,015,671	Tammie Green	418,969
José María Olazábal	969,900	Sherri Steinhauer	413,398
Corey Pavin	906,305	Kelly Robbins	396,778
Jeff Maggert	814,475	Betsy King	390,239
Hale Irwin	814,436	Meg Mallon	353,385
Scott Hoch	804,559	Elaine Crosby	344,735
Steve Lowery	794,048	Val Skinner	328,021
Mike Springer	770,717	Patty Sheehan	323,562
Bob Estes	765,360	Helen Alfredsson	277,971
Phil Mickelson	748,316	Jane Geddes	273,600
John Huston	731,499	Michelle McGann	269,936
Bill Glasson	689,110	Deb Richard	256,960
Brad Bryant	687,803	Judy Dickinson	246,879
Ernie Els	684,440	Hiromi Kobayashi	242,323
David Frost	671,683	Pat Bradley	236,274

SOURCE: Professional Golfers' Association, Ladies Professional Golfers' Association.

Appearance fees also play large roles in golfers' earnings. Witness the amounts paid to players just for showing up at the Alfred Dunhill Challenge in February 1995. Any player ranked in the top five received $150,000 for participating in the tournament. Players ranked between 6 and 10 received $50,000, while lower-ranked players received $25,000.

The rewards were even higher for participation in the January 1995 Dubai Desert Golf Classic, a tiny tournament held primarily for the entertainment of Dubai's millionaire prime minister Sheik Maktoum bin Rashin Al Maktoum. Six of the world's eight best golfers showed up not for the purse of $675,000 but rather for the appearance fees: $1.3 million divided six ways.

BOWLING

Professional bowlers still earn their money the old-fashioned way: they earn it. Although a handful of bowlers earn endorsement income for using a specific brand of ball, shoes, or gloves, because of bowling's limited television exposure, the amounts are fairly small. The majority of a bowler's income still comes from winning tournaments. And only a handful of professional bowlers can earn enough income from tournaments to make kegling their livelihood.

On the women's side, the Ladies Pro Bowlers Tour sponsors 22 open tournaments each year. The total prize money for each tournament is usually $60,000 (though a few events have purses of $70,000 and $75,000). The winner of each tournament takes home 18 percent of the total purse (or $10,800 for a $60,000 event), the second-place finisher gets 9 percent ($5,400), and third prize is 5.72 percent ($3,432). The rest of the purse is distributed in decreasing amounts to the bowlers placing fourth through thirtieth.

The rewards for men are considerably higher. The top 12 men all earned over $100,000 in 1994; some broke the six figure mark without winning a single tournament. (Like the women's tour, the Professional Bowlers Association tour rewards bowlers placing second, third, fourth, etc.) The difference, though, is that almost to a tee, each male bowler in the top 20 earned twice what the corresponding female bowler took home.

EARNINGS OF TOP BOWLERS, 1994

Men	Earnings	Women	Earnings
Norm Duke	$273,753	Aleta Sill	$126,325
Walter Ray Williams, Jr.	189,745	Anne Marie Duggan	124,722
Bryan Goebel	173,933	Tish Johnson	82,756
Eric Forkel	144,339	Marianne DiRupo	72,369
John Mazza	129,500	Carol Gianotti	68,039
Brian Voss	124,878	Tammy Turner	65,022
Parker Bohn III	121,885	Carolyn Dorin	62,117
Pete Weber	120,973	Kim Couture	61,978
Johnny Petraglia	115,070	Leanne Barrette	61,348
Justin Hromek	114,731	Sandra Jo Shiery	51,358
Steve Hoskins	106,234	Cheryl Daniels	50,247
Amleto Monacelli	102,875	Wendy Macpherson	45,166
Dave Husted	95,420	Debbie McMullen	44,772
Randy Pedersen	93,855	Kim Canady	44,354
David Ozio	89,162	Kim Straub	42,043
David D'Entremont	80,979	Jackie Sellers	41,571
Dave Traber	72,575	Darris Street	40,889
Bob Learn, Jr.	71,725	Dede Davidson	40,542
Butch Soper	67,873	Robin Romeo	36,118
Dennis Horan	65,638	Jeanne Naccarato	35,815

SOURCE: Professional Bowlers' Association, Ladies Pro Bowling Tour

HORSE RACING

Jockeys usually receive 10 percent of each winning purse, though occasionally, owners give guaranteed payments to top jockeys. Laffit Pincay, Jr., for example, received $50,000 to ride Groovy in one race in 1986.

EARNINGS OF TOP JOCKEYS, 1994

Jockey	Earnings	Jockey	Earnings
Mike Smith	$1,597,982	Chris Antley	$760,758
Pat Day	1,454,372	Laffit Pincay, Jr.	683,864
Gary Stevens	1,268,522	Robbie Davis	652,329
Jerry Bailey	1,151,591	Joe Bravo	637,626
Kent Desormeaux	1,129,724	Jorge Chavez	632,834
Chris McCarron	1,093,372	Shane Sellers	591,500
C. S. Nakatani	969,874	Mike Luzzi	568,809
Eddie Delahoussaye	863,349	Russel Baze	564,819
Jose Santos	832,994	Craig Perre	519,043
Alex Solis	771,041	Jorge Velazquez	487,474

SOURCE: *Daily Racing Form*

ENDORSEMENTS

The implicit message of endorsements has always been "Use this product and you'll be as successful as I am." In 1992, one advertiser finally came out and articulated those words with a campaign for Gatorade featuring Michael Jordan and the slogan "Be Like Mike; Drink Gatorade." The campaign was a huge success, at least until Jordan abandoned his role as basketball's greatest player to become one of baseball's worst players. But while this specific campaign had to be revised, Jordan's popularity as a spokesman did not wane. His return to the NBA in March 1995 (wearing jersey number 45 instead of his customary 23, in an effort to boost his merchandising even more) only increased his popularity.

The series of events demonstrates that while a level of athletic ability is necessary to command huge endorsement contracts, charisma and appeal to target audiences often plays a much larger role in who gets the big money. On or off the court, Jordan is still the king of endorsements, hauling down more than $30 million annually for hawking products ranging from Wheaties cereal to Hanes underwear to, of course, Air Jordan sneakers, which Nike continued to manufacture even while Jordan was playing baseball. But the two next-biggest endorsers in 1994 were golfers who hadn't won a tournament in years: Jack Nicklaus and Arnold Palmer. But because of their appeal to older consumers who remember the days when these former legends ruled the links, Nicklaus and Palmer each earned more than $13 million in endorsements. On the other side of the spectrum, Orlando Magic center Shaquille O'Neal's popularity with the under-25 set brought him more than $12 million in endorsements before he had won a single playoff game.

TOP ENDORSEMENT EARNINGS, 1994

Personality	**Sport**	**Endorsement Earnings, 1994 (million)**
Michael Jordan	Basketball	$30.0
Jack Nicklaus	Golf	14.5
Arnold Palmer	Golf	13.5
Shaquille O'Neal	Basketball	12.5
André Agassi	Tennis	9.5
Greg Norman	Golf	7.5
Joe Montana	Football	7.0
Pete Sampras	Tennis	7.0
Steffi Graf	Tennis	6.5
Charles Barkley	Basketball	6.0
Boris Becker	Tennis	5.0
George Foreman	Boxing	5.0
Wayne Gretzky	Hockey	4.5

SOURCE: *Forbes* magazine, December 5, 1994.

AMATEURS

The concept of amateurism was developed not in the ancient Greek Olympic games, but rather in nineteenth-century England as a way to prevent the working classes from competing against the aristocracy. And politics have continued to determine who is and is not an amateur ever since. The veil of amateurism was used to deny Jim Thorpe his gold medals in the 1912 Olympic decathlon and pentathlon because he had played semiprofessional baseball three years earlier. (In 1982, the International Olympic Committee voted to restore Thorpe's gold medals and presented them to his children in 1983.) For years, the Communist countries claimed they had no professional teams in any sport, and thus sent their best (read state-supported) athletes to international competition.

The admission of professional U.S. basketball players—the so-called Dream Team—to the 1992 games in Barcelona finally erased any pretense the Olympics might have had of amateurism. The average fan realized long before the International Olympic Committee did that even amateur athletes were being paid in some form or other to perform. But to adhere to the sham of Olympic amateurism, many athletes had to concoct elaborate schemes to earn a living while theoretically maintaining their amateur status. Meanwhile, because of the exposure provided from the televising of their competitions, "amateur" athletes were able to earn upwards of $1 million a year endorsing clothing and athletic equipment.

College Coaches

The income from television contracts has affected salary levels in what used to be called amateur sports just as it has in the professional arena. Since large schools can realize substantial profits by fielding teams good enough to be aired regionally or nationally, the pressure to win has made big-time college coaching as high-pressured and insecure a job as any in the pros. Football coaches were the first to experience this change, and today the minimum salary for an established person at a university that takes intercollegiate sports seriously is usually $50,000. Over the last decades, college basketball has become a major television attraction, and the predictable salary spiral has followed, with the biggest money being paid by those schools eager to develop winning teams in a sport other than football.

Anyone familiar with college athletics, however, knows that just as the players receive most of their benefits surreptitiously, so do their mentors. Virtually every football and basketball coach at a major university has his own television show, summer instructional camp, and guaranteed list of speaking engagements, not to mention such intangibles as ready access to the local business people, who are frequently alumni of the university. The legendary "Bear" Bryant earned $115,000 as athletic director and head football coach at Alabama, but he was known to be a millionaire based on his weekly television show, tie-in endorsements with advertisers, and real estate holdings. The situation is no different today: despite a base salary usually under $100,000, most big-time college football and basketball coaches end up taking home more than a half million dollars. And with speaking fees ranging as high as $25,000 a speech, a coach who makes a wide lecture circuit can easily boost his income over the $1 million mark.

The University of Miami's new football coach, Butch Davis, is a telling example of how profitable so-called amateur sports can be to a coach. Davis left a job as an assistant coach in the NFL to take over head coaching duties at Miami when Dennis Erickson left to become head coach of the Seattle Seahawks. Davis had been earning all of $120,000 in the NFL; at Miami, he'll take home $700,000 a year. (As for Erickson, you can be sure he didn't take a pay cut to leave a perennially strong college program to coach the perennially also-ran Seahawks.) The following table lists some salaries of well-known college football and basketball coaches. Keep in mind that these are average salaries, in which shoe contracts, speech fees, and other bonuses are spread out over several years.

ESTIMATED ANNUAL EARNINGS OF WELL-KNOWN COLLEGE FOOTBALL AND BASKETBALL COACHES

Coach	University	Sport	Average Annual Earnings
Rick Pitino	Kentucky	Basketball	$1,100,000
Mike Krzyzewski	Duke	Basketball	1,000,000
Dean Smith	North Carolina	Basketball	1,000,000
Lou Holtz	Notre Dame	Football	900,000
John Thompson	Georgetown	Basketball	900,000
Bobby Bowden	Florida State	Football	850,000
Bobby Knight	Indiana	Basketball	750,000
Butch Davis	Miami	Football	700,000
Tom Osborne	Nebraska	Football	700,000
John Cooper	Ohio State	Football	650,000
Nolan Richardson	Arkansas	Basketball	650,000
Bobby Cremins	Georgia Tech	Basketball	600,000
Joe Paterno	Penn State	Football	600,000
Howard Schnellenberger	Oklahoma	Football	550,000

While these salaries are typical for well-known college coaches, the vast majority of college coaches (even Division I programs) are not so famous. Many programs are strong only in one sport—quick! name the head football coach at Georgetown or the basketball coach at Nebraska—in large part because a big-name coach usually steers every available athletic department dollar to his program. Thus, national averages, even for football and basketball coaches, are much lower than the astronomical numbers in the above table.

A recent General Accounting Office (GAO) survey revealed that head football coaches averaged only $75,500 in base salary, but earned an average of $25,431 in university-provided benefits such as club memberships, houses, cars, etc., and $32,300 in outside income from shoe contracts, television shows, and summer camps. The situation was similar for men's basketball coaches, who earned an average of only $69,400 in salary, but added $19,995 in benefits and a whopping $38,686 in outside income. Because of all this additional income, a university's head football and men's basketball coaches are almost always better compensated than the school athletic director, who typically earns very little outside income.

Because women's sports programs typically attract less media attention than their men's counterparts, it is not surprising that coaches of women's basketball teams earn far less than the men's teams' coaches. What is surprising, though, is the discrepancy between male and female coaches of women's basketball teams. Women coaches of women's teams earned an average of $42,200 in 1991, while men coaches of women's teams earned only $35,900; but men took in $5,100 in benefits and $7,000 in outside income, compared to $4,900 and $6,500 for women. Only one of the 259 schools responding to the GAO survey had a woman athletic director; there were no women coaches of men's football or basketball teams. It's no wonder that many schools keep coaches' salaries a highly secretive matter. Some public institutions even go so far as to set up "foundations" which pay big-name coaches from alumni funds and other "donations," thus assuring complete privacy. Certainly they have a right to do this, but when coaches of the stature of Joe Paterno of Penn State and Bobby Knight of Indiana use the names, not to mention the facilities and resources, of publicly funded institutions to earn what must be very high salaries and yet refuse to disclose their basic incomes, some measure of the public trust (and probably the law) has been violated. And they are high.

Athletic Directors

The importance of athletics in college and university programs is clearly reflected in the salaries paid to athletic directors at these institutions of higher education. With a median salary of $55,162, athletic directors are some of the highest-paid student services officials, according to the College and University Personnel Association's 1994–95 *Administrative Compensation Survey.* Among administrators whose purpose it is to serve students directly, only the Chief Student Affairs Officer, the Director of Student Health Services (who is also a physician), and the Chief of Enrollment Management earn higher salaries. Gender discrimination is in evidence in this job category as well. At institutions where the athletic director's job is divided between men's and women's sports, the director of men's athletic programs earns about 10 percent more than the director of women's athletic programs, regardless of the sex of the office holder. This inequity continues despite federal legislation (Title IX) requiring colleges to devote equal funding to men's and women's athletic programs.

At many institutions where men's football or basketball programs consistently attract national attention (for example, Indiana in basketball, Penn State in football), the coach of the featured team also serves as athletic director. This not only makes the coach responsible to nobody except the head of the university but also effectively insures that the premier sport gets more of the athletic director's attention than any other sport at the institution.

SALARIES OF ATHLETIC DIRECTORS IN HIGHER EDUCATION

Type of Institution	Median Salary
Large Public Universities	$62,606
Large Private Universities	56,448
Private Religious Institutions	43,904
Two-Year (Junior) Colleges	45,563
All Institutions	$55,162

SOURCE: College and University Personnel Association, *Administrative Compensation Survey 1994–95* (1995).

Behind the Scenes

BEHIND THE SCENES IN TELEVISION

Some people still think television is a vast wasteland of worthless entertainment and offensive commercials; others view the tube as a quasi-divine instrument bringing mankind together in a "global village." No one, however, questions the simple fact that television has changed people's daily routines, while at the same time expanding their knowledge in ways not imagined only a few short decades ago. In America this has been accomplished essentially by a business-sponsored broadcasting system.

There are about 1,000 television stations in the United States. Of these, about 260 are run by nonprofit organizations, many located in universities, which is why they are usually referred to as "educational" stations. The others are called "commercial" stations because their owners make a profit from selling broadcast time to advertisers. Most of these commercial stations are linked together every night into four separate networks (ABC, CBS, NBC, and Fox) in order to provide advertisers with larger audiences, and audiences with better programming. In 1994 these stations and networks collected $10 billion in advertising fees.

Despite the size and scope of the industry, and the important role television plays in our daily lives, the business employs only about 100,000 people, 15,000 of them at the major networks. As in any business, most jobs are clerical or secretarial in the accounting and dataprocessing departments. Only a handful of people, perhaps 40,000, are directly involved with getting the news or entertainment onto our sets. For this reason there is intense competition for jobs in television, especially in large cities. However, the Department of Labor foresees expanded job opportunities in the field over the next decade because of the explosion in cable TV systems and the bright prospects for videotapes.

Broadcasting requires the skill and talents of many different kinds of people, from writers and directors to stagehands and lighting experts. Most of these jobs require union membership, but for that reason salary levels are relatively high. The most important television unions representing technicians at the networks and at major market stations are the International Brotherhood of Electrical Workers (IBEW), the National Association of Broadcast Employees and Technicians (NABET), and the International Alliance of Theatrical Stage Employees (IATSE). Nontechnical, behind-the-scenes people who are not considered management belong to the Directors Guild of America (DGA) or the Writers Guild of America (WGA).

Union contracts can be negotiated either with individual stations or with a network and its owned and operated stations for all staff jobs. Although there are differences between compensation at the networks and at the local stations, most technical people are paid close to the same rates. Salaries for other staff members will fluctuate, sometimes dramatically, from city to city or, in broadcasting lingo, market to market. And since most jobs in broadcasting exist on the local level, the job descriptions and salaries that follow are based on the organization of those stations. A few network salary figures are included.

Management

Every television station has at least three key managerial positions: general manager (also called station manager), sales manager, and program director. Although their duties will differ from station to station, the following general descriptions provide a clear idea of what each job entails. In this part all of these positions usually carry with them very hefty expense accounts.

General Manager/Station Manager—Basic responsibility is to run the station on a day-to-day as well as a long-term basis. Has final decision making power on all issues—from budgeting to programming—which affect the station's operation. All department managers or directors are answerable to him.

The average salary for station managers is $100,000 a year. Except in the smallest markets, almost all make over $60,000. The top people earn $200,000 or more.

Sales Manager—All commercial stations make all of their profits through advertising. The sales manager supervises the men and women who sell broadcast time to sponsors. This is frequently done through advertising agencies that represent large sponsors seeking local coverage. At large stations there are usually three sales managers—one for local sales, one for national sales, and one in charge of the whole sales operation who is known as general sales manager.

As you might expect, market size greatly influences salaries. In New York, $100,000 to $150,000 is not unheard of but $75,000 to $100,000 is tops in the middle market areas.

Program Directors—Initiate the development of all broadcasts for the station and then oversee their budgets and production. The producers of each program are answerable to the program director, who reports directly to the station manager.

Again, the size of the station and the market determine salary. An independent station tends to pay more because it does more of its own programming than stations affiliated with a network. The average salary of program directors is just under $50,000. In the top ten markets, however, most make over $80,000. Top pay in these areas is said to be between $100,000 and $150,000. In the smaller cities $40,000 to $50,000 was the average range.

Producers and Directors

Producer—Every show, whether it originates locally or comes from a network, has one person who is ultimately responsible for almost every phase of the program from concept through to finished product. Called the producer, he or she selects and works with the talent, instructs the director, and is frequently in charge of the show's budget. On major programs, including all those on the network, there is also an *executive producer* who is responsible for long-range planning and making sure the show does well in the ratings game. Big-time network programs such as *Today, 60 Minutes,* and *Good Morning America* will have producers and associate producers for each segment.

According to the National Association of Broadcasting, salaries for producers at local stations are the same as those for directors: the national average is about $45,000, but top markets often pay three times that amount (see the section on news producers). Since the networks reach much larger audiences, they hire the most talented people. The salaries therefore are much higher. Some of the best known even have agents. According to several New York–based agents, executive producers on the networks can make over $300,000 a year.

Director—On all live and taped shows (news, soap operas, game shows, interview programs, sporting events), the director sits at a long console and faces a row of television monitors which show him what is going on in the studio or on the field of play from different camera positions. On news broadcasts, there are also closed-circuit monitors where tape or film which has been edited that day will appear at the director's cue. The director's job is to choreograph all the elements of the broadcast: cue the studio cameras, give instructions to the stage manager on the floor to cue the talent, call for slides, film, or tape to be inserted in the control room and implement them on the floor.

There is a base salary for directors negotiated with the DGA, but there is no ceiling. Depending on demand, talent, and experience, a director can negotiate a handsome salary. Established soap opera directors, for example, can be paid $2,000 or more per episode. But the soaps are produced by networks, and the average salaries at local stations are much lower.

Associate Director—Sits next to the director and informs him what comes next in the broadcast. The AD keeps running time of the entire broadcast and on news shows counts down when videotape machines should roll tape. The AD informs the director when a commercial is coming up and how long it will run. After the broadcast the AD arranges for tapes to be made.

Salaries vary from market to market. At most network owned and operated stations the base salary is about $25,000 to start and rises to around $50,000 after three years.

Technicians

There are several specialized kinds of technicians needed at every station. Most network technicians earn about $20,000 to start with a top of about $35,000 after three years. Supervisors make $40,000 and up.

Technical Director—Physically implements the director's instructions at his cue by pushing a set of complex buttons on the console in front of him; i.e., he rolls tape machines, picks up camera shots. Salaries at the networks and at the major stations in large cities are in the $35,000 to $55,000 range.

Audio—Sits in a separate booth in the control room. Audio person wires the talent in the studio, tests and monitors their levels, as well as raises and lowers audio levels at the director's cue.

Video—Adjusts color levels and balances picture so that it is air-quality.

Chyron Operator—Types out names of people to be superimposed on the screen into a special machine and at the director's cue punches them up.

The ENG Crew—"Electronic news gathering" today uses a camera crew to shoot tape, not film, because it is cheaper and faster. The ENG crew consists of two people—one records the image and the other records the sound. These two positions can be interchangeable, although it is not all that common. Since the tape crew is always on call, their union contract provides for substantial overtime and holiday pay. Most tape technicians earn a good deal above their base salary. In most shops they are in the same union as other technicians. Many stations hire freelance people who receive about $200 a day.

Tape Editor—Screens the material on an electronic editing system. In news, unlike documentaries, the editor does not make major editorial decisions but takes notes on where the writer/associate producer or reporter wants the cut and which sound bites they want to use and pieces it all together with cover footage for narration. Again, tape editors are in the same union as technicians in most major market stations.

News Division

A large percentage of any station's payroll goes to supporting the people who bring us the local news. Below are the job descriptions and salaries for most of these positions. As with all jobs in broadcasting salaries vary widely based on the size of the market where the station is located.

News Director—Ultimately responsible for the image, format, and content of all news broadcasts. He or she answers directly to the general manager of the station. News directors' duties differ from station to station, depending on the size of the news staff, but they are usually involved with budgets, hiring the talent (reporters and anchorpersons), and acting as editor-in-chief in the newsroom. In top markets (Los Angeles, Chicago, etc.) their jobs are almost solely dependent on ratings, so there's a high turnover rate. Their salaries reflect this: According to several agents, news directors in New York City earn $70,000 at the smaller stations and as much as $100,000 to $150,000 at the major ones.

News Producer—On local news shows the producer decides on the order of presentation (the "lineup") for all the stories. He or she is responsible for making sure stories are complete and that they are properly integrated into the program. During the live broadcast, the producer sits in the control room with the director; any last-minute changes or on-the-air readjustments are the producer's responsibility. The average salary for news producers in third-market cities was about $45,000 in 1995.

In New York, Chicago, and Los Angeles, insiders claim, the producers of the evening news earn $100,000 or more. In these major markets there is also an *executive producer of news,* who takes responsibility for all local news broadcasts. Salaries range from $100,000 to $200,000 or more per year.

News Editors—Sometimes called *assignment editors* because they assign writers to particular stories. Also edit all copy that is scheduled for broadcast including reporters' scripts, and they write all necessary transitional copy to keep the show moving. In major markets they are all members of the Writers Guild, which establishes the base salaries. In New York, for example, the salary base is about $35,000 and news editors also receive a 15 percent premium for working nights.

News Writers—Members of the Writers Guild of America. At a top market station writers of 30-minute broadcasts for five-day-a-week strips earn between $97,810 and $141,668. In smaller markets, they make between $37,000 and $50,000, including overtime. According to inside sources, the top writers in big markets earn over $150,000.

News Desk Assistants—Situated in the middle of the newsroom, their responsibilities include fielding incoming phone calls from the public, the press, and public relations people, etc. They also check the newswires and distribute the copy to key newsroom personnel. Often their job also entails getting supplies, having machines repaired, etc. They are, in short, considered the newsroom gofers. Desk assistants do not usually make over $22,000 a year.

Other Key Personnel

At the end of almost every program a list of credits rolls up, usually too quickly to read, but below is a list of titles and descriptions most of us will recognize.

Graphic Artists—Throughout the day, the artists in graphics prepare visual elements that augment the broadcast—i.e., slides, charts, graphs, logos, etc. They prepare original material as well as duplicating or enlarging other artwork so that it is first-rate broadcast-quality. They also work with specialists on animation projects. Union agreements at a station in Washington, D.C., call for base pay of $283.50 a week to $377 a week after one year. The hourly rate is $9.43. The average salary for a graphic artist at a major top-market station, however, is about $36,000 a year, including overtime.

Lighting Director—Responsible for preplanning the lighting in the studio and ensuring that it is properly executed either during a taping or live broadcast. The latest IATSE figures for a lighting director at New York's PBS station is $969.46 per week; daily, $193.89.

Scenic Designers—Although they are highly paid, rarely work on a daily basis. They can design sets for special broadcasts, new shows, etc., as well as redesign old sets. Because of the nature of their work, they may not be needed daily. The most recent daily minimum rates for a scenic designer was $238 a day, $1,063 per week.

Scenic Artists—Do any necessary painting or primping of the set. The approximate rates from IATSE: chargeman (head) rate for scenic artists, $287.43 per day or $1,437.15 per week; journeymen, $234.36 per day or $1,171.80 per week.

Makeup Artists—Apply makeup and fix the hair of the news correspondents and anchorpeople in every broadcast. They work on the actors and actresses in the soaps, talk show guests, etc. Anyone who goes before a camera should be made up. In 1995, the average rate paid daily according to IATSE for stylists was $690 for television commercials, one of the highest paying segments of the business.

Stagehands—It is a union regulation that the studio cannot open up without three stagehands present. There are three types: electricians, carpenters, and prop people. They are basically responsible for checking sets and equipment before the broadcast begins, bringing props into the studio and moving them when necessary, etc. The most recent IATSE rate paid for studio head stagehand is $792.78 per week, or $46,274 annually. The average minimum rate for an assistant stagehand was $694.80 per week or $36,180 annually.

Stage Managers—Are on the floor of the studio and make sure that everything runs smoothly. He or she receives cues from the director and in turn cues the talent when to get off and on the set, when to start a news report, etc. In non-news broadcasts, the stage manager is responsible for supervising set changes. In large-market stations, the stage manager is usually a member of the Directors' Guild which negotiates minimum wage rates. Average salaries range from $16,800 to $31,500.

Researchers—At local stations researchers usually work in news. His or her job is to initiate stories, develop contacts, spot-check facts, and provide writers, reporters, and management with background information. They gather relevant audiovisual material to be incorporated in the broadcast. They also find interesting people to interview. They can work in the library, newsroom, and in the field. Although it is considered an entry level job in news, it sometimes leads to an associate producer's or writer's job.

At the networks there are many kinds of researchers. Some provide information on ratings, audience analysis, marketing, etc.; others work on particular shows finding background material, setting up interviews, even helping to develop new ideas.

At local stations, researchers earn $275 to $400. The networks pay better and one inside source says that senior research people earn as much as $45,000 to $50,000 a year, including overtime.

Production Assistants—Work on the daily rundown of a program, typing up the routine of the show, including the timing of each segment, the type of piece (film, tape) to be used, and any other production details that should be known. If the show is not seen daily, the production assistant works on long-range planning of the show until each piece fits into place. During the actual broadcast, they will sit in the control room and time the show.

On news programs, the production assistant is occupied throughout the day with coordinating graphics, slides, and names of people interviewed in each story to be superimposed on the screen during the report. The PA must coordinate the information he or she gets from the reporters, associate producers, etc., with the story lineup. As the day progresses and the show gets closer to airtime, the production assistant is responsible for "breaking script"; i.e., distributing a copy to everyone in the control room. Production assistants at CBS owned and operated stations are members of the Directors' Guild, so salaries are set by contractual agreement. Minimum salaries are approximately $18,000 to start and $22,000 after 30 months.

WHO MAKES WHAT IN THE FILM INDUSTRY

Are star actors being paid too much? Some analysts think so. Yet a basic rule is operating. Steven Spielberg once put it this way: "Whatever they're paying you, it's not enough." If the producers of *Waterworld* allowed Kevin Costner to run the movie's budget up over $150 million, it's because they expected to make even more than that as a direct result of his presence in the film. (They were wrong, of course.) This has been true since the earliest days of the movie industry. In the teens, Mary Pickford, Douglas Fairbanks, and Charles Chaplin (with D. W. Griffith) formed their own production company,

United Artists, at least in part because their legitimate fees were so extraordinarily high that other production companies couldn't pay them. For 30 years, long-term contracts helped to keep star salaries under control, but now that actors are free agents once again and movies are making money once again, the stars ask—and get—large fees. The producers, however, make even more. All of these fingers in the pot have driven up the cost of making movies—to an average of $50.4 million in 1994. And that's before Costner's 1995 film, *Waterworld.* In many cases it is still true that a star is the movie. People are paying to see Stallone, not the movie he's in.

Crew members and technicians make what appear to be good salaries (see the figures below), but remember that freelance work is different in nature from full-time employment. A cinematographer on a feature film can easily expect to make $2,000 or $3,000 per week, but this doesn't mean he or she is making $100,000 to $150,000 a year. The real annual income may be much less than half that, since the average shooting schedule for a film only lasts 12 weeks and even the successful freelancer may very well receive no more than two assignments a year.

Remember, too, that of the thousands of people that belong to any particular craft union, the majority are usually out of work. It's traditionally said that 85 percent of the Screen Actors Guild is unemployed at any one time.

With those provisos in mind, here are some of the basic pay rates for the various crafts and professions in the film industry.

Actors and Stars

The Screen Actors Guild represents extras: people who appear in movies and television shows and don't talk. There are only two minimum pay rates for extras and it's nearly impossible to make a career out of the job.

General Extras are paid a minimum of $65 per day as of 1995 under the Hollywood SAG contract. "Special Ability" Extras who can, for example, ride a horse, earn $75 per day.

The Screen Actors Guild also represents people who talk in movies. The basic day rate is $504 (plus a 12.5 percent payment for pension and welfare).

If an actor is hired for a full week's work that basic rate is $1,752. There is also a special three-day minimum of $1,276 for television work.

Multiple-pictures players (actors hired for more than one appearance) work for a starting salary that depends on the type of show:

30 minutes	$1,295 per week
1 hour	1,295
90 minutes	1,523
2 hours	1,797

Term players who get hired for the run of a half-hour production earn $1,752 a week for a guaranteed 13 out of 13 weeks; or $2,002 a week for a guaranteed minimum of 6 out of 13 weeks; and $2,336 a week for 6 weeks or less. For a one-hour production, the weekly rates are $2,105 for 13 out of 13 weeks, $2,350 a week for a minimum of 6 out of 13 weeks, and $2,747 a week for 6 weeks or less.

Of course these figures represent only the minimum allowed by contract. Many actors besides outright stars will be paid higher rates than these.

Salaries for the stars are, fittingly, astronomical. During the mid-1970s, Steve McQueen set a record by asking $3 million for any performance. He didn't work very often, but when he did, he got paid what he asked.

Many other star actors operate as co-producers and thus earn money as "bosses" as well as "workers." Any well-known actor will ask for and usually receive a percentage of the profits of the film, known in the trade as "points." Directors and even a few writers also commonly receive points. Other craftspeople haven't reached that level yet.

Sylvester Stallone, Arnold Schwarzenegger, Jack Nicholson, and Bruce Willis are generally regarded as the highest priced male stars. These actors garner anywhere from $10 million to as much as $20 million for a feature film (plus a hefty percentage of profits). Nicholson received $5 million for 10 days' work on *A Few Good Men.* Young Macaulay Culkin was paid $5 million plus 5 percent of the gross (a total of $16 million) for *Home Alone 2.*

Demi Moore, generally regarded as one of the highest priced female stars, received $12 million (plus a hefty percentage of profits) for *Striptease,* while Barbra Streisand received $3.5 million plus a percentage of profits for 10 weeks' work on *All Night Long.* Now she gets $6 million per film, as does *Basic Instinct* star Sharon Stone.

Actors and others who receive a percentage of the profits, by the way, are always careful that the contract reads in terms of percentages of the gross income from a film. "Net points"—percentages of profits after the studio and producers have deducted their expenses—always have a way of evaporating, even on very successful films.

Actors are also interested in the expanding uses of film product. Since 1960 every member of the Screen Actors Guild has shared in profits from television broadcast of films he has appeared in. "Residuals" can provide a small but steady income. The main point of the SAG strike of 1980 was to achieve a similar share of producers' profits from "supplementary markets"—videodiscs, videotape, pay television, cable, satellite, and so on. The actors won, and are now paid 3.6 percent of distributors' worldwide grosses on each film.

Writers

The Writers Guild of America sets standards and minimums for writers in film and television. Writers are the last in the chain to share directly in profits from a film (after producers, actors, and directors). Winston Groom, for example, sold the rights to his novel *Forrest Gump* to Paramount for $350,000 and three percent of the net profits. But even though *Gump* earned more than $350 million in 1994 alone, Groom didn't see a dime past his advance, as the studio claimed a $62 million loss on the film. Groom, understandably, has sued the studio for this all-too-common bookkeeping sleight of hand. Writers' fees are also often split. A writer who adapts a book or play for the screen will be paid less than the writer of an original screenplay. Writers, unlike directors, often work in teams and split fees. The fee structures under the WGA's Basic Minimum Agreement are as follows:

	1995–96		1996–97	
	High	**Low**	**High**	**Low**
Original Screenplay and Treatment	$73,992	$39,076	$76,582	$40,444
Original Screenplay Only	54,267	26,260	56,166	27,179
Nonoriginal Screenplay and Treatment	64,207	34,198	66,454	35,395
Nonoriginal Screenplay Only	44,399	21,369	45,953	22,117
Story or Treatment	19,736	12,822	20,427	13,271
Original Treatment	29,603	17,707	30,639	18,327
Rewrite of Screenplay	19,736	12,822	20,427	13,271
Polish of Screenplay	9,867	6,413	10,212	6,637

You want to know what a "polish" is? So do many screenwriters.

Television

Experienced television writers receive the following minimums under the WGA contract:

	1995–96		1996–97	
	Prime Time	**Nonprime Time**	**Prime Time[1]**	**Nonprime Time[2]**
30 minutes	$15,627	$8,099	$16,095	$8,382
1 hour	22,984	14,720	23,674	15,235
90 minutes	33,308	22,121	32,338	22,895
2 hours	43,822	28,991	42,546	30,006

[1]For 1997–98 rates, add 3 percent.
[2]For 1997–98 rates, add 4 percent.

Writers on weekly salaries at networks earn at least $2,500 per week, but there are few professionals in this category now. For both features and television, fees commonly exceed these bare minimums. A $200,000 salary is not uncommon for screenwriters with a track record; experienced screenwriters command three or four times that fee for feature films. Writers are less likely to get points than are directors, actors, or producers, but it does happen. Increasingly, writers are turning to producing in order to redress the financial imbalance between writer and director.

Studio Executives

Increasingly, studio executives either started out in the industry as agents or as MBAs. They tend to pay themselves quite well. A salary of less than $150,000 is now regarded as fit only for second- and third-level employees, and the many vice-presidents at the studios earn much more than that. Average salaries for the heads of production at major film companies exceed $500,000. The top executives at all the big studios earn over $2 million a year and with stocks and stock options they are worth five to ten times that amount. You can see why studios insist on a 35 percent cut as distribution fee; this sort of overhead mounts up.

In recent years the merger and acquisitions mania of the last decade came to Hollywood and, as in other business areas, had the effect of escalating salaries for key high-level personnel.

In 1989, for example, the Sony corporation agreed to pay Peter Guber and Jon Peters $750 million over five years to run Columbia Pictures which it had just purchased for $5 billion. Although this team had produced two huge hits (*Batman* and *Rain Man*), they in fact had never run a studio before. But what's often overlooked is the enormous sums earned by the executives at Columbia, a dismal failure in the year immediately prior to the sale. One industry source reported that the president received over $20 million, his second in command $13.5 million, another executive $10 million, and nine others at least $1 million.

U.S. Film Industry Employment and Salaries

In 1995, employment in the U.S. film industry topped 600,000 for the first time ever, according to the Bureau of Labor Statistics. And industry analysts say the number of people working on motion pictures is probably even higher because of the growing role of independent contractors, which is hard to track. Of course the prime beneficiaries of this explosion in the movie industry are the actors, directors, producers, editors, lighting technicians, stagehands, and electricians hired to work on feature films. The following figures show the minimum weekly salaries for those engaged in film production. (Note that these salaries are very rarely earned throughout the year—production work can be sporadic at the best of times.)

MINIMUM WEEKLY SALARIES FOR FILM WORK

Profession	Minimum Weekly Salary[1]
Director (Film with Budget Over $1,500,000)	$9,469
Director (Film with Budget $500,000–$1,500,000)	6,763
Director (Film with Budget under $500,000)	5,951
Art Director	2,524
Director of Photography	2,469
Costume Designer	2,040
Editor	1,927
Sound or Music Editor	1,405
Unit Production Manager	2,813
First Assistant Director	2,672
Key Second Assistant Director	1,791

[1]All figures are for a standard working week.
SOURCES: Industry Unions; 1995 contracts.

Directors

The Directors Guild of America negotiates for film and television directors. Their contracts with the film industry provide for minimum rates of pay as shown in the previous table. Most directors earn considerably more than the minimum rates of pay. Straight $2 million salaries are not unheard of for well-known directors; highly successful directors now get much more. James Cameron reportedly received $6 million for *Terminator II,* and Richard Donner got $4 million for *Lethal Weapon 3.* Like actors, star directors can also earn huge sums from the films in which they participate.

Television directors, like TV actors, are paid by the category of show.

Television directors will not command star salaries like feature film directors, but twice the minimum is not an uncommon salary. And there are substantial residuals. Directors of prime-time network shows get roughly 57 percent of their original fee each time the show is re-run. And aside from their work fee, feature film directors get a percentage of box office and videocassette sales.

MINIMUM WEEKLY PAY—DIRECTORS

Prime Time	Pay Rate
30 minutes	$14,337 for minimum 7 days
1 hour	$24,347 for minimum 15 days
90 minutes	$40,580 for minimum 25 days
2 hours	$68,170 for minimum 42 days

SOURCE: Directors Guild of America, 1995 Contracts.

MINIMUM WEEKLY PAY—DIRECTORS' ASSISTANTS

Title	Minimum Weekly Pay
Unit Production Manager	$2,813
First Assistant Director	2,672
Key Second Assistant Director	1,791
2nd Second Assistant Director	1,691
Additional Second Assistant Director	1,029

SOURCE: Directors Guild of America, July 1995.

Cinematographers

For several years now cinematographers—the people who actually photograph moving pictures—have been angling for admission to the charmed circle of producers, directors, writers, and actors. They haven't yet achieved this in terms of pay scales and percentages, but they are getting there in terms of publicity. Often the key bargaining points in a cinematographer's contract these days will have to do with getting their own mobile vans on location and guaranteed paid advertising rather than salary.

The American Society of Cinematographers contract ensures the following basic daily rates through July, 1996:

Director of Photography	$493.76
Camera Operator	302.26
Still Photographer	302.26
First Assistant Cameraman	218.72
Second Assistant	201.04
Film Loader	171.76

Top cinematographers will be able to earn $15,000–$22,000 per week, a salary which is comparable with that of decently paid writers; $25,000 per week with points is not unheard of.

Measured in terms of daily wages, cinematographers who work on television commercials do as well as or better than nearly all feature film DPs even if they aren't as well known. These rates go as high as $7,500 a day.

Editors

Editors have as much to do with the ultimate effect of a film as cinematographers, but they don't yet have the clout as a craft. This is reflected in lower pay scales. Film editors earn a minimum of $1,927 per week under the Motion Pictures Editors Guild contract, effective through July 1996. Assistants earn a minimum of $1,120. Sound effects and music editors earn at least $958. While it is possible for well-known editors to earn much more than this it is not common.

Composers and Musicians

Like cinematographers and editors, composers have been fighting for a larger share of the film pie in recent years. Like the Producers Guild, the Composers & Lyricists Guild is still fighting for recognition.

Top film composers like John Williams or Jerry Goldsmith will earn a minimum of $60,000 per feature film. Most composers earn half that, and low-budget features will go for as little as $25,000. A lyricist can expect $8,000 a song, and leading lyricists like Alan and Marilyn Bergman get much more.

For television, composers earn relatively more than you might expect, a reflection of the fact that so many television shows are produced with "wall-to-wall" music, unlike feature films where music is now usually intermittent. A half-hour sitcom will yield perhaps $2,500, a movie-of-the-week $12,000 to $15,000, a 4-hour miniseries $30,000.

Composers also share in performance royalties, but only actually receive half of this money (unlike their counterparts in the outside world); half goes to the producer.

Musicians are covered by an American Federation of Musicians videotape agreement which guarantees them $55.15 an hour for a minimum 2-hour call. A conductor will get double this amount. Different minimum rates exist for pay cable television, public television, documentary film, and basic cable television.

Film Designers and Artists

The recent success of animated full-length features (especially those from Disney) have put a premium on the skills of yet another group of players in Hollywood: the animators. Disney's success in this arena—*The Lion King* alone is expected to generate profits, including merchandising, of nearly $1 billion—has persuaded every major Hollywood studio to jump into the business of creating animated films. As a result, the once-sleepy field of animation has become one of the hottest career tracks in Hollywood. With the pool of talented animators too small to handle the burgeoning work, salaries for animators have skyrocketed. According to Tom Sito, president of the cartoonists' union that represents most Hollywood animators, average weekly salaries for animators with five years experience has just about doubled, from $1,000 in 1992 to close to $2,000 today. The top animators (such as those chosen to draw central characters like Pocahontas or the Little Mermaid) earn closer to $20,000.

Salary rates for other types of designers and artists in film and television follow.

WEEKLY PAY RATES FOR DESIGNERS AND ARTISTS IN FILM AND TELEVISION

	Minimum Weekly Salary	
Position	**Feature Film**	**Television**
Art Director	$2,524.00	$2,084.00
Assistant Art Director	1,950.00	1,702.60
Costume Designer	2,040.43	1,685.00
Assistant Costume Designer	1,250.00	958.75
Charge Scenic Artist	1,675.00	1,437.15
Journey Scenic Artist	1,350.00	1,171.80
Shop Person	900.00	746.05

SOURCE: United Scenic Artists Union, May 1995.

MINIMUM DAILY RATES FOR DESIGNERS AND ARTISTS IN TELEVISION COMMERCIALS

Position	Period	Rate
Art Director	day	$890.00
Stylist	day	690.00
Charge Scenic Artist	7 hours	350.00
	10 hours	650.00
Journey Scenic Artist	7 hours	320.00
	10 hours	594.26

SOURCE: United Scenic Artists Union, May 1995.

Entry Level Jobs

People who work in the offices of film companies often earn less than people of comparable skills would earn in other businesses. The competition even for secretarial positions is intense since the job is regarded as prestigious and glamorous.

Traditionally, one of the best ways to break into the industry (besides entry-level secretarial positions) is the job of story analyst. All production companies have to deal with thousands of scripts and novels each year. It is the job of the story analyst to read, summarize, and evaluate these potential properties. Very few story analysts have staff positions. Most are freelance and the pay scale is minimal, ranging from $35 to $100 per script or book covered. Since the coverage involves reading the property and writing two to 20 pages of summary and evaluation, even efficient story analysts earn less than established secretaries—and there are no fringe benefits.

BACKSTAGE

Behind the scenes of every play, whether it's staged on Broadway or in the local church basement, are all those unseen people who enable the show to go on. Some perform utilitarian tasks like moving scenery or making sure all the props are in order, while others are central to the creation of the world of verisimilitude that is the heart of theater: They design costumes, invent dance routines, and illuminate the stage and the actors in imaginative ways. Where they work and how much they get paid depends on where they are, what kind of theater the play is being performed in, and, for the creative staff, what degree of fame they have attained.

Stage Workers

This designation refers to almost everyone who works backstage, under the stage, high over the stage, behind the lights, or in the sound booth. Stage workers include skilled carpenters and electricians, as well as painters and people who only move scenery.

The International Alliance of Theatrical Stage Employees (IATSE) represents just over 60,000 stage workers throughout the country. Every professional theater, whether it houses a variety of art forms or specializes in opera, ballet, or theater, must hire union personnel. The minimum rates vary according to city and regions. New York City and Los Angeles are given below. Note that the designation "Department Head" refers to head carpenter, head electrician, etc.

MINIMUM RATES FOR STAGE WORKERS IN NEW YORK AND LOS ANGELES

Position	Weekly	Hourly
Department Heads	$1047	$36.75
Asst. Dept. Heads	923	30.31
Sound Crew	872	27.63
Lighting Crew	872	27.63
General Stagehands	800	24.85

SOURCE: IATSE, 1995.

Stage Managers

Stage managers, simply put, make sure that everything during rehearsals and performances runs smoothly on stage and off.

The first part of their job on a new play is to read the play and become familiar with it. After that, they help arrange for the theater, expedite auditions, coordinate rehearsals, supervise the hiring of the crew, and work with department heads and with the directors and designers. After the play opens, the stage manager does everything from handling union problems to prompting the cast during the performance. In effect, as far as the actors are concerned, the stage manager is director in absentia.

The rates below are the scale for stage managers who are represented by the Actors' Equity Association. The scale is minimum; with experience a stage manager can get from $50 to $150 a week more than scale, especially if he or she has worked over and over again with the same director.

MINIMUM WEEKLY PAY FOR STAGE MANAGERS ON BROADWAY[1]

	Musical	Drama
Stage Manager	$1643	$1413
First Assistant Stage Manager	1300	1154
Second Assistant Stage Manager	1086	NA

[1]Rates are as of June 1995.

MINIMUM WEEKLY PAY RATES FOR STAGE MANAGERS IN REGIONAL THEATERS[1]

Type of Theater[2]	Stage Manager		Asst. Stage Managers	
	Repertory	Nonrepertory	Repertory	Nonrepertory
A	$858	$858	$720	$717
B	728	658	657	558
C	683	629	581	529
D	614	543	509	447

[1]Rates effective through February 1996.
[2]For an explanation of A, B, C, D designations, see the earlier section "Actors."

Designers

A Broadway theater: The curtain opens and filtered night light glows on a bedraggled young woman selling flowers in front of a London playhouse. Music plays softly, Eliza Doolittle comes to life, and the audience becomes engrossed in *My Fair Lady*. But the ambience of the play is created by more than just the actors. What's before the audience is the result of collaboration among many people, with a major role played by unsung heroes—the scenic, lighting, and costume designers.

These are the creative artists who help translate the playwright's words and the choreographer's directions into a play and a ballet. Although their names appear in tiny type at the bottom of the playbill, they are essential to successful theater.

Designers are usually trained in special schools or in universities or through apprenticeships. They start out with small regional theaters or repertory companies and if they're lucky and very talented, work their way up to Broadway.

Most of the designers are represented by the United Scenic Artists Union. The pay tables that follow give the scale, which usually applies to beginners only. After some experience, designers can command a little more. The big names, of course, negotiate for as much as they can get.

Where the potential for big money comes in depends on royalties, which are fixed or variable. The fixed royalties generally apply to beginners and the middle-level designers. For each week the show runs, the designer gets a royalty of from $100 to $300 on Broadway and in big-city theaters, and from $35 to $75 Off-Broadway and in smaller theaters around the country. The royalty applies to the original show as well as any road companies, foreign tours, or dinner theaters.

Instead of a fixed royalty, the top names can command a percentage, usually from 0.5 to 1 percent, of the show's weekly gross. On a big Broadway musical that can be $5,000 a week or more. As with the fixed royalty, the top names get a percentage of the gross on any road companies or tours.

Added to this, the top designers usually work on as many as four or five shows a season. Frequently, a "hot" designer will do Broadway as well as Off-Broadway, where he or she can experiment more.

SET DESIGNERS

The best set designers are not simply interior decorators; they do not just paint pictures against which ballets are danced and dramas are acted. Whether it's building a drinking saloon in *Hello, Dolly!,* creating the manse of Norma Desmond in *Sunset Boulevard,* or evoking a steamy summer night for an Alvin Ailey number, the designer's job is to create a particular mood to blend with the acting.

Set designers, like lighting and costume designers, work closely with the director, deciding how to provide a suitable yet unobtrusive background for the action. They are also skilled in planning how scenery can be changed quickly with a minimum of noise and difficulty as well as how to create different scenes with only one basic set.

The legendary name in scenic design is Oliver Smith, who did the sets for *My Fair Lady, Hello, Dolly!,* and *West Side Story.* Today Robin Wagner is one of the current crop of most-sought-after set designers. He has done *Hair, Annie, A Chorus Line, 42nd Street,* and *Dream Girls.*

MINIMUM PAY RATES FOR SET DESIGNERS

Broadway	
Drama, Single Set	$ 7,501
Drama, Multiset	10,658
Musical, Single Set	7,501
Musical, Multiset	23,843

MINIMUM PAY RATES FOR SET DESIGNERS

Off-Broadway

	Seating Capacity		
	199 or less	**200–299**	**300–499**
Single Set	$1,414	$2,244	$4,215
Multiset	1,767	2,715	6,203
Unit Set with Phases	1,767	2,715	7,686

Regional Theater

	Seating Capacity				
	199 or less	**200–299**	**300–499**	**500–999**	**Over 1,000**
Single Set	$1,495	$2,048	$2,704	$3,353	$3,705
Two Sets	1,657	2,373	3,167	4,327	4,915
Unit Set with Phases	1,718	2,384	3,240	4,024	4,450
Each Additional Set	57	97	207	531	548

Ballet

	American Ballet Theater New York City Ballet Joffrey Ballet	**Standard Companies**
First Set	$5,135	$3,640
Second Set	1,510	946
Each Additional Set	1,005	708
Unit Set	5,140	3,480
Next 9 Phases	1,130	708

SOURCE: United Scenic Artists Union, 1995.

COSTUME DESIGNERS

Whether it's Shakespearean costume for a revival of *Hamlet,* a flowing dress for *Swan Lake,* or nineteenth century dresses for *The Heiress,* the costume designer has the task of carefully planning the clothes for both the play's character and the individual actor. Costumes play a major role in creating a character, and the designer's main job is to enhance the character without drawing too much attention to the clothes themselves.

A designer is well versed in different periods of clothing, which materials will hold up well or move well with dancers, how the outfit will look from the first as well as the last row, and, most important, how to use clothes to create a certain mood.

The amount of clothing a designer must plan can be staggering, especially in productions with 30 or 40 actors, singers, and dancers, many of whom change costumes for each act.

The best known costume designer is Theoni V. Aldredge, who has done dozens of Broadway shows. At one time, she had four Broadway hits playing simultaneously: *A Chorus Line, Annie, Barnum,* and *42nd Street.* A conservative estimate of her royalties from those shows was $15,000 per week.

MINIMUM PAY RATES FOR COSTUME DESIGNERS

Broadway Drama

Number of Characters	Pay
1–3	$ 4,066
4–7	4,066 + 317 Each
8–15	6,871
16–20	6,871 + 317 Each
21–30	9,395
31–35	9,395 + 317 Each
36 and Over	11,921

Broadway Musical

Number of Persons Onstage	Pay
1–15	$ 8,134
16–20	8,134 + 378 Each
21–30	16,265
31–35	16,265 + 378 Each
36 and Over	23,843

Regional Theaters

	Number of Costumes			
Theater Size	**10 or Fewer**	**11–20 Each**	**21–30 Each**	**31 or Over Each**
199 or Less	$1,495	$ 31	$31	$31
200–299	2,048	57	32	32
300–499	2,597	71	45	45
500–999	2,961	97	71	50
Over 1,000	3,705	121	80	71

MINIMUM PAY RATES FOR COSTUME DESIGNERS

Off Broadway

Number of Characters	Seating Capacity: 199 or Less	Seating Capacity: 200–299	Seating Capacity: 300–499
Drama			
1–3	10 or Less = $1,414	10 or Less = $2,009	$ 2,293
4–7			187 Each
8–15	More than 10 = 1,767	More than 10 = 2,362	3,846
16–20			187 Each
21–30			5,216
31–35			187 Each
36+			6,893
Musical			
1–15	NA	NA	4,611
16–20	NA	NA	225 Each
21–30	NA	NA	9,223
31–35	NA	NA	225 Each
36+	NA	NA	13,765

Ballet

	American Ballet Theater New York City Ballet Joffrey Ballet	Standard Companies
Minimum per Ballet	$2,625	$875
1–10 Each	Minimum[1]	Minimum[2]
11–25 Each	175.00 Each	120 Each
26–50 Each	120.00 Each	100 Each
51 and over Each	95.00 Each	78 Each
Repeats Each	52.50 Each	57 Each

[1]$265 each, whichever is greater
[2]Or $190 each, whichever is greater
SOURCE: United Scenic Artists Union, 1995.

LIGHTING DESIGNERS

After the sets and costumes have been designed, the next people called in are the lighting designers, who do a lot more than just decide where the lights will be hung. They work closely with the directors to plan lighting that will be exactly right for each moment of the play, enhancing the action, the mood, and the meaning. Lighting is even more important in ballet and dance, where scenery and costumes may be minimal.

MINIMUM PAY RATES FOR LIGHTING DESIGNERS

Broadway

Drama	
Single Set	$ 5,627
Multiset	7,995
Single Set with Phases	10,305
Musical	
Single Set	$ 5,627
Single Set with Phases	10,305
Multiset	17,883

Off-Broadway

	Seating Capacity		
	199 or less	**200–299**	**300–499**
Drama			
Single Set	$1,414	$2,009	$ 2,951
Multiset	1,767	2,362	4,338
Unit Set with Phases	N/A	N/A	5,383
Musical			
Single Set	NA	NA	$ 4,215
Multiset	NA	NA	13,765
Unit Set with Phases	NA	NA	7,686

Regional Theaters

	Seating Capacity				
	199 or less	**200–299**	**300–499**	**500–999**	**Over 1,000**
Single Set	$1,495	$1,852	$2,445	$2,961	$3,705
Multisets or Phases	1,657	2,083	2,754	3,420	4,366

MINIMUM PAY RATES FOR LIGHTING DESIGNERS

Ballet	Standard Companies
Full Length Ballet	$3,350
More than 1/3 of an evening	2,210
1/3 of an evening	1,100
Pas de un/trois	835

SOURCE: United Scenic Artists Union, 1995.

Lighting design is selecting what the audience, faced with an entire stage, will see at each moment, whether it's a crook of a finger, a smiling face, or the star in a big production number. The designer plots where the lights—what types and in what intensities—will be hung in a theater. He then cues the lights for every action so that after he completes his job an electrician can do the actual work during the run of a play.

Jules Fisher is one of the top lighting designers. He's done *Hair, Pippin,* and *Dancin'*. Tharon Musser is noted for creating *A Chorus Line*'s computerized lighting as well as that of *The Wiz.*

DESIGN ASSISTANTS

Most productions on Broadway or those staged by major ballet companies are so elaborate they require trained personnel to help the various designers. The union regulates their rates, too.

MINIMUM WEEKLY PAY RATES FOR DESIGN ASSISTANTS

	Broadway	Standard Ballet
Scenic	$885	$675
Costume	885	675
Lighting	885	675

SOURCE: United Scenic Artists Union, 1995.

Directors and Choreographers

The director's task, whether for dinner theater or a Broadway show, is to transform written dialogue and scenes into a lively art. Usually hired by the producer, the director is involved in the play from the very beginning. He functions as an artist, a teacher, and an executive. As an artist, he extracts the meaning from the play and changes it into physical action. As a teacher, he guides the actors through their paces. As an executive, he oversees and collaborates with the lighting, set, and costume designers, the makeup artists, and all the other craftspeople.

The director has the final say on who gets the lead, how the scenery is arranged, when the lights dim, how the actor crosses the stage, and all the other thousands of elements that go into bringing a play to life.

If the play is a musical, the director may also be the choreographer, like the late Bob Fosse (*Chicago, Dancin'*), Jerome Robbins (*West Side Story, Fiddler on the Roof, Gypsy*), or the late Gower Champion (*Hello Dolly!, 42nd Street*). The choreographer plots and coordinates all the dance numbers in a musical. Like a composer, the choreographer notes each step exactly so the number is performed the same on Broadway as it is years later in a summer theater.

The pay for directors and choreographers is a combination of a fee and a percentage of the weekly box-office gross. The fees listed below are minimum and can go much higher, especially for name directors like Hal Prince, Mike Nichols, Gene Saks, and Robert Moore. The percentage starts at 0.75 percent and can go as high as 5 percent for a sought-after director or choreographer. This amount can be substantial, as the weekly gross on a Broadway show can range between $150,000 and $400,000. If the director stages the national theater companies he gets an additional fee as well as the cut of the box-office gross. The choreographer also gets his weekly royalty from any touring companies.

Off-Broadway fees vary by theater size in the range shown below.

MINIMUM PAY SCALES FOR DIRECTORS AND CHOREOGRAPHERS

		Off-Broadway			
	Broadway	**A Theater (400–499 Seats)**	**B Theater (300–399 Seats)**	**C Theater (200–299 Seats)**	**D Theater (100–199 Seats)**
Director	$40,000 plus 1.5 percent	$10,058 plus 2 percent	$8,172 plus 2 percent	$8,172 plus 2 percent	$5,658 plus 2 percent
Choreographer	$33,250 plus 0.5 percent	$8,046 plus 1.5 percent	$6,539 plus 1.5 percent	$5,534 plus 1.5 percent	$4,526 plus 1.5 percent
Director-Choreographer	$73,250	$17,600 plus 2.75 percent	$14,302 plus 2.75 percent	$12,100 plus 2.75 percent	$9,902 plus 2.75 percent

SOURCE: Society of Stage Directors and Choreographers, collective bargaining agreement, 1995.

Photographers

Lots of people have a knack with a Nikon. But if you can break out of the weddings-and-graduation-photo racket, there's good money to be earned in high-fashion, magazine, and other commercial photography. But although the pay is pleasing, the field is extremely difficult to break into. It's competitive and the money's far from steady.

Putting caveats aside, the work is creative and challenging. Generally hired by magazines or advertising agencies, photographers help develop illustration or campaign ideas and then shoot them. The bulk of jobs are in magazine illustration and in advertising and marketing, with a variety of possible assignments that include television commercials, billboards, catalogues, and packaging. Think of the scope of freelance work possible next time you plow through glossy magazine ads, buy dog food, or choose a book by its cover.

"Probably the best place to break into photography is in magazine work," says Patti Harris, director of New York City's Freelancenter, a placement service for freelance photographers, illustrators, copywriters, and other artists. Which means that, geographically, New York, followed by Los Angeles and Chicago, holds the best opportunities for work in this field. New York also offers the advantage of being the nation's fashion capital. Jobs can also be found in other major cities with concentrations of advertising agencies.

RATE GUIDELINES FOR PROFESSIONAL PHOTOGRAPHERS

	Lower Range	Average	Upper Range
ADVERTISING[1]			
Consumer Magazine			
National	$ 750–1,250	$1,500–2,500	$2,000–3,375
Trade Magazine	500–675	1,000–1,350	1,350–1,800
Newspaper			
National	1,200	1,650–2,050	2,650+
Local	450–700	750–1,000	1,250+
Billboard			
National	1,400	1,850–2,125	2,500+
Local	550	700–825	925
Still for TV Commercial			
National	500	1,000	1,500
Local	275	400	500–750

RATE GUIDELINES FOR PROFESSIONAL PHOTOGRAPHERS

	Lower Range	Average	Upper Range
Brochure			
National	$ 375–450	$ 750–875	$1,500–1,750
Regional	225–325	450–625	900–1,250
Local	175–200	350–400	500–750
CORPORATE/INDUSTRIAL[2]			
Annual Reports	600	700–850	1,300+
Brochure	400	500–800	1,200+
Film Strip	400	600	900+
Record-Album Cover	450	1,350	1,600+
EDITORIAL			
Editorial Illustration (fashion, home products, magazine & book covers, etc.)	350	450–800	1,400+
Under 2 Hrs.; Magazines under 200,000 Circulation	250	300	350+
General Documentary (geography, travel, etc.)	350	400–500	700+
PUBLICITY & PROMOTION			
Basic Press Kit	250–300	300–350	600–750
Motion-picture Special	250–300	350–450	500–600
Senior Executive Portraits (PR sittings)	300	500–750	1,000–1,500
CATALOGUE/BROCHURE			
Covers (per version)	600–750	1,250	1,500–2,000[2]
Fashion Catalogue			
Per Single Figure	85	125–175	250–300
Per Day	750	1,250	1,500–2,000
CATALOGUE/BROCHURE			
Still-life Catalogue			
Per Single Product	75	150–300	1,000+[3]
Per Day	750	1,250	1,500–2,000
Brochure (also see above)			
Per Still Life	75–100	150–300	1,000+
Per Single Full Figure	125–150	200–250	300–350

RATE GUIDELINES FOR PROFESSIONAL PHOTOGRAPHERS

	Lower Range	Average	Upper Range
MISCELLANEOUS MEDIA[1]			
Posters			
Promotional	$ 350	$ 625	$ 950
Retail	300	425	575+
Calendars			
Advertising or Promotional	375	625	1,400+
Retail	325	500	800
Greeting Cards			
Advertising or Promotional	300		625
Retail	225		425
Murals (varies widely depending on size and placement)	550		2,500+
Jigsaw Puzzles	375		525

[1]Rate per assignment.
[2]When used.
[3]Highly complex.
SOURCE: American Society of Magazine Photographers; reprinted by permission.

PAY RATES FOR FREELANCE PHOTOGRAPHERS AT LARGE CONSUMER MAGAZINES

Magazine	Rate
Barron's	$150–$300 day rate
Esquire	$750 for color photo
Golf Digest	$100–$300 for transparencies
Good Housekeeping	$150–$1,000 for color transparencies
Harper's	$50 to $500 per photo
Motor Trend	$25–$500 for transparencies
Ms.	$75–200 per photo
National Wildlife	$300–$800 per photo
New York Times Magazine	$75 minimum for black & white photo
Sierra	$300 maximum for transparencies; more for cover
Ski	$75–$300 per photo
Sports Parade	$35 for transparencies; $50 for cover
Star	$150–$1,000 for color transparencies

SOURCE: Writer's Market, 1994

From what she's seen, Harris says, "Most photographers try to specialize in one area." Areas of concentration can include medical reports, fashion, people, still life, travel, editorial, and reportage.

An estimated 95,000 Americans work in all kinds of photography out of commercial studios. Since many photographers work as independent business people, there seems to be no available information on their annual incomes. We do know that the government employs 3,000 photographers in different capacities (including work for the armed forces), for whom the average salary is $24,000. For information on newspaper photographers, please see the section "The Newspaper" in Part VI.

High-fashion photography is undoubtedly the highest paid sector of the profession, with famous photographers receiving over $6,000 a job. These are closely followed by travel pictures and then still-life product shots. Most photographers work freelance, even the full-timers, often utilizing more than one agent or service to scout out and arrange jobs. The rates given above usually do not include the typical 25 to 45 percent additional markup for the agent's commission. Furthermore, additionally billable expenses include all film and processing, all location and transportation expenses, assistants, insurance, special equipment, overtime, and talent used in shoot.

III

The Five Standard Professions

In today's parlance the term "professional" is applied to all kinds of people from the highly trained or educated (engineers and teachers, for example) to those who have completed a short course of study required by the state (beauticians and real estate brokers, among others). Sometimes "professional" is used as a term of approbation referring to someone who is particularly good at his or her job, or to someone who acts with cool detachment when things go wrong on the job: "She didn't complain about the transfer to Boise; after all, she's a . . ." There are other uses too, but these should suffice to indicate why we decided to buck the contemporary trend and lump together the five occupations that have commonly been referred to as professions for most of this century: accountants, architects, dentists, doctors, and lawyers.

Only 2 percent of the workforce, about 3 million people, are actively engaged in these occupations. With the exception of accountants, they have all had to complete several years of rigorous postgraduate training followed by a period of low-paid apprenticeship. More often than not, they open their own offices and join an organization that sets standards for professional practice and provides essential information, including advice on setting fees. The latter is rather important because, with the exception of architects, membership in these professions virtually guarantees an income substantially above the national norm, frequently placing members among the top 10 percent of all income-earning families in America.

In the past the wealth and status of these professionals went unchallenged, the value of their work to society unquestioned. Only foreign radicals like George Bernard Shaw would refer to the professions as "conspiracies against the laity." The figures found in this section may lead you to the same conclusion, especially if you are a nuclear engineer, a physicist, a senior college professor, or in any occupation that requires years of preparation. If you are young and looking toward a career, however, these five professions are almost certain to remain sure roads to economic security despite shifting public opinion. One reason is that the norm for wages and income is established by people in private practice. So even if you work as a lawyer or accountant for a corporation or government agency, your salary is based, unofficially, of course, on what people earn on their own. Since there are no signs that Congress or the courts would sanction any legal limitations on fees for professional services, salary levels should remain very high.

ACCOUNTANTS

Gone is the old stereotype of an accountant with eyeshade and bifocals sitting hunched with pencil in hand over pages of tiny figures. Accountants today come equipped with calculators, computers, sophisticated management techniques, and more often than not, advanced degrees. About 1 million accountants work in the United States, and almost all of them work in the corporate sector. During the economic boom of the early 1980s, the number of accountants grew at a rate almost as remarkable as the salaries some of the top level accountants earned. In leaner times, less money abounds, but accountants are still needed to keep the books and find ways to cut costs. According to an annual survey by Robert Half International, the economy's steady growth through the mid 1990s means companies are hiring accounting and finance personnel in every region of the country and at every job level. In fact, the Bureau of Labor Statistics in 1994 ranked accounting among the ten fastest growing industries over the next 10 years. The biggest beneficiaries of this growth should be professionals with one to five years experience, whose starting salaries are growing even faster than the average for all accountants. Both corporations and public firms have begun relying more on these lower paid staff or junior accountants and less on highly rewarded middle managers. And according to Robert Half CEO, Max Messmer, many accounting firms are again using sweeteners like signing bonuses, relocation costs, and counteroffers (all of which had been largely abandoned during the 1990 to 1991 recession) to attract the most qualified candidates.

To keep payrolls at a lower level, both corporations and public firms are relying on staff or junior accountants with one to five years' experience rather than more highly paid middle managers. Other companies are hiring accountants on a part-time basis only. After laying off large numbers of people, the companies are finding they don't have enough accountants to get their work done, so they have to hire on a per diem basis.

In the most basic terms, what accountants do is prepare and analyze financial reports that provide managers with the information they need to make decisions. Within a company, for example, an industrial accountant can perform the following tasks, ranging from the simple to the complex: do bookkeeping in various departments, complete tax returns and audit reports, prepare cost analyses for new projects, determine cutoff return investments, and advise on mergers and corporate growth policy. On higher levels, such as treasurer, the accountant will make broad policy decisions on all financial operations.

In public accounting, most of the duties revolve around audits (examining a client's financial records and reports to judge their compliance with standards of preparation and reporting). The tasks include: reconciling cash, confirming receivables, observing and testing the taking of inventory, testing internal control and accounting records, preparing tax returns, researching and counseling clients on tax problems, and providing management consulting in the development of all financial operations and frequently in personnel policies, production, and computerbased information systems.

The accounting field is divided into four segments: About 60 percent work in industrial accounting, about 25 percent in public accounting, about 12 percent in government, and about 3 percent in education.

Industrial accounting—also called management, corporation, or internal accounting—goes on in businesses from multinational corporations to small companies where in-house accountants perform all the financial operations: the treasury, controllership, and internal-audit functions.

Titles and responsibilities vary from company to company, but in general the lower- and middle-level jobs include cost accountant, internal auditor, plant accountant, data processing specialist, systems and procedures manager, financial analyst, chief accountant, and budget director. Higher up the ladder are assistant controller, controller, treasurer, secretary, vice-president of finance, president, and chairman of the board. Every recent survey has found that about 30 percent of the chief executive officers of the largest U.S. corporations had accounting and financial backgrounds, more than any other business specialty.

Within industrial accounting the position of certified internal auditor is gaining more importance because of the increase in shareholder lawsuits resulting from alleged inaccurate financial reporting. The approximately 17,000 Certified Internal Auditors in the United States have college degrees, have completed a three-year apprenticeship in internal auditing, and have passed a four-part national exam.

Becoming a certified public accountant is not necessary in industrial accounting as it is in public accounting, but the CPA certificate usually commands a 10 percent salary increase over non-CPAs in comparable positions. CPAs must also serve an apprenticeship and pass a four-part national exam to be certified.

Public accounting in general is slightly more lucrative than industrial. Many of the 400,000 CPAs in the United States work for public accounting firms, ranging from giant worldwide firms with thousands of employees to small one-man offices. The public accountant's work entails financial audits, tax advice and preparation, and often management consulting. The audits require frequent travel to the client's headquarters or branches and long hours examining the company's books and records, usually with a team of experts from the public accounting firm.

Many of the big accounting firms want new employees to have at least a college degree in accounting and preferably an M.B.A., especially for management consulting; or a law degree, especially for taxation specialization. The career path starts with the junior or staff accountant position and progresses, if all goes very well, to senior accountant to manager to partner and, finally, to senior partner.

Personnel specialist Robert Half estimates that about 60 percent of public accountants leave their first job after three to five years if they fail to attain a supervisory position. After another 10 to 15 years, a large group exits without making partner. Source Finance, another personnel agency, estimates that only about 2 percent of the accountants who join a public accounting firm will make partner. Those who leave generally go to good positions in industrial accounting. In a big corporation, the CPA who made the switch can eventually make as much as or more than a partner at his old firm.

The approximately 110,000 accountants who work for municipal, county, state, and federal governments are usually not as well paid. Their duties are much the same as those of industrial accountants, except that the "company" is the government. A college degree and passing a civil service exam are both required for many government accounting positions.

All these accountants get their original training in schools and colleges from the 3 percent of accountants who are teachers. Many teach part-time and supplement their incomes with consultancy work and by serving on professional organization committees.

As in so many other areas, the number of women entering the accounting field has grown considerably over the last few years. In fact, starting in the late 1980s, more women than men earned bachelor's degrees in accounting. The Robert Half Agency has found that, unlike some other professions, women accountants are easier to place than men. Women were chosen over men, the agency found, three times out of four for 100 different job openings paying between $15,000 and $50,000.

Top-Level Accountants in Finance

The Robert Half Agency of New York provides the following national survey of high-level salary ranges in the financial field. Geographic differences can mean from 2 to 5 percent up or down, except for a few states like Alaska (plus 10 percent) or Florida (minus 10 percent), Arizona, New Mexico, Tennessee, and West Virginia (all of which are minus 9 percent). Within each state, an accountant who works in a city of one million or more people generally earns 5 percent more; if extensive travel is required, the job generally pays an additional 5 percent.

ANNUAL SALARY RANGES FOR TOP-LEVEL JOBS IN FINANCE

Title	Company Volume (Millions)	1995 Salary Range
Chief Financial Officer/Treasurer	to $ 50	$ 60,000–82,000
	50–100	72,000–93,000
	100–250[1]	92,000–142,000
	250–500[1]	138,000–235,000
	500+[1]	232,000–295,000
Corporate Controller	to $ 10[2]	$ 46,000–58,000
	10–50	52,000–67,000
	50–250[3]	67,000–89,000
	250+	82,000–134,000
Assistant Controller, Divisional Controller, Plant Controller, or Assistant Treasurer	to $ 10[2]	$ 40,000–49,000
	10–50[2,3]	42,000–53,000
	50–250[3]	50,000–62,500
	250+	58,000–77,750
Corporate Tax Managers	$50–250	$ 56,500–71,500
	250+	67,000–105,000

[1]Bonus and incentive compensation reflect an increasingly large part of an overall pay package at these levels.
[2]Add 10 percent for CPA.
[3]Add 10 percent for CMA.
SOURCE: Robert Half International, *1995 Salary Guide.* Reprinted by permission.

Industrial and Public Accountants

The following survey of private industry covers the salaries of accountants on six different levels. Accountant I, a beginning level job, includes such tasks as examining a variety of financial statements for completeness, reconciling reports and financial data with statements already on file, and preparing relatively simple financial statements. Accountant II is more experienced and performs such tasks as preparing routine working papers, schedules, exhibits, and summaries on financial conditions, and examines a variety of accounting documents for accuracy. Accountant III usually has charge of a segment of an accounting system or of an entire system. Duties entail developing nonstandard reports and statements, interpreting financial trends, projecting data, and predicting effects of change in operating programs. Accountant IV is usually in charge of an accounting operation and makes recommendations for new accounts, revisions in account structure, and changes in accounting procedures. Accountant V has duties similar to accountant IV but the department is larger and/or more complex. Duties include developing and coordinating new accounting systems, assuring accounting reporting systems are in compliance, and identifying and suggesting solutions for problem areas. Accountant VI does much the same except the department he supervises has unusually difficult and complicated problems. He also usually has complete responsibility for his department.

AVERAGE SALARIES OF ACCOUNTANTS IN PRIVATE INDUSTRY

Level	Number	Average Weekly Salary	Average Annual Salary
I	14,352	$ 499	$25,948
II	51,082	594	30,888
III	62,768	747	38,844
IV	28,963	966	50,232
V	8,477	1,245	64,740
VI	1,303	1,545	80,340

SOURCE: U.S. Bureau of Labor Statistics.

Median Salaries of Accountants and Analysts in Public and Internal Firms

The following survey gives salary ranges of internal and public accountants and of analysts in small, medium, and large firms. Large firms have more than $150 million in sales; medium firms have between $15 and $150 million in sales; small firms have less than $15 million in sales. Internal accountants perform general, audit, and cost work; public accountants perform audits and tax management services; analysts do financial, budget, and cost work.

PREVAILING STARTING SALARIES OF ACCOUNTANTS

Title	1995 Salary Range
General Audit and Cost Accountants, Internal—Large Firms[1]	
0–1 year experience	$27,000–30,000
1–3 years experience	28,000–36,000
Senior	36,000–44,000
Manager	43,000–63,000
General Audit and Cost Accountants, Internal—Medium Firms[1]	
0–1 year experience	$25,000–28,000
1–3 years experience	28,000–36,000
Senior	36,000–42,000
Manager	40,000–48,000
General Audit and Cost Accountants, Internal—Small Firms[1]	
0–1 year experience	$24,000–27,000
1–3 years experience	26,000–34,000
Senior	33,000–39,000
Manager	39,000–40,000
Financial, Budget, and Cost Analysts—Large Firms[1]	
0–1 year experience	$26,000–30,750
1–3 years experience	30,000–38,750
Senior	38,000–46,500
Manager	46,000–65,000
Analysts—Medium Firms[1]	
0–1 year experience	$25,000–29,000
1–3 years experience	28,000–36,750
Senior	36,000–42,750
Manager	42,500–54,000
Analysts—Small Firms[1]	
0–1 year experience	$23,500–27,000
1–3 years experience	27,000–33,000
Senior	33,000–38,750
Manager	38,500–50,000
Audit, Tax, & Management Services Public Accountants—Large Firms[2]	
0–1 year experience	$28,000–32,250
1–3 years experience	29,000–35,500
Senior	34,000–43,250
Manager	43,000–62,500
Manager/Director[3]	55,000–84,500

PREVAILING STARTING SALARIES OF ACCOUNTANTS

Title	1995 Salary Range
Audit, Tax, & Management Services Public Accountants—Medium Firms[2]	
0–1 year experience	$25,000–28,250
1–3 years experience	27,500–34,500
Senior	33,500–43,000
Manager[3]	45,000–62,500
Manager/Director[3]	56,000–80,000
Audit, Tax, & Management Services Public Accountants—Small Firms[2]	
0–1 year experience	$23,000–26,500
1–3 years experience	26,000–33,000
Senior	31,000–42,000
Manager[3]	42,000–57,000
Manager/Director[3]	31,000–73,000

[1]Add 10 percent for a graduate degree, an additional 10 percent for a CPA, and an additional 5 percent for substantial travel.
[2]Add 5 percent for a graduate degree; add 10 percent for a CPA.
[3]Subtract 5 percent if not a CPA.
SOURCE: Robert Half International, *1995 Salary Guide.* Reprinted by permission.

ARCHITECTS

Architecture, law, and medicine all promise a certain status as professions within our society. But in terms of financial reward, architecture is very much the poor relation. Moreover, the end of the building boom of the 1980s means that the situation is not likely to get any better in the near future.

Several theories exist to explain why remuneration is not commensurate with the prestige offered by the architecture profession. One of the more persuasive arguments is that architecture is a process, rather than a product, and as such, is not essential to the construction of a building. The role of the architect has been reduced by the introduction of design builders, contractors, and construction managers into the building process. Indeed, it has been claimed that only 20 percent of all building is from architects' designs. Architects need either to become indispensable to the building process or become increasingly entrepreneurial and, hence, control the building process. Architecture can be viewed as a generalizing profession; architects typically provide planning and consulting in addition to design services. A more extreme manifestation is the shift of architects toward entrepreneurship—as owners, developers, financers, builders, or construction managers.

Traditionally the field of architecture has been caught between the gentleman's art and the artisan's craft. As a profession, architecture is somewhat less than 200 years old, the image of professionalism being established by Benjamin Latrobe at the turn of the nineteenth century. The introduction of the first architecture school in 1865 at MIT paralleled the development of architecture as a profession.

Today, nationally accredited schools enroll some 20,000 students in both undergraduate and graduate programs, and award professional degrees to some 3,000 students annually. The National Council of Architectural Registration Boards is the federation of state registration boards that administers the professional examination sequence and currently recognizes approximately 65,000 registered architects. Nearly 10,000 prospective architects sit for the council's 4-day, 9-division annual architect's examination each year; the number who pass depends on the individual states. The American Institute of Architects represents the profession and boasts roughly 40,000 members. Of these, 34,000 are regular members and 6,000 are associate members—those who are waiting to become registered.

An architecture degree or registration does not necessitate a career as an architect, and what it means to be an architect seems to be undergoing fundamental changes. It has been claimed that close to 50 percent of architecture students end up in other fields. And while this figure is disputed, the decreasing role of the architect would suggest that it will be harder and harder for architecture graduates to find work until their numbers start decreasing as well.

To this day, architecture tends to remain locally based. Even in an age of increasing national and global business, most architecture firms are small (some 80 percent employ 10 or fewer and over 60 percent have only one architect on staff) and closely linked to their local economies and contacts within their communities. In the 1980s, this meant that as different regions of the country offered the opportunity to work, architects could relocate to follow the economy: from Texas to New England, from New England to California. But in a declining economy in which work is scarce everywhere, the advice to architects, especially established architects, is to stay put.

The salaries outlined below are meant to reflect the broad salary structure of those employed in architecture or architecture/engineering firms. Salaries will vary for those in allied design professions or other alternate careers. For example, in government service, architects are hired at federal, state, and local levels. In the federal government, architects are generally GS-11, 12, or 13 levels, where average salaries range from $40,000 to $60,000. Regional differences in salary become marked at state and local levels.

As a caveat, the following figures represent general salary ranges across a spectrum of firms. There can be no pretense that these figures are comprehensive. The variables within the industry (firms range from less than five employees to over one hundred) are too great to be summarized. Aside from variations in size of firms, in location, and in business cycles, there are fundamental differences in how the cost of an architect's services to a client can be determined. The American Institute of Architects recognizes several, including lump sum, direct cost plus compensation for overhead and profit, percentage of construction cost (varying with size and complexity of the particular job), cost plus fixed fees, and per diem rates.

Undoubtedly there are those earning less than the figures indicate, and it is generally acknowledged in the profession, as in other professions, that the top people—principals, partners, and owners—at the top firms are better compensated than might be suggested by these figures.

BASE SALARIES OF ARCHITECTS

Title	Average Salary	First Quartile	Third Quartile
Managing Partner/Principal	$74,691	$58,240	$85,000
Partner/Principal	77,759	60,000	85,000
Chief Architect/Dir. of Operations	66,013	48,000	75,600
Dir. Contract Admin.	55,972	56,000	70,500
Project Manager	51,185	45,000	57,401
Architect Level I	21,979	19,000	25,000
Architect Level II	26,846	24,000	28,600
Architect Level III	31,253	27,530	35,000
Architect Level IV	37,151	32,000	40,860
Architect Level V	41,892	36,200	47,320
Architect Level VI	48,632	41,750	55,016
Architect Level VII	53,023	44,000	58,483
Architect Level VIII	60,774	48,670	70,886
Architect, Dept. Head	68,260	57,000	77,418

SOURCE: D. Dietrich Associates, Phoenixville, PA. Copyright © 1994. Reprinted by permission.

Job Descriptions for Architects and Draftsmen

Architect I—The entry level of professional work, requiring a bachelor's degree in architecture and no experience, or the equivalent (to a degree) in architecture and no experience.

Architect II—At this continuing developmental level, performs routine architectural assignments under direct supervision. Works from designs of others, compiles data, performs design computations, makes quantity takeoffs and prepares estimates, prepares architectural plans and renaderings, consults manufacturers, evaluates materials, writes architectural specifications, and inspects architectural features of structures in the field. Limited exercise of judgment is required on details of work in making preliminary selections and adaptations of alternatives.

Architect III—Independently evaluates, selects, and applies standard architectural techniques, procedures, and criteria, using judgment in making minor adaptations and modifications. Assignments have clear and specified objectives and require the investigation of a limited number of variables. Performance at this level generally requires a minimum of one year architect II or related work experience.

Architect IV—A fully competent architect in all conventional aspects of the subject matter in the functional areas of the assignments: plans and conducts work requiring judgment in the independent evaluation, selection, and substantial adaptation and modification of standard techniques, procedures, and criteria; devises new approaches to problems encountered. Generally requires a minimum of two years' architect III or related experience. Registration as a licensed architect may be a requirement for certain positions.

Architect V—Applies sound and diversified knowledge of architectural principles and practices in broad areas of assignments and related fields. Makes decisions independently on architectural problems and methods. Requires the use of advanced techniques, and the modification and extension of theories, precepts, and practices of his field. Registration as a licensed architect is a requirement for most positions.

Architect VI—Has full responsibility for interpreting, organizing, executing, and coordinating assignments. Plans and develops architectural projects concerned with unique or controversial problems that have an important effect on major company programs. This involves exploration of subject area; definition of scope; selection of problems for investigation, and development of novel concepts and approaches. Maintains liaison with individuals and units within or outside organization, with responsibility for acting independently on technical matters pertaining to his field. Registration as a licensed architect is a requirement.

Architect VII—Makes decisions and recommendations that are recognized as authoritative and have an important impact on extensive architectural activities. Initiates and maintains extensive contacts with key architects and officials of other organizations and companies, requiring skill in persuasion and negotiation of critical issues. At this level, must exercise individual judgment in anticipating and solving unprecedented architectural problems, determining program objectives and requirements, organizing programs and projects, and developing standards and guides for diverse architectural activities. Registration as a licensed architect is a requirement.

Architect VIII—Makes decisions and recommendations that are recognized as authoritative and that have a far-reaching impact on extensive architectural and related activities of the company. Negotiates critical and controversial issues with top-level architects, engineers, and officers of other organizations and companies. Individuals at this level demonstrate a high degree of creativity, foresight, and mature judgment in planning, organizing, and guiding extensive architectural programs and activities of outstanding novelty and/or importance.

Architect Department Head (Nonpartner/Principal)—Provides technical and administrative supervision to the department to assure that the technical administrative, man-hour, and schedule targets of the department are met within the framework of established corporate policy and in accordance with applicable professional standards, design control procedures, corporate and division procedures, and design guides.

Junior Draftsman (Draftsman, Junior Technician, Professional Trainee)—A beginner requiring continuous close supervision, whose work is reviewed carefully upon completion for conformity to office standards. Normally a high school graduate with some drafting training but less than two years of experience.

SALARIES OF ARCHITECTURAL DRAFTERS AND DESIGNERS

Title	Average Salary	First Quartile	Third Quartile
Drafter Apprentice	$14,458	NA	NA
Drafter Level I	16,535	$15,600	$17,680
Drafter Level II	24,088	20,700	25,000
Drafter Level III	28,935	24,300	30,000
Senior Drafter	32,965	28,470	35,000
Job Captain	34,421	29,397	37,000
Junior Designer A	29,141	21,600	29,070
Junior Designer B	35,918	30,000	38,595
Designer	41,123	32,760	43,800
Project Designer	50,919	40,800	59,220

SOURCE: D. Dietrich Associates, Phoenixville, PA. Copyright © 1994. Reprinted by permission.

Junior Designer (Architectural Designer, Designer/Draftsman)—A design-sensitive draftsman handling design and/or drafting assignments on segments of a project under the direction and review of a more experienced designer. A recent graduate with limited (two to five years) training or experience.

Draftsman (Intermediate Draftsman, Architectural Draftsman)—A draftsman with sufficient work experience and/or technical training to work without supervision. The normal entry-level position for an inexperienced architectural graduate.

Designer (Architectural Designer, Design Development, Intermediate Designer, Project Designer)—Involved with segments of larger projects or smaller, less complex jobs, and with minimal supervisory responsibilities. Generally two to six years' experience with sufficient training and ability.

Senior Draftsman (Senior Architectural Draftsman, Assistant Job Captain)—Able to handle assignments of greater scope and complexity with minimum supervision. Several years (six or more) of progressively responsible experience.

Senior Designer (Design Job Captain, Project Designer)—Directs other designers on a project and consults regularly with the project manager, the officer or partner in charge of the project, and the client on matters concerning design. May fill a dual project-manager role on some projects of limited scope and complexity. Normally six or more years' experience.

Job Captain (Project Captain)—Responsible for producing the working drawings on projects and exercising independent professional judgment, but job teams assigned to his projects are small. Assists project manager and may also act as a senior draftsman on some projects.

Senior Job Captain (Deputy Project Manager, Project Manager)—Requires the exercise of independent professional judgment in coordinating the production of construction documents. Supervises a job team of consultants, draftsmen, and specification writers assigned to assist on a project. Normally possesses an architecture degree and may be registered.

Project Manager (Associate, Project Director, Project Architect)—Coordinates the efforts of technical and professional employees and manages the administrative and budget requirements of a job. Ten or more years of diversified experience in the field of architecture and typically an architecture degree and professional registration (although neither is absolutely essential).

Senior Project Manager (Senior Project Architect, Project Administrator)—Like a project manager, coordinates programming, design, production, and construction phases of a project but does so on a larger scale and for substantially greater compensation.

Principal Designer (Associate, Director of Design, Senior Project Designer, Director of Design Development)—One of a limited number of top-level, nonprincipal, design-oriented professional personnel in an office. May act as project manager or as overall project designer on the largest jobs, and participate in departmental staffing, in training and evaluation of design personnel, and in establishing design quality standards within the office. Generally has a degree and registration.

Increasingly Management-Oriented Titles

Program Coordinator—Develops functional and architectural programs for projects as required.

Chief of Design—Coordinates development of project from initial schematic stage through design development stages.

Executive Architect—Concerned with coordination and administration of all technical aspects of a project, client contact, and generation of new projects.

Related or Associated Job Titles

Specification Writer—Responsible for writing complete specifications and associated contract documents on a project. Collaborates with the job captain and project designer in establishing the content and format of the specifications and consults with the project team during the construction phase to ensure the proper execution of the work.

Field Superintendent (Field Representative, Construction Administrator)—Represents the architect and client on a job site to ensure construction meets the intent of the contract documents, generally in consultation with the job captain, project designer, and project manager.

Clerk of the Works (Field Superintendent)—Similar to the field superintendent in terms of experience and responsibilities but allegiance is to the owner/client and his compensation is controlled by the client.

Project Administrator—In charge of coordination and administration of all nontechnical aspects of a project, including contracts, fee schedules, selection of consultants, etc.

DENTISTS

Among the five professions, only dentists seem to have an inferiority complex. And not without reason. For most adult Americans, a visit to the dentist is associated either with middle-aged decay or with the remembrance of childhood terrors. Despite that we know how important their work is, how vital to good health, dentists are rarely afforded the same respect as doctors or even lawyers. To some people, dentists are simply failed medical students involved in boring work. No wonder all polls say the status of dentists is not very high.

One thing that does remain high for America's 183,000 professionally active dentists is the size of their incomes. The median net income of dentists in general practice was just under $120,000, according to a 1994 survey by *Dental Economics.* This is before-tax income and represents about 40 percent of the total money brought into the dentist's office (meaning that 60 percent of a dentist's gross income goes toward overhead). Incomes for dentists have increased by about 7 percent each year since 1991, or close to triple the rate of inflation over the same period. The survey also found that the median solo practitioner (representing more than three-quarters of all dentists) is 44 years old, practices 35 hours per week, has been in practice 17 years, and sees 50 patients per week. The median group practitioner is somewhat older (51), works about the same number of hours (36), sees about the same number of patients per week (53), but has been in business much longer (27 years) and earns correspondingly more ($180,000 for the group practitioner compared to $117,000 for the solo dentist).

The advantages of incorporation are as clear to dentists as they are to doctors: incorporated dentists averaged $138,231, while unincorporated dentists averaged only $89,639, according to a separate survey conducted by *Dental Management* magazine. Nevertheless, only about one third of all dentists are incorporated. It also pays to specialize. Although the majority of dentists (91 percent) are generalists, those who specialize in areas like oral surgery, orthodonture, and endodonture make about 50 percent more than dentists in general practice. And periodontists, who treat gums and the bones that support teeth, earn twice the average salary. But even general practice dentists earn extremely good money relative to other professions, higher even than the average lawyer's income (though salaries at the very top of the law profession can be much higher than the earnings of the best paid dentists). Considering that dental training lasts only four years, with one or two more for a specialty, dentists' incomes compare very favorably to that of many doctors. And patients rarely call in the middle of the night or complain about house calls.

The number of dentists increased appreciably in the 1970s after the federal government made a commitment to expanding the nation's dental schools. But starting in 1979, keen competition for jobs has led to a continuing decline of dental school enrollments, meaning that jobs (and more importantly, patients) should be somewhat easier to come by in the 1990s. Dentistry remains a man's world—only 8 percent of dentists are women, according to the American Dental Association—but the number of women is increasing at a rapid pace. Women dentist's incomes are also growing rapidly—about twice as fast as for men—but they still lag far behind their male counterparts'. According to the *Dental Economics* survey, women netted $82,300, compared with $119,997 for men. Of course, the median number of years in practice was only 10 years for women, compared to 17 years for men.

DISTRIBUTION OF DENTISTS

Category	Percent of All Dentists	Category	Percent of all Dentists
Age		***Years in Practice***	
Under 30	1.7	1 year or less	0.5
30–34	10.1	2–4 years	4.8
35–39	19.0	5–9 years	13.6
40–44	19.6	10–14 years	20.8
45–49	17.2	15–19 years	18.9
50–54	12.4	20–24 years	15.5
55–59	9.0	25–29 years	8.4
60–64	6.4	30–34 years	9.5
65 or over	4.6	35 years or more	8.0
Specialty		***Hours Practiced Weekly***	
General Dentists	91.4	25 hours or less	6.2
Orthodontists	2.2	26–30 hours	14.2
Pediatric Dentists	1.9	31–35 hours	40.1
Oral Surgeons	1.8	36–40 hours	32.1
Endodontists	1.1	41–45 hours	4.6
Periodontists	0.9	46–50 hours	2.4
Prosthodontists	0.7	51 hours or more	0.5

DISTRIBUTION OF DENTISTS

Category	Percent of All Dentists	Category	Percent of all Dentists
Annual Net Income		***Region***	
$ 50,000 or less	10.4	New England (CT, MA, ME, NH, RI, VT)	5.8
50,001–75,000	13.4	Middle Atlantic (NY, NJ, PA)	17.8
75,001–100,000	16.1	South Atlantic (DE, FL, GA, MD, NC, SC, WV)	15.6
100,001–125,000	16.0	East North Central (IL, IN, MI, OH, WI)	17.2
125,001–150,000	13.4	East South Central (AL, KY, MS, TN)	5.2
150,001–175,000	8.1	West North Central (IA, KS, MN, MO, NE, ND, SD)	7.2
175,001–200,000	7.0	West South Central (AR, LA, OK, TX)	8.6
200,001–250,000	8.1	Mountain (AZ, CO, ID, MT, NV, NM, UT, WY)	5.4
250,001–300,000	3.0	Pacific (AK, CA, HI, OR, WA)	16.3
300,001–350,000	2.0		
350,001–400,000	0.8	***Locale of Practice***	
400,001–450,000	0.8	Urban	25.3
450,001–500,000	0.2	Suburban	49.7
500,001 or more	0.6	Rural	25.0

SOURCE: *Dental Economics,* 1994 practice survey, October 1994.

It may seem that dentists are constantly trying to put themselves out of business by encouraging their patients to brush, floss, and gargle regularly, thus decreasing their need for dental care. But these efforts are more than offset by the growth of an elderly population that is more likely to retain its teeth than its predecessors. These older patients are much more likely to need maintenance on complicated dental work like bridges and implants. Dentists' prospects are also likely to be improved by the increasing number of people with dental insurance (up 300 percent since 1975!). And since half the population still fails to visit a dentist on a regular basis, the market for dental services is virtually endless.

DOCTORS

In a stark reflection of the current turmoil that has gripped the health care industry in the past few years, doctor's earnings dropped in 1993 for the first time in five decades. Average net income for physicians, which had reached its highest levels ever the year before, fell 8.3 percent to $140,840, according to a survey of more than 6,500 doctors by the journal *Medical Economics.* The reason for the drop in take-home pay was not revenues, which actually increased 2.4 percent, but a huge jump in practice expenses like payroll, office space, and malpractice insurance (which has more than tripled in price since 1982). The primary exception to this trend was the family practitioner, whose net income increased an average of 6.3 percent, and whose gross revenues jumped a whopping 14.8 percent over 1992. Nevertheless, more doctors are making less than $100,000, and fewer are making more than $250,000.

Many experts blame the explosion in managed care and health-maintenance organizations (HMOs) for doctors' declining incomes. As employers demand lower insurance premiums, the insurers refuse to pay doctors as much for their services. Of course, the insurance companies simply claim they are trying to deter the doctors from ordering unnecessary and costly tests and procedures.

Surgeons earn about 50 percent more than nonsurgeons. Among the surgeons, the best paid are orthopedic surgeons, who number 19,000 according to the American Medical Association, and whose average annual salary was $243,530 in 1993, according to *Medical Economics.* Radiologists, numbering 8,500, averaged $217,130. These doctors "read" X-rays, diagnosing patients' conditions. Radiologists have relatively low overhead and insurance premiums, so expenses do not take a big chunk of their income. The 34,000 specialists in obstetrics and gynecology placed next on the list, with an average salary of $198,000, followed by gastroenterologists ($193,060) and cardiologists ($192,800).

Most people are surprised to learn that the nation's 26,000 anesthesiologists rank very high in the income hierarchy, with an annual average salary of $191,450. The anesthesiologist's tasks are much more complicated than the layman thinks, and other doctors claim that it is tension-filled work, which in times of emergency can be the key to whether a patient survives an operation. Still, the figure seems very high and is perhaps best explained by the anesthesiologist's proximity to the surgeon.

With all the current talk about controlling the costs of health care, it's not surprising that some people are convinced that there are too many doctors in the United States. In fact, predictions of a doctor glut date back to the mid-1960s, when there were fewer than 300,000 practicing physicians, or one doctor for every 625 people. By 1992, the number of doctors had more than doubled to 653,062, according to the American Medical Association, or one doctor for every 394 people. In fact, some medical experts blame the decline in doctors' incomes on an oversupply of physicians: too many doctors are competing for too few patient dollars. The Department of Labor predicts rapid growth in the number of doctors over the next 10 years, since the number of medical school applicants (45,000) and graduates (16,000) continue to set all-time highs each year. These figures have sparked renewed calls to limit the number of doctors. In November 1995, the Pew Health Professions Commission recommended that medical schools slash their classes by 20 to 25 percent over the next 10 years.

Attempts to limit the number of doctors will most likely exacerbate what is already an inequitable distribution of medical care. Massachusetts, for example, had 337 doctors per 100,000 residents in 1990 (a function of the many teaching hospitals in Boston), while Maryland, New York, Pennsylvania, and Connecticut all had over 300. By contrast, Idaho, South Dakota, and Wyoming all had fewer than half that many doctors for every 100,000 residents. The heavy concentration of doctors in large metropolitan areas insures that people in rural and poor areas have far fewer doctors per capita, and consequently receive inferior medical care. Salaries are also lower in rural areas than in urban and suburban areas, thus perpetuating this imbalance.

To some degree, the law of supply and demand will help to correct this inequity. Younger physicians are looking toward rapidly growing areas in the South and West, where the patient pool is sure to expand and where competition won't be as strong as in cities like New York or Chicago. The federal government has also intervened, setting up a National Health Service Corps to repay the medical school loans (up to $20,000 per year for four years) of any doctor willing to undertake primary care duties in rural areas known as Health Manpower Shortage Areas. Since most medical school students have $50,000 to $60,000 in loans, it's easy to understand the attraction.

Other less obvious considerations can affect where doctors settle. In Washington, D.C., for example, there are almost five times as many psychiatrists per capita as the national average. This is not a reflection on the sanity of our nation's leaders, but is the result of federal workers being reimbursed for psychiatric care by their medical insurance. So add to the rule of supply and demand the fact that doctors settle where they can be sure of payment.

The number of medical specialists is also likely to change in the near future, since the government has determined that it is specialization that drives up the costs of medicine. More and more new doctors are being steered into general practice to serve as "gatekeepers" and diagnosticians. By providing financial incentives in the form of debt forgiveness for doctors who opt for family and general practice, federal and state governments will continue to fuel this development. According to the Association of American Medical Colleges, the trend is already evident in medical schools, where the percentage of students expressing an interest in pursuing general medicine rather than specialties has doubled since 1992.

A doctor's own business decisions also have a significant impact on earnings. Most accountants recommend that doctors incorporate to save money. Currently, about half of all doctors have done so, according to *Medical Economics*. More are expected to do so, since the advantages are clear. The average net income for an incorporated M.D. in 1991 was over 38 percent more than for the unincorporated doctor. The trend toward group practice will also encourage incorporation. Doctors who participate in at least one health maintenance organization (HMO) or managed-care plan also had higher net incomes than those who didn't.

PHYSICIANS' AVERAGE NET INCOME AFTER EXPENSES BEFORE TAXES

Type of Physician	Average Income
All Surgeons	$187,460
Orthopedic Surgeons	243,530
Radiologists	217,130
Obstetric/Gynecological Specialists	198,000
Gastroenterologists	193,060
Cardiologists	192,800
Anesthesiologists	191,450
Ophthalmologists	158,820
General Surgeons	152,050
All Nonsurgeons	$123,810
Internists	118,570
Pediatricians	111,510
Psychiatrists	109,410
Family Practitioners	109,160
General Practitioners	87,550
All Doctors	$140,840

SOURCE: *Medical Economics*, September 12, 1994. Reprinted by permission.

Keep in mind that these are all average figures and that a good number of doctors still earn upward of $500,000 (especially well-known surgeons, anesthesiologists, and radiologists in large hospitals). Most doctors who work on hospital staffs earn salaries greater than $100,000 (directors and chiefs of services generally earn about 25 percent more), but most also have income from outside practices and for consultations.

DOCTORS' AVERAGE OFFICE VISIT FEES, 1993

Type of Doctor	Fees for Established Patients	Fees for New Patients
All Physicians	$52.80	$ 90.90
General/Family Practice	40.60	58.80
General Internal Medicine	57.00	108.10
General Surgery	49.50	78.90
Pediatrics	45.90	71.00
Obstetric/Gynecological Specialists	62.60	93.10

SOURCE: American Medical Association, *Professional Expenses and Incomes of Physicians, 1994.* Reprinted by permission.

SALARY RANGES OF PHYSICIANS AND DENTISTS IN THE VETERANS ADMINISTRATION

Grade	Starting Salary	Maximum Salary
Director Grade	$78,122	$97,020
Executive Grade	72,136	91,935
Chief Grade	66,609	86,589
Senior Grade	56,627	73,619
Intermediate Grade	47,920	62,293
Full Grade	40,298	52,385

SOURCE: *Pay Structure of the Federal Civil Service, 1994,* (1995).

But all such discussion of doctors' incomes can be very misleading. Just thumbing through this book will reveal that many people earn just as much or more for work that is less demanding and certainly less valuable. No, money has never been, and probably never will be, the sole reason for enduring the often brutal regimentation that begins in premedical training and lasts through internship and residency, during which new doctors earn $30,000 a year for working 12 to 18 hours a day. Even after they establish a solid practice (usually not until after the age of 30), doctors lead abnormally stressful lives. They often work twice as many hours as most people, are subjected to constant interruptions of their free time, and are always expected to win the battle against disease and death.

While greed surely afflicts some doctors, many more forsake for years or even decades the pleasures and privileges their high-income status could bring. The majority of doctors provide some kind of charity care, be it free or reduced-fee care to indigent patients. According to the AMA, nearly two thirds of all doctors—but surprisingly only about half of pediatricians—participate in some form of charity care. On average, they spend three hours a week providing free care and 3.6 hours a week providing care at reduced fees.

DOCTORS' EARNINGS, 1993

Category	Average Salary
Type of Practice	
Solo	$123,380
Expense-Sharing	156,460
Partnership and Groups of 2 Physicians	150,790
Partnership and Groups of 3 Physicians	156,280
Partnership and Groups of 4 Physicians	177,660
Partnership and Groups of 5–9 Physicians	180,830
Partnership and Groups of 10–24 Physicians	204,750
Partnership and Groups of 25–49 Physicians	169,010
Partnership and Groups of 50 or more Physicians	154,630
Single Specialty Groups	184,510
Multispecialty Groups	152,180
Years in Practice	
1–2	$ 93,500
3–5	133,270
6–10	157,620
11–20	165,020
21–30	139,780
Over 30	102,580
Age	
30–34	$121,680
35–49	133,010
40–44	161,440
45–49	163,110
50–54	162,990
55–59	144,630
60–64	117,560
65–69	107,930
70 or over	75,380
Managed-Care Participation	
Doctor Participates in at Least One HMO	$148,610
Doctor Does Not Participate in at Least One HMO	$124,970

SOURCE: *Medical Economics*, September 12, 1994. Reprinted by permission.

DOCTORS' EARNINGS BY AREA AND REGION

Category	Average Salary
Area	
Urban	$140,980
Suburban	145,500
Rural	129,200
Region	
New England (ME, NH, VT, RI, MA, CT)	$140,310
Middle Atlantic (NY, NJ, PA)	137,350
South Atlantic (DE, D.C., FL, GA, MD, NC, SC, VA, WV)	145,250
East South Central (AL, KT, MS, TN)	151,680
West South Central (AR, LA, OK, TX)	150,000
West North Central (IO, KS, MN, MO, NE, ND, SD)	138,050
East North Central (IL, IN, MI, OH, WI)	133,550
Rocky Mountain (AZ, CO, ID, MT, NV, NM, UT, WY)	143,130
Pacific (AL, CA, HI, OR, WA)	130,120

SOURCE: *Medical Economics,* September 12, 1994. Reprinted by permission.

MEDIAN EARNINGS OF DOCTORS

Net Earnings	Percent of Doctors Earning This Amount
$400,000 or more	4
300,000–399,999	4
250,000–299,999	9
200,000–249,999	11
150,000–199,999	17
125,000–149,999	13
100,000–124,999	15
90,000– 99,999	5
80,000– 89,999	5
70,000– 79,999	4
60,000– 69,999	4
Less than $60,000	9

SOURCE: *Medical Economics,* September 12, 1994. Reprinted by permission.

Physicians remain members of an occupational group that continues to be held in the highest esteem. Doctors almost always rank near the top in Gallup polls of the most respected professions (though pharmacists and clergymen usually rank higher). This fraternity also remains an overwhelmingly male enclave: over 80 percent of doctors are men. Women are making inroads, though: fully one third of medical school graduates since 1989 have been women, and 30 percent of doctors under the age of 35 are now women. They are making similar progress on the salary front, especially in surgery. Female surgeons net about 90 percent of what male surgeons net, according to *Medical Economics,* even though their gross earnings are only 79 percent of their male counterparts'. But in nonsurgical fields, where women are twice as numerous, their net earnings are only two thirds of what men take home. That's a lot closer to the national average for all jobs: 70 female cents for every male dollar in 1992, according to the U.S. Department of Labor.

About two out of three doctors are in private practice, while 20 percent work fulltime in hospitals as interns, residents, or hospital-based specialists, like anesthesiologists. The remainder are engaged in teaching and research, or they work for government agencies, including the Veterans Administration, the National Institutes of Health, and the armed forces.

LAWYERS

Toward the end of Shakespeare's *Henry VI, Part Two,* Dick the butcher, one of the rebels against the king, utters the secret wish of so many plain folk throughout Western history. When they get power, Dick says, "The first thing we do, let's kill all the lawyers." While many people in contemporary America may still share Dick's sentiments, the task grows more difficult every year as the number of lawyers continues increasing at a rate much faster than the general population.

In 1950, when America's population was about 150 million, about 200,000 people (98 percent of them men) practiced law here, or one lawyer for every 750 people. By 1970, the great population boom added 50 million more people to the total, only 80,000 of them lawyers. But between 1970 and 1980, when the population increased by another 20 million, the number of lawyers more than doubled: the entry of 400,000 people into the legal profession made one lawyer for every 323 people. In 1995, there were more than 866,000 lawyers in the United States, or one for every 300 of America's 260 million people. About 37,000 new lawyers join the profession each year.

The explosion in the number of lawyers is due in large part to the fact that this can be a very lucrative profession. Median compensation for lawyers nationwide is $58,032, more than double that of most other occupations. Lawyers' incomes are 12 percent higher even than doctors' salaries. The average 1993 law school graduate took home close to $48,000 in his or her first year on the job, according to the National Association for Law Placement, going a long way toward repaying law school loans.

Although the bleeding that led many firms to lay off huge numbers of lawyers during the 1991–92 recession appears to have been stanched, the effects have been felt down the line. The number of lawyers isn't yet decreasing, but the rate of increase is finally slowing. Applications to law schools dropped to 78,000 in 1995, down from 94,000 as recently in 1991. And six months after graduation, 15 percent of 1994 graduates were still unemployed, compared with 9 percent in 1990, according to the National Association for Law Placement. The recession also led many firms outside of New York to move away from lock-step pay structures, making pay scales and bonuses more dependent on productivity and performance rather than simply on the number of years a lawyer has been with the firm.

Most single practitioners and small law firms deal with everyday legal problems like wills and trusts, small real estate deals, divorce and child custody, criminal matters, and incorporations. As the amount of work and money involved grows, the lawyers become more specialized and more expensive. Depending on the competition for clients, a lawyer's skill and prestige, and the complexity of the case, fees can range from $25 to $750 an hour, and vary widely even for the same work. *American Lawyer* magazine surveyed nine law firms on how much they would charge to sue a jewelry store for losing a wedding ring. The estimated costs ranged from $45 to $2,122.

A Maryland survey of lawyers' incomes ranked specialties on the basis of income. The results generally hold true nationwide. The most lucrative legal specialties, in descending order, were: labor law, insurance law, taxation, negligence-defendant, real property, corporate and business, administrative agencies, commercial bankruptcy, negligence-plaintiff, banking, savings and loans, wills, estates and probate, domestic relations, municipal government, and criminal law. In recent years, the field of environmental litigation has proven increasingly profitable; not to lawyers who defend America's natural resources, but rather to lawyers who find ways of preventing polluters from having to pay to clean up their environmental waste.

For all the high-priced lawyers, there are still thousands trying to get along in small private practices, making an average of $25,000 or less. Even in the growing field of legal clinics, lawyers are not well paid. Jacoby and Meyers, one of the largest such clinics, employs about 300 lawyers in 120 offices in six states: Arizona, California, Connecticut, New Jersey, New York, and Pennsylvania. Initial consultation fees at legal clinics range from about $25 to $35; the simplest legal procedures, like a personal bankruptcy or an uncontested divorce, costs about $1,000.

Women and the Law

Despite significant inroads by women, the legal profession remains very much a man's world. Women made up 23 percent of all lawyers in 1995, up significantly from the 3 percent they constituted in 1971. But a Price Waterhouse survey demonstrated that female lawyers earned less than their male counterparts at every level, despite comparable years of experience, billing hours, and practice settings. And although women constitute more than 40 percent of the people entering the profession, fewer than one in five new partners is female. This may be blamed in part on choices made by women, but according to a report by the American Bar Association, plain old gender discrimination remains as well: Lawyers of both sexes told the ABA's Commission on Women in the Profession that women lawyers were viewed as "insufficiently aggressive, uncomfortably forthright, [and] too emotional." Perhaps the most telling statistic is that 70 percent of male ABA members, but only 40 percent of female members, believe women have equal opportunities in the profession.

Lawyers' Earnings and Their Experience Level

The 1993 U.S. Bureau of Labor Statistics survey of lawyers' average weekly earnings in the private sector looked at six different levels of experience. The first level was for a lawyer in the first year of private practice; the last level was for a lawyer with extensive responsibilities. For purposes of comparison, we have approximated annual salaries by multiplying the average weekly salary by 52.

Experience Level	Average Weekly Salary, 1993	Average Annual Salary, 1993	Average Annual Salary, 1991
Level I	$ 807	$ 41,964	$ 40,302
Level II	1,007	52,364	48,113
Level III	1,319	68,588	61,568
Level IV	1,684	87,568	81,949
Level V	2,084	108,368	100,219
Level VI	2,602	135,304	125,855

Lawyers with Corporations

Over the past decade, spurred by complex litigation, high outside legal fees, and new government regulations, corporate law departments have grown by leaps and bounds. Corporate lawyers often specialize within their companies in energy, antitrust, or environmental law, as well as employment discrimination, product liability, toxic waste disposal, and pension funds. Pay at these corporations varies greatly with the kind of legal work performed and the nature of the company. For example, Philippe P. Dauman, the general counsel for Viacom, earned more than $2.2 million in 1994, while John Demos, Super Food Services Inc.'s general counsel, took home only $205,000, or slightly more than a seventh-year associate at a New York firm. Mr. Demos's earnings were much more typical for corporate lawyers; they earned a median income of $222,000 in 1994, exactly double the 1982 amount. Of course, in an area of the law that was once thought to be strictly the domain of those who failed to make partner at a major firm, none of these people can be said to be poor. The median salary for all nonsupervisory in-house attorneys was $85,500 in 1994, or double what it was in 1981.

Lawyers with Law Firms

The highest salaries for freshly minted lawyers are traditionally paid by large law firms in the major cities: Boston, New York, Washington, D.C., Chicago, Atlanta, Houston, and Los Angeles. The large firms entice prospective associates with salaries that range as high as $87,000 at New York's Wall Street firms. But to win such an offer, a lawyer must be in the top 10 percent of her class at one of the nation's elite law schools.

After signing on, associates usually work on a specialy like tax, labor, corporation, securities, real estate, entertainment, antitrust, estate, banking, or commercial law. After about eight years, the associates are told whether or not they have made partner. At this juncture, their salaries (which have on average nearly doubled since their first year) may jump dramatically into the high six-figure range, accompanied by better benefits and lots of prestige. As the accompanying table demonstrates, profits per partner at every law firm in the *National Law Journal*'s 1995 salary survey topped $212,000. And that survey didn't even include some of the most profitable New York firms, where profits per partner routinely top $1 million per year. Those who don't make partner sometimes stay on with the firm as associates, join a corporate law staff or government agency, or move to another firm.

PARTNER INCOME AT 32 LARGE LAW FIRMS, 1994

Firm Name and Principal Location	Number of Lawyers/ Partners	Gross Revenues	Profits per Partner
Anderson Kill Olick & Oshinsky (New York)	215/86	$ 84,327,000	$261,921
Baker & McKenzie (Chicago)	1642/500	544,000,000	389,000
Best, Best & Krieger (Riverside, CA)	112/52	28,770,500	206,700
Choate, Hall & Stewart (Boston)	167/71	63,263,000	300,000
Cooley Godward Castro Huddleson & Tatum (San Francisco)	174/64	64,900,000	330,000
Dorsey & Whitney (Minneapolis)	355/181	106,433,000	259,000
Dow, Lohnes & Albertson (Washington, D.C.)	125/55	51,700,000	420,000
Dykema Gossett (Detroit)	223/119	69,000,000	212,000
Gardere & Wynne (Dallas)	200/73	62,000,000	350,000
Gibson, Dunn & Crutcher (Los Angeles)	550/212	278,000,000	520,000
Graham & James (San Francisco)	272/127	97,000,000	266,000
Greenberg, Traurig (Miami)	222/98	80,400,000	360,000
Hale & Dorr (Boston)	256/113	109,500,000	405,000
Heller, Ehrman, White & McAuliffe (San Francisco)	319/152	120,000,000	273,000

Hughes Hubbard & Reed (New York)	240/80	78,000,000	325,000
Luce, Forward, Hamilton & Scripps (San Diego)	135/58	43,708,699	317,434
Manatt, Phelps, Phillips & Kantor (Los Angeles)	158/51	51,209,108	604,134
McDermott, Will & Emery (Chicago)	501/171	207,150,000	508,397
O'Melveny & Myers (Los Angeles)	538/184	256,897,000	605,000
Orrick, Herrington & Sutcliffe (San Francisco)	300/127	115,800,000	410,000
Patton Boggs (Washington, D.C.)	204/62	66,485,423	410,082
Paul, Hastings, Janofsky & Walker (Los Angeles)	378/134	15,650,000	420,000
Perkins Coie (Seattle)	322/133	10,386,700	265,000
Piper & Marbury (Baltimore)	279/107	85,738,000	255,000
Proskauer Rose Goetz & Mendelsohn (New York)	423/121	169,200,000	420,000
Shaw, Pittman, Potts & Trowbridge (Washington, D.C.)	269/110	85,000,000	315,000
Sheppard, Mullin, Richter & Hampton (Los Angeles)	222/100	81,600,000	303,000
Sonnenschein Nath & Rosenthal (Chicago)	377/130	118,000,000	340,000
Thompson & Knight (Dallas)	198/75	62,283,194	278,465
Winston & Strawn (Chicago)	430/85	146,000,000	451,000

SOURCE: *National Law Journal*. Reprinted by permission.

ASSOCIATES' SALARIES AT 30 SELECTED LAW FIRMS, 1993[1]

Firm Name and Principal Location	First Year	Fourth Year	Seventh Year
Arnold & Porter (Washington, D.C.)	$79,000	$86,000	$100,000
Baker & McKenzie (Chicago)	78,000	84,000–87,000	110,000–112,000
Brobeck, Phleger & Harrison (San Francisco)	73,500	76,500–87,000	100,000–117,000
Cahill Gordon & Reindel (New York)	85,000	133,000	174,000
Choate, Hall & Stewart (Boston)	68,000	79,000–91,500	96,000–118,000
Covington & Burling (Washington, D.C.)	72,000	90,000	108,000
Cravath, Swaine & Moore (New York)	83,000	130,000	180,000
Davis Polk & Wardwell (New York)	87,000	130,000	180,000
Dorsey & Whitney (Minneapolis)	58,000	74,000	87,500
Foley & Lardner (Milwaukee)	70,000	73,000–82,000	85,000– 95,000
Fulbright & Jaworski (Houston)	62,000	82,000	123,500
Hale & Dorr (Boston)	66,000	90,000	[2]
Holland & Hart (Denver)	56,500	57,000–63,000	69,000– 70,000
Holland & Knight (Miami)	57,000	69,000–74,000	93,500–109,000

Hunton & Williams (Richmond, VA)	65,500	76,000–82,500	90,500– 98,500
Johnson & Gibbs (Dallas)	61,000	73,000–77,000	93,500–103,000
Jones, Day, Reavis, & Pogue (Cleveland)	74,000	75,000	105,000
King & Spalding (Atlanta)	60,000	68,000–72,000	78,000– 93,000
Mayer, Brown & Platt (Chicago)	79,500	85,000–88,000	105,000–115,000
Morrison & Foerster (San Francisco)	74,000	83,000	102,000
Orrick, Herrington & Sutcliffe (San Francisco)	75,500	83,000	104,500
Paul Weiss Rifkind, Wharton & Garrison (New York)	85,000	129,000	172,000
Paul, Hastings, Janofsky, & Walker (Los Angeles)	75,000	84,000–94,000	111,000–149,000
Perkins Coie (Seattle)	56,500	61,000–80,500	71,000–103,000
Pillsbury Madison & Sutro (San Francisco)	74,000	80,000–97,500	98,000–113,000
Reed Smith Shaw & McClay (Pittsburgh)	70,500	70,500–73,500	81,000– 86,500
Sidley & Austin (Chicago)	81,000	87,000–90,500	105,000–125,000
Skadden, Arps, Slate, Meagher & Flom (New York)	85,000	130,000	178,000
Sonnenschein Nath & Rosenthal (Chicago)	75,500	82,500–91,000	99,500–111,000
Steptoe & Johnson (Washington, D.C.)	76,500	89,000–93,000	104,000–108,000

[1]Salaries include bonuses where applicable.
[2]Seventh-year associates are nonequity partners.
SOURCE: *The American Lawyer, AmLaw 100,* July/August 1994.

THE BIGGEST LAW FIRMS BY GROSS REVENUE, 1994

Rank/Firm	Number of Lawyers	Gross Revenue
1. Baker & McKenzie	1,667	$512,000,000
2. Skadden, Arps, Slate, Meagher & Flom	948	478,000,000
3. Jones, Day, Reavis & Pogue	1,034	346,000,000
4. Weil, Gotshal & Manges	635	318,000,000
5. Sullivan & Cromwell	374	299,000,000
6. Gibson, Dunn & Crutcher	580	283,000,000
7. Davis, Polk & Wardwell	404	270,000,000
8. Cleary, Gottlieb, Steen & Hamilton	464	263,000,000
9. Shearman & Sterling	512	256,000,000
10. Mayer, Brown & Platt	563	253,000,000

SOURCE: *The American Lawyer, AmLaw 100,* July/August 1994.

THE BIGGEST LAW FIRMS BY PROFITS PER PARTNER, 1994

Rank/Firm	Number of Partners	Profits per Partner
1. Cravath, Swaine & Moore	73	$1,410,000
2. Wachtell, Lipton, Rosen & Katz	54	1,350,000
3. Sullivan & Cromwell	101	1,275,000
4. Cahill, Gordon & Reindel	54	1,210,000
5. Davis, Polk & Wardwell	97	1,020,000
6. Simpson, Thacher & Bartlett	98	925,000
7. Cleary, Gottlieb, Steen & Hamilton	119	890,000
8. Weil, Gotshal & Manges	150	745,000
9. Wilkie Garr & Gallagher	106	720,000
10. Kirkland & Ellis	95	700,000

SOURCE: *The American Lawyer, AmLaw 100,* July/August 1994.

SALARIES OF PROFESSORS AT SELECTED LAW SCHOOLS

Law School	Assistant Professor	Associate Professor	Full Professor
American University, Washington College of Law	NA	$77,075	$102,050
Boston College Law School	$76,500	95,000	108,500
Brooklyn Law School	82,200	85,200	113,500
Univ. of California, Hastings College of Law	65,625	74,025	101,970
Creighton University School of Law	48,000	67,410	85,342
DePaul University College of Law	67,125	72,895	98,855
Howard University School of Law	NA	81,000	98,553
Indiana University School of Law (Indianapolis)	59,202	69,345	89,993
Loyola University School of Law (New Orleans)	60,180	66,780	78,750
McGeorge School of Law, Univ. of the Pacific	67,490	75,633	95,385
University of Miami School of Law	NA	81,761	110,560
University of Michigan Law School	78,500	NA	130,750
University of Mississippi School of Law	51,000	61,400	78,136
Univ. of Missouri-Kansas City School of Law	57,659	67,669	83,854
University of New Mexico School of Law	64,100	58,000	76,256
Northeastern University School of Law	75,875	82,975	107,550
Rutgers School of Law (Camden, NJ)	74,887	86,345	108,237
University of South Dakota School of Law	42,287	50,922	63,990
Vermont Law School	60,709	71,873	78,447
University of Washington School of Law	56,997	NA	86,886
West Virginia University College of Law	NA	62,466	77,410
Median Salary	$62,600	$72,000	$ 91,600

SOURCE: American Association of University Professors, *Annual Report 1994–1995.* Reprinted by permission.

SALARIES OF ATTORNEYS GENERAL IN SELECTED STATES, 1995

State	Entry-Level Position	Attorney General
California	$38,400	$102,000
Georgia	35,880	90,000
Illinois	27,048	93,333
Massachusetts	25,000	80,000
Michigan	35,182	111,200
New York	33,922	110,000
Pennsylvania	33,819	84,000
Vermont	26,520	61,025
Washington	30,000	92,000
Wyoming	31,500	75,000

SOURCE: *The Book of States 1994–95.*

SALARIES OF PUBLIC DEFENDERS IN SELECTED CITIES, 1995

City	Salary Range
Albuquerque, NM	$28,000– 58,400
Atlanta	37,841– 76,904
Billings, MT	27,771– 52,370
Charleston, WV	30,000– 59,500
Cheyenne, WY	26,736– 75,852
Chicago	32,772–105,000
Dallas	45,000–100,000
Detroit	35,997– 63,746
Fresno, CA	30,966– 93,000
Indianapolis	28,000– 65,000
Kansas City, MO	28,356– 73,008
Los Angeles	42,461–135,000
Miami	32,500–100,000
Milwaukee	36,187– 90,836
Nashville	29,462–109,915
New York	32,290– 64,795
Phoenix	35,700– 95,000
Provo, UT	35,000– 70,000
Seattle (King Co.)	35,300– 54,000
Spokane WA	26,700– 58,400
Topeka, KS	30,204– 61,020
Washington, D.C.	34,663– 84,885
Wilmington, DE	31,500– 73,700

SOURCE: *National Law Journal,* July 10, 1995. Reprinted by permission.

SALARIES OF PROSECUTORS IN SELECTED COUNTIES, 1995

County (Major City), and State	Salary Range
Baltimore County, MD	$33,108–108,180
Broward County (Fort Lauderdale), FL	23,000–100,212
Harris County (Houston) TX	35,472–104,440
Jackson County, MS	27,300– 73,000
Los Angeles County, CA	42,461– 96,829
Montgomery County, AL	33,882– 77,300
Multnomah County, (Portland), OR	32,573– 84,760
New York County (Manhattan), NY	32,000–115,000
St. Louis County, MO	30,833– 79,500
Suffolk County (Boston), MA	25,000– 72,500
Wayne County (Detroit), MI	34,885–101,710
U.S. Attorneys	$115,700
Assistant U.S. Attorneys	$28,400–107,300

SOURCE: *National Law Journal,* July 10, 1995. Reprinted by permission.

SALARIES OF CITY ATTORNEYS IN SELECTED CITIES

City	City Attorney	Assistant City Attorney
Albuquerque, NM	$ 67,000	$ 37,336
Alexandria, VA	107,500	39,112–57,782
Charlotte, NC	97,447	52,983
Chicago	108,420	35,975–80,532
Flint, MI	69,515	30,000–44,239
Harrisburg, PA	41,619–66,832	28,965–45,157
Lincoln, NE	48,100–92,600	26,300–41,500
Los Angeles	117,684	41,530–55,478
New York	110,000	38,760–65,545
Portland, OR	86,500	37,336–47,674

SOURCE: *National Law Journal,* July 10, 1995. Reprinted by permission

SALARIES OF LEGAL SERVICES LAWYERS, 1995

Service and Location	Staff Attorney	Executive Director
Idaho Legal Aid Services (Boise)	$22,000	$29,200–44,000+
Vermont Legal Aid (Burlington)	22,800–46,500	48,000
Ohio State Legal Services (Columbus)	26,900–45,300	80,000
New Hampshire Legal Assistance (Concord)	23,000–48,000	61,000
Gulf Coast Legal Foundation (Houston)	30,904–61,500	90,000+
Legal Aid of Western Missouri (Kansas City)	23,000	68,000–74,000
Florida Rural Legal Services (Lakeland)	28,000–53,000	NA
Nevada Legal Services (Las Vegas)	30,672–45,720	55,000–75,000
Dakota Plains Legal Services (Mission, SD)	23,500–36,500	47,817
Legal Services Corp. of Alabama, Inc. (Montgomery)	22,000–37,000	NA
Legal Aid Society of Middle Tennessee (Nashville)	25,500–59,500	64,500
Legal Services for New York City	30,900–59,750	72,000–99,000
Western Kentucky Legal Services	24,200–43,200	43,500
Community Legal Services (Philadelphia)	30,000–62,500	55,700–70,000
Pueblo County Legal Services (Colorado)	21,685–25,350	40,000
Central Virginia Legal Aid Society (Richmond)	25,500–54,000	66,000–69,000
Prairie State Legal Services (Rockford, IL)	23,000–39,000	50,000–75,000
California Rural Legal Assistance, Inc. (San Francisco)	26,000–48,500	79,000
Legal Services of Eastern Oklahoma (Tulsa)	25,500–47,871	60,000

SOURCE: *National Law Journal,* July 10, 1995. Reprinted by permission.

SALARIES OF PUBLIC INTEREST LAWYERS

Organization and Location	Starting Salary	Top Salary
American Alliance for Rights and Responsibilities (Washington, D.C.)	$60,000	$ 90,000
American Civil Liberties Union (New York)	28,750	75,000
Americans United for Life Legal Defense Fund (Chicago)	28,000	NA
Center for Individual Rights (Washington, D.C.)	$25,500–65,000	83,000
Chicago Lawyers Committee for Civil Rights Under Law	35,000	NA
Disability Rights Education Defense Fund (San Francisco)	30,000	50,000
Environmental Law Institute (Washington, D.C.)	30,000	150,000
Lambda Legal Defense and Education Fund (New York)	40,000+	60,000
Lawyers Committee for Civil Rights (Washington, D.C.)	31,000	NA
NAACP Legal Defense and Educational Fund (New York)	35,000	91,000
National Wildlife Federation (Washington, D.C.)	43,000	133,000

SALARIES OF PUBLIC INTEREST LAWYERS

Organization and Location	Starting Salary	Top Salary
National Women's Law Center (Washington, D.C.)	$37,000	$ 95,500
National Abortion and Reproductive Rights Action League (Washington, D.C.)	40,000	75,000
New England Legal Foundation (Boston)	25,000	95,000
Pacific Legal Foundation (Sacramento)	35,000	125,000+
People for the American Way (Washington, D.C.)	25,000	80,000
Public Citizen Litigation Group (Washington, D.C.)	25,000	70,000
Southeastern Legal Foundation (Atlanta)	35,000	70,000
Support Network for Battered Women (Mountain View, CA)	30,000	31,000
Trial Lawyers for Public Justice (Washington, D.C.)	30,000	100,000

SOURCE: *National Law Journal,* July 10, 1995. Reprinted by permission.

LEGAL ASSISTANTS (PARALEGALS)

Whatever kind of legal document you need—will, contract, separation agreement—chances are that if you go to a law firm for the service, the legal work will be done not by a lawyer but by a legal assistant. Legal assistants, also known as paralegals, perform all the same duties as lawyers except setting fees, giving advice, signing up new clients, or trying a case in court.

About 95,000 people are currently employed as legal assistants, and thanks to the mushrooming demand for legal services, the field is growing rapidly. The Bureau of Labor Statistics ranks it as one of the fastest growing professional occupations in America. By the year 2005, the number of legal assistants is expected to nearly double, a growth rate of about 5,000 jobs per year. The supply of paralegals has finally caught up with the intense demand for their services. So while the number of openings for legal assistants will continue to increase rapidly, competition for the jobs will be keen over the next decade. Whereas a significant number of currently employed legal assistants have only an associate's degree, there seems to be a trend toward more educational background as competition for these jobs grows.

According to the National Association of Legal Assistants, most job opportunities will be in major cities where the largest private law firms are centered. There will also be a great demand for paralegals in the federal government, especially in the Departments of Justice, Treasury, Interior, Health and Human Services, and in the General Services Administration.

The chief reason for the popularity of paralegals in both the public and private sectors is economic: paralegals can do most of the same work as lawyers but for a lot less money. Even the most inexperienced first-year associate earns more than double what a paralegal earns in an hour. The more work performed by paralegals, the greater the savings a firm can pass on to its clients.

Specifically, paralegals help draft legal documents like wills, mortgages, divorce papers, and trusts. They perform legal research; organize, index, and summarize documents and files; prepare different types of tax forms; draft organizational documents for corporations; and assist in all aspects of pretrial work for criminal and civil cases. Some paralegals are generalists, working on a civil case disposition one day and writing a brief for a felony trial the next. At large law firms, paralegals tend to specialize (as do lawyers) in one area, like real estate, labor law, litigation, corporate law, estates, or trusts. So prevalent is the use of paralegals that 25 states now have guidelines delineating the types of work they may and may not perform.

More and more people who work as paralegals are going through some kind of postgraduate training program, which can last anywhere from a few months to four years. The number of these programs is growing as fast as the profession—from about 300 just under two years ago to more than 600 today. The American Bar Association has approved 177 of these programs; graduates of such certified programs clearly have an advantage when it comes to finding jobs. In addition, the National Association of Legal Assistants offers a certification program culminating in a two-day exam. Salaries of paralegals certified by this test are about $2,000 higher on average than other legal assistants.

While paralegals don't earn wages comparable to lawyers, they can eventually make a good living. According to the Labor Department, salaries nationwide averaged over $28,300 a year. Starting salaries averaged $23,400, while paralegals with six to ten years' experience averaged $28,200 per year. A few senior paralegals, who manage entire departments in a big corporate firm earn upward of $50,000. The federal government paid new paralegals $18,000 to $23,000 in 1993; it paid highly experienced paralegals $37,600. Paralegals also received an average bonus of $1,700 per year, in addition to life and health insurance benefits. Employers of most paralegals also contribute to retirement or pension plans on their behalf.

Many large corporations have set up a paralegal services function within their law departments. According to the Administrative Management Society, the person in charge of that area is known as *legal assistant services manager,* and he or she is usually in charge of planning and coordinating the use of the paralegals, training new employees, and motivating and evaluating the entire staff.

IV

Science and Technology

Over the past forty years the American economy has created hundreds of thousands of jobs for scientists, engineers, and computer experts. Virtually everyone who entered these fields after securing a college degree found a good job and began a rewarding career. In the early 1990s, however, cutbacks in federal funding for scientific research reduced employment opportunities slightly, especially for those with doctorates who wished to leave affiliated-with-university research projects. Engineers, too, experienced some difficulty in the job market for the first time, but this does not yet appear to be more than a temporary problem. Despite many reports in the media describing the difficulties scientists and engineers are experiencing we think it important to emphasize that unemployment rates are still less than 2 percent in most parts of the country.

Most of the occupations in this section are concerned with the practical, that is to say business, applications of mathematical and scientific laws and theories. Whether these laws are applied in an established and venerable field such as civil engineering or in new fields like environmental or nuclear engineering, the one common denominator of all those in these fields is a high level of intelligence and intellectual curiosity. The salary levels for jobs in science and technology do not seem to give recognition to this requirement for higher than average brainpower, however; rather, salaries seem to move strictly by the laws of supply and demand. In the past, for instance, a drop in the price of oil to under $20 a barrel has had the predictable effect of putting many petroleum engineers out of work. Yet as the world continues to exhaust the supply of fossil fuels, rising oil prices may once again fuel a booming demand for those expert in extracting every last drop of oil from the earth. Likewise, events have cooled the demand for nuclear fuel and with it the prospects for nuclear engineers; but by the turn of the century, no one would be surprised if nuclear power generation were to make a comeback. In the meantime, environmental science and technology promises to be the fastest growing area of opportunity in the 1990s.

The moral of the story is that aspiring engineers and scientists with high earnings expectations should pick their fields with a view toward ones that are likely to grow because a degree in science or engineering is not necessarily a ticket to a lifetime of high earnings. In fact, while engineers and scientists tend to receive higher starting salaries than other college graduates, they do not, on average, earn more throughout their careers. Many reach a moderate earnings plateau relatively early in their working lives. This may be partly due to the fact that many in the field are project oriented and do not relish the supervisory and managerial roles that come with higher pay. It may also be that the caricature of the absentminded scientist is at least partially true—many very good scientists are not very good at the practical requirements of running a business. In this day of high technology, those who are good may end up running great ventures; however, whatever the case may be, the first priority of scientists and engineers is their science and their work, which they usually do well and without due recognition. For instance, the accomplishments of *Explorer* II in beaming back pictures of Neptune twelve years after launch are viewed rather matter-of-factly by most. But the spacecraft traveled billions of miles and arrived only 20 miles off its pinpoint target and was 20 minutes early. And it worked when it got there! This is certainly an accomplishment that deserves more recognition than it has gotten, and the subdued recognition that it did get illustrates that our society takes its scientific community largely for granted.

THE DISCIPLINES OF SCIENCE

The popular view of the American scientist is based on well-known caricatures. In the movies, or on television, scientists are usually depicted as absentminded or evil-minded, muddleheaded or pigheaded. If they are Americans, they are portrayed as easygoing but brilliant; Germans, humorless but brilliant; Russians, devious but brilliant. Whether their motives are humane or sinister, scientists are always shown to be in awe of their subject and of their own extraordinary powers. Skillful writers can blend all of these elements to reflect the ambivalent feelings most Americans have toward scientists.

On the one hand, our respect for scientific work borders on reverence, an attitude fostered by our early leadership in atomic and nuclear weaponry. But this reverence is tempered by our fear that scientists may have unlocked powers which could lead to our own destruction. Add to such fundamental misgivings a strong dose of ignorance concerning scientific methods and aims, and our ambiguous position becomes more understandable. How these factors might affect the relatively low compensation rates for scientists seems never to have been explored.

Only some 500,000 people in America are professionally engaged in nonmedical scientific activities. Many of these are in universities where they teach or do research and are paid under their school's established salary scale. Even at the best schools this means less than $100,000 a year for full professors. (See the section "University and College Professors" in Part I.) Some top-level researchers at prestigious institutions such as MIT and Cal Tech may control millions of dollars in federal research funds, but their personal compensation remains, at least according to the public record, based on their university salaries.

In the following pages will be found salary figures for scientists in private industry and public utilities, as well as state and federal governments. Although scientists are paid well at every level, their salaries should be compared to those in other occupations that require the same amount of educational experience (lawyers, accountants, engineers, for example). This may lead some readers to raise questions about the way work is rewarded in America: Why, for example, do top-level chemists and physicists make less than junior partners in large accounting firms? Should the work of the lawyer be better rewarded than that of the scientist?

It is certainly not within the province of this book to offer answers or to make recommendations regarding such questions. But it is necessary to point out what, in our opinion, are clearcut inequalities in pay structures. Salaries of scientists are sure to increase over the next decade, but whether they will reach the same levels as some jobs requiring less training and education remains to be seen.

Scientists' Salaries: An Overview

The range of salaries associated with a specific level—say, the entry rate for a scientist with a bachelor's degree—is somewhat narrow; the choice of scientific discipline, however, should not be dependent on anticipated earnings as much as personal desire. This narrow range of salaries exists especially in the early years of a career. Later, the differences become almost entirely a function of personal professional worth and employer need.

With this in mind, an excellent summary is available in the form of an annual publication prepared by D. Dietrich Associates, Inc., of Phoenixville, Pennsylvania, entitled *Survey of Scientific Salaries.* They have surveyed almost 10,000 scientists in both private industry and the federal government in virtually every part of the country. The table below summarizes some of their findings. They categorize scientists into eight levels—from the new college graduate to the department head.

A Scientist I is one with a bachelor's degree and no experience. Scientist II includes those with one year as a Scientist I or no experience and a master's degree. A Scientist III is a Scientist II after about one year or a Ph.D. with no experience. A Scientist IV is one who has been the equivalent of Scientist III for a year or two and has begun to prove himself capable of independent efforts with little to no day-to-day technical supervision. A Scientist V is recognized as an expert in his field—he usually supervises a small group of lower-level professionals and is contributory to higher-level decisions. A Scientist VI supervises Scientists I through V and has considerable responsibility for directing complex tasks. A Scientist VII makes decisions and recommendations on an authoritative level and is a leader and authority in his company. The Department Head provides overall supervision with regard to the technical, administrative, and scheduling aspects of the major programs in the company.

AVERAGE ANNUAL SALARIES OF SCIENTISTS BY LEVEL OF RESPONSIBILITY

Title	Average Salary	First Quartile	Third Quartile
Scientist I	$26,689	$24,250	$30,000
Scientist II	32,250	29,433	35,556
Scientist III	39,527	35,360	40,419
Scientist IV	47,875	41,080	50,000
Scientist V	59,123	48,568	62,103
Scientist VI	73,156	56,000	72,000
Scientist VII	80,511	63,040	84,500
Department Head	83,877	65,000	91,400

SOURCE: D. Dietrich Associates, Inc. *Survey of Scientific Salaries,* 1994. Reprinted by permission.

Chemists

Most chemists hold jobs in teaching, research, sales/marketing, and production/inspection. A bachelor's degree is sufficient to begin or continue in one's career, but an advanced degree is needed for most positions in teaching or research. Over the next decade, the job outlook for chemists is especially good in fields related to energy, pollution control, and health care.

There are four main fields of specialization: *analytical chemists* determine the structure, composition, and nature of substances and develop new techniques; *organic chemists* study the structure of all carbon compounds;

inorganic chemists study compounds other than carbon; *physical chemists* study energy transformations to find new and better energy sources.

At this time, there are about 92,000 chemists in the United States. Approximately 20,000 of them are in teaching. The rest work for manufacturing firms, state and local governments as well as the federal government (especially the Departments of Defense, Health and Human Services, and Agriculture).

With no experience, a chemist with a bachelor's degree can expect to start in the federal government at between $16,000 and $21,000, depending on academic record; with a master's degree, at about $25,000; and with a Ph.D., at about $35,000. The annual average salary in the federal government for experienced chemists is $52,000. The average starting salary in the private sector is $31,000 with a bachelor's; with experience a bachelor's degree brings about $39,000; a master's $42,000, and $53,000 for a Ph.D.

ANNUAL SALARIES OF CHEMISTS IN PRIVATE INDUSTRY, 1992

Level	Number of Chemists	First Quartile	Median	Third Quartile
I	4,414	$22,316	$27,092	$30,609
II	9,812	29,496	33,203	36,695
III	10,133	37,858	41,607	45,818
IV	8,810	46,399	50,427	55,529
V	6,824	57,422	61,377	65,990
VI	2,708	69,627	75,359	80,653
VII	691	81,642	87,815	94,167
Total	43,392			

SOURCE: Bureau of Labor Statistics.

Salaries of chemists in private industry are always included in an annual survey of pay conducted by the Bureau of Labor Statistics. Above are figures based on the salaries of over 40,000 chemists classified according to job levels as defined by the BLS. Generally speaking, these levels are based on experience, complexity of tasks, and supervisory responsibilities. Levels I and II, for example, are beginning positions in which chemists do routine testing and, although they may have the help of technicians, do not directly supervise anyone's work. Chemists at Levels III and IV, by far the largest number in the survey, are experienced employees who have specialized knowledge and who are expected to show "ingenuity" in evaluating unexpected problems. Chemists V and VI are the beginning of the supervisory chain of command where problem-solving and "originality" are the key elements of the job; these people frequently head small teams of researchers. At Level VII are chemists who in large companies supervise an entire segment of research and in smaller ones the entire program; others at this level are recognized as outstanding "creative" researchers who select problems and then supervise their analysis and solution. Level VIII chemists are usually top supervisory people, probably part of the upper echelon of management; not surprisingly, the government could not obtain sufficient salary data for this level.

Geologists

Geology is the study of the structure, composition, and history of the earth's crust. Most geologists' work centers on judging the suitability of construction sites and locating oil and other minerals and, to a lesser degree, predicting the possibility of earthquakes and their probable magnitudes. There are about 49,000 geologists in the United States today. Approximately 33,000 work in private industry and 6,400 in the federal government, and 10,000 teach in colleges and universities. The outlook is good, since new energy sources must be found and waste disposal sites and methods must be realized; but job growth will be about average for all occupations.

The main branches of geology are earth materials, earth processes, earth history, and what can be called new fields. There are several subdivisions of each: *Economic geologists,* for example, locate various minerals and solid fuels; *petroleum geologists* attempt to find oil and natural gas; *mineralogists* analyze and classify minerals and gems by composition and structure; *geochemists* study the chemical composition and changes in minerals and rocks; *palynologists* locate oil deposits by studying tiny organic fossils.

Geologists concerned with earth processes study the varied forces in the earth. *Volcanologists* study active and inactive volcanoes; *geomorphologists* study such forces as erosion and glaciation.

Among the earth historians, *paleontologists* study plant and animal fossils found in geological formations; *geochronologists* determine the age of geological formations by the radioactive decay of their elements; *stratigraphers* study the distribution and arrangement of sedimentary rock layers.

New fields in geology include the *astrogeologist,* who studies the geological conditions on other planets, and the *geological oceanographer,* who studies the sedimentary and other rock on the ocean floor and continental shelf.

In private industry (i.e., oil companies, mining companies, construction firms), starting salaries average about $28,000 per year with a bachelor's degree and $36,000 with a master's. The federal government (e.g., the Department of the Interior and the Bureau of Mines) start those with bachelor's degrees at about $25,000 per year, those with master's at about $28,000 and those with Ph.D.s at about $33,000. The average salary for geologists in the federal government is $50,000.

Life Scientists

Life scientists are so called because they study all aspects of living organisms. Most life scientists have jobs in zoos or botanical gardens, or are involved in medical research and food and drug testing. A bachelor's degree is at best an introduction to the field; a master's is the minimum requirement for most positions, and a doctorate is a necessity for advanced work.

The main branches of life science are the agricultural, the biological, and the medical. In most cases, however, life scientists take their job titles from the type of organism they study and by the activity they perform. Here are some examples:

The *botanist* deals primarily with plants and their environment; the *agronomist* is concerned with the mass development of plants by deriving new growth methods or by controlling diseases, pests, and weeds; the *horticulturist* works with orchard and garden plants.

Zoologists study the various aspects of animal life—its origin, behavior, and life processes. *Animal scientists* do research on the breeding, feeding, and diseases of domestic farm animals. *Anatomists* study the structure of organisms, from cell structure to the formation of tissues and organs. *Ecologists* explore the relationship between organisms and their environments. *Embryologists* study the development of an animal from a fertilized egg through the eventual birth. *Microbiologists* study microscopic organisms such as bacteria, viruses, and molds. *Physiologists* examine the various life functions of plants and animals under normal and abnormal conditions. *Toxicologists* and *pharmacologists* study the effects of drugs, gases, poisons, and other substances on the functioning of tissues and organs. *Pathologists* study the effects of diseases, parasites, and insects on human cells, tissues, and organs. *Health physicists* study the effects of toxic substances and nuclear radiation on humans and other animals and direct employers in the proper safeguards in the use of both.

There are about 150,000 life scientists in the country today. The agricultural sciences employ about 28,000, the biological sciences about 61,000; forestry and conservation sciences about 24,000; and the medical sciences about 27,000. About 25,000 are employed in teaching, while 52,000 work in government, especially in the Department of Agriculture. The remainder are employed in private industry, mostly in pharmaceutical, chemical, and food-processing firms.

Starting salaries in the federal government are about $18,000 to

$20,000, and $32,000 with a bachelor's, master's, and doctorate, respectively. Private industry pays less than 10 percent higher for life scientists; there is a slight salary bias toward the biological over the agricultural sciences. The outlook is good for those with advanced degrees, especially in environmental fields, but quite poor for those with only a bachelor's degree.

Physicists

Physics is the study of the mathematical nature and structure of the universe and the interaction of matter and energy in it. Most people in the field do some form of research. An advanced degree is virtually a necessity; those with only a bachelor's usually go into a related field such as engineering. All nonteaching physicists specialize in one or more specific branches. Some concentrate on the basic forces and particles in nature. These are the nuclear physicists, the atomic physicists, the elementary particle physicists, the molecular physicists, the plasma physicists. Some deal with a bigger picture. These specialize in optics, acoustics, fluids, electricity, magnetism, or thermodynamics.

There are about 22,000 physicists in the United States today, about 14,000 of whom teach and about 4,000 of whom are in private industry (manufacturers of chemicals, electrical equipment, aircraft, and missiles) and a few, less than 4,000, with the Department of Defense. The outlook is somewhat favorable for advanced-degree physicists in research and development. It should improve in the 1990s as many physicists retire.

In private industry, a physicist with a master's degree and no experience will start with about $34,000 per year; a Ph.D. will start at about $47,000. In the federal government, starting salaries are about $27,000, $30,000, and $40,000 per year for physicists with bachelor's, master's, and doctoral degrees, respectively; the average salary for an experienced physicist in the federal government is $63,000. In private industry the average is about $71,000.

INTERDISCIPLINARY SCIENCES

Just as there are many subdivisions of each category, so there are many overlappings. Paradoxically, as specialization has become the way of the world in science, that community has become more and more aware of the interactions among all scientific disciplines.

Biological Scientists

Biological scientists study living organisms and the relationship of animals and plants to their environment. Most of the 62,000 people in this occupation specialize in some area such as ornithology (the study of birds) or microbiology (the study of microscopic organisms). About half of all biological scientists work in research and development.

According to the College Placement Council, beginning salary offers in private industry to bachelor's degree recipients in biological science averaged about $25,000 a year in 1995. Biological scientists in the federal government averaged $47,000 a year in 1995. Only 10 percent of biological scientists earned over $62,000 in 1995.

Geophysicists

Geophysicists study the composition and physical aspects of the earth and its electric, magnetic, and gravitational fields. A bachelor's degree is usually sufficient to embark on a career in some branch of geophysics. The main branches of the field are the specialties of those who devote themselves to the solid earth, the fluid earth, the upper atmosphere, and other planets. *Exploration geophysicists* use seismic prospecting techniques to locate oil and other minerals; *seismologists* study the earth's interior and vibrations caused by man-made explosions; *geodesists* explore the size, shape, and gravitational field of the earth and other planets. *Hydrologists* study the distribution, circulation, and physical properties of underground and surface waters. *Geomagneticians* study the earth's magnetic field; *paleomagneticians* study the past magnetic fields from rocks or lava flows. *Planetologists* study the composition and atmosphere of the moon, planets, and other bodies in the solar system.

Increasingly, all these occupations are becoming known under the umbrella term *geoscientists,* which more accurately describes these scientists' roles in studying all aspects of the earth.

There are about 48,000 geophysicists or geoscientists in the United States today. About 20,000 of them are in private industry, especially in the petroleum and natural gas fields, and some are in mining or in private consulting. The rest are with the federal government as part of the U.S. Geological Survey, the National Oceanic and Atmospheric Administration (NOAA), or the Department of Defense. Starting salaries in private industries are $26,000 per year with a bachelor's degree, $29,000 with a master's degree, and $37,000 with a Ph.D. In the federal government, starting annual salaries for all geologists in managerial, supervisory, and nonsupervisory positions was $50,000; for all geophysicists it was $55,000; for all hydrologists it was $47,000; and for oceanographers at NOAA it was $55,000.

Meteorologists

Meteorology is the study of the atmosphere, its physical characteristics, motions, and processes, and the ways it affects the rest of the physical environment. Meteorologists usually work at jobs related to weather forecasting, air-pollution control, and prediction of climatic trends. Meteorologists who are devoted to the weather are called *synoptic meteorologists,* those devoted to research are *physical meteorologists,* and *climatologists* study the general trends of climate.

There are about 6,100 meteorologists in the United States today. Approximately 1,000 of them work in colleges and universities; private industry (e.g., airlines, weather consulting firms, meteorological instrumentation companies) employs about 3,000. The rest are employed in the federal government, mainly by NOAA.

In the federal government, an inexperienced meteorologist with a bachelor's degree can expect to start at $19,000 to $21,000 per year; with a master's degree, $26,000, and with a Ph.D., $38,000. An experienced meteorologist with the federal government will earn about $50,000 per year. Private industry starts meteorologists about 20 percent higher for each degree, and the annual salary range for experienced meteorologists is $50,000 to $60,000 per year. The outlook for meteorologists with advanced degrees is good, with jobs at the National Weather Service and in private industry expected to grow. The outlook for those with less than advanced degrees is poor.

Oceanographers

Oceanography is the study of the movements, physical properties, and plant and animal life of the oceans. Oceanographers usually hold jobs in fisheries development, mining and ocean resources, and weather forecasting. The minimum degree employable is a bachelor's, a master's is preferable, and a Ph.D. is often required for high level jobs.

There are two main branches of oceanography—biological and physical. *Marine biologists* study plant and animal life in the ocean; *limnologists* study freshwater aquatic life. *Physical oceanographers* study the physical properties of the ocean, such as waves, tides, and currents; *geological oceanographers* study the ocean's underwater mountain ranges, rocks, and sediments; *chemical oceanographers* study the chemical composition of ocean water and sediments, as well as chemical reactions in the sea.

There are only about 3,600 oceanographers in the country today, more than half of whom teach in colleges and universities. About 700 are employed by the federal government (Navy and NOAA); the rest are in private industry and state and local fisheries. The annual average salary of an oceanographer in the federal government was about $55,000 in 1995. The immediate outlook for employment in oceanography is not very good, with most openings being limited to replacement of the retiring.

Agricultural Scientists

Agricultural scientists study farm crops and animals and develop ways of improving their quantity and quality. They have played a vital part in the country's ever-rising agricultural productivity. Agricultural scientists normally practice in one of the following specialties: agronomy or the study of how crops grow; animal science or the study of livestock and poultry; food technology or the study of the chemical, physical, and biological nature of food; horticulture—the study of fruits, vegetables, and plants; soil science—the study of the characteristics of the soil; and entomology—the study of insects and their relation to plant and animal life.

There are over 25,000 agricultural scientists in the United States today. According to the College Placement Council, beginning salaries for graduates with a bachelor's degree averaged $24,000 to $27,000 in 1995. The average agricultural scientist employed by the federal government earned $54,000 in 1995.

JOB OPPORTUNITIES FOR SCIENTISTS

The job outlook for scientists will depend partly on two powerful and contradictory trends. On the one hand, the United States remains a highly technological culture dependent in many ways on its scientists' expertise; on the other hand, U.S. investment in research and development has begun to decline for the first time since the 1970s. This decline coincides with substantial increases by other countries, most notably Japan. Whether international competition in R&D will hasten American industrial decline or prompt a renewed effort to excel remains to be seen.

Predictably, certain specific fields will be affected more than others. According to Betty Vetter, executive director of the Commission of Professionals in Science and Technology, the most promising fields are electronics, lasers, and biotechnology. "There's particularly intense excitement in the biological sciences, especially with the new work in genetic engineering." In addition, she said that growing concerns about the natural environment will prompt scientific research and applications to solve problems of pollution and resource depletion.

Chemists—Job opportunities should be strong for the field overall for these reasons:

- The number of degrees granted in chemistry will not meet future demand
- Research and development will continually expand
- Demands for environmental protection will require increased attention from industry
- The chemical industry is much healthier than in the early 1980s
- Demand for innovative pharmaceuticals, biotechnology, and other technological breakthroughs will increase.

Through the year 2005 the Bureau of Labor Statistics estimates *new* annual job creation for chemists at about 1,000 a year at best.

Geologists and Geophysicists—In the past, most of this country's geologists have generally worked for the petroleum industry. Low oil and gas prices during the past decade have consequently suppressed need for scientists in this field. The U.S. Bureau of Labor Statistics anticipates that employment for geologists will grow only as fast as the average for all occupations through the year 2000. However, any substantial increase in oil and gas prices will create strong incentives for petroleum corporations to hire scientists once again. In addition, other job opportunities may occur in areas of groundwater monitoring, toxic waste management and cleanup, and geophysical research into other environmental issues.

Physicists and Astronomers—Slightly fewer than half of the nation's physicists are academic faculty members; the rest work for independent research and development laboratories, for the federal government, and for aerospace firms, electrical equipment manufacturers, engineering service firms, and the automobile industry. The job outlook for scientists in all these areas appears to be strong, although not consistently so. Many physicists—both academic and nonacademic—received their degrees during the 1960s and thus will approach retirement late in the present decade. On the other hand, the end of the Cold War and subsequent cuts in the U.S. defense budget will mean cutbacks in weapons-related R&D, with obvious implications for physicists in related fields.

Biological Scientists and Biotechnologists—Of the approximately 100,000 biological scientists in the United States at the previous decade's end, roughly one half held faculty positions in colleges and universities. Some 40 percent of the nonfaculty scientists work for federal, state, or local governments; most of the rest work for commercial or nonprofit research and development labs, hospitals, or the drug industry. For all these job categories, the job outlook is unusually bright. Biotechnology remains one of the most innovative fields anywhere in the sciences. Recombinant DNA and other techniques promise breakthroughs in agriculture, the pharmaceutical industry, medicine, and the environment. Most job growth will occur in the private sector.

Meteorologists—The overall outlook for scientists in this field is good for two main reasons. First, the National Weather Service, which employs most U.S. meteorologists, plans to increase its hiring over the next ten years. Second, the private sector will create many new jobs in response to needs for private weather forecasting services by farmers, commodity investors, transportation and construction firms, and radio and TV stations.

Agricultural Scientists—Over 40 percent of nonfaculty agricultural scientists work for federal, state, or local governments. Nonacademic agricultural scientists in the private sector generally work for commercial research and development laboratories, service companies, wholesale distributors, and seed or food products companies. The job outlook for agricultural scientists is good for several reasons: Enrollments in related curriculums have dropped considerably in recent years; a disproportionate number of current workers will be leaving the workforce; and advances in biotechnology will heighten the need for employees within the private sector.

ENGINEERING

by Robert L. Spring

Plato, in his *Theaetetus,* called a person with a hyperactive sense of wonder a potential philosopher. He never used the term "scientist." But a pure scientist is not so different from a philosopher. They both must have started with and retained that same inquisitive sense of wonder. While the philosopher is content to remain in the abstract, however, the scientist has an urge to scratch away at the concrete. The philosopher sticks with "roundness"; the scientist talks of spheres and elliptic hyperboloids.

The pure scientist gets closer to the world, but he still never quite talks about the one that we know. He's concerned with atoms and potential energy and entropy and relative time, and he is perfectly content to wallow there as long as he can prove his own theories and disprove everybody else's. A pure scientist has no more desire to build a bigger bridge or a smaller computer than the philosopher wants to quantify the electromagnetic forces binding the nucleus of the niobium atom. But they both wonder "why?"

While the philosopher and the pure scientist are questioning everything, a distant cousin is asking fewer questions and concentrating on answers. This person is known as the applied scientist. To the layman, applied science must sound redundant: What good is science if you cannot apply it? The applied scientist takes the world of the pure scientist and blends it with that of the layman. The applied scientist gave us television, stereo, and nuclear power; he quickened our travel, air-conditioned our homes, and put a man on the moon. An applied scientist is an engineer, the one who works to put it all together. He designs what the scientist says *can* work and the layman says *should* work.

In recent years, engineers have been regarded as saviors and killers, and everything in between, depending on where and when you went to school, who you voted for, and how much and which of the media you believe. During the 1960s, they were the golden boys who would help us catch up with the Russians; later they were the geniuses needed, as Tom Lehrer explained, to put "some clown on the moon." But during the Age of Aquarius people noticed that the air was becoming visible, and the water walkable. Anyone who smelled of "establishment"—and the engineer did—took the brunt of the blame. The 1970s then saw the advent of environmental engineering, especially as related to power engineering. The 1980s saw the power or energy production field as, in one way or the other, a major employer of engineers. It is certainly a rather large microcosm of the engineering world in general with respect to kinds of engineers employed and salaries paid. The 1990s seem to indicate a bleaker decade for a variety of engineers. None of the traditional fields are booming, and most are streamlining and concentrating on maintenance, good operations, and plant life extension. Environmental engineering is experiencing a major comeback and fire protection engineering has bloomed as a major new field.

But first, what is engineering? The *Encyclopedia Britannica* offers an excellent definition: Engineering is "the professional art of applying science to the optimum conversion of the resources of nature to benefit man." You may be surprised to see the word "art" in the brief, carefully worded definition, and most engineers would be too. Consider, however, a broader sense of "art" and "science." Science is an organized body of knowledge derived through observation of cause and effect; art, a systematic application of knowledge or skill in effecting a desired result. An engineer is as dependent on his judgment and imagination for solving problems as he is on his knowledge of physics, chemistry, mathematics, etc. The engineer must be both a scientist and an artist. He must possess the store of technical knowledge or science but he must also be imaginative enough to apply it to a particular problem as needed. And it must be done, as our definition above states, as an optimum application and benefit to man.

For example, automobiles would be fancier and cheaper if no safety factors were included; on the other hand they could be built with near-zero risk inherent in their use if an astronomical price tag could be placed on them. In the simplest of considerations, safety here is played against cost until a mixture is realized that is salable to the public and profitable to the seller. Social factors, economic factors, and health and safety factors must in all cases be interwoven with technical expertise to yield a final design. The engineer must weigh the importance of all these factors, plus a host of others (deadlines, regulations, resource availability, etc.) and play them against each other until the final product is the optimal blend.

So, essentially, the engineer exists to take the world of science, which is nature itself, and somehow apply it to accomplish a particular effect and to satisfy a particular need. The engineer does not generalize; he particularizes.

Let us hypothesize. In the suburbs of a very large American city, it has been forecast that, in ten years, more electrical power will be needed. Along with the lawyers, the politicians, the executives, and the other relevant people, the engineers are called in for expert advice and opinions. Society has a need and the engineers must come up with a solution. Build a power plant to supply, let's say, 1,000 more megawatts of electricity to the existing system serving Newburbia. The site must be found—an easy job if the plant is invisible and undetectable, in everyone else's backyard, and rates will not go up. What kind of fuel will be burned? Oil? Coal? Uranium? In the old days the engineers had a good deal of influence in this decision. Today, it's minimal, but they contribute technical support to the political, legal, environmental, and economic determination.

Now the Environmental Impact Statement must be written—and these have been known to fill small rooms. Plant design gets under way. Turbines, pumps, relays, boilers, thousands of feet of piping, tubing, wiring. The specifications are very complex: Is the equipment safety-related? Environmentally related? What special "extras" are needed? If it's a coal plant, design accessible storage space. If oil, ditto. If nuclear, make it capable of withstanding an earthquake, a tornado, a tsunami (seriously). There are still controls and instrumentation, redundant fail-safe components, inspections, quality assurance, fire protection, security, waste treatment, and, for coal or nuclear plants, waste packaging and shipment.

Now the structures must be built to house all this. What kind of floor do we put in to hold up a multiton turbine? The transmission lines must be designed to get the power where it's wanted. Don't forget the beautification plan and the permits and licenses and public-hearing testimony and checks and rechecks, and paper, paper, paper. The engineer survives and has, in turn, succeeded despite the "system."

Continuing within the framework of the example above, hundreds of engineers of various disciplines must be called on for their routine and not so routine problem-solving capabilities. Today's complex needs and desires demand a high degree of coordinated, specialized expertise. An individual can no longer stay abreast of rapid changes in a plethora of technological fields. He must concentrate on one aspect of engineering and stay more than superficially aware of what's going on in related fields; he can afford interest in unrelated fields little more than as a hobby. This was not always so.

In the distant past, in what not only Charlemagne but Caesar, Homer, and even King Tut would call the old days, there was civil engineering. The earliest engineer whose name has survived to our times was a civil engineer: He is Imhotep and he designed and supervised the construction of the step pyramid complex (a tomb plus associated temples and other buildings) for the third dynasty Egyptian pharaoh Djoser, also known as Horus Neterirykhet. That was 4,500 years ago; we still only theorize how it was all done. In later life Imhotep became a philosopher and was eventually deified.

Some Descriptions of Engineering Titles

Imhotep probably did all the conceptual work for Djoser's pyramid himself. He didn't consider himself a civil engineer—he was an engineer, a fulfiller of man's (albeit a man's) desire or, as the case may have been or appeared, need. He had a knowledge of physical science and the ability to apply that knowledge to a particular need. Granted, he needed only limited know-how; awareness of atomic structure would not have yielded a better pyramid, and, of course, it didn't have to fly or stay afloat. For thousands of years, civil engineers provided their citizenry, and, coincidentally, later generations, with the Sphinx in Egypt, the temples and "well-walled" cities of ancient Greece, the coliseum and aqueducts of Rome, the castles and cathedrals of medieval Europe, and more.

By the nineteenth century, the Industrial Revolution expanded the range of engineering to include mechanical engineering and, even later, chemical engineering and electrical engineering. Further hierarchies of specialization now include petroleum engineering, metallurgical and materials engineering, nuclear engineering, aerospace engineering, electronic engineering, industrial engineering, mining engineering. Each of these fields again splits up into more and more specialized branches of engineering.

To meet the needs of today, they all must work together, each on that aspect of the job for which he has been educated and trained but with knowledge of his own limitations and his fellow engineers' contributory efforts. Not only can no one branch of engineering expertise result in a finished product such as an automobile, a power plant, a spaceship, or even a fully functional modern office building, but the degree and complexity of the specialized knowledge needed for any of them is such that only a person skilled in a particular engineering discipline can, in truth, be beneficially utilized.

To get all of these highly trained experts to work together without getting in each other's way, without overemphasizing their own discipline and without ignoring important concerns outside their own area of expertise, is the job of *project engineer,* or *coordinating engineer.* He must have overall knowledge of what must be done, by whom, in what order, and on what detailed schedule. He could have been educated in any of the engineering fields of specialization; he should be experienced enough to have seen many projects come to fruition, successfully and unsuccessfully; he must possess at least superficial knowledge of the functions of all the disciplines that will be used. He must keep the mechanical and electrical engineers working on the same goal.

The *mechanical engineer* designs engines and motors and the turbine mentioned before. He sizes and lays out pipes that are needed to transport water, air, fine powders, or highly viscous liquid metals from one place to another for one reason or another. He considers the temperatures and pressures that he must deal with and finds or designs equipment with materials that are not only compatible but most efficient.

The *electrical engineer,* in as simple a statement as possible, is concerned with the most efficient way of getting electric power from one place to another. We've all seen transmission lines, electric circuits around the house, and maybe the insides of our televisions or stereos. They were all designed by the electrical engineer. He may not know what electricity is. He may not even care. But you can be sure he knows *how* it works. There's a lot of what he does we've only heard of, such as supplying power to the instruments on the likes of the Apollo project, recovering from a widespread urban blackout (what the utility business calls a "system disturbance"), and arriving at what we used to call an electronic brain.

The *civil* engineer, as mentioned above, gets things built. He takes on structures such as the Empire State Building, the Eiffel Tower, the Golden Gate Bridge, and the Statue of Liberty. Why don't they fall in a good wind, a small earthquake, a plane crash? Because of the civil engineer. Much of what he does we never see. The steel structure in a building of any size is designed by him. Such a problem varies in complexity: How do you do it on the San Andreas fault? Did you know the World Trade Center buildings sway? How must you build a wall or floor if it's half a mile under the Pentagon and it's supposed to withstand an all-out nuclear attack?

According to some people, much of this technology we've been talking about is polluting the earth. This is partially the realm of the *chemical engineer,* who takes the world of the chemist and utilizes his own artistic talents to apply it to the problems and needs of the everyday world around us. He knows that the water and the air can be made cleaner, and he knows how to do it. The chemical engineer does not concern himself solely with the cleanup but he applies his technology to satisfy our whims and needs in ways that do not pollute the environment.

The other branches of engineering are, for the most part, finer subsets of those we have been discussing. *Petroleum engineers* are specialized chemical engineers. *Environmental engineers* come from a variety of educational backgrounds, especially chemical and mechanical engineering. They devote their efforts to air and water quality as well as land use. *Metallurgical* and *material engineers* are mechanical engineers who study the internal structure of matter to be sure that materials are utilized to their fullest capabilities efficiently, and, more important, that they are not misused in design. *Aeronautical* and *astronautical engineers* do for planes and rockets and other space-travel components what *marine engineers* do for ships. Airplanes must be lighter than air; boats must be lighter than water; rockets must be able to counteract gravity for a sustained period of time. An important subdivision of mechanical engineering is *HVAC engineering.* The letters stand for Heating, Ventilation, and Air-Conditioning. If your office is like most and the AC works great in December and you've got a sauna in August, call up the HVAC engineer, who will explain how wonderfully it's designed and how poorly it's maintained. Not all temperature control is for the comfort of humans in office buildings. The HVAC engineer also works on computer rooms, museum displays, and spacecraft habitability.

Nuclear engineers, like environmental engineers, come from various engineering backgrounds. Many have been educated in physics or chemistry; more are mechanical, civil, or electrical engineers devoted to the design and/or operation of nuclear power plants. A combination of on-the-job training and further specialized education prepares them for the work. A fewer number are educated at the bachelor's level in nuclear engineering. The primary reason for the need of expanded training is that nuclear radiation, inherent in such a heat source, must be contained to the plant with no adverse health effects on the public or plant operating personnel. A nuclear engineer is, de facto, a nuclear *safety* engineer.

Fire protection engineers combine the talents of a variety of engineering disciplines. The fire protection engineer designs fire detection and suppression systems, is instrumental in providing fire prevention measures, and is often involved with the preparation of and compliance with relevant insurance and government codes and regulations. He/she evaluates the fire resistance of barriers such as walls and floors and will place limits on combustibles to be stored or used in specific sections of structures. Some of the tools of the fire protection engineer are mathematical modeling, computer simulation, and full-scale testing.

The list of engineering categories could go on forever—both legitimate categories and spurious ones. The trend is not to be a joiner of an existing engineering field but to invent a new one specifically devoted to your purposes. Some are abstractions like *process engineer, applications engineer,* or *systems engineer;* others pinpoint the function with titles like *traffic engineer, mining engineer,* and, believe it or not, *low-level nuclear rad waste engineer.* A purist may argue, but these are legitimate. Despite the fine-tuning of categorization, they are all engineers. They have been trained to be engineers by reason of their education and/or their job functions. Not so with many that are wrongly called engineers by employing euphemisms as the *sanitary engineer,* who is in fact a plumber, the *operating engineer,* who is a crane operator, and the *security engineer,* who is a night watchman or sells padlocks. Honorable professions all, but call them what they are and reserve the title "engineer" for those who do engineering.

An engineer has a college or university degree or the equivalent. These days, that pretty much means he *has* a college degree—a bachelor's, master's, or a Ph.D. The degree is usually called some kind of engineering as the fields discussed above, but not always. Physicists, chemists, and mathematicians have been known to "turn engineer," and at least a few major schools give a Bachelor of Applied Science degree for what most would call engineering. The significant thing is that the college-level training with certain basic coursework is there.

An engineer must be well trained in math. It is the language of science and engineering. Arithmetic and basic algebra are not sufficient; calculus is needed. The physical sciences are essential. General physics, electricity, magnetism, atomic structure, optics, statics and dynamics, thermodynamics, and general chemistry are basic. Elective courses provide the specialization necessary for the specific degree, such as electrical, civil, mechanical, etc.

Salaries of Engineers

Let's consider the engineer working as an engineer—no line supervisory responsibilities, no commissions, just the salaried engineer.

In 1995, he or she came out of college with a bachelor's degree and started at about $38,000 a year. The oil companies paid more; the poorer ones paid less. The span ran from about $30,000 to around $42,000. Theoretically, there was a small range in each company in which to take care of the top student, middle student, and the poorer student that no one admits to having a policy of hiring. Most come in at the high end of the range allowed by each company. In 1995 the entry rate at what we'll call the Sunshine Electric Utility, a large metropolitan supplier of electricity generated by nuclear and fossil fuels, was about 10 percent higher than it was three years before. This pretty much held true throughout the industry.

Engineers have done well over the years. Very few go on to extraordinarily high salaries. With the exception of the aftermath of the Apollo Project fiasco and the relatively gloomy situation today, engineers have rarely lacked for their choice of jobs at a living wage. The salaries are competitive, but at the imaginary utility, the quasi-socialist benefits add to the picture. Engineering salaries do and will continue to go up year after year. Today, new engineers just out of school do better against inflation in terms of yearly increases. Experienced engineers stay above water, but barely. Let's not lose perspective—they do better in absolute magnitude than many, probably most, occupations, but they are not by any stretch of the imagination living off the gravy. They work for the money they bring home; they're dedicated, so they often put in more hours than they are theoretically paid for; but, as said, they do make a living wage, and they will do better than many. In 1995, an engineer who has been at it for five years, probably at the same company, was earning anywhere from $45,000 to $60,000 a year.

A very significant point is that one can very easily become an engineer and advance little over the years in terms of salary. An engineer who does not do good engineering will not get good raises, and rightly so. On the other hand, a hotshot will do better. It's not a union job (yet); engineers are not paid for merely surviving. They must produce. They must use imagination. They should have good presentation skills. They must be able to tackle a job and come to a conclusion—not just a technically feasible one, but a safe, economical, and practical one. In every sense, the better an engineer is at this art, the better the financial reward. If more than good engineering talent is shown, he or she will go on to supervisory engineering work. As with other professions, this means seeing a bigger picture. Time spent behind the computer is minimized. Supervising means managing and handling people more than numbers. The well-roundedness of the engineer is called on to its fullest. A few more bucks are involved; on the average, say 30 to 40 percent more than the good, not best, engineer will see. In 1995 engineers with managerial responsibilities averaged about $100,000 per year.

A little summary: Engineering can be a rewarding profession. It will pay well. It can pay very well. It is not a millionaire-maker. It can, however, lay the groundwork for getting there. There's nothing or, at least, very little, that is automatic about it. A poorly planned education and/or a poor performance on the job will result in a lower but fair salary. Get that good education or make up for it later and apply common sense, sound engineering technology, imagination, good judgment and decision-making ability, reasonable presentation skills, and the rewards will be there—monetary rewards, the rewards of internal self-satisfaction, and a feeling of professionalism.

At this time the demand in many disciplines for newly graduated, inexperienced engineers is well below average. Employment in the engineering industry traditionally follows a "peaks and valleys" course. Recall that the engineer is called on to fulfill a need or desire of a segment of society at a particular time. Such needs and desires naturally fluctuate, so engineering opportunities and salaries, while not likely to see absolutely depressed conditions, will vary with economic circumstances.

Aerospace Engineers: Average starting salary $34,000

After five years, the average salary for aeronautical and astronautical engineers is about $44,000 and after ten years about $50,000. With a master's degree, salary does not tend to increase much, if at all, with five to ten years of experience; a Ph.D. will earn about 15 percent more than lesser degrees in this field. According to the Bureau of Labor Statistics, 73,000 aeronautical and astronautical engineers work in the United States today. A booming field 30 years ago, few young people are entering this field now, a situation that will make them a highly sought after commodity in the event of a surge in the U.S. aerospace program, which might be a while off due to reduced federal budgets.

Chemical Engineers: Average starting salary $43,000

After about five years working as a chemical engineer, one with a bachelor's degree earns about $50,000 yearly; after ten years a similarly educated chemical engineer with little to no supervisory responsibilities earns about $63,000. A master's degree does not appear to increase these figures significantly. One extra year of work brings a raise equivalent to the differential awarded the higher degrees. A Ph.D., however, can expect to earn 15 to 20 percent more than either. There are now about 50,000 chemical engineers in the United States. The chemical engineer will be assured of steady, interesting, and challenging work in the years ahead by reason of the large effort directed toward the minimization, cleanup, and eventual disposal—or, ultimately, recycling—of toxic wastes, and the development of synthetic fuels.

Civil Engineers: Average starting salary $34,000

A typical civil engineer without an advanced degree earns about $43,000 annually after five years in the field, after ten years, about $55,000. An advanced degree will mean a higher starting salary (usually 10 to 15 percent) at the beginning of a career, but after a few years it has little, if any, economic effect. There are about 199,000 civil engineers in various industries in the United States today. Until the day when all buildings are built and we need no more or better roads or bridges or subways, etc., the civil engineer will be as needed as ever. New materials, and the problems of constructing modern architecture in the future's high-population-density, limited-space-environment, will provide sufficient challenge to novices.

Electrical and Electronic Engineers: Average starting salary $39,000

After working for about five years as an electrical engineer with a bachelor's or master's degree, one earns about $45,000 per year. A Ph.D. in electrical engineering earns about $53,000 about five years after obtaining his degree. After ten years, these salaries increase to about $53,000 and $58,000, respectively, assuming no supervisory responsibilities. There are approximately 427,000 electrical/electronic engineers in the country today; this is by far the largest single engineering field in the United States—over 25 percent of all the engineers working in this country today are electrical or electronic engineers. Electricity is with us, and will be for quite a while, so those who can design the most efficient and progressive systems have a secure and profitable future.

Mechanical Engineers: Average starting salary $37,000

A mechanical engineer with no advanced degree and about five years of experience is earning about $47,000 annually; a master's degree picks this up a little but not much; a Ph.D. does less than would be expected, earning about $55,000 after an equivalent time since earning the bachelor's degree. After ten years, the Ph.D. seems to make about $63,000, while the lesser degreed ones make about 10 percent less or about $57,000 per year. Mechanical engineers are plentiful—the Bureau of Labor estimates that about 233,000 of them are working in the United States today. The outlook is, as it has been for years, very good. Despite what seems like a nuclear and electronic age, the mechanical engineer still tells us how to make things go. Most of our life continues to depend on mechanical goods; we just plug them in nowadays instead of winding them up.

Metallurgical and Materials Engineer: Average starting salary $37,000

After five years in one of these fields, one's salary is about $42,000 to $46,000, the higher figure more reflective of those with master's degrees. A Ph.D. is earning slightly more but has been working somewhat less than five years. After ten years, the metallurgical or materials engineer with a B.S. is up to about $55,000, with a master's to about $60,000 to $65,000, with the metallurgical engineer on the high side and the materials engineer on the low side; the Ph.D. in either would not be much higher. All of this assumes no supervisory responsibilities. There are about 18,000 metallurgical and materials engineers in the United States today and the field has been increasing of late. In aerospace technology and now certainly in the power production field, among others, materials are being used under pressures and temperatures so high that metallurgists and materials engineers have their work cut out for them indeed.

Nuclear Engineer: Average starting salary $37,000

After about five years in the industry, a nuclear reactor engineer's salary is up to about $43,000 to $46,000; ten years increases this figure to $56,000. Advanced degrees affect starting salaries as much as 10 to 15 percent but appear to have little direct effect on salary as the years of experience increase. There are about 18,000 nuclear engineers in the country today. In the early seventies, they were a highly sought-after commodity. The accident at Three Mile Island and the enormous publicity that followed has brought a flood of new regulations and along with it, more jobs and higher salaries for the relatively few who can fill them. That same accident, however, virtually halted new orders for reactors and cancelled many existing ones, and the disaster at Chernobyl has made things worse. As a result, nuclear engineers not employed by utilities or by the Nuclear Regulatory Commission are not faring very well in this relatively depressed job market.

Petroleum Engineer: Average starting salary $42,000

After five years of professional experience, a petroleum engineer is earning about $53,000; after ten years, about $67,000 per year. The difference in salary between a bachelor's degree and a master's is not apparent; a doctorate, however, is worth about 15 percent in terms of higher salary for nonsupervisory work. There are about 17,000 petroleum engineers in the United States today, 5,000 fewer than five years ago because the United States could not compete with lower priced foreign oil. The long-term trend may be away from oil in electric power production, but the transportation industry alone will support an enormous domestic petroleum industry, and prices should rise sufficiently to bring back a resurgence in the production of U.S. oil.

Fire Protection Engineer: Average starting salary $35,000

This is a relatively new engineering discipline and information on salaries of veteran fire protection engineers is sparse. At this time, a bachelor's degree commands a starting salary of about $29,000 to $35,000, and a master's would start at $35,000 to $42,000. There are about 3,000 fire protection engineers in the United States today, and the number is growing at a faster than average pace. Opportunities exist for fire protection engineers in industries such as insurance, power, automotive, chemical, construction, government, etc. The outlook is excellent, since the supply is still small and the demand growing rapidly.

Engineers in Private Industry: A Government Survey

Every year the U.S. Bureau of Labor Statistics surveys a wide variety of jobs in private industry. The study delineates various levels of experience and achievement for each occupation and provides detailed job descriptions and salary information for all levels. For engineers, eight levels are recognized in the survey. Here's a brief summary of the government's descriptions:

Engineer I—This is the entry level of professional work, requiring a bachelor's degree in engineering and no experience.

Engineer II—A continuing developmental level. Person performs routine engineering work requiring application of standard techniques, procedures, and criteria in carrying out a sequence of related engineering tasks. Requires work experience acquired at an entry-level position or appropriate graduate level study.

Engineer III—Independently evaluates, selects, and applies standard engineering techniques, procedures, and criteria, using judgment in making minor adaptations and modifications. Assignments usually include one or more of the following: equipment design and development, test of materials, preparation of specifications, process study, research investigations, and report preparation. Sometimes supervises or coordinates the work of drafters and technicians.

Engineer IV—Plans and conducts work requiring judgment in the independent evaluation, selection, and substantial adaptation and modification of standard techniques, procedures, and criteria. Devises new approaches to problems encountered. Work requires a broad knowledge of precedents in the specialty area and a good knowledge of principles and practices of related specialties. Usually works with only general supervisory instructions and may oversee work of a few other engineers.

Engineer V—Applies intensive and diversified knowledge of engineering principles and practices in broad areas of assignments and related fields. Makes decisions independently on engineering problems and methods and represents the organization in conferences to resolve important questions and to plan and coordinate work. Supervises, coordinates, and reviews the work of a small staff of engineers and technicians.

Engineer VI—Plans and develops engineering projects concerned with unique or controversial problems that have an important effect on major company programs. Plans, organizes, and supervises the work of a staff of engineers and technicians. As an independent researcher he or she often serves as a specialist in advanced theories to the entire staff.

Engineer VII—Makes decisions and recommendations that are authoritative and have an important impact on many engineering activities. Individuals have demonstrated creativity, foresight, and mature engineering judgment in anticipating and solving unprecedented engineering problems, determining program objectives and requirements, organizing programs and projects, and developing standards and guides for diverse engineering activities. Directs several subordinate supervisors or team leaders.

Engineer VIII—Makes authoritative decisions and recommendations that have far-reaching impact on extensive engineering activities. Negotiates critical and controversial issues with top-level engineers and officers of other organizations and companies. Often supervises the entire engineering program of a medium-sized company or an important segment of an extensive engineering program within a large corporation.

Department Head—Provides technical and administrative supervision, insuring that technical, administrative, and schedule targets of the department are met in accordance with professional standards, design control procedures, and engineering design guidelines.

Annual Salaries of Engineers in Private Industry

Title	Average Salary	First Quartile	Third Quartile
Engineer I	$30,967	$27,800	$33,748
Engineer II	34,700	30,680	39,000
Engineer III	39,526	36,701	44,970
Engineer IV	44,350	42,367	51,480
Engineer V	50,291	48,961	60,020
Engineer VI	59,697	57,874	68,699
Engineer VII	70,643	67,100	76,942
Engineer VIII	84,369	75,300	89,265
Department Head	85,582	77,574	96,231

SOURCE: D. Dietrich Associates, Inc. *Engineering Salaries Survey,* 1994. Reprinted by permission.

Job Opportunities for Engineers

The outlook for today's 1.5 million engineers is not so much mixed as it is murky and confused. Because of the recent collapse of the Soviet Union and the slow but inevitable reduction of America's bloated defense budgets, thousands of engineering jobs especially those in aerospace, will be lost in the near future, but how many will be replaced in other sectors of the economy—and how quickly—remains in the hands of the political budget makers. The passage of the gargantuan transportation bill unleashed tens of billions of federal dollars to local economies and created many jobs for civil engineers, design engineers, and the like, but just how other funds may be diverted from the research and development of destructive weapons to more productive pursuits is not entirely clear.

According to many experts the most promising fields for engineers in the 1990s will be those related to the protection of the environment. Literally tens of thousands of engineering jobs are being created for the management of solid waste, the cleansing of toxic waste sites, as well as the monitoring and controlling of industrial pollution. (Of course, older engineers will remember that in the 1960s nuclear power was the place to be, while in the 1970s petroleum engineers were in the greatest demand, both fields with limited demand today.) According to the Association of Environmental Engineering Professors, the universities are currently producing only about 2,000 of the 5,000 new engineers needed each year in this field. Employment opportunities exist throughout the country in both private industry (including the large corporations involved in oil exploration, chemical production, and several major environmental engineering firms such as CH2M Hill in Denver as well) and at the federal, state, and local levels of government as the enforcement of stricter pollution laws becomes essential for our future. Even the recent assault on environmental regulation launched by conservative Republicans in Congress has not reversed public opinion about this issue.

Chemical engineers will also benefit greatly from the "green movement." Many industries will be looking to chemical engineers to provide environmental experts, corrosion experts, etc., to supplement their staffs in the future.

For mechanical engineers the job market also looks encouraging although the Bureau of Labor Statistics believes that most opportunities will result from the need to replace many retiring engineers rather than from the creation of new jobs. Not surprisingly, then, most of the literally hundreds of ads for mechanical engineers we found in 1995 were for those with five or more years of experience.

While the outlook is not exuberant, there are more employment opportunities for experienced electrical and electronics engineers than for most other engineering disciplines. The power industry—utilities, independent power producers, and their suppliers—has been stagnant for some time, but some parts of the country are hiring. Two other strong fields for electrical engineers include medical electronics and telecommunications.

Aerospace engineering and the companies devoted to it are as depressed as one would expect given diminishing defense and space-related budgets. It will be a while before these industries recover and become strong sources of employment, but it will happen.

The nuclear engineering field, which employs a wide variety of engineering disciplines, as well as those with nuclear training and experience, has been in a lull but is starting to bounce back. The power reactor business has, over the last 10 to 20 years, been the principal employer of nuclear engineers. Since, however, no new units have been ordered since the Three Mile Island accident and several under construction have been cancelled, licensees (the owners and operators of the reactors) have not increased their need for nuclear engineers except in the areas of operations and maintenance. They have, however, maintained that need for a high-quality engineering staff, since safety and downtime are of vital importance.

The Nuclear Regulatory Commission (NRC), the overseeing regulator of the industry, has been seeking and hiring engineers in anticipation of the retirement of existing personnel who joined them in large numbers in the 1950s and 1960s, when the business was starting in earnest, and then again in the 1970s, when a multitude of engineers became available at the end of the Apollo Project.

Within the next 5 to 10 years, the NRC expects a rebirth of activity in the regulatory arena due to the need to review plans for new units of a standardized design as well as applications for renewal of existing 40-year licenses which will start to expire around the turn of the century. Both these activities will require a large resource allotment by the NRC and the utilities as well as by contractors to both.

The Department of Energy is also seeking to hire nuclear engineers for both the cleanup of the waste generated by government reactors used to produce weapons-grade material and for safe, renewed operation of reactors (e.g., Savannah River in South Carolina) to be used for such in the future.

HOW TO CONDUCT YOUR OWN JOB SEARCH

The preceding description of opportunities for engineers may strike some as a bit optimistic. We believe, however, that our own research has demonstrated that there are jobs available, and we suggest the following approach to anyone seeking a job in this field.

An excellent and current source of information is any technical journal or magazine, usually published monthly. Examples include *Mechanical Engineering, Electrical World, Machine Design, Chemical Engineering News, Aviation Week and Space Technology Power, Nuclear News,* and *Graduating Engineer Magazine.* Each of these and others in more specific fields are available in any large public library or technical library, and each has a standard section entitled something like "Employment Opportunities." The articles and editorials in these trade publications should not be ignored—they occasionally include a discussion of a specific discipline or company that is currently in a strong growth period and may, therefore, be a source of immediate employment. This awareness of the company's current undertakings can be beneficial and discussion provoking at a job interview.

A very important source of current engineering employment opportunities is the *On-Line Career Line,* which provides job seekers with a listing of available engineering positions with a variety of companies. A computer and a modem are all that's required; there are no fees and anonymity is possible if desired. This system allows you to learn the background (including employee benefits) of those companies with openings, and to leave a resume electronically on-line so that the system can forward it to the employers of your choice. There are often several hundred jobs listed.

Note that actual application to a specific company is not handled by the On-Line Career Line, but names, addresses, and phone numbers are made available for direct contact. This system is updated each week to assure currency. Hookup to the system is accomplished by dialing (via modem) (802) 297-1912. The password to be typed in when prompted is NEWJOB. To resolve problems or ask questions, prompt and courteous help is provided by humans at (802) 297-9334.

WHERE THE JOBS ARE

Our own research has indicated that no particular region of the country will have significantly greater demand for engineers beyond that dictated by population growth and economic development. But we did discover that some organizations were more apt to hire engineers than others.

For example, a major source of engineering opportunities exists today in consulting firms. These companies vary in size from a handful to thousands of engineering employees. The small- to medium-sized firms (less than 200 to 300 employees) are more stable and require substantial overtime when times are good but do not generally lay off employees when the work falls off. Frequent travel may be involved, and weekly to monthly time away from home is often part of the job. Larger consulting firms are similar with regard to travel and time away from home, but they are not known for stability or commitment to their employees. The peaks and valleys of contracts on hand dictate the number of engineers employed.

These consulting firms market their services to large, more stable engineering organizations in just about every field and discipline. They provide several crucial services including long- and short-term supplementary manpower for staff augmentation; they also contract for a specific project and handle it "cradle-to-grave" with minimal client supervision, or they will simply provide specific expertise when required by an organization who does not keep such a specialty on their engineering staff. Marketing ability is often a job requirement as strong as engineering expertise. The larger consulting companies include Stone & Webster, California-based Bechtel, Inc., and Science Applications, Inc. The trade journals are informative as to when these companies are hiring.

There are also many openings today for various position levels, including department heads and deans, in the university environment. Salaries will generally be less than equivalent experience would yield in industry, but there *are* many jobs available in this sector every year.

Finally, there are many engineering job opportunities these days outside the United States. The Leslie Corporation in Houston, for example, has placed many mechanical engineers in jobs in Saudi Arabia. A program called USAID Electrification for the Atlantic Coast places experienced electrical engineers for remote area work in Nicaragua. In Japan many industries have a strong interest in American engineers especially in the fields of chemicals, electronics, automobiles, communications, information, shipbuilding, food, and pharmaceuticals. For further information on such opportunities, as well as in-depth insight into living and working there, consult *Working in Japan: An Insider's Guide for Engineers,* available from the American Society of Mechanical Engineers (ASME) Order Department at 1-800-843-2763 (fax 201/882-1717) for $19.95 for ASME members and $24.95 for nonmembers.

Engineering Technicians, Science Technicians, and Drafters

The ever-increasing importance of science and technology in all areas of the workplace has helped to create a strong job market for engineering technicians, science technicians, and electrical and electronic technicians. These people assist scientists and engineers in research and development of various equipment by setting up experiments and calculating results. Technicians in production test product quality and monitor procedures. Some work as manufacturers' field reps, advising buyers on the installation or maintenance of complex machinery. Others simply sell or service the equipment.

Engineering and science technicians usually require a post–high school training, often in a technical institute or a junior or community college. Many receive on-the-job training while serving in the armed forces. Others, especially science technicians, attend a four-year college.

Related to the work of science technicians and engineers is drafting. Drafters prepare detailed drawings from the rough sketches and specifications made by scientists, engineers, architects, and designers. They are also expected to specify materials to be used, procedures to be followed, and any other information needed to carry out the job. Drafters usually specialize in a particular field, such as mechanical, electrical, aeronautical, civil, or architectural drafting.

Applicants for drafting positions are expected to have two years of post–high school training in a technical institute, junior, or community college. Some receive their experience in the armed forces. Pertinent courses for a career in drafting include mathematics, physical sciences, and mechanical drawing, with some training in engineering and industrial technology a plus.

HOURLY WAGE RATES FOR DESIGNERS AND DRAFTERS, 1995

Title	Average Hourly Wage	First Quartile	Third Quartile
Drafting			
Level I	$ 9.74	$ 7.83	$10.91
Level II	10.55	9.50	12.57
Level III	12.74	11.30	14.70
Level IV	15.40	13.32	16.53
Drafting Supervisor	15.54	14.22	20.36
Designer			
Level I	16.19	14.65	16.55
Level II	17.92	16.00	19.54
Level III	20.01	18.78	21.34
Level IV	25.36	21.20	26.32
Design Manager	26.52	23.31	29.17
Application Analyst	21.13	18.25	23.32
Autographics Supervisor	20.46	17.50	23.60
Lead Operator	17.68	16.30	20.09
Senior Operator	16.69	13.00	18.27
Operator	13.28	11.92	14.90
Assistant Operator	10.44	8.82	12.39
Clerk	10.13	8.80	11.08

SOURCE: D. Dietrich Associates. Reprinted by permission.

Increasingly complex design problems associated with the information age will greatly increase the demand for drafting services in the coming decade, although some say this growth may be offset by the rising use of CAD (computer-aided design) systems, which cut down a drafter's work time. So far, however, the predicted layoffs have not for the most part occurred, and drafting remains a field worthy of serious consideration.

Opposite are salary figures compiled by D. Dietrich Associates for drafters at five different levels. Drafter I works under close supervision, traces or copies finished drawings, and makes revisions. Drafter II prepares drawings of simple, easily visualized parts or equipment from sketches or marked-up prints. Drafter III prepares various drawings of parts and assemblies, including sectional profiles, irregular or reverse curves, hidden lines, and intricate details. Drafter IV prepares complete sets of drawings which include multiple views, detail drawings, and assembly drawings. Drafter V performs unusually difficult assignments requiring considerable initiative, resourcefulness, and drafting expertise.

Job Descriptions for Drafters

DRAFTING/DESIGNER POSITION CLASSIFICATION DESCRIPTIONS

Drafting, Apprentice—Trainee assignment to learn the basic drafting skills and techniques.

Drafting, Level I—Entry level with high school drafting training or other appropriate basic-level drafting experience. Copies sketches, layouts, and drawings prepared by others.

Drafting, Level II—Entry level for individual with some specialized technology relating to drafting or engineering such as associate degree or experience as Level I. Copies detailed plans and drawings.

Drafting, Level III—Experienced draftsperson able to perform nonroutine and complex drafting assignments that require the application of standardized drawing techniques. Works independently with occasional advice from supervisor and may direct the efforts of less experienced draftspersons.

Drafting, Level IV—Involved in planning the graphic presentation of complex items having distinctive design features that can differ significantly from established drafting precedents. May recommend minor design changes. May direct the preparation of drawings by other drafting personnel of lesser experience.

Drafting Supervisor—Coordinates the work activities of a group of (five or more) drafters of various levels of capability to ensure that time schedules and quality of work are maintained. Works with professional staff in scheduling work and assigning drafting support staff to their projects. Normally requires an experienced drafter with 10 or more years of experience.

Designer—Involved in application of engineering fundamentals to engineering design; will select and recommend procedures in design and prepare preliminary designs for engineer's approval. Works independently on design projects in support of design engineer and will often coordinate drafting efforts on projects.

Senior Designer—A designer with significant years of engineering experience and proficiency.

COMPUTER-AIDED GRAPHICS DRAFTING GROUP CLASSIFICATION DESCRIPTIONS

Application Analyst—Explore, develop, and administer electronic graphics coupled with associated data for the production of design computer drafting. Train and assist workstation users in drawing techniques, input sketch preparation, clarification of standards, drawing verification, and revision and checking of output. Requires degree in engineering graphics or associate degree with four years of computer graphics experience.

Supervisor, Autographics—Responsible for quality and productivity of subordinate operators and the review of work for conformance to standards. Implements new methods and procedures. Provides coordination of operations with source departments for equipment utilization, drawing development, and work processing. Requires three to five years of computer graphics experience with drafting or graphics course work at technical school or college level.

Lead Operator, Autographics—Provides supervisor with assistance in maintaining efficient daily operations by resolving problems of other operators and handling difficult operating tasks. May analyze incoming material and develop drafting methods for most efficient production.

Should have three years of computer graphics experience with some applicable technical schooling.

Senior Operator, Autographics—With minimal supervision will operate autographics input station using digitizer, console unit, disk storage, and preprogrammed material to develop finished drawings. Able to maintain and increase proficiency in operations and recommend new methods and procedures. Accuracy, quality, completeness, and schedule adherence can be independently maintained at this level of experience. Requires two to three years of experience in computer graphics with some technical schooling.

Operator, Autographics—Under general supervision will operate with proficiency autographics input station using digitizer, console units, disk storage, and preprogrammed material to develop finished drawings. Can analyze sketches, notes, and other input material to determine best approach to complete drawing. Will operate plotter to transfer developed drawings from disk or tape storage to reproducible medium. Responsible for input-output of drawings from mag tape and/or disk. Requires one and a half to two years of computer graphics experience with some technical schooling.

Assistant Operator, Autographics—Under close supervision and instruction will learn proficiency in operation of autographics input station. Assignments should progress in difficulty as proficiency is increased. All work at this level will be fully reviewed and checked. Requires one year of drafting experience.

Clerk, Autographics—Responsible for logging in/out work requests and maintaining all records and files of work requests. Maintain files and records within the group and provide typing and clerical skills of competent proficiency.

COMPUTER TECHNOLOGISTS AND PROFESSIONALS

The information-processing industry changed dramatically during the 1980s with the spread of one item—the microprocessor—and its packaging into the personal computer. In 1980, while most white-collar workers had access to reports produced by large computers, the majority performed their jobs using some combination of telephone, copy machine, and typewriter. By the end of the decade the personal computer had placed the computing power of a small mainframe on the desktop.

The promise of the 1990s is that the computing power on the desktop will be multiplied at least tenfold. This will make computers an even more important part of American business. In the early 1990s the continued growth in sales of all types of computer equipment (including the instant success of portable computers), despite a deep economic recession, should bode well for the rest of the decade.

Still, it is not the industry itself that provides the key to job growth for highly trained computer people. It is virtually every business in America, large and small, that has come to depend on the power of the computer that employs most of the key personnel. The two most important jobs—programmers and systems analysts—remain reliable paths to regular employment, high wages, and eventually power and influence.

Systems analysts and programmers work in offices in almost every industry. The most profitable futures for both analysts and programmers will be in financial services (including banks, investment houses, and insurance companies), retailing operations, airlines, hotels and other travel industries, and industries that rely on a high level of customer service to generate business.

The outlook for the future continues to be exceedingly positive in every area of the country. Every prediction through the first decade of the next century is for continued growth.

In 1994 1.35 million people were employed as software engineers, systems analysts, and other computer professionals, a rise of 87 percent (from 719,000) in just 10 years. Moreover, official federal government estimates for the next decade predict another astonishing increase of 55 percent (compared to 22 percent employment growth for the entire economy). According to *Computerworld* demand for computer professionals jumped 45 percent between 1993 and 1994. Below is a summary of the federal government's projections for the next decade.

Computer Systems Analysts

The increasing use of computers by businesses of all kinds means that demand for systems analysts should grow much faster than the national average for all jobs by the year 2005. However, increasing specialization within this field means that competition for jobs will increase, threatening those who do not have specialized computer training or experience. Nevertheless, the number of systems analysts is expected to grow nearly 80 percent, to 829,000 by the year 2005, up from 463,000 in 1990.

Computer Programmers

Further automation of offices and factories, coupled with advances in health and medicine, will make the job of programmer ever more important through the 1990s. Jobs for programmers should grow much faster than the national average by the year 2005, according to the Department of Labor. Competition for jobs is high. Jobs for both systems and applications programmers should be particularly plentiful in data-processing service firms, software houses, and computer consulting businesses.

There were 565,000 computer programmers in 1990; the number is expected to swell 56 percent to 882,000 by the year 2005. Like systems analysts, programmers must keep abreast of changing technology and train and retrain constantly. Most of them can find work in every area of the country.

Operations Research Analysts

This job combines business savvy with extensive knowledge of computers. Generally speaking, these people are problem solvers who utilize mathematical models to present managers with a series of possible outcomes that will help them make more informed decisions. They are employed in most industries, and their numbers are expected to increase by over 70 percent, from 57,000 in 1990 to 100,000 by 2005. Salaries range from $50,000 to $100,000. The requirements for employment are a fairly rigorous training in mathematics or quantitative methods with a strong knowledge of computer programming.

JOB DESCRIPTIONS IN DATA PROCESSING

First, an overview of the three basic divisions in DP.

Systems Analysts—The systems analyst provides management with the information and computer processes necessary to meet different organizational goals. Systems analysts design or improve operational systems and periodically evaluate and revise existing ones. They prepare detailed descriptions of the tasks a computer system will have to perform—for example, estimating the stress during monsoon season on a bridge to be built in the tropics.

Computer Programmers—Once the systems analyst details what the computer's tasks are to be, programmers tell it how to do them. To continue with our bridge project, the programmer is told that the computer will have to retrieve data stored in another computer, organize it in a certain way, and perform needed calculations. He or she then breaks down each of those steps into a series of instructions coded in one of the computer languages.

Computer Operators—These specialized workers physically operate the computer console, entering data to be processed with instructions to the computer ("input") and retrieving final results ("output"). They run the program, producing the numbers needed in order to build that bridge.

JOB DESCRIPTIONS IN DATA PROCESSING: BY TITLE

Management

Corporation Director of Data Processing—The top executive for all computer processing.

Manager of Database Systems—Plans, organizes, and controls all activities of database systems, their design, and integration.

Manager of Data Processing—Directly supervises personnel, administration, and data processing. Oversees all three divisions of data processing work.

Assistant Manager of Data Processing—Assists in planning, organizing, and controlling the three divisions of DP.

Project/Team Leader—Plans, organizes, and controls all facets of work on a particular assigned project.

Systems Analysis and Programming

Manager of Systems Analysis/Programming; Lead Systems Analyst/Programmer; Senior Systems Analyst/Programmer; Systems Analyst/Programmer; Systems Analyst/Programmer Trainee—These positions cover both the analysis and programming functions.

Systems Analysis

Manager of Systems Analysis—Analyzes how data processing is applied to user problems; designs effective and efficient solutions.

Senior Systems Analyst—Confers with users to define data processing projects, formulates problems, designs solutions.

Systems Analyst—Assists in devising computer system specifications and record layouts, with guidance and instruction.

Applications Programming

Manager of Applications Programming—Responsible for the development of effective, efficient, well-documented programs.

Lead Applications Programmer—Assists in planning, organizing, and controlling section activities.

Senior Applications Programmer—Works with program designs or specifications.

Junior Applications Programmer—Assists in the review and analysis of detailed systems specifications and the preparation of the program instructions.

Applications Programmer Trainee—Learns to program, working under direct supervision. This is the entry level.

Systems Programming

Manager of Systems Programming—Plans and directs the activities of the operating system–programming section; assigns personnel to projects.

Lead Systems Programmer—Assists in planning, organizing, and controlling the activities of the operating system–programming section.

Senior Systems Programmer—May specialize in the support, maintenance, and use of one or more major operating systems; is able to work at the highest level of programming.

Systems Programmer—Assists in the review and analysis of detailed systems specifications and the preparation of the program instructions.

Trainee—Learns programming and other routine work of the department, under direct supervision. This is the entry level.

Data Communications Manager—Responsible for design of data-communications networks and installation and operation of data links.

Data Communications Operator—Operates and/or monitors, under supervision, various communication devices related to the information-processing system.

Computer Operations

Manager of Computer Operations—Responsible for the operation of computers, including scheduling, assignment of operators, and monitoring of efficiency.

Lead Operator—May be responsible for the operation of large-scale computers during a complete eight-hour shift or for the operation of a remote site.

Senior Computer Operator—May be responsible for all operations on a medium-scale computer or for console operator of a large machine.

Computer Operator—Assists in computer monitoring and control; able to work on own on several phases of operation.

Computer Operator Trainee—Usually assigned to mounting magnetic media, loading printers, or working on a peripheral subsystem, always under direct supervision.

Computer Input/Output Control Manager—Schedules and controls all data entering the DP system, and the editing and balancing of reports coming from the system.

AVERAGE ANNUAL SALARIES OF COMPUTER PROFESSIONALS BY INDUSTRY

Title	Manu-facturing	Banking/ Financial Services	IS Services	Retail	Govern-ment	Medical/ Legal Services	Trans-portation/ Utilities	Education	Construction/ Mining Agriculture	Other Services
CIO/VP	$115,829	$121,481	$139,336	$99,576	$93,136	$102,089	$161,352	$80,771	NA	$117,731
Director	78,473	92,538	88,839	48,557	71,456	63,226	77,792	61,812	$85,000	79,634
Manager/Supervisor	57,299	60,590	66,454	56,999	57,636	47,527	57,623	49,403	54,375	61,535
Application Development Manager	62,913	64,523	64,564	59,350	58,128	57,252	61,315	51,893	60,000	63,684
Application Designer	54,765	55,996	50,486	42,741	51,410	40,870	51,481	41,383	48,000	53,622
Application Developer	47,186	53,495	46,139	40,848	46,422	40,416	48,018	42,023	35,000	49,173
Project Manager	52,735	59,276	60,369	56,962	53,379	48,711	58,346	46,822	65,000	58,062
Project Leader	50,323	60,502	53,658	50,890	50,089	44,368	50,878	47,697	NA	55,157
Senior Systems Analyst	49,561	52,770	51,411	46,788	48,173	42,498	50,880	40,789	62,586	52,969
Systems Analyst	42,361	45,683	42,638	43,021	40,656	37,968	43,378	36,014	45,000	45,411
Senior Programmer Analyst	43,599	45,541	43,604	42,216	46,769	42,497	42,624	36,619	37,381	44,756
Programmer	36,431	38,913	34,865	32,744	36,108	30,457	33,806	30,926	30,000	37,715
Computer Operator	26,411	28,825	23,323	24,397	27,347	22,579	26,679	26,205	20,286	27,060
Data Entry Clerk	19,976	22,005	19,022	18,376	22,434	18,167	24,762	17,739	NA	21,402
Administrator	53,308	60,773	52,710	55,954	49,798	42,539	54,374	53,010	58,000	47,897
Database Analyst	47,390	51,166	50,184	41,955	46,616	37,603	44,953	41,865	48,000	43,573
Network Manager (LAN/WAN)	52,066	57,921	50,987	44,531	50,621	48,722	50,601	40,133	50,000	50,011
LAN Manager	45,227	51,363	50,615	38,329	48,042	38,279	46,198	34,547	43,952	45,620
Network Engineer	41,905	42,597	43,606	35,033	42,957	36,552	42,008	46,191	40,000	44,015
Help Desk Manager	43,100	43,743	48,127	39,073	43,267	38,195	43,664	35,432	50,000	43,213
Technical Support Analyst	36,464	38,714	40,391	35,764	38,039	29,528	37,450	30,506	47,025	35,469
Computer Hardware Engineer	39,255	42,442	40,683	39,787	40,904	31,603	37,146	37,838	40,000	42,946
PC Technician	31,643	35,217	31,905	35,813	32,044	27,511	29,332	27,304	NA	33,715

NA: Not Available.

SOURCE: *Datamation* magazine, annual salary survey, October 15, 1994. Reprinted by permission.

AVERAGE ANNUAL SALARIES OF COMPUTER PROFESSIONALS BY COMPANY SIZE

Title	Under $50 Million	$51 Million–$500 Million	$501 Million–$1 Billion	Over $1 Billion
CIO/VP	$93,983	$104,497	$130,412	$130,606
Director	65,657	76,927	81,169	89,501
Manager/Supervisor	52,898	56,783	56,740	64,850
Application Development Manager	57,222	60,889	60,924	64,494
Application Designer	48,452	51,717	49,533	53,254
Application Developer	45,955	46,133	45,994	49,710
Project Manager	52,641	54,943	56,237	58,385
Project Leader	50,702	50,850	51,889	56,197
Senior Systems Analyst	48,051	48,523	50,876	51,181
Systems Analyst	38,432	42,633	42,826	43,405
Senior Programmer Analyst	42,438	44,207	42,685	44,852
Programmer	33,766	35,148	34,694	38,251
Computer Operator	26,102	25,073	28,069	28,277
Data Entry Clerk	19,472	21,150	21,533	22,532
Administrator	49,039	50,532	56,265	54,390
Database Analyst	43,593	45,417	47,447	47,398
Network Manager (LAN/WAN)	45,073	50,054	53,937	53,994
LAN Manager	38,768	45,890	46,969	48,360
Network Engineer	38,379	40,670	44,020	46,037
Help Desk Manager	36,636	41,494	43,303	49,574
Technical Support Analyst	34,500	36,108	36,654	39,461
Computer Hardware Engineer	39,874	38,305	38,274	43,571
PC Technician	29,026	30,806	31,850	35,464

SOURCE: *Datamation* magazine, annual salary survey, October 15, 1994. Reprinted by permission.

AVERAGE ANNUAL SALARIES OF COMPUTER PROFESSIONALS BY LOCATION

Title	National Average	Washington, D.C.	Boston	New York	Florida	Chicago	Texas	Los Angeles	San Francisco
CIO/VP	$111,495	$99,000	$112,679	$109,265	$92,095	$103,460	$103,500	$153,385	$113,583
Director	76,380	73,805	83,184	70,519	68,730	74,818	71,957	84,526	86,898
Manager/Supervisor	57,246	55,709	59,625	57,080	49,678	57,058	49,248	62,562	65,440
Application Development Manager	61,006	59,052	67,792	58,773	55,071	57,397	54,712	65,341	69,962
Application Designer	51,408	58,000	53,300	48,389	46,815	44,686	45,688	55,526	58,760
Application Developer	47,210	47,080	53,364	45,055	42,092	41,360	41,011	51,242	52,085
Project Manager	55,691	55,453	63,345	53,058	50,065	52,364	53,904	56,731	58,541
Project Leader	52,667	51,138	68,727	47,278	45,927	49,925	46,456	56,263	55,034
Senior Systems Analyst	49,621	50,250	59,683	48,406	43,172	47,301	44,263	50,297	53,697
Systems Analyst	42,166	40,926	47,545	41,532	35,795	41,021	38,690	42,895	47,990
Senior Programmer Analyst	43,912	43,375	47,858	42,136	38,615	40,132	40,592	49,249	48,505
Programmer	35,481	34,693	40,063	33,430	30,340	32,905	33,025	40,781	39,404
Computer Operator	26,130	27,056	30,593	23,451	21,597	24,095	23,677	29,633	29,896
Data Entry Clerk	20,821	19,016	22,250	19,075	17,700	20,416	19,430	23,254	23,964
Administrator	52,508	48,940	64,556	55,316	40,738	50,679	45,736	52,618	56,691
Database Analyst	46,410	44,923	55,000	49,427	41,838	41,042	40,585	46,045	50,687
Network Manager (LAN/WAN)	50,466	49,932	55,227	51,400	43,740	50,267	44,749	50,981	54,704
LAN Manager	45,460	43,494	51,345	43,826	39,865	43,094	44,081	47,574	49,059
Network Engineer	42,471	39,917	44,000	40,714	38,231	43,364	38,463	42,760	49,253
Help Desk Manager	42,624	38,000	41,572	42,138	40,027	40,973	38,350	43,840	51,926
Technical Support Analyst	36,559	33,126	40,828	33,943	35,729	38,366	35,602	36,567	39,323
Computer Hardware Engineer	39,638	34,200	39,143	39,074	39,700	37,692	36,033	40,643	48,866
PC Technician	31,614	27,696	35,909	29,847	29,259	31,160	29,413	32,188	36,902

SOURCE: *Datamation* magazine, annual salary survey, October 15, 1994. Reprinted by permission.

COMPARATIVE DATA PROCESSING SALARIES, 1965–1995

Title	1965	1975	1985	1990	1995
Director of Data Processing	$19,000	$22,500	$48,000	$64,000	$76,000
System Analyst Manager	14,000	19,000	37,000	52,000	61,000
Systems Analyst	10,400	17,200	32,000	37,000	46,000
Programmer Analyst	10,500	14,800	28,000	33,000	39,000
Programmer	9,100	14,000	22,000	27,000	32,000

SOURCE: Robert Half Associates, *1995 Salary Guide.* These figures are average of data from large, medium, and small installations. Reprinted by permission.

COMPUTER CAREERS IN THE 1990s

by Christopher D. Stack[1]

Data processing is one of the strongest functional areas in which to develop a career as well as a good springboard from which to launch a career in another, sometimes distantly related, field of interest. It has gone through explosive, virtually unmanaged growth in the past three decades, but it is finally showing some signs of maturing. Not that the growth won't continue, but it won't be as strong. The industry appears to be settling down to the degree that there is finally some structure and reason to the growth. There are some disadvantages and pitfalls for the unwary, and they must be recognized and anticipated to avoid launching a career that will eventually reach a dead end.

The discipline of data processing or MIS (management information systems) or IS (information systems) or IRM (information resource management) shows no sign of a slowdown in its steady increase in importance and influence in the business world or for that matter, in the social, cultural, medical, and other worlds. Throughout our society we see a rise in the demands for computer literacy. It is difficult to use a phone, perform a banking transaction, or run a household appliance without a passing acquaintance with computers and microprocessors. But, more importantly, it is almost impossible to perform any job in today's economy without interfacing with a computer.

Growing Influence Breeds a Need for Change

Businesses are requiring a facility with PCs from employees in disciplines far removed from the technical. Throughout industry, there is a rise

[1]Chris Stack was executive vice president of William Stack Associates, a New York executive recruiting firm. He has 15 years prior experience as an MIS professional.

in the recognition of the value of the information resource, that body of data that becomes more than the sum of its parts through computerized organization, analysis, and access. Companies are beginning to recognize this information as more than an historical record, but in fact as a critical element in their ability to differentiate their products. This importance is being reflected in the tendency of a growing number of companies to establish the position of chief information officer, the senior data processing executive in the company reporting to the president or CEO. The position now has strategic business importance in its own right and no longer reports to the controller or the chief financial officer. The influence of data processing in business has never been greater, and the signs are that it will continue to grow.

However, this new influence demands new skills of the field's practitioners and has imposed some unsettling changes on them. The growing familiarity of the general public with computers and their use in daily life has meant an increased demand for responsiveness from the professionals to the questions and needs of the user public. The reliance on technological mystification and audience naivete to avoid hard or inconvenient questions doesn't work for computer professionals anymore. Seldom can an MIS manager sidestep having to make a complicated explanation by saying, "You wouldn't understand it. It's too technical." Now the MIS manager not only has to make the explanation: It has to be comprehensible. In other words, the MIS manager must now enter the mainstream.

Computer Operations as Part of the Corporate Information Utility

As the mystique of computers is diluted by growing familiarity, DP departments themselves are coming under greater and greater pressure to meet budget constraints and scheduling deadlines. Planning, cost awareness, and adherence to established standards are the norm now. The freewheeling days of galloping along full speed ahead and ignoring anyone trying to impose restraints because they cramp your style are gone. This growing adherence to standards has also resulted in MIS departments coming under increasing pressure to quantify the value they are adding to the business. Each computer decision is treated as a business decision, not as something that falls outside the rules because it's involved with MIS. The data processing departments are finding themselves increasingly competing for corporate capital and having to justify their capital expenditures by the same yardsticks as do others.

The New MIS Professional

All of this means that there is a change in the types of skills needed from MIS professionals today. Demand is increasing for those with a general business background. Companies still want people who primarily can solve computer problems. However, they also want people with sufficient business experience, or at least a broad-based background, to put MIS systems into the business framework in which they must function. The data processing department can no longer function in a vacuum. The shift in emphasis to structured design and coding, the highly sophisticated software now available at even the PC level, and the power of fourth generation languages has caused a corresponding shift in emphasis to an understanding of the problems to be solved rather than the techniques commonly used in solving them.

Thus, there are inherent traps in the industry today that those considering or working in the field should be aware of. Structured programming and fourth generation languages with their emphasis on easily maintainable code have the ironic effect of making programmers a commodity. A concentration in a particular speciality leads to more and more environments in which development work is done by hired guns, independents who are brought in on a temporary basis to do a specific job and who are sloughed off as soon as the job is over. In some very large operations, such as General Motors, computer operations' maintenance are being contracted to outside organizations like EDS. This can also make it difficult to keep skills current and to stay abreast of the technology. For instance, if you are in demand because you have a certain, very esoteric speciality, you will be encouraged to take advantage of that specialization and won't be exposed to the developing technology that may eventually make your specialty obsolete.

These trends have a number of implications for those who desire to pursue the field of data processing.

- First, build your technical knowledge, stay current with the developing technology, but don't fail to focus on the business climate.
- Know about the environment in which the technology will be applied. Understand the business reasons for the problems you're solving and the business basis for the solution.
- Don't assume that the DP skills alone are sufficient to keep you in demand. Broaden your base of knowledge.
- Don't fall into the trap (perpetuated by many headhunters) of building your career by changing employers at frequent intervals. It's alluring because you can raise your salary rapidly, but you develop no track record, and you can just as rapidly price yourself out of the market. Why should a company pay you $30,000 to do something when it can just as easily get a $25,000 person to do the same thing? There will always be newer, cheaper, (and often more current) talent coming along.
- Finally, take an active interest in the development of your own career. A career doesn't take care of itself, and unless you are lucky

enough to find a mentor to take you in hand, your career will founder without some firm guidance. Make a periodic appraisal of where you are, what the next step is, and what you need to get there. Then fill that gap. Think in terms of job satisfaction and career progress rather than just salary when you consider a change. Let your superiors know that you are interested in your future with the company and discuss your career with them. Use performance reviews to constructive ends. Too many people in data processing believe that they are special, that they don't have to worry about their careers because they have this or that particular ability. That never has been true, and it's becoming less and less true every day.

Career Paths in MIS

In planning your career in MIS, it is important to recognize that different career options exist. There are three different career paths within data processing: operational, software, and managerial. They demand different training, different backgrounds, and different levels of skill. They also have different career potentials. Within the three, there are opportunities for everyone at any level.

Operational—The operations jobs in data processing include all those positions that get the work done. They are the people who prepare the information for processing, who run the machinery, and who maintain it. Brief descriptions of major operational job categories follow.

Keypunch and data entry operators provide the computers with the information they need to know in order to be useful. Sitting at a terminal and in direct contact with the computer, they type information into the system. Often they will receive information back from the computer about the data. They may be recording sales statistics, coding banking transactions, entering customer orders, enrolling welfare clients, or any of a myriad of other tasks. Some data entry positions require knowledge of the industry or product line, others require substantial customer contact, still others are purely routine and undemanding. These positions exist in nearly every large and many small companies as well as within government agencies and educational institutions.

Computer operators actually run the computers. They work in the computer rooms, turning the machines and various programs on and off. They oversee the security and backup procedures to make sure the data kept on the computers is safe and up to date. They perform routine maintenance on the equipment. The computer operators will generally not have much exposure to the business itself, focussing mainly on the operation of the equipment. However, the potential to move into other areas of data processing is fairly good, and this can be a good stepping-stone in a data processing career, especially for someone with a limited educational background. The final category of the operational side of computing is the service and repair of DP equipment. These people are generally employed by the manufacturers or distributors of computers and peripheral equipment such as printers, scanners, storage media, telecommunications equipment, and the like. A technical ability is a must, and constant technical update training is necessary. The training, however, is almost always done at the expense of the employer and is highly pragmatic; theory is kept to a minimum. There is a constant demand for these practitioners, and as the PCs become more and more widespread, the need for technicians to repair them grows correspondingly. Opportunities for advancement are excellent as are the possibilities for making lateral moves into related fields.

Software—Software professionals in data processing are those who plan and create the computer software as well as maintain it. They include *programmers, systems analysts, MIS consultants,* and the *customer service/support people* who help others use their products. They can be generally classified into two categories: systems and applications. The systems side is concerned with the software that allows the computer to be programmed to solve an application problem. It includes such software as operating systems, language compilers (for Fortran, COBOL, Pascal, C, and many others), file handlers, database systems, and the like—the programs that are the building blocks of computer programming. The applications side is concerned with taking the products created by the systems side and using them to solve real world problems. Thus, a systems group might write a COBOL compiler to translate a COBOL program for a specific computer. An applications group would then use this compiler in writing a program in COBOL to do a company's inventory control. Systems professionals focus more on the operations of the computers themselves. Applications professionals focus more on the specific real world problems to be solved. Of course these distinctions are not so finely drawn, and there are many people who fall into some middle ground, but the contrast is nonetheless useful.

Within these two broad areas there is still a similar job structure. *Programmers* write the actual code that makes up a computer program using computer language. They are under the direction of *systems analysts* who design the structure of a system, often composed of hundreds of program modules. Analysts work with the general concept of the problem to be solved and the constraints imposed by the computer and must have a good understanding of programming, but they may themselves not do any actual coding. *Consultants* generally are a hybrid of programmer and analyst with some additional abilities thrown in. They advise a series of clients on MIS problems facing them and may perform a whole gamut of tasks from programming to planning to cost justification. Each consultant brings something different to the profession and has a particular set of skills to offer. Finally, within the classification of software professionals are the customer service/support specialists. These generally come from the ranks of analysts that have responsibility for developing a certain piece of software, and they are experts in its use. They serve as a resource to the end users, and either working over the telephone or going out into the field, they help ensure that the software is used in the most effective and constructive ways possible.

All of the career possibilities within the software category require the technical bent of a computer programmer. A penchant for logical analysis, for structure, and for abstraction is essential. An undergraduate degree in a technical field such as electrical engineering or data processing is becoming more and more common in the industry to gain entry-level jobs, but there are still those who break into the field by taking a practical course in computers and programming or simply through acquiring the skills on their own. Despite what the schools would like you to believe, the body of knowledge necessary to be a computer programmer is relatively small; the analytical mind-set is much more important and cannot really be taught. Any software professional must also be prepared to continue to learn. As the technology advances, so does the necessity to acquire new knowledge, to master new techniques, and to stay abreast of changes in the industry. The career path is fairly direct through the technical levels and eventually leads to either a senior technical position, a highly esoteric specialty, or into the managerial ranks. It is a very competitive field but one with potentially high rewards.

Managerial—The managerial ranks of the data processing field include those who direct the efforts of all of the preceding categories. They oversee the structure, mission, allocation of resources, and, most important, planning of the MIS function within a company. Of most importance to these individuals is the transition in focus from what the information systems can do to what the business needs are. The managers of the MIS function must be the intermediaries between the professionals and the line and staff managers whose operations MIS supports. However, the critical skill is business management rather than technical. For this reason, technical background is not necessary for senior MIS management. Technical knowledge is helpful in facilitating communication with technical subordinates, but the business skills are the most essential to the equation.

The managerial career path can lead to the senior MIS position in the company. With growing frequency, this position carries a title like chief information officer and has strategic planning responsibility and reports to the president or CEO. As the information resource continues to gain in importance and influence, the path from MIS management to senior line management will become more and more common.

Systems Integrators (the hybrid)—Bridging the gaps between software, hardware, and service industries are the systems integrators. The Information Technology Association of America (ITAA) has said that one of the best areas of opportunity in the computer field is that of systems integration. In their words, "A systems integrator designs and develops information systems that automate key operations for private businesses or government agencies [managing] the entire process from design and development, through purchasing, implementation, training and management." They state that the use of systems integration by the private sector is growing 29 percent a year and that it is already a $5.8 billion industry. This discipline requires a careful blending of a multitude of technical skills as well as managerial ones. Systems integration teams can be found as stand-alone companies and as units within large corporations. Most of the Big Six accounting firms have IS development groups that are, in fact, systems integration divisions. EDP has made a huge business out of the systems integration function with a strong focus on facilities management. Again, these large companies are the most likely prospects for employment, and they can be found across the country.

How to Begin Your Job Search

There are several places one can look for assistance in a job search in the computer industry. Trade periodicals such as *Datamation* and *Computer World* can be valuable sources of information about the companies that are likely prospects. The Association for Computing Machinery (ACM) has headquarters in New York but has local chapters all across the country; it too can be a clearinghouse for job information both formally and informally.

More specific to job openings, there are a number of tools worth considering in a search. Newspaper advertisements are a fruitful source of leads. Local papers as well as regional editions of *The Wall Street Journal* and the *National Business Employment Weekly* (a compilation of regional *Wall Street Journal* listings) are all good sources and periodically have special editions or separate sections devoted to jobs in the computer industry. The advantage to these ads is that you have eliminated the first problem of a job search: locating a job you want or a company that's hiring.

Another source is the job fairs held in and around major cities around the country at regular intervals. Here, many potential employers come to meet job seekers. They will generally have a shopping list in mind and will be looking for specific talents, but someone with a good skill set has a considerable chance of finding a match. It has the advantage of bringing the principals face-to-face early on in the process. Information about these fairs can be found in local papers, trade journals, and from the job fair organizers themselves. One of the largest of these companies is BPI Tech Fair in Minneapolis.

A third source of job information is the recruiting industry. Recruiters, or headhunters, find the candidates for a company that has an opening to fill. Retainer recruiters accept assignments only on an exclusive basis and are paid for conducting the candidate search, not just for finding the final candidate. However, they work only at the high end of the job spectrum: positions that pay $80,000 to $100,000 and up. Contingency recruiters take up the rest of the market, and most recruiters who specialize in computer jobs fall into this category. These firms learn of a job opening and compete with each other to fill it. Only the firm that makes the placement gets a fee. Competition is fierce, and often only cursory thought is given to the appropriateness of the match. For that reason, the job seeker should take care to control use of his or her name by a contingency recruiter. Don't authorize a recruiter to send your resume to anyone without describing the proposed job and company to you first. Then you decide whether it sounds appropriate and if so allow your name to be submitted as a candidate *for that one job only.* Make the recruiting firm repeat the process for every job that it wants to recommend you for. Don't listen to the recruiter who says you're tying his hands by making him contact you first each time. He is only trying to avoid a situation called "prioring." If some other recruiter submits your name to the same company and you are hired, the recruiter who had the prior submission of your name is the one to be paid. Thus, for an unprincipled recruiter, the best plan of action is to get your name in front of every company possible regardless of the appropriateness of the job so that if you are hired later, even for another job, he will have the prior. Some unpleasant squabbling over fees can arise from this practice and employment opportunities have been hopelessly confused and sometimes lost because of shoddy recruiting. This is why the epithet "headhunter" is sometimes appropriate. There is no reason not to use a recruiter or better yet, several of them, but be sure *you* control the process.

A final way to go about finding work in the computer industry is through so-called "body shops." These are companies that hire computer professionals that they in turn farm out to other companies for temporary assignments. Often the assignments are project based and usually last for at least a few months, often much longer. The advantage to the company using body shop personnel is the ability to hire just for a short-term need without having any long-term commitment to the individual. The advantage to the body shop is the markup taken on the salary of the professional placed. The advantage to the individual is the flexibility to work when and as long as desired and the chance to avoid being locked in to a boring set of responsibilities that never changes.

To find both reputable recruiters and good body shop operations, ask friends and acquaintances at any large computer-user company what firms their personnel staff uses. Speak directly to human resources people about the advantages and drawbacks of specific firms and individuals. A little bit of leg work can make all the difference between finding the right company to help you and sowing the seeds of dissatisfaction and disappointment.

Finally, there are databases available to employers containing resumes of computer technologists. Individuals can submit their resumes for no charge and be listed according to their skills and interests. Usually, individuals can specify firms their resumes should not go to, to avoid a current employer finding out about a job search. The ACM has established a relationship with Business People Inc./BPI Tech Fair in Minneapolis to maintain a database of the ACM members who wish to be listed, and BPI will extend this listing opportunity to anyone in the computer field.

Note: Under no circumstances should you pay to be listed in a database or for a recruiter to find you a job. Those that charge individuals are unethical.

The Geographical Picture

Geographically speaking, the only strong growth areas of the country seem to be in the Northwest, in and around Seattle, and in those cities where a particular high-growth producer or provider has established a base of operations such as Austin, Texas, where Dell Computer Corporation is headquartered. Silicon Valley has been hard hit by resizing within the industry. Boston's Route 495 circle has been devastated both because the minicomputer industry which was spawned there has been mortally wounded by the microcomputer growth and by real trouble in the area's financial and real estate markets.

New York is typical of most large cities on the east and west coasts. While there is still a continuing need for computer personnel in support of the operations of the city's businesses, the need is tempered by the health of those businesses. Furthermore, as real estate prices remain high relative to prices in the surrounding exurban area and as communications costs decrease while the speed and accuracy of communications increase, there is a growing trend toward moving operations out of downtown business centers. In many cases, these operations are being moved to entirely different areas of the country. This is a trend that will almost certainly continue.

NEW CAREERS IN THE COMPUTER WORLD

Over the past few years, there has been a significant rise in job opportunities in the new world of computer-based entertainment, education, and information research. The dramatic improvement in CD-ROM technology combined with the rapid increase in the power of personal computers to create a new world generally called *multimedia.* Major book publishers and software companies rushed to establish production departments that could create realistic games, put the whole encyclopedia on one disc to make research as easy as a keystroke, and in general began a whole new method of presenting educational material in an enjoyable way.

In 1994, the emergence of the Internet and its now-famous World Wide Web ("The Web") presented an entire new region for job creation: cyberspace. All this term means is the vast world of interconnected computers that allows people to communicate or to access information from Websites or from commercial on-line services like America OnLine. The recent introduction of new technology that allows Web developers to create and users to access information in multimedia formats has only added to the excitement over the potential for on-line communication. It will also mean the addition of thousands of new jobs for people with special computer skills.

Multimedia[1]

Unless you've spent the past few years in a monastery under a rigid code of silence, you've probably heard of the term "multimedia." Originally little more than a computer industry buzzword, ten parts hype to one part reality, it has become the label for one of the most exciting technical developments in years—a development that's bursting with professional and entrepreneurial opportunities, especially if you enjoy working at the intersection of art and technology.

Only a few years ago, most personal computers weren't powerful enough for the real-time processing of sound, graphics, and text—the multiplicity of media in multimedia. But the advent of much more powerful microprocessors, the tiny silicon computing engines that drive PCs, changed all that, and it is now possible to buy a multimedia computer for as little as $1,500, including built-in stereo speakers, a color monitor, and a CD-ROM drive. About five years ago, you would have had to pay several times that sum just for a CD-ROM drive—and a slow one at that.

The enormous popularity in multimedia computers (almost all PCs now include built-in CD-ROM drives) has been matched by a boom in CD-ROM publishing. Thousands of discs are being issued every year. Many of them are little more than computerized adaptations of encyclopedias and other reference works, but an increasing number are original creations, devised expressly to take advantage of the CD-ROM's extraordinary interactive properties. Not surprisingly, games, such as the best-selling *Myst* an engrossing treasure hunt set in a hauntingly archaic future, are the most popular—and perhaps the most innovative—genre. Like movies before the advent of sound and color, the CD-ROM is very much in its infancy, a long way from technical and artistic fulfillment.

A small but rapidly growing CD-ROM publishing industry has arisen in only a few years. Many of the established software houses, such as Microsoft and Broderbund, have set up CD-ROM departments. Being part of big and

---

[1]Portions of this section were prepared by Stan Augarten, author of *Bit by Bit: An Illustrated History of Computers* (Ticknor & Fields, 1984), and *State of the Art: A Photographic History of the Integrated Circuit* (Ticknor & Fields, 1983).

wealthy companies, these groups are relatively large and well-funded, and publish a dozen or more titles a year. But most CD-ROM outfits are quite small, founded on a prayer and a shoestring to exploit the enormous technical and commercial potential of this new medium. Few of them have more than a dozen employees, and they usually issue only two or three titles a year. But dozens of such companies have popped up, mostly located in and around New York, Boston, Seattle, and San Francisco, just north of Silicon Valley.

The CD-ROM isn't the only medium of multimedia expression, although it's perhaps the most popular. Once offering no more than text, the Internet and other computer networks are increasingly adding graphics and sound to their presentations. For example, one site on the World Wide Web, the multimedia portion of the Internet, offers a tour of the Louvre, the great Parisian art museum, with dozens of color photos accompanied by detailed captions. There are thousands of sites on the World Wide Web, many of them put there by companies that hired consultants or highly specialized firms to do the work.

Because the multimedia publishing business (both CD-ROM and online) is so new, no reliable employment statistics exist. At most, the industry probably contains no more than ten or twenty thousand people. As in the movie business, a relatively small number of employees are on staff, while the majority are freelancers, working on an hourly, project-by-project basis. But the business' growth line resembles a hockey stick, and many thousands of full-time and freelance jobs will undoubtedly be added in the coming years, especially when TV set-top boxes—gadgets designed to bring multimedia to television—are introduced.

Most of the people in CD-ROM and related multimedia endeavors gravitated into the field from the computer industry, while others came from print publishing and movie or TV production. These are still the best routes into the field, whether your interest lies in the business or technical side. If you're a student or another brand of outsider, however, you can prepare yourself for a job in the field by attending one of the growing number of multimedia programs at schools around the country. Some of these are degree-granting programs open only to matriculated students, but others simply give completion certificates and are thus open to almost anyone, even high school students. (In the pragmatic world of multimedia, hands-on experience and ability is usually more important than a degree.) By virtue of its proximity to Silicon Valley, San Francisco State University has one of the largest nondegree multimedia programs, with some eighty classes (as of the spring of 1995). Many of them, such as "Graphic Design for Multimedia on the Mac" and "Lingo Architecture and Programming," are quite technical, offering solid experience in the latest multimedia tools. You don't have to buy your own equipment, since the school has a couple of well-equipped computer labs, but the courses are expensive, ranging from $75 to $725 each. (Incidentally, the Macintosh is still the machine of choice in multimedia production, and Lingo is the programming language for Macromedia Director, the most popular multimedia authoring software; Lingo programmers are very much in demand.)

Job Descriptions in Multimedia

Here is a list of the major technical job titles in multimedia and a brief description of the work involved. For more information about multimedia opportunities, see *Careers in Multimedia* by Ken Fromm (Ziff-Davis Press, 1995). For details about the latest developments in multimedia, see *NewMedia,* a monthly trade magazine published in San Mateo, California; for subscriptions, call (609) 786-4430.

Creative Director—Supervises all design and production, making sure that the final product meets the company's standards and budget. The creative director usually has strong technical skills and a fine creative mind.

Project Manager—Responsible for the production of a specific CD-ROM or other multimedia project, such as an Internet site. Working under the creative director, the project manager orchestrates the entire production effort, supervising (and often hiring) the designers, writers, artists, and programmers and making sure the project is finished on time and on budget.

Game Designer/Instructional Designer—A specialist in the design of games or educational software. For the latter, a background in education, educational psychology, or instructional technology is particularly useful.

Writer/Editor—Writes or edits the script or text. A game may require a script to be narrated by actors; a nonfiction work will require a text, often adapted from a book.

Graphic Artist—Creates the artwork. Graphic artists usually specialize: some do animation, others static graphics, and still others video. Graphic artists must be adept with such applications as Adobe Photoshop, which is widely used to modify photographs, and Adobe Illustrator, used to create graphics.

Software Designer/Programmer—Writes the software code that makes everything work. A good programmer usually knows several programming languages, such as Lingo, C, and C++, and a variety of authoring applications, such as Macromedia Director, Apple HyperCard, and Asymetrix ToolBook.

Tester—An entry-level position, the tester plays the game (or other multimedia creation) over and over again, searching for bugs and other incongruities.

Digitizer—Scans words and images into the computer. Cleans or removes extraneous materials from images and sizes them to fit the final product.

Interface Designer—Designs the overall look of the CD-ROM. Usually has a background in page design in magazines or advertising.

Artist-Illustrator—Oversees the creation of artwork for the entire CD-ROM. Often consults with designer on interface. Usually has a design background from advertising or publishing.

ESTIMATED ANNUAL SALARY RANGES FOR JOBS IN MULTIMEDIA

Position	Estimated Annual Salary Range
Design	
Producer/Account Manager	$100,000–$125,000
Director	100,000– 125,000
Editor-in-Chief	60,000– 75,000
Art Director	60,000– 75,000
Software Director	60,000– 65,000
Interface Designer	60,000– 65,000
Sound Designer	60,000– 65,000
Production	
Chief Programmer	$60,000–$ 75,000
Production Manager	50,000– 60,000
Sound Folio Artist	40,000– 50,000
Writer	25,000– 30,000
Artist-Illustrator	25,000– 30,000
Digitizer	25,000– 30,000
Proofreader	20,000– 25,000
Researcher/Permissions	20,000– 25,000
Production Secretary	20,000– 25,000

SOURCE: *CD-ROM Professional*, July, 1995; industry executives.

Cyberspace

Unlike CD-ROMs, which are still a fixed medium despite their technological superiority to reams and reams of paper, the world of cyberspace is a fluid one. So fluid, in fact, that nobody is exactly sure how many people are using it. Estimates of 20–25 million users have been popularized in some quarters and generally accepted as close to the truth. If the number of users continues to double every year, as has been the case over the past five years, every home in America will be wired by the end of the century.

Of course, this kind of growth isn't likely to be sustained—only a third of all U.S. households even have a computer, much less a modem—but that hasn't deterred every media outlet, publisher, perfume manufacturer, and nonprofit organization from rushing to set up an electronic soapbox. The main shopping center for these endeavors is the World Wide Web, a spiderweb of links that uses a hypertext programming language to transmit compressed multimedia words and images quickly over phone lines.

But the question of what to put on a company's Web site, and how to present it has given rise to an entirely new profession: the *Web site designer.* The relative openness of the Web means that almost anybody with a computer, a scanner, a few graphics programs, and a working knowledge of the Web's basic writing tool (known as HTML, or hypertext markup language), can design a Web site from his or her basement. But the designers who can deliver the most interesting information and most entertaining graphics are beginning to find themselves in short supply.

The exact number of Web site designers is no easier to ascertain than the size of the Internet community, especially since even the most established companies have been in business for only a few years. In broad terms, Web site designer salaries start at about $30,000 for a college graduate with basic skills. A sophisticated programmer who oversees the design, content, and use of a busy Web site is known in many companies as the *Web master,* and earns anywhere from $75,000 to $100,000. In large companies with extensive Web sites, the Web master oversees several designers, programmers, and writers the same way a magazine publisher oversees writers, editors, photographers, and page designers.

The explosion in the number of Web sites has also given rise to a corresponding increase in the number of people needed to review each site. Several companies now produce Web guidebooks, either in printed form or as an on-line service. To keep track of the hundreds of new sites joining the World Wide Web each week, these companies hire writers known as *Web site reviewers.* These are usually freelancers fresh out of college, who earn anywhere from 10 to 25 cents per word, or $10–$25 per 100-word review. According to one Web directory publisher, the average review takes about a half hour to write, making this a more lucrative field than one might imagine.

There is a richer, more intellectual side to this new electronic world. The huge amount of information on the Web has helped create a demand for people with librarian-like skills for researching. Sometimes called "cybrarians," or simply on-line searchers, these people provide information for a fee to businesses who don't have the time or the skill to locate what they need. Over 600 people already belong to the Association of Independent Information Professionals, but the number is rising.

V

Key White-Collar Jobs

At first glance the occupations contained in this section may appear to be an unorthodox grouping, especially if one is accustomed to standard delineations of white-collar jobs and blue-collar jobs, or service-sector and production-sector jobs. Those designations are helpful to economists and sociologists, to be sure. But the characteristics common to the jobs found here make this section especially relevant to those planning a career. For these jobs usually require a college education, they pay well, they exist in every major corporation, and the government predicts good opportunities for all of them over the next decade.

This career orientation requires extensive entries that include job descriptions and salary information for entry-level to senior and vice-presidential positions. Where it was possible, we also included salary figures from different industries. Special attention was given to government pay levels in personnel and purchasing, since they are large and essential areas in the public employment sector. Interested readers should also be sure to consult the sections on accountants (in Part III) and computer professionals (in Part IV).

The section begins with a look at those executives who have made it to the top levels of the corporation. A detailed list of compensation figures for leaders of America's major corporations highlights this profile.

We devote the next section to describing typical white-collar jobs at large and mid-sized companies. At one point, these jobs were synonymous with ironclad job security and rising salaries. However, beginning in the 1980s, white-collar jobs became targets for corporate cost cutting, starting with so-called staff and support jobs. White-collar operating jobs became the target of further cost cutting as the 1990s approached with methods such as "increasing spans of control," "outsourcing basic support service," and "reengineering processes" finding their way into management's lexicon. Many supervisory and managerial jobs have been eliminated as a result. In fact, white-collar workers were laid off as often as blue-collar workers during the last recession, and those jobs have not come back in many cases or have come back at lower salary levels. There are numerous case histories describing $100,000 managers becoming entrepreneurs struggling to break even or reentering the corporate world at one half to two thirds of their former salaries.

In today's environment, the white-collar worker must develop transportable skills and knowledge within one's functional area. For example, an ideal plant manager today is one who understands and can apply modern quality-control theory, not one whose chief skill is managing people. The ideal inventory-control manager is one who can manipulate data to perform "just in time" techniques efectively. Among the most desirable human resource specialists are those who can design and administer diversity programs. Administrative and people skills are still required, but they must be closely tied to specific expertise for two reasons. First, the skilled white-collar generalist, the "manager" of yesterday, is on the endangered list, having been declared a surplus species at least five years ago. Second, with job security a tenuous proposition at best in today's work environment, and with large numbers of white-collar workers pounding the pavement at any given time, employers are more pointedly specifying the skills and experience they need to fill a vacancy and are using lack of these as a disqualifying factor in the hiring decision. Also, having special skills can help promote one's career with the service companies to whom the corporations are outsourcing as well as enable the white-collar worker to move into a smaller company environment or strike out on his or her own.

Ironically, while this reengineering of the corporate landscape has done much to change the vocabulary and job skills of the white-collar worker, there is growing evidence that downsizing has done little if anything to improve corporate bottom lines. According to a 1995 study by the San Francisco-based Wyatt Co., of 531 downsizing companies, only 46 percent increased earnings, only 34 percent increased productivity, and a mere 33 percent improved customer service. Kenneth DeMeuse, a business professor at the University of Wisconsin in Eau Claire performed a similar study, and found that companies that downsized had no better (and in many cases worse) profit margins than similarly situated companies that did not reengineer their workplaces.

THE AMERICAN CHIEF EXECUTIVE

Our look at executive compensation starts at the top. There is probably no subject in the field of compensation that has been more controversial over the past 10 years than the growing compensation of the chief executive officers of America's top corporations. According to Graef S. Crystal, a vocal critic of CEO pay, the pay of American CEOs increased by 400 percent from 1970 to 1990. This has created a vast gulf between CEO pay and the pay of all other workers.

This gap is evident in the following statistics cited by Crystal in his book, *In Search of Excess,* published in 1991. After adjustment for inflation, the average pay of the American worker declined by 14 percent over the 20-year period from 1970 to 1990 and by 5 percent in the 1980s when the high inflation of the previous decade was brought down to more reasonable levels. At the same time in the same inflation-adjusted dollars, the average CEO pay tripled. In 1974, the typical CEO earned 35 times the pay of the average manufacturing worker. In 1990, that same CEO earned roughly 120 times the pay of the average manufacturing worker and about 150 times the pay of the average worker in manufacturing and service combined. When changes in the tax code are taken into effect, CEO compensation is shown to have increased by 400 percent, while the decrease in real worker pay declined only slightly less—13 percent. According to Crystal, the average CEO in Japan in 1990 earned 16 times the average worker; in Germany, 21 times. Such comparisons raise many issues.

Crystal has cited three trends that are driving American executive compensation to such dizzying heights. According to Crystal:

- U.S. senior executives are paid so much in excess of U.S. workers as to raise questions of equity, and even decency. And the excesses have continued to grow in the 1990s.
- U.S. senior executives are paid far in excess of their counterparts in other countries. And that gap has continued to grow also, although there is some evidence that Canadian and European executives have caught on to the inflated American compensation plans.
- U.S. senior executives are insulating themselves from pay risks to an alarming degree. While CEO effectiveness and compensation plans are being increasingly questioned by large stockholders such as Calpers, there are very few scenarios in corporations today that could devastate the CEO's pay package, while there are an almost infinite number of scenarios that could materialize to enrich the top executive.

At the extremes, the compensation of the best paid CEOs does seem outlandish, although current numbers are paltry when compared to the recent past. Topping the list of the highest compensated CEOs, as published by *Business Week,* is Morton International CEO, Charles Locke, who earned $25.9 million in 1994. This compares with the 1991 champion of short-term compensation, Roberto Goizueta of Coca-Cola, who earned $59 million in salary, bonus, and stock grants, and the 1991 champ of combined short- and long-term compensation, Anthony J. F. O'Reilly of H. J. Heinz, whose combined compensation stemming from salary, bonus, and the exercising of stock options totaled $74.8 million.

Bowing to pressure from the public, as well as from influential shareholders, more corporations in the 1990s have adopted a pay-for-performance approach by shifting a greater proportion of the CEO's compensation into stock options. *Business Week* reports that boards of directors will also be moving toward rewarding chief executives based on a formula that ties compensation to stock appreciation. Compensation via increased stock options or a percentage of stock appreciation can mean even greater upside rewards for CEOs, while their base short-term compensation package may be expected to remain extremely high in most cases. For example, Lawrence Bossidy, chairman of Allied Signal, was working under a contract that provided him with a base pay of $2 million in salary and a guaranteed minimum bonus of $1.85 million. In addition, Bossidy's potential gain on stock options granted is estimated to be more than $100 million over 10 years.

According to *Business Week,* Travelers chairman and CEO Sanford Weill has what is described as one of the most generous compensation packages. Weill, who earned $12.2 million in salary and bonus in 1994, has an unusual "reload" feature in his stock option plan. Each time he exercises an option he receives a new one to replace the one exercised. In 1991 to 1993, Weill received options on 6.9 million shares. In 1994, he was given a reload on about 525,000 of those shares. In contrast, typical CEO option grants range from 100,000 to 250,000 in any given year. This has resulted in estimated "paper profits" to Weill of $185 million from options granted between 1991 and 1993. On the other hand, Travelers' market value under Weill's stewardship has risen from $1 billion in 1986 to $12.3 billion now. Weill's defenders say that he has a right to share in the share owners' gains because without him there would have been no such gain. However, considering that the average 1994 CEO compensation for the 350 largest American companies was $14.8 million, does not Weill's compensation seem excessive by comparison? In his own defense, Weill can show that the company has prospered. That cannot be said of some of his peers on the highest paid list.

The tables on the following pages list the top 20 CEOs in terms of total long-term and short-term pay for 1994, the top 10 non-CEOs compensation-wise, and the top two executives at 100 of America's largest corporations.

Regardless of the debate over executive compensation, the clear trend is ever upward. *The Wall Street Journal* reported this fact in a special supplement on April 13, 1995. The *Journal* attributed the current upward trend to "rising profits, directors' pursuit of outside talent, and reduced public criticism." The *Journal* reported that the median increase in CEO cash compensation in 1994 was 11.4 percent, on top of an 8.1 percent increase in 1993. The average increase for all white-collar workers, by contrast, was a mere 4.2 percent. What seems to be missing from that report and the debate that still rages, if less publicly, is a sense of proportionality on the part of boards and CEOs. Compensation committees of the boards of directors that set CEO compensation packages are usually quick to point out that whatever the pay package, it is required to hold on to the particular executive who would otherwise be moving to greener pastures. But is the average CEO really that mobile? Does an extra half-million dollars, or even a million, mean that much when the CEO is earning so much already? One suspects that ego has more to do with setting the CEO's compensation. CEOs are highly competitive people with huge egos to whom being tops in their industry or tops in compensation in America may be a tangible, satisfying goal. And in general, the bigger the company (especially in corporations with revenues over $400 million), the more lucrative the CEO's compensation package. The CEOs also usually select the compensation consultant who advises the compensation committee.

THE TOP CEOs IN TERMS OF LONG-TERM COMPENSATION

Executive/Company	Estimated Value of Nonexercised Stock Options ($ Million)
Michael Eisner/Walt Disney	171.9
Wayne Calloway/Pepsico	64.6
Lawrence Ellison/Oracle	60.5
Eckhard Pfeiffer/Compaq	54.4
Paul Fireman/Reebok	54.0
Gordon Binder/Amgen	49.6
William McGuire/United Healthcare	49.3
Roberto Goizueta/Coca-Cola	46.4
James Donald/DSC Communications	41.2
Andrew Grove/Intel	36.1
John Tolleson/First USA	35.8
Reuben Mark/Colgate-Palmolive	33.1
Daniel Tully/Merrill Lynch	31.0
Edward McCracken/Silicon Graphics	29.9
Carl Reichardt/Wells Fargo	28.3
Harry Merlo/Louisiana Pacific	27.8
Albert Dunlap/Scott Paper	23.3
John Welch/General Electric	22.6
Roy Vagelos/Merck	21.6

Estimates are based on the stock price at the end of the company's fiscal year.
SOURCE: *Business Week,* April 24, 1995

These days, even executives at levels below CEO are taking home salaries to make even the best-paid baseball player jealous. The most celebrated of lieutenants is of course Michael Ovitz, who left the helm of his own Creative Artists Agency to take a job at Disney valued at approximately $100 million over five years.

HIGHEST PAID LIEUTENANTS

Officer	Company and position	Total compensation (millions)
Millard S. Drexler	The Gap: President and Chief Operating Officer	$15.6
John C. Sites	Bear Stearns & Co.: Executive Vice President	13.6
Warren J. Spector	Bear Stearns & Co.: Executive Vice President	12.8
Constantine L. Hampers	W.R. Grace & Co.: Executive Vice President	11.3
Henry A. Schimber	Coca-Cola Enterprises: President and Chief Operating Officer	10.3

SOURCE: Graef Crystal

Whatever the driving forces behind the typical CEO's appetite for rewards, it seems safe to assume that, while wages or salaries for the average American worker are losing ground to inflation, CEO compensation will continue to far outstrip inflation. A recent headline in *Newsday* summed up the differing perspective between the top of the corporation and the rank and file this way: "Citicorp's Reed Gets a Crummy 5 Percent Raise." The accompanying article points out that John S. Reed, Citicorp's Chairman and CEO, received a raise of less than 5 percent in cash and compensation in 1994, despite the fact that the bank had record earnings. The pay included a $1.275 million annual salary and a cash bonus of $3 million, which means that Mr. Reed's "crummy" raise surely exceeded what 99 percent of Citicorp's workers made all year in 1994. To his credit, Mr. Reed was not quoted as calling his increase "crummy" and he may even admit that there have been years in which he was overcompensated, given Citicorp's past roller-coaster results. But the word does sum up the attitude of many CEOs.

The following tables list the top 20 CEOs in terms of total long-term and short-term pay for 1994, the top 10 non-CEOS compensation-wise, and the top two executives at 100 of America's largest corporations.

THE 20 HIGHEST PAID CEOs . . .

Name	Company	1994 Salary and Bonus	Long-term Compensation (in Thousands)	Total Pay
Charles Locke	Morton International	$12,042	$13,886	$25,928
James Donald	DSC Communications	8,208	15,618	23,826
Carl Reichardt	Wells Fargo	2,671	13,941	16,612
Reuben Mark	Colgate-Palmolive	2,358	13,412	15,770
Eckhard Pfeiffer	Compaq Computers	5,050	9,642	14,692
James Cayne	Bear Stearns	7,666	6,906	14,572
Hugh McColl	Nationsbank	3,000	10,725	13,725
Lawrence Bossidy	Allied Signal	3,633	8,756	12,389
Louis Gerstner	IBM	4,600	7,753	12,353
Sanford Weill	Travelers	3,903	8,266	12,169
Maurice Greenberg	American International Group	3,750	8,330	12,080
Roberto Goizueta	Coca-Cola	4,371	7,683	12,054
Warren Batts	Premark International	2,366	9,611	11,977
Charles Knight	Emerson Electric	2,015	9,738	11,753
James Mellor	General Dynamics	2,691	8,533	11,224
Michael Eisner	Walt Disney	8,019	2,638	10,657
Robert Kidder	Duracell International	1,349	9,280	10,269
W. J. Sanders III	Advanced Micro Devices	4,660	5,773	10,433
Kenneth Lay	Enron	2,486	7,653	10,139
Steven Walske	Parametric Technology	726	8,179	8,905

. . . AND 10 WHO AREN'T CEOs

Samuel Geisberg	Chairman, Parametric Technology	$ 1,402	$16,943	$18,345
Gary Stimac	Senior VP, Compaq Computer	1,000	14,228	15,228
John Chambers	Executive VP, CISCO Systems	345	14,681	15,026
Alan Greenberg	Chairman, Bear Stearns	10,981	3,591	14,572
Lawrence Lasser	President, Putnam	11,320	368	11,688
George Berkow	Executive VP, United Healthcare	1,351	9,141	10,492
William Murray	Chairman, Philip Morris	2,150	6,063	8,213
William Shanahan	President, Colgate-Palmolive	1,297	6,397	7,694
Gerald Montry	Senior VP, DSC Communications	1,747	5,887	7,634
Robert Greenhill	Chairman, Smith Barney	5,080	2,129	7,209

SOURCE: *Business Week*, April 24, 1995. Reprinted by permission.

TOP EXECUTIVE PAY AT MAJOR AMERICAN CORPORATIONS

Company	Type of Business	Title	1994 Compensation (in Thousands)	Long-Term Compensation (in Thousands)
AETNA LIFE & CASUALTY	Nonbank Financial	Chairman, President, CEO	$ 1,075	—
		Executive VP	700	219
ALUMINUM CO. OF AMERICA	Metals and Mining	Chairman, CEO	1,450	1,437
		Executive VP	674	672
AMERICAN BRANDS	Tobacco	Chairman, CEO	2,113	2,333
		President, COO	1,118	1,130
AMERICAN EXPRESS	Nonbank Financial	Chairman, CEO	3,077	1,800
		President	2,255	1,793
AMERITECH	Telecommunications	President, CEO	1,544	244
		Vice Chairman	1,028	264
AMOCO	Natural Resources	Chairman, President, CEO	864	1,020
		Vice Chairman	520	263
AMR	Airlines	Chairman, President, CEO	636	2,792
		Executive VP, CFO	540	2,863
ANHEUSER-BUSCH	Beverages	President, CEO	2,172	—
		Executive VP, CFO	1,091	—
APPLE COMPUTER	Office Equipment and Computers	President, CEO	934	—
		Executive VP	604	—
ATLANTIC RICHFIELD	Natural Resources	Chairman, CEO	2,449	14
		President, COO, CEO	1,438	12
AT&T	Telecommunications	Chairman, CEO	3,499	1,886
		Executive VP	1,725	503

TOP EXECUTIVE PAY AT MAJOR AMERICAN CORPORATIONS

Company	Type of Business	Title	1994 Compensation (in Thousands)	Long-Term Compensation (in Thousands)
BANK AMERICA	Banks and Bank Holding Companies	Chairman, President, CEO	$ 3,142	$ 348
		VP, CFO	1,750	—
BEAR STEARNS	Nonbank Financial	President, CEO	7,660	6,906
		Chairman	10,981	3,591
BOEING	Aerospace	Chairman, CEO	1,445	1,026
		Executive VP	792	571
BRISTOL-MYERS-SQUIBB	Drugs	President, CEO	1,910	332
		Chairman	2,523	570
CAMPBELL SOUP	Food Processing	Chairman, President, CEO	1.810	81
		Senior VP, CFO	600	—
CAPITAL CITIES/ABC	Publishing, Radio, and Television Broadcasting	Chairman, CEO	1,361	7,481
		President, CFO, COO	593	2,194
CATERPILLAR	General and Special Machinery	Chairman, CEO	1,573	192
		Vice Chairman	1,037	1,515
CBS[1]	Publishing, Radio, and Television Broadcasting	Chairman, President, CEO	1,000	987
		President-Subsidiary	2,167	—
CHASE MANHATTAN	Banks and Bank Holding Companies	Chairman, CEO	3.424	1,289
		President-Bank	1,079	516
CHEMICAL BANKING[1]	Banks and Bank Holding Companies	Chairman, CEO	2,496	1,271
		President	1,871	595
CHEVRON	Natural Resources	Chairman, CEO	1,700	1,403
		Vice Chairman	995	787

CHRYSLER	Automotive	Chairman, CEO	3,324	21,830
		President, COO	2,448	869
CHUBB	Nonbank Financial	Chairman, CEO	1,393	289
		President	920	193
CIGNA	Nonbank Financial	Chairman, President, CEO	1,723	222
		Executive VP, CFO	997	118
CITICORP	Banks and Bank Holding	Chairman, CEO	4,275	825
	Companies	Vice Chairman	1,850	524
COCA-COLA	Beverages	Chairman, CEO	4,371	7,682
		President, COO	1,168	2,620
COLGATE-PALMOLIVE	Personal Care Products	Chairman, CEO	2,359	13,412
		President, COO	1,297	6,397
COMPAQ COMPUTER	Office Equipment and	President, CEO	5,650	9,642
	Computers	Senior VP	1,000	14,228
CORNING	Miscellaneous	Chairman, CEO	1,555	1,079
	Manufacturing	President	1,176	791
DEERE	General and Special	Chairman CEO	1,659	1,719
	Machinery	President, COO	1,091	1,409
DELTA AIRLINES	Airlines	Chairman, President, CEO	484	—
		Executive VP-Operations	260	—
DIGITAL EQUIPMENT	Office Equipment and	President, CEO	900	—
	Computers	Vice President	978	—
DOW CHEMICAL	Chemicals	President, CEO	1,635	1,590
		Senior VP	900	459
DUPONT	Chemicals	Chairman, CEO	2,025	1,693
		Vice Chairman	1,448	698
EASTMAN KODAK	Leisure Time Industries	Chairman, President, CEO	3,901	2.064
		Executive VP	1,107	—
EXXON	Natural Resources	Chairman, CEO	1,866	1,614
		President	1,370	1,740

TOP EXECUTIVE PAY AT MAJOR AMERICAN CORPORATIONS

Company	Type of Business	Title	1994 Compensation (in Thousands)	Long-Term Compensation (in Thousands)
FEDERAL EXPRESS	Service Industries	Chairman, President, CEO	$ 1,204	—
		Executive VP	949	$ 510
FIRST CHICAGO	Banks and Bank Holding Companies	Chairman, CEO	1,769	3,067
		Executive VP	921	2,576
FORD MOTOR COMPANY	Automotive	President, CEO	7,733	267
		Vice Chairman	4,613	974
GENERAL DYNAMICS	Aerospace	Chairman, CEO	2,691	8,533
		Executive VP	1,242	279
GENERAL ELECTRIC	Conglomerates	Chairman, CEO	4,350	3,259
		Vice Chairman	2,125	—
GENERAL MILLS	Food Processing	Chairman, CEO	850	60
		Vice Chairman	706	68
GENERAL MOTORS	Automotive	President, CEO	3,425	2,689
		Executive VP	1,800	1,417
GEORGIA-PACIFIC	Paper and Forest Products	Chairman, CEO	3,686	466
		Executive VP	3,125	—
GILLETTE	Personal Care Products	Chairman, CEO	2,000	2,645
		Executive VP	827	273
GOODYEAR TIRE & RUBBER	Tires and Rubber	Chairman, CEO	2,190	1,014
		Vice Chairman, President, COO	1,483	633
GTE	Telecommunications	Chairman, CEO	2,004	698
		Vice Chairman, President GTE-Tele.	1,526	398

HALIBURTON	Oil Service and Supply	Chairman, CEO	1,200	—
		Vice Chairman, COO	843	463
HERSHEY FOOD	Food Processing	Chairman, CEO	897	357
		President, COO	678	276
HEWLETT-PACKARD	Office Equipment and Computers	Chairman, President, CEO	1,179	2,182
		Exec. VP, CFO	6,861	1,045
HEINZ (H.J.)	Food Processing	Chairman, President, CEO	895	824
		Senior VP	425	396
HILTON HOTELS	Food and Lodging	Chairman, CEO	1,000	—
		President, COO	942	—
HONEYWELL	Instruments	Chairman, CEO	1,062	109
		President, COO	974	—
IBM	Office Equipment and Computers	Chairman, CEO	4,600	7,753
		Vice Chairman	2,300	—
INTEL	Electrical, Electronics	President, CEO	2,102	—
		Executive VP, COO	4,555	—
INTERNATIONAL PAPER	Paper and Paper Products	Chairman, CEO	2,069	1,212
		Executive VP	800	430
ITT	Conglomerates	Chairman, President, CEO	4,249	—
		Executive VP	1,263	—
JOHNSON & JOHNSON	Drugs	Chairman, CEO	1,893	—
		Vice Chairman	1,562	529
J.P. MORGAN	Banks and Bank Holding Companies	Chairman, CEO	2,310	1,959
		President	1,950	1,817
KELLOGG	Food Processing	Chairman, CEO	1,489	—
		Executive VP	717	—
LEOWS	Nonbank Financial	Co-Chairman, Co-COO	1,937	26
		President, COO	697	20
MARRIOTT	Food and Lodging	Chairman, President, CEO	1,434	134
		Executive VP	835	148

TOP EXECUTIVE PAY AT MAJOR AMERICAN CORPORATIONS

Company	Type of Business	Title	1994 Compensation (in Thousands)	Long-Term Compensation (in Thousands)
MATTELL	Leisure Time Industries	Chairman, CEO	$ 1,782	$ 5,775
		President, COO	1,361	3,245
MCDONNELL DOUGLAS	Aerospace	Chairman, CEO	1,610	—
		President, CEO	979	4,657
McGRAW-HILL	Publishing, Radio, and Television	Chairman, CEO	1,603	1,046
	Boradcasting	President, COO	966	489
MCI COMMUNICATIONS	Telecommunications	Chairman, CEO	1,819	896
		President, COO	970	713
MERRILL LYNCH	Nonbank Financial	Chairman, CEO	4,840	1,059
		President, COO	3,200	626
MINNESOTA MINING & MFG.	Miscellaneous Manufacturing	Chairman, CEO	1,226	1,704
		Executive VP	699	948
MOBIL	Natural Resources	Chairman, President, CEO, COO	1,408	1,460
		Chairman, CEO	367	5,220
MOTOROLA	Electrical, Electronics	Vice Chairman, CEO	1,985	—
		President, COO	1,490	2,964
NEW YORK TIMES	Publishing, Radio, and Television	Chairman, CEO	1,365	336
	Broadcasting	President	1,101	267
NIKE	Textiles, Apparel	Chairman, CEO	968	—
		President, COO	792	—
OCCIDENTAL PETROLEUM	Natural Resources	President, CEO	3,419	2,421
		Executive VP	1,155	425

PEPSICO	Beverages	Chairman, CEO	3,064	—
		Vice Chairman	1,427	1,340
PHILIP MORRIS	Tobacco	Chairman, President, CEO	1,904	5,973
		Chairman	2,150	6,063
PHILLIPS PETROLEUM	Natural Resources	Chairman, CEO	1,581	345
		President, COO	742	309
PROCTER & GAMBLE[1]	Personal Care Products	Chairman, CEO	2,290	565
		President	1,614	1,093
RALSTON PURINA	Food Processing	Chairman, CEO	1,340	—
		Vice President	464	—
READER'S DIGEST ASSOCIATION	Publishing, Radio, and Television Broadcasting	Chairman, CEO	2,170	873
		President, COO	1,059	491
REEBOK INTERNATIONAL	Textiles, Apparel	Chairman, President, CEO	2,000	—
		Executive VP, CFO	1,108	2,517
RJR NABISCO HOLDINGS	Tobacco	Chairman, CEO	5,061	—
		Chairman, CEO, Subsidiaries	2,798	255
SALOMON	Nonbank Financial	Chairman, CEO	1,000	4,369
		Executive VP	1,048	3,042
SARA LEE	Food Processing	Chairman, CEO	1,736	237
		Vice Chairman, CFO	927	—
SCHWAB (CHARLES)	Nonbank Financial	Chairman, CEO	3,273	—
		President, COO	1,321	1,578
SCOTT PAPER	Paper and Paper Products	Chairman, CEO	3,576	3,855
		Senior VP	599	2,316
SEARS ROEBUCK	Retailing (Nonfood)	Chairman, President, CEO	1,658	—
		Chairman, CEO-Subsidiary	2,080	—

TOP EXECUTIVE PAY AT MAJOR AMERICAN CORPORATIONS

Company	Type of Business	Title	1994 Compensation (in Thousands)	Long-Term Compensation (in Thousands)
TEXACO[1]	Natural Resources	President, CEO	$ 1,532	$ 1,279
		Chairman	1,033	707
TEXAS INSTRUMENTS	Electrical, Electronics	Chairman, President, CEO	1,928	2,090
		Vice Chairman	995	921
TIME WARNER	Publishing, Radio, and Television Broadcasting	President, CO-CEO	5,180	—
		Executive VP, CFO	2,011	—
UNION CARBIDE	Chemicals	Chairman, CEO	1,838	4,129
		President, COO	953	340
UNITED HEALTHCARE	Services Industries	CEO	2,687	0
		Executive VP, CFO	1,351	9,141
UPJOHN[1]	Drugs	Chairman, CEO	1,531	587
		President, COO	911	153
WALT DISNEY	Leisure Time Industries	Chairman, CEO	8,019	2,638
		President, COO	2,677	—
WARNER LAMBERT	Drugs	Chairman, CEO	1,686	2,554
		President, COO	1,117	125
WMX TECHNOLOGIES	Services Industries	Chairman, CEO	2,597	—
		President, COO	2,029	—
XEROX	Office Equipment and Computers	CEO	3,392	3,433
		Executive VP	1,958	360

[1]May include data from a preliminary proxy.
SOURCE: Corporations proxy statements, 1995.

THE AMERICAN EXECUTIVE COMPENSATION SYSTEM

Lest our look at executive compensation become totally jaundiced by the megapay of the corporate elite, we will now take a more balanced look at executive compensation.

The Total Compensation Package

For the top officers of every corporation, salary is only one aspect of what is referred to as the total compensation package.

TYPICAL EXECUTIVE COMPENSATION PACKAGES IN LARGE CORPORATIONS

	Top Management	Middle Management	Lower Management
Title	Chief Operating Officer	Division Manager	Division Controller
Base Salary	$750,000	$200,000 to $300,000	$80,000 to $120,000
Annual Bonus Expected Maximum	50 percent of base to 100 percent of base	40 percent of base to 80 percent of base	25 percent of base to 50 percent of base
Capital Accumulation	25,000 nonqualified stock options plus 50,000 performance units	7,500 nonqualified stock options	2,000 nonqualified stock options
Retirement Benefits	Company pension plus supplemental benefits to equal 65 percent of final average 5-year gross pay (salary plus bonus)	40 to 50 percent of final average 5-year gross pay	40 to 50 percent of final average 5-year gross pay
Life Insurance	Three times base	1.5 times base	1.5 times base
Major Medical and Dental	Company group plan plus supplemental	Company group plan	Company group plan

TYPICAL EXECUTIVE COMPENSATION PACKAGES IN LARGE CORPORATIONS

	Top Management	Middle Management	Lower Management
Perks	Car, luncheon club, country club, personal tax and financial planning advice	Possibly a car, a luncheon club or a country club	None

SOURCE: Peat, Marwick, Mitchell & Co.

EXECUTIVE COMPENSATION: AN ACTUAL SAMPLE

(Executive recruited into company)

Age:	53
Company:	Fashion industry related, with $650 million in sales
Contract:	3 years, 8 months
Annual salary:	$300,000
Front-end bonus:	$175,000 with cash or deferred-payment option. (Cash was taken.)
Annual incentive bonus:	0 to 50 percent of salary, determined by success in meeting mutually determined goals.
Stock grant:	30,000 shares given at market value of NYSE closing price on the first day of work.
Pension:	Guaranteed annual pension of 65 percent of final year's pay starting at age 65. No vesting for first three years of employment; 40 percent vesting at start of fourth year; additional added vesting at 10 percent annually thereafter.

Miscellaneous:	Personal choice of leased, Cadillac-value car, all expenses included. Membership in luncheon or athletic club of choice.
Insurance:	Fully paid medical insurance; plus all other medical expenses for family not covered with maximum of $10,000 a year. Group life insurance of $750,000. Long-term disability insurance of $5,000 a month, exclusive of social security benefits. Travel insurance: $600,000.
Personal accounting and legal services:	Up to $5,000 a year.
Termination Agreement:	If contract not renewed by company, executive receives $50,000 a year for ten years; plus additional vesting in pension plan to equal 6 years, or 60 percent of benefits at age 65.
Relocation:	All expenses with mortgage provision to keep payments constant, company also agreed to lend up to $100,000 as down payment with interest rate of 5 percent. No principal payment for three years at which point the loan could be rolled over.

SOURCE: Wells Management. Reprinted by permission.

Elements of the Compensation Package

Executive compensation depends, predictably enough, on the size of the corporation and the kind of business that it does. In theory, the most talented people end up working for the largest companies, so they usually earn the most money. Historically, the automobile, oil, and food industries paid their top people the most, but today aerospace electronics, communications, computers, and entertainment are right up there with them and may have surpassed them in some cases. The common elements of these compensation packages are described below.

SALARIES AND BONUSES

While every person's contract is different, almost all of them contain provision for compensation over and above base salary. The most common form of additional cash payment is the annual bonus, which is at least partially tied to how well the company performs. Most top executives, however, have minimum bonus clauses that pay off no matter what the record.

Different companies use bonuses in different ways. In some firms, base salaries are deliberately kept low, with extra compensation as high as 200 percent or more of base pay. This ties performance directly to compensation. In other companies, a higher base salary is set to pay for average-to-good executive performance and bonus compensation used to reward outstanding achievement. Still another method is to tie the bonus to a five-year performance goal, which if met, brings a very big payoff.

STOCK OPTIONS AND STOCK APPRECIATION RIGHTS

Nine out of ten companies provide stock-related plans, but usually only 1 to 3 percent of the company's employees receive these perks. Stock options offer the recipient the right to purchase a specified amount of stock at today's price at some future date. The time limit usually set for exercising the option is almost always ten years with restrictions placed on exercising the options during the first three or four years. If the stock price rises, the executive can make a substantial profit by exercising his or her options at the appropriate time. If the stock price declines, he or she simply chooses not to exercise the option, and loses nothing. A stock appreciation right is usually part of a long-term plan whereby a unit of so-called phantom stock is held at a specific market price for an executive. If the stock price rises above that level, the executive can cash in on the gain without having to put up any money. With stock options, the executive must provide cash for the purchase of the shares.

DEFERRED PAYMENTS

It is not uncommon today for executives to receive deferred payments other than stock options as a part of their cash compensation to be paid in future years. This amount is normally expressed as a percentage of base compensation, typically ranging from 25 to 50 percent of combined salary plus cash bonus. This is not a deferral of a portion of those amounts. Rather, it is an addition.

RETIREMENT PAY AND TERMINATION PAY

Even when a successful executive comes to the end of his career, the possibility of hefty earnings does not necessarily fade away. In addition to their pensions and retirement plans, many executives have deferred payments still owed to them, sometimes tied to stock and sometimes tied to base compensation. At the very top of the executive ladder, moreover, retired executives get themselves hired on as consultants to the corporations they just left. For instance, when Harold F. Geneen retired as CEO of ITT almost a decade ago, he received a retirement package of over $450,000. It consisted of $250,000 for consulting fees, $112,000 in deferred payments provided by his employment contract, and $130,000 provided by the company's retirement plan. Today every chairman who retires receives at least $2 million.

However, the biggest retirement perk for executives is when companies enlarge the base of compensation to include both base salary and bonuses to the base to which the earned retirement percentage is applied.

In a relatively new method of compensating a retiring CEO, RJR Nabisco reportedly bought Charles Harper an annuity estimated at a principal amount of $11 million. Since the annuity was taxable, RJR also paid Harper's $5.5 million tax bill. This munificence was in addition to his cash compensation of $10.5 million for 1994 and his regular pension payout of $1 million annually.

Compensation consultants commented that this arrangement is unusual. Normally such a fund is set up in-house and is taxable only when proceeds flow to the retired executive. The risk to the beneficiary is that the fund can be terminated if he is fired or leaves of his own volition prior to retirement. In this case, Harper owns the annuity. A similar annuity was set up for Louis Gerstner while he was at RJR. Presumably, he took it with him to IBM.

William Alley, CEO of American Brands, is one of the few other CEOs with a similar arrangement. His annuity is estimated to be worth $9.5 million and American Brands is said to have paid about $4.7 million in taxes for Alley.

What if the executive does not last in the corporation until the day of his or her retirement? Today most executives have termination pay clauses written into their contracts. These usually pay one to two years' salary if the executive is fired within three to five years. This relatively new form of executive compensation is a result of the increasingly precarious nature of life at the top of the corporate ladder. Failure to meet set goals for whatever reasons, "bad chemistry" with the board of directors, and the current terrible business climate are all cited as reasons for the sharp increase in the numbers of executives who have been booted out after periods as short as a few months. In this there is really no distinction between competency and incompetency. Short of committing a felony, the executive fired for failing to perform is treated no differently from one who is laid off because of an acquisition.

Finally, many fired executives also get a chance to work for their former company as management consultants. Although the rationale always given is that the fired executive is an excellent planner but a poor implementer, the true reason for creating the job is to secure the executive's secrecy in confidential corporate affairs.

PERKS: HIDDEN COMPENSATION

Derived from the word "perquisite," whose meaning has evolved since the Renaissance from something that could be demanded to indicate something given over and above what is deserved, "perk" has become a standard part of today's business language, especially at the executive level. Every manager from the middle of the corporate pyramid to the top receives some kind of extra rewards in addition to salary and bonus. The most common perks given to executives today include:

- Company car and free parking facilities (the very top executives in large corporations always have chauffeurs)
- Free use of corporate-owned apartments and vacation homes
- Country club memberships and fees
- Luncheon club membership and/or expense account for entertaining
- Personal financial counseling
- Low-interest loans
- Travel expenses for spouse on business trips
- Free insurance: life insurance up to $1 million and more, 100 percent medical and dental coverage, up to $5,000 a month disability
- Pension: up to 65 percent of the average pay over the final five years of work

Not too long ago perks were considered simply tax-free amenities that helped to ensure the loyalty of the corporation's most prized employees. In today's highly unstable business world, however, perks have become less of a factor in attracting people or convincing employees to stay. Perks still are expected and once given they are difficult to take away. Still, in the new era of cost cutting many companies have taken steps not only to trim executive jobs, but also to slim down executive perks. The table below depicts the overall status of executive perks in the United States.

	Percent of Companies Offering Perk	Percent of Employees Eligible
Airline VIP-club Membership	34	1.2
Chauffeur Service	40	0.1
Communications Equipment	22	0.2
Company Car	68	1.1
Company Plane	63	0.3
WATS Line (Home Use)	11	0.3
Country Club Membership	55	0.5
Estate Planning	52	0.6
Executive Dining Room	30	1.3
Financial Counseling	64	0.6
Financial Seminars	11	2.8
First-class Air Travel	62	0.7
Health Club Membership	19	0.7
Home Security System	25	0.2
Income Tax Preparation	63	0.7
Legal Counseling	6	0.6
Loans (Low-Interest/Interest-Free)	9	3.2
Luncheon Club Membership	55	0.8
Personal Liability Insurance	50	1.0
Physical Exam	91	6.5
Reserved Parking	32	1.0
Spouse Travel	47	1.0

GOLDEN PARACHUTES

During the acquisition and buyout fever of the 1980s, golden parachutes became a subject that sparked as much debate as the level of executive compensation does today. Corporations faced with takeover and those that may have felt vulnerable drew up special "termination compensation agreements," more commonly known as "golden parachutes," for top executives. The purpose of a parachute is to cushion the fall of a corporate executive pushed out the door as a result of such action. The cushion is usually a deep pile of cash and benefits. Two to three years' salary and, in some cases, hefty bonuses are now common.

Golden parachutes have made some executives millionaires many times over. They have also raised substantial issues concerning conflict of interest and greed. For instance, F. Ross Johnson, CEO of RJR Nabisco, and E. A. Horrigan, vice chairman of the same company, reportedly received parachutes estimated at $53.8 million and $45.7 million, respectively, when the company was sold to Kolberg, Kravis and Roberts, a New York investment firm. The sale was actually set in motion when a management group led by Johnson made an offer to do a leveraged buyout at a price below what was considered fair market value and substantially below the price finally realized. The insiders' offer may well have been accepted without question had it not been for a few diligent outside directors. In the end, the shareholders of RJR Nabisco realized higher value, but the whole affair raised some serious questions. For instance, can a group of executives objectively evaluate alternatives to selling their company when they know they will personally profit handsomely from the sale? Or when they are personally involved in the bidding? Does the existence of a golden parachute represent a temptation to put the company into play? Also, can other shareholders expect their boards, like the RJR board, to stand up and ensure a maximized price in other instances?

EXCESSIVE EXECUTIVE PERKS

In the not too distant past when reports of executive abuse of privilege in the form of excessive perks would surface, corporate boards seemed to look the other way. Ross Johnson was legend in the 1980s for his use of corporate jets to suit personal whims as well as excessive use of other perks at company expense, e.g., flying his personal chef all over the world. However, the unrivaled king of the use of perks was Steve Ross, the late CEO of Time-Warner. Ross lavished gifts on his corporate officers and directors, friends, and himself all paid for by the company treasury. Ross reportedly even paid (with Time-Warner funds) for expensive art selected by his wife to hang in their apartment. Given that a strong CEO can dominate a company board and that the CEO's business and personal persona frequently merge in his day-to-day activities, it is relatively easy for directors to rationalize almost any expenditure as being for the good of the company. In the cases above, the directors did just that.

In 1995 in a very highly publicized case at Morrison Knudsen, an engineering and construction company based in Boise, directors took a different tack and staged a coup against the CEO. The directors forced the resignation of CEO William Agee. This case was said to epitomize two principles of CEO power. First, once he is installed, it is extremely difficult to dislodge a CEO. Mr. Agee was said to have managed the company into near insolvency, yet his compensation kept rising, and until sometime in 1994 there had not been a whimper of protest from the board which consisted, with one exception, of Agee's friends. Second, a CEO with selling talents and a friendly, docile board has a license to abuse corporate resources for his own comfort and aggrandisement: Agee was reported to be running the company a majority of the time from his estate in Pebble Beach, CA. He reportedly spent company money ($7,050) for a near-life-size portrait of himself and his wife which hung at company headquarters in Boise. He is also said to have had Morrison Knudsen pay for legal expenses incurred by his wife, to have used the corporate jet for personal purposes on many occasions, and to have charged the company for many of the expenses associated with maintaining his home in California. Still, Mr. Agee lost his job because of bad business results and a loss of confidence with his senior managers, and not because he had plunged his hand too deeply into the corporate till. Even though rumors of Mr. Agee's excesses had existed for years, it is doubtful that his board would have pulled back the extra perks that he had taken on his own as long as profits continued to flow.

Executive Compensation in Mid-sized Companies

The compensation statistics below are from a study of mid-sized companies in California conducted by *California Business* and KPMG Peat Marwick published in 1990. While some allowances must be made for regional differences, the results present a comprehensive view of compensation in companies with $100 million of revenue or less. While this study has not been updated, we believe the relative differences to be valid still.

TOTAL CEO COMPENSATION BY COMPANY SIZE[1]

Revenues (Millions of Dollars)	Percentile (Thousands) 25th	50th	75th
5–10	$105.0	$150.0	$217.3
10.1–15	105.8	143.0	199.8
15.1–25	120.0	163.0	250.0
25.1–50	123.0	175.0	309.0
50.1–100	168.0	220.0	295.0

[1]Financial institutions excluded.

TOTAL CEO COMPENSATION BY INDUSTRY

Industry	Percentile (Thousands) 25th	50th	75th
High-Tech Manufacturing	$120.0	$170.0	$247.0
Other Manufacturing	110.0	144.0	210.0
Wholesale/Retail Trade	93.0	132.0	223.0
Financial Services	92.0	151.5	192.8
Other	108.8	154.0	225.0

SENIOR EXECUTIVES TOTAL COMPENSATION BY COMPANY SIZE

Median Compensation Revenues (Millions of Dollars)	COO	(Thousands) CFO	CMO[1]
5–10	$ 87.5	$ 60.0	$ 70.0
10.1–15	90.0	70.0	83.0
15.1–25	113.8	78.5	90.0
25.1–50	110.0	90.0	100.0
50.1–100	123.5	104.0	117.0

[1]COO, Chief Operating Officer; CFO, Chief Financial Officer; CMO, Chief Marketing Officer.

SENIOR EXECUTIVES TOTAL COMPENSATION BY INDUSTRY

Industry	COO	Median Compensation (Thousands) CFO	CMO
High-Tech Manufacturing	$104.0	$90.0	$95.0
Other Manufacturing	100.0	70.0	92.5
Wholesale/Retail Trade	92.0	66.5	80.0
Financial Services	64.0	76.0	62.0
Other	117.5	91.0	86.0

PROFILE OF THE MEDIUM-SIZED COMPANY CEO	
Median Total Compensation	$150,000
Median Base Salary	$120,000
Percent Receiving Bonus	70.9
Median Bonus (of those receiving one)	$45,000
Percent Receiving Long-Term Incentives	30.5
Median Age	51
Median Years as CEO	8
Median Years with Company	14
Median Number of Positions with Company	2
Median Number of Employers Last 10 Years	1
Formal Titles:	
Percent CEO	50.9
Percent Chairman of the Board	20.9
Percent President	69.8
Percent Shareholders in Company	69.7
Percent Owning 50 Percent or More of Company	26.5
Percent Owning 100 Percent of Company	9.5

Compensation of the Chief Financial Officer

CFO MEAN COMPENSATION BY COMPANY SIZE

Company Revenues (millions of dollars)	Base Salary	Bonus (Thousands)	Total Compensation
<10	64.5	17.2	81.7
10–14.9	70.4	21.6	92.0
15–24.9	75.0	16.5	91.5
25–49.9	90.9	28.9	119.8
50–99.9	104.1	33.4	137.5
100–249.9	125.0	36.9	161.9
250–499.9	148.6	53.4	202.0
500–999.9	164.4	67.9	232.3
more than 999.9	174.9	56.4	231.3

SOURCE: *CFO Magazine,* June 1994. Reprinted by permission.

CFO PAY AS A FUNCTION OF INDUSTRY

Industry	Salary	Bonus	Total Compensation
	Thousands		
Agribusiness	83.5	16.7	100.2
Business Services	89.6	52.8	142.4
Communications	110.0	22.2	132.2
Construction	99.9	30.5	130.4
Education	109.5	5.0	114.5
Entertainment/Media	166.2	22.0	188.2
Financial Services	108.7	40.4	149.1
Health Care	108.9	23.0	131.9
High Tech	110.0	47.1	157.1
Insurance	127.8	45.7	173.5
Manufacturing (Nondurables)	114.6	34.2	148.8
Manufacturing (Durables)	101.8	32.5	134.3
Oil & Gas	115.3	89.2	204.5
Utilities	124.4	49.6	174.0
Real Estate	113.5	43.8	157.3
Retailing	123.3	38.3	161.6
Transportation	111.4	27.4	138.8
Wholesale/Distribution	91.3	30.1	121.4

SOURCE: *CFO Magazine,* June 1994. Reprinted by permission.

According to *CFO Magazine,* the top-earning chief financial officers in terms of cash earnings in 1993 earned between $400,000 and a little over $1.1 million. The 12 highest paid financial executives in 1993 and their cash compensation are listed below.

TOP EARNING CFOs, 1993

Name	Company	Base Salary	Cash Bonus	Total Annual Company
Joseph T. Casey	Litton Industries	$500,011	$635,000	$1,135,011
Gary C. Valade	Chrysler	325,417	680,000	1,005,417
Ronald J. Arnault	Atlantic Richfield	650,780	320,000	970,780
Jerry C. Ritter	Anheuser-Busch	523,000	433,000	956,000
Robert J. Weeks	Mobil	575,000	380,000	955,000
William C. Lusk Jr.	Shaw Industries	519,750	400,000	919,750
Stanley A. Seneker	Ford Motor	396,250	400,000	796,250
Robert G. Dettmer	Pepsico	445,769	302,200	747,969

TOP EARNING CFOs, 1993

Name	Company	Base Salary	Cash Bonus	Total Annual Company
Hans G. Storr	Philip Morris	565,000	168,000	733,000
John W. Baxter	AlliedSignal	387,500	345,000	732,500
Robert M. Hernandez	USX	375,000	325,000	700,000
C. Richard Wagoner Jr.	General Motors	675,000	0	675,000

SOURCE: *CFO Magazine,* June 1994 (as disclosed in 1993 fiscal year proxy statements). Reprinted by permission.

Boards of Directors

Every large corporation has a board of directors whose essential function is to give advice and consent to the management team. The power and influence of this board vary from company to company, ranging from purely ceremonial to almost dictatorial. The size and composition of most boards are, however, fairly uniform.

According to the Korn/Ferry annual survey, the average company had 12 directors in 1994, the same number as in 1990. On average, three directors come from within the company and the other nine come from outside. These outside directors usually have very similar backgrounds and experience. Senior executives of other large corporations sat on 82 percent of all boards of directors; retired corporate executives sat on 88 percent. Former government officials sat on 52 percent, and commercial bankers sat on 34 percent. Women's presence on corporate boards continues to grow, as 63 percent of boards have at least one woman director, up from 52 percent in 1987.

Most corporations pay their directors an annual retainer (averaging $22,423 in 1994) as well as a per-meeting fee ($1,124). Many companies pay the directors the fee even if they don't attend the meetings. Total compensation for directors was $31,415 in 1994, up from $26,190 just four years earlier. More than 90 percent of the companies in the Korn/Ferry study paid directors additional amounts for serving on any of several board committees. Committee fees averaged about $1,000 per meeting; committee chairmen generally receive a retainer of $4,000 to $5,000 per year. When committee fees are taken into account, board members averaged $39,707 in total corporate largesse for their services. Half the boards surveyed allow directors to defer their fees until retirement (mostly for tax purposes), 45 percent provide a pension or retirement plan in addition to this deferred income, and a third provide stock options and/or stock grants.

AVERAGE PAYMENTS TO MEMBERS OF BOARDS OF DIRECTORS, 1994

Type and Size of Company	Annual Retainer Plus per-Meeting Fee	Committee Meeting Fee[1]	Committee Chairman's Retainer	Total Annual Compensation[2]
Industrials				
$600 million–$999 million	$25,490	$ 902	$2,995	$34,936
$1 billion–$2.999 billion	29,583	917	3,673	36,029
$3 billion–$4.999 billion	34,791	993	4,186	42,594
$5 billion and over	41,111	1,048	6,259	49,700
Banks	26,866	845	4,515	37,074
Other Financial Institutions	36,390	4,058	7,303	49,705
Insurance Companies	34,437	935	3,811	44,200
Retailers	32,245	1,022	4,811	36,452
Service Companies	30,839	1,034	3,946	40,505
Average of all Companies	**$31,415**	**$ 947**	**$4,610**	**$39,707**

[1]For regular committee members. Committee chairmen receive slightly higher committee fees in addition to their annual committee retainer.
[2]Based on responses of outside directors; proxies do not state this information.
SOURCE: Korn/Ferry International, *Board of Directors, 22nd Annual Study, 1995*. Reprinted by permission.

Some celebrated examples made even more money for sitting on corporate boards. At American Express, directors including Henry Kissinger received $64,000 retainers in 1994, plus 1,000 shares of stock, an annual $30,000 pension, $50,000 in free life insurance, $300,000 of accidental death coverage, and a half-million-dollar gift to a chosen charity upon death. If this were not enough, board committee chairmen received an additional $10,000. All of this beneficence is needed in the eyes of the company to attract and retain a top-notch slate of directors. At Baltimore Gas & Electric, nonemployee directors receive lifetime pensions equal to their annual retainer of $18,000; at Sprint, directors get a $35,000 annual retainer paid for up to 10 years *after they retire from the board.* In anticipation of shareholder protests, some companies are changing their directors' compensation programs. Travelers now pays its directors a flat fee. But the amount, $75,000, isn't likely to keep any of its directors from buying that new Range Rover this year.

So what do these companies get in return for showering their directors with amounts of money that must be considered extravagant by even white-collar standards but are a pittance when compared to the annual compensation packages these directors receive at their own companies? Companies in the Korn/Ferry survey averaged eight board meetings a year in 1994, up from seven in 1993. Outside directors spent an average of 163 hours per year attending, preparing to attend, and traveling to and from board meetings. That comes out to roughly $244 per hour per director. For the company, the costs are even higher, since average payments don't include the amounts spent on life insurance, pension plans, charitable donations, and flying the directors to company headquarters eight times a year. This last item can be quite expensive, especially considering that 19 percent of boards had at least one non–U.S. citizen as a director.

HUMAN RESOURCES

Human resources, once known simply as personnel, encompasses all areas of a company's dealings and relationships with its employees, from the hiring of new staff members to planning programs to assist people when they leave the company. Human resources also covers: training, compensation and benefits (including but not limited to health care), labor relations, corporate safety and security, and in many companies in-house communications.

More than 400,000 individuals are employed in this field, which has grown dramatically in status and importance over the last decade. And despite all the corporate downsizing in the 1990s, the experts forecast above-average job opportunities in human resources over the next few years. That's because more and more corporate managers and executives are beginning to realize that the best run, most successful large companies in America are those that take special care of their employees' needs. In these corporations, the personnel function is a service for, not just an obligation to, the workers. How best to utilize the talents of the staff and how to win its loyalty are functions more appreciated and valued by the best places. Because of their success, these attitudes are likely to spread.

The increasing importance of the training staff within human resources departments is one example of management's changing views. Teaching standardized company procedures to all levels of employees, from clerks to middle-level managers, helps corporations cope with high turnover rates and frees veteran employees from an instructional burden that often hampers their own work. Frequently, employers look for people with educational or teaching backgrounds to fill these slots. "The need and importance of keeping workers abreast of changing technologies has required companies to maintain and enforce their entire corporate training and development programs," says Helen Bensimon of the American Society of Training. In addition, many companies hire training people on a freelance basis (see the separate entry called "The Training Staff" in this section).

The field of human resources is constantly changing, but between now and the end of the century, the positions most in demand will be compensation specialists, employee benefits administrators, and employee relations administrators. The area of cultural diversity, once limited to fulfilling affirmative action obligations, is expected to grow significantly in importance as it deals with the growing influx of foreigners in the workplace and the interests and needs of minority workers.

Salaries in human resources continue to vary widely, probably because of the variety of positions contained under this grouping—the following chart provides salary information for a total of 58 different positions in human resources—and because of the variety of industries in which these people work. The median 1992 salary for all specialists in human resources was $32,000; for managers it was $37,000. The lowest 10 percent earned under $17,000 while the highest 10 percent topped $64,000. Salaries for personnel specialists in the federal government start at $18,300 for a person with a bachelor's degree and three years of experience in human resources.

Below are a wide range of salary levels compiled from several sources, including the federal and state governments, and the Society for Human Resources Management. In conjunction with William M. Mercer Inc. of Deerfield, Illinois, the Society produces the best and most accurate survey of salaries in personnel every year, as well as an excellent set of job descriptions and salary information for mostly large corporate personnel departments.

AVERAGE ANNUAL SALARIES IN CORPORATE HUMAN RESOURCE DEPARTMENTS

Title	Average Salary	Average Minimum[1]	Average Maximum[1]
Vice President, Administration[2]	$153,900	$118,700	$189,300
Top Human Resource Management Executive[2] (with industrial relations)	148,800	115,700	180,000
Top Human Resource Management Executive[2] (without industrial relations)	130,200	100,300	160,900
International Top Human Resource Management Executive[2]	115,300	80,900	133,000
Total Top Quality Executive	100,800	72,300	113,500
Top Corporate Labor/Industrial Relations Executive[2]	100,100	75,700	115,900
Top Corporate Organizational Development Executive	96,000	70,900	112,000
Executive Compensation Manager	92,500	69,000	126,000
Top Corporate Compensation and Benefits Executive	88,400	67,200	106,100

AVERAGE ANNUAL SALARIES IN CORPORATE HUMAN RESOURCE DEPARTMENTS

Title	Average salary	Average Minimum[1]	Average Maximum[1]
Top Division, Subsidiary or Regional Human Resource Executive	$ 87,000	$ 70,000	$111,100
Top Corporate Employee Relations Executive	80,600	61,600	96,800
International Compensation and Benefits Manager	78,100	56,700	88,900
Human Resource Planning Manager	75,300	56,400	89,100
Top Corporate Security Manager	73,700	57,900	90,000
Labor Relations Supervisor	70,900	54,100	82,600
Top Corporate Safety Manager	70,400	54,200	84,100
Training and Organizational Development Manager	70,400	53,800	84,300
Human Resource Director (in small organization)	69,700	57,200	87,900
Compensation Manager	69,700	53,900	84,300
Employee Benefits Manager	68,300	54,200	84,200
Total Quality Manager	68,000	52,900	81,700
Equal Employment Opportunity Manager	65,100	52,800	82,600
Management Development Manager	64,400	51,100	80,400
Plant/Branch Human Resource Manager (union facility)	64,300	51,900	79,900
Group Insurance Manager	64,000	50,800	79,000
Human Resource Information System Manager	61,600	48,000	74,800
Employee Communications Director	60,800	47,800	74,100
Employment and Recruiting Manager	59,900	48,300	75,300
Employee Assistance Program Manager	59,700	45,700	69,500
Plant/Branch Human Resource Manager (nonunion facility)	59,700	46,900	73,200
Employee Training Manager	57,700	46,300	72,400
Work and Family Program Manager	56,600	44,700	71,600
Labor Relations Generalist	53,000	41,500	62,400
Managerial and Executive Recruitment Specialist	50,700	41,600	65,900
Safety/Security Supervisor	48,900	40,000	61,100
Manager, Office Services	48,800	41,900	63,800
Workers' Compensation Supervisor	47,400	40,100	61,400
Benefits Planning Analyst	46,800	37,800	58,000
Generalist	46,400	35,000	54,100
Safety Specialist	46,100	36,800	55,700
Senior Compensation Analyst	45,800	36,800	56,500
Equal Employment Opportunity Specialist	45,500	37,200	57,200
Employee Assistance Program Counselor	45,000	35,900	54,500

AVERAGE ANNUAL SALARIES IN CORPORATE HUMAN RESOURCE DEPARTMENTS

Title	Average salary	Average Minimum[1]	Average Maximum[1]
Plant/Branch Human Resource Administrator	$ 44,800	$ 34,700	$ 54,000
Wellness Program Manager	43,800	36,800	64,900
Senior Training Specialist	43,600	36,900	56,600
Professional/Technical Recruitment Specialist	42,100	34,600	53,300
Compensation and Benefits Administrator	40,900	34,000	51,600
Human Resource Information System Specialist	40,400	31,700	48,500
Associate Training Specialist	37,700	29,600	45,100
Industrial Nurse	37,400	30,600	46,300
Benefits Administrator	37,100	31,800	48,500
Compensation Analyst	36,500	30,100	46,200
Recruiter	34,100	28,600	43,700
Entry Level Generalist	33,200	27,600	42,300
Security Specialist	30,800	31,900	48,500
Benefits Clerk	26,200	21,500	31,900
Personnel Assistant	25,800	21,500	31,800

[1]Not all companies report minimum and maximum salaries, so figures in this column may be based on smaller sample sizes than the average salary column.
[2]Salary does not reflect bonus, which reflects a large percentage (more than 25 percent) of total compensation.
SOURCE: William M. Mercer Inc., *1995 Human Resource Management Compensation Survey.*

Job Descriptions

UPPER MANAGEMENT

Vice-President, Administration—Responsible for planning and directing corporate staff functions in support of the operations. Specific responsibilities may include human resources, purchasing, management information systems, long-range planning, budgeting, and finance. Manages administration activities for corporate properties and facilities. May act as chief advisor or liaison to executive vice-president, president, and/or chief operating officer in order to plan, evaluate, and recommend overall corporate strategies.

Top Human Resource Management Executive—Develops, implements, and coordinates policies and programs encompassing all, or nearly all, aspects of human resource management, including employment, labor relations, wage and salary administration, training, placement, safety and health, benefits, and employee services. Originates policies and monitors activities affecting all operations and locations of the company. May be responsible for community and/or public relations activities.

Top Corporate Personnel Executive—Develops, implements, and coordinates policies and programs encompassing all, or nearly all, aspects of personnel for salaried (nonunion) employees, including employment, salary administration, training placement, manpower planning and development, employee benefits, and affirmative action programs. Originates policies and monitors activities affecting all operations and locations of the company. May report to top human resource management executive, the CEO, or other corporate general management.

MANAGEMENT

International Top Human Resource Executive—Develops, implements, and coordinates policies and programs encompassing all, or nearly all, aspects of international human resource management including employment, labor relations, wage and salary administration, training, placement, safety and health, benefits, and employee services. Originates policies and monitors activities affecting all international operations and locations of the company.

Top Divisional/Regional Human Resource Executive—Develops and implements human resource policies and programs within the policy guidelines formulated by the top corporate human resource executive and top management. Usually receives guidance and counsel from the corporate human resource function.

Top Corporate Security Manager—Develops and administers policies to protect corporate facilities, properties, and employees which may include computer security system and employee identification card system. Selects and supervises outside protective services contractors and in-house security guards. Typically reports to human resource executive or corporate management. This job does not include safety responsibilities.

Top Corporate Safety Manager—Develops and administers policies and programs to insure all facilities are in compliance with OSHA and other safety and health requirements and that employee safety programs are developed and carried out. May also be responsible for highway safety where applicable. Typically reports to human resource executive or corporate management. This job does not include security responsibilities.

Top Corporate Employee Relations Executive—Directs the establishment and maintenance of satisfactory labor-management relations, union avoidance and decertification efforts, and the formulation and administration of the company's labor relations policy, subject to top management guidance and approval. Represents management in labor relations, including the negotiation, interpretation, and administration of collective bargaining agreements, directly or through subordinates, and administration of grievance procedures. May include responsibilities for programs designed to improve the quality of work life and employee satisfaction. Typically reports to top unit or corporate human resource executive.

Top Corporate Organizational Development Executive—Directs the development and implementation of corporate programs to better develop and utilize human resources. Major responsibilities may include: internal consulting; management assessment and development; performance measurement; management utilization and development needs; consultation with managers on motivational strategies, human performance problems, personal career development, and stress reactions; employment research and attitude surveys; job enrichment applications; long-term human resource plan and management succession. May supervise employment and recruiting function. Typically reports to top corporate human resource executive or top corporate personnel executive.

Top Corporate Compensation and Benefits Executive—Responsible for all compensation and benefits programs for all employees including design, implementation, and administration of programs. Compensation duties often include job descriptions, job evaluation, performance appraisal, merit and other salary increases, wage and salary surveys, incentive plans, and stock option and other executive programs. Benefits responsibilities often include life, health, and disability insurance programs, profit-sharing and retirement programs, and personnel practices. Often responsible for selection and supervision of benefits consultants, brokers, trustees, and necessary legal assistants.

Human Resource Director—Develops and administers policies and programs covering several or all of the following: recruitment, wage and salary administration, training, safety and security, benefits and services, employee and labor relations, and personnel research. Supervises small human resource department in small- to medium-sized firm. Typically reports to senior management.

LABOR RELATIONS

Labor Relations Supervisor—Establishes and maintains satisfactory labor-management relations, formulates and administers the company's labor relations policy subject to top management guidance and approval, and represents management in labor relations, including the negotiation, interpretation, and administration of collective bargaining agreements. Responsible for administering grievance procedures. May be responsible for developing union-avoidance programs at nonunion facilities and for coordinating decertification activities at union facilities. May include supervision of quality of work life programs.

Labor Relations Generalist—Assists in administration of company's labor relations policies. May be involved in negotiations, administration of collective bargaining agreements, and administration of grievance procedures. This exempt position typically reports to plant/branch human resources manager or labor relations supervisor.

EMPLOYEE RELATIONS

Equal Employment Opportunity Manager—Develops, implements, and recommends equal employment and affirmative action programs which are in keeping with corporate objectives and which insure compliance with the current legal requirements. Maintains statistics necessary to monitor the effectiveness of the programs and alerts top management to difficulties encountered in attaining and maintaining compliance with established policies. Communicates policies and affirmative action programs to employees, top management, the public, and government agencies. May direct processing of complaints and company defense before administration or judicial proceedings. Typically reports to top employee relations or top corporate personnel executive.

Human Resource Information System Manager—Designs, develops, tests, and directs ongoing administration of the human resources information system including selection of software and hardware. Supervises maintenance and processing of employee records. Human resource information system may be on microcomputer, minicomputer, mainframe, or a combination. Develops recurring or special reports as requested. Typically reports to top employee relations executive or top unit or corporate human resource executive.

Employee Assistance Program Manager—Develops, implements, and directs company-wide employee assistance programs. Researches, investigates, and evaluates existing methods and approaches in the field of employee assistance programs. May also investigate treatment facilities and their staffs in order to maintain an up-to-date reference resource and information on current treatment philosophy. May design and implement own programs and procedures. Produces in-house publication of information on corporate employee assistance programs and procedures. May assist in effectively resolving employee job performance problems through performance evaluation, documentation, and counseling. Typically reports to top corporate employee relations executive.

Employee Communications Director—Manages the company's employee communications programs. Areas of responsibility may include preparation and publication of several or most of the following: company newsletters, management reports, brochures, employee handbooks, materials for employee conferences and seminars, internal directories, etc. May provide assistance in management speech writing, may also be involved in corporate–public/community relations programs. Normally reports to top employee relations executive.

ORGANIZATIONAL DEVELOPMENT

Employment and Recruiting Manager—Establishes procedures for recruitment and placement. Directs the exempt and nonexempt recruiting, interviewing, selection, and placement of applicants for employment. Directs design and placement of employment advertising. Responsible for relations with outside employment agencies and recruiters. Supervises testing and training programs. Assures that equal employment opportunity goals are attained. May direct new employee orientation, inprocessing, exit interviews, outplacement, and employee counseling.

Recruitment Specialist—Interviews and recommends placement of candidates for entry-level and experienced positions. Seeks out sources of candidates including colleges, technical schools, and job fairs. May travel extensively. Typically reports to employment and recruiting manager or top human resource executive of own organizational unit.

Human Resources Planning Manager—Develops short- and long-range strategic plans for effective recruitment, development, and utilization of human resources. Projects current and future company-wide staffing and organizational requirements. Establishes and maintains human resource planning, control, and reporting activities. Advises with departmental managers on the preparation of departmental human resource plans. May also contribute to top corporate strategic planning process. Typically reports to the top corporate organizational development executive.

Training/Organizational Development Manager—Analyzes and determines training needs of the company and formulates and develops plans, procedures, and programs to meet specific training needs and problems. Develops and constructs training manuals and training aids or may supervise their development by outside suppliers. Plans, conducts, and coordinates management inventories, appraisals, placement, counseling, and training, and coordinates participation in outside training programs by company employees. Typically reports to top organizational development executive or top human resource executive (corporate or own unit).

Employee Training Manager—Analyzes and determines training needs; administers plan, procedures, and programs to meet training needs and problems. Constructs training manuals and aids. Supervises or conducts special courses designed for training selected groups of company employees. Typically reports to training/organizational development manager, top organizational development executive, top unit, or corporate human resource executive.

Management Development Manager—Plans, conducts, and coordinates special studies of existing management staff and possible replacements. Conducts investigations to ascertain the executive training and developmental needs. Develops and directs approved management training programs. Typically reports to training/organizational development manager, top organizational development executives, top unit, or corporate human resource executive.

COMPENSATION AND BENEFITS

Executive Compensation Manager—Designs, implements, and administers compensation programs for officers and key executives. Programs may include perquisites, short- and long-term incentive plans, stock option plans, long-term capital accumulation, special benefit programs for executives (such as deferred compensation, supplemental life insurance, and low-interest loans), in addition to executive salaries. May coordinate financial counseling, executive relocation, and tax return preparation for executives. Conducts and participates in surveys of competitive executive compensation.

International Compensation Manager—Develops, implements, and administers compensation programs for international personnel, to include expatriates and third country nationals (may be responsible for local nationals). Programs include salary administration, tax equalization, differentials, allowances, and employee benefits. Provides guidance to international management and may take policy level direction from them. Typically reports to top compensation and benefits executive, top international human resource executive, or top corporate human resource executive.

Employee Benefits Manager—Designs and administers retirement, profit-sharing, thrift, group medical-surgical, disability, and life plans. Often responsible for selection and supervision of benefits consultants, brokers, trustees, and necessary legal assistance. Ensures that the firm retains a competitive benefits posture in the marketplace. Typically reports to top corporate compensation and benefits executive, top unit, or corporate human resource executive.

Compensation and Benefits Administrator—Administers compensation and benefits programs. May administer any or all of the following programs: life, health, and disability insurance programs; profit-sharing, pension, and other retirement programs. Typically reports to top corporate compensation and benefits executive or local human resource management.

Compensation Manager—Directs the design, implementation, and administration of compensation programs including job evaluation, salary administration, annual and long-term management cash incentives, sales compensation and differential incentive, and perquisite and supplemental pay programs. May coordinate stock option, perquisite, deferred compensation, and other executive programs. Administers performance appraisal and salary administration programs.

AVERAGE ANNUAL SALARIES OF HUMAN RESOURCES PERSONNEL IN PRIVATE INDUSTRY

Job Title/Grade	Number of Employees	Average Salary
Personnel Clerks/Assistants		
I	3,441	$ 15,659
II	8,541	19,266
III	5,912	22,937
IV	2,102	27,599
Personnel Specialists		
I	3,355	$ 25,364
II	18,495	28,343
III	31,316	35,681
IV	20,447	46,326
V	5,631	58,672
VI	501	73,265
Personnel Supervisors		
I	2,996	$ 48,391
II	4,330	61,099
III	2,084	78,489
IV	442	96,964
Directors of Personnel		
I	1,797	$ 45,618
II	3,472	59,188
III	1,699	77,780
IV	425	101,922

SOURCE: U.S. Department of Labor, Bureau of Labor Statistics, 1992.

ANNUAL SALARIES OF STATE PERSONNEL DIRECTORS

State	Salary	State	Salary
Alabama	$98,525	Montana	$ 50,014
Alaska	72,468	Nebraska	60,800
Arizona	76,000	Nevada	68,000
Arkansas	62,466	New Hampshire	50,955
California	95,052	New Jersey	100,225
Colorado	77,800	New Mexico	59,277
Connecticut	72,681	New York	90,832
Delaware	80,700	North Carolina	77,289
Florida	68,116	North Dakota	47,316
Georgia	84,870	Ohio	67,766
Hawaii	85,302	Oklahoma	59,661
Idaho	65,125	Oregon	76,332
Illinois	52,752	Pennsylvania	75,900
Indiana	66,950	Rhode Island	72,283
Iowa	68,250	South Carolina	73,462
Kansas	68,808	South Dakota	64,742
Kentucky	70,000	Tennessee	71,388
Louisiana	86,616	Texas	48,552
Maine	62,462	Utah	58,504
Maryland	85,027	Vermont	52,000
Massachusetts	73,156	Virginia	NA
Michigan	85,952	Washington	90,057
Minnesota	67,500	West Virginia	38,976
Mississippi	73,614	Wisconsin	77,160
Missouri	56,461	Wyoming	50,000

SOURCE: Council of State Governments, *The Book of States,* 1994–95.

MANAGEMENT CONSULTANTS

Consultants are the gypsies of the business world, moving from assignment to assignment without putting down roots. This fact creates problems. To the career consultant there is no permanency. He or she is hired for the expertise and objectivity they bring to a situation. After performing the task at hand, they are summarily let go while the client goes about using or implementing the particular product of the consultant's work. So consultants cannot point to any particular enterprise other than the project work performed as their own. From the client side there can be a mistrust of consultants because at least in theory they are not held closely accountable for their work. The idea that the consultant just pushes ideas, meaningful or not, is a lament that can stem from poor consulting work or it can be an excuse for not cooperating with the consultant.

The role of the consultant is to come into a situation in which a client is unsure or inexpert and recommend actions or provide assessments. There are many different types of situations and so the specific use of consultants can vary widely. Therefore there are many different shapes and sizes of consultants. At the top of the list are the well known, old line management consulting firms such as McKinsey &.Co., and Booz, Allen, Hamilton who practice consulting on a broad list of business operating and strategic issues. There are also firms, large and small, as well as individuals whose practice centers on single aspects of business such as sales productivity or marketing strategy. And there are firms which may specialize in specific disciplines, such as the MIS function.

A wide variety of practitioners also exists. Anyone with some degree of business experience or an expert field can hang out a consulting shingle. The number of one- to two-person consulting operations may well exceed a hundred thousand. Many small firms also exist, filling special niches and usually serving medium- and small-sized companies. These may serve specialized needs like engineering studies or providing expert opinion, or they may give generalized advice. There are also consulting divisions in larger companies, such as the major accounting firms, which use the special expertise of the organization as a wedge to get other kinds of consulting work. The largest firms have national and international practices with staffs that number in the thousands.

The top general management consulting firms are very exclusive clubs. These firms normally hire consultants directly from the top graduate schools of business and then train them in their own methodology and traditions. Competition for the best graduates is stiff and starting salaries in the $65,000 to $75,000 range are common. The new consultant then has five to seven years to make it to the first partnership level or leave. Not more than one in five is expected to pass the test.

While the titles of the working levels in a consulting firm are different from firm to firm, the pecking order follows a logical progression that indicates length of experience and relative ranking. What follows is a discussion of a typical structure in a top-rate consulting firm. The titles are not a foolproof indication of either standing or compensation. Some well-known firms have few partners, perhaps only the founders; yet the same titles are used. Use the information accordingly.

A brand-new consultant may be referred to as an Associate for the first two years or so. The progression is then to Senior Associate, a title which indicates three to five years experience and the ability to do more complex and independent work. The Senior Associate may supervise others as well. Around the five-year mark, the consultant who is making satisfactory progress may become an Engagement Manager with the responsibility to lead a consulting team on a particular client project. The best may then become Senior Engagement Managers, leading several study teams or a very large project team. This is a prelude to being considered for junior partnership. Around the seven-year mark the very best will be considered for appointment as junior partners, sometimes titled Principals. Partnership brings with it responsibility for marketing the firm and its services as well as the leadership of client projects. The final step some time later is to senior partnership or Director.

Compensation for the few who run the full course can be extremely rewarding. As mentioned, starting salaries at the best firms easily exceed $70,000. A bonus opportunity of up to 40 percent and noncontributory profit-sharing may be included. Progress up the entry-level ranks brings generous increases in base salary. In general, more experience means that the firm can charge more for an individual's services and therefore the individual shares in the increasing fee structure. Junior partnership brings a salary often in the $150,000 range plus bonus and the right to purchase shares in the firm. These shares give the partner a claim against the assets of the firm. The shares can be sold when the individual leaves. Senior partners may earn a base compensation in excess of $300,000 plus the other compensation incentives.

Independent consultants work on a different structure. They are self-employed, although much of their work may come from established firms on a subcontract basis. Generally these consultants can command fees between $400 and $1,000 a day. Some well-known professionals may receive over $2,000 a day. Most are on the lower end of the scale. When the independent works on his or her own, the fee is maximized because there is no one to split it with. Of course self-employed is one step away from being unemployed, so many hedge their bets by working in close association with others as subcontractors. By pooling talents, marketing is easier; more resources can be brought to bear on an assignment, and different talents and backgrounds are made available. So there are advantages even though a portion of the fee (up to 50 percent) may be sacrificed.

By working for themselves consultants also sacrifice benefits provided by the large firms, so the fees gained are not free and clear. To cover these overheads as well as protect against lost cash flow during idle periods, the independent is in a constant struggle to maximize fees. Still, despite the insecurity, independents exist because they are not the type of people who are comfortable working for large organizations. They like the intellectual challenge of consulting as well as the personal freedom of movement the independent road brings.

When thinking about career consultants remember a familiar but corrupted form of the old Bernard Shaw saw, "He who can does; he who cannot consults." Consultants seem to get much of their satisfaction from advising rather than doing. New MBA graduates who get into the profession do so because it is normally a ticket to a good second job high in the management ranks of a client company. Those who remain consultants or who return to the profession are unique individuals. (Here we distinguish between the truly professional consultants and those who are doing the work because they can't find anything else.)

Consultants are different most of all because they normally have been blessed with higher than average intelligence. These highly intelligent people also possess a great deal of self-confidence and have faith in their ability to handle any situation presented. They are very analytical and objective by nature. They thrive on exposure to the lofty areas of corporate policy and executive decision-making. Many career consultants are workaholics who may spend undue amounts of time on the road. To many a fourteen- to sixteen-hour workday and a six- or seven-day work week is common.

While some may bill themselves as general management consultants and others as specialists, all have certain areas where they are normally more expert. Some may have special knowledge or experience in a specific industry or group of industries. Others may be expert on specific functions such as advertising or compensation. All the good ones are quick to learn and keep their knowledge updated.

Consulting also requires a great deal of tact, even while debating a point or telling someone they have misinterpreted data. A consultant must be good at making presentations and quick on his or her feet, able to refute objections with finality. And he or she must be able to enlist cooperation while exerting leadership. Part of this overall ability to handle people and situations arises from the expertise and experience of the consultant, but part of it is a talent that can't be taught.

While consulting is a potentially lucrative profession, it is not an easy one to prosper in. It requires a disposition toward the intellectual side of business, a natural curiosity about how things are working and how they should work. This must be coupled with an ability to be unbiased and analytical. For those who have the talent the rewards are substantial.

There are many large consulting firms which have gained national prominence over the years. Some generalist firms like McKinsey and Company, and Booz, Allen, Hamilton are multinational in scope with offices around the world. Other large firms like John Diebold and Associates, which specialize in specific fields, are also very large and broad in reach. In the 1980s the large accounting firms such as Coopers & Lybrand and Peat Marwick Main Hurdman started large consulting practices. Employment opportunities vary among the large firms. Some will hire research associates directly out of college and provide a career path into consultancy for the best and brightest of these people. Others hire only from graduate schools into consultant-level positions. The accounting firms usually require an accounting background even on the part of their consultants. Some are looking for industry-specific or functional expertise, such as computer systems or inventory management on which they can leverage. All are looking for very bright, imaginative people.

Beyond the very large and well-known firms there are literally thousands of smaller firms with a wide variety of needs. These consulting companies tend to specialize in specific areas of knowledge and expertise, and do not usually hire trainees. To land a job with any of these requires a demonstrated track record in an industry or a functional area and in most cases prior consulting experience.

THE LARGEST U.S. MANAGEMENT CONSULTING FIRMS, 1995

Company	Management Consulting Revenues	Number of Consultants	Revenues per Consultant[1]
Ernst & Young	$830,000,000	4,300	$193,000
McKinsey & Co.	600,000,000	1,300	461,500
Mercer Consulting Group	553,000,000	4,355	127,000
Andersen Consulting	518,800,000	12,405	41,800
Towers Perrin	510,400,000	2,749	185,700
Arthur Andersen	503,600,000	NA	NA
Deloitte & Touche	491,000,000	3,409	144,000
Coopers & Lybrand Consulting	480,000,000	3,800	126,300
KPMG Peat Marwick	410,000,000	2,500	164,000
Hewitt Associates LLC	384,600,000	2,567	149,800
Booz-Allen & Hamilton	340,000,000	1,700	200,000

[1]Calculated by *The American Almanac of Jobs and Salaries* to the nearest thousand.
SOURCE: ©*1995 Consultant News,* Reprinted with permission of Kennedy Publications, Fitzwilliam, N.H.

Among the consulting specialties most in demand are computers, human resources, marketing research, inventory control, telecommunications, and manufacturing efficiency. Consultants who specialize in computers advise clients on the use of computer systems, the development of programs and applications, and, generally, how to use computer systems to enhance operating efficiency. Consultants in human resources perform a wide variety of services from doing comparative compensation studies to designing training programs. Marketing research is a very large and special area that is described below. Experts in inventory control advise companies on modern-day techniques for reducing inventory costs, such as just-in-time inventory stocking. Telecommunications consultants aid businesses in selecting telephone and data communications equipment and services. They also monitor expenditures and make recommendations on reducing costs. Consultants in the area of manufacturing efficiency advise clients on making their equipment and manufacturing processes as efficient as possible. There are many other specialties as well.

Compensation for specialists averages close to $1,000 per day. Unless the specialty is particularly arcane or the specialist is well known, the specialist generally earns less than the generalists who practice strategy consulting.

MARKET RESEARCHERS

When C. Wright Mills wrote of the changing world of business after World War II in *White Collar* (1951), he mentioned market research only in passing and did not cite the field as a major category in the book's index. However, the future importance of market research was clearly indicated in the following passage from *White Collar:* "Before high-pressure salesmanship, emphasis was upon the salesman's knowledge of the product, a sales knowledge grounded in apprenticeship; after it, the focus is upon hypnotizing the prospect, an art provided by psychology."

The underpinning of this "hypnosis" of the American buying public is frequently provided by market research analysts—a work force of approximately 30,000 men and women employed not only in independent market research organizations, but also in manufacturing companies, advertising agencies, media enterprises, university research units, and government agencies.

Independent market research organizations may be found in large- and medium-sized cities—wherever there are central sales and manufacturing offices, but the largest tend to cluster in major cities; for example, A. C. Nielsen, Arbitron, and Burke Marketing are all in New York.

The market researcher provides businesses with information about the needs and desires of the buying public, attempting at the same time to shape that information into future trends. The basic tools for this information gathering and trend projecting are surveys and interviews. The market researcher collaborates with statisticians and trained interviewers—all working together to monitor and shape not only buying habits but basic thinking and motivation as well. After the information and data have been collected and analyzed, the market researcher determines what action should be taken: changes in advertising to improve sales, searches for new markets, efforts to reach a new segment of the population, attempts to improve the public's discernment of the faltering image of anything from a bar of soap to a soapbox politician.

AVERAGE SALARIES FOR MARKET RESEARCH WORKERS, 1988–94

Title	Average Salary 1994	Average Salary 1988	Percent Change 1988–94
Market Research Director	$80,860	$61,300	32%
Assistant Director	67,560	50,700	33.3
Senior Analyst	45,770	40,300	13.6
Statistician	50,380	45,400	11.0
Analyst	36,740	31,100	18.1
Field Work Director	25,430	32,300	−21.3
Librarian	35,000	31,200	12.2
Junior Analyst	23,120	24,900	−7.1
Clerical Supervisor	31,300	22,600	38.5
Full-Time Interviewer	16,100	17,000	−5.3
Tabulating and Clerical Help	22,930	19,700	16.3

SOURCE: American Marketing Association, *1994 Survey of Marketing Research.*

A market research trainee usually has a bachelor's degree in marketing or economics with strong background in mathematics, statistic survey design, and computer science. To advance, graduate work in business administration or a related field is frequently required. Some marketing positions require specialized knowledge or skills related to the particular product or service being promoted. Finally, for more and more market research work, strong training in computer technology is helpful.

Market research trainees usually perform a great deal of clerical work along with basic research—transcribing data and tabulating questionnaire and survey results. Junior analysts help to conduct surveys and questionnaires, along with writing reports on the results. Senior analysts assume responsibility for specific market research projects. At the top of the ladder is the manager and then the director; they have overall supervisory responsibility.

Market research requires considerable quantitative skill along with the creativity to break new ground by analyzing buying habits and the underlying motivation. As the backseat driver for business, the market researcher must also be skilled in written and oral communication.

PUBLIC RELATIONS

In his 1952 book on the growing field he helped develop, Edward Bernays wrote, "Public relations is vitally important today because modern social science has found that the adjustment of individuals, groups, and institutions to life is necessary for the well-being of all." He explains that "because technology has advanced more rapidly than human relations, society has been unable to cope with accelerated technological advances." Public relations, he concludes, is "the new profession of adjustment."

Since then, the growth of the public relations industry has more than kept pace with technological advancement. Public relations workers may, for example, act on behalf of medical research institutes in bringing possible new cancer cures like interferon to public attention. They may present the pros and cons of nuclear power to the press and public in the energy debate. Whatever the organization being represented, the public relations department is the place where technical concerns and developments are filtered through communications experts for public dissemination, usually via the mass media.

What in 1952 was a field struggling for respectability is now a part of the American way of life that employs over 100,000 people, mostly in large media-center cities. They work for nonprofit organizations, large corporations, and independent consulting firms.

But "public relations" is a term that covers a wide range of communications functions. PR people act as two-way information centers, promoting their clients to the targeted public through the media and also providing feedback to the clients along with advice about how a particular move might impress the public. PR workers are concerned with publicity, trying to keep their employers in the limelight, or, in the case of certain big companies and their executives, out of it. Their work is closely allied with the news media and actually accounts for a significant percentage of news stories and features. Today's press release can be and often is tomorrow's newspaper article.

PR representatives can be book, record, or film promoters; government or corporate spokespersons; college fund-raisers; or lobbyists in Washington. Whatever subject matter they handle, they must be strong communicators, dealing with telephone inquiries, maintaining thriving press contacts, and otherwise interacting with the public in a way that is courteous, creative, and, one hopes, informative.

The traditional entry into public relations was via journalism, and today media training is still an advantage to the PR job seeker. But many people also enter the field with educational backgrounds in English, sociology, economics, political science, or business administration. Some corporations look for PR representatives with expertise in the business of the company itself, such as finance, energy, or heavy industry.

A 1993 survey by *Public Relations Journal,* a monthly magazine, showed the following earnings by job groupings:

MEDIAN SALARY BY JOB TITLE

Title	Region East	Midwest	South	West
Account Executives, Representatives, Associates, Assistants	$34,143	$28,054	$31,393	$30,688
Account Supervisors, Group Managers, Other Supervisors	54,874	46,902	45,284	48,389
Senior Counselors, Partners, Senior Vice-Presidents, Executive Vice-Presidents	81,684	63,846	56,332	66,837

MEDIAN SALARY BY PR ACTIVITY, 1993

Industry	Salary
Investor Relations	$66,707
International	62,240
Environmental Affairs	54,920
Issues Management	54,420
Technology	50,718
Government Relations	54,595
Crisis Management	52,508
Public Affairs	51,926
Corporate Communications	50,634
Generalist	49,108
Research	47,763
Employee Relations	46,142
Media Relations	46,765
Special Events	45,224
Marketing	45,345
Community Relations	45,445
Publicity	44,893
Advertising	43,416
Fund-raising/Philanthropy	39,676
Public Relations Education	43,674
Publications/Brochures	34,678
Other	43,089

SOURCE: *Public Relations Journal,* 1993 salary survey. Reprinted by permission.

MEDIAN ENTRY-LEVEL PR SALARIES, 1993

Type of Employer	Salary
Corporation	$23,400
Nonprofit	20,980
Public Relations Firms	19,210
All Respondents	21,310

SOURCE: *Public Relations Journal,* 1993 salary survey. Reprinted by permission.

MEDIAN SALARIES BY EXPERIENCE

	Median Salary	Percent over $40,000	Median Bonus Size
All Respondents	$46,204	52	$ 3,081
Men	58,477	71	5,074
Women	39,542	37	2,238
1–4 Years Experience			
Men	30,117	13	827
Women	25,886	5	802
5–9 Years Experience			
Men	44,300	48	2,657
Women	37,509	25	2,108
10–14 Years Experience			
Men	60,190	79	4,758
Women	46,242	53	3,450
15–19 Years Experience			
Men	65,690	88	7,547
Women	55,893	74	4,574
20 plus Years Experience			
Men	70,015	88	12,604
Women	58,487	74	4,908

SOURCE: *PR Journal,* 1993. Reprinted by permission.

TEN LARGEST PUBLIC RELATIONS FIRMS, 1994

	1994 Net Fees	Number of Employees
1. Burson-Marsteller	$192,491,000	1,700
2. Shandwick	160,100,000	1,813
3. Hill and Knowlton	139,300,000	1,227
4. Communications Int'l Group (formerly Omnicom)	111,720,434	1,183
5. Edelman Public Relations Worldwide	74,908,804	819
6. Fleishman-Hillard	73,898,000	622
7. Ketchum Public Relations	55,405,000	487
8. Ogilvy Adams & Rinehart	39,055,000	411
9. Robinson Lake/Sawyer Miller/Bozell	37,800,000	250
10. The Rowland Co.	35,000,000	301

SOURCE: J.R. O'Dwyer Co; Inc. Reprinted with permission.

Nonprofit Organizations

Into this category falls an alphabet soup of groups and foundations, colleges and universities, hospitals, and the largest employer of them all, federal, state, and local governments. About 33 percent of all public relations personnel work for government on all levels. In the federal government their median salary is $45,400, although at major departments (State, Defense, etc.) and agencies they are often classified at the GS-15 level, which carries an average salary of over $75,000. In state and city governments press aides, or "directors of communications," for governors and mayors frequently earn over $50,000, depending on the size of the government.

Public relations specialists are also finding well-paying positions in colleges and universities. According to a detailed salary survey published annually by the College and University Personnel Association, the chief PR officer at large public universities (over 20,000 students) usually earns in excess of $70,000, while the director of the university's information office makes more than $60,000.

For the most part, salaries are lower in the nonprofit area. The nonprofit agency can be a good place to begin a career in public relations. It's a way to receive valuable training and experience before moving into the more competitive—and lucrative—jobs in agencies or large corporations. Of course, many people choose to remain in this sector of the occupation. Applying their communications skills to an organization whose goals and work personally interest them—a consumer group, for example, or a health research foundation—can bring great job satisfaction. And in the top-level jobs, salaries are very respectable, often surpassing $100,000.

Independent Agencies

About 23 percent of those answering the PRSA survey work as consultants in PR agencies or in advertising agencies and a few as independents. Not surprisingly, New York City is the major center for public relations firms: Of the 4,000 PR firms listed in the national Yellow Pages, 70 are in Manhattan. Other large cities—such as Los Angeles, with 300; Washington, D.C., with 250; Chicago, with 225; and San Francisco, with 150—are strong areas for jobs in public relations.

In 1993 the median salary at PR counseling firms was $53,728. People working in the PR section of advertising agencies command a median salary of $41,066. Solo practitioners reported a median of $43,101.

The entry-level position is that of Assistant Account Executive, with a typical salary between $19,210 and $23,400. These workers mainly write press releases "pitching" their client, then follow them up with telephone calls. They're also on hand to help with the legwork in campaigns planned by senior consultants. That could involve activities ranging from hand-delivering releases to making arrangements for a promotional luncheon.

After three or so years, promotion to Account Executive may come, with a median salary expectation of $35,715. Employees at this level deal exclusively with clients and propose and plan publicity campaigns. Promotion to the next level, Account Supervisor, can bring a median salary in the neighborhood of $55,500. Vice-presidents tend to earn roughly $62,600 although some go as high as $80,000. People on the very top of the 15 most successful counseling firms may be making between $50,000 and $100,000 (group vice-president or manager) or even between $100,000 and $200,000 (firm principals), according to Marshall Consultants.

And don't forget the so-called "superflacks," individual public relations consultants handling big clients in such publicity-conscious spheres as show business and politics. Media whiz kids have kept Broadway shows from closing after poor reviews, gotten unusual films like *The Postman* national attention (and good box-office receipts). Superflacks handle clients on monthly retainers that run from $3,000 to $10,000, sometimes more.

Corporations

The largest number of people in public relations, 42 percent, work for corporations, with top salaries in many large companies inching their way toward dizzying heights.

In the nation's top 25 corporations (over $8 billion in sales), PR executives are part of management's highest echelon. Divisional PR heads and those running corporate staff services earn between $50,000 and $125,000 annually. Vice-presidents in charge of corporate communications make between $80,000 and $190,000. The annual compensation package for a senior vice-president at a *Fortune* 100 company can run as much as $200,000 to $300,000.

The corporation is not the place to start but to consider after several years of organization or agency experience. "Corporations for the most part do not offer entry-level positions," says Marshall Consultants' Judith Cushman. "They want applicants who have some background and experience so they can handle the structure and constraints of a corporation." The job includes corporate communications (such as writing brochures and company newsletters); handling employee, government, investor, and press relations; involvement with community affairs; attention to international issues; and any other facets of the company's public dealings and actions.

MEDIAN PR SALARY BY INDUSTRY, 1993

Industry	Salary
Industrial/Manufacturing	$62,363
Utility	52,672
Scientific/Technical	44,351
Public Relations Counseling Firm	53,728
Media/Communications	48,473
Financial/Insurance	49,602
Government	44,019
Solo Practitioner	43,101
Association/Foundation	43,388
Health Care	41,550
Transportation/Hotels/Resorts/Entertainment	41,843
Miscellaneous Services	47,915
Education	41,008
Advertising Agency	41,066
Miscellaneous Non-Profits/Museums	32,910
Religious/Charitable	35,545
Other	41,618

SOURCE: *Public Relations Journal,* 1993 Salary Survey. Reprinted by permission.

The Speech Writer

Most of the *Fortune* 1000 companies have a need for people who can craft words for their top executives when they are before the public eye speaking at trade shows and conventions or before business and charitable organizations or in other public arenas such as committees of the Congress. Somewhere around 50 percent of these companies employ full-time speech writers. Others use people provided by their public relations firms or independent speech writers. Typically speech writers are also charged with producing text for the companies' annual reports and other special publications. Salaries for in-house speech writers range from $70,000 to more than $120,000. Freelance speech writers may command from $1,000 to $10,000 for a thirty-minute speech.

PURCHASING AGENTS

According to the CEO of a major industrial corporation, the three most important characteristics of the purchasing agent are honesty, integrity, and unpopularity. The reason becomes apparent when one realizes that purchasing people, on average, spend half the income of the company for which they work.

About 300,000 people are employed in purchasing in the United States today. These individuals are responsible for buying the goods and services necessary for the running of their company; regardless of its type and size, every company must make certain purchases nearly every day. It is the purchasing agent's job to procure materials, supplies, and equipment of the best value for the best price. Additionally, a purchasing department may monitor other departments to see that they stay within budget when purchasing supplies. Purchasers constantly work to reduce costs.

Openings in purchasing have been projected at nearly 15,000 per year for the next ten years. Salaries in purchasing also reflect an occupation growing in size and importance. In a recent survey of purchasing compensation by *Purchasing* magazine, two out of three respondents describe their current salary as "equitable." The findings of the survey suggest that talent counts more than title in determining compensation. Although salaries vary from industry to industry and according to the size of the firm, a large firm does not always promise a larger paycheck. What usually matters, especially at the executive levels, is the volume of purchases necessary.

Studies show that about a third of all purchasing personnel receive regular bonuses, and these beneficiaries include buyers, not just top management. Thus, bonuses, generally about 10 percent of the base salary, are a major factor to be considered in assessing purchasers' compensation.

The National Association of Purchasing Management delineates five categories of "buyers," the broadest job title within purchasing. These areas are General Products Buyer, Construction Buyer, Production Materials or Components Buyer, Raw Material or Commodity Buyer, and Governmental and Institutional Buyer. The type of work and qualifications for purchasers in the public sector are not necessarily different from those in private industry, but most government positions are regulated by Civil Service requirements. Moreover, because federal, state, and local governments spend almost $100 billion a year acquiring goods and services, opportunities for purchasers abound there. Most federal purchasing is concentrated in the military and the General Services Administration; the local level has state, municipal, and county buyers.

Jobs in Purchasing

Duties within purchasing jobs often are not strictly confined to a designated job title. Depending on the size of the purchasing department, titles may vary from company to company while duties will overlap. Often the title Purchasing Agent serves as a general term for any position in a purchasing department. Listed below are job descriptions for the most commonly used titles in the field. These titles supply a guideline to a purchasing department ladder, but keep in mind that a multitude of responsibilities can be assigned to employees with the titles Purchasing Agent or Buyer.

Vice-President/Director of Purchasing—Depending upon the size of the company, the top purchasing position usually bears one of these titles. Primarily an administrative position, responsible for coordinating, directing, and planning all aspects of the purchasing department.

Materials Manager/Purchasing Manager—These positions usually combine two functions: buying and supervising subordinates' buying activities. In addition to their own buying responsibilities, they also train new buyers and advise assistant purchasing managers.

Purchasing Agent—Responsible for inventories and supplies of necessary materials, for buying goods and services, and for determining the best sources from which to buy. Often the purchasing agent will confer directly with manufacturers and suppliers.

Purchasing Analyst—Compiles and analyzes data to determine the feasibility of purchasing products, determines price objectives, keeps up to date on price trends and manufacturing processes. Sufficient data was not available for salary range determination for this position, but generally salaries are equivalent to those of purchasing agents.

Buyers—Many levels of buyers exist, and responsibilities of a particular buyer will depend upon the size of the company and the experience of the buyer. In general, buyers will perform some or all of the aspects required in determining, analyzing, negotiating, delivering, supplying, and procuring necessary goods and services. Most companies have senior buyers, buyers, and junior buyers positions.

Salaries in Purchasing

Since people working in the purchasing area usually begin as buyers, that seems a good place to start. Every year the Bureau of Labor Statistics surveys four basic categories of buyers and labels them in its typical way, I through IV. The first two levels are responsible for purchasing "off-the-shelf" materials, while III and IV deal with specialized items, some made-to-order, and usually of a technical nature. The figures below are for private industry only.

AVERAGE ANNUAL SALARIES OF BUYERS IN PRIVATE INDUSTRY

	Number in Survey	Average Salary
Buyer I	7,463	$24,766
Buyer II	22,575	31,032
Buyer III	20,595	40,344
Buyer IV	5,355	47,997

SOURCE: Bureau of Labor Statistics.

In the federal government buyers at these levels usually have the following GS ratings:

I	GS-5	$18,340–$23,839
II	GS-7	22,717– 29,530
III	GS-9	27,789– 36,123
IV	GS-11	33,623– 43,712

ANNUAL SALARIES OF STATE DIRECTORS OF PURCHASING

State	Salary	State	Salary
Alabama	$49,972	Colorado	$69,528
Alaska	NA	Connecticut	NA
Arizona	66,313	Delaware	53,000
Arkansas	62,466	Florida	70,145
California	82,164	Georgia	60,744

ANNUAL SALARIES OF STATE DIRECTORS OF PURCHASING

State	Salary	State	Salary
Hawaii	$50,364	New York	NA
Idaho	46,301	North Carolina	$67,701
Illinois	55,656	North Dakota	NA
Indiana	55,510	Ohio	65,686
Iowa	50,482	Oklahoma	53,140
Kansas	57,576	Oregon	62,784
Kentucky	NA	Pennsylvania	61,301
Louisiana	61,692	Rhode Island	78,191
Maine	50,024	South Carolina	44,157
Maryland	40,959	South Dakota	55,307
Massachusetts	73,156	Tennessee	55,284
Michigan	46,520	Texas	56,238
Minnesota	67,484	Utah	35,538
Mississippi	43,392	Vermont	48,131
Missouri	56,461	Virginia	83,459
Montana	35,996	Washington	60,660
Nebraska	NA	West Virginia	38,976
Nevada	40,752	Wisconsin	59,193
New Hampshire	36,134	Wyoming	47,500
New Jersey	86,100	District of Columbia	NA
New Mexico	49,314		

SOURCE: Council of State Governments, *The Book of States, 1994–95.*

Average Salaries in Purchasing

The best salary survey in the field is published by *Purchasing,* a monthly periodical devoted to the ins and outs of the business. The 1995 *Purchasing* survey found that the average salary in purchasing was $49,700, up 4.6 percent from 1994's average of $47,500. Salaries were highest in the Northeast (the average buyer salary in Wilmington, Delaware, was $81,000), and lowest in the Plains states (buyer salaries in Oshkosh, Wisconsin, averaged $31,400). Purchasing remains very much a man's world both in numbers—men outnumber women three to one—and in earnings. Men continue to earn about 30 percent more than women in purchasing, a trend that has remained constant over the past 15 years. Education and certification also played a large role in purchasing salaries. Purchasing professionals with a college degree, as well as "certified purchasing managers" each earned about $13,000 more than their less educated or noncertified counterparts.

AVERAGE SALARIES BY REGION

Region	Average Salary, 1995	Percent Increase Since 1994
New England (CT, ME, MA, NH, RI, VT)	$50,500	—
Middle Atlantic (DE, DC, NJ, NY, PA)	56,800	+9.9%
Southeast (AL, AR, FL, GA, KY, LA, MS, NC, SC, TN, VA, WV)	49,200	+5.4%
Great Lakes (IL, IN, MI, OH, WI)	49,800	+9.5%
Plains States (IA, KS, NE, MN, MO, ND, SD)	39,100	−7.1%
Southwest (AZ, NM, OK, TX)	51,200	+5.8%
West (AK, CA, CO, HI, ID, MT, NV, OR, UT, WA, WY)	51,200	+2.1%

SOURCE: *Purchasing Magazine*, December 14, 1995. Copyright © Cahners Publishing Co. Reprinted by permission.

PURCHASING SALARIES, 1995

Category	Average salary		
	All	Men	Women
Job Title			
Buyer	$ 32,500	$ 35,700	$ 29,700
Senior Buyer	44,400	46,100	40,900
Purchasing Agent	39,200	42,100	34,500
Purchasing Manager	54,300	56,400	45,100
Materials Manager	59,400	60,600	52,300
Materials Director	75,900	81,300	38,300
Subcontract Administrator	48,400	46,900	44,800
Purchasing Director	77,400	78,400	65,700
Vice President of Purchasing	102,500	104,200	38,000
Age			
20–24	$ 27,300	$ 27,200	$ 27,400
25–29	32,700	37,500	29,700
30–34	42,100	44,900	37,300
35–40	45,900	49,600	37,100
41–50	52,700	57,100	40,700
Over 51	60,300	66,900	40,600
Experience (in years)			
3 or fewer	$ 41,000	$ 46,900	$ 33,500
4–6	41,900	47,300	31,800
7–10	45,300	49,600	37,400
11–15	52,500	57,300	41,600
More than 15	57,800	61,200	42,500

PURCHASING SALARIES, 1995

Category	Average salary All	Men	Women
Education level			
No degree	$ 40,900	$ 47,100	$ 34,200
B.S. (liberal arts)	50,300	53,600	37,500
B.S. (business)	47,900	50,100	39,700
B.S. (technical)	57,000	59,000	45,800
M.B.A.	74,400	76,900	56,600
Other graduate degree	55,100	58,200	44,500
Company Size (sales)			
Less than $2 million	$ 31,300	$ 35,200	$ 25,500
$2–$10 million	34,700	37,400	30,100
$11–$20 million	39,600	43,500	32,600
$21–$50 million	44,300	49,000	34,800
$51–$125 million	49,200	52,500	40,000
$126–$250 million	52,000	59,900	34,700
$251–$500 million	55,700	59,100	41,700
$501 million–$1 billion	53,600	56,200	47,100
More than $1 billion	64,500	68,400	47,800
Industry			
Primary Metals	$ 61,500	$ 64,900	$ 36,300
Chemicals	60,000	64,100	47,400
Paper	85,400	67,800	41,700
Transportation	58,000	61,700	38,400
Financial Services	57,100	57,400	56,400
Food, Tobacco	54,800	59,200	36,100
Petroleum	54,500	57,400	46,100
Public Utilities	53,900	57,700	45,300
Transportation Equipment	53,000	57,200	40,600
Printing, Publishing	52,700	61,600	40,600
Stone/Glass/Clay	51,500	63,700	27,000
Furniture	50,700	57,000	31,800
Electrical Equipment	49,400	54,500	36,600
Rubber	48,500	54,400	42,500
Construction	47,900	52,300	32,100
Instruments	46,300	45,700	47,500
Fabricated Metals	46,100	50,100	33,100
Wholesale	44,700	47,500	32,900
Miscellaneous Manufacturing	44,300	50,800	35,300
Energy	43,600	54,400	31,000
Machinery (Excluding Electric)	40,500	43,200	35,100
Textiles, Leather	36,700	39,900	29,300
Lumber	33,000	32,000	33,500

SOURCE: *Purchasing Magazine*, December 14, 1995. Copyright © Cahners Publishing Co. Reprinted by permission.

CITIES WITH HIGHEST AND LOWEST AVERAGE PURCHASING SALARIES, 1995

City	Average Salary	City	Average Salary
Highest Salaries		**Lowest Salaries**	
Wilmington, DE	$81,000	Oshkosh, WI	$31,400
New York, NY	80,500	Mankato, MN	32,800
El Paso, TX	74,700	York, PA	33,900
Lehigh Valley, PA	74,700	Canton, OH	34,200
San Francisco, CA	74,000	Seattle, WA	37,000
Greenville, SC	68,600	Kalamazoo, MI	37,000
Newark, NJ	66,800	Des Moines, IA	37,300
New Haven, CT	65,900	Oklahoma City, OK	34,900
South Jersey, NJ	65,900	Ogden, UT	38,400
Fort Wayne, IN	65,100	Portland, OR	38,700
Stamford, CT	64,400	Rockford, IL	39,400
Detroit, MI	63,900	Orlando, FL	39,400
Rochester, NY	63,500	Wichita, KS	39,900
Memphis, TN	61,200	Mansfield, OH	41,000
Toledo, OH	60,200	St. Paul, MN	41,700

SOURCE: *Purchasing Magazine*, December 14, 1995. Copyright © Cahners Publishing Co. Reprinted by permission.

THE SALES FORCE

One of the largest occupational groupings in the United States, sales is also the one with the largest number of projected new jobs in the coming decade. There were 3.6 million people employed full-time in retail sales in 1990, according to the Department of Labor; by 2005, that number should increase to more than 4.5 million.

The rewards of sales vary widely by industry, ability, and geography. Starting salaries for part-time retail sales jobs is minimum wage, but in areas where employers have trouble attracting and retaining workers, wages are much higher. The following chart shows median weekly earnings for sales workers in six industries.

Information on many of these jobs—those in real estate and financial services, for example—can be found in other parts of this book. Here we will be dealing exclusively with sales personnel in manufacturing and service industries.

Industry	Median Weekly Earnings
Motor Vehicles and Boats	$479
Hardware and Building Supplies	323
Radio, Television, Hi-fi, and Appliances	415
Furniture and Home Furnishings	354
Apparel	255
Parts	319
Other Commodities	269

SOURCE: U.S. Department of Labor, Bureau of Labor Statistics, *Occupational Outlook Handbook, 1994–95.*

The Sales Professional

For 30 years, Willy Loman, Arthur Miller's confused and pathetic character in *Death of a Salesman,* has been regarded as the prototype of the American salesman. But the days of the drummer, like Willy "riding on a shoeshine and a smile," have long since passed. According to a survey by the Dartnell Corporation, today's salesperson:

- is male (only 26 percent of salespeople are women, up from 7 percent in 1982)
- is 37 years old (the median age of the entire population is 44)
- has a college degree (62 percent)
- will stay with his or her current company for close to 7 years
- makes 3.6 sales calls or visits per day
- works about 45.5 hours per week
- earns $30,000 in an entry-level job, $40,000 as an intermediate salesperson, and $53,300 as a senior level salesperson
- receives an average of $6,838 in benefits from his or her employer

The earnings of sales professionals have obviously also changed dramatically, as businesses have come to realize the importance of competent, well-trained people, especially in highly competitive industries. The following table lists base salaries and total compensation levels for 10 sales positions by product type and by company size.

AVERAGE TOTAL CASH COMPENSATION FOR SALES PERSONNEL BY TYPE OF PRODUCT OR SERVICE AND BY COMPANY SIZE

	Base Salary/Total Compensation									
Group	Top Marketing Executive	Top Sales Executive	Regional Sales Manager	District Sales Manager	Senior Sales Rep	Intermediate Sales Rep	Entry Level Sales Rep	National/ Major Account Manager	National Account Rep	Major (Key) Account Rep
By Type of Product or Service										
Consumer Products	$ 68,900/ 84,400	$ 59,600/ 75,900	$51,100/ 64,000	$46,600/ 57,900	$34,900/ 46,500	$26,700/ 35,800	$22,900/ 28,300	$55,300/ 68,400	$51,000/ 61,500	$48,500/ 57,000
Consumer Services	61,900/ 84,800	52,800/ 71,200	48,600/ 71,700	48,000/ 67,900	35,200/ 48,000	27,100/ 35,000	22,400/ 28,400	53,400/ 78,400	61,000/ 76,800	45,400/ 57,800
Industrial Products	72,700/ 94,300	66,400/ 87,400	50,800/ 65,400	50,900/ 70,300	40,300/ 56,600	32,100/ 42,500	24,300/ 32,700	58,800/ 77,200	55,400/ 65,900	43,300/ 52,100
Industrial Services	68,800/ 94,900	63,700/ 85,600	49,600/ 71,700	50,900/ 72,800	38,400/ 60,900	29,100/ 41,900	23,100/ 32,600	53,900/ 76,700	57,800/ 68,900	44,400/ 51,500
Office Products	68,100/ 83,400	60,500/ 79,500	50,600/ 64,400	48,600/ 64,700	33,700/ 47,600	28,100/ 37,900	21,800/ 27,300	59,000/ 79,000	55,100/ 69,100	41,400/ 49,400
Office Services	75,200 105,100	58,000/ 82,000	49,400/ 69,200	54,600/ 89,500	36,800/ 54,700	27,000/ 37,100	21,300/ 27,700	56,200/ 79,900	NA	37,500/ 44,300

By Company Size

Under $5 million	$ 52,100/ 65,100	$ 40,400/ 53,000	$30,300/ 42,000	$44,700/ 51,500	$30,400/ 39,800	$23,700/ 30,400	$19,700/ 24,500	NA	$27,000/ 30,000	$36,600/ 43,900
$5 million–$25 million	65,200/ 83,500	61,100/ 83,000	43,000/ 56,600	39,100/ 62,800	36,700/ 53,500	28,500/ 38,400	22,500/ 30,200	$37,900/ 46,000	37,800/ 42,800	35,000/ 47,600
$25 million–$100 million	85,200/ 111,000	68,500/ 85,200	54,500/ 67,700	45,900/ 53,900	42,700/ 59,600	31,100/ 41,800	25,300/ 30,400	54,200/ 72,000	45,700/ 54,800	40,600/ 47,000
$100 million–$250 million	104,500/ 126,100	101,100/ 131,100	64,400/ 95,000	57,200/ 87,600	42,900/ 71,100	33,300/ 48,500	26,000/ 40,600	65,700/ 80,000	54,100/ 71,200	49,400/ 60,400
Over $250 million	111,700/ 167,600	95,100/ 139,100	74,000/ 97,800	62,600/ 88,700	51,400/ 72,700	44,200/ 62,200	33,200/ 43,900	68,900/ 99,200	59,900/ 74,400	56,100/ 68,800

SOURCE: The Dartnell Corporation, *Sales Force Compensation 1994–95*. Copyright © 1995 The Dartnell Corporation.

Salary vs. Commission

In any corporate sales job the role of commissions cannot be ignored, since virtually every company attempts to reward its sales staff for any increase in volume. Even when the company's official policy is to pay salespeople a straight salary, it usually has some short-term incentives such as a small bonus or a free trip. According to the Dartnell Corporation, the straight salary plan works best when it is difficult for management to determine which person on the staff actually made the sale; or when the product involved has a broad, cyclical sales pattern, which would leave the sales staff with virtually no income during the fallow periods if only a commission were used. Unfortunately, this plan also rewards nonproducers.

Those corporations using a straight commission plan usually want to provide the greatest incentive to their salespeople while maintaining a predictable sales cost in relation to sales volume. This method of compensation has fallen out of favor recently because it leads to high personnel turnover and a downgrading of the service aspects of selling—a key element for strongly established companies.

For these reasons, many corporations have installed a combination plan that provides a fixed salary plus an incentive feature. This helps to establish continuity in the sales force, yet allows the top producers to earn more and encourages everyone to develop new business. The figures below show that such plans are now prevalent throughout American businesses. On average, those on the hybrid plan earn slightly more than those working solely for commission. Salespeople on salary only earn significantly less. Outstanding sales personnel on commission or straight commission usually achieve markedly higher compensation at the high end of the scale, but they must prove themselves anew each year.

Most salespeople working for corporations get the same fringe benefits as other employees, and many get additional ones that are important to their work and beneficial to their personal and family lives as well. The most common of these special benefits is a company car, but many salespeople also get fringe benefits worth as much as 40 percent of their pay.

After learning the business, some salespeople choose self-employment. Many insurance agents work for themselves, selling policies written by various firms. (See the section on insurance in Part VI.) Manufacturers' representatives work the same way, handling products that complement one another but do not compete.

Self-employment has the benefit of independence, the risks associated with working solely on a commission basis (no sales, no pay), and the prospect of substantial income if all goes well. Typically, the manufacturer who turns to agencies to sell its products sees immediate market penetration as a major benefit. An agency in place with established customers can bring in business almost immediately. Also, manufacturers see longevity as an important factor. Manufacturers' agents are business partners who grow with their principals and maintain a steady presence in a territory. Compared with the fairly rapid turnover seen with salaried factory people, this stability is a critical factor today, as competition is intense and getting worse.

The Manufacturers' Agents National Association, a trade group in Laguna Hills, California, periodically surveys its members about the commissions they earn. The figures beginning on page 383 are reprinted from the Association's latest survey of sales commissions. It is important to understand, however, that there is no such thing as a "standard" commission, nor should there be. Commission rates vary widely from industry to industry and even within individual industries. For example, some products require special installation and service; when this is part of the picture, commission rates are higher. Many agents also do more than simply sell products for the companies they represent. Some provide warehousing facilities, while others do extensive engineering consulting. On the other hand, products in the mature part of the marketing cycle require less effort to sell. And of course, regardless of overall trends, there are usually considerable variations for the same product from territory to territory because of unique competitive conditions. Thus the accompanying figures represent not a standard, but a snapshot, or an average based on considerable national and territorial variations.

AVERAGE COMPENSATION LEVELS FOR SENIOR SALES REPRESENTATIVES, BY INDUSTRY

	Type of Pay Plan			
Industry	Paid by Salary Only	Paid by Incentives Only	Paid by Both Salary and Incentives	Average Total Cash Compensation for All Plans
Aerospace Equipment	$57,500	NA	$52,600	$52,600
Agriculture, Forestry and Fishing	NA	NA	37,100	48,600
Banking	NA	NA	62,100	59,900
Business Services	65,400	$ 71,700	53,600	59,100
Chemicals	72,500	56,500	74,400	64,000
Communications	NA	64,800	73,200	63,800
Construction	NA	66,700	50,800	57,000
Educational Services	NA	66,700	56,000	81,800
Electronics	62,000	40,000	61,800	70,300
Fabricated Metals	54,600	95,500	71,100	67,400
Food Products	65,000	NA	60,100	61,400
Furniture and Fixtures	NA	62,200	19,900	50,100
Health Services	NA	36,000	34,700	38,000
Holding and Other Investment Offices	NA	NA	60,300	48,000
Hotels and Other Lodging Places	NA	NA	39,600	39,700
Instruments	47,500	NA	62,100	66,400
Insurance	31,800	79,200	75,600	58,700
Machinery	51,200	125,000	59,400	61,800
Manufacturing	35,000	115,800	66,000	56,700
Office Equipment	NA	NA	49,700	52,200
Paper and Allied Products	NA	72,700	62,300	60,400
Primary Metal Products	57,700	51,700	60,600	55,200
Printing and Publishing	58,800	68,400	59,500	59,000
Real Estate	NA	38,100	44,000	38,200
Retail	40,000	48,400	36,900	40,600
Rubber/Plastics	50,000	46,200	51,600	50,500
Stone, Clay and Glass Products	NA	NA	70,400	70,400
Textile Mill Products	40,000	NA	65,300	43,800
Transportation Equipment	50,000	NA	58,000	50,000
Trucking and Warehousing	NA	56,700	92,500	47,900
Utilities	45,200	NA	50,000	46,800
Wholesale (Consumer Goods)	41,300	62,800	45,500	48,100
Overall	**$50,000**	**$64,000**	**$56,500**	**$55,600**

SOURCE: The Dartnell Corporation, *Sales Force Compensation Survey, 1994–95*. Reprinted by permission.

AVERAGE COMMISSIONS FOR MANUFACTURER'S REPRESENTATIVES

Product Market	Selling to: End User	OEM	Distributor
Abrasives	17.17%	12.38%	7.03%
Advertising Products and Services	15.00	15.00	10.00
Aerospace and Aviation	10.44	6.05	NA
Agriculture/Chemicals	17.50	4.00	4.00
Agriculture/Equipment and Machinery	9.17	5.77	7.38
Appliances	8.75	4.80	4.00
Architects and Interior Designers	9.13	NA	8.30
Arts and Crafts	13.25	9.00	7.75
Automation/Robotics	9.40	9.72	11.63
Automotive/Aftermarket	13.75	5.12	6.80
Automotive/OEM	8.90	4.67	6.25
Builders/Contractors	12.90	6.25	7.99
Building Materials and Supplies	10.05	4.90	6.50
Castings and Forgings	5.78	4.54	4.50
Chemicals/Industrial	12.87	10.59	8.60
Chemicals/Maintenance	22.50	9.50	10.06
Coatings	13.53	9.79	9.92
Computer Hardware, Software, and Peripheral Equipment and Supplies	11.72	6.77	10.00
Construction Equipment and Machinery	10.75	6.23	7.77
Controls and Instrumentation	14.81	10.61	12.04
Electrical/Consumer	13.59	4.75	7.03
Electrical/Technical and Industrial	12.47	8.12	9.44
Electronic/Communications, Audio-Visual, and Professional Products	12.59	6.65	8.25
Electronic/Components and Materials	7.92	6.16	6.85
Electronic/Consumer Products	7.38	7.00	6.13
Electronic/Technical Products	11.61	8.29	9.00
Energy	11.00	4.50	8.50
Engineering/Design	19.05	9.22	7.00
Environmental	12.79	12.54	9.60
Fasteners	5.63	5.22	6.89
Floor and Wall Coverings	8.72	15.75	9.22
Food/Beverage Chemicals	12.50	12.50	NA
Food/Beverage Processing	16.08	12.10	NA
Food/Beverage Products and Services	8.88	NA	5.00
Food/Beverage Service Equipment	9.75	6.50	8.23
Furniture and Furnishings	12.88	4.50	7.72
Gas, Oil, and Petroleum Products and Services	11.09	11.50	9.25
Glass Industry/Raw Materials and Products	13.45	8.65	5.50
Government	9.32	6.30	NA

AVERAGE COMMISSIONS FOR MANUFACTURER'S REPRESENTATIVES

Product Market	Selling to: End User	OEM	Distributor
Graphics/Printing Equipment and Supplies	13.25%	5.34%	7.50%
Hardware/Houseware	5.70	5.01	6.76
Hazardous Waste/Material Handling	12.27	9.30	7.00
Health and Beauty Aids	NA	NA	3.50
Heating, Ventilation, Air Conditioning	14.58	8.32	9.99
Heavy-Duty Truck-Trailer Equipment	6.63	5.04	6.36
Home Improvement	5.50	6.00	5.77
Import-Export	13.34	8.50	8.25
Industrial Equipment and Machinery	12.89	10.40	9.91
Industrial Supplies	15.58	7.60	8.36
Injection Molding, Parts, and Supplies	10.73	6.01	9.90
Jewelry	11.50	9.00	6.50
Kitchen/Bath	6.50	4.50	7.00
Lawn and Garden	3.75	4.37	6.39
Lighting	NA	5.10	8.45
Lubricants	9.10	8.72	8.83
Lumber Industry	20.00	7.59	6.10
Machining Equipment and Services	10.91	6.19	7.58
Maintenance Supplies	16.42	7.75	7.93
Marine	13.42	6.50	6.79
Material Handling	11.85	9.25	8.35
Medical Equipment, Supplies, and Services	12.27	6.97	5.48
Metals/Processing, Fabricating, Assemblies and Products	8.85	5.99	9.20
Metals/Raw Materials	5.36	3.42	3.20
Mining	13.42	8.75	10.25
Mobile Homes, Accessories and Supplies	NA	4.88	5.00
Office Supplies and Equipment	10.00	5.34	8.50
Optical Equipment and Supplies	10.82	7.38	10.00
Packaging and Plastics	10.21	7.22	7.82
Paints and Varnishes	20.00	8.80	7.11
Paper Industry	12.97	8.70	7.13
Pharmaceutical	12.50	13.25	NA
Photographic Equipment and Supplies	8.00	6.34	6.00
Plastics	9.10	5.60	7.97
Plumbing	21.50	6.80	7.42
Pollution and Purification Products and Services	12.56	13.65	15.00
Powdered Metal/Parts and Components	14.67	5.13	6.75
Power Transmission	8.16	7.17	7.33
Process Equipment	12.04	11.57	17.44
Pumps	16.29	10.33	10.35

AVERAGE COMMISSIONS FOR MANUFACTURER'S REPRESENTATIVES

Product Market	Selling to: End User	OEM	Distributor
Recreational Vehicle/Aftermarket and OEM	5.84%	5.07%	5.00%
Recreational Water Products/Services	6.50	5.88	16.85
Recycling	11.17	15.00	5.00
Refractories	11.17	NA	5.50
Refrigeration and Cold Storage	11.13	7.34	8.20
Rental Equipment and Supplies	10.00	NA	16.56
Retail Consumer Products and Services	10.00	NA	6.25
Roofing Materials and Supplies	7.80	4.50	5.21
Rubber Products	12.14	5.97	5.67
Safety, Emergency and Security Products	16.82	12.40	10.24
Scientific Research Equipment and Supplies	13.33	10.00	11.34
Screw Machine Products	6.07	5.15	5.29
Sporting Goods, Supplies and Accessories	7.75	5.88	7.30
Stampings	6.34	5.10	6.29
Steel Mills and Foundries	9.88	7.01	2.29
Telecommunications Equipment, Services and Supplies	12.67	4.00	8.67
Textile/Apparel Trade	9.75	5.50	NA
Textile/Industrial	12.00	5.00	6.00
Toys, Gifts and Novelties	8.80	10.75	7.40
Transportation	5.00	6.17	NA
Tubing	7.46	4.77	4.10
Utilities	13.33	10.25	NA
Waste Handling/Processing	11.91	7.38	8.00
Water/Wastewater Treatment Equipment Products and Services	11.39	11.13	10.84
Welding	12.50	6.25	8.21
Wood/Woodworking	10.88	8.40	6.11

SOURCE: Manufacturers' Agents National Association, *1994 Survey of Sales Commissions.*

Sales Executives

Sales also offers superb opportunities for advancement, and the pay at the top is excellent. In past years, *Sales & Marketing Management* magazine conducted surveys of leading companies and reported the salaries and other compensation paid to their top sales and marketing executives. Following are the earnings of the top executive at 100 leading companies, from the last annual compensation survey of *Sales & Marketing Management.*

Below are the results of the last *Sales & Marketing Management* magazine survey; although several years old the basic information remains relevant.

SALES AND MARKETING EXECUTIVE COMPENSATION BY SIZE OF COMPANY

Company Revenues	Average Compensation, 1991
$1 Billion and More	$266,000
$500 Million to $1 Billion	203,000
$100 to $500 Million	160,000
Less than $100 Million	132,000

ANNUAL EARNINGS OF THE TOP 100 SALES AND MARKETING EXECUTIVES

Company	Title	Total Cash Compensation
Durable Goods		
Comdisco	Executive VP/Pres. Marketing	$1,650,000
Xerox Corp.	Executive VP, Marketing and Customer Operations	755,492
Stone Container Corp.	Executive VP	643,480
A.G. Edwards	Vice Chairman/Director, Sales and Marketing Division	455,849
BMC Software	Senior VP, Sales and Marketing	440,218
Data General Corp.	Vice Chairman/Exec. VP, Int'l Sales and Services	435,000
Advanced Micro Devices	Senior VP and Chief Marketing Exec.	327,609
Bandag	Senior VP, Sales and Marketing	315,738
Analog Devices	VP, Sales and Marketing	279,594
Snap-On Tools	Senior VP, Sales	267,875
Wallace Computer	VP Sales	248,529
La-Z-Boy Chair Corp.	Senior VP, Sales and Marketing Dir.	248,410
Huffy Corp.	VP, Marketing	211,417
Conseco Industries	VP, Sales	203,774
Texlon Corp.	VP, North American Sales	201,083
National Presto Industries	Vice Chairman/Director of Sales	200,000
Franklin Electric	VP, Sales and Marketing	199,666
Floating Point Systems	VP, Marketing, Sales and Services	179,200
Inter-Tel	Senior VP, Sales and Marketing/Pres., Inter-Tel Equipment	176,993
Network Systems Corp.	VP, Sales and Marketing	172,360
Bohemia	VP, Marketing	162,372
Applied Magnetics Corp.	Executive VP, Sales and Marketing	162,000
Varco	VP, Sales and Marketing	162,000
Hutchinson Technology	VP, Sales and Marketing	160,196
Intermetrics	VP, Corporation Marketing	142,833
Gateway Communications	VP, Sales	142,499
Sage Software	VP, Marketing	131,707
CPT Corp.	VP, Sales	127,200
Sage Software	VP, Sales, Southern Region	124,943
Printronix	VP, North American Sales	124,487
DH Technology	VP, Sales and Marketing	123,103
CTS Corp.	VP, Sales and Marketing	122,954

ANNUAL EARNINGS OF THE TOP 100 SALES AND MARKETING EXECUTIVES

Company	Title	Total Cash Compensation
Hughes Supply	VP, Sales and Marketing/Regional Manager	$ 119,533
L.B. Foster	VP, Sales	116,131
Twin Disc	VP, International Marketing	109,000
CPT Corp.	VP, Marketing/Engineering and Customer Service	107,366
Twin Disc	VP, Marketing	104,000
Washington Scientific Industries	VP, Contract Manufacturing Division, Marketing and Corporation Planning	101,312
Datakey	VP, Sales and Marketing	87,421
	VP, Commercial Marketing	85,542
Terminal Data Corp.	VP, Sales	83,015
Nondurable Goods		
Colgate Palmolive	Executive VP, Specialty Marketing	601,833
Shaw Industries	VP, Marketing	586,444
Ross Stores	Executive VP, Merchandise and Marketing Director	463,248
Tyson Foods	Senior VP, Sales and Marketing	444,215
Wal-Mart Stores	Executive VP, Merchandise and Sales	425,000
L.A. Gear	VP, Sales	368,796
Super Valu Stores	Senior VP, Marketing	337,416
William Wrigley, Jr.	Group VP, Marketing	333,997
Forest Laboratories	Executive VP, Marketing	322,500
Tyco Toys	Senior VP, Sales	265,277
Diamond Shamrock	Senior VP/Group Executive Marketing	254,670
Agmen	VP, Sales and Marketing	248,082
A. Schulman	VP, North American Sales	244,792
Family Dollar Stores	Senior VP, Merchandise and Sales	209,455
Cagles	Senior VP, Processing and Marketing	205,715
Fretter	Senior VP, Western Region	200,550
Duplex Products	Senior VP, Sales and Marketing	184,133
Thorn Apple Valley	Senior VP, Sales	173,882
Quaker State Corp.	Director and Executive VP, Executive VP, Marketing and International Sales	172,845
WD-40	VP, Sales	162,500
Handelman Company	Executive VP, Sales	159,034
R.G. Barry Corp.	VP, Marketing and Sales	147,500
Champion Parts	VP, Sales and Marketing	141,805
Longview Fibre Co.	Senior VP, Paper Sales	129,323
Super Food Services	Executive VP, Marketing	125,769
Cagles	VP, Sales and Marketing	122,261

ANNUAL EARNINGS OF THE TOP 100 SALES AND MARKETING EXECUTIVES

Company	Title	Total Cash Compensation
Seneca Foods Corp.	Senior VP, Sales	$ 119,275
Kiddie Products	VP, Sales	113,224
Artistic Greetings	VP, Marketing	108,885
Eagle Food Centers	Senior VP, Sales and Marketing	104,934
American Vanguard Corp.	VP/Director of Marketing, Amvac Chemical Corp.	85,327
Services		
I.C.H. Corp.	Director/Senior Executive VP, Marketing and Real Estate	700,476
Gannett Co.	Executive VP, Marketing/Publishing, *USA Today*	600,000
Carnival Cruise Lines	Senior VP, Sales and Marketing	593,000
Golden Nugget	Executive VP, Marketing and Hotel Operations	475,000
A.G. Edwards	Vice Chairman/Director, Sales and Marketing Division	455,848
Circus, Circus Enterprises	Executive VP, Marketing	426,006
Browning-Ferris Industries	Vice Chairman/Chief Marketing Officer and Director	418,100
USAir	Executive VP/Executive VP, Marketing	353,077
Turner Broadcasting System	VP, Broadcast Sales	339,377
Yellow Freight System of Delaware	Senior VP, Marketing	326,844
Airborne Freight	Executive VP, Marketing Division	308,035
Alfa Corp.	Executive VP, Marketing	258,685
Consolidated Freightways	Director of Corporate Marketing	258,224
Standard Register	VP, Form Sales	256,847
The M/A/R/C Group	Executive VP/President, Targetbase Marketing	184,360
First Federal of Michigan	Executive VP, Marketing Division	171,229
GTE California	VP, Sales	164,580
United Illuminating Co.	Senior VP, Marketing	154,900
General Computer Corp.	VP, Sales	153,387
Tech/Ops Landauer	VP, Marketing	146,250
Piedmont Natural Gas Co.	Senior VP, Marketing	126,295

ANNUAL EARNINGS OF THE TOP 100 SALES AND MARKETING EXECUTIVES

Company	Title	Total Cash Compensation
Freymiller Trucking	VP, Marketing	$ 122,587
Carolina Freight Co.	Executive VP, Marketing	114,689
United Cities Gas Co.	VP/Senior VP, Gas Supply and Marketing	96,986
General Computer Corp.	Executive VP, Marketing	91,533
Keegan Management Co.	National Sales Director	72,347

SOURCE: *Sales & Marketing Management* magazine, November 1991. Reprinted by permission.

The Marketing Staff

While businesses rely on their salespeople to bring in revenues, salespersons in large companies are normally supported by a marketing staff which does everything from preparing fancy sales brochures to designing sales promotion programs to developing new or improved products and much more. In general, the larger the company, the larger the marketing organization and the more important the marketing role. Typical management positions in marketing include brand or product manager, sales promotion or support manager, advertising manager, and market research manager. The orientation of the work done by the marketing staff tends to be more strategic than the tactical orientation of the sales force.

There are basically two distinct career paths in marketing—one involving direct entry into the marketing disciplines, the other gaining entry via the sales function. In small and medium-sized companies there are likely to be no separately identified marketing functions. In these companies salespeople perform the marketing functions on a part-time basis. The roles of sales and marketing are thus combined and selling receives most of the emphasis. In these companies the career path for someone with a bent for marketing definitely has a sales bias; i.e., while the need for marketing skills may be recognized by the organization, people are promoted largely based on their sales abilities.

Employees of large companies may also find themselves on a career path toward marketing via sales. At IBM or Xerox, for example, an aspiring marketing manager will usually find himself or herself in the field selling long before getting the opportunity to work in a marketing capacity. This approach makes sense in situations where products and markets are highly complex. Managers in such markets are expected to understand them from the ground up. By starting as a salesperson, they acquire a detailed understanding of what makes people buy, and this understanding permits them to then function effectively in the marketing role.

In consumer product companies, where the emphasis in marketing is on the ultimate user of the product, it is common to hire and train product and brand managers directly from graduate school. Procter & Gamble is particularly renowned for hiring and training professional product and brand managers. Its development program, which is very intense and packed with pressure to perform, has been the envy of the consumer products industry for years. P & G's approach has in fact been copied by more than one of its rivals.

These companies typically hire MBAs as assistant brand or product managers at starting salaries of $40,000 to $60,000. Basically, these managers are responsible for increasing sales of their assigned product or brand. This means planning and executing retail and trade promotions as well as advertising campaigns, evaluating product packaging and positioning, assessing the potential of product improvements and new products, tracking and analyzing sales, etc. The brand manager must pull all of these elements together into a cohesive program, sell that program to various parts of the company, and then implement it. This requires a great deal of analytical ability, a capability to distill large volumes of data into meaningful groupings of information, a personal style that communicates persuasively orally and in writing, and, most of all, an underlying feel for the intangible forces that affect relative success or failure in highly competitive markets.

The challenge to those beginning their careers in consumer marketing is to rise from assistant manager to manager within two to three years. A brand or product manager wields much power and influence. Budgets can run into millions of dollars. Those who are successful in attaining the manager level can earn $70,000 or more before the age of 30. While this is not financial success of 1980s Wall Street dimensions, it is still substantial compensation for someone who has been in the business world for less than five years. Also, progression through the product and brand management ranks can lead directly to compensation of the levels shown previously in this section. In fact, in a recent poll more than 40 percent of today's CEOs cited sales and marketing as the best route to the top ranks of American business.

The Training Staff

In 1940 a small group of sales executives wanted to change attitudes toward buying in the United States. Realizing the need for good teaching personnel to ensure companies of ethical yet highly persuasive salesmanship, they founded the first national society of training directors. The American Society of Training Directors (ASTD) was formed in 1945, and today (under the name American Society of Training and Development) it has over 50,000 members. It also publishes a journal and provides one- and two-week courses of instruction at its own institutes.

Originally the ASTD's emphasis was on the training of manufacturing and marketing personnel. While training in those two fields continues, many other fields of employment now have training programs as well, including government, utilities, and finance. The programs range in scope from introductory sales techniques to safety courses for school bus drivers, and from basic office procedures to lessons in word processing techniques. Some training personnel even teach stress management with Zen and yoga methods. Corporate awareness of the need for carefully planned training programs to provide essential instruction to employees has grown, and the increased costs of mismanaging human resources has become apparent; these factors have led companies to place greater value on the function of the trainer and to increase the number of training positions available.

Trainers work with on-the-job trainees both at the actual corporation site and at training centers, to which corporations send their employees. The optimum training system is one that encompasses instruction, evaluation, and implementation; therefore, trainers' jobs consist of elements within all these areas. The most common training job titles are listed below, followed by each title's annual salary range.

AVERAGE ANNUAL SALARIES OF THE TRAINING STAFF BY POSITION

Title	Average Salary
Executive-Level Training Manager	$70,650
Training Manager (company with five or more full-time trainers)	58,731
Training Manager (company with one to four full-time trainers)	51,121
One-Person Training Department	44,341
Management, Career, Organization Development Specialists	43,121
Training Instructional Designer	43,128
Classroom Training Instructor	39,336
Personnel Manager	52,482

SOURCE: *Training* magazine, 1994.

The training occupation is currently undergoing substantial changes, and trainers' responsibilities and spheres of involvement are expanding due to the increased demand for trainers within both traditional fields and new fields of employment. In all probability the training occupation will continue to grow markedly in the upcoming years, as will trainers' salaries.

VI

Jobs and Salaries in Representative Businesses

This section contains job descriptions and salary information for occupations that exist only in specialized businesses. Actuary, bank teller, flight attendant, and media planner, for example, are jobs found only in the insurance, banking, airline, and advertising businesses, respectively. Obviously, not every distinct enterprise could be included, but we did manage to get a good mix of large industries employing hundreds of thousands of workers with relatively small businesses that are recognized as extremely powerful and influential (the brokerage firm and the advertising agency, for example).

Note that office jobs found in every business establishment, such as secretary, typist, and keypunch operator, are not included here. See the section "Office Staff" in Part VIII.

THE ADVERTISING AGENCY

Few facts reveal the extraordinary growth of America's so-called mass-consumption society as vividly as those dealing with the advertising business. In 1950, as the postwar economy began to heat up, American business spent $5.7 billion to advertise its goods and services, just about double the 1930 figure. By the late 1980s, the total money spent on advertising had increased to over $120 billion. And in 1993, total advertising spending was more than

$138 billion. Advertising has in fact become such an integral part of our business system that more than 50 corporations now spend over $100 million a year to place their ads and commercials in broadcast, print, and outdoor media. The vast majority of these dollars get filtered through that uniquely American business known as the advertising agency.

According to *Advertising Age* magazine, there are about 6,000 large and small agencies currently in operation and employing most of the 125,000 people engaged directly in advertising. Most agencies make most of their money by charging their clients a commission of 15 percent of the total fee billed by the newspaper, magazine, or radio or television station. This can amount to quite an impressive sum. The three biggest U.S. advertisers in 1993 (Procter and Gamble, General Motors, and Philip Morris) each spent more than a billion dollars on advertising their various products.

During the 1980s, the merger mania that played such a key role in American business finally struck the advertising world. As a result, several well-known agencies were folded into others, giving birth to the so-called superagency, like the worldwide Saatchi & Saatchi Company, whose U.S. agencies include Backer Spielvogel Bates, Campbell Mithun Esty, and Cliff Freeman & Partners among others. By the 1990s, these mergers had translated into lost jobs, 7,600 in 1991 alone. Agencies outside of New York weathered the recession far better than those on Madison Avenue. Job growth is expected to be greatest in sales promotion departments and in agencies that specialize in health care.

JOBS WITHIN ADVERTISING AGENCIES

To understand the hierarchy of an advertising agency, one must understand the advertising and marketing process. When a client places advertising for its product into review, each ad agency's accounts and marketing departments evaluate the product's potential in the marketplace. If the agency wins the account, the heads of the accounts, marketing, and creative departments formulate an advertising plan or campaign, which involves an advertising concept, a schedule, and a budget. Each department then assumes responsibility for designated tasks (see below for detailed descriptions of those responsibilities) and goals. All three departments are regulated by a fourth department: office management and finance. That group makes sure the three groups adhere to their schedules and budgets and integrates all efforts to reach a mutual end, which is the introduction or sale of a product.

Governing the four agency arms—creative, accounts, marketing, and office management—is the agency president and board of directors. These executives are customarily seasoned veterans of the Madison Avenue wars. The structure of the presidency and governing board is specific to each agency and determined by the size of the agency, the dollar volume in which it trades, and the diversity of its accounts and interests.

What follows is a department-by-department breakdown of agency jobs, progressing from department head down the company ladder.

Accounts Department

This department is responsible for dealing with the client in all aspects of the campaign; it is the agency's "public face" and, in terms of expense accounts and the social sphere, is the most visible department.

Accounts Manager—Responsible for overseeing and guiding the course of new business and accounts and supervising the management of existing accounts by working with a staff of account executives. Helps create budgets and project schedules, answers to board of directors or agency president.

Accounts Supervisor—Mediates between account executives and management; works with other department supervisors to meet schedules and agency goals. In a large agency, supervisors may be responsible for related items (e.g., packaged goods or food accounts) or for one client's spectrum of products (e.g., Procter & Gamble's soaps, lotions, and instant coffee).

Account Executive (AE)—As a liaison between client and agency, the AE meets client needs without compromising the agency's creative concepts or budget. Part of the job entails wooing (and winning) prospective accounts, as well as maintaining happy relations with existing accounts. This is a high-visibility position, and good AEs advance quickly in the corporate ranks. There is a high turnover of AEs, as an account succeeds or fails. A good AE is a valuable agency asset; as a result, perquisites, performance incentives, and bonuses are granted in accord with the AE's track record.

Senior AE and Junior AE—Titles which, in larger agencies, denote greater (or lesser) experience and expertise. Senior AEs usually are responsible for a staff. Salaries are scaled according to rank.

AE Trainee—Largely a little-thanks, prove-yourself position for an individual who has excelled in an entry-level spot and wants to rise in the agency. Projects are assigned rather than self-determined.

Marketing Department

This department is responsible for market analysis, consumer research, product evaluation, and ultimately providing the data and statistical insight to create an advertising campaign.

Marketing Manager—Integrates the media research and sales promotion department efforts; works with staff to implement ads that maximize existing market potential and utilize agency resources; works with creative and accounts managers to formulate campaign. Answers to agency president and/or board of directors.

Media Director—Responsible for supervision of staff, planning, and scheduling; authorizes the purchase of air time on television and radio, or newspaper and magazine space for ads; usually works with AEs and clients to develop ad plan.

Media Planner—Responsible for a specific medium; e.g., television, radio, print, or specialty advertising (display, direct response, etc.). Analyzes media options and selects best ad forum; develops media plans and strategies. Frequently the titles *Associate* or *Assistant Media Director* are used.

Media Buyer—Negotiates and procures time and space, deals with media representatives, evaluates and selects media markets (networks, programs) to suit a campaign.

Operational Media Staff—In close conjunction with buyers, they handle agency paperwork (requisitions, invoices, memos, etc.) and media correspondence. This is often an entry-level position.

Research Director—Responsible for the accumulation, preparation, and presentation of research findings, statistics, and market analysis data to marketing and accounts staff (and occasionally to the client). Supervises and assigns research staff projects.

Research Analyst—Responsible for the design and execution of statistical analyses of a product's salability; they also supply data to corroborate ad claims, and perform product-related tests and studies.

Market Researcher—Analyzes existing market and projects market potential; advises media and creative staff on ad choices; provides statistics on the consumer, general economics, and the marketplace.

Media Researcher—Analyzes media options, then suggests most effective media to sell the product; projects media trends.

Junior/Senior Research Analyst—Again, these titles denote seniority in the agency and reflect a salary variance equivalent to the rank. Senior staff usually head a group and supervise group effort.

Sales Promotion Manager—Supervises and coordinates sales and promotion staffs; designs sales strategy once market has been targeted.

Sales Representative—Responsible for ad sales (both projected and actual) in an assigned region. Operating on national, regional, and local scales, working with sales staff, sales representatives implement sales strategies previously outlined by the sales manager and the client, in conjunction with the AE. Sales reps are also valuable agency members, and experienced individuals accumulate contacts that simplify negotiations and give the agency a favorable position in good markets. Sales reps are on salary and receive commissions which act as production incentives.

Promotion Staff—These individuals, working with AEs and creative department staff, design, manage, and enact promotional events, direct-response mail campaigns, consumer incentives (coupons, special "deals"), and in-store and display ads, as well as manufacture elaborate schemes and public events designed to draw attention (and business) to the product.

Creative Department

The creative department is the most diverse and complicated facet of the agency. Following is a skeleton structure of a hypothetical creative department; in the industry, no two are identical, but all fill the same function: to create, design, and produce advertising art and copy.

Creative Director—Responsible for all copy, art, and production work; works with marketing and accounts directors (and, rarely, the client) to formalize ad concept; guides department staff to meet goals.

Copy Supervisor/Group Head—Helps create advertising languages, supervises writing staff, develops ideas with art director, writes copy for select accounts or creates central ideas to be written out in detail by copy staff.

Copywriter—Writes advertising for print media, scripts for radio and television commercials, and sales promotional material for sales department.

In larger agencies there is also a *senior copywriter* responsible to copy supervisor and creative director for ad copy on one or a related series of accounts; supervises copy staff. Works in conjunction with senior art staff members to integrate copy and art for presentation to management and client. A *junior copywriter* proofreads ad copy and may write incidental copy or participate in group writing projects; this is an entry-level position.

Art Director—Works with copy supervisor, AE, and art staff to produce ad art, storyboards (for television commercials), magazine layouts, and other visual media (speciality advertising).

Commercial Artists, Designers—Perform the actual drawing of ads; design and lay out ad pages; work with photos, copy, and other visuals to create ads.

Paste-up, Mechanical Artists—Construct (paste-up) boards for print media; construct models and dummy material for client and management review and approval.

Storyboard Artists—Create television storyboards—frame-by-frame setups of the television commercial as it will be shot, incorporating director's camera angles, set designer's specifications, and other production variables.

Commercial Production Staff—Each agency has its own system for commercial production. A large Madison Avenue agency may employ a full-time casting department (*casting director* and *assistants*) and a television and radio commercial production department (in-house *directors, producers,* and *technicians*). A smaller or regional agency may bring in casting and production personnel for a specific commercial; still others maintain steady freelance relationships with a roster of commercial talent.

Traffic Department Staff—The size of the traffic department depends on agency size; usually a traffic supervisor is responsible for a traffic staff. In larger agencies, of course, the staff is more diverse; in smaller houses, one or two people may be the entire department. Essentially, traffic personnel tie together all the odd threads of the creative department to keep the ad on schedule and reasonably within budget. They handle paperwork flow, keep tabs on progress of creative department projects, coordinate department efforts, and handle freelance assignments and internal memoranda.

Office Management and Finance Department

This department is responsible for the inner agency workings as well as paying outstanding accounts and billing for agency services; oversees total agency expenditures and maintains budgets.

Department Manager—Responsible for internal agency checks and balances: keeping departments within budgets and on schedule. Oversees agency financial operations, including payments to media and expense accounts; employee relations and personnel; and general administration.

Estimators—Estimate print, radio, and television spot advertising costs; generalize network and production estimates.

Planners—Anticipate and plan for new business, agency expansion; adjust existing schedules to reflect actual timetables. Planners can be responsible for a facet of a department (for instance, the copy end of the Creative Department) or for the entire department.

Senior Planners—Supervise and guide a planning team and integrate individual plans to formulate a total projection for management; their salary is commensurate with their responsibility, seniority, and expertise.

Broadcast Forwarders—Working with shipping estimates and schedules, responsible for trafficking broadcast copy to various media outlets.

Coordinators—Plan, schedule, and coordinate media traffic flow; buy office and art supplies; coordinate use of marketing, sales/promotional, and creative materials.

Talent Payments Staff—Pay commercial and freelance design talent: actors, directors, artists, technicians, etc.

Billers—Bill clients for agency services (e.g., commercial production costs, advertising pages, newspaper copy).

Some Entry-Level Positions

The advertising industry is mercurial, with a high turnover in agency staff, creating a serious and competitive job market. Entry-level positions exist throughout the industry, but they are scarce and tough to get because of stiff competition. Additionally, current economic trends dictate that agencies trim their "trainee" and "intern" programs substantially; thus, the advertising neophyte is faced with a bleak, tight job arena. If an entry-level spot is open, the most prized skill across the board is, alas, typing. Candidates are sought who are meticulous and detail-minded, as well as strong in language and math skills. Usually a first agency job will be working as an assistant (or a glorified "gofer"), learning department operations, and looking after the loose odds and ends of a superior's efforts. Some examples of entry-level positions follow.

Creative Department, Production Assistant—Gal/guy Friday with general office skills; position offers the opportunity to learn print, television, and/or radio production, as well as art production; growth potential.

Creative Department, Assistant Copywriter—Clerical and editorial (proofreading) work; strong language skills needed for limited writing; career interest fostered.

Marketing Department, Advertising Assistant, Sales—Heavy telephone work and typing, work with sales reps, some client contact.

Marketing Department, Media Assistant—Trainee can learn media operations, buying, planning, and scheduling; job involves preparation of graphs and client presentations.

AVERAGE TOTAL COMPENSATION IN ADVERTISING AGENCIES (BY AGENCY SIZE)

Title	Average	Agency Size (billings in millions)			
		Under $50	$50–99	$100–249	$250+
Executives					
Chairman/CEO	$166,700	$118,800	$302,500	$286,000	$246,800[1]
COO/CFO	124,300	108,200	151,700[1]	100,000[1]	222,400[1]
President	121,900	115,300	207,000[1]	265,000	450,000[1]
Partner	103,900	103,200	123,300[1]	169,000	NA
Executive VP	125,000	88,500	118,500	128,400	143,800
Vice-President	80,300	66,200	80,000	89,800	86,300
Supervisor	54,200	48,100	58,000	53,300	61,000
Senior	48,100	40,800	49,100	54,900	51,600
Junior Assistant	33,600	30,300	37,900	43,900	36,000
Other Departments					
Headquarters/ Holding Co.	130,800	107,500	176,600	200,400	246,800
Creative	85,900	71,400	88,100	116,500	94,200
Account Services	76,700	55,500	78,700	89,100	88,100
Media	69,900	51,000	73,900	70,900	82,300
Administrative/ Financial	65,800	51,700	84,200	82,400[1]	73,800

[1]Small sample size.
SOURCE: *Adweek* magazine, May 1994. Reprinted by permission.

THE AIRLINES

The airline industry has been in almost constant upheaval ever since the passage of the Airline Deregulation Act, in 1978. No longer compelled by the Federal Aviation Administration (FAA) to fly unprofitable low-density routes, airlines dropped them in favor of competing for the more heavily traveled and profitable routes. The less-traveled routes have been filled by commuter airlines, which fly smaller planes in short hops between regional airfields and the major airport hubs. In most cases, the major airlines have bought up these smaller carriers.

The business rationale for deregulation was to allow the major airlines to fly hub to hub in order to improve profitability. But in the end, cutthroat competition led to mountainous losses, widespread labor unrest, and the eventual destruction of several companies that had been mainstays of the airline industry, including Eastern, Pan Am, and Braniff. Many other carriers were forced to seek bankruptcy protection in order to stay operational (America West, TWA, Continental, and Northwest, among others). Today, there are only three major airlines in the United States—American, United, and Delta—and each is now an international carrier with well-established routes purchased from the defunct airlines. So despite extraordinary losses of billions of dollars during the early 1990s, these three companies should thrive in the years ahead. Other carriers like USAir and Continental have been struggling but should benefit from a rebounding economy. The strongest regional carrier for many years has been Southwest Airlines in Phoenix.

Airline industry analysts are predicting growth rates of 5 percent for the next several years. Some believe that by the year 2000, international travel will nearly double as Europe opens its borders and Asia becomes a more popular destination for tourists and business people alike. The impact of this kind of growth on the job opportunities will, in the end, be quite favorable as more flights will require more mechanics, more pilots, and more attendants, both on the ground and in the air. Keep in mind, however, that the competition for these jobs will be very strong. In fact, the most recent projections indicate a downsizing trend—including significant job and wage cuts—among the big three airlines that will not be offset by the growth of small, no-frills regional carriers. The medium-sized carriers will survive in this market only by teaming up with foreign airlines: Northwest with KLM Royal Dutch Airlines; USAir with British Airways; and Continental with Air Canada. These alliances will prevent further erosion of jobs, but they are not likely to produce any new positions in the United States in this troubled industry.

Working for the airlines has several positive aspects including good benefits and very inexpensive travel opportunities. But unless you are a pilot or first officer, the pay is moderate at best, a condition that is not likely to be ameliorated by intense competition for scarce jobs.

Pilots

The Airline Pilots Association (ALPA), which represents pilots at most major airlines (American, which has an in-house union, is one exception), estimates that some 60,000 active pilots fly for the scheduled airlines.

Being a pilot is a competitive, demanding job. Training takes years, and advancement comes on a strict seniority basis and is run very much along military lines. This can partly be attributed to the fact that many pilots receive their training and original FAA licenses from the armed services—which also helps explain why there are still so few women commanding large aircraft.

Three positions control the cockpit. The captain, also called the pilot in command, does the bulk of the actual flying and has overall responsibility for the safety of the craft, crew, passengers, and cargo. The first officer or copilot, assists and relieves the captain in the operation of the aircraft. He shares a percentage of the flying, and monitors certain systems during the flight. The second officer, or flight engineer, rarely engages in any actual flying. The monitoring of the aircraft's electronic and mechanical system is his responsibility.

AVERAGE SALARIES OF COMMERCIAL AIRLINE CAPTAINS AND FIRST OFFICERS

Airline	First Year Captain	Maximum Captain Pay	Average First Officer Salary (6th year)
American[1]	$153,700	$206,350	$92,500
Continental[1]	101,200	133,000	62,700
Delta	151,600	208,000	93,000
Northwest	133,500	192,700	80,300
United	146,500	208,200	89,800

[1]Pilots for American and Continental airlines are represented by an in-house union, not the ALPA.
SOURCE: AIR, Inc.

Starting salaries for pilots are about $31,961, according to Airline Information Research, Inc. (AIR, Inc.), a research group that publishes ALPA contracts. That's for about 86 flight hours each month. Salaries rise dramatically for pilots after the first year on the job. The average first officer earns about $82,393 and the average captain's salary is over $133,000, according to AIR, Inc. Some senior captains (those who have worked for the airline for 30 years) earned as much as $165,000. Generally, pilots who work outside the commercial airlines earn lower salaries. Generally, pilots who fly jet aircraft earn higher salaries than pilots who fly propeller planes.

Employment of pilots is sensitive to cyclical swings in the economy. During recessions, when declines in air travel force airlines to curtail their number of flights, they may temporarily furlough pilots. The 1990–1991 recession, coupled with fears of flying because of the war in the Persian Gulf, caused a severe drop in air travel and forced the airlines to lay off nearly 7,000 pilots. The rest of the decade should be better, though: Future Aviation Professionals of America anticipated about 52,000 to 62,000 new jobs for pilots by the end of the decade. As of April 1995, AIR, Inc. reports that five of the major airlines—including Northwest, Southwest, and United—were hiring pilots.

Flight Attendants

After much fuss and many lawsuits, the stewardess has become a flight attendant—chosen without regard to sex, race, religion, marital status, or even the amount of makeup worn. Flight attendants are considered the airline's personal representatives. They greet passengers as they board the plane, serve meals and beverages, assist with information concerning connecting flights, and, at the end of the flight, complete paperwork relating to cabin maintenance, in-flight catering and sales, and, if necessary, incidents.

Nearly 100,000 flight attendants work on the scheduled airlines, logging an average of 75 to 85 hours in flight each month. These hours do not include time spent on the ground en route or in preflight checking of supplies. Furthermore, before acquiring a regular run, all flight attendants serve on reserve duty, lasting from three months to two years, during which time they must be on constant call.

Salaries for flight attendants are outlined in the following table.

REPRESENTATIVE MONTHLY AND YEARLY SALARIES OF FLIGHT ATTENDANTS[1]

	Base Starting Salary		6th Year Salary		Maximum Salary (After number of years in parenthesis)	
Airline	**Monthly**	**Yearly**	**Monthly**	**Yearly**	**Monthly**	**Yearly**
Majors						
American	$1,325	$15,902	$1,924	$23,098	$3,005 (16)	$36,055 (16)
United	1,374	16,490	2,369	28,427	2,958 (15)	35,501 (15)
TWA	1,069	12,825	1,526	18,306	1,902 (12)	22,824 (12)
Nationals						
Hawaiian	1,064	12,762	1,882	22,581	2,327 (20)	27,927 (20)
Alaska	1,091	13,095	2,102	25,218	3,069 (13)	36,825 (13)

REPRESENTATIVE MONTHLY AND YEARLY SALARIES OF FLIGHT ATTENDANTS[1]

	Base Starting Salary		6th Year Salary		Maximum Salary (After number of years in parenthesis)	
Airline	Monthly	Yearly	Monthly	Yearly	Monthly	Yearly
Regionals						
Piedmont	$1,067	$12,789	$1,588	$19,053	$1,912 (15)	$22,941 (15)
Flagship	825	9,900	1,275	15,300	1,275 (10)	15,300 (10)
West Air	908	10,890	1,352	16,227	1,501 (9)	18,009 (9)

[1]All rates effective February 1995; based on 75 hours of flying per month. Domestic rates shown. International rates are higher.
SOURCE: Association of Flight Attendants.

Airplane Mechanics

The roughly 64,000 industry mechanics perform scheduled maintenance on all aircraft systems and equipment at periodic intervals. They put each aircraft through a checklist of functions before each flight, and complete inspections required by the FAA. Several levels of advancement exist within this occupation which is represented by the International Association of Machinists and Aerospace Workers.

In 1994 the median salary of aircraft mechanics was $36,868. Mechanics who worked on jets generally earned more than those working on other aircraft. The top 10 percent of all aircraft mechanics earned over $46,166 a year. Airline employees and their immediate families receive reduced fare transportation on their own and on most other airlines. Beginning aircraft mechanics employed by the airlines earned from $11.13 to $16.55 an hour. Earnings of experienced mechanics ranged from $16.93 to $22.98 an hour. Mechanics employed by the federal government averaged $32,500 a year in 1992.

Mechanic—Their job is as described above. Mechanics are responsible for their own work but do not supervise others; nor are they required to test and inspect parts on completed aircraft except as necessary to test their own work.

Lead Mechanic—A mechanic who, as a working member of a group, leads, directs, and approves the work of other employees. Must hold valid federal licenses.

Lead Inspector—Assigned at maintenance bases to the work of overall inspection of aircraft during major repairs and overhauls. At the airport, lead inspectors handle preliminary and final inspection during heavy maintenance checks. They perform the required "critical item inspection" before takeoff at airport stations. Must hold valid federal licenses. Average hourly wages for these jobs declined slightly from 1993 to 1994 as union members accepted stock in lieu of rate increases:

	1993	**1994**
Mechanic	$21.89	$20.17
Lead Mechanic	23.07	21.23
Lead Inspector	23.07	21.75

Added to these base figures are license premiums, which can add from $.50 per hour for the first license held, to a maximum of approximately $2.60 for holding several, depending on the airline. Also, shift premiums can add $.51 to $.58 per hour for working night or rotating shifts. There are across-the-board cost-of-living increases almost each year.

Reservation or Ticket Agents

In recent years these two jobs have been consolidated into one. Agents may be based in large central offices or at ticket counters in airports and sales offices. They answer telephone inquiries and book customer reservations on a computer terminal on which they record passenger reservation information. At the airport, they accept luggage, ticket it, and give boarding passes. Agents also stand at the gate, helping passengers board and working with flight attendants to ensure that all necessary equipment is on board the flight.

The following hourly wages are for Northwest Airlines.

	1986	**1987**	**1988**	**1992**
Beginning	$10.23	$10.64	$11.01	$10.25
10th Year	16.26	16.91	17.70	17.70

Agents received a 4 percent salary increase in 1986, and a 3.5 percent increase in 1987 under contracts with the now defunct Brotherhood of Airline and Railway Clerks. In 1992, under a contract with the Association of Machinists and Aerospace Workers, first year wages fell 7 percent, and 10th year wages increased by only 2 percent since 1988. At one time the top pay tier was reached after seven years on the job; it now requires ten years' seniority.

The following are 1992–93 wages for reservation and ticket agents at various airlines. Raises have been very small over the last few years.

	Northwest	Delta	American
Beginning	$10.25	$ 7.13	$ 6.25
10th Year	17.70	17.43	16.25

Baggage Handlers and Skycaps

Known officially as station agents, these people work for the different airlines, not for the airport. Station agents handle the loading and unloading of baggage and air freight; assign passengers with baggage, wheelchairs, and the like; place the disembarking ramp for passengers and freight; and aid the aircraft into position at the ramp. For these tables note that all shifts have different salary schedules; night work receives extra pay.

	Northwest	Delta	American
Beginning	$ 8.76	$ 7.13	$ 6.25
10th Year	17.25	17.43	16.25

THE BANK

Banking is a major American enterprise whose activities influence the daily lives of all of us. Just about everybody has a bank account, and anyone who works gets paid through one. Bank accounts are used for everything from simple identification to proof of one's credit standing. The bank itself is a source of capital for anything from a family home to a company's production plant. Banks stand for prosperity and thrift, as well as conservatism in everything from interest rates and dress codes to the salaries of their employees.

The spectacular savings and loan debacle of late 1980s and the recession of the early 1990s pitched the banking industry into depression early in this decade. Bailing out the S&Ls has already cost the American taxpayer close to $100 million and is expected to cost more than $500 million in total. But since 1992, low interest rates have kept banks riding a wave of good fortune. The drop in banking employment—the Bureau of Labor Statistics estimates that 50,000 jobs were lost in 1991 alone—leveled off, with some experts anticipating a slight increase in bank workers in 1995. An estimated 2.1 million people in the United States work in some form of banking, the majority for America's 12,000 commercial banks, making banks one of the largest employers of American workers. Meanwhile, profitability and productivity both increased dramatically between 1991 and 1994.

The prognostications for the future are not so rosy, however. In an effort to control inflation, the Federal Reserve raised the discount rate seven times in 1994 alone, causing demand for mortgages and other consumer banking products to plummet. And the consolidation of banks, like the megamerger between Manufacturers Hanover and Chemical banks, has also eliminated the need for some employees whose functions were duplicated. The Commerce Department estimates that the number of banking jobs will continue to decrease by as much as a quarter of a million by the year 2000. It's no surprise, then, that many analysts believe that there will be only 8,000 banks in the United States by the end of the century.

More than 80 percent of banking jobs are tedious, low-paying clerical jobs such as teller, accounting clerk, or proof machine operator. The federal government projects that most of the job openings in the banking industry will come in these areas, not because of job growth, but because of the high turnover rates. And no wonder. Banks usually pay their clerks less than those in other industries, and the work is hardly stimulating. The Bureau of Labor Statistics describes the teller's job succinctly as "a series of repetitive tasks and prolonged standing." The federal government predicts that 45,000 of the more than 500,000 teller jobs are open each year.

Bank clerks and tellers are usually required to have a high school diploma, but exceptions are made. Tellers earn as little as $12,000 in small banks, and their salaries rarely top $19,000. If clerks or tellers stay with a bank for a long time, they can attain a supervisory role in some branch of operations. But unless they seek further education, their chances of joining the nation's 250,000 bank officers are nonexistent.

Bank officers are hand-picked from colleges, universities, and sometimes from graduate schools and are then trained within the bank for up to two years. They begin on different pay scales from clerks and ascend a different ladder of advancement.

The information that follows was gathered from a number of industry and government sources and pertains to commercial banks alone, which comprise the largest segment of the industry. In general, Federal Reserve banks pay about the same as commercial banks, but mutual savings banks and savings and loan institutions pay less. Salaries for similar jobs can vary from 5 to 20 percent between savings and loan associations and commercial banks.

Bank Officers

The standard unwritten rules governing salary levels apply to bank officers as much as to anyone: The older you are, the more years of education you have, and the more years of service you have, the more you get paid. And as the figures demonstrate, the size of the bank, in terms of total assets, also affects officers' salaries significantly.

A word of caution: Don't be surprised by the paltry figures. Bank officers' salaries are known to be comparatively low. Excellent benefits and job security, combined with work that is not considered very high-pressured are the compensatory elements. In addition, like all bank employees, officers are virtually guaranteed mortgage loans and personal loans, and at a slightly reduced rate of interest.

Below are job descriptions for just about every kind of bank officer; they are derived from those given by the Bank Administration Institute. The chief executive officer and second-ranking officer are not included on the grounds that their functions are managerial in the broadest sense of the term.

Bank Investment Officer (Senior)—Overall responsibility for investment of bank funds.

Bond Department Manager—Acquisition of treasury and agency securities; maintains the bank's portfolio.

Branch Manager (Small, Medium, Large)—Responsible for all phases of branch operation, including personnel, business transactions, customer relations, and branch finance.

Business Development Officer (Senior)—Same as New Accounts. A sales representative for the bank. Solicits new accounts; sells new services to old and new accounts, such as payroll preparation and time deposits.

Commercial Credit Department Manager—Develops credit studies for loan officers, financial analysis, review and control of loan portfolio.

Correspondent Bank Officer (Senior)—Establishes and coordinates acquisition of demand deposit accounts with correspondent banks. (For example, when a bank in Indiana wants to clear checks through or borrow cash from a New York bank, it contacts the correspondent bank officer.)

Financial Officer (Chief)—Prepares and interprets reports for top management, fiscal reports, federal reserve and government reports, and internal budgets.

Installment Loan Collection (Collector, Manager)—Day-to-day personal accounting; reviews credit ratings and applications; deals with delinquent accounts.

Installment Loan Department Manager Officer—Services customers seeking car loans, boat loans, trailer loans, etc.

International Banking Officer (Senior)—Recommends overall policy for international division; develops new and existing services to accounts overseas and intergovernmental loans.

Loan Officer, Commercial—Makes and services loans to businesses.

Loan Officer, General—In smaller banks this one person makes and services a variety of business and individual incorporated loans.

Loan Officer, Mortgage (Department Manager, Jr.)—Studies risk and then approves or rejects mortgage loans, either personal or commercial or both.

New Accounts, Officer/Representative—See Business Development Officer.

Personal Banking Manager Officer—Sits on "the platform" in a branch office across from the tellers; provides customers with information; certifies checks; waives overdrafts or individual customers; sometimes acts in a supervisory capacity.

Trust Department Officer (Senior)—Oversees personal and corporate trusts and securities administration. Develops new trust business and coordinates investments.

Most of the salary figures that follow have been extracted from a salary survey, published annually by the Bank Administration Institute. Salaries have been rounded off to the nearest 100 and do not include annual bonuses. Nationally, bonuses average from about 6 percent of base salary (for an officer trainee with a bachelor's degree in a bank with assets of $73.5 million) to over 30 percent of base salary (for the chief executive of a bank with over $1 billion in assets). There are three tables: one listing salary ranges in banks, a second showing average base salaries of officers of banks with assets over $1 billion, and a third listing average base salaries of officers in banks with assets of $100 million and lower.

SALARY RANGES FOR BANKING PERSONNEL, 1995[1]

Position	Salary Range, 1995	Percent Change from 1994
Senior Vice-President/Head of Lending	$194,000–$209,000	2.0
Division Lending Head	92,000–129,000	1.8
Commercial Lender		
1–3 Years Experience	42,500– 54,000	2.7
3 or More Years Experience	56,000– 82,500	2.6
Commercial Real Estate Mortgage Lender	51,000– 70,500	1.7
Residential Real Estate Mortgage Lender	33,500– 44,000	2.6
Consumer Loan Officer	32,000– 45,750	2.3

SALARY RANGES FOR BANKING PERSONNEL, 1995[1]

Position	Salary Range, 1995	Percent Change from 1994
Investment or Merchant Banker/Corporate Finance	$ 53,000– 71,500	2.0
Executive Professional Lender		
1–3 Years Experience	36,000– 46,000	2.5
3 or More Years Experience	48,000– 64,000	2.3
Loan Review Officer	45,000– 56,000	1.0
Loan Workout Officer	57,750– 80,000	1.7
Branch Manager	36,000– 46,000	2.5
Branch Administrator	42,000– 54,000	2.1
Marketing Director	68,000– 93,000	2.5
Asset/Liability Investment Manager	55,000– 77,000	2.3
Operation Officer	38,000– 49,000	2.4
Corporate Trust Officer	38,500– 49,000	2.3
Personal Trust Officer	35,000– 45,000	1.9
Employee Benefits Trust Officer	35,000– 44,750	2.2
Trust Investment Officer	45,000– 55,000	2.0

[1]Figures are for banks with assets of $1 billion or more. Deduct 5 percent for banks with assets of $500 million to $1 billion; deduct 10 percent for banks with assets of $100 million to $500 million; deduct 15 percent for banks with assets of $100 million or less.
SOURCE: Robert Half International, *1995 Salary Guide.*

AVERAGE BASE SALARIES OF OFFICERS IN LARGE BANKS[1]

Job Title	Weighted Average Salary	Salary Range
Management		
Chief Executive Officer	$297,300	$208,100–390,300
Chief Operating Officer	169,600	155,100–250,900
Chief Financial Officer	137,100	100,100–150,100
Director of Marketing	72,700	54,100– 90,100
Business Development Officer	35,800	31,200– 53,800
Bank Investment Officer	62,200	46,800–111,000
Head of Data Processing/Information Services	76,300	56,100– 90,500
Head of Operations	87,800	74,300–113,300
Head of Retail Banking	113,900	87,100–146,000
Branch Administration Manager	59,300	48,800– 75,100
Branch Manager I	32,400	29,200– 35,800
Branch Manager II	39,500	34,400– 44,700

AVERAGE BASE SALARIES OF OFFICERS IN LARGE BANKS[1]

Job Title	Weighted Average Salary	Salary Range
Loan Department		
Commercial Loan Dept. Manager	$ 91,400	$ 75,000–107,600
Senior Commercial Loan Officer	57,400	49,400– 71,400
Commercial Loan Officer	43,100	34,200– 50,300
Consumer Loan Dept. Manager	72,400	47,300– 89,000
Senior Consumer Loan Officer	42,000	36,600– 49,000
Consumer Loan Officer	31,400	28,200– 37,500
Mortgage Loan Dept. Manager	67,500	55,500– 90,100
Senior Mortgage Loan Officer	37,100	30,100– 50,000
Mortgage Loan Officer	25,200	22,100– 34,400
Trust Department		
Senior Trust Officer	$ 52,100	$ 41,500– 61,000
Trust Investment Officer	51,700	41,600– 59,500
Senior Personal Trust Officer	52,100	41,500– 61,000
Junior Officers		
Assistant Branch Manager I	$ 24,300	$ 22,000– 27,100
Assistant Branch Manager II	27,300	24,200– 31,600
Personal/Private Banker Officer Trainee	23,900	21,400– 36,800

[1]Banks with assets of more than $1 billion.

SOURCE: Bank Administration Institute, *Cash Compensation Survey 1994*. Reprinted by permission.

AVERAGE BASE SALARIES OF OFFICERS IN SMALL BANKS[1]

Job Title	Average Weighted Salary	Salary Range
Management		
Chief Executive Officer	$118,400	$100,000–132,100
Chief Operating Officer	77,600	61,000– 90,000
Chief Financial Officer	69,200	55,100– 81,500
Director of Marketing	40,200	32,100– 46,400
Business Development Officer	34,200	25,000– 38,400
Bank Investment Officer	44,700	30,600– 51,900
Head of Data Processing/Information Services	40,700	33,000– 48,000
Head of Operations	45,800	35,000– 56,200
Head of Retail Banking	53,600	42,500– 57,300
Branch Administration Manager	44,400	35,000– 48,200
Branch Manager I	29,900	24,000– 31,600
Branch Manager II	38,000	30,200– 44,800

AVERAGE BASE SALARIES OF OFFICERS IN SMALL BANKS[1]

Job Title	Average Weighted Salary	Salary Range
Loan Department		
Commercial Loan Dept. Manager	$ 65,000	$ 54,600– 71,500
Senior Commercial Loan Officer	51,700	43,100– 57,900
Commercial Loan Officer	44,900	33,600– 42,500
Consumer Loan Dept. Manager	46,000	36,900– 53,200
Senior Consumer Loan Officer	34,400	29,700– 40,700
Consumer Loan Officer	27,700	24,700– 30,500
Mortgage Loan Dept. Manager	47,900	38,300– 55,500
Senior Mortgage Loan Officer	36,500	30,000– 42,800
Mortgage Loan Officer	27,500	22,600– 32,500
Trust Department		
Senior Trust Officer	$ 43,000	$ 31,500– 44,700
Trust Investment Officer	37,000	31,000– 42,000
Senior Personal Trust Officer	43,000	31,500– 44,700
Junior Officers		
Assistant Branch Manager I	$ 20,800	$ 17,500– 23,100
Assistant Branch Manager II	24,000	21,300– 27,000
Personal/Private Banker Officer Trainee	22,400	19,000– 27,200

[1]Banks with assets of $100 to $249 million.
SOURCE: Bank Administration Institute, *Cash Compensation Survey, 1994.* Reprinted by permission.

Tellers and Clerks

Ever since the arrival of the automated teller machine (ATM), or cash machine, the human teller has become a dying breed. As the number of ATM transactions has quadrupled in the past 13 years, the number of tellers has dropped by more than 20 percent, from a high of 561,000 in 1982 to 441,000 in 1994, according to the Bureau of Labor Statistics. And if the big banks have their way, those numbers will keep moving in the same directions. The mathematics aren't hard to fathom: It costs the average bank 28 cents to process an ATM withdrawal (65 cents if the ATM transaction is at a networked bank), while that same transaction costs an average of $1.15 with a human teller.

AVERAGE ANNUAL EARNINGS OF BANK CLERKS AND TELLERS

Job Title	Large Banks[1]		Small Banks[2]	
	Weighted Average	Salary Range	Weighted Average	Salary Range
Accounting Clerk I	$15,100	$14,600–19,000	$16,100	$13,700–17,900
Accounting Clerk II	18,300	17,600–22,400	19,000	16,600–20,800
Loan Officer I	31,500	27,400–42,000	30,600	26,400–36,000
Loan Officer II	48,400	41,400–60,000	43,700	39,300–51,000
Clerk/Processor				
Loan Department	$15,700	$15,200–20,700	$16,600	$15,000–18,400
Mortgage Department	19,300	17,000–23,300	18,000	16,100–20,000
Commercial Loan	19,200	16,500–21,700	17,900	15,000–18,700

Bookkeeping and Operations				
Clerk I	$15,000	$13,500–17,000	$14,100	$12,600–15,700
Clerk II	17,800	16,700–19,700	16,400	14,700–18,900
File Statement Clerk	14,800	13,300–15,900	13,500	11,300–15,500
Proof Operator	13,300	12,500–15,800	14,400	12,700–16,100
Check Processing Clerk	15,300	13,700–17,400	14,900	12,700–17,000
Wire Transfer Clerk, Safe Deposit Clerk	16,800	14,500–17,600	15,200	13,200–16,800
Data Entry	16,100	14,000–17,600	16,100	13,000–17,500
Head Teller	18,300	16,900–19,700	17,900	16,000–19,700
Teller I	13,900	12,700–14,900	13,500	11,700–14,200
Teller II	16,000	14,400–17,700	14,700	13,600–16,200
Teller, ATM	18,200	15,900–19,300	15,800	12,800–17,000
Teller, Note Loan	17,400	15,000–20,900	16,300	14,500–17,500
Teller, Vault	16,100	14,500–18,200	16,800	14,900–18,000
Teller, Part-time	14,400	13,500–15,900	13,900	11,900–15,000

[1]Banks with assets of more than $1 billion.
[2]Banks with assets of $100 to $249 million.
SOURCE: Banking Administration Institute, *Cash Compensation Survey, 1994.* Reprinted by permission.

Human tellers haven't quite (and probably won't ever) gone away like the full-service filling station or the neighborhood drug store. In the summer of 1995, customers raised a fierce protest when Citibank attempted to impose teller fees for customers who insisted on using a human teller for transactions they could have performed at an ATM. And some tellers will always be needed to perform tasks like changing money, issuing certified checks, and accepting coin deposits.

But tellers' roles and numbers will be sharply reduced over the next 10 years. Some banks, including Citibank, are extending free electronic banking services to their customers to encourage them to do their banking over the information superhighway. Others are seeking to expand their use of direct deposit, which reduces their need for tellers to cash checks. First National Bank of Chicago succeeded in foisting a $3 fee on customers for teller transactions. But perhaps the greatest reduction in tellers will result from shrinkage. Changes in interstate banking laws are expected to cut the nation's 10,000+ banks by 50 percent within a few years. And the number of branches, currently more than 54,000, will also be halved.

There are several different kinds of tellers and a wide variety of clerks serving various functions. The best-paid tellers are the *note tellers,* who draft contracts, calculate renewal notes and mortgages, and pay dividends. *Commercial tellers,* also known as paying and receiving tellers, are the most common type. They cash checks and handle deposits and withdrawals. *Head tellers* are supervisory personnel who help train new paying and receiving tellers and who answer most of the difficult questions. According to the Bank Administration Institute, they earn an average of $16,000–$19,800 per year.

There are also different kinds of bank clerks, and the pay scale is generally the same for all of them: low. The more a clerk knows about processing and recording information, the better his or her salary should be, regardless of the job titles. The Bureau of Labor Statistics lists the following clerical categories.

Country Collection Clerks—Sort thousands of pieces of mail daily and determine which items must be held at the main office and which should be routed to branch banks.

Exchange Clerks—Service foreign deposit accounts.

Interest Clerks—Keep records on interest-bearing items.

Mortgage Clerks—Type legal papers dealing with real estate upon which money has been loaned.

Proof-Machine Operators—Use equipment that sorts checks and deposit slips, adds their amounts, and records the tabulations.

Reconcilement Clerks—Process financial statements from other banks to reconcile differences.

Sorters—Separate checks, deposit slips, etc., into different batches and tabulate them.

Transit Clerks—Sort checks and drafts on other banks.

Trust Securities Clerks—Post investment transactions made by trust officers on behalf of bank customers.

THE BROKERAGE FIRM

The lucrative business of buying and selling stocks, bonds, mutual funds, and other instruments of capital formation is carried on by a relatively small number of people. The entire securities industry employs over 240,000 people, many of them in the 5,300 firms registered with the National Association of Securities Dealers. Both the number of employees and number of firms peaked (at 260,000 and 6,700, respectively) before falling precipitously after the 1987 stock market crash. When the stock market rebounded, so did employment, which has been increasing along with the Dow Jones industrial average since 1990. The number of firms started rebounding in 1993.

Securities dealers vary in size from well-known giants in the industry like Merrill Lynch or Prudential to small two-room office operations whose names are familiar only to a handful of investors. Regardless of size, the majority of firms are located in New York City. The number of employees in the big national full-line firms has fluctuated from year to year, but employment by discount brokers has more than doubled, from 4,800 in 1988 to 9,800 in 1993.

Anyone who has had experience looking for a job in this business, especially on Wall Street itself, knows that there are two related obstacles to finding one: the relatively small size of the industry and the blatant nepotism that pervades every area. Because the pay is so good (even retail brokers *average* over $128,000 a year), and the work is clean and mostly respectable, the continual scandals notwithstanding, it's not surprising or unusual that the relatives of those on the inside have the first crack at these jobs.

The job market looks better today than it has since October 1987 when the Dow plunged more than 500 points and the industry began a major contraction, reducing the workforce by 50,000 over the next three years. Since then, the Dow Jones Index has surged to record levels, avoided radical swings, and helped bring greatly increased pretax profits to most securities firms. Increased business on the global level also brought hefty profits and helped the market see new future possibilities. Recent setbacks, in 1994 to 1995, especially in bonds and in emerging markets, has hurt profits and caused sporadic employee layoffs. But generally speaking the surge in market activity should keep employment levels rising.

A very important reason for the dramatic increase in market activity was the lowering of interest rates at entry level. Many investors began taking their money out of banks, where it was earning less than 5 percent interest, and sought higher returns in stocks, mutual funds, collateralized mortgages, and a whole host of products that were once the province of only the most sophisticated players. As a result, many of the largest firms—including Merrill Lynch, Dean Witter, and Smith Barney—have been increasing their staffs of retail brokers. Others have resumed their training programs to meet future needs.

The most prestigious and best paying jobs are in sales, trading, research, and underwriting. In fact, average salaries in these areas are probably the highest of any nonprofessional group in the country. In other words, a person can make a great deal of money in a brokerage firm without a formal education or long arduous training. Although an M.B.A. has become a prerequisite in research and corporate finance, savvy, guts, and a quick wit remain the best qualifications for the high-paying, pressure-packed jobs of trader and broker.

Brokers

According to the Securities Industry Association, there are currently 91,000 registered brokers in the United States. Brokers act as agents for people buying or selling securities and collect a fee for that service. Brokers are known in the industry as registered representatives, or account executives, and sometimes simply as salespersons. Brokers usually specialize in one type of security and are therefore known as stockbrokers, bond brokers, etc. They also specialize in retail sales (with individuals as clients) and industrial sales (with associations or corporations as clients). A few work right on the floor of the stock exchange and are called, appropriately enough, floor brokers.

Brokers receive a commission on the fee their firms charge for all transactions. Since a firm's fee varies with the type of security and the size of the transaction, so does the broker's commission. Retail brokers often collect 35 to 40 percent of the gross fee; institutional brokers collect a lower percentage because they deal with larger blocks of security, but they also usually get large bonuses. First Boston, for example, pays 15 percent, and Merrill Lynch 13 percent to their brokers.

Beginning brokers usually start with a salary and lower commission. As they become experienced, the commission rises and the salary remains the same or drops, often to a point at which a broker is working on a straight commission. Because pay depends on an individual's production, income for brokers varies wildly. Incomes run literally from $10,000 to $3 million, but the Securities Industry Association reports the following average income figures for 1993:

Institutional Brokers	$305,000
Retail Brokers	$129,000

While the prosperity of the mid-80s brought brokers' compensation to record high levels, the postcrash environment on Wall Street just a few years later reduced the pay of brokers to a considerable degree. Between 1989 and 1992 the Securities Industry Association reported that average broker compensation rose from $79,000 to $90,000. Thanks to the surge in trading activity by small investors, spawned by an improved economy, that average is rising very rapidly.

And as salaries have risen, so have the number of brokers. There are currently 91,000 in the United States, according to the SIA, as compared to only 73,700 in 1990. The number is still down from 1987, when over 102,000 Americans held this title. But many industry watchers predict the demand for brokers will further increase as more and more employees are being asked to make their own retirement decisions, a role that in the past was often filled by employers.

Traders

Traders use their firm's capital to buy and sell securities and earn money on fluctuations in the marketplace. There are traders for different types of securities: corporate bonds, municipal bonds, etc. Most traders are paid a salary plus bonus, but because the industry places heavy emphasis on individual performance, that bonus can run anywhere from 10 percent to 200 percent of one's salary.

A bonus is meant to reflect the amount of money a trader makes for a firm. Some brokerage houses pay a "production bonus," which is a fixed percentage of a trader's annual output. If a firm's production bonus is 10 percent and a trader makes $600,000 for that firm, then he or she will make $60,000 as a bonus. In some firms, bonuses are more arbitrary and less systematic. A 50 percent bonus might be granted to all traders in a good year, regardless of each trader's performance. There is at least one firm in New York that offers bonuses strictly on the basis of seniority. In general, large firms tend to pay higher salaries and lower bonuses and small firms tend to do just the opposite.

The pitfalls of this bonus system were exposed in February 1995, when 28-year-old trader Nicholas Leeson risked more than $29 billion on the Japanese stock market in an attempt to win huge profits for his firm and a correspondingly gigantic bonus for himself. But he lost $750 million on the trade—Leeson fled to Germany before anybody had realized what he had done—and caused the collapse of his firm, Barings PLC, Britain's oldest and one of its most venerable investment firms. To forestall such a collapse in the U.S., federal banking regulators issued a set of guidelines in late 1995 that limit the pay of traders who take excessive risks. The guidelines don't make trading in derivatives and emerging markets any less volatile or risky, but they should deter individual traders from making a big, speculative bet in hopes of earning a hefty bonus.

The average salary for a beginning (or assistant) trader is $30,000–$40,000. The average salary for a senior (or head) trader is $75,000–85,000. Industry employees estimate that with bonuses, average compensation can run well over $150,000. At the top end of the scale is a large cluster of total pay between $400,000 and $850,000. At the largest firms, however, the compensation at the top is usually over $1 million a year. In the 1992 scandal at Salomon Brothers, for example, it became public knowledge that senior partners (all of whome were traders) made no less than $2 million each and as much as $6 million.

Research

Behind every broker who makes the big sale and every trader who makes the right move stands a small group of experts working without fanfare in the research department. Their jobs consist of studying stocks and bonds, usually in specific areas such as automobiles, oil, or steel. Known as *security analysts* or *stock analysts,* they issue reports on the current value of these securities and predict the effects of national economic trends on their growth potential.

In today's extraordinarily competitive marketplace the importance of analysts has never been greater. This is why, when prestigious Wall Street firms decide to spend millions of dollars on television advertising, they often single out the work of their excellent research departments on all the commercials. Tough competition also explains the rise of independent investment counselors devoted only to research. Some analysts have achieved such fame and respect among investors that their predictions are accepted as facts the moment they are made.

Analysts receive their training on the job, but an increasing number now come into the business armed with an M.B.A. This trend has helped increase starting salaries to as much as $65,000 for "junior analysts" or "research analysts" and $75,000 for those with a few years of experience. The industry average for experienced analysts is $150,000, according to a Wall Street recruiter.

Senior analysts, sometimes called managing directors of a firm's research department, often earn over $200,000 a year; the top directors earn as much as $300,000. Their base salary is only between $100,000 and $200,000, but bonuses can run as high as three times that figure. In the past few years, as corporate takeovers, leveraged buyouts, and merger-mania have made research ever more important, the elite analysts have been able to induce the big houses into bidding wars for their services, sending their salaries skyrocketing. "When analysts are instrumental in pulling in underwriting business, they get big bonuses," former analyst Nancy Zambell told the Wall Street Journal. "Then they're no longer making $250,000. They're making $1 million and up." Merrill Lynch paid three analysts $1.2 million each to lure them away from other firms. Jack B. Grubman, one of Wall Street's top telecommunications analysts, received a two-year, $5-million deal for jumping from Paine Webber to Salomon in 1994.

Corporate Finance

In large brokerage firms, the principal activity of this department is called "underwriting." When a brokerage house or investment bank purchases an entire new issue of stocks or bonds from a corporation or government (state or municipality, for example) in order to distribute them to the marketplace, that firm is said to "underwrite" those securities, thus guaranteeing their sale. For this service, the investment bankers who handle the transactions take a commission of only .05 percent. Of course, when you deal with sums in the hundreds of millions of dollars, even such a small percentage can translate into a substantial amount of money.

Underwriting these so-called "initial public offerings" (IPOs) requires knowledge of research and finance and a thorough understanding of the economic status of the nation. For this reason, virtually all employees entering the field today have an M.B.A. degree or broad experience in several phases of the business. The high salaries reflect those requirements. In good years, bonuses range from 25 percent to more than 100 percent of salary. In recent years the number of IPOs has risen to record levels making this department one of the most desirable in the business. With bonuses running into the high six figures it is easy to understand why.

Operations

During the late sixties and early seventies, the securities industry learned just how vital "back-office" operations were to the business. The inability to process and record hundreds of thousands of daily transactions actually helped to sink some important brokerage firms, and only the advent of the computer saved others. Today the stock market alone easily handles trading days of 250 million shares or more, and the operations function is completely in the hands of the computer people. But the human factor in the orderly transfer of all securities remains the clerks and so-called "cage" personnel.

The "cage" is the area of a brokerage house where securities are received, stored, or transferred. Because so many stocks and bonds are negotiable this is a highly secured operation which in the past was actually encased in a mental cage. *Cage clerks* who receive and deliver (R&D) stocks and bonds, or do stock recording, or transfer securities, or "box" them for storage in the vault are paid starting salaries of $14,000 to $18,000 and between $22,000 and $25,000 with experience. Supervisors earn between $25,000 and $50,000.

Other clerical personnel such as *dividend clerks, clearance clerks,* and *purchase and sales (P&S) clerks,* are all paid at about those same levels. *Margin clerks,* people who keep track of customers' accounts to make sure they have not purchased more on credit than is legally allowed, usually earn $18,000 to $24,000 with experience. So-called *compliance clerks* who check that transactions are completed according to all rules and regulations are paid at the same rates.

In large brokerage firms, there are department heads for all of these services. The *purchase and sales director,* for example, is in charge, among other things, of computing taxes and commissions on all transactions; the *stock loan manager* lends out the firm's excess securities to other houses; the *wire manager* supervises teletype and other lines of communication; the *new accounts manager* and *credit (or margin) manager* do what one would expect. All usually earn between $25,000 and $45,000 including bonus.

The highest paid people in operations are the computer experts. The chief systems analyst for a large firm, for example, will earn anywhere from $50,000 to $75,000, and the head of programming from $80,000 to $100,000. (See the section on computer professionals in Part IV for comparative figures in other industries.)

The New York Stock Exchange

We should also mention the stock exchange itself, which employs fewer people but provides some of the industry's highest incomes. The New York

Stock Exchange (one of several exchanges in the United States) is a primary marketplace. Major companies list their stocks there, and those who wish to purchase or sell those stocks do so through somebody "on the floor" of the exchange. People who conduct these floor transactions must own a seat on the exchange. (A seat is a license or permit to deal stock.) Seats on the New York Stock Exchange are few in number and are very expensive. Most investment firms of the sort mentioned earlier in the chapter have salaried agents called floor brokers to conduct their business on the exchange. However, there are those who work on the exchange exclusively. They are:

Specialists, who are traders with exclusive responsibility for a stock or group of stocks listed on the exchange. They are charged with maintaining an orderly and fair market for those stocks. Floor brokers of investment firms and other traders go to the specialist in a particular stock in order to find the buyer or seller they require for a transaction in that stock. The specialist is required to purchase a certain percentage of any offer if there are no other buyers. Obviously this requires an enormous amount of capital, and most specialists have been in business for decades in order to amass that leverage. The right to specialize is awarded by the Board of Governors of the exchange and is determined by the board's perception of the ability of a specialist to afford the position and by its belief that the specialist will act responsibly in that position. In other words, the system operates on the old-boy network, so specialists are often wealthy to begin with, and they continue to increase their wealth as key operators in the marketplace.

Traders, like specialists, invest their own capital but do not specialize in any particular stock. They simply trade up and down the market and make money on the fluctuations of stock prices. These traders are usually organized as small partnerships or firms, but there are also a few individuals who own their own seats and trade their own inventory of stock.

As is the case with the industry in general, the individual determines the strength of his or her income. There are no salaries as such for freelance brokers, traders, or specialists; they make money according to their ability in the marketplace and, to a certain extent, upon their luck. Spectacular stories about income crop up continually in the business press, magazines, and the grapevine. In general, though, an average annual salary figure for a member of the New York Stock Exchange is estimated at around $1 million.

The New York Stock Exchange also has a structure of corporate employment which includes a president, vice-presidents, treasurers, etc. The chief executive officer makes over $600,000 a year.

Wall Street's Top Earners of 1994

While most of the public discussion about pay levels in the United States focuses on outrage over the high salaries of professional athletes or the golden parachutes paid to failed CEOs, the extraordinary annual earnings among the elite of the world of finance are rarely mentioned. The most obvious reason for this is that the audiences for Larry King, Rush Limbaugh, and their colleagues do not understand hedge funds, leveraged buyouts, and the like, and so don't want to learn how men like George Soros or Henry Kravis make tens of millions of dollars annually while the real wages of most Americans continue to decline.

Over the last few years, *Financial World* magazine has published an annual list of the top 100 Wall Street earners based on public records and its own educated guesswork. All these financiers are men, almost all are white, and almost all were wealthy even before they started working on Wall Street. They use their own capital or their firm's to make more money, sometimes by creating new corporations, but mainly by moving it in and out of securities funds or bond funds, or by helping companies they own stock in find an investor who will pay more for the stock than its current price. We realize that this is a simple explanation, but it's not too far from the mark.

WALL STREET'S TOP 20 EARNERS, 1994

Name	Firm	Estimated Earnings (Millions)
1. Thomas Lee	Thomas H. Lee Co.	$170
2. George Soros	Soros Fund Management	70
3. Robert Bass	Keystone	60
4. B. Gerald Cantor	Cantor Fitzgerald	55
5. Sam Fox	Harbour Group	45
6. Paul Tudor Jones II	Tudor Investment	45
7. Michael David Weill	Lazard Frères	32
8. Monroe Trout, Jr.	Trout Trading	31
9. Andrew Fisher	Salomon, Inc.	30
10. Dennis Keegan	Salomon, Inc.	30
11. Robert Stavis	Salomon, Inc.	30
12. Theodore Forstmann	Forstmann Little	29
13. James Simons	Resistance Technologies	22
14. John Childs	Thomas H. Lee Co.	21
15. Richard Rainwater	Rainwater & Co.	21
16. James Wolfensohn	James D. Wolfensohn, Inc.	21
17. Steven Cohen	SAC Capital Management	20
18. Shigeru Myojin	Salomon, Inc.	20
19. Stephen Posford	Salomon, Inc.	20
20. Samuel Zell	Private Investor	20

SOURCE: *Financial World* magazine. Reprinted by permission.

THE RETAIL TRADE

The department store, once the definitive symbol of American consumerism, stood until the late 1980s as the cornerstone of retailing. As a monolith of consumerism that was unique to America, the department store dominated the urban and suburban landscapes as the center of convenience in a culture where people depend so heavily on their cars. In recent times, the department store has declined, only to be replaced by large chains and discounters as well as specialty retailers. Large chain stores, such as K-Mart and Wal-Mart, with their broad selection of merchandise at discounted prices, as well as specialty chains, such as The Gap and The Limited, dominate national retailing today the way department stores like Macy's and Nordstrom dominated regional retailing in their heyday.

The local mall has become what the department store was for years—a one-stop shopping center that conveniently saves time, gas and money. The typical mall with its large anchor store—more often now a discount "superstore"—may house specialty stores, old-fashioned department stores, and chain stores, all competing for the same customers. In this environment, department stores have narrowed the number of products they carry and refocused on high margin products. They have resorted to frequent markdowns to keep their customers loyal, selling 60 percent to 80 percent of their merchandise on sale in 1994. Despite these efforts, even affluent shoppers have moved away from the department store to the specialty stores and the large discount chains. The latter stores have taken advantage of the weaknesses of the department stores' approach to merchandising. The specialty stores typically sell within a narrow product range (e.g., Footlocker sells only sneakers), but offer a far wider selection within their specialty categories. The discount stores offer less service and fewer upscale products, but takes advantage of a reborn cost consciousness in the American consumer of the 1990s.

Despite these changes in the retailing landscape which place a premium on lowering costs, such as inventory building, merchandising, and selling, job growth in the retail trade remains strong. While many of these jobs are at the low-wage sales associate level, there are many opportunities to move up the ranks. We will concentrate here on the specialty chain in discussing these career opportunities. The titles, job descriptions, and salaries/wages shown are generally transferable across all retailing.

In most specialty chains, the buying decisions and merchandising decisions are made at company headquarters and not at the store level. There are several levels of management in these organizations, and they are divided into two distinct categories of activities—merchandising and operations. Merchandising management positions include: general merchandising managers, divisional merchandising managers, buyers, and assistant buyers. In addition to these corporate merchandising positions, those positions that are actually involved in the operation of the stores are: regional or zone managers, district or area managers, store managers, assistant managers, visual merchandisers, and the sales staff.

For management positions in retail, a college degree is preferred but not required. Prior experience in retail is also looked upon favorably.

Jobs in Merchandising

General Merchandising Manager (GMM)—GMMs have vice-presidential status and have overall responsibility for one of the three divisions above. While not involved in actual buying, they coordinate buying and selling activities. They plan sales promotions, determine quantity of merchandise to be stocked, and decide markups and markdowns. GMMs report directly to the store's chief executive officer.

Divisional Merchandise Manager (DMM)—Reporting directly to the GMM, the divisional merchandise manager is responsible for one or more classifications of merchandise. For example, there's a DMM in charge of juniors (coats, dresses, sportswear); a DMM overseeing furniture, carpeting, and lamps; another for cosmetics and accessories, and so on. The DMM's first duty is to achieve the profits and sales set for his or her department by management. With the help of the three to seven buyers under his or her supervision, the DMM keeps stock of merchandise, its display, replenishment, and sales movement.

Both GMMs and DMMs are usually college graduates these days, some with degrees in fashion merchandising, others simply with years of experience as buyers, the usual path of advancement. Salaries vary widely, with the biggest difference due to the store's volume. In a large majority of stores, executives' annual earnings include a bonus for meeting or exceeding sales goals.

general merchandise manager	$60,000 to 200,000
divisional merchandise manager	50,000 to 120,000

Buyer—Buyers seek out and purchase all the items stocked by a retail store, from canned soup to mothballs to Christian Dior suits. They do often lead glamorous lives, traveling four to five days each month or more to trade and fashion shows, sometimes around the world. They return with items past experience or market research or their own fashion instincts indicate will sell at way above original cost. About 150,000 buyers work in retail stores around the country, mostly in major metropolitan areas.

Generally, they have college degrees, although their training comes from the store where they start out as assistant buyers. Earnings vary by location and volume, but most buyers make between $40,000 and $80,000.

Assistant Buyers—While training (usually for about a year) to become buyers, assistant buyers must also grapple with much of their division's daily paperwork: processing purchase orders, checking invoices on material received, keeping account of stock. The salary range for senior and junior assistant buyers is $20,000 to $50,000.

Jobs in Retail Operations

Zone or Regional Managers—In large regional or nationwide retail operations, zone or regional managers supervise large geographic regions composed of two or more districts or areas. They mainly oversee the activities of the district or area managers who report to them. They also implement and oversee company policies and enforce company standards. By virtue of their experience, zone or regional managers also perform troubleshooting in their operations. Salaries for zone or regional managers range from $45,000 to over $100,000 plus incentives.

District or Area Managers—District or area managers are in charge of a group of stores, usually ranging from 3 to 10 stores. District managers supervise store managers and define their responsibilities. They channel corporate information to their stores. They also help solve any problems that the store manager may be having trouble dealing with. District managers meet frequently with store managers and their staffs to insure that the stores are being run to company standards. They set and track the stores' sales and budget goals, and suggest and help implement merchandising techniques to promote sales. District or area managers' salaries range between about $40,000 and $70,000. Incentive programs may add to these salaries.

Store Managers—Store managers are in charge of all aspects of daily operations within the store. Along with the district or zone manager, they set the sales and budget goals and make sure the staff is achieving these goals. Store managers are also in charge of employee incentive programs to keep their staffs motivated. Store managers work closely with their assistant managers, defining their responsibilities and delegating the daily activities of the store. A major part of the store manager's job consists of educating the staff on performing their jobs and on matters of corporate policy. Salaries for store managers range between $24,000 and $45,000. Companies also frequently incentivize store managers in achieving or beating their sales goals.

Assistant Store Managers—Assistant managers basically help with the day-to-day operations of the store, like merchandising, supervising, scheduling, serving customers, and assuring that customer service guidelines are followed. They also help with the implementation of company programs. Assistant managers supervise those employees who do pricing, ticketing, and restocking. Some assistant managers are paid on a salary basis, but most are paid on an hourly basis. The wages usually range from $5.00 to $12.50 per hour, depending on the size of the store, its location, and the experience level of the assistant manager. Some companies also offer incentive programs to assistant managers.

Merchandisers—Some very large retail stores have merchandising managers within the store; in others, merchandisers travel from store to store within a district or area. Usually working with a company recommended store and display layout, merchandisers create displays that appeal to customers. This job is very important because the placement and display of goods has a big impact on customer buying patterns. Merchandisers must have a special talent—the ability to visualize displays that will attract customer interest and make the merchandise attractive. Hourly wages are $5 to $10, but those who travel from store to store receive salaries ranging from $21,000 to $30,000.

Sales Staff—Retail businesses employ over three million salespeople. Sales workers' major priorities are customer service and selling. They present product features and benefits and answer any questions. They also help with the daily maintenance of the store as well as unpacking goods, price ticketing, and placing them on the display floor. Sales staffs are normally paid on an hourly basis with wages ranging from $5 to $12. Some companies also pay commissions on sales. In some cases, commissions can double earnings.

HOTELS AND MOTELS

More than 1.5 million people work in hotels and motels—a figure that continues to rise along with the growth of tourism and business travel. The range of salaries is enormous. Bellhops make as little as $3.31 an hour before tips; general managers make more than $100,000 a year after bonuses. More than half the employees work in the service area, which includes food service, housekeeping, and personal services. About 20 percent do clerical work as telephone operators, secretaries, and front office staff. General managers, restaurant managers, bar managers, and executive housekeepers make up another 13 percent; the rest work as salespersons, skilled workers (electricians, plumbers, etc.), and general staff.

One's education and the size and whereabouts of the hotel or motel affect salaries. A laundry worker in New York, for example, can make twice as much as a telephone operator in Atlanta. The manager of a hotel with over 1,000 rooms might make three times as much as the manager of a motel with 60 rooms. Graduates of a hotel management school earn between $17,000 and $22,000 in their first job.

HOTEL OCCUPANCY AND ROOM RATES, 1990–94

	Occupancy Rate (Percent)		Average Room Rate	
Category	**1990**	**1994**	**1990**	**1994**
Region				
New England	57.9	60.6	$74.30	$ 78.11
Middle Atlantic	63.0	66.5	78.05	54.03
South Atlantic	61.7	65.4	58.19	62.09
East North Central	58.5	63.4	53.04	58.38
East South Central	60.1	65.7	43.51	49.51
West North Central	60.4	64.2	43.64	50.72
West South Central	59.3	64.2	49.40	56.10
Mountain	63.6	67.3	55.22	62.58
Pacific	65.3	64.7	70.11	73.06
Price				
Luxury	65.9	72.0	$90.44	$109.83
Upscale	61.6	68.0	62.16	74.32
Mid-Price	59.1	65.3	47.92	56.78
Economy	65.3	62.1	52.12	44.21
Budget	61.7	61.6	33.29	33.99
U.S. Average	**61.8**	**65.2**	**$58.70**	**$ 63.63**

SOURCE: American Hotel and Motel Association, *Lodging Outlook Survey, 1994* (1995).

Like the rest of the travel industry, jobs in the hotel and motel industry are subject to fluctuations in the economy's health. Business travel, which accounts for the majority of hotel stays, is one of the first items to be cut from corporate budgets during a recession, thus creating even harder times for people who work in hotels and motels. This trend is illustrated by hotel occupancy rates, which dropped to 60.9 percent during the 1991 recession, but have since rebounded to 65.2 percent in 1994. This rate is still below the 68 percent occupancy rate considered the baseline for sustained profitability, but the industry continues to show signs that it is emerging from the recession in good health. For one, the higher the cost of the hotel, the higher the occupancy rate. This is in contrast with the situation four years earlier, when occupancy rates were highest among economy hotels and lowest among basic and upscale hotels, suggesting that travelers were cutting down the scale of their trips rather than canceling them outright. By geographic region, occupancy is consistently highest in the mountain states and lowest in New England.

Room rates are another reflection of the health of the hotel industry. And they too are on the rise. They jumped 8.6 percent, from $61.30 in 1993 to $63.63 in 1994. As might be expected, rates are highest in urban areas and in the geographic areas (i.e., New York in the Middle Atlantic, Los Angeles and San Francisco in the Pacific region) where the biggest and most expensive cities are located.

Jobs in Hotel and Motel Management

Job descriptions in the services area—maids, bellhops, and laundry workers—are really unnecessary, but some of the managerial positions should be defined.

General Manager—Manages, through subordinate managers, all aspects of the hotel's or motel's activities.

Resident Manager—Lives on the premises, reports to the general manager, and supervises all hotel activities except those of the food and beverage department.

Food and Beverage Manager—Reports to general manager. Supervises food, banquet, and beverage service through subordinate managers.

Front Office Manager—Supervises front office personnel. Compiles daily a revised weekly, monthly, and yearly rooms forecast. Handles guest complaints, schedules employees' work assignments.

Front Office Reservations Manager—Reports to Front Office Manager. Responsible for reservations, operations, and coordination of rooms forecast.

Controller—Supervises accounting personnel, cashiers, auditors; in charge of payroll, credit, and accounting departments. Compiles financial statements.

Executive Housekeeper—Supervises all maids, porters, cleaners, and window washers. Orders supplies and fabrics. Determines room redecorations and prepares work schedules.

Chief Engineer—Supervises all mechanics, tradesmen, and other maintenance personnel. Purchases maintenance and fire equipment.

Sales Manager—Supervises a sales force to promote maximum transient, convention group, and banquet business. Prepares sales reports and plans sales quotas.

Because salaries for management personnel are frequently tied to a bonus system based on sales and profitability, the table below is divided according to hotels that pay a bonus and those that don't. All of these jobs have small perquisites, too: Some companies, for example, provide rooms for their general managers and meal discounts to all managerial employees.

ANNUAL SALARIES OF HOTEL/MOTEL MANAGERS

Position	First Class Hotels	Standard Hotels	Suites Hotels	Economy Hotels	All Hotels
General Manager with Maintenance					
Average Minimum Salary	$73,082	$56,571	$58,423	$33,942	$59,106
Average Maximum Salary	74,341	57,181	58,431	34,071	59,737
General Manager without Maintenance					
Average Minimum Salary	87,496	47,133	46,160	35,114	54,949
Average Maximum Salary	90,804	47,315	46,160	36,400	55,984
Resident Manager					
Average Minimum Salary	46,067	38,751	26,626	24,186	33,532
Average Maximum Salary	46,471	39,336	30,639	24,278	35,158
Front Office Manager					
Average Minimum Salary	27,613	25,208	19,619	17,477	25,278
Average Maximum Salary	28,565	25,418	19,619	18,256	25,783

ANNUAL SALARIES OF HOTEL/MOTEL MANAGERS

Position	First Class Hotels	Standard Hotels	Suites Hotels	Economy Hotels	All Hotels
Reservations Manager					
Average Minimum Salary	$24,277	$20,748	$17,240	$14,750	$22,749
Average Maximum Salary	24,557	20,864	17,240	14,750	22,962
Controller					
Average Minimum Salary	42,569	35,010	24,926	17,439	38,362
Average Maximum Salary	43,500	35,082	24,926	17,439	38,917
Executive Housekeeper					
Average Minimum Salary	27,490	23,479	26,017	19,285	24,410
Average Maximum Salary	28,216	23,582	27,017	19,437	24,831
Chief Engineer					
Average Minimum Salary	35,572	29,350	31,593	18,378	31,165
Average Maximum Salary	36,500	29,479	32,214	18,962	31,660
Director of Sales and Marketing					
Average Minimum Salary	46,234	34,479	39,424	22,316	38,585
Average Maximum Salary	47,148	35,115	39,696	22,684	39,245
Senior Sales Manager					
Average Minimum Salary	29,546	24,695	26,738	23,295	26,457
Average Maximum Salary	31,588	26,536	29,650	23,295	28,515
Sales Manager					
Average Minimum Salary	23,630	22,027	24,267	23,287	23,515
Average Maximum Salary	27,793	23,482	26,484	23,287	26,477
Security Director					
Average Minimum Salary	26,414	23,583	NA	17,000	25,118
Average Maximum Salary	27,063	23,583	NA	17,000	25,490
Personnel Director					
Average Minimum Salary	36,206	30,815	22,656	22,500	31,750
Average Maximum Salary	36,629	30,827	22,903	27,000	32,006
Director of Food and Beverages					
Average Minimum Salary	44,873	35,592	38,301	22,123	38,754
Average Maximum Salary	46,435	35,797	38,509	23,373	39,439

ANNUAL SALARIES OF HOTEL/MOTEL MANAGERS

Position	First Class Hotels	Standard Hotels	Suites Hotels	Economy Hotels	All Hotels
Executive Chef					
Average Minimum Salary	$42,811	$33,628	$32,796	$28,000	$38,259
Average Maximum Salary	43,598	33,686	33,593	28,000	38,771
Executive Steward					
Average Minimum Salary	24,848	20,223	NA	NA	24,287
Average Maximum Salary	25,282	20,223	NA	NA	24,668
Restaurant Manager					
Average Minimum Salary	23,156	21,426	22,508	13,000	22,314
Average Maximum Salary	25,502	22,490	23,874	13,000	24,034

SOURCE: American Hotel and Motel Association, Hospitality Industry Compensation Survey, August 1991.

THE INSURANCE INDUSTRY

The insurance industry is a vast and financially powerful sector of the U.S. economy. In 1992 alone premium receipts totaled over 319 billion for life insurance, and 228 billion for property and casualty insurance (including 104 billion for auto insurance). The industry is also one of the largest employers in the country with just under 2.5 million people employed, approximately half of them in clerical positions.

The employment situation has been stable recently, but most analysts believe that demand for insurance products will continue to increase, thereby creating solid, long-term future job growth. Despite the 1991 failures of four huge life insurance companies—Executive Life, First Capital, Monarch, and Mutual Benefit—the insurance industry's worst crises appear to be over. An industry-wide shakeout is unquestionably in progress, yet its rigors may boost as many companies as it burdens. Strong insurers such as Northwestern Mutual, Prudential, New York Life, and Metropolitan Life will gain more policyholders from weaker firms.

In addition, demographic variables—conspicuously the aging of the baby boom generation—will raise demand sharply for products that provide retirement income and health care insurance. Health insurance seems likely to provide one of the strongest sectors of growth. Elected officials now voice concern over the plight of uninsured and underinsured citizens; even Americans with adequate coverage may upgrade their policies in response to escalating health care costs. Underwriters, adjusters, investigators, and claim workers seem likely to benefit from ongoing growth in this sector of the industry. Since insurance companies require large clerical staffs to function, growth in clerical job categories is also probable.

Actuaries

Actuaries are the architects of the insurance industry. Insurance agreements of every kind—life, casualty, and health—as well as industry pension plans are all the designs of insurance actuaries. If you ever got hot under the collar because as a 25-year-old your automobile insurance rates were nearly twice as high as those of a friend only three years older, then you have actuaries to blame. They are the ones who have studied and assimilated the statistics which prove that drivers under 25 are apt to pay more attention to the radio than the road. But whatever they decide, their findings are the results of an incredible amount of research and deduction. Probabilities of injury, sickness, death, and unemployment in certain industries and certain surroundings, situations, and living conditions, and property loss from fire, theft, or natural disaster, are all carefully studied by actuaries, and their calculations of loss determine what premium rates for insurance policies should be. This task is not easy, since rates must be fair and competitive but still sufficiently high to cover all possible claims and expenses.

Approximately two thirds of all actuaries work in the insurance industry, with the rest employed by consulting firms and rating bureaus to gather information for smaller insurance companies that don't employ actuaries of their own. About 90 percent of actuaries work in life insurance; the rest work in casualty, property, and other types of insurance.

Actuaries are the highest paid professionals in the insurance field, with average annual salaries of $22,000 to $26,000 for beginners who have not taken their actuary exams, $24,000 to $28,000 for those who have completed their first exam, and $26,000 to $30,000 for those who have completed both actuary exams. Salaries for new associates certified by the Society of Actuaries average between $25,000 and $48,000 per year, while actuaries who become fellows of the society average between $47,000 and $57,000. Experienced fellows can earn $100,000 a year or more.

Estimates of the number of actuaries range from 15,000 to 20,000, but almost every source predicts fast job growth in this profession. The growth of the working-age and new family population (i.e., the baby boom generation) who are the bulk of insurance consumers means that life and casualty providers should see increased business. And as the health care debate continues, the need for actuaries to figure out exactly who will pay for insurance (and how much they should pay) in the future will be acute.

Two other factors contribute to an optimistic outlook for actuaries through the next decade. First, the National Academy of Insurance Commissioners requires that insurance companies keep an actuary on staff to provide opinions about loss reserves and other financial issues affecting firms' financial solvency; second, the role of the actuary is broadening to include more managerial and marketing duties within the insurance industry. Jim Murphy, executive vice-president of the American Academy of Actuaries, believes these two factors bode well for actuaries' employment. "There's a significant need for the technical knowledge that actuaries possess, and the focus on competition and expenses these days also means that actuaries will be needed to plan and react to industry changes."

George Bundschuh, president of New York Life Insurance Co., says there is always a need for good agents. "But most people starting as such have had prior experience elsewhere in the business world. You don't often see people right out of school, because one needs a network of people to sell to.

"It's also a very tough job," he concedes, "though it can be quite lucrative. And you can make your own hours—it's not a nine-to-five job.

"Agents have the most success when they sell to their peers, so they generally 'grow up' with their clients," he says. "As the client gets older, earns more money, and needs more insurance, that's when the agent really does well."

Claim Representatives

Under the title *claim representative,* also called *claim approver,* there are actually two separate and distinct jobs. A claim representative is either a *claim adjuster* or a *claim examiner.* Each works toward a speedy and agreeable settlement of all claims, but there the similarity ends. Basically, adjusters have desk jobs. They settle claims by using various reports, physical evidence, and the testimony of witnesses. But examiners are assigned to the investigation of questionable claims or those that exceed reasonable amounts. They work in the field. Their method is much the same as a police investigator's or a private eye's. They interview medical specialists and in other ways check for accuracy and honesty.

About 125,000 people work as claim representatives, and the majority of these work for insurance companies that sell property and liability coverage. Adjusters earn a median salary of $27,104. Examiners, on the other hand, receive a median annual salary of $41,100. Claim supervisors in casualty companies and life insurance companies have median earnings of $45,534, and claim managers, $58,240.

Underwriters

The persons who examine and decide which risks their company will take are called underwriters. They must analyze numerous sources—applications, backgrounds, medical reports, actuarial studies—and then make the decision themselves. It is one of the most responsible positions a person can have in the industry. Underwriters may correspond with policyholders and their agents, and they may frequently accompany the agents when they call on their clients. Nearly 100,000 people hold this position in the insurance field, and about 75 percent of them are property and liability underwriters. Underwriters with life insurance companies, however, make more money. With two to four years of experience, a life underwriter can earn a median salary of $40,000 a year. Senior personal and commercial underwriters make $55,000 on average. Underwriter supervisors in property and liability insurance average about $67,200 a year, managers about $80,000.

Agents and Brokers

Insurance agents and brokers are the persons who actually sell the policies to the individuals and businesses that wish to insure themselves against future losses and accidents. About 415,000 agents and brokers sell some kind of insurance in the United States. About half are in life insurance, and most of the remainder sell property and liability insurance. They are employed either as agents of insurance companies or as brokers, independent insurance businessmen who may represent one or more insurance companies in order to place their clients with the policies that best meet their particular needs.

During the training period, agents net about $2,100 a month for as long as six months or more. Thereafter, most are paid on a commission that is dependent upon the type and amount of insurance they sell. Those who have been in the business for several years net a median of $75,000 a year in commissions on new policies. Some highly successful ones (about one in five of those with over 10 years of experience) bring home over $150,000 a year. More than in any other position in the insurance field, the salary for agents and brokers can be self-determined.

Clerical Workers

Those who hold clerical positions within the insurance industry basically perform the same duties as they would in the administrative offices of any business. Records must be kept so premium payments, services, and benefits are all up-to-date. For this purpose, secretaries, stenographers, accounting clerks, typists, office machine operators, and general office workers are all needed. Some companies use titles such as *premiums ledger card clerk* (a bookkeeping function usually equivalent to accounting clerk), or *policy evaluation clerk* (typing and proofreading approved policies), but the pay scales are the same as for standard office jobs.

Altogether, they make up about 50 percent of all the people employed in the industry. Pay for clerical workers in the insurance field varies from city to city, company to company, and position to position. In 1994 on the average, file clerks made between $15,000 and $18,000 a year; accounting clerks, $20,000 to $35,000; secretaries, $25,000 to $35,000; and experienced computer operators, $19,000 to $35,000. (For more information on the salaries of office workers, see the section "The Office Staff" in Part VIII.)

THE MAGAZINE

After a decade of tremendous growth, the magazine industry went into a tailspin in the early 1990s. Venerable titles like *House and Garden* folded, advertising revenues decreased for many top magazines, newsstand sales flattened, and subscribers, without the lure of free gifts like sneaker phones and calculators, were harder to attract than ever.

By 1995, the industry showed signs of rebounding, with small increases in advertising profits and subscription sales. However, the manner in which magazines operated and profited was forever changed, like so many other industries that made it over the recessionary wall. Subscribers no longer get an almost-free ride on the backs of advertisers, who refuse to pay hefty page rate increases each year. Newsstand buyers find magazine cover prices have skyrocketed, to an average cost of $4 an issue. Editors expanded their duties to include attracting advertisers and marketing the magazine through mediums from department stores to on-line services to cable-TV shows. Editorial staffers are now expected to be proficient with computers, especially desktop publishing programs.

Despite the competitive field, the industry continues to attract new players. More than 11,150 magazines were published in 1994, earning about $8.5 billion in advertising revenues. Most of those revenues were earned by a select group of about 600 top consumer and business magazines, the most successful of which were directed at targeted audiences. Two of the hottest magazines, *Men's Health* and *Details,* were aimed at the 20-something generation, readers previously ignored by the major magazines. *Cooking Light* and *Victoria* were highly specific—one serving women's practical needs, the other women's pleasurable needs. Other hot publications, such as *Worth,* capitalized on trends like the increased financial concerns of aging baby boomers. Hundreds of other, less glamorous, niche publications maintain a steady readership and profit by narrowly focusing their editorial content. The largest subscription magazine, *Modern Maturity,* caters to retired persons. Dozens of small magazines, like *Fly Fisherman* and *Military History,* depend on loyal audiences.

The success of these niche publications attracted more than 800 start-up magazines in 1994 to an already crowded field, most targeting a selective readership interested in computers, crafts, sports, automobiles, or music. While these magazines do indeed help readers carve a better decoy, cook a more tender chicken, climb a career ladder, comprehend mutual funds, or catch a husband, their primary goal is to deliver readers to advertisers.

Magazines make money through both advertising and circulation. For decades advertising revenues constituted the bulk of the profits, sometimes up to 70 percent, but the recession changed all that. In 1994, circulation accounted for 52 percent of revenues, while advertising pulled in 48 percent. Magazines make money through circulation by putting together a selective collection of articles and photographs on a weekly, monthly, or quarterly basis, hoping to attract a large number of readers. Magazines sold on newsstands and in supermarkets earn a higher profit for publishers because they share the revenues only with distributors and retailers. Magazines sold through subscription are less profitable because of the high costs of getting and keeping readers through direct mail. By the time they pay for a direct mail campaign, postage, billing, and other mailing costs, publishers very often lose money in the first year of a subscription.

In circulation, both quality and quantity count. The quality refers to the readers, who are measured by both demographics—age, income, education, geographic area—and psychographics—lifestyles, hobbies, intellectual pursuits. Quantity applies to numbers—how many readers the magazine attracts week in and week out.

Magazines use the quality and quantity of their readership to draw advertisers, trying to convince them that their magazine is read by the very same customers the advertisers are trying to attract to their products. With the right quality of reader, even small circulation publications can win advertisers. *American Lawyer,* for example, is attractive to luxury car makers not for its circulation quantity (relatively small) but rather for its quality (average income $350,000).

The reason profits from advertising have drastically declined is because advertisers are unwilling to pay the "sticker price" for ad rates, demanding instead negotiated page rates. In addition, while advertising budgets have not increased substantially, magazines face increased competition from other new magazines. The slice of the advertising pie has gotten thinner and thinner.

Some magazines, called controlled circulation magazines, make money only through advertising. The magazines deliver a highly desirable audience—doctors, business executives, airline passengers, moviegoers—that advertisers want to reach. The readers are generally happy to get a free magazine that contains useful information. Magazines are also divided into two categories by editorial coverage: consumer and trade. Consumer publications, like *TV Guide, Sports Illustrated, Newsweek, Good Housekeeping,* and other magazines most of us receive at home, are geared to reader's personal interests and make their money by appealing to a wide general audience. Trade publications, meanwhile, like *Ad Age* and *Publishers Weekly,* are not generally available on newsstands and have a very high subscription price. But because their editorial content is narrowly tailored to an audience that often considers the publication required reading in the industry, trade publications can charge higher rates for their advertising.

Magazine staffs are usually divided between the editorial side and the business side, which is comprised of advertising, circulation, and production departments. Thousands of small publications exist where a half dozen or fewer staffers perform both editorial and business duties. About 600 magazines, audited by the Audit Bureau of Circulation, account for more than 75 percent of all magazine circulation and advertising. The following listing describes the typical staff structure at these magazines.

The Executives

Publisher—Supervises all activities of advertising, circulation, and production and manufacturing departments. Involvement with the editorial department is usually minimal unless he or she is also the editor, in which case he or she sets the magazine's editorial policy. Basically the publisher's job is to make sure the magazine makes a profit. If the magazine is incorporated, the publisher is usually president or executive vice-president of the corporation as well. At most large consumer magazines where the publisher is a salaried employee, the salary is anywhere from $50,000 to $400,000 a year. Publishers of magazines in the Time/Life Group (*Sports Illustrated, Fortune, People, Entertainment Weekly,* etc.) tend toward the upper end of that range.

Editor—Has ultimate responsibility for the magazine's entire editorial content, including art, text, and cover of the magazine. If publisher is not also editor, plays leading role in determining editorial policy. Along with the managing editor, the editor must make sure each issue of the magazine is acceptable, on time, and within budget. The editor is also the magazine's figurehead. On some major publications where the editor must spend much of his or her time making public appearances and doing other essentially promotional activities, where he or she is in charge of a group of publications, or where he or she is both editor and publisher, the day-to-day operations of the magazine may be turned over to an executive editor.

Managing Editor—Coordinates editorial, art, and production departments to insure that the magazine is put out on time and in an acceptable form. Oversees the copyediting and proofreading staff to make sure the magazine is factually and grammatically correct. The managing editor may also be responsible for keeping the editorial department within its budget, and usually has a large say in the magazine's content.

Art Director—Oversees all art and editorial design work for the magazine, including illustrations and photography. Supervises art staff and controls art budget and works with production manager and printing house to insure that printing quality is acceptable and colors are accurate. Oversees art production and heads photography and illustration departments.

Assistant Art Director—Designs editorial page layouts, supervises illustrators, photographers, and typographers. Works with editors to arrange photography sessions. Pastes up editorial pages and prepares them for the printer.

Editorial Department

Senior Editor—Supervises a major editorial department. Sometimes senior editors have specific titles, such as sports editor, fashion editor, fiction editor, and so on. The senior editor is responsible for all writing from the department and supervises lower level editors, freelance writers, and sometimes photographers. Some senior editors also write articles and regular columns, but most don't have time.

Bureau Chief—Supervises a staff of writers in a field location, assigns stories for them to cover, and usually does some reporting as well. In one-person bureaus, the bureau chief does *all* the reporting. In places where there is not enough news to keep a full-time reporter busy, the magazine may employ a *stringer,* who follows and reports on noteworthy events, but is usually paid on a per-article basis.

Staff Writer—Writes articles, columns, and other features for the magazine, usually in a particular subject area. The degree of autonomy varies widely; some staff writers have all their assignments dictated by an editor, but more famous ones may enjoy a free choice of subjects.

Sometimes people who are, in effect, staff writers are called contributing editors: But sometimes that title signifies nothing more than a contractual agreement giving the magazine first dibs (''right of first refusal'') on anything the author writes.

Assistant Editor/Associate Editor—The line between these two titles is often vague and may depend on little more than seniority and salary. On larger publications, assistant and associate editors work in one department or subject area of the magazine. They assign and edit articles, sometimes organize photography shootings, and maintain an expertise in their subject area by attending press conferences and trade shows and keeping up with what's written about it. They write most of the magazine's incidental copy (article titles, photo captions, and so on) and occasional feature articles, and may be assigned a regular column.

Copy Editor—Goes over all editorial copy for grammar and adherence to the magazine's stylistic rules. Checks all facts for accuracy. Prepares all copy for typesetter, proofreads all typeset copy, and works with managing editor to establish and maintain production schedule.

Editorial Assistant—This is the entry-level position, primarily a secretarial and clerical job. It is usually thought of as a preparation for higher responsibilities. In addition to typing manuscripts into a computer, filing, answering phones, and fetching coffee, editorial assistants may also write short pieces, proofread, fact-check, help generate ideas for articles, have an occasional stab at editing an article or column, and do other small editorial tasks.

Advertising Sales Department

Advertising Sales Director—Supervises the advertising sales department and is responsible for having the department meet goals and quotas set by the publisher. The advertising sales director helps set the prices the magazine charges for advertising space, and may have considerable latitude in offering discounts and making other policy decisions. He or she supervises branch managers and other advertising sales staff, and is in charge of recruiting and training new sales personnel. Advertising sales directors depend on incentives more than anyone else in publishing.

Research Director—Through the use of surveys, statistical analysis, and other research techniques, the research director develops profiles of the magazine's actual and potential readership, in order to learn how the magazine is perceived, improve its image, and draw new readers. The research director's statistics about readers are a major tool in selling space to advertisers.

Regional Sales Manager—Is responsible for the sale of advertising accounts in a certain geographic area, and usually operates out of the area assigned, rather than out of the magazine's main office. Sometimes supervises a sales staff.

Advertising Sales Representative—Sells advertising space to clients; opens new accounts and services current ones. Makes presentations to clients and advertising agencies concerning the magazine's audience and the effectiveness of its advertisements. May suggest ways to adapt an advertising campaign to the magazine's readers or region.

Circulation Department

Circulation Marketing Director—Plans and directs all circulation marketing efforts to maximize profits from circulation; supervises analysis, planning, budgeting, and execution of all subscription and newsstand sales programs; is responsible for maintaining the magazine's circulation at the optimum level.

Subscription Manager—Subscriptions are also usually handled by outside companies, called fulfillment houses. In addition to coordinating activity with the fulfillment house, the subscription manager develops short- and long-term plans for improving subscription circulation, and supervises the solicitation of new subscriptions through cards in the magazine, advertisements elsewhere, direct-mail campaigns, and other sales techniques.

Newsstand Circulation Manager—Few magazines handle their own newsstand sales; most work through outside companies, called distribution houses. The newsstand circulation manager coordinates activity between the publisher and the distribution house. He or she determines how many copies will be printed for newsstand sale and how many will be allocated to each region, and makes regular reports on newsstand sales.

Production and Manufacturing

Manufacturing and Distribution Head—Negotiates contracts with vendors, typesetters, printers, and engravers; supervises and coordinates their activities to make sure agreements are kept and the magazine is manufactured and distributed properly and on time; supervises all activities of the production and manufacturing department.

Traffic and Distribution Director—Responsible for the delivery of printed magazines by rail, truck, and mail to distribution houses, fulfillment houses or subscribers, and other destinations. Prepares distribution budgets, monitors costs, and is responsible for the observance of freight tariffs, postal regulations, and other government regulations.

AVERAGE SALARIES AT LARGE CONSUMER MAGAZINES

Title	Average Salary	After
Section Editor	$52,580	flat
General Editor	42,900	flat
Associate Editorial Director	32,552	flat
Writer-Editor, Staff Correspondent	32,500	1 year
Editor	32,214	3 years
Associate Editor	31,326	6 years
Art Editor	27,040	3 years
Rewrite Chief Copy Chief	27,040	3 years
Head, Subscription and Statistical Services Division	39,534	4 years
Circulation Manager	27,917	3 years
Subscription Manager	25,155	3 years
Key Punch Operator	26,267	3 years
Proofreader	18,980	2 years
Tape Librarian	18,980	2 years

SOURCE: The Newspaper Guild, 1994.

AVERAGE SALARIES OF RESEARCHERS AT SELECTED MAGAZINES

Magazine	Average Salary	After
Time	$32,136	1 Year
Macleans	30,798	3 Years
Scientific American	23,777	3 Years
Newsweek	23,194	3 Years

SOURCE: The Newspaper Guild, 1994.

AVERAGE SALARIES FOR EXECUTIVES AT CONSUMER MAGAZINES

Category	Editor	Managing Editor	Senior Editor	Art Director
Region				
Northeast	$58,717	$52,207	$45,145	$47,530
South	46,791	33,593	40,315	35,418
North Central	56,217	39,328	38,227	38,208
West	43,911	36,365	39,174	37,122
Sex (4–10 years experience)				
Male	37,806	40,405	43,686	37,478
Female	52,900	34,856	36,157	36,151
Age				
29 or younger	31,420	30,957	34,411	32,375
30–39	52,125	40,947	43,553	40,357
40–49	58,172	57,007	41,254	43,957
50 or older	70,284	60,209	46,867	NA
Circulation				
Up to 49,999	57,404	37,763	42,257	35,812
50,000–99,999	66,530	37,001	36,157	38,553
100,000–499,999	53,731	49,935	46,640	43,940
500,000 or more	124,178	69,198	49,889	NA
Range				
Highest salary	443,000	210,000	76,000	115,000
Lowest salary	13,080	21,500	17,500	16,000

SOURCE: Magazine Publishers of America, *Folio: 1994 Editorial Salary Survey.*

Production Director—Assists in negotiating printing, typesetting, and engraving contracts, and establishes production schedules; oversees and coordinates technical matters and scheduling between editorial and advertising production; and has the final responsibility for quality control. The demand for good production directors has increased considerably in the past few years, and with it their average salary.

Production Manager—Is responsible for providing finished mechanicals of the entire magazine to the printer on time for printing; oversees quality and accuracy of printing and binding, and acts as liaison with paper suppliers; maintains production schedule and proper flow of materials, and tries to minimize costs.

Paper Purchasing Manager—Negotiates contracts for the purchase of paper for printing the magazine; maintains paper inventory at optimum levels; locates new sources of paper.

THE NEWSPAPER

First came television, then VCRs and cable, now the home computer. For decades, newspapers have competed with formidable foes, all of which have eroded their readership. To stave off these challenges, newspapers have broadened their definition of news, adding sections like "Living," "Home," "Business," and "Science," and have expanded coverage of entertainment, restaurants, and sports. Publishers, many in cities without a competing paper, have been successful in producing profitable newspapers targeted at well-educated, affluent readers sought by advertisers. There are more than 1,500 dailies and nearly 900 Sunday newspapers, with circulations ranging from a few thousand to well over a million. The number of Sunday editions has been increasing in recent years even as the number of daily papers (and total newspaper circulation) has dropped precipitously. As recently as 1980, there were 1,745 daily papers with a combined circulation of more than 62 million. Circulation of daily papers has dropped every year since 1987; all of the decline has come from folding evening papers, whose numbers and circulation have dropped every year since 1975.

In the mid-90s, newspapers face new competition from cyberspace in the form of on-line services and other outlets on the Internet. In this case, newspapers are not fighting the competition, they're joining them, with their own Internet "home page" and on-line services. The Newspaper Association of America reports that more than 60 major newspapers have on-line services and about 30 are planned for 1995. From the *San Jose Mercury News,* to the *Chicago Tribune,* to *The Tampa Tribune,* to Long Island's *Newsday,* newspapers are providing readers with on-line previews of the next day's paper and extended coverage of top news stories. Readers can talk back to editors and reporters about stories as well as access information from previous issues. Most newspaper publishers are uncertain whether the on-line services will be financially successful. But they don't want to be left in a ditch off the information superhighway, so they cruise down a road that could lead nowhere or to a pot of gold.

The on-line services have created new types of jobs with titles like *content provider* and *content designer.* Both these positions require the ability to integrate different types of information and merge text with graphics, video, and sound for an on-line "package." Some newspapers have created departments to hire and train these new wave journalists. *The Washington Post,* for example, has a new department dubbed the Digital Ink Co., which advertises job openings on the Internet. One New York financial paper recently hired a journalist just to report on Internet developments in the securities industry.

The more traditional reporter's worklife has also been changed by technology. Computer skills are a given; reporters are also expected to use online research for everything from searching local real estate records to retrieving U.S. Census documents to checking computerized data banks in Australia. Electronic bulletin boards offer a new way to get comments for stories and to develop sources.

Modern technology is not the only development to leave a lasting mark on the newspaper industry. The women's movement, as well as sex discrimination lawsuits, has also brought change to the business. The number of women in the newsroom has shifted dramatically since 1970, when only a small percentage of reporters and editors were women. Today, more than half the nation's 58,000 editorial employees are women, and most journalism schools report that the majority of students are women. However, only about 8 percent of J-school graduates find jobs with newspapers, according to the latest annual survey by the Ohio State Journalism Department. About half pursue careers in unrelated fields, while the rest go into corporate communications, public relations, advertising, and broadcasting.

Newspapers' increased attention to the diversity of their editorial staff indicates that women and minorities will find it easier to land a job in newspapers, even though total newspaper employment—including advertising, circulation, production, and other staff—is down about 30,000 from its all-time high of 479,000 in June 1990. But total female employment in all segments of newspaper operations has held steady at just over 200,000 for the past seven years, even as male employment has declined (from 270,000 in 1987 to 246,900 in 1993). These figures suggest that older male employees—typesetters, darkroom assistants, and pressmen—are retiring and being replaced by new technologies like digital photography and desktop publishing, rather than by new employees. The U.S. Department of Labor predicts that job growth for newspapers will be about average through the year 2005. Most editorial openings will be created by people leaving to retire or switch to less stressful, less time-consuming work.

While technology has created new jobs and recast other positions, in many aspects, the reporter's worklife remains unchanged. Most reporters start out on small weekly or daily newspapers where they cover everything from crime to community boards to cooking contests. Newspaper reporting is not a nine-to-five job; it's a lifestyle that often requires long hours and not very glamorous travel. Editors try to hire reporters with tenacity, initiative, creativity, a nose for news, and an ability to deal with all types of people from the homeless to the famous. A high energy level coupled with strong self-motivation are requirements for success. After several years on a small paper, most reporters move up to either a larger paper or an editing slot. Career advancement depends on good clips (published stories) and good contacts with both newsmakers and editors at other papers.

WEEKLY SALARIES OF NEWS STAFF AT SELECTED NEWSPAPERS

Newspaper	Copydesk Top Minimum (After Years Employed)	Reporter Top Minimum (After Years Employed)
Baltimore Sun	$946.00 (6)	$916.00 (5)
Boston Herald	801.50 (2)	791.63 (4)
Buffalo News	893.08 (5)	883.42 (5)
Chicago Sun-Times	988.36 (5)	955.90 (5)
Denver Post	753.00 (5)	738.00 (5)
Detroit News	761.54 (4)	750.54 (4)
Eugene Register-Guard (OR)	815.70 (6)	799.81 (5)
Harrisburg Patriot, News (PA)	653.75 (4)	623.75 (4)
Jersey City Journal	681.19 (flat)	650.03 (4)
Lansing State Journal (MI)	595.00 (5)	579.86 (5)
Lynn Item (MA)	695.65 flat	608.00 (4)
Manchester Union Leader (NH)	756.23 (6 months)	746.23 (3)
Norristown Times Herald (PA)	698.92 (5)	683.44 (5)
Pawtucket Times (RI)	615.90 (1)	610.00 (4)
Pittsburgh Post-Gazette	898.00 (3)	898.00 (5)
Pottstown Mercury (PA)	765.00 flat	701.05 (5)
Providence Journal-Bulletin	871.50 (4)	835.19 (4)
St. Louis Post-Dispatch	946.26 (5)	933.76 (5)
Salem (MA) *News*	629.56 (5)	610.61 (4)
San Diego Union	859.01 (6)	832.76 (6)
San Jose Mercury News (CA)	904.94 (6)	887.44 (6)
Seattle Times	779.28 (5)	773.69 (5)
Sioux City Journal (IA)	561.82 (5)	541.64 (4)
Toledo Blade	862.91 (2)	824.08 (4)

SOURCE: The Newspaper Guild, 1994.

Small or large, most newspapers operate in the same manner. Reporters generate stories either through their own sources or from assignment editors, who specialize in coverage of different sections of the paper like local, state, or national news, sports, or lifestyles. Reporters cover the story by doing research, which can include reading past stories on the same topic, searching databases of other publications and information sources, or telephoning sources. While many reporters do most of their news gathering over the phone, often they cover a story in person, armed with paper, pen, and tape recorder. Reporters "file" stories either in the office or from an outside location on a laptop computer hooked by modem to the newspaper. In either case, once completed, the story, usually of a predetermined length, goes first to the desk editor, who works with the assignment editor.

WEEKLY SALARIES OF DISTRICT CIRCULATION MANAGERS FOR SELECTED NEWSPAPERS

Newspaper	Top Minimum (After Years Employed)	Newspaper	Top Minimum (After Years Employed)
The New York Times	$1,269.00 (4)	*Denver Post*	$699.00 (4)
Toledo Blade	824.08 (4)	*Albany Times-Union*	678.22 (4)
Minneapolis Star Tribune	820.50 (5)	*Portland Press Herald*	666.60 (4)
Long Beach Press-Telegram	794.53 (4)	*Duluth News-Tribune*	655.71 (5)
Seattle Times	775.79 (4)	*Manchester Union Leader*	651.82 (3)
San Diego Union	774.77 (5)	*Salem News* (Mass.)	564.61 (2)
Boston Herald	743.09 (3)	*Terre Haute Tribune-Star*	438.02 (5)
St. Louis Post-Dispatch	722.60 (5)		

SOURCE: The Newspaper Guild, 1994.

After the editor reads the story and makes corrections or changes, the copy goes to the copy desk, where a *copy editor* checks for errors in grammar, spelling, and facts and prepares it for the typesetter. At many papers, the copy editor also writes the headline. The story then goes to the composing room, where it is set in type by a printer on a tape that feeds into an automatic composing machine. The copy that comes out of the composing machine is ready to be pasted onto page-sized boards. More and more newspapers are using computers to paste up their pages—basically a very sophisticated desktop publishing program—meaning that no paper is used to create the newspaper until the final product is printed. The boards, whether pasted up by hand or computer, then go to a photoengraver, who takes a picture of them. The picture is converted into a curved plate by the stereotyper and put on a high-speed press by the pressmen, and out comes the morning newspaper. This, of course, is a simplified version of the whole process, which varies from newspaper to newspaper.

Reporters working for daily newspapers who were members of the Newspaper Guild had starting salaries ranging from about $17,576 to nearly $37,502 in 1994. According to the guild, experienced reporters averaged about $39,600. Virtually all experienced reporters earned over $30,056 a year, while the top contractual salary was $65,988. A number of top reporters on big-city dailies earned more. In general, newspaper salaries increase proportionately to the circulation of the newspaper.

Copy editors and assistant editors follow reporters on the salary scale. At many newspapers, these workers make about 10 percent more than the reporters and reach the salary ceiling more quickly. An assistant managing editor responsible for several departments at a large newspaper makes upward of $85,000, while salaries for managing editors at large papers usually top $100,000.

WEEKLY SALARIES FOR ADVERTISING SALES STAFF AT SELECTED NEWSPAPERS

	Top Minimums		
Newspaper	**Ad Sales, Display**	**Ad Sales, Classified Outside**	**Ad Sales, Classified Inside**
Albany Times-Union	$ 651.21	$ 651.21	$471.30
Baltimore Sun	832.76	832.76	663.00
Boston Herald	840.88	840.88	566.80
Denver Post	738.00	699.00	461.00
Duluth News-Tribune	655.71	655.71	397.14
Manchester Union Leader (NH)	768.62	768.62	660.83
Memphis Commercial Appeal	769.60	665.78	567.20
Philadelphia Inquirer	1,000.00	1,000.00	741.58
Sacramento Bee	649.00	649.00	463.71
San Diego Union	832.76	832.76	639.41
San Francisco Chronicle	887.44	887.44	694.58
San Jose Mercury News (CA)	887.44	887.44	694.58
Seattle Times	725.39	725.39	607.95
St. Louis Post-Dispatch	933.76	933.76	671.95
Toledo Blade (OH)	824.08	824.08	564.66
Washington Post	891.80	891.80	580.40

SOURCE: The Newspaper Guild, 1994.

Reporters, writers, and editors for the major news wire services crank out news almost as fast as it happens. Most newspapers rely on wire service copy for national and international news they are unable to cover themselves. Average salaries vary widely among the major news services. The minimum weekly salary at United Press International is $683.69 (a reflection of the company's poor fiscal health), while at Reuters, it's $991.34. Minimum salaries at the Associated Press range from $813.50 in Albany, Chattanooga,

Peoria, St. Louis, and Yakima, Washington, to $856.50 in Boston, San Francisco, and Los Angeles. (Minimum AP salaries in New York and Washington, D.C., were $893.50).

WEEKLY SALARIES FOR VARIOUS ADMINISTRATIVE POSITIONS FOR SELECTED NEWSPAPERS

Newspaper	Librarian Minimum (After Years Employed)	Clerk Minimum (After Years Employed)	Copy and Office Person Minimum (After Years Employed)
Baltimore Sun	$ 678.00 (5)	$460.00 (5)	$402.00 (5)
Boston Herald	831.11 (1)	461.08 (3)	362.39 (2)
Buffalo News	927.77 flat	421.36 (3)	361.59 (1)
Chicago Sun-Times	748.05 (5)	439.52 (3)	361.58 (1)
Cleveland Plain Dealer	663.01 (3)	480.77 (3)	446.97 (1)
Denver Post	830.00 (5)	338.00 (3.5)	317.00 (3.5)
Detroit Free Press	670.29 (4)	495.61 (4)	NA
Detroit News	695.29 (4)	495.61 (4)	417.24 (1)
Indianapolis Star	468.00 (3)	384.75 (3)	300.50 (flat)
Long Beach Press-Telegraph (CA)	534.79 (3)	432.81 (1)	396.80 (flat)
Manchester Union Leader (NH)	566.02 (2)	534.34 (3)	458.32 (1)
Minneapolis Star Tribune	732.00 (2)	462.00 (4)	397.75 (6 months)
New York Times	1,099.00 (4)	608.97 (2)	413.18 (1)
Philadelphia Inquirer	605.13 (5)	488.40 (4)	476.02 (3)
Pittsburgh Post-Gazette	643.00 (2)	485.00 (3)	357.00 (1)
San Francisco Chronicle	664.57 (4)	458.81 (2)	406.70 (15 months)
Seattle Times	592.72 (4)	431.73 (2)	362.85 (2)
St. Louis Post-Dispatch	540.42 (4)	413.60 (3)	291.82 (1)
Toledo Blade	571.98 (3)	447.77 (2)	393.96 (6 mos)
Washington Post	891.80 (2)	443.10 (2)	409.20 (1.5)

SOURCE: The Newspaper Guild, 1994.

THE PUBLISHING HOUSE

Despite the ubiquitous presence of books in our lives (not in our homes, of course, just on TV with Oprah, Phil, and Geraldo), book publishing is a relatively small industry. In 1993, book shipments totaled nearly $23 billion, while employment stood at only 75,000 nationwide. So anyone who feels he or she must have a job in this so-called glamour industry should take a hard look at the various areas of the business to see which offer the best opportunities. They should also look into the fast developing field of electronic and multimedia publishing.

In recent years, sales of adult hardcover and paperback trade books have been growing while sales through book clubs have been down for a number of years. In educational publishing, college textbook sales have been flat, but school publishing has been very profitable. The most successful areas of general publishing have been children's books (up 37 percent between 1987 and 1994, but slowing down in 1995), religious books and Bibles, and of course computer books of all kinds, especially those about the internet and those written for "dummies." IDG Books, the publisher of that well-known series, is located in Foster City, California; they claim to have sold over 9 million copies of their books.

The U.S. publishing industry has been in transition for over a decade. After dealing with the effects of corporate takeovers, publishers had to navigate the 1991 to 1992 recession. Currently, book publishers, who have been burdened by overspending on advances to authors, overproduction of titles, and overoptimistic printings, are pruning their lists and trimming their staffs as well. New book outputs rose from nearly 47,000 in 1990 to over 49,000 in 1992, but fell 14 percent to just over 42,000 in 1993, according to the R. R. Bowker Company.

Among the major reasons for this decline has been the sudden but very real commitment to electronic publishing, both multimedia (CD-ROMs) and online (the internet). A heavy investment in these new technologies, as well as in new—and often highly paid—staff have already helped to draw off some of the capital normally earmarked for books. Many, if not most, of the new jobs being created in publishing today are in the new electronic divisions established in such old-name houses as Macmillan, Random House, and Time Warner. Even the venerable 500-year-old Oxford University Press has opened electronic media departments both in the United States and England. (See the section on "Electronic Publishing" for more details.)

Geographically New York City is still the publishing center of the country, but many regional and specialty publishers have been started around the country. For example, there is a large enclave of publishers in the San Francisco Bay area, and small publishers and university presses abound in the rest of California, Colorado, and other Rocky Mountain states. Other new job opportunities have appeared as several foreign publishers have been opening offices in New York. So too are some well-known multimedia developers, although San Francisco and Los Angeles remain the major centers for this activity.

Below are descriptions of a wide variety of jobs that exist in all large publishing houses. Most require a bachelor's degree and virtually all require some knowledge of computers. Anyone seeking employment in this field should acquire as much knowledge of the leading software programs

(WordPerfect, Word, etc.) as possible. Knowledge of specialized programs such as PageMaker, QuarkXPress, and other Macintosh-related products will be a major help in securing employment. The anecdotal evidence would indicate that the book publishing industry is moving to Macs en masse although most large houses still use IBMs for their accounting and word processing needs.

Editorial Department

Acquisitions Editors—Frequently called senior editors, their primary responsibilities are deciding what books the company will publish, negotiating with writers and their agents to decide how much they will be paid, and working with writers to insure that manuscripts are turned in on schedule and in reasonably good condition. Once the manuscript comes in and is accepted, the editor shepherds the book through the various stages of production; he or she also attends sales and publicity meetings to explain why the book deserves more advertising and why the company's sales people should push it harder to bookstore owners. Responsibility for actual editing—i.e., marking manuscripts with a pencil—varies considerably from editor to editor.

Assistant and Associate Editors—Work is similar to that of senior editors except that they usually handle fewer books and less prominent authors, and have less autonomy in deciding what books they will acquire and in negotiating fees. The last two functions are often reviewed closely and sometimes taken over by senior editors. In many houses the assistant or associate editor only reads and edits manuscripts that are under contract.

Editorial Assistants—Often they are treated as glorified secretaries, and the main evidence of their glorification is that they are paid less than secretaries. However, many times this position does serve the function of an apprenticeship, which was its original intention. In addition to typing letters and contracts, filing, and related tasks, editorial assistants are sometimes permitted to read unsolicited manuscripts and give their recommendations for rejection or acceptance.

Developmental Editor—Often the impetus to produce a book comes not from an individual author but from the publisher, as in the case of many textbooks and reference books. In this case the so-called developmental editor takes a much more active role in the writing of the book: He or she will find the writers, explain to them in detail what is required, edit the work closely, and often write some of the material.

Production Editor—Sometimes called a managing editor, coordinates activity between editors, designers, copy editors, typesetters, and other people necessary to prepare a manuscript for printing. He or she establishes a production schedule, makes sure it is followed, and often sets and supervises the editorial budget.

Copy Editor—Reads manuscripts for grammatical accuracy, consistency of style, phrasing, word use, and logical consistency. Also usually proofreads galleys, repro, and mechanicals (the initial boards from which printing plates are made) to see that the typesetters and paste-up artists have followed the editor's instructions.

Advertising, Sales, and Publicity

Publicity Director—It is the publicity director's job to make sure the company's books receive attention in the media. Toward this end he or she sends out copies of newly published books to publications likely to review them, tries to get authors on TV and radio shows, and arranges other engagements for authors, such as autographing sessions in bookstores and lecture tours of colleges.

Publicist—Under the supervision of the publicity director, performs essentially the same job, except that he or she may deal with less important authors and books, or may be restricted to a specific aspect of publicity.

Copywriter—Writes material intended to sell books. This includes advertising copy, press releases, and the laudatory plot synopses found on the inside flaps of book jackets and called "flap copy."

Marketing Director—Is in charge of the overall effort to sell published books. On the basis of projected sales, he or she decides how many copies of a book will be printed and how and where they will be distributed, oversees the sales staff, and decides how and where books will be advertised.

Advertising Director—Places advertisements in selected publications, such as book review supplements of newspapers and journals aimed at the book's intended audience, and in the case of bestsellers and other mass market books, with TV and other media. A few publishers still prepare their own advertising rather than rely on agencies, so here the advertising director also supervises the writing and design of ads and helps set the advertising budget for each book.

Sales Manager—Supervises the sales staff, makes sure they receive all the necessary materials such as press releases and news of new publications, receives their reports and orders for new books, and generally coordinates their activities with those of the rest of the company.

Salespersons—Spend most of their time on the road, visiting bookstore owners and gently persuading them to buy as many books as possible and to display them as prominently as possible. Then they make follow-up visits to make sure the books and other materials (such as those large cardboard display stands, called "dump bins") have arrived satisfactorily. Salespeople also report back to the main office their customers' comments on the quality of service, what kinds of books they are asking for, and other information. Because of the knowledge they thus acquire of the book market, salespeople are sometimes promoted to editors.

Subsidiary Rights Director—A book's circulation seldom ends with its hardcover sales. It may be sold to a book club, a movie company, or a paperback publisher, parts of it may be reprinted in magazines, or all of the above may happen. The subsidiary rights director, usually in concert with the author's agent, promotes and manages these sales. Over the past decade, as subsidiary rights contracts for top books have climbed into the millions of dollars, "sub-rights" directors have become increasingly important at major publishing houses. They now exercise a strong influence over the acquisition of new books and the advances paid to writers based on the chances of subsequent sub-rights sales.

Subsidiary Rights Assistant—Usually handles a specific area of sub-rights sales, such as magazines, foreign rights, or book clubs.

Production Department

Art Director—Determines what the book will look like. Along with the acquisition editor and production director, he or she selects the typeface, book size, paper, jacket design, display type, and other elements of the book's design. The art director also procures the necessary illustrations and photographs (sometimes these are supplied by the author) and determines how they will be placed in the book. Finally, he or she supervises illustrators, freelancers, and paste-up artists.

Managing Editor—See Production Editor under "Editorial Department."

AVERAGE ANNUAL SALARIES IN PUBLISHING HOUSES

	Company Revenues			
Department and Title	**under $1 million**	**$1 million–9.9 million**	**$10 million–99.9 million**	**$100 million or more**
Editorial				
Editorial Director/Editor-in-Chief	$37,267	$ 61,616	$101,638	$125,856
Executive Editor/Managing Editor	42,979	35,567	60,921	73,059
Editor	36,125	36,200	37,000	34,450
Associate Editor	NA	20,100	28,000	29,550
Production/Development Editor	NA	54,600	71,500	65,333
Copy Editor/Proofreader	NA	NA	NA	41,850
Editorial Assistant	16,000	19,200	22,950	19,500
Sales and Marketing				
V.P. Sales and Marketing	$60,000	$ 54,650	$102,000	$130,832
Publisher	99,250	55,000	183,500	116,800
Associate Publisher	24,900	54,500	NA	161,332
Sales Director/Manager	42,250	44,317	75,113	75,791
Marketing Director/Manager	25,650	41,839	49,714	70,438
Promotion Director/Manager	NA	32,200	52,000	45,667
Sales Rep/Account Manager	NA	40,032	45,157	54,785
Marketing/Sales Assistant	30,000	32,000	32,700	21,250
Publicity Manager/Director	NA	50,000	53,600	95,000

AVERAGE ANNUAL SALARIES IN PUBLISHING HOUSES

	Company Revenues			
Department and Title	**under $1 million**	**$1 million–9.9 million**	**$10 million–99.9 million**	**$100 million or more**
Management				
President/CEO	$58,366	$154,918	$381,000	$454,000
Executive/Senior Vice President	24,500	94,500	100,000	216,400
V.P. General Manager	NA	79,666	122,250	155,000
V.P. Finance/Controller	30,000	66,257	150,625	134,759
V.P. Production/Operations	NA	73,300	70,600	116,667
Business/Office Manager	27,500	38,500	80,400	72,333
Operations				
Distribution Manager/Fulfillment Director	$29,500	NA	NA	$ 68,000
Production Manager/Director	39,867	$ 41,975	$ 68,900	73,425
Art Director	NA	35,500	39,900	85,000
Accounting/Credit Manager	NA	32,000	47,450	NA
Rights				
Sub Rights Director/Manager	NA	$ 45,000	$ 58,300	$ 51,600
Licensing Director/Manager	NA	NA	NA	48,900
International Rights Director/Manager	NA	45,000	NA	NA

SOURCE: *Publishers Weekly* Magazine, July 31, 1995

Traffic Manager—Large publishing houses with complex production schedules often require a traffic manager to keep track of everything. The traffic manager oversees the flow of work between the editorial and art departments, the typesetter, and the printer; sets schedules; and keeps records of what stage of development each project is in. The traffic manager's job is similar to the production editor's, and indeed the two often work closely together; but the production editor's concern is primarily with the needs of the editorial department, while the traffic manager coordinates work among all departments.

Production Director—Supervises the work of the production department, sets a budget for the preparation and printing of each book, and negotiates contracts with typesetters, printers, paper manufacturers, and other suppliers.

ELECTRONIC PUBLISHING

This is such a new field that the standard government information sources on jobs and job availability have not yet produced the kind of hard data that can be found in all the other parts of this book. But a search of the want ads in major newspapers in New York and California, as well as in *Publishers Weekly* reveals that jobs are being created in this area, and that many of them can be found in the traditional publishing houses. In addition to their own staffing, many well-known names, including Houghton- Mifflin, Simon & Schuster, and Random House have also made direct investments in the major multimedia development companies. Strong commitments by major corporations mean that the new technologies are being viewed seriously as the future of the business.

There are currently two areas of electronic publishing to consider: the CD-ROM and the on-line world (often called the information superhighway, or cyberspace). Publishers are interested in both because both enable publishers to create products that do essentially the same thing that books have been doing for five centuries: namely, transmitting information, knowledge, and beauty to readers in a pleasing, easy-to-use format.

The first signs that the computer was going to cause a revolution in the publishing business could be glimpsed as early as 1991, when the value of CD-ROM technology first became apparent to publishers of law books, dictionaries, and encyclopedias. The ability to store vast amounts of information and find it almost instantly was of great use to researchers, writers, marketing specialists, lawyers, and, of course, the most sophisticated of all information consumers, librarians. Publishers with strong connections to this latter group—Bowker, Facts on File, Gale, and Houghton Mifflin—learned quickly that the CD-ROM would be a valuable and profitable means of publishing their works.

During the early 1990s, as the personal computer grew dramatically more powerful each year, several innovative companies, including Voyager and Broderbund, began to produce CD-ROMs that included music and video as well as text. Suddenly the possibilities of *multimedia* as a learning tool of extraordinary power became apparent to every publishing concern, and soon the market was being flooded with all kinds of CD-ROMs, most of dubious quality. Some, however, achieved instant success (*Cinemania,* from Microsoft, and *Compton's Interactive Encyclopedia,* for example), demonstrating the depth of a serious market. For job seekers, the news that CD-ROM drives are now built into every new personal computer can only mean strong growth for the future.

So too do the latest developments on the Internet. For a short while, multimedia was the sole province of the CD-ROM developer. But by 1994, new developments in software allowed for the addition of sound, color, photography, and video to be accessed over that part of the Internet called the World Wide Web. With at least 10 million people already on the Internet and millions more projected over the next few years, a new medium is being created out of existing media. (See also in Part IV, "New Careers in the Computer World.")

Jobs in Electronic Publishing

According to Ralph Protsik, a leading Boston management recruiter, those book publishers that have moved into multimedia are struggling to set up new job categories that make sense for a publishing house. Below are his descriptions and salary range estimates reprinted from the July 1995 issue of *CD-ROM Professional.* But he forewarned that this industry is very fluid right now and some titles may not be universally applicable.

Academic Alliance Manager ($60,000–$90,000)—Establishes relationships with key software purchasing decision-makers at colleges and universities. Provides marketing support to text-oriented sales staff. Seeks potential co-development projects.

Director, New Media ($100,000–$300,000)—Creates the company's strategic plan for multimedia product. Defines company's market and product mix. Staffs and manages department. Takes lead role in business development, including acquisitions and partnerships.

Director, Special Sales ($60,000–$90,000)—Identifies and exploits nontraditional marketing and distribution channels, e.g., computer stores, consumer electronics stores, warehouse clubs, mass market sellers, and others. Assists marketing director with pricing, packaging, licensing, and bundling decisions.

Manager, Acquisitions and Licensing ($50,000–$80,000)—Investigates products to purchase, license, and co-develop. Negotiates contracts. Develops revenues through licensing of company's products.

Manager, Applications Programming ($50,000–$70,000)—Customizes underlying software to match the content of multimedia products.

Online Marketing Manager ($45,000–$70,000)—Establishes a marketing presence for the company on the Internet. Creates and administers a home page. Uses the Internet and online services to generate market research data and to promote the company's product.

Producer ($45,000–$100,000)—Manages team of internal and external programmers, graphic and interface designers, animators, and others assembled to produce a particular multimedia product. Defines budgets and schedules. Assumes overall responsibility for the product.

Technical Director ($80,000–$150,000)—Overall technical advisor to the multimedia team. Manages internal programmers and external developers. Develops underlying architecture and supervises the application programming of the generic software engine. Administers QA testing and technical support operations.

VII

Jobs and Salaries in Health Care

In 1980 the nation reached a milestone of sorts when for the first time in its history slightly more than half of all its citizens were past the age of 30. With birth rates and fertility rates remaining at very low levels, the median age of the population has continued to rise throughout the decade: in 1990 it was 33.0 years and by the year 2000 it will be 36.4. By 2010, 14 percent of the U.S. population will be over 65, up from under 10 percent in 1970, and 11 percent in 1980. A continuously aging society will cause many dramatic changes in the future, not the least of which will be the need for an expanded workforce in the health care field.

Over 6 million people are currently employed in health care jobs, but by the year 2000 the federal government estimates 8.5 million will be. Jobs for registered nurses are expected to increase by 700,000; and by 340,000 for licensed practical nurses; 119,000 for medical assistants; over 125,000 for therapists; and 433,000 for nursing aides, orderlies, and attendants. Employment in the health care field has grown fastest in physicians' and surgeons' offices—which added 200,000 jobs between 1988 and 1990. During that same period 409,000 hospital jobs were added.

Almost every occupation in health care will have higher than average growth in the 1990s including the highly paid managerial positions. With hospitals forced to deal with cuts in government support, and with new types of health care organizations (HMOs, PPOs) growing across the country, management and accounting skills are more highly valued than ever before. According to the U.S. Department of Labor the biggest portion of the growth—some 700,000 jobs—will occur in the demand for registered nurses by the year 2005. The requirement for licensed practical nurses is expected to grow by 269,000. Other occupations expected to experience triple-figure growth are physicians and surgeons; therapists, nursing aides, orderlies, and attendants; and medical assistants. Almost every occupation in the health care field will experience higher than average growth in the 1990s (see the table on the next page).

But it is important to keep in mind that these figures were compiled before the full impact of for-profit medical centers and serious cutbacks in federal funding could be measured. We know now that many hospitals are being forced to reduce staff across the board; some are openly replacing highly trained registered nurses with licensed practical nurses simply to save money, while other reports indicate that nurses are being asked to perform the tasks of respiratory therapists and the like.

The future pay structure in the industry is hard to predict. No one is quite sure whether wage rates will increase as society places a higher value on health care work or stay about the same as cost-saving pressures predominate. Although we might normally expect to see some heavy upward pressure on earnings as the demand for workers grows, the need to control the skyrocketing overall cost of health care will possibly exert an equal downward pressure. An increasingly strong union movement among nonprofessional employees—especially in public hospitals—will make for some confrontations regarding wage rates.

At the same time the importance of hospital administrators—executives, accountants, marketing, and public relations specialists—has grown in direct proportion to the requirement that hospitals (and the rapidly growing HMOs) become part of contemporary corporate culture. As most Americans are forced to accept less health care service at greater personal cost, the salaries of administrators soar, especially in the publicly held, for-profit health maintenance organizations. In 1994 the average cash compensation for chief executives in the HMO industry was $255,000, but as the accompanying table indicates the highest paid executives made much more because of their stock option plans (see the entry on "the American Executive" for an explanation of how these plans work). Even Graef Crystal, the foremost executive compensation expert, pronounced these compensation awards "monstrously large . . . among the highest in any industry." So while many doctors, nurses, and technicians are all asked to take salary reductions, the people demanding that health costs be reduced are reaping huge salaries while providing investors with hefty returns.

The true impact of this peculiarly American approach to caring for the sick and dying may not be known for a while, but for now the anecdotal evidence clearly points to a much reduced system aimed at those with good health care coverage and with wage rates relatively stable.

TOTAL COMPENSATION OF CEOS IN THE HMO INDUSTRY, 1994

CEO	HMO	Cash and Stock Options (Millions)
Stephen Wiggins	Oxford Health Plans	$36.4
Norman Payson	Healthsource	15.5
Daniel Crowley	Foundation Health	13.7
Roger Greaves	Health Systems International	8.9
Malik Hasan	Health Systems International	8.8
William McGuire	United Healthcare	6.8
Leonard Abramson	U.S. Healthcare	5.6
George Jochum	Mid Atlantic Medical Services	3.7

SOURCE: Corporate reports.

EMPLOYMENT GROWTH FOR HEALTH CARE WORKERS, 1990–2005

Occupation	Employment[1]		Average Annual Increase	Net Increase
	1990	2005		
Dental Assistants	176,000	236,000	4,000	60,000
Dental Hygienists	97,000	137,000	2,666	40,000
Dieticians and Nutritionists	45,000	56,000	730	11,000
Medical Assistants	165,000	287,000	8,133	122,000
Nurses				
Registered	1,700,000	2,500,000	46,670	700,000
Licensed Practical	644,000	913,000	17,933	269,000
Nurses Aides, Orderlies	1,300,000	1,900,000	40,000	600,000
Psychiatric Aides	100,000	134,000	2,267	34,000
Pharmacists	169,000	204,000	2,333	35,000
Pharmacy Assistants	83,000	101,000	1,200	18,000
Physicians Assistants	53,000	72,000	1,267	19,000
Podiatrists	16,000	23,000	466	7,000
Technicians				
Clinical Lab	258,000	321,000	4,200	63,000
EEG	7,000	11,000	266	4,000
EKG	16,000	15,000	None	−1,000
Emergency Medical	89,000	116,000	1,800	27,000
Medical Records	52,000	80,000	1,866	28,000
Nuclear Medicine	10,000	16,000	400	6,000
Opticians	64,000	88,000	1,600	24,000
Radiologic	149,000	252,000	6,866	103,000
Surgical	38,000	59,000	1,400	21,000
All Other Paraprofessionals and Health Technicians	409,000	588,000	11,933	179,000

EMPLOYMENT GROWTH FOR HEALTH CARE WORKERS, 1990–2005

Occupation	Employment[1] 1990	2005	Average Annual Increase	Net Increase
Therapists				
Occupational	36,000	56,000	1,333	20,000
Physical	88,000	155,000	4,533	68,000
Recreational	32,000	45,000	866	13,000
Respiratory	60,000	91,000	2,066	31,000
Speech	68,000	91,000	1,533	23,000
All Others	26,000	40,000	933	14,000
Therapy Assistants	55,000	89,000	2,266	34,000

[1]Based on U.S. Department of Labor, Bureau of Labor statistical projections for a moderately growing economy and industry.

SOURCE: U.S. Department of Labor, Bureau of Labor Statistics, *Monthly Labor Review,* November 1991.

HOSPITAL ADMINISTRATORS

At the center of America's health care system are the approximately 6,500 hospitals that every year admit almost 35 million patients and provide $256 billion worth of services, more than 38 percent of the nation's total health care bill. This is big business by anyone's definition, but every prediction indicates that many hospitals will close and many more will merge their services as the federal government cuts back its financial support for Medicare. The crucial problems most hospitals face today are the same ones that other businesses must cope with, including strict, ever-changing government regulations, stiff competition for patients, and spiraling costs. As in other businesses too, a new breed of specially trained personnel is bringing important changes to the way hospitals are run.

The complex task of managing a hospital falls to the administrator, sometimes known as president, chief executive officer, or executive vice-president. The administrator's duties and salary vary considerably, according to the size of the hospital. At a small rural hospital with less than 100 beds, an administrator will earn an average of $90,000 and have a finger in everything from deciding how often the floors should be waxed to planning a redesign of the emergency room. At a big-city medical center with about 500 beds, an administrator will earn $225,000 on average and will spend some of his time managing associate and assistant administrators who take care of the day-to-day operation. Good-sized chunks of time are given to raising funds for new construction; lobbying with local, state, and federal officials; presenting proposals to government watchdog committees; conferring with physicians and the board of directors on whether to buy a multimillion dollar piece of equipment. At the same time, a good administrator tries to keep the high-priced medical specialists as well as the lowly interns happy. While the administrator spends hours in meetings, his subordinates see that all the departments—from admissions to purchasing to X ray—are running smoothly. In most hospitals, all the medical departments are also headed by a physician who oversees all the strictly medical areas.

The Department of Labor classifies about 257,000 persons as health service managers. Under this title fall government and nongovernment hospital administrators as well as managers of nursing homes and health-maintenance organizations. A sizeable number are employed by government agencies that analyze regional health care needs, by insurance agencies, by hospital associations, and by consulting firms. The Department of Labor estimates that job openings in the field will grow much faster than average through the year 2005.

Because the medical field has grown increasingly sophisticated in its use of management techniques, many hospitals require job seekers to have a master's degree in business or health administration. A survey by *Modern Health Care* magazine found that almost 70 percent of hospital administrators held advanced degrees. Salaries among top hospital administrators vary widely by geography—New England executives earn as much as 70 percent more than their counterparts in Arizona, Colorado, Idaho, and other mountain states. The shifting nature of hospital services is reflected in several changes in the salary structure of administrators as well. The strongest growth areas are outpatient services (the heads of those departments saw a 9 percent increase in 1995) and public affairs/public relations (which saw about 7 percent raises).

MEDIAN TOTAL COMPENSATION OF HOSPITAL ADMINISTRATORS, 1995
(in thousands of dollars)

		(By Number of Employees[1])			
Title	**All Facilities**	**0–599**	**600–1199**	**1200–2199**	**Over 2200**
Medical Affairs Director	$182.3	$139.6	$150.0	$185.4	$190.3
Administrator/CEO	165.5	110.1	167.4	207.3	233.7
Assoc. Administrator/ COO	110.0	72.2	106.6	146.3	160.1
Chief Financial Officer	105.3	76.7	99.3	129.6	151.0
Head of Nursing Services	88.0	66.2	90.0	101.3	108.2
Head of MIS	71.3	45.2	64.6	75.0	84.6

[1]Full-time equivalents (FTEs).
SOURCE: *Modern Health Care*, executive compensation survey, June 1995. Reprinted by permission.

MEDIAN TOTAL COMPENSATION FOR SELECTED HOSPITAL ADMINISTRATORS, 1995

Department Executive/Mgt	1995 (Thousands of Dollars)	1994	Percent Change
Administration			
General Counsel	$104.0	$114.2	−8.9%
Public Affairs	86.6	81.7	6.0
Development	75.6	73.3	3.1
Planning	75.0	74.1	1.3
Marketing	63.6	59.7	6.5
Quality Assurance	56.5	54.5	3.7
Public Relations	51.6	48.0	7.5
Financial			
Controller	$ 70.1	$ 67.9	3.2%
General Accounting	50.5	49.5	0.2
Business Office	55.4	54.4	1.8
Admitting	40.1	39.8	0.1
Budget Planning	50.9	51.0	−0.1
Risk Management	51.3	51.4	−0.2
Medical Records	50.9	49.2	3.4
General Services			
General Services	$ 80.0	$ 77.5	5.8%
Food/Dietary Services	53.2	52.8	0.8
General Service/ Supply	40.3	40.0	0.8
Linen Services	38.9	36.8	5.7
Patient Care			
Ancillary Patient Care	$ 85.5	$ 83.8	2.0%
Pharmacy	69.7	67.9	2.6
Clinical Lab	58.7	57.9	1.4
Radiology	58.0	57.1	1.6
Nuclear Medicine	46.1	45,7	0.1
Rehab Services	66.7	62.8	6.2
Physical Therapy	58.0	57.2	1.4
Occupational Therapy	51.3	50.9	0.1
Speech Therapy	49.2	48.5	0.2
Respiratory Therapy	52.3	52.0	0.1
Chaplain	48.8	47.3	3.2
Social Services	50.7	49.1	3.3
Outpatient Services	62.4	57.0	9.5

SOURCE: *Modern Health Care,* executive compensation survey, June 1995. Reprinted by permission.

NURSES

As a nation our commitment to first-rate health care is unrivaled, or at least we believe that to be the case. But today a strong possibility exists that our system of caring for the sick could be threatened by the low social and economic status of health care personnel. Their work may have a high social value, but as long as their services are not productive or profitable in the traditional sense they will always have to struggle for higher wages. No better example of this premise exists than the historic role of nurses in American life.

The image of kind, saintly women ministering to the needs of the sick and dying has been a constant theme in Western art, and the ideals embodied in those representations are part of our cultural heritage. Over the last century women continued to play a vital role as leaders in the fight for better health care. Equally important were the services women performed as low-paid workers in financially troubled hospitals. This situation continued into the 1980s. According to the American Nurses' Association, increases in maximum salaries for nurses have failed to keep up with inflation in eight of the last seventeen years; and increases in nurses' starting salaries have been outstripped by inflation nine times.

Such low salaries for such highly responsible work had an extremely adverse affect on the profession. By 1980, for example, more than 25 percent of all nurses had left the field completely; and according to *RN* magazine, only 60 percent of all nurses were working at any given time; moreover, 90,000 to 100,000 nursing vacancies existed nationwide, leaving 88 percent of all hospitals with nursing jobs unfilled. The acute shortage of nurses had become such a serious matter that some hospitals were recruiting personnel from overseas. They paid their plane fares, as well as their lodging for 30 days. A California hospital even offered a free Hawaii vacation to any nurse who would sign a one-year contract. Some hospitals hired professional recruiters to lure experienced people to such places as Detroit, Minneapolis, and Corpus Christi. (The fee for this service can run as high as $1,000 per placement.)

Traditional economic theory says that these circumstances should have immediately driven up nurses' wages. But in fact this did not happen in any dramatic way. The hospital industry argued that the already staggering costs of modern hospital care wouldn't allow for any dramatic increase in labor costs, especially since the government was bearing so much of the cost. Unlike manufacturing or other service industries, these costs could not be continually passed on to some mythical consumer who decides whether or not to purchase the article or service based on its price. One result was that nurses, like teachers, began to seek better working facilities in lieu of higher pay. Those hospitals in poorer areas were thereby left with the biggest staff shortages. Not surprisingly, the rash of nurses' strikes in 1980 and 1981 took place mostly in large cities and for the most part were touched off by issues such as forced overtime because of understaffing.

Only a short time before most nurses believed a strike was irresponsible, perhaps even immoral. But over the years many joined unions (some even belong to the Teamsters), while statewide nurses' associations and even nurses employed by public hospitals have used the strike, or more frequently the threat of one, to win better pay agreements. Still, during the 1980s the shortage of nurses continued to grow as more left the profession and few students entered nursing programs. By January of 1988 the situation had reached crisis proportions with hospitals listing more than 20,000 nursing vacancies nationwide, a full 10 percent of the positions available. The shortage was not only nationwide, but affected every clinical area. It was particularly marked on unpopular shifts and in critical care units. The situation was deemed so critical by some hospitals that they were paying bounties of up to $10,000 for each new nurse hired.

The sources of the nursing shortage are both economic and social. With nursing pay scales under pressure from government cost containment programs, nursing salaries did not keep up with those of their technical counterparts. Starting salaries for nurses range from $28,000 to $35,000. In 1991, nurses on average only earned a maximum of $33,696; and it generally took them a maximum of eight to ten years to reach that level.

Big city hospitals responded to the challenge. In January 1991, pay for starting registered nurses exceeded $29,000 in five cities (New York, Boston, Los Angeles, Washington, D.C., and Philadelphia) and maximum pay in those cities' hospitals went as high as $56,000.

Meanwhile, the high rates paid to nurses finally attracted enough new people to the nursing profession to prompt *RN* magazine to declare an end to the nursing shortage in its October 1993 survey of the profession. Nurses' salaries increased 9 percent between 1991 and 1993—a healthy growth rate for most professions, considering that the cost of living index rose only 6 percent over that same period, but nothing compared to the 35 percent increase in nursing salaries between 1987 and 1991. And in anticipation of health care reform, many hospitals are leaving vacancies unfilled or using lower paid LPNs to provide care formerly given by RNs.

Despite the changes, the employment outlook for nurses remains good. The Department of Labor continues to project much faster than average growth throughout the year 2005. According to the Bureau of Health Professions, more than half a million new nurses will be needed on top of the 1.8 million RNs who were working in 1992. In fact, one of every five new jobs in the health care industry will be for nurses. The aging population, which is responsible for fueling most of the growth in the health care industry, will especially benefit nurses, especially home health care nurses.

Growth will also be strong for nurses in physicians' offices, clinics, HMOs, ambulatory centers, and nursing homes. Hospitals, where two of every three RNs currently work, will experience the slowest growth, as the number of inpatients is not expected to increase. That's primarily a result of fiscal austerity by insurance companies, who are refusing to pay for overnight stays for all but the most serious procedures. The one major change in the profession will be the increase in part-time work (without benefits, of course).

Part-Time Work for Nurses

About one in four nurses works part-time, according to *RN* magazine. Part-timers work an average of 24 hours a week; their hourly salaries are about $1.00 higher than their full-time counterparts (to make up for their lack of benefits). But they take home an average of only $25,620, or $14,000 less than what full-time nurses earn over the course of a year. A closer look at the demographics of each group helps explain why part-timers can afford to pass up this income. Nine out of ten part-time nurses are married, with an average household income of $62,580, or more than $3,000 higher than average household incomes for full-timers, less than two thirds of whom are married. These figures suggest that many part-time nurses work because they want to work, not because they need the money.

ESTIMATED HOURLY RATES OF SENIOR NURSES IN PRIVATE HOSPITALS

Nursing Supervisior	$22.00–31.00
Head Nurse	21.00–29.00
Nurse Anesthetist	28.00–31.00
Nurse Practitioner	21.00–30.00

SOURCE: U.S. Department of Labor, Bureau of Labor Statistics 1991 study.

Job Description of Registered Nurses

Registered Nurse—Provides professional nursing care to patients in hospitals, nursing homes, clinics, health units, private residences, and community health organizations. Assists physicians with treatment, assesses patient health problems and needs, develops and implements nursing care plans, maintains medical records. May specialize, e.g.: nurse anesthetist, nurse practitioner, industrial nurse, psychiatric nurse, clinical nurse specialist.

Nursing Supervisor—A registered professional nurse who directs and supervises nursing services in more than one organized nursing unit or operating room.

Head Nurse—A registered professional nurse who is responsible for nursing services and patient care in a single nursing unit.

Nurse Anesthetist—Recommends and administers general anesthetics intravenously, topically, by inhalation, or by endotracheal intubation.

Nurse Practitioner—A registered nurse responsible for providing continuous and comprehensive nursing care in collaboration with a physician and/or other members of a health care team. This position requires additional preparation beyond requirements for licensure which typically includes a master's degree in nursing science.

Staff Nurse—A registered nurse who employs special skills, knowledge, and judgment in caring for patients within an organized nursing unit. Gives medication, administers highly specialized therapy using complicated equipment, observes and reports on patient's condition, and maintains all medical records therein.

Job Level Descriptions of Nurses

Level I: Provide standard nursing care.

Level II: Assignments involve comprehensive nursing care.

Level II specialists: Typically work in intensive care or critical care units.

Level III: Provide advanced nursing care beyond specialized patient care.

AVERAGE HOURLY RATES FOR REGISTERED NURSES, 1993

	Hourly Pay	
	Full-time	**Part-time**
By Shift		
Day	$18.10	$18.50
Evening	17.60	18.30
Night	17.40	19.30
Rotating/Other	16.90	18.50

AVERAGE HOURLY RATES FOR REGISTERED NURSES, 1993

	Hourly Pay	
	Full-time	**Part-time**
By Service		
Medical/Surgical	$17.10	$17.90
Operating/Recovery Room	17.60	18.50
OBGYN/Newborn	17.40	18.50
Emergency Room/Outpatient	17.90	19.10
Critical Care	17.90	18.80
By Region		
New England (CT, ME, MA, NH, RI, VT)	$19.20	$19.00
Mid-Atlantic (DE, NJ, NY, PA)	18.60	19.70
South Atlantic (FL, GA, MD, NC, SC, VA, WV)	17.50	17.60
Mid South (AL, KY, MS, TN)	16.30	NA
Southwest (AR, LA, OK, TX)	17.00	NA
Great Lakes (IL, IN, MI, OH, WI)	17.20	17.60
Plains (IA, KS, MN, MO, NE, ND, SD)	16.10	16.50
Rocky Mountains (AZ, CO, ID, MT, NV, NM, UT, WY)	16.70	NA
Far West (AK, CA, HI, OR, WA)	20.70	21.80
By Location		
Urban	$18.00	$18.70
Suburban	18.30	19.30
Rural	16.10	16.60
By Hospital Size (Number of Beds)		
Under 100	15.70	16.10
100–299	7.70	18.80
300–499	18.20	19.20
500 or more	18.30	19.10
By Type of Hospital		
Community Nonprofit	17.50	18.20
Private Nonprofit	18.10	18.10
Private for Profit	17.30	18.80
University	18.20	NA
Public (VA, State, County, etc.)	17.60	NA
By Number of Years in Practice		
Less than 3	14.70	16.00
3–5	16.30	18.10
6–10	17.50	18.50
11–15	18.80	18.90
More than 15	19.10	19.00

SOURCE: *RN* magazine, October 1993. Reprinted by permission.

VETERANS ADMINISTRATION NURSES: NUMBER EMPLOYED AND AVERAGE SALARIES

Grade	Number Employed	Average Salary
I	7,742	$36,070
II	18,934	44,282
III	6,261	54,421
IV	467	64,868
V	145	89,293
Unspecified	2	50,651
Total	33,551	$44,760

SOURCE: Office of Personnel Management, *Pay Structure of the Federal Civil Service* (1994).

PHYSICIAN ASSISTANTS

While some nurses, especially the nurse practitioner and the nurse clinician, are carving out roles for themselves that allow a greater participation in patient-care decisions, a small group of health care specialists, called physician assistants, has been doing just that for about twenty years. The idea of using medically trained people (nurses and military medics, for example) to perform the physician's routine tasks surfaced in the mid-sixties when dire predictions of a doctor shortage ran rampant. By 1970 there were about 100 specially trained P.A.s (as they are called) but by 1982, however, there were about 10,000, with 40 percent of them serving in rural areas (counties of less than 50,000), where doctors are still hard to find. And today, P.A.s number more than 52,000; about 35 percent of them serve rural areas.

Most P.A.s work under the direct supervision of a licensed physician, although a growing number, now about 40 percent, work in hospitals and clinics. The P.A.'s duties include taking down patient histories, giving physical examinations, ordering laboratory tests, and assisting during complicated medical procedures such as cardiac catheterizations. Some P.A.s specialize in assisting surgeons or pediatricians, or working in a hospital emergency room; in those cases their duties are more elaborate.

Training to be a P.A. takes two years in one of the nation's 57 approved educational programs. Many of the trainees are college graduates and about 80 percent have had extensive experience in health care, usually as a nurse or medical technician. Predicting the future job opportunities for this occupation is a bit tricky. Official government sources say that a continued doctor glut could severely diminish the need for physician assistants. However, since doctors traditionally refuse to settle in rural areas (only 8 percent live in counties of less than 50,000), this problem will most likely not affect the P.A.s who work there. In addition, as medical practice grows more specialized, and more technologically oriented, the need for trained people to assist in the daily routines could, or perhaps should, increase.

CHARACTERISTICS OF PHYSICIAN ASSISTANTS

	Percentage of All Physician Assistants		Percentage of All Physician Assistants
Ethnicity		*Highest Degree Attained*	
White	90.6	Doctorate	0.7
Black	3.9	Masters	12.0
Hispanic	3.0	Bachelor	71.9
Asian/Pacific Islander	1.8	Associate	9.1
American Indian/Alaskan	0.7	Certificate	6.2
Gender		*Years in Practice*	
Male	57.7	Less than 1 year	4.4
Female	42.3	1–3 years	18.0
		4–6 years	16.8
Age		7–9 years	13.6
25 or under	1.2	10–12 years	15.9
26–30	12.0	13–15 years	13.1
31–35	17.4	16–18 years	11.0
36–40	21.1	19 or more years	7.2
41–45	23.2		
46–50	16.9	*Income (Full-Time)*	
51–55	5.4	Less than $30,000	0.8
56–60	1.9	$30,000–39,999	8.2
Over 60	0.9	$40,000–49,999	30.1
		$50,000–59,999	28.4
Region		$60,000–69,999	15.5
Northeast	24.0	$70,000–79,999	7.7
North Central	18.7	$80,000–89,999	5.0
Southeast	25.8	$90,000–99,999	2.3
South Central	12.3	$100,000 and over	3.0
West	17.3	*Average Salary*	*$56,568*
Overseas	2.0	*Median Salary*	*$53,234*

SOURCE: American Academy of Physician Assistants, *1994 Membership Census Report,* February 1995. Figures may not add up to 100 percent because of independent rounding.

Given their extensive training and experience, physician assistants, like almost all health care workers except for doctors, receive relatively low pay. According to a survey by the University of Texas Medical Branch, median earnings for P.A.s working a 40-hour week were $41,038 in October 1992. A more recent survey, taken in 1994 by the American Academy of Physician Assistants, found the median salary to be $53,234. For new graduates, the median salary was $44,176.

NURSES' AIDES AND ORDERLIES

Over 1.3 million people work as aides, orderlies, or attendants in our hospitals and nursing home facilities. Their tasks include taking temperatures, giving baths, making beds, transporting patients from one part of a facility to another, etc. According to the Department of Labor, median annual earnings of nurses' aides were about $13,800 in 1992. The middle 50 percent earned between $11,000 and $17,900. The middle 80 percent (all of whom had level II experience) earned an average of $15,787. Orderlies in hospitals earned an average of $15,121 in October 1992, according to a survey by the University of Texas Medical Branch. Nursing homes paid certified nurses' aides median annual salaries of $11,500 in 1993.

LICENSED PRACTICAL NURSES

Over the next decade, this will be one of the fastest growing jobs in the nation. According to the federal government, jobs for LPNs will grow by more than 260,000 by the year 2005. There are currently more than 665,000 LPNs working in hospitals, nursing homes, private homes, doctors' offices, and now more frequently in HMOs. They do everything from keeping records and giving alcohol rubs to administering prescribed medicines and taking patients' vital signs. Their willingness and ability to perform a wide variety of jobs has made LPNs a crucial part of the emerging lower-paid health care workforce. In addition, because so much of contemporary medicine is administered in the home, the numbers of part-timers will increase significantly, as in other parts of the American economy.

According to the Bureau of Labor Statistics, hourly wages for LPNs vary by region, from $9.00 to $10.00 in the South to $13.00 to $15.00 in the North and West. Those with more experience earn slightly more. Several other surveys indicate that LPNs earn an average annual salary in the $22,000–$26,000 range, with a top salary of $30,000–$35,000.

HEALTH TECHNICIANS

Almost 550,000 people work as technicians and technologists in the medical and allied health fields. Health technology is a rapidly growing field. Advances in diagnosis and treatment of disease have created jobs that did not exist 10 or 15 years ago, and given the extent of research going on in this country alone, this trend will clearly continue. In addition, the combination of recent population growth, better medical plans, and the public's greater, if not obsessive, health consciousness has led to an increase in regular physical examinations and the routine tests which are a part of them. This has meant excellent job growth for health technicians throughout the 1980s and 1990s.

A technician must complete high school and at least two years of college, or a specialized program in the field. The American Medical Association's Committee on Allied Health Education and Accreditation approves these programs, which are available in vocational schools, junior colleges, and hospitals. On-the-job training is equally important. A cardiopulmonary technologist, for example, needs 6 to 12 months of training for proficiency in invasive tests (when substances such as chemical dyes or tubes enter the patient's body) and 3 to 6 months for proficiency in one noninvasive test.

Technicians can be certified by passing examinations administered by their associations. Most hospitals and clinics prefer to hire registered technicians, and there is some evidence that they receive higher salaries than their nonregistered counterparts. The most striking fact about salaries in this field, however, is the enormous difference between pay on the West Coast as compared to the rest of the country.

Job Descriptions of Health Technicians

It is difficult to standardize job descriptions because the degree of responsibility varies so much depending on the job setting. The descriptions that follow attempt to summarize the usual duties of each technician.

CLINICAL LABORATORY PERSONNEL

Clinical laboratory personnel work in the laboratories of hospitals, clinics, and research institutions, in private laboratories, and in doctors' offices. With the exception of the medical technologist they work under the supervision of the laboratory director.

Certified Laboratory Assistant—Performs a variety of routine tests and procedures including collecting blood specimens, typing blood, and preparing slides.

Medical Laboratory Technician—Performs more complex tests than those handled by the certified laboratory assistant, but only those which do not require a great deal of technical knowledge.

Medical Technologist—A skilled general laboratory scientist who performs the chemical, microscopic, and blood-analysis tests that require the exercise of independent judgment and the responsibility of diagnosis. Often runs private laboratories and may also specialize in one aspect of laboratory research.

SURGICAL TECHNICIANS AND PERFUSIONISTS

These technicians work only in the hospital setting, under the direction of the surgeon performing the operation in which they are involved.

Surgical Technician—Prepares the operating room and organizes the supplies used during surgery. In some instances assists the surgeon by holding instruments and cutting stitches.

Perfusionist (Extracorporeal Technologist)—Operates the heart-lung machines that take over for the patient's own blood circulation during open-heart surgery. Must know the limitations of every piece of equipment and be able to keep it working properly during surgery.

INSTRUMENT TECHNICIANS

The following technicians work with technical instrumentation. They work in hospitals, clinics, and private offices, and are primarily involved with the diagnostic side of medicine. Dialysis technicians, radiation therapy technologists, and nuclear medicine technologists are involved with treatment of disease.[1]

EKG (Electrocardiogram) Technologist—Performs heart testing under a physician's supervision. Attaches the electrodes to the patient's body and adjusts them to obtain different records of heart action.

EEG (Electroencephalograph) Technologist—Uses equipment to measure and record the brain's electrical activity. Attaches the electrodes to the patient's head, monitors the test, and prepares a descriptive report of the tracing for the physician.

Cardiopulmonary Technologist—Performs diagnostic tests on the lungs and heart. In noninvasive procedures the technologist has the same duties as an EKG technologist, but in invasive tests injects the patient with

[1]SOURCES: Bureau of Labor Statistics, *Health Careers Guidebook;* American Medical Technologists; American Society of EEG Technologists; American Society of Radiologic Technologists.

chemical dyes, or inserts tubing. Must carefully monitor the patient to be able to recognize heart or respiratory failure.

Ultrasound Technologists (Diagnostic Medical Sonographer)—Uses complex equipment to direct high-frequency sound waves into specific areas of the body to determine abnormalities. Selects and operates the equipment and must have enough knowledge of anatomy to recognize abnormalities.

X-ray Technician—Takes X-ray film for use in diagnosis of medical problems.

Radiation Therapy Technologist—Assists physicians in treatment of patients with prescribed doses of radiation.

Nuclear Medicine Technologist—Participates in activity involving radioactive drugs used for the diagnosis and treatment of medical problems. Calculates and administers the correct dosages of drugs and is involved with the safety procedures required when using them.

Dialysis Technician—Prepares and maintains the dialyzer that performs kidney functions for the patient. Also takes blood tests and monitors the patient's vital signs.

EMERGENCY MEDICAL TECHNICIANS

Emergency medical technicians are trained to provide immediate care to the critically ill or injured. They are often the first people to treat the victims of an accident or illness and as such must determine the nature of the injury and decide on the sequence of emergency treatment. Depending on their level of training they may treat shock, control bleeding, apply splints, or assist in childbirth.

The State Emergency Medical Services Directors estimate that there are 450,000 emergency medical technicians and emergency medical technician-paramedics in the United States, many of whom work on a voluntary basis.

There are three ratings for emergency medical technicians.

Emergency Medical Technician (Non-Ambulance)—Works as nurse, nurse's aide, and orderly. Must complete an 81-hour course in emergency medical care and have three months of patient or health care experience. There is no evidence that these technicians receive additional compensation for having this training. In fact, many hospitals are requiring their employees, at all levels, to take a certain amount of emergency medical training in order to remain on staff.

AVERAGE ANNUAL SALARIES OF EMERGENCY MEDICAL TECHNICIANS, BY TYPE OF EMPLOYER, 1993

Employer	Paramedic	EMT-Basic (Ambulance)	EMT-Intermediate (Nonambulance)
Private Ambulance Services	25,606	19,383	20,060
Hospitals	24,944	18,845	21,088
Fire Departments	34,994	31,141	30,914
All Employers (Mean)	**$28,079**	**$22,848**	**$22,682**

SOURCE: *Journal of Emergency Medical Services.*

AVERAGE SALARIES OF HEALTH CARE WORKERS IN THE FEDERAL GOVERNMENT

Title	Number Employed	Average Salary
Physicians' Assistants	1,910	$46,488
Nurses	43,285	43,181
Nursing Assistants	15,159	20,814
Occupational Therapists	712	40,469
Physical Therapists	583	42,728
Corrective Therapists	536	34,622
Rehabilitation Therapists' Assistants	886	23,379
Nuclear Medicine Technologists	152	34,156
Medical Technologists	5,604	36,423
Medical Technicans	2,238	23,327
Pathology Technicians	525	28,232
Diagnostic Radiology Technicians	3,145	29,826
Medical Instrument Technicians	2,177	27,286
Pharmacy Technicians	3,575	21,150
Speech Pathologists and Audiologists	742	46,999
Health System Administrators	630	71,326
Medical Record Technicians	3,211	22,010
Dental Assistants	2,954	20,879
Dental Hygienists	342	26,931

SOURCE: Office of Personnel Management, *Occupations of Federal White-Collar and Blue-Collar Workers,* September 1993.

Emergency Medical Technician (Ambulance)—Works on ambulance and with rescue or military services. Must complete the 81-hour course plus six months of emergency ambulance rescue service, and must renew certification every two years.

Emergency Medical Technician (Paramedic)—Usually works on mobile intensive care vehicles, under a physician's direction, using voice contact from a medical center. A paramedic must first be registered as an "emergency medical technician—ambulance," and then complete a special training program in advanced life support, ranging from 800 to 1,500 hours, and six months of field experience. Paramedics work for police and fire departments, and private and municipal ambulance services. Emergency medical technicians who work for police and fire departments receive the same salary as patrol officers or firefighters.

PHYSICAL THERAPISTS

Physical therapists work as part of a health team to help people cope with muscle, nerve, joint, and bone diseases or injuries. They perform tests for muscle strength and motor development and plan treatment for patients in cooperation with a physician. Physical therapists use various procedures to relieve pain and strengthen muscles, including exercise, massage, electrical stimulation of paralyzed muscles, and hot and cold compresses.

Physical therapy is one of the fastest growing occupations of the 1990s, with job opportunities expected to grow by 76 percent (or 4,000 jobs per year) between 1989 and 2005. As the field expands, it will grow in specialization. Specialty areas include neurology, pulmonary therapy, musculoskeletal therapy, sports medicine, and prevention. In addition to the increasing levels of specialization, the field has also changed in terms of its competency standards. Over 100 colleges now offer degrees in this field, and a B.S. degree has quickly become a minimum requirement. Competition to enter the best programs (the University of Vermont's, for example) is very stiff. The American Physical Therapy Association now requires a postbaccalaureate degree for certification.

The American Physical Therapy Association surveyed its membership and found the typical physical therapist to be a white 31-year-old female with a B.S. in physical therapy working in a hospital, treating 14 to 19 patients each day. There are approximately 88,000 physical therapists currently practicing. Both the Department of Labor and the American Physical Therapy Association report a shortage of physical therapists and, like many other health care professionals, poor distribution of those already employed.

A physical therapist may be on staff at a facility like a hospital or nursing home, or may be self-employed and contract out to work at such a facility for a set fee. Self-employed physical therapists often make more than $30 per hour. The average salary for physical therapists was $37,638, according to a survey by the University of Texas Medical Branch.

OCCUPATIONAL THERAPISTS

Occupational therapists plan and participate in goal-related therapy for people who are physically or psychologically impaired. They involve patients in activities suited to their individual needs, ranging from jewelry making and weaving to vocational training. But whatever the activity, the goals are the same: to help the patient adjust to everyday living in spite of his or her handicap.

Roughly 60 percent of all 40,000 occupational therapists work with people who have physical disabilities. Their activities are designed to improve motor skills, strength, and endurance. The remaining 40 percent work with patients with psychological problems, and in this case activities are designed to develop communication skills, motivation, and concentration, and to improve ability to function in a group situation.

AVERAGE ANNUAL SALARIES OF OCCUPATIONAL THERAPISTS BY YEARS OF EXPERIENCE, 1993

Years of Experience	Occupational Therapists	Occupational Therapy Assistants
0–1	$34,404	$22,734
1–2	36,126	23,263
3–4	38,987	23,867
5–6	40,949	24,873
7–9	43,293	25,440
10–14	45,891	27,595
15 or More	46,455	27,821
All Therapists	**$42,245**	**$25,348**

SOURCE: The American Occupational Therapy Association.

Occupational therapists must have a college degree and six to nine months of clinical experience to be eligible for professional registration. In addition to their knowledge of the physical sciences and psychology, they must have experience in teaching manual and creative skills and be knowledgeable in a variety of educational subjects and recreational activities.

Hospitals are the single largest employers of occupational therapists.

Approximately 40 percent of all occupational therapists work in short-term, long-term, and psychiatric hospitals. Other places of employment include rehabilitation centers, nursing homes, community mental health programs, day-care centers, and schools.

The accompanying tables show average annual salaries for occupation therapists and occupational therapy assistants by years of experience, highest educational degree, primary function, and employment setting. The average salary for all occupational therapists in 1993 was $42,245; for certified occupational therapy assistants, it was $25,348.

AVERAGE ANNUAL SALARIES OF OCCUPATIONAL THERAPISTS BY HIGHEST EDUCATIONAL DEGREE, 1993

Degree Level	Occupational Therapists	Occupational Therapy Assistants
Associate	NA	$24,430
Baccalaureate	$40,866	28,025
Masters	46,138	34,055
Doctorate	59,307	NA
Other	41,320	26,374

SOURCE: The American Occupational Therapy Association.

AVERAGE ANNUAL SALARIES OF OCCUPATIONAL THERAPISTS BY PRIMARY FUNCTION, 1993

Function	Occupational Therapists	Occupational Therapy Assistants
Administration	$52,265	$31,752
Consultation	44,261	23,761
Direct Service/Treatment	39,714	24,812
Public Relations/Marketing	48,655	31,165
Research	48,867	NA
Supervision	44,220	27,062
Classroom Teaching	44,513	26,393
Fieldwork Teaching	46,337	NA
Other	42,009	27,750
Department Head	45,015	25,477
Nondepartment Head	38,643	24,895
Highest Therapist in Facility	45,548	25,154
Generalist	41,378	24,780
Specialist	42,424	25,515

SOURCE: The American Occupational Therapy Association.

AVERAGE ANNUAL SALARIES OF OCCUPATIONAL THERAPISTS BY PRIMARY EMPLOYMENT SETTING, 1993

Setting	Occupational Therapists	Occupational Therapy Assistants
College, 2 Year	$45,779	$29,137
College or University, 4 Year	48,793	NA
Community Mental Health Center	37,870	24,361
Day-Care Program	36,528	22,424
Developmental Center	39,124	NA
Early Intervention Program	36,297	NA
Health Maintenance Organization	45,382	NA
Home Health Agency	45,059	28,678
Hospice	35,611	NA
General Hospital–Neonatal Intensive Care Unit	42,713	NA
General Hospital—Psychiatric Unit	40,647	25,947
General Hospital—Rehabilitation Unit	39,493	24,118
General Hospital—All Other	41,876	25,056
Pediatric Hospital	40,450	26,678
Psychiatric Hospital	41,615	27,748
Outpatient Clinic, Freestanding	42,863	25,279
Physician's Office	44,206	NA
Private Industry	48,424	33,017
Private Practice	52,769	27,915
Public Health Agency	43,857	26,857
Rehabilitation Hospital or Center	41,201	26,008
Research Facility	47,517	NA
Residential Care Facility/Group Home/ Independent Living Center	42,476	25,090
Retirement or Senior Center	46,611	24,879
School System	38,093	21,814
Sheltered Workshop	36,251	22,778
Skilled Nursing Home/Intensive Care Facility	44,132	25,194
Vocational or Prevocational Program	43,011	23,258
Voluntary Agency	37,431	23,463
All Therapists	**$42,245**	**$25,348**

SOURCE: The American Occupational Therapy Association.

SPEECH THERAPISTS AND AUDIOLOGISTS

Speech therapists and audiologists provide help to people with speech and hearing problems resulting from brain injury, partial or total hearing loss, cleft palate, or emotional illness. A speech therapist diagnoses and evaluates one's speech and language abilities and conducts treatment programs designed to restore or develop a patient's communication skills. He may teach patients to correct a lisp or stutter or to recover speech following a stroke or after a hearing impairment is corrected.

An audiologist assesses the degree of hearing impairment and plans and conducts rehabilitation programs. He is involved in hearing-aid selection auditory training, and teaching speech reading.

Although there are some jobs for people with bachelor's degrees, state and federal agencies as well as school systems and hospitals prefer to hire someone with a master's in one of the specialities. In fact, almost 80 percent of all 68,000 speech pathologists and audiologists have a master's degree. Speech pathologists and audiologists may have a variety of credentials, including a state license, certification by the American Speech and Hearing Association, and teaching credentials. Because speech and hearing are interrelated, a therapist must be familiar with both fields to be competent in one. Dual certification in both speech pathology and audiology is common, and a therapist holding dual certification generally earns more than one certified in one specialty.

Average salaries in this field are relatively low, considering the level of education required. According to a 1992 survey conducted by the American Speech, Language and Hearing Association, the average salary of speech-language pathologists in hospitals and medical centers was $34,000, while the average salary of audiologists was $35,782.

Most speech pathologists and audiologists in public schools are classified as teachers or special education teachers and are paid accordingly. Teacher salaries vary widely by state—from under $25,000 in North and South Dakota to over $40,000 in New York and New Jersey. The average teacher salary was $34,313 in 1991–92.

PHARMACISTS

Although pharmacists' duties vary depending on their place of employment, their principal responsibility remains the same: to compound and dispense medication ordered by physicians or other authorized prescribers. A pharmacist must be familiar with the effects of drugs on people and have thorough knowledge of the procedures for testing drug purity and strength. Physicians rely heavily on the pharmacist for information on prescription drugs.

To become a pharmacist, one must have at least a B.S. degree in pharmacy. The bachelor's program involves five years of college study. Some colleges offer an integrated program which includes liberal arts and professional training, while others require one or two years of preprofessional study before entering the professional college. All states have strict laws about licensing and registering pharmacists, although the regulations vary. All states require graduation from an accredited school of pharmacy, and most states require an internship before being eligible for registration. All pharmacists must pass an examination given by the board of pharmacy in the state where they choose to practice.

AVERAGE BASE SALARIES OF PHARMACISTS, BY PRACTICE SETTING, 1994

Category	Independent Pharmacy	Pharmacy Chain	Hospital
Region			
East	$51,400	$56,800	$54,600
South	47,400	53,000	53,700
Midwest	47,600	54,700	51,900
West	52,700	57,500	60,500
Sex			
Male	$50,700	$52,200	$55,200
Female	45,100	53,600	52,300
Job Title			
Store Manager	$51,100	$55,700	NA
Chief Supervising R.Ph.	52,100	55,700	NA
Staff	46,300	53,300	$49,800
Director	NA	NA	58,600
Age			
Under 36	$49,300	$54,400	$50,400
36–45	49,200	55,700	56,500
46 and over	48,700	54,600	55,600

SOURCE: *Drug Topics* magazine, March 20, 1995. Reprinted by permission.

About 163,000 people work as pharmacists according to the Department of Labor. Three-fifths of them work in community pharmacies and receive a salary. Another quarter work in hospitals, health maintenance organizations (HMOs), nursing homes, and clinics. The remainder are self-employed. Pharmacists worked an average of 40 hours per week in 1992, with self-employed pharmacists working closer to 50 hours per week. About one in seven pharmacists works only part-time. Jobs for pharmacists are expected to grow faster than the national average for all occupations through the year 2005, due in large part to an aging population's increasing need for drugs and medications.

Salaries of pharmacists are influenced by the location, size, and type of employer; the education and professional attributes of the pharmacist; and the duties and responsibilities of the position. Pharmacists working in chain drugstores had an average base salary of $54,900 per year in 1994, while pharmacists in independent drugstores averaged $49,000, according to a biannual survey by *Drug Topics* magazine. Salaries were higher for pharmacists in discount drugstores ($58,000), supermarkets ($54,400), HMOs ($56,600), and hospitals ($54,300). Pharmacists in these businesses also tend to receive more benefits that those in independent drugstores. In general, the highest salaries were paid on the West Coast. Pharmacists who own their own business often earn considerably more than salaried pharmacists. Total compensation (which includes bonuses, overtime, and profit-sharing proceeds) boosted the average pharmacist's salary by about $4,000.

In hospitals, pharmacists are employed at several levels. There is almost always a chief of pharmaceutical services, several assistant supervisors, and a group of staff pharmacists. Salaries of hospital pharmacists depend on the number of beds in the hospital.

MEDICAL PRACTITIONERS

There is a wide range of occupations in the field of medicine, from technicians to physicians. Somewhere in between are the four professional groups discussed here: chiropractors, optometrists, podiatrists, and midwives. The first three of these are called "doctors" (Dr. of Chiropractics; Dr. of Optometry, O.D.; and Dr. of Podiatric Medicine, C.P.M.) and earn their degrees by attending professional colleges. Yet they often do not command the same respect or salaries as M.D.s.

Opportunities in these fields are increasing, as they are in all health professions. Podiatry is the least crowded of all health occupations, but the demand for podiatric services is steadily rising, no doubt partly because of the nationwide obsession with fitness and its resultant problems. Chiropractors are also seeing more patients than ever before. There is now wider public acceptance of chiropractic treatment, and most insurance plans, including Medicare, Medicaid, and workmen's compensation, provide coverage for these services, leading people to consult chiropractors rather than orthopedists.

Chiropractors

A chiropractor diagnoses a patient's health problems in the same way as a physician: by interviewing the patient and by conducting a physical examination, an X-ray examination, and laboratory tests. It is in the area of treatment where chiropractors differ from medical doctors.

In chiropractics, the emphasis is on the spine and its position. Treatment consists mainly of chiropractic adjustment; that is, the manipulation of the body, especially the spinal column. Chiropractors are not permitted to perform surgery or dispense prescription drugs, although they can advise the patient to begin a nutritional program which always includes vitamins.

The academic training program for chiropractors consists of six years of study. A two-year preprofessional (liberal arts) program must be completed before admission to the chiropractic college. The professional curriculum consists of two years of science courses and two years of clinical work under supervision. All states require chiropractors to be licensed, and many states require practicing chiropractors to take continuing education courses throughout their careers. The Bureau of Labor Statistics estimates that job growth prospects in the 1990s will be very good.

Almost all (74 percent) of the country's 50,000 chiropractors are self-employed or work as part of a chiropractic health group. According to a survey conducted by the American Chiropractic Association, the median income for chiropractors was $70,000 in 1992 after expenses.

Optometrists

Optometrists are trained to examine, diagnose, and treat conditions of the vision system. They perform a variety of tests to detect eye problems and prescribe corrective or contact lenses as a means of treatment. Optometrists may not prescribe drugs or perform surgery; that's done by ophthalmologists.

All schools of optometry require at least two years of college prior to admission, although most students complete all four years of college prior to entering the professional program. Programs leading to the O.D. degree are four years in duration. Optometrists must be licensed in the states in which they choose to practice. Traditionally, most optometrists have been men, but this is changing dramatically. About 40 percent of the entering classes in schools of optometry are women. In 1990, the Department of Labor predicted faster than average growth in this field through the next decade; but by 1992, it revised this forecast to indicate only average growth because advances in technology and optometrists' productivity had allowed each optometrist to see more patients. Moreover, this is an industry with an extremely low turnover rate: almost every job opening in optometry will result from the death or retirement of a practicing optometrist.

Although some optometrists are employed by nursing homes and clinics, and an increasing number now work in the new "vision centers," by far the majority of the 31,000 licensed optometrists are self-employed. Salary and income data are limited. According to the American Optometric Association, net earnings of new optometry graduates in their first year of practice averaged about $50,000 in 1992. The mean net income of all practicing optometrists in 1992 was approximately $80,000, while the median net income was $75,000.

AVERAGE SALARIES OF OPTOMETRISTS AND PODIATRISTS IN THE FEDERAL GOVERNMENT

Title and Grade	Number	Average Salary
Associate Grade	1	$38,129
Full Grade	11	52,357
Intermediate Grade	36	58,619
Senior Grade	55	71,458
Chief Grade	73	86,764
TOTAL	**176**	**$73,485**

SOURCE: Office of Personnel Management, *Pay Structure of the Federal Civil Service, 1994.*

Podiatrists

According to the American Podiatric Association, there are 14,700 licensed practitioners of the care and treatment of feet. As with other medical practitioners, podiatrists rely on examinations, laboratory tests, and X rays to determine the nature of the problem, which may range from simple corns to fractures and tumors. Unlike the other practitioners in this section, podiatrists do prescribe medication and do surgery on foot bones and muscles even though they are not M.D.s.

A podiatrist has completed two to four years of college and a four-year professional program that includes two years of classroom study and lab work and two years of clinical training. Most podiatrists serve a hospital residency before beginning a practice.

Most podiatrists are self-employed, although a growing number are entering partnerships and group practices. Average net income of podiatrists in 1993 was $100,287, according to a survey by the American Association of Colleges of Podiatric Medicine, a figure that is closer to the salaries earned by doctors than those earned by other types of practitioners discussed in this chapter. However, salaries vary greatly with years of experience and location of practice. For example, in the Northeast, where most podiatrists are concentrated, competition for patients is fierce, and lower salaries reflect it. An aging population (with tired feet) will contribute to a demand for podiatrists that will increase faster than the national average through the year 2005. Some estimates put podiatrist growth rates as high as 50 percent over this period. Job openings will result primarily from growth, as very few podiatrists leave the field before they die or retire.

Midwives

There has been a growing trend, at least among a certain set of people, toward a return to having babies at home. But economic and cultural deprivation, especially in rural areas, have also contributed to an increase in the number of pregnant women who truly need the assistance of trained people. According to the American College of Nurse-Midwives, about 4,500 trained midwives are working in the United States today. They frequently contribute their help on the basis of a small donation, but for those who can afford to pay, the charges range from $900 to $1,200 per birth, including prenatal care. Average salaries for midwives range from $40,000 to $70,000, depending upon the area in which they practice. Midwives in large urban areas command the highest salaries.

DENTAL ASSISTANTS AND DENTAL HYGIENISTS

The demand for good dental care has increased as the public has become educated about the importance of oral hygiene. In order for dentists to increase their productive capacity, they must rely on the services of dental assistants and dental hygienists.

Dental assistants work "chairside," sterilizing instruments, arranging them on trays, and handing them to the dentist as needed. They also prepare solutions and process X rays. It is not unusual for an assistant to perform clerical duties as well, such as keeping patient-treatment records and bookkeeping. A dental assistant may also perform expanded functions, which vary by state and which may include treating the teeth to make them more resistant to decay and making impressions of the mouth. In states where it is legal, assistants may also clean and polish teeth and make uncomplicated repairs on dentures.

There are accredited programs for dental assistants in community colleges and vocational schools, but many dentists hire assistants right out of high school and conduct their own training. Certification is optional and not a requirement for employment.

There are currently about 183,000 dental assistants in the United States; the Bureau of Labor Statistics predicts that this number will grow by almost 100,000 by the year 2005. Progress in the field of dental medicine will continue to fuel demand for all dental occupations, because as people retain their natural teeth longer, they will continue to need to clean, maintain, and repair them. The outlook is particulary bright for dental assistants because dentists are relying on them to perform routine tasks that they or their hygienists once had to perform themselves.

Fully one third of all dental assistants worked only part-time, according to the Department of Labor. Median weekly earnings for full-time assistants were $332 in 1992, according to the American Dental Association. That breaks down to $9.20 an hour.

A dental hygienist is a more highly trained technician. A hygienist must complete a two-year program after high school or college and must obtain a state license before he or she can be employed. In some states continuing education is required to maintain licensure.

Dental hygienists working in private practice remove scale from teeth, treat teeth to make them resistant to decay, take X rays, and perform laboratory tests. They also advise the patients on the proper way to take care of their teeth and give instruction about the correct way to brush and use dental floss. Their expanded functions, again governed by the state, may include administering local anesthetics, performing curettage (scraping under the gums), and placement and removal of temporary fillings.

About half of all dental hygienists work part-time—usually fewer than 35 hours a week—meaning that only 70,000 to 80,000 hygienists were needed to fill the 108,000 positions available for hygienists in 1992, according to the Department of Labor. Some hygienists work for a different dentist each day of the week. Job growth in this field is expected to be rapid, as dentists turn more tasks over to hygienists. Younger dentists are even more likely than older ones to rely on hygienists. According to a survey by the American Dental Association, dental hygienists who worked 32 hours a week or more averaged $609 in 1991. That translates into an average hourly wage of $18.50.

PSYCHOLOGISTS

Psychology, the study of the human mind, is, according to its practitioners, a science which provides us with information on intelligence, mental capacity, and the effect of emotions on health and behavior. Over 144,000 people work in the field of psychology, most of them in the areas of research and counseling.

Experimental psychologists are the largest group working in research. These are the people who conduct experiments designed to study some aspect of animal and/or human behavior, such as learning or perception. Though experimental psychologists may work in private laboratories or in industry, they most often hold teaching positions at colleges or universities. Their salaries are listed in Part I in the section "University and College Professors."

The second area of psychology and, not surprisingly, the most familiar to the general public, is counseling. An estimated 34 million Americans annually seek professional help for their problems. In addition to the 40,000 practicing psychiatrists in the United States, there are, according to the American Psychological Association, 58,000 clinical psychologists and psychiatric social workers (see the section "Social Workers" in Part I) and 12,500 counselors vying for the estimated $13 billion spent annually for psychological services.

ANNUAL SALARIES OF STATE DIRECTORS OF MENTAL HEALTH DEPARTMENTS[1]

State	Salary	State	Salary
Alabama	$ 72,514	Nebraska	$ 82,424
Alaska	72,468	Nevada	75,348
Arizona	77,000	New Hampshire	56,842
Arkansas	68,303	New Jersey	85,037
California	95,052	New Mexico	59,893
Colorado	69,528	New York	102,235
Connecticut	78,732	North Carolina	93,993
Delaware	91,300	North Dakota	53,880
Florida	72,100	Ohio	89,232
Georgia	96,000	Oklahoma	88,691
Hawaii	74,880	Oregon	84,096
Illinois	78,839	Pennsylvania	75,400
Indiana	82,394	Rhode Island	86,328
Iowa	76,856	South Carolina	87,087
Kansas	63,360	South Dakota	73,784
Louisiana	160,000	Tennessee	79,956
Maine	77,896	Texas	93,868
Maryland	75,236	Utah	64,979
Massachusetts	77,547	Vermont	71,489
Michigan	87,236	Virginia	99,345
Minnesota	76,734	Washington	79,596
Mississippi	72,152	West Virginia	70,000
Missouri	78,623	Wisconsin	47,773
Montana	52,008	Wyoming	65,662

[1]Not all states have this position.
SOURCE: The Council of State Governments, *The Book of the States, 1994–95.*

A clinical psychologist works directly with patients to uncover information that will help them understand and correct their problems. Methods of treatment vary. Some psychologists specialize in psychoanalysis, the Freudian technique of curing neuroses by talking about dreams, fantasies, etc., and by the transference of emotions to the analyst. This type of therapy often involves an unwavering commitment in time and money, since patients must attend sessions weekly, or from two to five times a week, for several years, often for a very high fee. The cost of a 50-minute session ranges between $50 and $140 depending on the analyst and the city in which he or she practices. Short-term therapies based on Freudian principles are also available, and psychologists who treat patients in this way usually charge $50 to $120 for a 45-minute session. Another method of treatment is called behavior modification. The psychologist attempts to help the patient correct undesirable behavior or habits through conditioning. Fees for an individual session range from $40 to $120, depending again on the therapist and the location of the practice. Group sessions, which are usually used when modifying eating or smoking habits, cost from $25 to $60 per person.

Most opportunities exist for psychologists with doctoral degrees. A clinical psychologist must usually complete an internship in conjunction with his or her program. All states require psychologists to pass licensing examinations, and in order to qualify for the examination one must have a doctorate. All graduates of professional psychological institutes or graduate schools or universities are called therapists, as are all mental health workers, regardless of the degree they hold. There are, however, countless others who call themselves therapists—sex therapists, marriage counselors, crisis therapists—who on closer inspection would be found to have little or no professional training. There is no real monitoring system in this profession, and therefore, it is essential for a person seeking help to know as much as possible about a therapist's educational background.

Society's ever-increasing acceptance of the value of psychological counseling has helped to make this one of the fastest growing occupations in the country. And the U.S. Department of Labor predicts that the spiraling growth will continue through the year 2005, with about 5,000 new positions available each year until then. Most of the jobs will be for clinical psychologists working in community mental health centers, nursing homes, and drug and alcohol abuse programs. And because of the high level of education required for entry into this field, turnover in the profession is low, meaning that most jobs will result from growth or the need to replace retiring psychologists. The AIDS epidemic will also bring a stronger demand for specialized psychological services. So, too, will the needs of the aged, whose growing numbers are affecting all health care services.

According to the American Psychological Association (APA) increased opportunities for psychologists are also expected to occur in schools and in corporations as industrial psychology grows in importance in the human resources sector. In addition, with the rise in the willingness of third-party insurers to cover some of the costs of therapy, more and more psychologists are expected to enter private practice (approximately one in six psychologists is self-employed). Finally, a surprising number of college and university teaching positions will be available over the coming years since over 20 percent of the current faculty are over the age of 55.

MEDIAN ANNUAL SALARIES FOR PSYCHOLOGISTS BY EMPLOYMENT SECTOR AND PRIMARY WORK ACTIVITY, 1993

Category	Median Annual Salary	Category	Median Annual Salary
Employment Sector		*Primary Work Activity*	
Universities and Four-Year Colleges	$48,500	Research and Development	$57,500
Other Educational Institutions	50,300	Teaching	45,400
Private for-Profit Institutions	65,900	Management, Sales, and Administration	60,900
Private Nonprofit Institutions	52,400	Computer Applications	60,900
Federal Government	59,000	Other	50,100
State and Local Government	49,500		
All Psychologists with Doctoral Degrees			*$51,700*

MEDIAN SALARIES FOR PSYCHOLOGY INSTRUCTORS WITH DOCTORAL DEGREES, 1993

Setting and Rank	Median Annual Salary
University Psychology Department	
Full Professor	$60,000
Associate Professor	42,000
Assistant Professor	35,000
University Research Center/Institute	
Full Professor	$73,000
Four-Year College Psychology Department	
Full Professor	$50,000
Associate Professor	37,000
Assistant Professor	34,000
Two-Year College	
Full Professor	$54,000
Associate Professor	47,000
Lecturer/Instructor	39,000

MEDIAN SALARIES FOR PSYCHOLOGY INSTRUCTORS WITH DOCTORAL DEGREES, 1993

Setting and Rank	Median Annual Salary
Medical School Psychiatry Department	
Full Professor	$71,000
Associate Professor	51,500
Assistant Professor	38,000
University-Affiliated Professional School of Psychology	
Full Professor	$54,000
Freestanding Professional School of Psychology	
Full Professor	$52,000
Other Professional School	
Full Professor	$58,000
Associate Professor	46,000

SOURCE: The American Psychological Association, *1993 Salaries in Psychology.*

One note of caution for those not familiar with this profession: All supervisory positions, and most of meaningful responsibility, require a doctoral degree; many entry-level positions require a master's degree. On the positive side the APA estimates that the unemployment rate for psychologists is less than 1 percent.

According to the National Science Foundation, the median earnings of a psychologist with a doctorate is $51,700 for work in hospitals, schools, prisons, etc. The table below shows median annual salaries by place and kind of work. Those with an independent practice usually earn 20 to 30 percent more than the median.

In the federal government, the average starting salary for a psychologist with a bachelor's degree ranged from $18,300 to $22,700 in 1993, depending on academic credentials. Counseling psychologists with a master's degree and a year of counseling experience started at $27,800. Clinical psychologists with a doctorate and one year of internship started at $33,600 or $40,300, again depending on academic credentials. The average salary for all psychologists in the federal government was $54,400 in 1993.

MEDIAN SALARIES FOR CLINICAL PSYCHOLOGISTS WITH DOCTOR'S DEGREES BY SETTING AND EXPERIENCE, 1993

Setting and Years of Experience	Median Annual Salary
University Counseling Center	
2–4	$34,000
5–9	40,000
10–14	55,500
Public General Hospital	
2–4	$46,000
5–9	46,000
10–14	57,500
Private General Hospital	
2–4	$44,000
5–9	49,000
10–14	60,000
15–19	57,000
20–24	62,000
Public Psychiatric Hospital	
2–4	$42,000
5–9	46,000
10–14	48,000
15–19	50,000
20–24	51,500
VA Hospital	
2–4	$48,000
5–9	52,000
10–14	58,000
15–19	60,000
20–24	62,000
30+	63,000
Individual Private Practice	
2–4	$50,000
5–9	63,000
10–14	75,000
15–19	85,000
20–24	80,000
25–29	75,000
30+	75,000
Group Psychological Practice	
2–4	$50,000
5–9	69,000
10–14	75,000
15–19	80,000
20–24	80,000
25–29	75,000
30+	71,000
Medical-Psychological Group Practice	
2–4	$60,000
5–9	67,500
10–14	83,000
15–19	75,000
20–24	92,000
25–29	90,500
Outpatient Clinic	
2–4	$42,000
5–9	44,000
Community Mental Health Center	
2–4	$38,000
5–9	40,000
15–19	48,000
20–24	49,000
HMO	
5–9	$60,000
10–14	67,500
15–19	67,500
20–24	65,500
Specialized Health Service	
5–9	$50,000
Other Human Service Setting	
2–4	$40,000
5–9	54,000

SOURCE: The American Psychological Association, *1993 Salaries in Psychology.*

Job Level Descriptions of Professional and Administrative Workers in Private Hospitals[1]

Pharmacist I—Applies pharmaceutical principles and concepts to conventional problems; may perform additional administrative duties and/or supervise nonprofessional pharmacy staff.

Pharmacist II (Senior Pharmacist, Pharmacy Supervisor)—First line supervisor of Pharmacists I, staff pharmacists in a specialty field, and staff generalists with a broad experience in total pharmacy operations.

Physical Therapist I—Works under general supervision; seeks technical advice in solving nonroutine problems; may provide technical direction to nonprofessional staff.

Physical Therapist II—Independently evaluates, plans, and carries out a full range of treatments with complex therapeutic objectives with procedures that require highly specialized knowledge and skill.

Medical Technologist I—Performs a limited variety of standard but specialized medical laboratory tests and nonroutine procedures; reviews, analyzes, and records test results.

Medical Technologist II (Senior or Lead Medical Technologist)—Performs and analyzes wide range of specialized tests and nonroutine procedures; establishes quality controls; troubleshoots and modifies existing procedures; implements protocols for new procedures; may supervise lab technicians.

Job Level Descriptions for Hospital Technical Support Occupations[1]

Licensed Practical Nurse (LPN) I—Provides standard nursing care requiring some latitude for independent judgment and initiative to perform recurring duties.

LPN II—Provides nursing care requiring an understanding of diseases and illnesses sufficient to communicate with physicians, registered nurses, and patients.

[1]SOURCE: U.S. Department of Labor, Bureau of Labor Statistics, January 1991.

LPN III—Can immediately recognize and respond to serious situations, sometimes prior to notifying a registered nurse, though any deviations from guidelines must be approved by a supervisor.

Nursing Assistant I—Performs simple personal care and housekeeping tasks requiring no previous training.

Nursing Assistant II—Performs common nursing procedures, in addition to providing personal care.

Nursing Assistant III—Performs a variety of common nursing procedures. Work requires prior experience or training and some latitude for exercising independent initiative of limited judgment.

Diagnostic Medical Sonographer—Operates diagnostic equipment which produces ultrasonic patterns and positive pictures of internal organs for use by doctors in diagnosing disease or monitoring pregnancy.

Respiratory Therapist I—Administers a variety of prescribed therapeutic and diagnostic respiratory therapy procedures.

Respiratory Therapist II—Independently administers a variety of complex respiratory therapy treatments and diagnostic procedures.

Medical Laboratory Technician I—Performs routine or standardized tests following detailed written procedures.

Medical Technician II—Performs a variety of complex tests. Exercises judgment in applying written procedures.

VIII

Jobs and Wages in the Workaday World

The title of this part is our own invention, it has no standing whatsoever with economists, with sociologists, or even with employment agencies. Yet in this section can be found the occupations and wage levels of some 20 million Americans. Most of these jobs are traditionally classified as white-collar or blue-collar; some would be called skilled, but most unskilled; some are unionized, others not; some are held almost exclusively by women, others predominantly by men. But certain essential characteristics common to them all made this present grouping especially appropriate to this book.

First of all, none of these jobs, save electricians, is represented by large, national unions whose power is centered in one industry and which can therefore dramatically affect wage levels. Nor are any of these jobs predominantly in the public sector where job security and benefits are very good. On the other hand, none of these jobs requires a college degree or extensive formal training, so there is no elaborate hierarchical structure such as distinguish those occupations commonly referred to as careers. Finally, the pay for these jobs is normally calculated as an hourly or weekly wage rate rather than on an annual salary basis. As a result of all these factors, the annual income from these jobs is very rarely above $30,000 and very frequently below $18,000.

Most of the jobs represented in this section need little or no description, since the work involved will be familiar, at least in a general way, to all readers. Although barbers, electricians, plumbers, etc., follow procedures we're not aware of, most of us know the function these people serve. (Where this is not the case, information is, of course, provided.) The jobs are organized in two different ways. Some of the most common are grouped under general headings: "Building Trades Workers," "The Office Staff," "Restaurant Workers," etc. These are followed by a simple alphabetical listing that should enable quick and easy reference.

For other jobs that fit in this basic category but are located in different sections, see the index for baggage handlers, bank clerks, bank tellers, bellhops, insurance clerks, farm workers, nurses' aides, and orderlies.

BUILDING TRADES WORKERS

The term "construction worker" actually encompasses workers in as many as a dozen occupations related to the construction of houses and buildings. Together, the country's bricklayers, carpenters, electricians, plumbers, painters, and unskilled construction workers total more than 3.7 million laborers. More than half are unionized, and about one in four is self-employed. Because there is no one employer that dominates the construction industry the way General Motors or U.S. Steel dominate their respective industries, construction unions are largely decentralized. The union headquarters may publish guidelines and average wages for specific areas of the country, but local chapters are free to negotiate their own contracts. All unions (except the building laborers' union) have apprenticeship programs which are usually administered by the locals in conjunction with building contractors. Most apprenticeships last from three to five years.

No other sector of the economy feels the immediate effect of a recession more quickly than construction. In the last recession, people, as always, stopped buying new houses, so housing starts (a key indicator of the economy's health) declined—and rapidly too. And with commercial vacancy rates hovering around 20 percent, due to a tax code that encouraged wealthy citizens to invest in office space that no one needed, construction jobs dropped by 310,000 in 1991 alone.

Since then, however, the construction industry has rebounded to the point that the Department of Labor still predicts average to better than average growth in almost all construction occupations through the year 2005. Although demand has slowed for new construction, the need to improve the nation's infrastructure—repairing and maintaining roads, bridges, tunnels, and buildings—will more than offset this decline in demand. Nevertheless, unemployment among construction workers in the past 30 years has remained fairly consistent at double the overall rate and will continue to in the future. Moreover, because construction work is subject to the weather, most construction workers do not work a full year. As a result, the hourly or weekly wages given in this section cannot be extrapolated to yield average annual incomes. The exception is maintenance construction workers, who work full-time in buildings or power plants. They usually earn less per hour, but their employment is steady and they work even when cold weather stops other construction work. Figures are supplied at the end of the entry.

Bricklayers

Bricklayers—some of whom are represented by the International Union of Bricklayers and Allied Craftsmen and others by the Bricklayers, Masons, and Plasterers International Union of America—number about 139,000, according to the Department of Labor. Median weekly earnings for bricklayers in 1992 were $480. Beginning apprentices are usually paid about 50 percent of the journeyman rate; apprenticeships usually last about three years.

Although the number of bricklayers (and their earnings) was down significantly from 1990 levels, jobs for bricklayers are still expected to grow about as fast as the average for all occupations through the year 2005. Population and business growth will create a need for new factories, schools, and hospitals. The popularity of brick exteriors will continue to stimulate demand for bricklayers' work.

Building Laborers

Building laborers unload trucks, carry materials, dig ditches, erect scaffolds, and do other routine tasks to assist more specialized construction workers. There is no apprenticeship, but many laborers do enter training for specific building crafts. There are more than half a million; all are represented by the Laborers' International Union of North America.

Carpenters

Carpenters are the largest group of building trade workers in the country, numbering just under 1 million. Because wood is such a versatile material, carpentry is divided into many specialties. Construction carpenters are classified as either "rough" carpenters—those who build scaffolds; frameworks, forms for concrete, bridges, and other large structures—or "finish" carpenters—those who build stairs, put up moldings and paneling, lay floors, and so on. Carpenters in factories (making furniture, for instance) may specialize in specific machines, such as sanders, trim saws, rip saws, and plywood presses. Carpenters also work with glass, fiberglass, plastic, and other building materials.

About 40 percent of carpenters are self-employed. Although most employers recommend that prospective carpenters learn their trade through a formal apprenticeship, the number of programs is limited. Thus, only a small proportion of carpenters acquire their skills this way. The rest learn through informal apprenticeships, vocational education, or on-the-job training under the supervision of experienced workers. The five major carpenters' unions, the biggest of which is the United Brotherhood of Carpenters and Joiners of America, sponsor and administer three- to four-year apprenticeship programs that combine on-the-job training with classroom instruction. First-year apprentices generally make no more than 50 percent of what an experienced carpenter earns. By their fourth year of apprenticeship, the trainee receives 90 to 95 percent of the journeyman's rate. Scheduled increases in salary stop at the end of the apprenticeship, but, in general, the more experience carpenters have, the more money they earn. Specialties requiring finer work, such as cabinetmaking, pay better than other types of carpentry. The union does not set nationwide pay levels, but rather leaves it up to the local chapters to negotiate each contract individually. This practice results in a wide range of salaries.

The median weekly earning of carpenters who were not self-employed was $425 in 1992. Like other construction occupations, carpentry's growth is subject to the number of new housing starts. The increased use of prefabricated components should decrease the need for carpenters, meaning that this field will grow no faster than the average for all occupations. If building activity picks up dramatically, however, so should carpentry. Moreover, because the industry is large and turnover is high, the number of job openings for carpenters is usually higher than for other construction and craft occupations.

Electricians

According to the Bureau of Labor Statistics, there are about 518,000 electricians in the United States today. More than half are employed in the construction industry. Others work as maintenance electricians in just about every industry. One tenth of electricians are self-employed. Almost all electricians belong to the International Brotherhood of Electrical Workers, which administers apprenticeship programs for aspiring electricians. A typical apprenticeship program provides at least 144 hours of classroom instruction each year and more than 8,000 hours of on-the-job training. Earnings for electricians are among the highest earned by skilled workers: Median weekly earnings were $550 in 1992. Maintenance electricians in metropolitan areas earned about $16 an hour.

Electricians' unemployment rate is usually lower than the rate for other construction workers—at times less than half as high as the rate for bricklayers, stonemasons, and roofers. Their employment is also less subject to the weather or cyclical swings in the economy. Nevertheless, their jobless rate is still tied to the level of new construction.

Jobs for electricians are expected to grow about as fast as the national average. Increasing use of computers, automation, and robots will necessitate rewiring (or in the case of new construction, wiring) by experienced electricians. Job turnover in this field is low, but a large number of openings is expected, because a large number of electricians are beginning to reach retirement age.

Painters

About half of the country's 440,000 painters and paperhangers are self-employed, about double most other construction occupations. Most painters belong to the International Brotherhood of Painters and Allied Trades. Apprenticeships in painting usually involve three years of on-the-job training and 144 hours of classroom instruction in topics like color harmony, use and care of tools and equipment, surface preparation, application techniques, paint mixing and matching, blueprint reading, wood finishing, and safety. Median weekly earnings for painters who were not self-employed were about $376 in 1992. Maintenance painters earned about $15.26 per hour. Paperhangers generally earn more than painters. Jobs for painters and paperhangers will grow faster than the national average through the year 2005.

Plasterers

There are about 32,000 plasterers in the country; about one third of them are self-employed. Their numbers declined in the past as more and more builders switched to drywall construction, which is cheaper than plastering and requires less skill. But that decline has reversed in the 1990s, as newer, cheaper, and easier-to-install types of plaster have made the material more attractive to builders.

Two unions represent plasterers: the Operative Plasterers' and Cement Masons' Association of the United States and Canada, and the Bricklayers and Allied Craftsmen International Union. Apprentices, who must work for four years before becoming journeymen, usually start at half the journeyman's base rate. The average plasterer made between $15 and $33 per hour in 1992. Jobs for plasterers are expected to increase—albeit slowly—as more people realize that plaster is much more durable and attractive than drywall. Plasterers will also be needed to renovate plasterwork in older structures and to create special architectural effects like curved surfaces.

Plumbers and Pipe Fitters

Plumbing, pipe fitting, and steam fitting are often considered the same trade, and people who work primarily in one may easily switch to another. All three involve installing and maintaining conduits for fluids. Plumbers, of course, work with water pipes in homes, schools, and so on. Pipe fitters work with industrial pipes that carry a variety of materials, like oil, gas, and hot water. Steamfitters, of course, specialize in steam pipes. Workers in all three trades number about 351,000.

Apprenticeships usually involve four to five years of on-the-job training and 144 hours of classroom instruction in topics like drafting and blueprint reading, mathematics, applied physics and chemistry, and local plumbing codes and regulations. Apprentices usually begin at about 50 percent of the wage rate paid to experienced plumbers or pipe fitters, and their salaries increase periodically as they improve their skills. Many plumbers and pipe fitters are members of the United Association of Journeymen and Apprentices of the Plumbing and Pipe Fitting Industry of the United States and Canada. Median hourly earnings for plumbers and pipe fitters were $18.05 in 1992. In general, wage rates tend to be higher in the Midwest than in the Northeast and South. Plumbers are expected to be victims of their own efficiency throughout the next decade, because the plastic pipes and fittings now being installed are much easier to use and need less maintenance than their older metal counterparts. The job market for plumbers is less cyclical than for other construction workers, because maintenance, rehabilitation, and replacement of existing systems provide jobs for plumbers even when construction activity declines.

Roofers

By definition, roofers work outdoors in all kinds of weather. It is not surprising, therefore, to find that roofers have the highest accident rates of all construction workers. They risk slipping and falling from scaffolds, ladders, and roofs, and, especially during the summer, they can get burned by the hot roofing tar that holds the shingles, insulation, or other coverings in place on the roof. Severely cold, rainy, or snowy weather can reduce the number of days they are able to work.

There were about 127,000 roofers in 1992. Almost all wage and salary roofers work for roofing contractors. About 40 percent of roofers are self-employed, and the majority of self-employed roofers specialize in residential work. Most roofers acquire their training through informal apprenticeships with experienced roofers or through three-year apprenticeship programs administered by locals of the United Union of Roofers, Waterproofers, and

Allied Workers. The program requires 144 hours of classroom training in subjects like tool use, arithmetic, and safety, as well as 1,400 hours of on-the-job training.

Turnover among roofers is high because of the hot, dirty, strenuous nature of the work. Many roofers leave the trade for other construction occupations that are less difficult and dangerous. As a result, job openings for roofers should be plentiful through the year 2005. Roofs need repair more often than other parts of a building, and so keep roofers in business throughout downturns in new construction. About 75 percent of all roofing work is repair.

Median weekly earnings for full-time roofers were $315 a week in 1992. According to a survey by the *Engineering News Record,* average hourly earnings (including benefits) for union roofers were $23.63 in 1992. Salaries were highest in New York City and lowest in Atlanta. Apprentices start at about 40 percent of what experienced roofers earn.

Maintenance Mechanics

Most craft workers specialize in one kind of work; general maintenance mechanics are jacks-of-all-trades. They repair and maintain mechanical equipment, machines, and buildings; work on plumbing, electrical gear, air-conditioning and heating systems; and install, maintain, and repair specialized equipment and machinery. They also do routine preventive maintenance to correct defects before equipment breaks or buildings deteriorate.

General maintenance mechanics held about 1.15 million jobs in 1992. Unlike many other jobs in the trades, jobs for maintenance mechanics are expected to grow throughout the 1990s. Earnings in this field vary widely by industry, geographic area, and skill level. The median salary was $9.37 per hour in 1992; it was about $9.90 an hour in manufacturing businesses and about $8.75 in nonmanufacturing businesses. Wages are generally highest in transportation companies and public utilities and lowest in service firms. On average, workers in the Midwest and Northeast earned more than those in the West and South.

AVERAGE HOURLY RATES OF MAINTENANCE TRADES WORKERS IN 15 CITIES

City	General Maintenance Workers	Maintenance Electricians	Maintenance Machinery Mechanics	Maintenance Motor Vehicle Mechanics	Maintenance Pipe Fitters
Atlanta	$ 9.82	$16.21	$13.55	$14.88	$18.89
Baltimore	9.66	15.64	14.86	14.18	18.40
Boston	11.12	17.83	16.50	16.23	18.19
Chicago	10.99	19.25	16.93	17.67	20.93
Dallas	9.20	14.70	15.01	14.97	NA
Denver	9.24	17.55	15.12	15.61	NA
Detroit	11.33	20.22	19.25	17.04	20.41
Houston	8.70	17.27	15.87	13.68	17.77
Los Angeles	10.42	19.64	17.12	18.25	20.37
Miami	8.56	15.12	14.52	13.64	14.88
New York	13.78	22.77	17.88	19.14	21.25
St. Louis	9.77	17.93	15.13	14.48	17.83
San Diego	9.05	19.20	16.69	16.60	NA
San Francisco	10.46	25.64	—	19.50	NA
Seattle	10.75	19.26	18.86	18.28	NA

SOURCE: Bureau of Labor Statistics, *Occupational Compensation Survey, National Summary, 1993.*

THE OFFICE STAFF

In the United States today, the Department of Labor estimates that there are:

- 3.3 million secretaries
- 2.1 million bookkeeping, accounting, and auditing clerks
- 1.2 million typists, word processors, and data entry keyers
- 904,000 receptionists
- 409,000 billing clerks
- 314,000 switchboard operators
- 257,000 file clerks
- 128,000 personnel clerks
- 115,000 stenographers

Clerical and secretarial occupations are among the lowest paid white-collar jobs available anywhere. This is no new development, but rather an old and venerated tradition: Bob Cratchit was a clerk for Ebenezer Scrooge; Herman Melville's Bartleby was a scrivener, or copyist. Typical modern salaries range from as low as $12,400 for a clerk in the federal government to $36,000 for a secretary in private industry. It is rare for office workers to make over $40,000, although some executive secretaries, whose duties include much more than the usual typing, filing, and answering the phone (see job descriptions, below) can earn upward of $50,000 in private industry. For additional salary statistics based on a nationwide survey, see the table, "Average Annual Salaries of Office Workers in Private Industry" later in this section.

EMPLOYMENT LEVELS AND PERCENTAGE GROWTH FOR SELECTED ADMINISTRATIVE SUPPORT OCCUPATIONS, 1992–2005

Job	Estimated Employment, 1992	Projected Employment, 2005	Percentage change, 1992–2005
Adjusters, Investigators, and Collectors	1,185,000	1,552,000	31
Clerical Supervisors and Managers	1,267,000	1,568,000	24
Computer and Peripheral Equipment Operators	218,000	271,000	24
Credit Clerks and Authorizers	296,000	174,000	−41
General Office Clerks	2,688,000	3,342,000	24
Information Clerks	1,333,000	1,762,000	32
Hotel and Motel Desk Clerks	122,000	172,000	40
Interviewing and New Accounts Clerks	175,000	209,000	19
Receptionists	904,000	1,209,000	34
Mail Clerks and Messengers	271,000	297,000	10
Material Recording, Scheduling, Dispatching, and Distributing Occupations	3,558,000	4,013,000	13
Dispatchers	222,000	268,000	21
Stock Clerks	1,969,000	2,156,000	10
Traffic, Shipping, and Receiving Clerks	824,000	971,000	18
Record Clerks	3,573,000	3,777,000	6
Billing Clerks	409,000	421,000	3
Bookkeeping, Accounting, and Auditing Clerks	2,112,000	2,185,000	3
Brokerage Clerks and Statement Clerks	88,000	93,900	7
File Clerks	257,000	305,000	19
Library Assistants and Bookmobile Drivers	114,000	134,000	18
Order Clerks	300,000	313,000	4
Payroll and Timekeeping Clerks	165,000	165,000	0
Personnel Clerks	128,000	160,000	25
Secretaries	3,324,000	3,710,000	12
Stenographers and Court Reporters	115,000	113,300	−2
Telephone Operators	314,000	225,000	−28
Typists, Word Processors, and Data Entry Keyers	1,238,000	1,192,000	−4

SOURCE: *Occupational Outlook Quarterly,* spring 1994.

The largest major occupational group, this collection of office support and clerical jobs is expected to grow at about the same rate as the national average for all jobs. Technological advances are expected to decrease the demand for stenographers, typists, word processors, and data entry keyers, while the demand for information clerks is expected to grow substantially. By the year 2005, jobs for receptionists will grow the fastest, at 47 percent, while the market for general office clerks should increase by the most jobs, 670,000. Typists and word processors will lose more than 100,000 jobs. Overall, the industry should grow about 12 percent, from just under 22 million in 1990 to about 24.84 million in 2005, according to the Department of Labor. The size of this industry and rapid turnover within the industry should mean lots of job openings through the end of the millennium.

Secretaries

In the movie *9 to 5,* Dolly Parton played a teased-hair, stiletto-heeled babe who was smarter than her mean, leering boss. She eventually triumphs over him and turns their office into a kinder, gentler workplace. While many secretaries may be smarter than their bosses, the rest of the scenario plays out only in the movies. The workplace has not been kind to secretaries over the past decade.

The 3.4 million secretaries in the United States in 1994 comprised 2.8 percent of the workforce, down dramatically from 3.7 percent a decade earlier. Computers, of course, have made the biggest dent in the need for secretaries. The one boss–one secretary ratio no longer exists, except in the upper management ranks. Now most secretaries work for several bosses, each with competing demands.

In the recessionary downsizing, many secretarial jobs were cut, and the trend continues. IBM announced that the first targets in a company-wide salary review would be 120 senior secretaries, some of who made more than $70,000. They were told to expect pay cuts of up to 36 percent, by mid-1996, bringing their pay more in line with that of other corporate secretaries, who, according to IBM, earn in the $40,000 range. (Of course, there was no mention of a pay cut for IBM's chairman and chief executive Louis V. Gerstner, Jr., who earned $12.4 million in salary, bonuses, and other compensation in 1994.)

Even the title "secretary," considered sexist or demeaning by some, has changed. Now the preferred title is "executive assistant," "administrative assistant," and "clerical staffer." The "assistant" title usually means more money, upward of $30,000 in major cities. The title also means more skills are expected: from e-mail to fax to spreadsheets to word processing.

But those high-paying, prestigious job are scarce. For most secretaries without advanced skills, the job generally is low-paying and a dead end. Most secretaries make under $25,000, with median annual earnings of $19,916, according to the Bureau of Labor Statistics.

Obviously the more responsibility, the higher the pay.

The Administrative Management Society, one of the best sources for information about salaries and benefits for office employees, makes the following distinctions among the various levels of secretaries:

Executive Secretary/Administrative Assistant—Performs a full range of secretarial and administrative duties for high-level member of executive staff; handles project-oriented duties and may be held accountable for the timely completion of these tasks; relieves executive of routine administrative detail. Position requires an in-depth knowledge of company practice, structure, and a high degree of technical skills.

Secretary, Level A—Performs an unlimited range of secretarial duties for middle-management personnel or for more than one individual; composes and/or takes and transcribes correspondence of a complex and confidential nature. Position requires a knowledge of company policy and procedure, and above-average secretarial and administrative skills.

Secretary, Level B—Performs a limited range of secretarial duties in a small company or for a supervisor in a larger firm; may take dictation and transcribe from notes or dictating equipment with speed and accuracy; screens calls, makes appointments, handles travel arrangements, answers routine correspondence, and maintains filing systems.

Legal Secretary—Performs an unlimited range of secretarial duties for one or more members of the firm, usually a junior, senior, or managing partner; takes and transcribes dictation with a high degree of speed and accuracy. Position requires knowledge of the specific legal terminology within the attorney's area of specialization, i.e., litigation, probate, corporate, etc. May utilize word processing equipment.

Jobs for secretaries are expected to grow more slowly than the national average for all jobs. But there are always opportunities for well-qualified and experienced secretaries. Several hundred thousand positions turn over each year, as secretaries transfer to positions of greater responsibility or leave the labor force. The trend toward secretaries assuming more responsibilities also means that their ranks should grow at the expense of the managers and professionals who formerly performed these duties.

Below are some examples of average salaries in major cities.

AVERAGE WEEKLY SALARIES OF SECRETARIES IN 15 CITIES

City	Level I	Level II	Level III	Level IV	Level V
Atlanta	$359	$415	$507	$581	$697
Baltimore	380	421	484	533	599
Boston	426	472	528	613	718
Chicago	427	469	538	616	729
Dallas	399	469	525	605	724
Denver	372	439	489	590	667
Detroit	478	481	571	615	765
Houston	403	475	533	639	804
Los Angeles	495	523	586	647	778
New York	453	501	583	683	826
Miami	368	442	470	563	682
St. Louis	364	415	489	570	698
San Diego	425	471	526	610	709
San Francisco	494	511	562	633	777
Seattle	434	474	516	604	710

SOURCE: Bureau of Labor Statistics, *Occupational Compensation Survey, National Summary, 1993.*

File Clerks

The work of the file clerk varies in complexity from simple filing to maintaining a large and varied filing system and keeping computerized records of filed materials. Advanced level file clerks may even supervise a staff of lower level clerks. File clerks held about 257,000 jobs in 1992. They are found in nearly every sector of the economy, though 80 percent work in services; finance, insurance, and real estate; and government. The average file clerk earned $15,700 in 1992 (slightly less in the federal government), though salaries vary considerably by geography, industry, and responsibility.

AVERAGE WEEKLY SALARIES OF CLERKS IN 15 CITIES

	Accounting Clerks				General Clerks				Personnel Clerks		
City	I	II	III	IV	I	II	III	IV	I	II	III
Atlanta	$315	$375	$442	$521	NA	$303	$429	$382	$412	$465	$531
Baltimore	333	366	411	493	$269	290	359	411	414	472	NA
Boston	NA	396	442	516	NA	326	398	456	440	490	591
Chicago	277	382	426	514	292	332	391	475	NA	479	NA
Dallas	NA	320	429	503	273	324	385	418	384	462	NA
Denver	317	356	420	520	271	305	374	455	392	449	NA

AVERAGE WEEKLY SALARIES OF CLERKS IN 15 CITIES

City	Accounting Clerks				General Clerks				Personnel Clerks		
	I	II	III	IV	I	II	III	IV	I	II	III
Detroit	265	370	455	618	263	334	408	495	432	502	NA
Houston	320	360	451	551	288	325	408	453	428	511	556
Los Angeles	NA	405	453	531	NA	393	450	509	458	522	641
New York	316	410	464	579	NA	362	395	445	418	526	617
Miami	272	345	423	497	NA	NA	366	400	NA	NA	NA
St. Louis	298	350	403	491	241	304	361	433	379	458	NA
San Diego	NA	374	427	526	NA	307	397	474	NA	480	NA
San Francisco	NA	415	505	541	369	393	460	546	490	537	NA
Seattle	NA	370	432	514	295	307	393	470	NA	NA	NA

SOURCE: Bureau of Labor Statistics, *Occupational Compensation Survey, National Summary, 1993.*

Accounting Clerks

Accounting Clerks record their companies' financial transactions in ledgers; maintain financial records; and are responsible for the accuracy, completeness, and consistency of those records. The Bureau of Labor Statistics divides accounting clerks into four classifications. Level I and II clerks perform simple bookkeeping tasks under close supervision, while Level III and IV clerks' jobs "require a knowledge and understanding of established and standardized bookkeeping and accounting procedures," including double-entry bookkeeping. They may also supervise lower level accounting clerks. There were more than 2 million people working as bookkeeping, accounting, or auditing clerks in 1992. One fourth of them worked in the wholesale or retail trade industries.

BOOKEEPERS' SALARIES, 1995

Title	Salary Range
Full Charge/Controller (Financial Statements)	$30,250–37,500
Full Charge (General Ledger)	25,750–32,750
Bookkeeper/Assistant (up to General Ledger)	22,500–27,000
Accounting Clerk	19,500–24,500
Accounts Receivable/Payable Supervisor	29,500–36,000
Payroll Manager	29,000–38,500
Payroll Clerk	20,000–24,500

SOURCE: Robert Half International, *1995 Salary Guide.* Reprinted by permission.

Accounting clerks frequently do the same tasks as bookkeepers, and it would seem likely that the two levels recognized by the Bureau of Labor Statistics would correspond roughly to the titles "assistant bookkeeper" and "full charge bookkeeper" as they are advertised in the newspapers. Oddly, they do not. Whereas an accounting clerk can expect to earn no more than $24,500, a full-charge bookkeeper's salary starts at over $30,000 and may range as high as $37,500, according to the Robert Half International Salary Guide (see table). If one wishes to pursue this profession, it is obviously better to call oneself a bookkeeper than an accounting clerk. For more information, see the "Accountants" entry in Chapter III.

Personnel Clerks/Assistants

The great importance of personnel and/or human resources departments (see also the section in Chapter V: Human Resources) has created many new clerical jobs in this area. The Bureau of Labor Statistics defines this job as providing "clerical and technical support to personnel professionals or managers" who deal with all aspects of employment, from recruiting to compensation and benefits, to termination of company employees. The responsibilities of clerks/assistants range from checking that job applications are filled out properly, checking references of new employees, and eventually interviewing prospective job candidates. Senior people must have an excellent knowledge of the company's entire personnel policy.

Purchasing Assistants

People in this job assist the buyers and purchasing agents described in Chapter V. Like the human resources department, purchasing has become an increasingly vital function in companies of every size and description. The entry-level purchasing assistant's job is primarily a clerical one, requiring fact checking by rote, routing, and filing functions. After gaining some experience (and depending on the boss's flexibility), assistants handle daily routine ordering and eventually advise the supervisory staff about the suitability of supplies and the quality of materials. At the highest levels, people in these jobs earn over $35,000 a year.

Receptionists and Switchboard Operators

At all but the largest companies, the receptionist and the switchboard operator are the same person. This person is usually required to do some of the typing and light clerical work. Salaries for receptionists are usually on a par with those of general and file clerks—about $13,000 to $15,000—though salary progression is uncommon. Many companies use the receptionist position as a stepping-stone to jobs with more responsibility. Because of this, and because of the tedium involved in this position, turnover among receptionists is high. Many receptionists leave the labor force when they leave their jobs, either to return to school, to tend to household duties, or to retire. There were 904,000 receptionists in 1992. Job openings for receptionists should be plentiful in the coming years, not only because of the high turnover but also because so many receptionists work in the service industry, which is expected to continue its strong growth through the end of the century. Doctors' and dentists' offices, law firms, temporary help agencies, and consulting firms should all have high demand for receptionists.

In large companies, operating the switchboard is often a full-time job in itself. In 1992, more than 300,000 people made answering the phone their primary responsibility. One fourth of these people worked for national or local phone companies. The remainder were employed in hospitals, hotels, department stores, or other large companies. Operators for telephone companies like AT&T and the Bell Operating Companies (a.k.a. the Baby

AVERAGE WEEKLY SALARIES OF SWITCHBOARD OPERATORS/RECEPTIONISTS AND COMPUTER OPERATING PERSONNEL IN 15 LARGE CITIES

	Word Processors			Key Entry Operators		Switchboard Operators/ Receptionists
City	I	II	III	I	II	
Atlanta	NA	$447	$523	$341	$398	$344
Baltimore	$396	435	NA	319	371	332
Boston	NA	448	551	361	455	390
Chicago	395	457	533	303	381	354
Dallas	424	445	532	307	373	346
Denver	NA	435	485	311	NA	338
Detroit	357	481	588	334	NA	363
Houston	360	461	515	307	373	321
Los Angeles	471	491	616	349	425	357
New York	NA	502	586	NA	439	407
Miami	342	419	598	323	399	316
St. Louis	323	NA	512	291	363	323
San Diego	380	456	580	NA	400	328
San Francisco	NA	538	663	384	478	423
Seattle	NA	478	552	340	422	351

SOURCE: Bureau of Labor Statistics, *Occupational Compensation Survey, National Summary, 1993.*

Bells) earn considerably more than other operators. That is primarily because they are almost all members of one of two unions: the Communications Workers of America (CWA) or the International Brotherhood of Electrical Workers. Average salaries for CWA operators were around $560 in 1992. For nonunionized operators, it was $385. Automation is expected to replace much of the work currently performed by operators, so employment prospects in this field are dire.

Computer Operating Personnel

After the 1 million-plus systems analysts and programmers have drawn up plans and instructions in a language their computers can understand, some 296,000 workers are needed to keep the machines functioning smoothly. Some of these people are *key entry operators* who work at keypunch machines or key-operated magnetic tape or disc encoders which "translate" data into a form suitable for computer processing. The Bureau of Labor Statistics describes the work as "routine and repetitive" at the first level, but requiring "experience and judgment" at the higher level. (From the salary figures in the table later in this section titled "Average Weekly Salaries of Office Workers in Private Industry," these qualities don't seem to be worth very much.) Despite the generally strong growth patterns in employment among computer operating personnel, the future of the key entry operator isn't encouraging. The predictions are that improved technology will eliminate much of their function.

Just the opposite is true for *computer operators,* who are also commonly known as *console operators.* Rapidly changing computer technology is not only making these machines more powerful, it is also making them accessible to more and more businesses. The result will be a significant net increase in jobs over the next decade for an occupation many experts said had reached the saturation point.

Computer operators are usually required to have a high school diploma, and most have received special training in the field before they are hired. This training may have been acquired in high school, in a community college, in the military, or in an accredited institution offering courses in this area. In addition, many firms transfer employees from other departments and provide on-the-job training for them.

The Department of Labor recognizes six different levels of expertise among all computer operators. Levels I and II are essentially trainee positions, while Level VI requires knowledge of program language and an ability to assist programmers in developing systems or modifying programs. In between, Levels III to V carry out the basic tasks of computer operating: loading the equipment with tapes, cards, etc.; starting and overseeing the machine;

responding to the computer's instructions, including "error messages"; and maintaining a record of work.

Employment is expected to decline sharply as data centers become automated and as more computing is done on personal computers. For salary figures, see the tables at the end of this section. (See also "Computer Technologists and Professionals" in Chapter IV.)

Typists, Word Processors, and Data Entry Keyers

When the first edition of this book was published, the word processor's job was one of the most important in the modern office. Today, the word processor's importance has diminished as the majority of the office staff has become computer literate and word processing is integrated into the duties of almost every employee, from receptionist to CEO. In offices nationwide—not to mention private homes—the word processor, a catchall term, has replaced the typewriter. The reliance on computers has meant that secretaries with word processing abilities are in high demand, and those who lack this ability often learn it quickly on the job.

The Department of Labor classifies word processors with typists and data entry keyers when keeping employment statistics. Because so many typists now work on computers, the differences between them are growing more and more slight. Data entry keyers do less literate work, like filling out forms that appear on a computer screen or entering lists of items or numbers. Together, these three occupations accounted for nearly 1.2 million jobs in 1992 in every sector of the economy. Forty percent worked in educational institutions, health care facilities, law offices, temporary agencies, and word processing service bureaus. They earned an average of $20,000 in 1992. Word processors, meanwhile, earned an average of $23,000. In the federal government, clerk typists and inexperienced data entry keyers started at $13,400 and averaged $18,800.

Although the amount of text to be processed and entered is tremendous and growing, increasing automation and restructuring of work processes should enable fewer typists, word processors, and data entry keyers to handle the increased workload. There should be little change, therefore, in the total number of people employed in this field. However, job openings should be plentiful since turnover in these jobs is high. The one threatening factor is the amount of work being sent overseas where labor costs are dramatically lower.

AVERAGE WEEKLY SALARIES OF OFFICE WORKERS IN PRIVATE INDUSTRY

Job Title and Level	Number Surveyed	Average Salary
Accounting Clerks I	13,973	$291
Accounting Clerks II	156,105	350
Accounting Clerks III	102,296	426
Accounting Clerks IV	27,551	526
Computer Operators I	4,531	336
Computer Operators II	31,739	423
Computer Operators III	25,799	539
Computer Operators IV	6,514	647
Computer Operators V	387	762
General Clerks I	10,939	254
General Clerks II	68,825	302
General Clerks III	84,176	384
General Clerks IV	36,159	476
Key Entry Operators I	65,699	307
Key Entry Operators II	35,280	394
Personnel Clerks/Assistants I	1,346	314
Personnel Clerks/Assistants II	5,856	390
Personnel Clerks/Assistants III	6,105	473
Personnel Clerks/Assistants IV	1,490	542
Secretaries I	53,060	379
Secretaries II	88,920	418
Secretaries III	123,664	520
Secretaries IV	57,751	611
Secretaries V	12,384	745
Switchboard Operators/Receptionists	95,783	327
Word Processors I	10,793	360
Word Processors II	22,551	435
Word Processors III	4,644	546

SOURCE: Bureau of Labor Statistics, *Occupational Compensation Survey, National Summary, 1993.*

MACHINING OCCUPATIONS

More than 2 million people are employed in machining occupations. Machine tools are used to shape metal, and metal parts are the bricks of mass production, since, according to the Bureau of Labor Statistics, "nearly every product of American industry, from cornflakes to turbines, is made either using machine tools or using machines made by machine tools." Machine tools are extremely precise and are often designed for specific tasks by the people who operate them. The design of machines and their functions is the part of machining that is most interesting and lucrative. The operation of machinery after it has been produced and adjusted can be tedious, especially if the machines are designed to do all of the work.

There are four different categories of machine workers, although in smaller shops, the distinctions are not as clear-cut as in large ones. Employment in machining occupations is expected to grow no faster than the average rate for all jobs, and in many cases is expected to decline. As machines become more sophisticated, they will do more of the work themselves. Most jobs are found, of course, in places with lots of factories, such as Los Angeles, Chicago, New York, Philadelphia, Boston, San Francisco, and Houston.

All-Round Machinists

There are about 359,000 all-round machinists working today, down from 386,000 in 1992; the number is expected to continue decreasing slowly over the next decade. These are skilled workers who have often completed a four-year formal apprenticeship (about 8,000 shop hours and 570 hours in the classroom). A high school science or vocational degree is preferred by most employers. Workers must be able to operate a variety of machines using a variety of metals. Besides shaping metal, they must also know how to calculate precise measurements (sometimes down to a millionth of an inch) so that the pieces they produce will be perfect.

Working conditions in most machine shops have improved from the sweatshop image that many people still harbor. Work areas are now well lit and ventilated; more sophisticated equipment makes less noise. However, the enormous energy and cutting speed required to chop up blocks of metal can produce red-hot, molten pieces that sometimes fly through the air. Machinists are required to wear protective clothing and goggles while they work.

Earnings of all-round machinists compare favorably with those of other skilled workers. In 1992, their median weekly earnings were about $492; the top 10 percent made more than $750 a week.

Metalworking and Plastics-Working Machine Operators

These 1.4 million employees can be separated into two groups: those who set up machines for operation and those who tend the machines while they operate. Setup workers (or setters) need to know how the machines operate, so they generally have more training and are more skilled than those who simply operate the machines. Regular operators are usually identified by the kind of machine they run, for example, a screw machine operator or lathe tender. Half of these workers are machine tool cutting and forming machine setters or operators, and another 8 percent are sheet-metal workers. About 35 to 40 percent of setup workers and operators are represented by unions.

Median weekly earnings for metal- and plastics-working machine operators were $413 in 1992; the top 10 percent earned over $697. Employees who worked in the industries of transportation equipment ($633), primary metals ($590), machinery ($525), fabricated metal products ($475), and plastics materials and resins ($433), earned considerably more than the average. Jobs in this area are expected to decline through the year 2005 as firms move factories (and jobs) to other countries where labor is cheaper and as fewer laborers are needed to tend more machines.

Tool and Die Makers

Tools and dies are the parts of equipment used by other machining workers to mass produce metal parts. Tool makers produce "jibs" and fixtures that hold metal while it is being shaved, and measuring devices to gauge the precision of the parts produced. Die makers produce metal forms or dies for stamping out pieces of metal. These jobs are most like those of instrument makers except that tool-and-die makers specialize in one type of product. Tool and die makers work in machine shops but usually in separate, quieter areas called toolrooms. Four years of apprenticeship is the norm. The Bureau of Labor Statistics says that "many tool and die makers become tool designers and others may open their own tool and die shops." About 138,000 people are employed as tool and die makers, a number that is likely to decline as businesses increase their use of numerically controlled (or automated) machine tools.

Millwrights

Millwrights install machinery, not just in the production of metal parts but in all industries, from textiles to printing. Installation includes construction of foundations and platforms for machines, which means that a millwright has to read blueprints and be able to use installation tools (torches, crowbars, power tools, etc.) and direct the operation of cranes and other equipment. Millwrights sometimes train as apprentices for as many as eight years, but many follow a four-year course of job and classroom instruction similar to that of all-round machinists.

Most of the 73,000 millwrights are employed full-time by large manufacturers, but a fair percentage are employed by contractors and construction companies, and this means that many are frequently out of work when the economy is in a downward trend. Median earnings of full-time millwrights were $596 in 1992.

AVERAGE HOURLY EARNINGS OF MACHINISTS IN 15 CITIES

City	Maintenance Machinists	Tool and Die Makers
Atlanta	$17.49	$16.72
Baltimore	16.24	18.12
Boston	17.57	18.31
Chicago	18.57	16.72
Dallas	15.53	15.48
Denver	17.16	NA
Detroit	17.10	19.84
Houston	18.71	15.29
Los Angeles	17.76	19.05
New York	NA	NA
Miami	19.15	NA
St. Louis	18.21	18.85
San Diego	16.62	18.23
San Francisco	NA	NA
Seattle	18.29	NA

SOURCE: Bureau of Labor Statistics, *Occupational Compensation Survey, National Summary, 1993.*

MATERIAL MOVEMENT WORKERS

These are the people in the background, working to ensure that items move quickly and safely from point A to point B. Material movement workers represent over 35 million members of the workforce. Generally members of large unions, workers in these occupations tend to earn wages on a par with or even better than national averages for blue-collar jobs. However, the future employment outlook varies for the different occupations in this field because of increased mechanization and automation. Here are descriptions of several of these occupations.

Forklift Operators

Because of strict union regulations, forklift operators don't actually manually load or unload material from ships, trucks, or railroad cars. That job is left to material handlers (see below). Rather, forklift operators stack crates in warehouses and load and unload trucks and boxcars only when their machinery is required. Many forklift operators work in the electronics manufacturing industry, although opportunities also exist on the docks, in freight yards, and in any other field where warehouses are to be found. The employment outlook for this occupation is about average for nonsupervisory positions.

Material Handlers

Many material handlers, also known as stevedores or handling laborers, work in the motor vehicle and equipment manufacturing field. They load and unload parts and raw materials from railroad cars, ships, and trucks. That makes them the first people on the assembly line. Material handlers are members of the UAW (United Automobile, Aerospace, and Agricultural Implement Workers of America).

Shipping and Receiving Clerks

These clerks record all shipments sent out and received. Shipping clerks have the final responsibility for merchandise before it leaves the company to go to a customer. They must check to see that an order has been filled correctly and that it is well packaged and bears the proper postage. Then they must supervise its loading onto delivery trucks.

Receiving clerks handle similar tasks in reverse. They inspect incoming merchandise to make sure an order has been correctly filled and billed. They may direct goods to the department that ordered them within the company. Receiving clerks must be adept at record keeping, too, in order to assist with inventory computations.

There are about 824,000 shipping and receiving clerks in the country. Employment opportunities are expected to grow about as fast as the national average for all jobs. Median weekly earnings in 1992 were between $350 and $370. These clerks generally receive no more than standard benefits.

Warehouse Specialists

Sometimes known as stock clerks, warehouse specialists are given a list of all the part numbers and quantities needed by a customer. They go through the warehouse filling the order, and then take it to be packed and shipped. Their earnings are generally a bit higher than those of shipping and receiving clerks.

AVERAGE HOURLY WAGES OF MATERIAL MOVEMENT WORKERS IN 15 CITIES

City	Forklift Operators	Material Handling Laborers	Shipping/ Receiving Clerks	Warehouse Specialists	Truckdrivers			
					Light	Medium	Heavy	Tractor Trailer
Atlanta	$10.25	$ 8.36	$ 9.99	NA	$ 8.05	NA	NA	NA
Baltimore	12.80	9.30	9.86	$11.51	6.57	$12.82	$10.23	$13.11
Boston	12.30	10.87	11.07	11.20	NA	15.14	13.87	14.90
Chicago	11.51	12.68	10.02	11.63	NA	16.58	15.68	16.42
Dallas	10.28	NA	9.41	9.68	NA	NA	9.20	14.08
Denver	12.12	NA	10.65	NA	NA	15.41	13.48	13.52
Detroit	15.98	13.55	12.60	13.62	NA	NA	15.30	14.70
Houston	9.82	5.87	8.67	10.58	7.06	NA	9.79	12.98
Los Angeles	11.46	NA	9.99	11.67	8.11	14.18	13.48	14.52
Miami	8.24	NA	8.85	NA	6.73	NA	9.98	13.00
New York	NA	NA	NA	NA	12.31	NA	NA	18.36
St. Louis	13.20	NA	9.94	NA	7.87	12.85	12.09	15.03
San Diego	12.25	4.60	8.77	11.04	7.67	14.24	14.03	13.48
San Francisco	NA	12.54	11.93	13.09	8.64	NA	NA	19.05
Seattle	13.58	NA	11.11	13.00	9.39	11.34	15.67	16.19

SOURCE: Bureau of Labor Statistics, *Occupational Compensation Survey, National Summary, 1993.*

MECHANICS, INSTALLERS, AND REPAIRERS

It's heartening to know that in this land of disposable everything, there are still large numbers of people whose workday is spent fixing, mending, and repairing. There are quite a few occupations falling under the mechanics and repairers category, in which a total of nearly 4.6 million Americans work. The unemployment rate for mechanics, in particular, tends to be much lower than that for blue-collar workers generally, so the work is basically steady and less subject to seasonal layoffs. Most of these jobs are not unionized, although there is frequently some licensing qualification. Training usually comes in the form of apprenticeships. Earnings are commensurate with experience, with highly skilled workers earning wages considerably above average for nonsupervisory positions.

Although these jobs tend to have longer than usual work weeks, employees often work with minimal supervision, and many are self-employed.

The various occupations in this category evidence one of the widest fluctuations of growth within a single industry. Increases in the use of data processing equipment and biomedical equipment will bring with them a corresponding need for people to repair and install them. At the same time, labor-saving advances should cause a decline in employment for installers and repairers of telephones, televisions, and other types of communications equipment.

Overall, America's 4.5 million mechanics, installers, and repairers should grow 16 percent by the year 2005, according to the Department of Labor. Jobs for computer and office machine repairers should grow by 30 percent; meanwhile, telephone installers and repairers should see their numbers decline by half. Statistics for all jobs within the industry follow.

MECHANICS, INSTALLERS, AND REPAIRERS, 1990–1992, BY TYPE

	Employment	
Job	**1990**	**1992**
Aircraft Mechanics and Engine Specialists	122,000	131,000
Automotive Body Repairers	219,000	202,000
Automotive Mechanics	757,000	739,000
Diesel (Bus and Truck) Mechanics	268,000	263,000
Electronic Equipment Repairers, Total	370,000	398,000
Computer and Office Machine Repairers	159,000	143,000
Communications Equipment Mechanics	125,000	108,000
Commercial and Industrial Electronic Equipment Repairers	73,000	68,000
Electronic Home Entertainment Equipment Repairers	41,000	49,000
Telephone Installers and Repairers	47,000	40,000
Elevator Installers and Repairers	19,000	22,000

MECHANICS, INSTALLERS, AND REPAIRERS, 1990–1992, BY TYPE

Job	Employment 1990	1992
Farm Equipment Mechanics	48,000	47,000
General Maintenance Repairers	1,128,000	1,145,000
Heating, Air-conditioning, & Refrigeration Technicians	219,000	212,000
Home Appliance and Power Tool Repairers	71,000	74,000
Industrial Machinery Mechanics	474,000	477,000
Line Installers and Cable Splicers	133,000	273,000
Millwrights	73,000	73,000
Mobile Heavy Equipment Mechanics	104,000	96,000
Motorcycle, Boat, and Small Engine Mechanics	50,000	46,000
Musical Instrument Repairers and Tuners	9,000	12,000
Vending Machine Servicers and Repairers	26,000	20,000
Bicycle Repairers	15,000	14,000
Camera and Photographic Equipment Repairers	7,000	7,600
Electric Meter Installers and Repairers	14,000	13,000
Electromedical and Biomedical Equipment Repairers	8,000	9,500
Precision Instrument Repairers	50,000	45,000
Riggers	14,000	12,000
Tire Repairers	81,000	80,000
Watchmakers	7,000	94,000
TOTAL	**4,361,000**	**4,515,100**

SOURCE: *Occupational Outlook Handbook,* 1994.

Heating, Air-conditioning, and Refrigeration Mechanics

Wherever large numbers of people live, work, or play, some system for keeping them cool in hot weather and warm in cold weather is an integral part of the building and its maintenance. Heating, refrigeration, and air-conditioning mechanics are skilled workers who repair, install, and maintain the complex systems that fill these functions.

Some mechanics specialize in one kind of equipment or a particular task, such as installation or repair. Others handle all facets of a building's climate-control system, as well as doing such maintenance work as overhauling the air-conditioning system in the winter and making sure pipes are clear and ducts clean for heating. There are about 212,000 mechanics in this classification; about half of them worked for cooling and heating contractors. A little over 20 percent were self-employed. The remainder were divided among the federal government, hospitals, office buildings, and other organizations that operate large air-conditioning, refrigeration, or heating systems.

Because of the increasing sophistication of air-conditioning, refrigeration, and heating systems, employers are beginning to rely more on mechanics with technical school or apprenticeship training. Apprenticeship programs, lasting 4 to 5 years and combining on-the-job training with 144 hours of classroom instruction, are administered by locals of various different unions, including the Air-conditioning Contractors of America, the Mechanical Contractors' Association of America, and the National Association of Plumbers, Pipe Fitters, and Cooling Contractors. In addition, many secondary and postsecondary technical trade schools, junior colleges, and the U.S. armed forces now offer one- to two-year programs in heating, air-conditioning, and refrigeration. Despite the development of all these programs, however, a sizable number of heating, air-conditioning, and refrigeration mechanics continue to learn their trade on the job.

Earnings in this field vary with experience, skills, and geographical location. Median weekly earnings in 1992 were $474 for full-time mechanics. And although turnover in this field is very low, job openings are expected to be plentiful as a result of faster than average growth. The continued pattern of U.S. migration from the rust belt to areas in the South and West (where central cooling systems abound) should also help job prospects in this field.

Home Appliance Repairers

Back in nineteenth-century England, a band of workers, fearful they would soon be losing their jobs to machines and frustrated by the newfangled things, joined forces under Ned Ludd and smashed all the equipment they could lay their hands on. The Luddites had their day or two in history, but with time, workers grew accustomed, or at least resigned to, the mechanized workplace; they, and everyone else, eventually saw it happen to their homes as well. American homes are a gadget heaven, with appliances existing to vacuum, clean clothes, wash dishes, make toast, blend food, dry hair, dry lettuce, chop onions, fry perfect hamburgers, mow lawns, and brush teeth—and that's a conservative listing. (With all these time-saving devices, want to guess how much less time a homemaker spends on weekly chores today than did her counterpart 90 years ago? Answer: exactly one minute.)

However, as everyone knows, appliances are fair-weather friends. Some corollary to Murphy's law dictates that the icemaking machine must break down, with the air conditioner, in July; the blow-dryer on prom night; and so on. Luckily, there are heroes in these scenarios. They are appliance repairers.

There are about 74,000 people working as home appliance and power tool repairers, with little change expected over the next two decades. Most repairers are employed by independent appliance stores and repair shops.

Many work, too, for gas and electric utility companies, department stores, and in service centers operated by appliance manufacturers.

Repairers, who often take vocational classes for background training, also receive on-the-job training, sometimes up to three years' worth before becoming fully skilled on very complicated machinery. They must be adept with mechanical and electrical work so as to be able to determine what exactly is wrong with an appliance and how to fix it or replace a used or defective part. Some appliance repairers make house calls, bringing all their tools along to repair an item on the spot, or to install an appliance and explain its use.

According to the Department of Labor, earnings for appliance repairers vary widely by skill level, geographic location, and type of equipment serviced. On average, experienced repairers earned $467 per week in 1992. Trainees earned less and senior technicians earned more than the range extremes. Salaries tend to be highest in large firms and for those servicing gas appliances.

Automobile Mechanics

There are some who consider finding an honest, reliable automobile mechanic more vital than finding a reliable family doctor. Mechanics test-drive a car or use testing equipment to locate a problem on a car that a customer has brought in. Once the problem has been determined, mechanics make the needed repair or adjustment or replace a part that is worn. They also perform such routine maintenance as oil changes and tune-ups.

Probably the vast majority of auto mechanics are generalists, able to deal with just about any kind of car repair. However, some specialize in such narrower areas as automatic transmissions, automobile air-conditioning, automobile radiators, auto glass, brakes, tune-ups, mufflers, wheel alignments, and front-end adjustments.

There were 739,000 automobile mechanics in 1992, with job openings expected to increase apace with the national average over the next decade. Qualified mechanics should find work wherever they go, as opportunities exist all over the country. Mechanics with the most training, especially training in basic electronics, should find the most job prospects and the highest salaries.

Most mechanics receive all their training on the job, with their earnings increasing as their skills and experience do. Some independent repair shops and large auto dealers offer apprenticeship programs. The majority of all mechanics are employed by franchised dealerships like Ford or GM service shops, which employ eight or nine mechanics on the average. Other jobs exist in gasoline service stations, auto repair shops, and department stores' automotive service centers.

Median weekly earnings of auto mechanics were $408 in 1992. Many experienced mechanics also receive a commission related to the labor cost charged to the customer. Many employers guarantee a minimum weekly salary in case the amount of work drops in a given week. Auto mechanics belong to one of several unions: the United Auto Workers, the Teamsters, and the International Association of Machinists and Aerospace Workers.

Industrial Machinery Repairers

Industrial machinery repairers work in factories repairing broken machinery and doing preventive maintenance. They're experts in diagnosis, being able to tell by the mere sounds and shakes of a piece of equipment just what is ailing it. They then disassemble it and make the necessary repair or replacement of the damaged part. Since service and general overhauls must go on even if machinery is idle or running at low capacity, industrial machinery repairers are not usually subject to seasonal layoffs or slow work periods.

There are now about 477,000 workers in this trade. They are employed in a wide variety of industries, ranging from coal to paper to machinery to food products. Work can be found all over the country, although of course most jobs exist in the more industrialized states. This is a highly unionized occupation, with mechanics belonging to different unions, depending on what industry they're working in. Most industrial repairers belong to the United Steelworkers of America, the UAW, the International Association of Machinists and Aerospace Workers, or the International Union of Electrical, Radio, and Machine Workers.

Job opportunities are forecasted to decline as more firms move to automated production equipment. All job openings will result from retirement or the need to replace workers who leave the field or the labor force. According to the Department of Labor, median weekly earnings of most industrial machinery repairers were $498 in 1992.

Shoe Repairers

Here's one trade that profits when economic times are hard—and not because many people look "down at the heel." It's just that people are more interested in repairing or maintaining shoes they already own than in spending money on new ones. Shoe repairers reheel, make new soles, replace insoles, and restyle old shoes by dyeing uppers and changing heels. They also do a miscellany of other tasks, such as mending handbags, tents, and luggage, stretching shoes, and fixing zippers.

According to the Bureau of Labor Statistics, shoe and leather workers held about 22,000 jobs in 1992; about 4,000 were self-employed. Inexpensive imports have made the cost of replacing shoes and leather goods cheaper or more convenient than repairing them, thus reducing the demand for shoe and leather repairers. However, repair of more expensive, high-end products will continue to grow, as will demand for repairers of custom-made and orthopedic shoes. An increase in the population over 75 years old, the group most likely to need orthopedic shoes, should expand the market for this type of shoemaker and repairer. The trade is nonunionized, with many of its workers running their own shops, often squeezed into tiny spaces in alleyways between other stores. Salary information is therefore limited. Generally, beginning workers earn no more than the minimum wage. Store owners earn substantially more.

RESTAURANT WORKERS

More than 6.5 million people work in the restaurants, bars, pizza places, and chili joints, etc., that seem to have sprung up in every nook and cranny of every little town, large urban area, and suburban mall. Despite recent tough times in the $260 billion industry, every analyst in every state as well as all the forecasters in Washington, D.C., project very strong growth in this sector of the economy. In fact, the Bureau of Labor Statistics expects that fully 6 percent of U.S. employees (some 8.7 million people) will work in eating and drinking establishments. Average annual growth should top 1.9 percent, well above the average for the rest of the labor force.

The most important question, though, is what kind of establishment will they be working in? The strongest current industry trend is an enormous surge in the fast-food sector, which provides hundreds of thousands of minimum-wage and low-paying jobs. The big three burger joints—McDonald's, Burger King, and Wendy's—all reported dramatically improved sales in 1991. Meanwhile, the number of sit-down restaurants has declined dramatically, from 379,000 in 1989 to 269,000 today according to Restaurant Consulting Group, Inc. in Evanston, Illinois. These two facts seem to suggest that people are treating themselves to inexpensive meals even though they cannot afford a night out at a so-called white-tablecloth restaurant. Restaurateurs can take heart in a recent Gallup survey in which 45 percent of adults said they would eat out more often if they had the money.

The restaurants that seem most likely to prosper will be those that cater to cost-conscious baby-boomers with children. Chili's, Buffets Inc., and Cracker Barrel Old Country Store are examples of this type of restaurant. But of course the best (and most expensive) restaurants, like New York's Lutèce or Los Angeles's Spago, are always booked solid, no matter what the economy.

Bartenders, Waiters, and Bus Persons

The vast majority of the nation's 2.6 million bartenders, waiters, and busboys (of both sexes, also called dining room attendants) work part-time. Indeed, few admit to this being their career. Flexible hours and low educational and training requirements make this an attractive option for actors, musicians, writers, and students seeking to pay their rent while pursuing their careers. Most waiters and waitresses are in their late teens or early twenties and have little or no work experience. Bartenders generally have some form of training (usually obtained through a vocational course that may or may not help with job placement) and are expected to be familiar with state and local laws concerning the sale of alcoholic beverages; consequently, they often earn more than waiters and buspersons.

Salaries in all these positions are subject to lower minimum wage requirements than all other jobs, because food service workers make such a large proportion of their money from tips. Salaries within each job category vary widely depending on the prices charged by the restaurant, the number of people served, and whether or not waiters share some portion of their tips with the bartenders and/or the busboys. And because so many restaurant workers are paid off the books (and therefore don't necessarily report all their income to the IRS), they may tend to underreport their incomes to Department of Labor interviewers as well. Bear that fact in mind as you read the following median weekly salaries for full-time restaurant workers, according to a 1992 Bureau of Labor Statistics survey:

Position	**Median Weekly Earnings**
Busboys	$210
Waiters and Waitresses	$220
Fast-food Waiters or Attendants	$220
Bartenders	$250

Thus, it is clear that for every bartender who boasts of taking home $200 in tips alone on a single Saturday night, there are hundreds of restaurant workers toiling at a rate a lot closer to the minimum wage (or at least telling this to the government).

In addition to their salaries and tips, most restaurant workers receive free meals from their employers (though after working there for a few weeks, many such employees report that they'd rather go hungry than eat the food served in their restaurant). But generally, only full-time workers receive benefits like paid vacation, sick leave, or health insurance. That may change as the service industry continues to expand and restaurants seek to keep qualified workers from jumping ship. For example, Starbucks, the Seattle-based coffee bar giant, provides full medical benefits to any employee who works as little as 20 hours per week. The company has found that the amount it spends on benefits (about $1,275 per year) is far less than the cost of rehiring and training new employees (about $3,000). Restaurant service workers in the largest restaurants and hotels belong to unions, the principal ones being the Hotel and Restaurant Employees International Union and the Service Employees International Union.

Cooks and Chefs

The Department of Labor counts more than 3.1 million people working as cooks of all kinds, ranging from short-order cooks to pastry bakers. Their wages vary as much as do their tasks, from the $4.25 per hour earned by fast-food fryers to the $75,000 plus per year earned by executive chefs in first-rate restaurants. In between are cooks, whose median hourly earnings were $6.57 in 1992, according to the National Restaurant Association; bread and pastry bakers whose median earnings were $6.25; assistant cooks ($6.00); and short-order cooks ($5.99). Chefs who develop a following often end up as partner or sole proprietor of their own restaurant, where their income depends on the establishment's success. Some employers provide their employees with uniforms and free meals, but federal law allows them to deduct the fair value of these meals from their workers' salaries.

MEDIAN ANNUAL SALARIES OF CHEFS IN HOTELS IN THE U.S. AND CANADA[1]

	U.S. Hotels		Canadian Hotels		
Category	250–500 Rooms	500+ Rooms	150–250 Rooms	250–475 Rooms	475+ Rooms
Executive Chef	NA[2]	NA	$36,000	$56,000	$51,000
Gourment Restaurant Chef	$44,000	$44,000	32,000	50,000	38,000
Executive Sous Chef	33,000	42,000	30,000	40,000	37,000
Pastry Chef	32,000	37,000	30,000	32,000	36,000

[1]Rates are for full-service hotels with a minimum average room rate of $130 in the U.S. and $100 Canadian in Canada.
[2]NA = not applicable: no comparable position.
SOURCE: American Hotel & Motel Association.

To some degree, the number of jobs for cooks and chefs is reliant on a strong economy, as people tend to eat out more often (and in more expensive restaurants) when the economy is healthy. Nevertheless, jobs for chefs and cooks are expected to grow rapidly irrespective of the health of the economy because of population growth and increased leisure time. In addition, as more and more women enter the workforce, fewer people are at home preparing dinner, making a meal in a restaurant as much of a convenience as a treat. Jobs for cooks and chefs in restaurants, especially those offering more varied menus, are expected to grow the fastest; jobs for cooks and chefs in nursing homes will be equally strong, followed by openings in institutions like schools, hospitals, and other cafeterias.

REPRESENTATIVE JOBS IN THE WORKADAY WORLD

Precision Assemblers

Assemblers staff the production lines, putting together the different parts of manufactured items. Each worker is stationed at a set point along a moving conveyor belt, completing his or her task in the production of a single, finished product. Assemblers, therefore, all work with different equipment and use different skills. Floor assemblers work on heavy machinery on shop floors and often use power tools, such as power drills or soldering irons, to fasten equipment. Bench assemblers do more detailed work or sometimes are responsible for a complete subassembly, such as the whole motor of a vacuum cleaner.

Out of the 1 million-plus assembly line workers who assemble the parts of manufactured goods, the elite are the 334,000 who are employed as precision assemblers. Precision assembly requires a great degree of accuracy. The precision assembler must be able to interpret detailed specifications and instructions and apply independent judgment as opposed to the simple repetitive jobs of the majority of assembly line workers. Precision assemblers are usually involved in the manufacturing of durable goods.

The Department of Labor estimates that jobs for precision assemblers will decline over the next decade as companies automate their factories and move assembly operations to countries like Mexico, the Philippines, and Malaysia, where labor is vastly cheaper. But not all precision assemblers can be replaced by a machine or a third-world laborer. The jobs that require the most precision and skill and the least repetition—and those that involve assembly of irregularly sized parts—will survive best.

Median weekly earnings for precision assemblers were $318 in 1992. Wages were much higher for unionized assemblers working in companies manufacturing automobiles, aircraft, and electronic equipment: Median weekly earnings ranged from $400 to $600. The biggest unions representing assemblers are the International Association of Machinists and Aerospace Workers; the International Union of Electrical, Radio and Machine Workers; and the United Automobile, Aerospace and Agricultural Implement Workers of America.

Barbers and Cosmetologists

The haircutting profession has come a long way since the day when men whistled for "shave and a haircut, two bits." Today, nine out of every ten haircutters are "cosmetologists," who offer many more services than the traditional barber of yesteryear, who seems to be going the way of the candy-striped pole and the 25-cent haircut. In addition to cutting hair, the cosmetologist (also known as a beautician or stylist) shampoos, styles, and colors hair, advises customers how to care for their hair, performs treatments that make straight hair curly or vice versa, and provides scalp massages and treatments. Some also do manicures, makeup, and electrolysis. It is the rare barber (and never a cosmetologist) who still offers a razor-and-strap shave.

The Department of Labor estimates that there were 746,000 cosmetologists and barbers in 1992. The vast majority worked in a beauty salon or a "unisex" salon, though most of the 70,000 or so barbers remaining still work in traditional barbershops. About four-fifths of barbers and half of all cosmetologists are self-employed; about one in three haircutters works part-time. Every state requires barbers and cosmetologists to be licensed, though qualifications for a license vary from an eighth-grade education in some states to rigorous physical and educational requirements in others. Public and private vocational schools offer training programs that last 6 to 12 months, usually followed by an apprenticeship of one to two years. Reciprocity agreements between many states allow haircutters to practice in a different state without having to retrain.

Jobs for hairstylists should grow faster than the national average for all jobs through the year 2005, as population growth and an increasing number of women entering the labor force should increase demand for hairstyling services. Cosmetologists will account for all of these jobs; barbers' employment is expected to decline. Opportunities will be best for haircutters offering the widest array of services, for men and women alike.

Because so many haircutters are self-employed, salaries vary depending on the success of the establishment. Non-self-employed barbers and cosmetologists receive income either from commission (usually 50 to 70 percent of the price of the service) or from wages and tips. According to a limited survey by the Department of Labor, barbers and cosmetologists earned between $20,000 and $30,000 in 1992. Barbers generally earn about 30 to 35 percent more than cosmetologists or stylists.

Custodial Workers

There are about 3 million people working as building custodians; about one third of them work part-time. Also called janitors or cleaners, custodians keep schools, stores, office buildings, hospitals, factories, and apartment houses clean and in general repair. In addition to such chores as cleaning and waxing floors, vacuuming carpets, dusting, and washing windows, custodians also do maintenance tasks including basic painting and carpentry, minor plumbing, lawnmowing, and exterminating.

Good opportunities exist for work as a custodian, especially in part-time and evening shifts. Jobs are found all over the country but are concentrated in cities with lots of large buildings. As most cleaners learn their skills on the job, no special education or training is required. However, in places where there is more than one maintenance worker, a high school diploma can help improve the chances of promotion to a supervisory job.

AVERAGE HOURLY WAGES OF JANITORS AND GUARDS IN 15 CITIES

City	Janitors	Guards, Nonmanufacturing	Guards, Manufacturing
Atlanta	$ 6.12	$6.19	NA
Baltimore	7.09	6.69	NA
Boston	8.60	7.17	$12.30
Chicago	8.16	6.52	11.89
Dallas	5.70	6.49	11.28
Denver	6.48	6.14	12.55
Detroit	9.56	6.16	12.33
Houston	5.24	6.02	12.44
Los Angeles	7.35	6.83	11.62
Miami	5.75	6.07	7.61
New York	11.76	NA	11.09
San Diego	7.88	6.15	NA
San Francisco	10.37	7.13	11.73
Seattle	9.33	6.80	NA
St. Louis	6.43	6.11	11.22

SOURCE: Bureau of Labor Statistics, *Occupational Compensation Survey, National Summary, 1993.*

Guards

More than 800,000 guards, working for security services or for privately run police forces, provide protection and surveillance for such varied institutions as banks, factories, college campuses, office buildings, hotels, and individuals. Their duties include visitor registration, traffic control, and identification during business hours. During off hours, they perform as caretakers, making rounds of buildings and facilities to protect against any number of potential problems from fires to robbery or spying. Guards who are members of one of the two major guard unions earn slightly more than the average of $6.00 per hour for all guards. Guards with specialized training earn nearly double this amount.

The Bureau of Labor Statistics uses the classifications I and II to differentiate those guards who are specially trained, always armed, and in good physical shape from the run-of-the-mill security person who stands around supermarkets and is rarely armed. Since most Class I guards are hired by manufacturing companies and Class II guards by nonmanufacturing companies, we have used only those designations in the table.

Cashiers/Retail Clerks

There are about 2.7 million people working as cashiers, almost all of them under the age of 25. As the size of this population continues to shrink throughout the 1990s, openings in this occupation will be plentiful. Cashiers work at the register in a variety of stores as well as in theaters and offices. In addition to working with cash, they may perform bookkeeping functions, wrap and bag purchases, and act as receptionists. The work is entry level, requiring little or no previous work experience or educational requirements, though a high school diploma is preferred.

The United Food and Commercial Workers International Union represents about 5 percent of cashiers and retail clerks. Their salaries are considerably higher than the vast majority of clerks who earn little more than the federal minimum wage of $4.25 per hour. In addition, more than half of cashiers work only part-time. Their earnings do not figure in the median weekly salary of $219 for full-time cashiers. Because of the shrinking labor pool for cashiers, many employers are using higher wages, additional benefits, and flexible schedules to attract and keep cashiers on staff.

Meat Cutters

Meat cutters, who also cut and debone fish and chicken, work in supermarkets or wholesale food outlets preparing meats for purchase. Tasks include dividing meat into primal cuts, trimming fat, removing bones, and in some stores, stocking meat display cases and serving customers.

There are about 349,000 meat cutters in the United States; 220,000 of them are skilled butchers, the majority of whom work in retail grocery stores.

Meat cutters can find work in almost every American town or city; a high school diploma is not even required, though it is preferred. Training is usually on the job, although some trade schools offer apprenticeship programs. Many meat cutters are represented by the United Food and Commercial Workers Union.

Butchers and meat cutters had median weekly earnings of $310 in 1992; the highest 10 percent earned over $630 per week. Meat cutters are usually among the highest paid employees in the grocery store. They also receive paid vacation and sick leave, and health and life insurance. Union meat-cutters also have pension plans.

IX

Special Groups

This section has been intentionally designed as a hodgepodge, a catchall that gives the book a broader scope by enabling important topics to be included. How, for example, do the earnings of women and minorities stack up against those of white males? In addition, recent trends in the salary levels of college graduates and newly minted M.B.A.s can also be found here.

THE TEMPORARY WORKER

The task of counting the nation's temporary workers has always been a difficult one, primarily because of the difficulty of defining what makes an employee temporary. Some seasonal work, such as ski instructor or migrant farm worker, is by nature temporary, since the job lasts only as long as the weather. Other temporary workers, such as contract engineers or secretaries, may work a full work week every week of the year, but at a different business each week. So it was not until 1995 that the Bureau of Labor Statistics even undertook to estimate the number of temporary workers in the U.S.

The results of the survey—6 million people hold jobs they do not consider permanent—surprised many analysts, who had expected the number would be higher. The report allayed some economists' fears of a disposable workplace, where not only secretaries, receptionists, and tax accountants, but also lawyers, nurses, computer programmers, and executives could be hired only when needed from a temporary agency. The BLS survey reported that about 1.2 million temporary workers are affiliated with a temporary help agency. Temporary workers are also more likely to be female or black, and are about 20 percent less likely than full-time workers to have health insurance.

The benefits to a company of using temporary work are obvious: temps earn slightly more in hourly wages than do full-time employees, but usually do not accrue the benefits that accompany full-time employment. In some companies, a benefits package, including health insurance, disability or workers' compensation, life insurance and a pension plan, increase the cost of having a full-time worker by as much as 35 percent. The company also has no long-term obligations to temporary workers and can let them go at a moment's notice without having to pay severance or unemployment insurance. Anybody who has tried to fire a union member or other employee with some amount of job security doesn't need to be told how important that flexibility is. So the hiring of temporaries can be a boon for any company where demand for labor is volatile. For years, companies have used temporary workers during periods of peak work and heavy vacation; in the current downsizing labor market, companies that have laid off full-time workers are finding they still need people to do the work, and as a consequence are resorting to temps.

From the worker's point of view, the temps who choose not to have a permanent position talk about how much they cherish the "convenience" or "freedom" offered by temporary work. They may find themselves in a situation where temporary work is a good source of income while they look for something more permanent. Others may view a temporary assignment as a door opener for permanent work. And there are also workers who value the ability to specify where and when they will work. In all, though, only about one third of temporary workers said they prefer their situation to a permanent job.

These sentiments are not shared, however, by unemployed stockbrokers working as temporary secretaries in order to put food on the table. The pay these workers earn from temping is usually enough to survive on—notwithstanding the 33 percent cut that the temporary agency gets for placing the temp—but the lack of benefits, especially health insurance, is daunting for many.

As in many other areas of our economy, supply and demand have combined to create a strong market for temporary help. Rates for temporaries in a profession, because they do not include benefits, can be quite high. Doctors may receive upwards of $300 per day while on temporary assignment; lawyers and computer experts can command more than $100 per hour. In some cases, temporary workers do earn benefits like paid holidays, vacation and sick days. A separate Department of Labor survey found that 75 percent of temps got a week of paid vacation if they worked more than 1,500 hours (42 weeks at 35 hours per week) and two weeks if they worked a full 40-hour week for 50 weeks. About 25 percent received at least partial support for the cost of their health insurance. These benefits are typically paid by the agency that places them, rather than the company that hires the temp.

The average temporary work assignment lasts up to two months with only 14 percent of the assignments lasting longer. Those that last longer usually involve professional services. Of course, the temporary worker absorbs the loss of income for any downtime between assignments.

AVERAGE HOURLY EARNINGS FOR TEMPORARY WORKERS, BY OCCUPATION, 1994

Position	Number of Workers	Average Hourly Earnings
All Occupations	**1,122,165**	**$ 7.74**
White-collar Occupations	**547,671**	**$ 9.37**
Professional Specialty and Technical	75,265	17.68
Professional Specialty	33,236	24.11
Commercial/Graphic Artists	1,712	17.63
Computer Systems Analysts	1,779	28.75
Designers	8,351	23.04
Engineers	10,243	28.54
Registered Nurses	6,164	21.98
Technical Writers	1,377	22.71
Technical	42,029	12.60
Computer Programmers	2,492	25.40
Drafters	5,821	13.64
Electrical and Electronic Technicians	6,853	10.32
Licensed Practical Nurses	4,908	14.30
Executive, Administrative, and Managerial	9,124	17.22
Accountants and Auditors	4,323	13.96
Accountants	4,220	13.96
Auditors	103	13.83
Marketing and Sales	31,513	6.61
Cashiers	3,397	5.72
Product Promoters	9,082	6.43
Telemarketing Sales Workers	9,041	7.18
Clerical and Administrative Support	431,769	7.96
Bookkeepers, Accounting, and Auditing Clerks	18,332	8.30
Computer Aides	249	9.44
Computer Operators and Printer Operators	4,217	10.63
Customer Service Workers	18,068	7.81
Data Entry Operators	57,416	7.15
General Office Clerks	90,182	6.78
Inventory Clerks	4,683	6.59
Receptionists	39,733	7.07
Secretaries	61,353	9.49
Typists and Word Processors	57,173	9.85

AVERAGE HOURLY EARNINGS FOR TEMPORARY WORKERS, BY OCCUPATION, 1994

Position	Number of Workers	Average Hourly Earnings
Blue-collar occupations	**444,895**	**$ 6.02**
Precision Production, Craft, and Repair	47,354	7.23
Assemblers, Electrical and Electronic Equipment	32,495	6.60
Machine Operators, Assemblers, and Inspectors	111,593	6.26
Assemblers, Other than Electrical and Electronic	73,092	5.97
Transportation and Material Movement	10,853	7.03
Motor Vehicle Operators	7,164	7.34
Handlers, Equipment Cleaners, Helpers, and Laborers	275,095	5.67
Construction Laborers	10,503	5.39
Helpers	6,768	5.93
Equipment Cleaners and Vehicle Washers	1,282	5.43
Laborers, Other than Construction	194,030	5.64
Material Handlers	62,512	5.80
Service Occupations	**56,624**	**$ 6.28**
Janitors and Cleaners	10,220	5.67
Maids and Housekeepers	2,912	5.26
Nursing Aides, Orderlies, and Attendants	23,387	7.01
Nursing Aides and Attendants	28,121	7.02

SOURCE: U.S. Bureau of Labor Statistics, *Occupational Compensation Survey: Temporary Help Supply Services, November 1994* (1995).

Full-time workers at temporary agencies who are responsible for hiring and placing temporary workers generally work on commission. Salary information for these employees, therefore, is highly variable and highly competitive, according to Bruce Steinberg, spokesman for the National Association of Temporary Services. The agent interviews and screens candidates for temporary positions at large companies and receives a percentage of the temp's earnings. The agency commission can run as high as half the total cost to the company seeking temporary help. It is not hard to understand, therefore, why some temps are dismayed to learn that they are receiving only $10 per hour when the company is paying the agency $20 for their services. About 20,000 people work full-time in temporary agencies. That number increases (as do the number of temporary workers) around the end of each decade, when the federal government hires large numbers of temporary workers to carry out the decennial census.

THE DAY-CARE WORKER

With the increase in single-parent families and families where both parents work, day care has become a fact of life in almost every American community. Today, there are over 200,000 day-care business establishments caring for more than 10 million children in America and employing close to a million day-care workers. The number of day-care workers is expected to grow by nearly 50 percent by 2005, according to the BLS.

About one in four institutions is affiliated with a religious institution. The rest are divided among schools and preschools, local and national chains, centers run by business firms for their own employees, and small mom-and-pop operations. Because so many centers are of this last variety (and consequently file no financial reports), total revenues generated in this burgeoning business are not known. Salary information is equally hard to find. In general, though, pay is on the low end. According to the Bureau of Labor Statistics, median weekly earnings for full-time salaried child-care workers were $260, with the top 10 percent earning over $460.

AVERAGE SALARIES OF CHILD CARE WORKERS, 1988–92[1]

	1988 Salary		1992 Salary		Percent Change
Category	**Hourly**	**Annually**	**Hourly**	**Annually**	**1988–92**
Lowest Paid Assistant	$5.16	$ 9,030	$5.08	$ 8,890	−1.5
Highest Paid Assistant	5.98	10,465	6.05	10,587	+1.2
Lowest Paid Teacher	6.35	11,112	6.50	11,375	+2.4
Highest Paid Teacher	8.19	14,332	8.85	15,488	+8.0

[1]All figures in constant (1992) dollars.
SOURCE: National Center for the Early Childhood Work Force, *National Child Care Staffing Study Revisited*, 1993.

A 1992 survey by the National Center for the Early Childhood Work Force, a research and advocacy project in Washington, D.C., corroborates these depressing results. The center found that the highest paid teachers at day-care centers, most of whom have college-level training in early childhood education, earned an average of $8.85 an hour, or less than $15,500 per year. Adjusted for inflation, that is only a 66 cent increase over the highest salary in 1988. Meanwhile, the salary of the highest paid assistant teacher increased all of 7 cents over the same four-year period, while the lowest paid assistant's salary declined 8 cents (1.5 percent) between 1988 and 1992. It's no wonder, then, that turnover in this field averages 40 percent each year. By comparison, turnover among public school teachers is less than 6 percent per year. Child care providers who work in public schools have salaries and turnover rates that are more commensurate with those of public school teachers than with day-care workers.

The growing number—and notoriety—of child abuse and molestation scandals surrounding disreputable day-care centers has led many states to adopt licensing requirements that regulate caregiver training. Educational requirements can range from a high school diploma to a college or post-graduate degree in childhood development. Many states require a Childhood Development Associate credential, offered by the Council for Early Childhood Professional Recognition, which also administers a training program.

FARMERS AND FARMWORKERS

Nothing symbolizes the unparalleled abundance of America more strikingly than the richness and diversity of our food supply. So fertile is the land and so efficient the agricultural system that our farms not only feed more than 260 million Americans as well as millions more overseas, we actually pay farmers to limit their production so prices won't collapse. Moreover, unlike more agrarian countries where up to 40 percent of the population may work in agriculture, the United States needs less than 2 percent of its people to produce such extraordinary results. In the history of farming, interestingly enough, can the principal source of America's industrial strength be found.

In 1776, when the "embattled farmers" began their revolution against the British, more than 95 percent of the 3 million colonists were directly involved in agriculture. By 1900, only 42 percent of the nation's 70 million people lived on farms. By 1950, the population had doubled to 150 million people, but the farm population had dwindled to 23 million, or just over 15 percent of the total population. Today, fewer than 5 million people live on farms even though the population has nearly doubled again since 1950. The number of people who actually work on farms is even less: In 1993, 2.6 million people worked on farms, about half as many as in 1970.

There are just over 2 million farms in the United States today, covering just under a billion acres of land. While more than 67,000 farms are of the giant commercial (over 2,000 acres) variety, the vast majority remain moderate-sized family-run operations. However, the average farm size continues to increase dramatically, from under 430 acres in 1982 to 470 acres in 1992. There are more than 412,000 farms of 10 to 50 acres, an additional 311,000 with 50 to 100 acres, and another 334,000 farms of 100 to 179,000 acres. As such, they remain as vulnerable to the vagaries of weather and politics as they have been throughout history. And unlike most other sectors of the economy, where income generally follows a gradual upward progression, farm income continues to fluctuate dramatically. Since 1986, however, gross and net farm income have both increased gradually every year, even as government payments to farms have decreased. Nevertheless, median income for farm families ($30,809) continues to lag behind that of nonfarm families ($34,300). However, median income by household (a different statistical measure than family income) was about the same for farm and nonfarm households.

Earnings for farmworkers, which once varied widely by age, race, and geographic region, are now fairly uniform across the country. According to the U.S. Department of Agriculture, median weekly earnings for the 848,000 hired farmworkers were $200 in 1992. Earnings were highest among those 35 to 44 years of age (who had median earnings of $250) and among those who had completed more than 12 years of school ($275); it was lowest among women (who had median weekly earnings of $175, compared to $216 for men), non-Hispanic blacks ($190), and workers between the ages of 15 and 19 ($100).

THE MIDDLEMEN: AGENTS, AUCTIONEERS, AND BROKERS

People who make their livings by representing the interests of another person to a third party are commonly referred to as middlemen or go-betweens. Their jobs consists of bringing buyers and sellers together (auctioneers and brokers) or of finding outlets for the work of people with special talents (agents). In both cases their chief function is negotiating a fair price or fee, and both earn their money by taking a percentage of that figure. Below are examples of both kinds of jobs, some commonplace, others slightly offbeat.

Executive Recruiters

In Europe they proudly proclaim themselves "headhunters." In America where the term is considered pejorative, they call themselves "executive search consultants." In either case, the profession is one which has raised a good deal of controversy. Many feel that headhunters are vultures setting out to steal well-trained, relatively happy bodies from their corporations with a siren's song of high pay and unlimited advancement. And, according to the critics, they don't do the job very well, often coaxing naive managers into situations that are doomed to failure. The executive recruiter takes the view that much like the broker he is putting buyer and seller together. One thing is certain, recruiting is a profession that can be very lucrative.

Recruiters get paid for work performed much like the salesman. The recruiting firm usually receives one third of the total first-year compensation of the selected candidate as its fee. Of this amount the recruiter who actually makes the placement receives 40 percent of the proceeds—or more if he or she brought the search assignment through the door. Much like the large law or consulting firms, compensation may grow if the recruiter plays a supervisory role or is a partner in the firm.

There can be vast differences in compensation and the nature of the work depending on the type of firm and the market for its service. Recruiters always work for the client company and their fees are paid by the hirer not the hired. This distinguishes recruiting firms from employment agencies. The arrangement with the client differs, however, according to the type of firm—contingency or retainer. Contingency firms operate much like employment agencies. They are given the right along with a number of other firms to search for candidates to fill vacancies. The hiring company pays the fee only to the firm which finds the person finally hired. The retainer firm, on the other hand, is granted an exclusive right to search for appropriate candidates: Progress payments are made, so the retainer firm receives up to 75 percent of its fee regardless of whether it completes the search or not.

As a rule, contingency firms operate at the lower end of the compensation spectrum, where quantity and speed rather than quality are the keys to success. Given the need to perform to get paid, the contingency world is highly competitive and some may be highly unprincipled in meeting the pressure. On the retainer side where the search may reach the proportions of finding a new CEO for IBM or American Express and compensation packages may be expressed in the upper 6 or 7 figures, quality, discretion, and judgment are emphasized. Here the process is more deliberate and the potential rewards per search are much higher. This type of search is a careful process of rooting out the most appropriate, best qualified people to fill demanding positions rather than running a list of qualified people past a client.

Given our rule of thumb on compensation—40 percent of the one third that the firm receives—ample compensation can be earned on either side of the industry. In general, the contingency recruiter has to make more placements, but there are more to be made. Since contingency firms work at the low end of the market, the average first-year compensation may be only $36,000. So in order for the recruiter to earn $75,000, it would take about 16 successful placements.

On the retainer side, where the average package is normally in the $100,000 to $200,000 range, it may take only half as many placements to reach the same range of income. An experienced retainer recruiter should be able to complete 8 to 12 searches a year. Thus the recruiter who completes 8 searches at $100,000 each would make about $100,000. This is about the industry average, according to *Executive Recruiter News,* an industry publication. For partners-level consultants at the upper end, compensation ranges from $300,000 to $500,000. The accompanying chart details revenues and billings per recruiter for the 10 largest U.S. firms. The compensation figures are derived by multiplying the billings per recruiter by the 40 percent commission.

Obviously most search firms are smaller than the 10 listed in the table, and a majority are operations of less than three people, grossing less than $1 million per year. But the estimates provide a good guide nonetheless, since size of billings in total has very little to do with individual compensation. Of more importance is the average fee value of the searches undertaken. There are many firms where that value exceeds $100,000. Since an experienced recruiter ought to be able to close one search a month, it would not be uncommon for the average professional in a small firm to earn as much or more than those at the larger firms, provided business is good.

REVENUES, BILLINGS, AND EARNINGS AT THE 10 LARGEST U.S. RETAINED SEARCH FIRMS

Firm Name	Total Revenues	Billings per Recruiter	Estimated Compensation per Recruiter[1]
Korn Ferry International	$102,200,000	$577,401	$231,000
Heidrick & Struggles, Inc.	86,900,000	886,735	354,700
SpencerStuart	69,700,000	967,361	386,900
Russell Reynolds Associates	61,700,000	582,075	232,800
Lamalie Amrop International	28,300,000	577,551	231,000
Paul Ray Berndtson	26,500,000	602,273	240,900
A.T. Kearney Executive Search	22,500,000	459,184	183,700
Ward Howell International	16,500,000	458,333	183,300
Egon Zehnder International	14,100,000	742,105	296,800
Witt/Kieffer Ford Hadelman & Lloyd	12,200,000	338,889	133,600

[1]Compensation figures calculated by *The American Almanac of Jobs and Salaries.*
SOURCE: © 1995 *Executive Recruiter News,* Reprinted with permission of Kennedy Publications, Fitzwilliam, NH.

Literary Agents

In a recent interview, Perry Knowlton, head of the Curtis Brown Ltd. Literary Agency, gave a condensed explanation of the agent's role as publishing middleman. "It seems to me that 50 years ago publishers looked down on agents and didn't want to have anything to do with them. Nowadays, publishers would almost rather work with an agent. He leaves the relationship between the editor and the author relatively free of all the nastiness of the business aspects of writing."

Agents represent authors to publishers. They evaluate proposals or manuscripts and, if they deem them salable, submit them to the most suitable publishers for consideration. The right house is not automatically the one offering the highest advance, either: Agents have been known to choose a house offering less if the editor is enthusiastic enough about the product to stay behind it through all phases of the publishing process or if he or she has the right reputation for a special kind of book.

Once upon a time, book projects were submitted to only one publisher at a time. Nowadays, agents routinely send even first novels to several houses simultaneously, complete with response datelines. Some 20 years ago, "superagent" Scott Meredith revolutionized the business with the introduction of the auction. Since then, it has become common practice to send properties to ten or more publishers, giving them the choice of telephoning a bid on the appointed day or offering an earlier preemptive bid instead.

Once a sale is made, agents run a fine-tooth comb through contracts, which tend to arrive in a standard form that gives the publisher most of the advantages unless marked otherwise. Later, agents often become involved in subsidiary rights sales, such as magazine excerpts, TV and film deals, and paperback contracts. In between, there's a lot of hand-holding and encouragement.

Successful literary agents usually combine a knowledge of book publishing with an instinct for public taste that is often more finely honed than that of many editors. When agent J. Garon took on John Grisham, for example, his work had already been turned down by many publishers. But Garon believed in the author and persevered. After receiving a super deal from Doubleday, through Garon's efforts, Grisham's tepid novels have become international bestsellers in hardcover and paperback, and have been made into high-budget movies as well.

Agents' earnings come from commissions, the standard rate being 10 percent of all the author's earnings from the book, including advance and royalties. Many now take 15 percent, but why any author would pay an agent 50 percent more than most people charge is a mystery. Many smaller agents also deduct expenses made on a client's behalf. The individual nature of the business makes it impossible to gauge earnings with any accuracy. It's only safe to say they range enormously, often getting better with time. Literary agenting usually does not pay off for the first year or two, before books sold to publishers are actually printed and capable of earning royalties, and before agents establish the reputation that brings them money-generating clients. But the ultimate possibilities are dazzling. Before his death in 1993, Meredith said published estimates that his aftertax income was $300,000 were "low." When you look at just part of his extensive and impressive client list you believe him. It includes Norman Mailer (for whom Meredith negotiated a $4 million deal), Taylor Caldwell, Carl Sagan, Abba Eban, Arthur C. Clarke, and the estates of Eugene O'Neill and P. G. Wodehouse.

Models' Agents

Models' agents arrange bookings for their listed models. When advertising agencies, clothing designers, department stores, and others requiring the use of a model have an opening, they contact an agency, sometimes several. The agency then sends the models fitting the client's requirements on what is often termed a "go-see."

The four biggest modeling agencies are in New York City: The Eileen Ford Agency, Wilhelmina, Women, and Elite Model Management. They are the largest because they represent the most famous models. The Eileen Ford Agency boasts such big names as Christy Turlington, Bridget Hall, Lauren Hutton, Cheryl Tiegs, and Margaux Hemingway. Among the cream at Elite (whose owner John Casablancas, has been locked in a much-published model tug-of-war with both Wilhelmina and Ford) are the ubiquitous über-model-*cum*-actress-*cum* MTV talk show host Cindy Crawford, model/actress/makeup endorser Isabella Rosellini, model/restaurateur/novelist/singer Naomi Campbell, and Linda Evangelista, who is content to do nothing but model (to the tune of $3 million a year). The top models at Women are *Sports Illustrated* swimsuit issue covergirl Elle Macpherson and Kate Moss, the skin-and-bones pioneer of Calvin Klein's "waif look." Wilhelmina's top models include Shaun Casey and Kim Alexis, who does much work for Almay and Maybelline.

These agents wield a double-edged sword in earning their money. Standard commissions are 20 percent from the model plus 10 percent from the client. In other words, if a booking comes in for a $1,000 assignment, the agency bills the client for $1,100 and also deducts $200 from the check handed the model, who receives $800. When you consider that percentage on a $15,000 assignment, which is what the top models earn for a day of fashion shooting or runway work, or on a $100,000 payment for a major fashion show, the net result is a not untidy profit, even after the telephone bills have been paid.

Real Estate Agents and Brokers

Like other types of agents, people in real estate embody the hustle-to-get-ahead nature of hard-core free enterprise. This is the business of the mythical Florida land scheme, and in which 1 in 18 Californians holds a real estate license.

Previously one of the faster growing occupations, jobs for real estate agents and brokers are not expected to grow any faster than the average rate through the year 2005. There are just under 400,000 agents and brokers in the United States today. The vast majority of these are sales agents, independent sales workers who contract out their services to real estate brokers in return for a portion—usually half—of the agency's commission on the sale of property. Brokers, who number about 70,000, are independent business people who buy and sell real estate for others, and in some cases rent and manage properties for a fee. Brokers may also help prospective buyers line up financing for their purchase in order to facilitate a sale.

An additional 44,000 people work as *real estate appraisers,* who provide unbiased estimates of a property's value and quality. This is the fastest growing occupation in the real estate industry, with an expected growth of 25 percent by 2005.

All 50 states and the District of Columbia require prospective agents to be a high school graduate, be at least 18 years old, and pass a written test of their knowledge of property laws and real estate transactions, in order to receive a realtor's license. Most states also require classroom training of at least 30 hours for a sales license and 90 hours for a broker's license. Brokers generally also need anywhere from one to three years of selling experience before they can apply for the broker's license.

The standard commission on the sale of a house is 6 percent. Traditionally, this figure is presented to sellers as if it were a legislated rate. However, the commission is negotiable; and in the present climate of frenzied buying and selling, it's often slashed as part of the broker's competition to obtain listings. On the other hand, if a firm can receive an exclusive listing, giving its brokers exclusive showing rights for a set period of time, commissions can rise to 10 to 15 percent. Some agents routinely charge higher commissions on properties valued under $150,000.

The money can be excellent—if you can survive the first year. Newcomers go through brief, intensive training, and then, according to Long Beach, New York, agent Doris Newalk, "You don't get to sell houses until you've been there six months to a year. You handle rentals at first, for a small percentage, but that cannot support you. You need another job or another wage-earner in the family for that first year."

Because industry averages reflect not just the long-time agent but also the large number of people who leave the business after less than a year, salary averages are low. So even though median earnings for full-time agents were about $19,000 a year in 1990, the agent who has been in the business for at least a few years earns a figure closer to $50,000. And as in all sales jobs, what you earn depends on what you sell. According to the *New York Times,* top agents selling Manhattan's and Los Angeles's choicest co-ops, town houses, and condominiums earn upwards of $200,000. Brokers had a median gross personal income (after expenses) of $50,000 a year according to the Department of Labor.

There is a small but aggressive movement afoot in the industry to sell houses not for the traditional commission but for a straight flat fee instead.

The savings to sellers can be substantial. A broker who asks a flat $2,000 fee for selling a $100,000 house, for example, will save the owner $4,000. Flat-rate brokers make their profit from the wider volume of sales.

This approach has met resistance from other brokers, to say the least. Gina Williams, a Los Angeles broker who began a service for a straight $1,995 fee, at first found her method obtained lucrative results. Her listings went from 35 in the first month of business to 70 two months later. Suddenly her troubles began. She, and her clients, received obscene telephone calls and found their homes' For Sale signs hacked to bits. Then she started receiving death threats (including threats to her children's lives), pieces of garbage were strewn on her lawn, and her office was firebombed. She brought a lawsuit against the San Fernando Valley Board of Realtors and others. In the meantime, Williams is keeping a low profile, selling condominiums for a developer. But the flat-fee idea continues to win converts, with new brokerage firms opening yearly around the country. Opportunities exist particularly in San Francisco, Boston, New York, Chicago, and various Sun Belt cities, especially Phoenix, Tampa, and Dallas, where population increases continue to exceed the national average.

Another approach fast winning adherents in the western and southwestern United States is the buyer's agent, who receives his or her commission from the person seeking to buy a house rather than from the seller. Unheard of as little as ten years ago, buyer's agents now number close to 40,000, sparking the ire of traditional seller's agents, who are reluctant to share their commissions.

Sports Agents

Most people representing professional athletes have two things in common: They are lawyers, and they are very well heeled. Just a glimpse at the lists of sports stars' salaries in Chapter II of this book will reveal why sports agents make so much money. The standard agent's fee for contract negotiation is 5 percent, which amounts to $100,000 on a $2 million contract, a commonplace figure for today's sports superstars. Some agents with several multimillion dollar athletes in their stable often wield substantial power in professional sports; at times their ability to shape team rosters and payrolls exceeds that of a team's general manager. For example, it was rumored that agent David Falk urged Xavier McDaniel to leave New York and accept an offer from the Boston Celtics because Falk was worried that McDaniel would have turned the Knicks into a serious title threat to the Chicago Bulls, whose star player, Michael Jordan, is Falk's bread and butter. Of course, since Falk also represents Knick's center Patrick Ewing, the rumors were probably little more than conjecture by a few sportswriters, but it's not hard to imagine other agents being motivated solely by the interests of their most profitable clients.

The proliferation of multimillion dollar contracts for athletes has filled the sports pages with the names of as many agents as stars. Many agents specialize in one particular sport, though they usually have a few clients in each sport. Falk specializes primarily in basketball; Jerry Kapstein and Richard Moss are among the best known baseball agents; Leigh Steinberg's stable of athletes contains mostly football players, most of whom are quarterbacks.

Agents in other sports like golf and tennis may not be household names, but when their clients bring in millions of dollars each year, the agents still profit from it. Golf and tennis agents generally receive 10 percent of the player's winnings and as much as 25 percent of endorsement income. For well-known players like Jimmy Connors or John McEnroe, who may not be at the top of their games, endorsement income often far outstrips winnings, making the agent's percentage substantial. For more information about endorsements, see the entry in Chapter II: "In the Public Eye and Behind the Scenes."

There are other middlemen in sports. In boxing, managers usually receive 33 percent of their fighters' prizes, while trainers receive about 10 percent. There are exceptions, however, especially when a fighter hits it big. Mike Tyson, for example, dumped manager Bill Cayton (who received only 20 percent of Tyson's prizes) in favor of an arrangement with fight promoter Don King. Fighters Larry Holmes and Michael Spinks managed themselves. Former heavyweight champion, Riddick Bowe, is managed by Rock Newman, who was relatively unknown until Bowe wrested the title from Evander Holyfield.

Travel Agents

For many years, the deregulation of the airline industry made the professional travel agent irreplaceable. The dizzying array of options that opened to travelers—a simple flight from New York to Los Angeles suddenly could present a choice of four or five airlines and six or seven fare options—almost necessitated exploiting a travel agents' skills at finding the cheapest and most convenient itinerary. And the price to the consumer—nothing—was right.

Ironically, though, today's deregulated airline industry may now spell the travel agents' death knell. For while deregulation no doubt has reduced the cost of air travel, it has also resulted in the establishment of three megagiants (American, Delta, and United), that increasingly dictate prices and fees in the industry. So when Delta, American, and Northwest airlines all announced in February 1995 that they would no longer pay travel agents the customary 10 percent commission on airline tickets, but would instead cap commissions at $50 for a domestic round-trip ticket, many agents felt powerless to do anything about it. And in order to survive, most agents responded by saying they would have to pass on the fees to their customers instead (and by filing an antitrust lawsuit, which is still pending, against the major airlines).

Business travelers will probably be exempted from the new customer fees, as will frequent and valued clients who do large amounts of business with one travel agency. But it remains to be seen whether casual travelers will continue to use travel agents to book low-cost airline tickets if the price of their tickets is augmented by a travel agent fee ranging from $10 to $25 per ticket. In the computer age, many consumers now have as much (or sometimes more) travel information at their fingertips as some travel agents, and comparing fares can be as simple as checking a few addresses on the Internet. And for consumers without home computers, airline ticket kiosks installed in more than 800 supermarkets and pharmacies nationwide are available to help them make their travel decisions and even purchase tickets along with their cosmetics and comestibles.

Not all the news for travel agents is so dire, however. In the wake of the airlines' decision to limit fees, other segments of the travel industry have announced that they will raise the travel agent's commission. Carnival Cruise Lines, for example, said it would raise the agent's take from 10 to 12 percent. Amtrak announced that on short-term promotions, the agent's commission would be as high as 15 percent instead of the 10 percent it now awards. And the Hotel Reservations Network, a nationwide hotel booking service, said it would double its 5 percent agent's commission to 10 percent. Also, commissions on international airfares, which range from 8 to 11 percent, were not affected by the airlines' recent reduction.

It's no wonder, then, that many agents are predicting that selling airline tickets will be a much smaller portion of what they do in the future. According to the American Society of Travel Agents, airline tickets constituted 61 percent of travel agency revenues in 1992. Today, industry officials say, the percentage is closer to the low 50s and it is expected to decline even further. Moreover, with agency commissions running at over $1 billion per year at the biggest airlines (making it their third biggest expense after salaries and fuel), the airlines may not lament some drop-off in business from travel agents, especially if those same customers book their tickets directly. Currently, only about one in five customers books airline tickets without a travel agent.

There are about 250,000 travel agents working in 32,500 agencies across the United States. And even though close to 3,000 agencies go broke every year (nearly three times as many as in 1987), job opportunities for travel agents are expected to expand much faster than average for all jobs, as business and leisure travel continue to grow. Some estimates place growth in this industry at over 80,000 jobs over the next 10 years.

The number of jobs in this field is heavily dependent on the health of the economy, as travel is one of the first things businesses and individuals cut back on during hard times. Most agents at travel agencies are salaried, but some work as independent contractors. Those who have been in the business long enough to develop a following may work at an agency's offices but receive a portion of the agency's commissions (sometimes as high as 50 to 70 percent of what the agency receives). Others may work through, but outside, an agency's offices or as part-timers. These agents may receive 25 to 50 percent of the agency's commission in lieu of salary. About 9 out of 10 agents work for an agency; the rest are self-employed.

Earnings for travel agents are determined by many factors, including experience, sales ability, and the size and location of the agency. According to *Travel Weekly* magazine, beginning travel agents earned about $12,000 in 1992, while experienced agents earned anywhere from $15,000 to $25,000. Those numbers are not appreciably different from salaries earned by travel agents in 1986. Salaried agents usually have standard benefits like health and disability insurance and paid vacations.

Self-employed agents pay their own benefits, but they make considerably more than the averages printed above. However, the investment required to start an independent travel agency is estimated to be approximately $50,000 to $75,000.

Something which must be considered, however, are the travel benefits that come with the job. These can include discounts as high as 75 percent off domestic travel and the same off international flights after one year in the business. Hotels also offer many concessions to agents, including free rooms during off-peak season.

Even with these benefits, the salary and income figures are surprisingly low. Brian Huggins, of Travel Age East, found several explanations for the rather low figures. "The business is a people-intensive one of high expenses—telephone, promotion, and labor—and low monetary return." A large number of people working as travel agents are women who are not primarily family wage earners but who enjoy the work for the considerable travel benefits offered. Many young people also work for agencies for the same reason.

"Most men in this business are agency owners," says Huggins, "and agency owners are the only people in the field who do make good money." As usual, this fact of business life is a tough one to change. In an industry dominated by family operators, many agency owners were brought into the business by relatives who were already in travel. One assumes that in the future, more daughters will have both the interest and the opportunity to inherit the family business.

Job opportunities for travel agents will be available in most regions of the country, but according to P. Jason King, president of Yours in Travel

Personnel Agency, most travel agent jobs will be found on the East Coast, particularly in Boston, New York City, Washington, D.C., and Florida. California, Chicago, Dallas, Denver, and Phoenix will also offer good opportunities. Strong growth in managerial, professional, and sales occupations—the people who travel the most on business—should also spark an increase in sales for travel agents, especially those with corporate clients. Travel agents with foreign language skills will also thrive in the coming years.

Agencies that are best able to adapt to the changing travel environment will have the most success in the 1990s. That means creating specialized itineraries to places like Disney World, the Grand Ole Opry, or the Great Barrier Reef. It also means catering to specialized audiences like senior citizens, music aficionados, honeymooners, or the environmentally conscious. And it also means cruises, cruise, cruises. Agents typically receive a 12 percent commission on cruises, which sell for several thousand dollars per person. Because of the high dollar volume involved, more than 800 travel agencies now sell cruises exclusively. As more airlines continue to cut their commissions, this trend can only be expected to continue.

Auctioneers

The auction has long been a popular way of selling all kinds of things from rare works of art to parcels of real estate, household goods, even livestock. The National Auctioneers' Association, a trade group with 6,000 members, estimates that the number of auctioneers has doubled in the last decade. One reason for the increase is the possibility of good pay. The head of a Missouri school of auctioneering estimates annual income to be about $40,000 to $50,000 for a successful auctioneer.

As with all middleman jobs, the auctioneer takes a percentage of the total sale as a commission for his efforts. For real estate the figure is usually 6 percent; for household sales, 20 percent or more.

WRITERS

The term "writer" carries with it a lot of cultural baggage, some of it dragged along from the nineteenth century, some from the era when Fitzgerald and Hemingway were supposedly forging a modern American sensibility. Images of the writer as a lonely artist or indefatigable scholar are ones we all absorbed in school, probably to the detriment of our own development: Who, after all, could measure up? On the other hand, at that age who knew that people actually had jobs as writers that didn't require psychic immolation and an unwavering commitment to Art and Knowledge?

For most professionals, however, today as well as in the past, writing is not so much a creative exercise as it is a skill, a way to make a living, a career like banking or engineering. Writers who work on a freelance basis for magazines, for example, must be able to adapt their styles to the publication's needs. Until the writer has a reputation in a particular subject, he or she will have to cover a variety of topics for several magazines. Technical writers, on the other hand, must acquire knowledge in complex subjects such as chemistry or medicine so that their writing and editing skills can be used to communicate information to the public or to business leaders.

For young college graduates the question of whether to pursue a career as a writer is not a simple one. Some observers say that jobs for writers will be plentiful. In a society where the rudimentary forms of literacy are supposedly declining faster than enrollments in English literature classes, one would think the skill of writing would be marketable. But others insist that the "crisis" in literacy is a media-created myth, since the number of books and magazines have proliferated over the last decade in unprecedented fashion. In fact, not only are more people reading more than ever before, more writers are generating more words than society can possibly absorb. Although almost 50,000 new books are published each year, publishers tell of receiving literally thousands of unsolicited manuscripts which not only don't get read, but frequently are returned unopened. Magazine editors, too, say they receive more articles and suggestions than ever before.

Just how many writers or would-be writers there are may be impossible to ascertain. Professional groups such as the Writers Guild and the Authors Guild, both of which require at least a modicum of success for membership, account for only 15,000 people. But other signs, such as the 100,000-plus circulation of *Writer's Digest* and the brisk sales of an annual publication called *Writer's Marketplace,* indicate that a large number of people are looking for realistic, professional advice about how to make money as a writer. Many of them are, of course, disguised as editorial assistants and copy editors in publishing houses, or as accountants and housewives who work on their computers in spare hours. What they have in common, however, is the tenacity to pursue very demanding work without guarantee of reward.

This section focuses on writers who produce material for books and magazines, and it ends with a short discussion of the fast-growing field of technical writing. For those readers interested in other kinds of writing jobs, see in Chapter II the sections "Who Makes What in the Film Industry" for scriptwriters and "Behind the Scenes in Television" for television news writers; still more information can be found in Chapter V in the section "Public Relations" and in Chapter VI in the section "The Newspaper."

Writers of Books

If you've written your first book, or even part of one, and are looking to find a publisher, the best advice anyone can give you is to find a literary agent who likes your work well enough to represent it (see the previous section, "The Middlemen"). So many manuscripts are being written today that editors find it almost impossible to properly evaluate unsolicited work. Most editors now rely on a small enclave of New York City–based agents to screen the works of would-be writers. But even if you do find a willing agent, there are some basic items in every publisher's contract that every writer should know about, mainly because they all affect one's income. Whether you write fiction or nonfiction, reference books or textbooks, and whether your words appear between cloth or paper covers, the following terms are relevant to your work: *royalties, advances against royalties,* and *subsidiary rights.*

Royalties

In those forms of publishing designed to make a profit, the author usually receives from the publisher a percentage of the take based on the list price of each book. On clothbound trade books (the ones you see in bookstores), the standard royalty clause is 10 percent on the first 5,000 copies sold, 12.5 percent on the next 2,500, and 15 percent on everything after 7,500 copies. So, for example, if a $15 book sold 10,000 copies the author would earn $17,812; if it sold 50,000 copies the figure would be $107,812, and if it became a bestseller and sold 200,000 copies, the author would earn $445,312.

Royalties on paperbacks are always lower, because the margin of profit is smaller, or at least that's what the publishers say. On trade paperbacks such as the one you're reading, royalty rates range from 6 percent of the list price to 10 percent, rarely going any higher. Trade paperbacks, the fastest growing form of publishing, are priced above $8.95 and are usually sold in bookstores or department stores. Mass-market paperbacks are the least expensive and are distributed through candy stores, drugstores, and airport shops as well as traditional book outlets. Royalty rates for mass-market paperbacks vary greatly depending on the author. A standard royalty arrangement for an author not considered a star property is 6 percent of the list price on the first 150,000 copies, 8 percent on 150,000 to 500,000, and 10 percent thereafter. Perennially bestselling authors such as James Michener reportedly receive 15 percent on every paperback copy.

College textbook publishers usually pay royalties based on the book's net price—i.e., what the bookstore paid for it, which is usually 20 percent less than the list price. Standard royalty rates are 12 percent of net, rising to

15 percent and then 18 percent depending on the projected sales rates. College publishers will frequently try to pay less, but with some prodding most are willing to follow these guidelines.

Advance Against Royalties

When a publisher decides to take on a project, he or she will usually pay the author a lump sum of money called an advance. The practice developed to help struggling authors eat and pay the rent while they finished their books. It has evolved into the most important point of negotiation for books sought by several publishers.

Strictly speaking, money given "in advance" of publication is actually a no-interest loan, since authors are required to pay it back through their royalties after the book is published. No royalties are paid until the advance has been earned back through actual sales of the book. If the book does not sell in sufficient quantities, however, the author is not required to pay back any of the advance money.

Most advances are paid in two installments—half on signing of the contract, half on delivery of the final manuscript. When the sum exceeds $20,000 or so, it is often paid one third on signing, one third on delivery of half the manuscript, and one third on delivery of the rest.

Authors and their agents are, of course, enamored of large advances, but not just for immediate gain. In theory a big advance means that the publisher will do much more promotional work so that the book sells and the lump sum can be recouped. In today's economic and cultural climate, however, agents claim that the size of the average advance is declining. A very good project rarely brings over $75,000 they say. Supposedly this is because so much big money is going to what publishers believe will be the boffo bestseller, often an imitation of a book already on the bestseller lists. New American Library for example, paid an unprecedented $800,000 for a first novel called *Woman's Work* which the publisher claimed would "do for the advertising business what *Scruples* did for the fashion business" (whatever that was). While many publishers keep searching for derivative works, most first novels and serious nonfiction books bring advances of $5,000 to $25,000.

Until recent years advances of over $1 million have been paid only to such established writers as Norman Mailer, John Irving, and Arthur C. Clarke. Today any writer who has had a bestseller commands millions in upfront payments. Robert Ludlum, John Jakes, Len Deighton, Jean Auel, Tom Clancy, Ken Follett, and Jeffrey Archer now sign multibook deals for $10 to $15 million. In 1995 Clive Cussler entered this exclusive circle when he signed a two-book deal for $14 million (for United States and Canadian rights *only*).

Stephen King, however, can demand $10 million *per* book. The enormous success of romance novels has also brought the big advance to the most read authors of that genre as well: Barbara Taylor Bradford and Danielle Steel all command over $6 million for each book.

Among nonfiction writers Kitty Kelley has been the highest paid in recent years. She reportedly received over $2 million for her scathing biography of Nancy Reagan and nearly $5 million for a book about the British royal family.

Celebrities of any type—actor, athlete or business person—can almost always obtain a substantial advance for their autobiographies. In recent years Marlon Brando ($5 million), Mia Farrow ($3 million), General Norman Schwarzkopf ($5 million), Magic Johnson ($5 million for two books), and Sam Walton ($4 million) were the biggest money winners. And the O.J. Simpson double murder trial made millionaires of prosecutors Marcia Clark and Christopher Darden, who, despite failing to win a conviction, signed book deals valued at $4 million and $2 million respectively.

In any kind of publishing the key to obtaining a large advance—say, one over $100,000—is to get more than one publisher interested in the project. The book is then auctioned off to the highest bidder. Even a first-time author (with a skillful agent), can negotiate an advance approaching $1 million if he or she succeeds in getting several publishers to bid against each other. Most trade publishers today often pay higher advances than they could ever realistically expect to recover through sales alone. For books with very good sales prospects the publisher counts on income from subsidiary rights to make up the difference and then some.

Subsidiary Rights

Most material written to appear in book form can usually have a life outside that medium. All writers should know that in exchange for putting up the capital, publishers expect to share in any income derived from any other printed version of the work.

Magazines and newspapers are obvious examples of media that thrive on reprinting excerpts from books. Sometimes they choose whole chapters, sometimes rewritten summaries of whole sections. The author is almost always paid for this, but the sum depends on the size of the excerpt, the nature and circulation of the periodical or newspaper, and, of course, the reputation of the writer and the topicality of the subject. In addition, if the publication acquires the rights to publish the excerpt before the book appears (these are called "first serial rights") it usually must pay more than if the book is already available ("second serial rights"). If you are a writer without an agent, you should know that publishers usually split second serial fees 50–50, but for first serial rights the writer keeps 90 percent.

Two traditional, and frequently very lucrative, sources of subsidiary rights income are simply reprints of the existing work after it is published. First, if a clothbound trade book is picked up by one or more book clubs, especially the two largest, Book-of-the-Month Club and the Literary Guild, the author will receive another advance as well as royalties on every copy of the club's edition. Second, if the publisher licenses another house to do a paperback version of the work, the author receives another advance and royalties. For bestselling books or those expected to be bestsellers, these deals can be very lucrative.

Over the past five years or so the blockbuster paperback sale has diminished in visibility and importance as large hardcover publishing houses have merged with or acquired the major paperback houses. Now almost all of the megadeals include all rights including paperback. The largest paperback sales in recent years were for Terry McMillan's *Waiting to Exhale* ($2.6 million), Robert Harris' *Fatherland* ($1.8 million) and Gail Sheehy's *The Silent Passage* ($1 million).

Of increasing importance to authors is the value of their work overseas. Many of the largest publishers—Penguin USA, HarperCollins, Random House—are now international corporations while others (most notably Bantam Doubleday Dell) are owned outright by large foreign publishers. All these houses seek world rights for their properties and authors (and their agents) and often must struggle to obtain fair market prices for these rights. Most publishers will give the author 75 percent of monies received from a foreign publisher but if they are selling books to their own company, be it in London or in Australia, they try to pay the author as little as possible.

As a result, most agents try to retain foreign rights, preferring to hire an agent who specializes in this field. Germany, Japan, the United Kingdom, France, Spain, and Holland are all excellent markets for U.S. titles and their total advances can reach $100,000 to $300,000 quite easily.

And with Hollywood waiting to cannibalize on the success of any bestseller, the movie rights fees for a popular page-turner can often outweigh the earnings from the book. Stephen King, John Grisham, and now *Bridges of Madison County* author Robert James Waller have all profited even more handsomely from the movie versions than from the books they were based on. But perhaps the most curious example is that of Nicholas Evans, who received a $3.2 million book deal for his novel *The Horse Whisperer* only *after* he had negotiated another $3.2 million from Hollywood Pictures for the film rights.

The other burgeoning areas are audio and electronic publishing (CD-ROM especially). Most publishers try to retain 50 percent of all the monies but strong resistance has begun to set in as these new media begin to become commonplace. Now publishers who retain these rights are merely acting as the author's agent so a 20 to 50 percent fee should be more than adequate.

Magazine Writers

Most magazine articles are written by freelancers, not staff writers, who produce mostly service copy—blurbs about clothes and other merchandise featured. The reasons are twofold. The first is cost; it is much cheaper to pay a one-shot fee to a freelancer than an annual salary and benefits. The other reason is originality. Editors, chained to their desks, rely on freelancers to spot emerging trends, uncover topical issues, and sniff out stories. The pay for all this work ranges from dismal to dazzling, depending on the circulation and reputation of the magazine.

Magazine writing requires the ability to come up with fresh, original story ideas and then follow through with good research, reporting, and writing. Many writers break into the field with a 1,000-word department article, also known as a front- or back-of-the-book piece, which covers specific topics like health, personal finance, or education. Usually writers need an established track record, demonstrated by "clips" from smaller publications, before they are assigned major features, running from 1,000 to 5,000 words. With 11,000 magazines in the United States, covering virtually every field and interest, there are lots of opportunities for writers to begin at small publications.

To get an assignment, a writer must first understand a magazine's niche. Each of the dozens of women's magazines, for example, believes it carves out an editorial market no one else covers. A frequent reason for a rejection letter is that the idea is not clearly targeted for that particular magazine's readers. Editors lament, "Do freelancers actually *read* our magazine?"

A story is usually proposed in a query letter, which describes the idea, outlines the research and reporting, and gives the writer's credentials. Many magazines will only consider queries, automatically rejecting completed manuscripts. If the idea is accepted, the writer signs a contract agreeing to do the piece for a specified amount on deadline. If the writer is new, often the editor will assign the piece on speculation (or spec), meaning that the magazine will consider the finished piece but is not obligated to buy it.

The payment can range from 20 cents a word to $4 a word, depending on the writer's reputation and the publication. *The New Yorker* is reported to pay some of its marquee writers upward of $20,000 for a 10,000 word piece. *Vanity Fair,* especially during the Tina Brown era, paid name writers about $10,000 for an exclusive story. For an established freelancer without a national reputation, the going rate is about $1 a word, although some magazines will pay up to $2 a word. Most offer a kill fee of 20 to 25 percent if a contracted piece is not used.

While some people do make a living writing for magazines, it is a difficult life that requires persistence, hustle, and a high energy level, not to mention talent. Many freelancers supplement their magazine income by writing for corporations, public relations firms, educational publishers, and other less glamorous outlets.

REPRESENTATIVE PAYMENTS FOR MAGAZINE ARTICLES

Magazine	Payment
American Way	$850 and up for 1,000 to 3,500 words
Cat Fancy	$35 to $400 for 500 to 3,000 words
Good Housekeeping	$1,500+ for 1,500 to 2,500 words
Outdoor Life	$350 to $600 for 1,000 words; $900 to $1200 for 2,000 words
Parenting	$500 to $2,000 for 1,000 to 3,500 words
PC World	$50 to $2,000 for 1,500 to 2,500 words
Playboy	$500 for department (1,000 words); $3,000+ for feature (3,000 to 7,000 words)
Soap Opera Digest	$150 to $500 for 1,000 to 2,000 words

Source: *The Writer's Market,* 1995.

Ghostwriters

Some call them hacks, some call them godsends, but there's no doubt that many people do call on ghostwriters for assistance in literary ventures. And they have been with us a long time: It's thought that Roman emperor Nero's speeches were ghosted by Seneca, that *The Autobiography of Ulysses S. Grant* was written by Mark Twain, and that even Washington's Farewell Address was prepared by Alexander Hamilton. More recent items of speculation include *The Autobiography of Malcolm X:* How much was written by Alex Haley? And what part was Theodore Sorensen's contribution to John F. Kennedy's *Profiles in Courage?*

Ghostwriters' clients are a varied lot. They include gothic romance publishing houses, politicians, scientists, celebrities, and wealthy narcissists looking to tell their story whether or not anyone will buy it.

Today, many ghostwriters work as part of an agency. S. J. Michelson, 73, employs 200 from his New York–based service. According to *The New York Times,* Robin Moore, credited with *The French Connection, The Green Berets,* and *The Happy Hooker,* farmed out most of the 45 or so books published under his name in the last ten years.

If the credit is elusive, the money is quite tangible in ghosting. Several established writers will tackle most projects for between $1,000 and $6,000 in a flat-fee arrangement. Where books are involved, most ghosts opt for what has become the standard in publishing: 50 percent of the author's earnings. For major books the ghostwriter frequently receives a large fee or advance. Michael Novak, for example, received $80,000 for *Iacocca* (Iacocca himself made $6 million); Novak, however, has become the most sought-after "ghost" and now gets full billing with the authors (including Tip O'Neill and Nancy Reagan) and probably half the royalties.

Technical Writers

Technical writers work for industry, government, and nonprofit organizations, translating technological terms and facts into easily understood language. They produce instructional aides, training manuals, and public relations brochures. Technical writers may also prepare reports to corporate stockholders or work with scientists in preparing complex documents or research papers.

There are more than 25,000 technical writers and editors working in America in just about every industry. Federal, state, and local government agencies employ large numbers of technical writers, as do large companies in the chemical, computer manufacturing, aerospace, aviation, electronics, and pharmaceutical industries.

According to the Society for Technical Communication, a professional organization of more than 15,000 technical writers, the average salary for technical writers and editors was $42,469 in 1995. Starting salaries ranged from $22,178 to $43,200, and top salaries for senior management writers and editors ranged as high as $63,000. Salaries were highest in New England and on the West Coast, and lowest in the midwestern states of Kentucky, Ohio, Indiana, and Michigan. Technical writing is also a good career for women: They earned 93 cents per men's dollar, compared to an average of 70 cents for all other occupations. This is a significant increase from the society's 1988 survey, when women earned 86 cents per men's dollar.

SALARIES FOR TECHNICAL WRITERS

Category	First Quartile	Average Salary	Third Quartile
Total	**$35,000**	**$42,469**	**$50,000**
Employment Level			
Entry Level	$25,000	$30,721	$34,750
Mid-Level, Nonsupervisory	33,000	39,694	45,000
Mid-Level, Management	39,800	46,608	52,500
Senior Management, Nonsupervisory	42,875	49,044	55,065
Senior Management	44,500	54,100	60,950

SALARIES FOR TECHNICAL WRITERS

Category	First Quartile	Average Salary	Third Quartile
Education			
Bachelor's Degree	$33,000	$41,213	$48,000
Master's Degree	37,308	44,865	52,000
Doctorate	40,250	46,357	50,750
Industry			
Computer Industry	$36,000	$43,709	$50,270
All Other Industries	32,812	40,732	47,000
Sex			
Female	$34,750	$41,986	$48,260
Male	35,000	43,637	51,000
Age			
20–29	$29,000	$34,033	$39,300
30–39	35,000	40,978	45,750
40–49	37,911	45,248	51,900
50+	42,000	48,464	54,000
Years of Experience			
Less than 2	28,780	$36,714	$44,000
2–5	30,112	36,062	40,425
6–10	36,000	42,223	47,566
11+	42,000	49,444	55,075

SOURCE: Society for Technical Communication, *1995 Salary Survey.*

WOMEN'S WAGES

Three decades of affirmative action have opened doors for millions of women, although not as wide as hoped by many. Now, affirmative action programs are coming under attack not only from the Republican Congress but also from President Clinton, who wants a critical "review" of the legislation. In California, a lobbying group is attempting to abolish the state's "preferential treatment" laws by referendum. And a 1995 *Wall Street Journal*/ABC poll found that two out of three Americans oppose affirmative action.

Is this another form of backlash? Why the opposition to helping women and minorities get ahead? Critics cite varying causes. One is a perception that the numbers of groups covered by affirmative action have expanded beyond women and minorities to the disabled, homosexuals, and other underrepresented people. Many executives complain that "white men need not apply" is an unstated requirement for many job openings. Others argue that unqualified women and minorities have been promoted over men. Anecdotes circulate like the (true) tale of the National Forestry Services quest for "unqualified applicants" to fill $20,000-a-year jobs so it could meet its quota of 43 percent female workers.

Women's groups counter that while substantial progress has been made there's still a long way to go before they achieve pay and job equity with men. The 1993 median income for all men workers was $30,407, while women's was $21,747. More than 60 percent of working women are mired in low-paying clerical and sales jobs. In simple terms, in 1993, working women averaged 72 cents for every dollar earned by men. In the last 30 years, the wage gap has narrowed by only 12 cents. At that rate, it will take women another 66 years before they close the gap, according to the National Committee of Pay Equity, a lobbying group.

One area where women are actually pulling ahead of men is in university administration: Women deans now earn more than their male counterparts. But not all university personnel come close to achieving pay equity. Despite the increased national attention to women's college basketball, only 32 percent of women's coaches earn more than $60,000, as compared with 88 percent of men's coaches.

While the outlook is grim for women in low-paying jobs, women with education and skills have fared much better. In corporate America, pay for women managers and professionals has risen dramatically in comparison with men's compensation. *Working Woman* magazine reported that the average pay for women executives rose 18.3 percent in the 15-year period ending in 1993, while salaries for their male counterparts rose only 1.7 percent. Women executives earn between 80 and 90 cents for every dollar earned by male executives. Unfortunately, part of the progress is due to men's falling salaries, caused by downsizing and layoffs.

When the title is office manager or assistant vice-president, women hold 45 percent of those positions, according to a 1995 report by the federal Glass Ceiling Commission. Women have successfully navigated middle management, particularly in the finance, real estate, and insurance industries. However, when the nameplate reads vice-president or above, it's a man behind the title, most likely a white man. While they constitute 43 percent of the workforce, white men hold 95 percent of senior management positions at *Fortune* 500 companies. Women who do make it to the top are found most often in female ghettos in personnel and public relations, not in operations or line positions that lead to CEO. They hit the "glass ceiling" of corporate life beyond which they cannot rise. More than 50 percent of managers in a

Working Woman survey complained of this invisible barrier to their careers.

While corporations often boast of a commitment to diversity, the reality is very different. "There is a difference between what corporate leadership says it wants to happen and what is actually happening," noted the Glass Ceiling Commission, a bipartisan panel formed to investigate the problems. In a report issued in spring 1995, after conducting hearings and research, the commission found that a glass ceiling exists because "of the perception of many white males that they are losing—losing the corporate game, losing control, losing opportunity." Women's careers are also limited because they frequently are not chosen for international assignments or training programs, often because male bosses believe that women will not spend large periods of time away from their families or will not relocate.

Some of these bosses are not wrong in their perceptions. *The Wall Street Journal* reported that the inability to balance career and family demands has led to a 25 percent turnover among female executives. A Labor Department survey of 250,000 women found that major concerns included reducing job stress and balancing work and family. In an effort to achieve a balance, many women find themselves on the much-maligned mommy track, trading less work time and pay for the catch-22 of more family time but less career advancement and prestige. Some experts believe that until companies alter their macho take-no-prisoners culture and adopt a gentler, employee-friendly attitude, the glass ceiling will remain shatterproof.

In an effort to overcome the sexist bias in major corporations, many women have dropped off the corporate fast track to set up their own shops. The number of women-owned business grew from 6.3 million in 1992 to 7.7 million in 1995, employing more than 15.5 million people, according to a report by Dun & Bradstreet and the National Foundation for Women Business Owners. Impressive in an era of downsizing is the fact that the number of women-owned businesses with more than 100 employees has grown by nearly 20 percent since 1991. While many of these women "inherited" the companies from their fathers, joined family businesses, or took over after a family member's death, the women remained at the helm, refusing to pass the torch to the next male in line. The increased number of women-owned business also reflects the growing trend toward midcareer self-employment.

The outlook for the millennium is promising. The percentage of women working hit 58.8 percent in 1994, continuing a slow, steady increase, while the participation of men continued its long-term slide to 75.1 percent. ("Keeping house," however, is still the number one reason women gave for not working.) In comparison, 30 years ago, 82 percent of men worked, compared with 39 percent of women. The number of women in the pipeline continues to gush, from college, where they make up 55.5 percent of the students, to graduate school, where they are 56.4 percent, to law school, where they constitute 43 percent, to medical school where 42 percent of the class of 1997 are women.

Encouraging news is also found in cyberspace, where many new jobs are being created in software and on-line design. By their nature, software companies often have less hierarchical organizational structures in their attempts to encourage creativity. *Working Woman* magazine put "on-line multimedia content developer and services marketer" on the top of its list for best careers for women in the year 2005. Other careers included advanced-practice nurse; physical therapist; practice care manager; human resources manager; special education teacher; bank financial services manager; independent financial planner; hotel general manager; travel agent; paralegal, labor, employment, or environmental lawyer; and environmental engineer. These jobs reflect that a third of all new jobs in the next decade will be in health, business services, or social services. The worst careers? Because of both diminished job growth and low satisfaction, the careers that made the list include child and elder care provider, telemarketing sales representative, word processor, switchboard operator, and bank teller.

OCCUPATION OF THE CIVILIAN LABOR FORCE BY SEX

Occupations	Total	
	Male	Female
Managerial and Professional Specialty Occupations	16,154,739	15,112,106
Executive, Administrative, and Managerial Occupations	8,448,483	6,170,674
Professional Specialty Occupations	7,706,256	8,941,432
Technical, Sales, and Administrative Support Occupations	14,184,207	24,341,533
Technician and Related Support Occupations	2,366,641	2,020,767
Sales Occupations	7,334,643	7,098,126
Administrative Support Occupations, Including Clerical	4,482,923	15,222,640
Service Occupations	6,919,021	9,648,536
Private Household Occupations	29,077	534,841
Protective Service Occupations	1,754,500	330,275
Service Occupations, Except Protective and Household	5,135,444	8,783,420

OCCUPATION OF THE CIVILIAN LABOR FORCE BY SEX

Occupations	Total	
	Male	Female
Farming, Forestry, and Fishing Occupations	2,597,829	507,566
Precision Production, Craft, and Repair Occupations	12,701,437	1,329,863
Operators, Fabricators, and Laborers	13,983,231	4,993,431
Machine Operators, Assemblers, and Inspectors	5,185,397	3,450,107
Transportation and Material Moving Occupations	4,594,570	504,404
Handlers, Equipment Cleaners, Helpers, and Laborers	4,203,264	1,038,920
TOTAL	*66,986,201*	*56,487,249*

SOURCE: U.S. Department of Commerce, 1990 Census.

PERCENT OF FEMALE WORKERS IN SELECTED OCCUPATIONS, 1975–1994

Occupation	Women as Percent of Total Employed		
	1975	1985	1994
Airline Pilot	—	2.6	2.6
Auto Mechanic	0.5	0.6	1.0
Bartender	35.2	47.9	55.1
Bus Driver	37.7	49.2	47.0
Cab Driver, Chauffeur	8.7	10.9	10.3
Carpenter	0.6	1.2	1.0
Child-Care Worker	98.4	96.1	97.3
Computer Programmer	25.6	34.3	29.3
Computer Systems Analyst	14.8	28.0	31.4
Data Entry Keyer	92.8	90.7	83.8
Data Processing Equipment Repairer	1.8	10.4	18.0
Dentist	1.8	6.5	13.3
Dental Assistant	100.0	99.0	96.6
Economist	13.1	34.5	47.4
Editor, Reporter	44.6	51.7	48.8
Elementary School Teacher	85.4	84.0	85.6
College/University Professor	31.1	35.2	42.5
Garage, Gas Station Attendant	4.7	6.8	5.2

PERCENT OF FEMALE WORKERS IN SELECTED OCCUPATIONS, 1975–1994

Occupation	Women as Percent of Total Employed		
	1975	1985	1994
Lawyer, Judge	7.1%	18.2%	24.8%
Librarian	81.1	87.0	84.1
Mail Carrier (Postal Service)	8.7	17.2	34.0
Office Machine Repairer	1.7	5.7	2.1
Physician	13.0	17.2	22.3
Registered Nurse	97.0	95.1	93.8
Social Worker	60.8	66.7	69.3
Telephone Installer, Repairer	4.8	12.8	16.8
Telephone Operator	93.3	88.8	88.8
Waiter/Waitress	91.1	84.0	78.6
Welder	4.4	4.8	4.4

SOURCE: U.S. Department of Labor, Bureau of Labor Statistics, *Employment and Earnings* (monthly) January issue.

EMPLOYMENT STATUS OF THE POPULATION BY SEX, 1960–1994 (numbers in thousands)

Year	Civilian Noninstitutional Population[1]	Total in Workforce	Percentage of Population	Number Employed	Employment/ Population Ratio[2]	Percentage of Unemployed
			Total			
1960	117,245	69,628	59.4%	65,778	56.1	5.5%
1965	126,513	74,455	58.9	71,088	56.2	4.5
1970	137,085	82,771	60.4	78,678	57.4	4.9
1975	153,153	93,775	61.2	85,846	56.1	8.5
1980	167,745	106,940	63.8	99,303	59.2	7.1
1985	178,206	115,461	64.8	107,150	60.1	7.2
1990	188,049	124,787	66.4	117,914	62.7	5.5
1991	189,765	125,303	66.0	116,877	61.6	6.7
1992	191,576	126,982	66.3	117,598	61.4	7.4
1993	193,550	128,040	66.2	119,306	61.6	6.8
1994[3]	196,814	131,056	66.6	123,060	62.5	6.1
			Male			
1960	55,662	46,388	83.3%	43,904	78.9	5.4%
1965	59,782	48,255	80.7	46,340	77.5	4.0
1970	64,304	51,228	79.7	48,990	76.2	4.4
1975	72,291	56,299	77.9	51,857	71.7	7.9

EMPLOYMENT STATUS OF THE POPULATION BY SEX, 1960–1994 (numbers in thousands)

Year	Civilian Noninstitutional Population[1]	Total in Workforce	Percentage of Population	Number Employed	Employment/ Population Ratio[2]	Percentage of Unemployed
1980	79,398	61,453	77.4%	57,186	72.0	6.9%
1985	84,469	64,411	76.3	59,891	70.9	7.0
1990	89,650	68,234	76.1	64,435	71.9	5.6
1991	90,552	68,411	75.5	63,593	70.2	7.0
1992	91,541	69,184	75.6	63,805	69.7	7.8
1993	92,620	69,633	75.2	64,700	69.9	7.1
1994[3]	94,355	70,817	75.1	66,450	70.4	6.2
			Female			
1960	61,582	23,240	37.7%	21,874	35.5	5.9%
1965	66,731	26,200	39.3	24,748	37.1	5.5
1970	72,782	31,543	43.3	29,688	40.8	5.9
1975	80,860	37,475	46.3	33,989	42.0	9.3
1980	88,348	45,487	51.5	42,117	47.7	7.4
1985	93,736	51,050	54.5	47,259	50.4	7.4
1990	98,399	56,554	57.5	53,479	54.3	5.4
1991	99,214	56,893	57.3	53,284	53.7	6.3
1992	100,035	57,798	57.8	53,793	53.9	6.9
1993	100,930	58,407	57.9	54,606	54.1	6.5
1994[3]	102,460	60,239	58.8	56,610	55.3	6.0

[1]Age 16 and over.
[2]Civilians employed as a percentage of the civilian noninstitutional population.
[3]Data for 1994 are not directly comparable with data for previous years because of a major redesign of the Current Population Survey questionnaire and collection methodology and the introduction of 1990-census-based population controls, adjusted for the estimated undercount.
SOURCE: U.S. Department of Labor, Bureau of Labor Statistics, *Employment and Earnings* (monthly), January issue.

The Top Workplaces for Mothers

Working Mother magazine annually ranks the 100 best companies based on their salaries, child-care options, family-friendly benefits, and advancement opportunities for women. The top ten companies for 1994 were:

AT&T
Barnett Banks, Inc.
Fel-Pro, Inc.
Glaxo, Inc.
IBM
John Hancock Mutual Life Insurance Co.
Johnson & Johnson
Lancaster Laboratories, Inc.
NationsBank
Xerox Corporation

THE BEST PAID WOMEN IN CORPORATE AMERICA, 1994

Rank, Name	Position, Company	Total Compensation[1]
1. Rena Rowan	Executive Vice-President, Jones Apparel Group	$4,030,000
2. Sherry Lansing	Chair, Paramount Motion Pictures	3,000,000
3. Carol A. Bartz	Chair, CEO, and President, Autodesk	2,570,000
4. Linda Wachner	Chair, CEO, and President, Warnaco Group	2,360,000
5. Marion Sandler	Co-CEO, Golden West Financial	2,030,000
6. Jill Barad	President and CEO, Mattel Toys	1,790,000
7. Lucie Salhany	CEO and President, Fox Broadcasting	1,500,000
8. Ellen Gordon	President, Tootsie Roll Industries	1,300,000
9. Patricia DeRosa	President, Gap Kids	1,060,000
10. Nicole Eskenazi	Executive Vice-President, Bernard Chaws (1993)	1,040,000
11. Antonia Sosta	Group Executive, Household International	935,276
12. Carol F. St. Mark	President, Pitney Bowes Logistics Systems and Business Services	921,206
13. Sally Frome Kasaks	CEO, Ann Taylor	901,505
14. Carol Bernick	Executive Vice-President, Alberto-Culver	894,758
15. Turi Josefsen	Executive Vice-President, U.S. Surgical Corp.	835,080
16. Jane Shaw	President, Alza (1993)	830,000
17. Laurel Cutler	Global Director of Marketing and Planning, Foote, Cone & Belding	758,078
18. Carolyn Murphy	Senior Vice-President, CNA Insurance Company	730,523
19. Bernice Lavin	Vice-Chair, Secretary, and Treasurer, Alberto-Culver	719,477
20. Judy Lewent	CEO and Senior Vice-President, Mesck	668,844

[1]This listing is comprised exclusively of employees of public companies. Earnings include salary, bonuses, and other cash compensation, and value of options exercised.
SOURCE: *Working Woman* magazine, 1994 salary survey.

OCCUPATIONS WITH GREATEST INCREASES AND DECREASES IN THE GENDER WAGE GAP, 1983–1991

	Women's Earnings per Men's Dollar		
Occupation	**1983**	**1991**	**Change**
Secretaries	77¢	97¢	+20¢
Bill Collectors, Social Welfare Clerks	58	74	+16
Designers (Clothes, Graphic, Furniture)	53	69	+16
Mechanics, Repairers	89	104	+15
Police, Guards, Firefighters	70	84	+14
Personnel Trainers, Labor Relations Specialists	66	80	+14
Bank Tellers, Proofreaders, Statistical Clerks	80	92	+12
Mathematicians, Computer Scientists	75	86	+11
Purchasing Agents, Buyers	63	74	+11
Public Relations Specialists	74	84	+10
Financial Managers	64	59	−5
Lawyers	89	75	−14
Physicians	82	54	−28

SOURCE: *Working Woman* magazine, 1993 salary survey.

FEDERAL WHITE-COLLAR WORKERS: AVERAGE ANNUAL SALARIES, BY SEX, 1994

Occupation	**Men's Salaries**	**Women's Salaries**
Administrator	$74,839	$57,817
Architect	51,197	46,167
Attorney	70,896	63,343
Cartographer	44,810	42,769
Chaplain	48,670	42,311
Chemist	55,162	45,902
Clerk-Typist	21,898	19,170
Computer Operator	28,473	26,918
Computer Specialist	48,657	42,929
Dentist	80,882	62,717
Doctor	82,212	79,200
Economist	60,809	51,162
Engineer, Aerospace	59,261	50,163
Engineer, Chemical	54,995	47,252
Engineer, Civil	53,610	44,195
Engineer, Electrical	42,887	45,293
Engineer, General	63,408	53,383
Engineer, Mechanical	51,951	45,537

FEDERAL WHITE-COLLAR WORKERS: AVERAGE ANNUAL SALARIES, BY SEX, 1994

Occupation	Men's Salaries	Women's Salaries
Engineer, Nuclear	$58,668	$50,275
Engineer, Petroleum	56,221	49,807
Engineering Technician	38,601	30,554
Internal Revenue Agent	51,054	43,578
Librarian	48,015	44,289
Library Technician	24,512	23,623
Management and Program Analyst	53,150	44,285
Mathematician	56,639	49,530
Medical Technologist	36,862	36,211
Messenger	18,262	20,139
Museum Curator	39,361	35,811
Nurse	42,703	43,242
Nursing Assistant	20,676	20,890
Paralegal	41,621	36,165
Pharmacist	50,150	47,193
Photographer	33,981	28,958
Physicist	64,400	54,071
Psychologist	57,300	48,223
Secretary	22,177	24,294
Security Guard	22,270	21,585
Social Insurance Claims Examiner	39,366	35,811
Social Worker	43,191	40,043
Statistician	55,444	47,862
Telephone Operator	18,881	19,225
Veterinary Scientist	51,901	47,247
Writer and Editor	45,560	37,674

SOURCE: Office of Personnel Management, *Occupations of Federal White-Collar and Blue-Collar Workers*, September 1993.

INCOME AND EARNINGS OF MINORITIES

With all the talk on Capitol Hill and in statehouses across the country about reforming or even dismantling affirmative action programs, one might be tempted to think racial discrimination in the workplace had been eradicated. But while the situation is a lot rosier for minorities than it was just 30 years ago (not to mention two hundred years ago, when black slaves were declared the equivalent of three fifths of a person), there are plenty of indicators that employment opportunities and rewards are still greater for whites than for blacks. Whether or not that is an argument for continuing affirmative action in its present form is debatable, but it is surely an argument against completely dismantling programs that open doors to a group of people who continue to be the victims of workplace discrimination. Here are just a few indicators:

- Minorities currently make up 21 percent of the workforce, but in no industry do they make up more than 13 percent of managers, and in many industries, fewer than 1 in 100 managers is a minority, according to the federal Glass Ceiling Commission, a bipartisan panel studying diversity in the workplace. Overall, minorities hold less than 3 percent of senior-level (vice-president and above) jobs in corporations.
- Black men's annual earnings are 74 percent of what white men earn, the same as they were in 1975. Hispanic men's earnings were 64.8 percent, down from 72.1 percent in 1975. And while earnings for black and Hispanic women have increased in proportion to white men's salaries over the same time period, they have not increased as fast as their white women counterparts. Their earnings have therefore decreased in relation to white women's salaries.
- Median household income for blacks, adjusted for inflation, declined in 1993 to $21,542 from $22,253 in 1980, while it increased for whites to $39,300 from $38,458. The difference between median incomes of blacks and whites in 1993 was $17,758, or double what the difference was in 1979. Median incomes for Hispanic households also declined, from $25,838 in 1980 to $23,654 in 1993.
- Unemployment rates for blacks is consistently double the rate for whites, regardless of the country's economic prosperity. Black unemployment dropped below the 10 percent mark in December 1994 for the first time since 1972. But 34.6 percent of blacks between the ages of 16 and 19 are unemployed, compared with 14.7 percent of white youths.
- The percentage of blacks below the poverty level was 33.1 in 1993, about the same as it has been every year since 1968. Meanwhile, the percentage of whites has fluctuated, from a high of 18.1 percent in 1959, to a low of 8.4 percent in 1973, and back up to 12.2 percent in 1993. The percentage of Hispanics below the poverty level (21.6 percent in 1973) has also fluctuated, but has recently been on the upswing, reaching an all-time high of 30.6 percent in 1993.

Such statistics speak the kind of stark truth no political rhetoric can capture because they reveal deep-rooted patterns of social and cultural discrimination that remain immune to any attempts at mere economic adjustments.

The nation's 30 million black people constitute just over 12 percent of the population. Of the 14 million blacks in the workforce, about 22 percent are in service occupations (double the percentage of whites), while 29 percent hold blue-collar jobs. Among the 48 percent who are white-collar workers, only 13 percent of black males were employed in managerial or professional specialty occupations, or about half the rate for white males. As a result, many are leaving the corporate environment in favor of their own business; the number of minority-owned businesses has risen by as much as 50 percent in recent years according to some reports.

The most important of the so-called other groups are the 22 million people of Hispanic origin who constitute 9 percent of our official population. Of these, 60 percent are of Mexican origin, 12 percent are of Puerto Rican origin, and 5 percent are of Cuban origin, so the vast majority of Hispanic Americans are from groups with established communities in this country. This may help to explain why median family incomes for people of Hispanic origin (who may be of any race) is higher than that for blacks. Of course the incredible growth in the number of illegal aliens from Spanish-speaking countries (especially Mexico) means that income and population statistics regarding people of Hispanic origin are suspect at best.

MEDIAN ANNUAL EARNINGS BY RACE, SEX, & HISPANIC ORIGIN

	Earnings as a Percentage of White Men's Earnings				
Year	**Black men**	**Hispanic Men**	**White Women**	**Black Women**	**Hispanic Women**
1975	74.3%	72.1%	57.5%	55.4%	49.3%
1980	70.7	70.8	58.9	55.7	50.5
1985	69.7	68.0	63.0	57.1	52.1
1990	73.1	66.3	69.4	62.5	54.3
1993	74.0	64.8	70.8	63.7	53.9

SOURCE: National Committee on Pay Equity.

Conservative estimates of the illegal alien population run as high as 6 million people living and working here on a regular basis, most of them providing cheap labor in the agricultural fields of California and Texas, the sweatshops of New York City, and the kitchens of hotels and restaurants around the country. Others work in individual households as housekeepers, maids, and gardeners, paid off the books so that their income is untaxed and so their employers don't have to pay social security, unemployment and disability insurance, or payroll taxes. Because they have no legal rights, illegal aliens are usually paid less than the minimum wage, and, of course, they are never a threat as potential union members.

INCOME OF INDIVIDUALS AND FAMILIES BY RACE AND HISPANIC ORIGIN, 1973–93

	1973			1993		
Category	**White**	**Black**	**Hispanic**	**White**	**Black**	**Hispanic**
INDIVIDUALS						
Median Income[1]						
Male	$25,878	$15,653	$18,981	$21,981	$14,605	$13,689
Female	8,642	7,801	8,119	11,266	9,508	8,100
Percentage Below the Poverty Line	8.4	31.4	21.9	12.2	33.1	30.6
FAMILIES						
Median Family Income	$38,559	$22,254	$26,680	$39,300	$21,542	$23,654
Percentage of Families with Income[2]						
Under $5,000	1.6	5.5	2.8	2.5	10.7	5.8
$5,000–$9,999	4.3	13.7	8.5	4.8	15.1	12.1
$10,000–$14,999	6.2	14.0	11.0	6.6	11.4	12.5
$15,000–$24,999	15.1	23.6	24.6	15.1	18.6	22.2
$25,000–$34,999	17.2	15.9	19.1	15.1	13.7	16.6
$35,000–$49,999	24.4	15.4	19.0	18.8	12.9	14.0
$50,000–$74,999	20.7	8.9	11.7	20.6	10.9	11.4
$75,000 to $99,999	6.4	2.2	2.3	8.6	4.2	3.1
$100,000 and over	4.1	0.8	0.9	8.0	2.4	2.4

[1]For year-round full-time workers over 15 years old with income.
[2]Income levels in constant (1993) dollars.
SOURCE: U.S. Census Bureau, *Money Income of Households, Families, and Persons in the United States, 1990,* 1992.

Of the 10 million people of Hispanic origin in the workforce, only about 13 percent work in managerial and professional specialty occupations, while about 23 percent work as operators, fabricators, and laborers, and another 19 percent work in service occupations, which are usually low paying. Nearly 20 percent of Hispanic males work in precision production, craft, or repair occupations.

EMPLOYMENT STATUS OF THE POPULATION BY RACE AND HISPANIC ORIGIN, 1960–1994
(Numbers in Thousands)

Year	Civilian Noninstitutional Population[1]	Total in Workforce	Percentage of Population	Number Employed	Employment/ Population Ratio[2]	Percentage of Unemployed
			White			
1975	134,790	82,831	61.5%	76,411	56.7	7.8%
1980	146,122	93,600	64.1	87,715	60.0	6.3
1985	153,679	99,926	65.0	93,736	61.0	6.2
1990	160,415	107,177	66.8	102,087	63.6	4.7
1991	161,511	107,486	66.6	101,039	62.6	6.0
1992	162,658	108,526	66.7	101,479	62.4	6.5
1993	163,921	109,359	66.7	102,812	62.7	6.0
1994[3]	165,555	111,082	67.1	105,190	63.5	5.3
			Black			
1975	15,751	9,263	58.8%	7,894	50.1	14.8%
1980	17,824	10,865	61.0	9,313	52.2	14.3
1985	19,664	12,364	62.9	10,501	53.4	15.1
1990	21,300	13,493	63.3	11,966	56.2	11.3
1991	21,615	13,542	62.6	11,863	54.9	12.4
1992	21,958	13,891	63.3	11,933	54.3	14.1
1993	22,329	13,943	62.4	12,146	54.4	12.9
1994[3]	22,879	14,502	63.4	12,835	56.1	11.5
			Hispanic[4]			
1975	NA	NA	NA	NA	NA	NA
1980	9,598	6,146	64.0%	5,527	57.6	10.1%
1985	11,915	7,698	64.6	6,888	57.8	10.5
1990	14,297	9,576	67.0	8,808	61.6	8.0
1991	14,770	9,762	66.1	8,799	59.6	9.9
1992	15,244	10,131	66.5	8,971	58.9	11.4
1993	15,753	10,377	65.9	9,272	58.9	10.6
1994[3]	18,117	11,975	66.1	10,788	59.5	9.9

[1]Age 16 and over.
[2]Civilians employed as a percentage of the civilian noninstitutional population.
[3]Data for 1994 are not directly comparable with data for previous years because of a major redesign of the Current Population Survey questionnaire and collection methodology and the introduction of 1990-census-based population controls, adjusted for the estimated undercount.
[4]Hispanics may be of any race.
SOURCE: U.S. Department of Labor, Bureau of Labor Statistics, *Employment and Earnings* (monthly), January issue.

THE NEW COLLEGE GRADUATE

Although it should be obvious to readers of this book that a college education is required for virtually every job that has long-term high earnings potential, it may come as a surprise that only about 25 percent of the American workforce has finished college. However, the percentage of college graduates is increasing, as is the market for their skills. An average of one million people a year have been graduating from four-year colleges and universities since 1980, according to the Department of Education. That number is expected to increase through the year 2005, even as the college age population shrinks. The Department of Education predicts that one of every three 22-year-olds will be a college graduate in 1996, compared with one in five in 1980.

While the increase in college graduates will create a more educated population, it won't do anything to help the glut of college graduates in the job market. Although the percentage of jobs requiring a college degree has been increasing steadily, it hasn't kept pace with the number of college graduates. Between 1984 and 1992, there were an average of 1.2 million college graduates competing for 940,000 jobs each year, leaving a surplus of 180,000 graduates. From 1992 to 2005, the Department of Labor projects an annual average of 1.4 million job seekers for 1.05 million jobs, a surplus of 350,000 collegians. Looked at another way, one of every four college graduates over the next 10 years will not be able to find a job requiring a college degree.

EMPLOYMENT GROWTH BY REQUIRED EDUCATION, 1992–2005

	Employment		Change, 1992–2005	
	Actual	Projected		
Occupation Type	**1992**	**2005**	**Number**	**Percent**
All Jobs	121,099,000	147,482,000	26,383,000	21.8%
Jobs Requiring a College Degree	23,770,000	33,296,000	9,526,000	40.1
Executive, Administrative and Managerial	6,905,000	9,276,000	2,371,000	34.3
Professional Specialty	12,115,000	17,091,000	4,976,000	41.1
Technicians	1,169,000	1,806,000	637,000	54.5
Sales Representatives and Supervisors	2,198,000	3,060,000	862,000	39.2
All Other	1,383,000	2,062,000	679,000	49.1
Jobs Not Requiring a College Degree	97,329,000	114,186,000	16,857,000	17.3

SOURCE: Bureau of Labor Statistics, *Occupational Outlook Quarterly,* Summer 1994.

Few of these college graduates should find themselves on the unemployment lines, however. Instead, many will accept jobs that don't require a college degree. This phenomenon, known as "educational underutilization," or "underemployment," is illustrated by the occupation of construction and building inspectors. Between 1984 and 1990, the number of college graduates in this profession more than doubled, not because the job became more complex (though this is true in small part) but rather because college graduates were available. Underemployment often has its own corrective effect: Once a college graduate fills a position, it often becomes a job requiring a college degree for all succeeding workers in that job. Underemployment may also be responsible for the fact that real hourly wages (i.e., adjusted for inflation) for college graduates declined 1.6 percent between 1989 and 1991, according to figures from the Department of Labor.

Nevertheless, job prospects will continue to be better for those with degrees than those without. Over their lifetimes, college graduates continue to earn about 40 percent more than those without degrees, and the gap is widening. Median annual earnings for college graduates were $37,000 in 1992, compared with $21,000 for high school graduates. College graduates have much lower unemployment rates too: an average of 3 percent each year, compared with 8 percent for high school graduates.

Job prospects for college graduates will be best in the occupations that currently employ the largest numbers of graduates: teacher, computer systems analyst, engineer, scientist, registered nurse, physician, physical therapist, social worker, and human service worker. Other fast-growing occupations for college graduates are accountant and financial manager.

The following table puts the value of education in its starkest terms of dollars and cents. Over a lifetime, college graduates can expect to earn nearly twice what a mere high school graduate will earn, and a person with a professional degree like a doctor or lawyer can earn more than double the lifetime income of a college graduate.

ESTIMATED LIFETIME EARNINGS BY EDUCATION LEVELS

Highest Level of Education Completed	Estimated lifetime earnings
Some High School	$ 609,000
High School Graduate	821,000
Some College	993,000
Associate's Degree	1,062,000
Bachelor's Degree	1,421,000
Master's Degree	1,619,000
Doctorate Degree (Ph. D.)	2,142,000
Professional Degree	3,013,000

SOURCE: U.S. Bureau of the Census, *Educational Attainment in the United States, March, 1993* (1994).

BACHELOR'S DEGREES AWARDED BY SEX AND AS A PERCENTAGE OF THE 23-YEAR-OLD POPULATION, 1870–1993

Year	Total	Males	Females	As Percentage of All 23-Year-Olds
1870	9,371	7,993	1,378	NA
1880	12,896	10,411	2,485	NA
1890	15,539	12,857	2,682	NA
1900	27,410	22,173	5,237	1.9%
1910	37,199	28,762	8,437	2.0
1920	48,622	31,980	16,642	2.6
1930	122,484	73,615	48,869	5.7
1940	186,500	109,546	76,954	8.1
1946[1]	136,174	58,664	77,510	5.6
1950	432,058	328,841	103,217	18.2
1955	285,841	182,839	103,002	15.1
1960	392,440	254,063	138,377	18.2
1965[2]	493,757	282,173	211,584	19.4
1970	792,317	451,097	341,220	21.8
1975	922,933	504,841	418,092	24.9
1980	929,417	473,611	455,806	21.8
1985	979,477	482,528	496,949	23.0
1990	1,049,657	491,488	558,169	28.2
1991	1,094,538	504,045	590,493	30.1
1992	1,136,553	520,811	615,742	30.6
1993	1,165,179	532,881	632,298	30.3

[1]Figures for 1945 not available.

[2]Data before 1965 include first professional degrees but do not include Alaska or Hawaii.

SOURCE: U.S. Department of Education, *Digest of Education Statistics* and unpublished data.

AVERAGE YEARLY SALARY OFFERS MADE TO BACHELOR'S DEGREE CANDIDATES FOR ALL TYPES OF EMPLOYERS

Function	Average Offer	Function	Average Offer
Finance		Investment Banking (Corp. Finance)	$29,414
Accounting (Public)	$28,961		
Accounting (Private)	26,650	Investment Banking (Mergers and Acquisitions)	30,885
Auditing (Public)	29,375		
Auditing (Private)	26,561		
Commercial Banking (Consumer)	23,820	Investment Banking (Real Estate)	26,633
Commercial Banking (Lending)	25,446	Investment Banking (Sales and Trading)	26,410

AVERAGE YEARLY SALARY OFFERS MADE TO BACHELOR'S DEGREE CANDIDATES FOR ALL TYPES OF EMPLOYERS

Function	Average Offer
Financial/Treasury Analysis	$29,625
Portfolio Management/ Brokerage	27,585
Insurance (Underwriting)	25,976
Insurance (Claims)	24,497
Communications	
Design/Graphic Arts	$21,237
Media Planning	20,592
Reporting	17,761
Production	21,324
Public Relations	20,772
Writing/Editing	21,856
Marketing	
Advertising	$20,983
Brand/Product Management	25,491
Buyer/Merchandising	25,010
Customer Service	22,110
Distribution	24,565
Market Research	24,416
Purchasing	24,372
Sales	25,324
Public Administration	
Executive, Legislative, and General	$23,972
Finance, Taxation, Monetary Policy	24,545
Economic Programs	24,515
Law Enforcement	24,306
Military	24,988
National Security	26,268
Urban/Regional Planning	23,500
Engineering	
Bioengineering	$31,079
Design/Construction	31,190
Environment/Sanitation	31,204
Manufacturing/Industrial	$34,937
Systems/Programming	33,576
Power Systems	34,294
Software Design and Development	34,654
Hardware Design and Development	35,545
Research and Development	34,953
Testing	34,716
Process Engineering	39,364
Project Engineering	34,818
Quality Control	29,432
Other Engineering	33,810
Industrial Hygiene/ Occupational Safety	34,100
Social Services	
Administration	$20,907
Counseling	18,511
Fund-raising/Development	17,234
Social Work	19,385
Computer Science	
Computer Programming	$30,335
Information Systems	29,642
Systems Analysis and Design	31,060
Health Care	
Administrative	$23,931
Dietitian	27,980
Medical Technology	25,645
Nursing/Personal Care	28,408
Occupational Therapy	33,765
Pharmacist	46,378
Physical Therapy	28,900
Radiation Therapy	32,229
Respiratory Therapy	35,000
Speech Pathology/ Audiology	21,060
Other Health Related	22,132

AVERAGE YEARLY SALARY OFFERS MADE TO BACHELOR'S DEGREE CANDIDATES FOR ALL TYPES OF EMPLOYERS

Function	Average Offer	Function	Average Offer
Other Functional Areas		Management Trainee	23,897
Actuarial	$34,770	Mathematician/Statistician	26,354
Agricultural/Natural Resources	22,115	Paralegal	19,900
Architecture	23,831	Research (Nontechnical)	22,684
Consulting	31,158	Research (Technical)	26,396
Human Resources/Industrial Relations	23,229	Training	21,609

SOURCE: National Association of Colleges and Employers, *Salary Survey, 1994.* Reprinted by permission.

AVERAGE YEARLY SALARY OFFERS MADE TO BACHELOR'S DEGREE CANDIDATES FOR ALL TYPES OF EMPLOYERS

Curriculum (Proportion of Total Offers)	Average Offer	Curriculum (Proportion of Total Offers)	Average Offer
Business (44 percent)	$28,372	*Education (3 percent)*	
Accounting	25,102	Elementary Education	$21,139
Business Administration	27,179	Pre-elementary Education	16,641
Distribution Management	27,643	Physical Education	22,759
Economics and Finance	21,856	Special Education	21,485
Hotel/Restaurant Finance	24,215		
Human Resources (Including Labor Relations)	29,178	*Home Economics (1 percent)*	
Management Information Systems	24,584	Textiles and Clothing	$22,964
Merchandising Management	22,534	Home Economics	21,146
Real Estate	23,933		
		Engineering (31 percent)	
Communications (3 percent)		Aerospace and Aeronautical Engineering	$30,860
Advertising	$21,153	Agricultural Engineering	32,857
Communications	22,324	Architectural Engineering	29,652
Journalism	20,906	Bioengineering and Biomedical Engineering	29,239
Public Relations	21,101	Chemical Engineering	39,204
Telecommunications/Broadcasting	20,785	Civil Engineering	29,809
		Computer Engineering	33,842

AVERAGE YEARLY SALARY OFFERS MADE TO BACHELOR'S DEGREE CANDIDATES FOR ALL TYPES OF EMPLOYERS

Curriculum (Proportion of Total Offers)	Average Offer
Electrical/Electronic Engineering	$34,840
Environmental Engineering	33,066
Industrial Engineering	33,257
Mechanical Engineering	35,051
Metallurgical Engineering	33,429
Mining (Including Geological)	32,638
Nuclear Engineering	33,603
Ocean Engineering	20,900
Petroleum Engineering	38,286
Safety Engineering (Occupational)	24,600
Systems Engineering	37,400
Textile Engineering	20,333
Engineering Technology	30,509
Industrial Technology	32,157
Humanities and Social Sciences (7 percent)	
Foreign Languages	$23,205
Letters (Including English)	21,360
Visual and Performing Arts	21,252
Other Humanities	23,519
Criminal Justice	22,827
History	23,361
Political Science/ Government	24,369
Psychology	20,488
Sociology	21,490
Other Social Sciences	23,023
Agriculture and Natural Resources (1 percent)	
Agribusiness	$23,137
Animal Sciences	$22,381
Plant Sciences	23,154
Natural Resources	21,901
Other Agricultural Sciences	24,980
Computer Sciences (5 percent)	
Computer Science	$31,783
Computer Programming	31,330
Information Sciences	30,975
Systems Analysis	33,218
Health Sciences (2 percent)	
Allied Health	$30,649
Health Sciences	24,886
Nursing	28,594
Pharmacy	46,108
Sciences (3 percent)	
Actuarial	$33,315
Architectural and Environmental Design	24,385
Biological Sciences	22,804
Chemistry	28,128
Environmental Sciences	22,563
Geology and Geological Sciences	25,459
Mathematics	28,221
Physics	28,117
Other Physical and Earth Sciences	20,740
Polymer Science	25,930

SOURCE: National Association of Colleges and Employers, *Salary Survey, 1994*. Reprinted by permission.

WHEN SEEKING YOUR FIRST JOB

by Edward J. Dwyer, Jr.[1]

Many first-time job seekers spend endless time agonizing over making the right choice. For those who have decided at age sixteen that medicine or law or carpentry is the profession they want to pursue, the choice is relatively easy when it comes time to start working. These people have had a clearcut goal and have gone through the necessary preparation to achieve it. But most students don't feel strongly about any particular field, so the need to make a choice can trigger an excruciating personal debate. At times this uncertainty can even stop them from making any decision at all.

There is no need for the first job decision to be such a source of anxiety. There are a set of rational steps that a person can take when embarking on the process. There are also certain attitudes that one should bring into the process to inject a sense of reality and provide a framework for making the decision.

First of all we should say right up-front that picking a first job does not constitute making a lifetime choice. Joseph L. Dionne, the president and CEO of McGraw-Hill, started his worklife as a high school teacher and coach, for example. Nick Buoniconti, who was the middle linebacker on the Miami Dolphins' Super Bowl championship teams, became a lawyer and player agent before he took over running the American Tobacco Company. Many a degreed lawyer has never practiced law. Conversely there are English majors who have found themselves in charge of technical operations. In fact one of the best market research consultants specializes in high-tech, using to the hilt his master's degree in library science. So when starting out you need not find the situation that you must fit for the rest of your working days. Nor will it necessarily be one for which your college education is particularly apropos.

It should be a situation which will help you build a career or profession, however. This means finding a job that will help you to start building transportable skills. Also, you should go into your job search with the notion that you want to find something that makes sense for the next two years at least. This is the minimum amount of time in which you can become well-grounded and practiced in those skills. Then too it gives you time to build some concrete accomplishments. With this in mind then you should target a meaningful job in a good company in an attractive industry. So you will have to put some effort into doing your homework, but more about that later.

No matter what direction you may take you will succeed and find satisfaction predominantly from hard work. So you should pick a functional

[1]This article was written expressly for this book by Edward J. Dwyer, Jr., a highly successful management consultant and executive recruiter.

field and an industry that strongly interest you. Since you will be putting a minimum of seven hours a day five days a week into the job you may as well spend the time performing activities that you find interesting and challenging. No one performs well over any length of time carrying out activities that they consider mere drudgery or routine. Those who get the promotions are those who bring enthusiasm and contribution to the job. While there is a certain level below which you may not be able to subsist, compensation should not be your most important criterion for judging the right situation. Survey after survey has shown that a vast majority of successful people who are happy with themselves and their jobs find the work itself to be their main source of satisfaction rather than their compensation. So you should try to find work that you feel is interesting and important.

Even though we have just dismissed compensation as the prime motive for job selection, we do want to make one point clear. You can garner from the pages of this book what the pay scales are by type of jobs and industries. One major implication that can be drawn here is that pay is not uniform by job category or across different size companies or different industries. You can get a reasonable idea of what you might expect as a new job seeker given your background, the type of position you seek and the industry in which you seek it. The key here is to have reasonable expectations. History majors with no work experience cannot command thirty thousand dollars in starting salary. So if you are a history major set your sights accordingly, because there is nothing worse than going into the job market with an inflated sense of one's own value. It can only lead to dissatisfaction and make the search very long and painful.

Getting Started

Now the homework part. The starting point for any job search is with yourself. You really have to know the kind of person you are and match your strong and weak points, likes and dislikes, knowledge and interests, etc., with the various opportunities that are in the job market. Standardized psychological tests are of limited value at this point. Such tests may help in directing you away from certain fields for which you would have little aptitude and interest, and generally toward ones in which you have both. But these tests won't help you decide specifically on banking versus brokerage or marketing versus sales. When trying to find your own focus as it relates to starting a career, there are a number of questions to ask yourself: "Who am I?" and "What would I like to do?" and "What do I want to get out of my career?" Your answers to these will tell you a lot about what you should aspire to be and not be. For instance, if you take rejection of your ideas and suggestions highly personally, you shouldn't look to a career in sales where even those most successful in selling the best products hear "yes" less than half the time. Or if retiring at age fifty is one of your goals, you had better be aiming at the fast track.

There is no set approach. You can make up your own questions to find your own personal profile or get suggestions from articles and books. A personal profile is simply a guide to help you take inventory. Rating each attribute on a scale of 1 to 5 is usually of benefit as well. Be as objective as possible; try to see yourself as others see you. Once you've taken this inventory you should look at the career fields you are considering versus the attribute areas and see how you match up. Since you may have little or no experience upon which to base judgments about career fields and their requirements, consult the media as well as your college placement office for help. And don't neglect to use any personal contacts you may have who are experienced in industries you may be interested in.

Targeting the Right Opportunities

Having taken inventory you should then start doing research to find which industries, companies, and jobs will most likely provide the kinds of intellectual, psychic, social, and monetary rewards you seek. If you do not see yourself working as the product manager in charge of promoting the newest flavor in pudding pops, stay clear of marketing in food companies. You may see yourself as a salesman, but of what? You may be in a hurry to achieve that universal symbol of great success—six figures—so you want to find industries which have a reputation for allowing young people the opportunity to achieve that level quickly.

Most importantly, whatever your aspirations, aim for a situation that will allow you to start growing your skill and knowledge base in terms of gaining your career goals. If you are an engineer you may be tempted to go to work on a project that involves very lengthy and detailed work, such as designing and installing factory automation equipment for the furniture manufacturing industry. This is fine as far as it goes, but what might you be doing five years from now? You may want to become an expert in the detailed engineering work involved in installing such systems and you may see this aspect of the work as highly interesting and rewarding. On the other hand, you may see your first engineering job as a necessary stop on your career path to management responsibility. The attractiveness of a given job situation will depend on your longer range goals. In summary, certain companies and positions will fit you and your needs better than others. Finding the right ones will depend on how well you've prepared yourself.

Above all approach the selection as a two-year decision. You should be ready to ask yourself and your prospective employers where you might be in two years. The picture you should have in your mind should have two dimensions: (1) the inventory of skills and experiences you will have acquired as well as the transferability of these, and (2) the level of responsibility you should have gained and the opportunity to achieve concrete results. (The most transferable assets of all are the latter.) See if this agrees with your own picture of where you want to be, and whether or not other recent graduates have achieved this at these companies.

Now ask the same question about the five-year timepoint. The key here is that your first job is not likely to be your last, so you want to assure yourself that the progress you make will not be lost if you move on. Still you do not want to change companies too often even early in your career, so the two-year horizon provides some stability as you set sail on your shakedown run. Furthermore, you want to have a reasonable gauge of the progress you may have made should you decide not to move elsewhere.

A few words about selecting the appropriate industries and businesses to target: Given the current shakeout in American industry, job security is not what it used to be and probably won't be again. To say that the most promising opportunities are in growth industries is both obvious and oversimplified. To begin with, most large companies are portfolios of new and promising businesses, along with growing ones, mature ones, and declining ones. This is true even if the company concentrates in a highly attractive industry such as computers. Your choice of industry is important because industry knowledge is an important commodity that you can carry with you for the rest of your career to your own major benefit. So naturally you want to move into a business in an industry that has long-term potential. But don't be fooled; potential does not necessarily mean high-flying growth. Many high-flyers go out of business very quickly and many old-line companies go on seemingly forever. Choose an industry that interests you and that has stability based on an extended future and on an environment where you can hone your skills.

The Interview Process

Naturally, before you get as far as weighing job offers you must first go through an interview process, probably consisting of three or four separate sessions. The most important piece of advice to follow during the interview is to be yourself. The interviewer knows you are green. He or she is not looking for anyone to come in and bowl them over. The interviewers are looking for aptitudes, attitudes, social presence, and other intangibles that may indicate a bright and constructive future for you in their company. The appearance, courtesy, self-assurance, and intelligence you display in the process are more important than what you've done. So you don't want to fake it. The interviewers can easily spot insincerity and lack of candor. There is no surer way of not being invited back.

Remember also that the interview is a two-way street as far as information gathering goes. Don't be afraid to ask questions. You want to learn as much pertinent information about the company as they are learning about you. And you want to see if they're faking it. One problem about the interview process is that you are both trying to put on your best face, so often the less attractive side only surfaces after hiring. It is always best to get as much information as you feel you would need to make a decision, even down to visiting a potential work location and talking to people on the job if negotiations start to get serious.

Just remember that there is no certainty. This is not a science. Feelings may count more than anything else when you make your final decision. If in your gut the situation looks questionable, no amount of information will be enough to convince you otherwise, so don't take the job. Do not let lack of information or 100 percent assurance freeze you into indecisiveness. Take your best shot and then get to work.

Again, we want to remind you that choosing your first job is not a lifetime decision. Choosing an industry and general career path on which you can build for the rest of your working life will help you make the quickest progress toward your career goals since each successive move will build on already acquired strengths. So you should, by all means, take the time to prepare yourself by inventorying yourself and matching your strengths and interests with target industries, companies and jobs.

Even so, your early career decision may come down to circumstance. If you can't find a situation that meets your requirements completely, you may be forced to settle for the best of the offers on the table. This decision will have the most effective long-term result if you make it on the basis of being a short-, not long-term decision.

Getting Off to a Good Start

There are three questions we can pose that address the issues you should be concerned with once you get the job:

- What does and what should one do in the first days, weeks, and months of a new job?
- How does one become an effective, accepted, and even respected member of the new organization?
- How long must the apprenticeship last?

In a series of sessions with graduating M.B.A. students Bill Stack, a noted executive recruiter and president of William Stack Associates, posed these questions to his audience. His answers are equally appropriate for any level of graduate. What follows is based on the advice that Stack gave.

To begin with you should have a clear understanding of why you were hired. The principal reason you have received a job offer is your proven ability to learn. Your employer is prepared to teach you. This will be direct, practical, and immediate learning. The success with which you learn your new job will have immediate tangible results: pace of progress, money, position, and level of responsibility. At this stage the rewards are earned by the most effective learner.

Your attitude should be one of interest and of enthusiasm. Be cooperative too. Strive to do every assignment well, going the extra, unasked-for yard. Be alert to the group's goals and the group discipline needed to achieve those goals. Ask for help from those who know the job, the procedures, the company. Ask pertinent questions, but don't ask unnecessary ones. A low verbal profile from the novice is highly desirable. Quiet self-reliance is a more highly prized quality than is challenging questioning. It is easy to cultivate hostility or at least irritation by needless questioning or challenging the system before demonstrating competence. Worse yet is the practice of picking others' brains and then regurgitating the words as one's own. Be deliberate rather than headstrong; be a problem solver, not a problem.

In the initial period you have one very strong and unique advantage. No one expects a great deal from you in the way of immediate productivity. In fact, most of your associates will assume that you won't be of much help for several months at least. If, through patient, quiet, and persistent effort you do achieve some modest success the impact of this upon your fellow employees will have considerably more effect than at any other time in your career: In fact, you have all the cards in your hand to play a winning game right from the beginning.

The Fast Track

If you aspire to move into management and if you hope to win your way to top management responsibility you are embarking on a very challenging, rigorous, interesting, and exciting career. It requires good business judgment, an eye for the big picture, tremendous physical stamina, the willingness to sacrifice one's personal satisfactions for the good of the organization, and a single-minded drive to succeed. So choosing the fast track really involves more than the simple wish to be judged as a success in the business world; it is the conscious choice of a lifestyle that is dominated by one's work, accompanied by the unceasing drive to do the best possible job and get to the top.

While progress in this quest demands superior performance at all times, realization of such high aspirations can be very elusive. The competition is tough and sometimes unethical. One's good standing can be very fragile in this heady atmosphere where big responsibilities may breed big egos. One mistake and a promising career can be torpedoed very quickly. Advancement on the fast track also usually requires the active support and sponsorship of senior management. A minor disagreement on a particular course of action has caused the crash of more than one high-flyer because it bruised a higher-up's ego. So tact and the willingness to submerge one's individualism come into play. Furthermore, there is a large element of luck and serendipity involved. So one can spend all his or her energies in producing superior results, pleasing the right people, and moving up the ladder, and still not realize the top rung.

Regardless of what your ultimate aspiration may be you will enjoy your work more and realize greater satisfaction if you strive to do the best you can. Advancement comes most assuredly from such an approach. Taking a deep and active interest in your company's business produces a high degree of self-satisfaction, whether you are lucky enough to advance to the top or not. Furthermore, there is no more challenging time as the present for American business. There are few, if any, corporations whose markets are not being redefined or challenged by technology and competition. An explosion of new methodologies, new knowledge, new technologies, new products, and new markets are at work today. Just the heightened availability of information and computing power are forcing major changes. The new workers entering the business world today have a hidden advantage in that they better understand and feel more comfortable with this information base than any previous generation. This fact alone gives the work environment a much more positive perspective for the recent graduate. So you don't need to become president of the company or even come close to have an exciting and rewarding career. And you will probably be happier and more fulfilled if you approach your job with this in mind.

The People on the Job

As soon as you enter the business world you are in competition either explicitly or implicitly. Your work will be judged in relation to your associates and your potential for advancement will be assessed accordingly. Assessment of job performance for the sake of bonuses and raises is normally done objectively, although the amount granted is usually based on relative performance. Assessment of potential and selection for advancement is essentially a subjective process, however. Though companies spend millions of dollars a year on assessment centers and the like to give the appearance of objectivity, this is mainly form rather than substance. The subjectivity, in fact, can never be eliminated. So if you are tapped for advancement in any but a pure seniority system, it is because you have done your job better than some co-worker with whom you were in competition. If you are working to get a better job, you can be certain that one or more other people are striving for the same thing. Hence only your very best effort will get you there.

Unfortunately the best person doesn't always win. Often in an organizational environment, ability, industry, intelligence, and good business sense, among other estimable qualities don't carry the day. Other factors such as ultimate potential, strength in a particular functional area, such as marketing, or even physical appearance may be the deciding factors. In some cases it may be the relative power of the person who is advocating one candidacy over another—good old corporate politics. Business isn't always fair; the top candidate doesn't always win. The successful career person is the one who realizes this and continues undaunted. Complaints about lack of fairness will not win the appointment, but continued hard work usually does. He or she rests secure in the knowledge that sooner or later their ability will show and be rewarded.

This does not mean that everyone you meet in the business world is a shark looking for the first sign of blood. On the contrary, most of the people you meet will be dedicated, honest, friendly, and cooperative. You will meet all kinds of people with widely varying backgrounds, educational levels, and personal values. It is important for you to know that your success will depend to a great degree on your ability to relate to all of them equally well. Business is a team sport and no matter how high you go you are still a member of the team and ever more dependent on it.

In fact one trait shared by nearly every successful manager is the ability to achieve optimum results from subordinates. Not just the good subordinates, but all subordinates. A good manager knows just how far to push each individual. Often the effective manager will ask a subordinate for, and get, more than the individual may have thought he could provide. It is this process of challenge and leadership in handling people that is perhaps the biggest key to success.

The Boss

What about your boss? Will he or she be noble, kind, and helpful? Probably not. In fact, you will probably find that the boss from whom you learn the most will be impatient and totally unreasonable in his demands on you. He will accept no excuses and won't ask for your opinion; he'll just tell you what to do. Lots of times this may not make much sense to you. While you may rightly wonder what you are doing in such a situation working for an autocrat whose instructions may not seem to be the best course, try to see it from the boss's point of view. Inherent in the boss-subordinate relationship is the fact that he or she is playing on a bigger field of operations than yours. If you look at the situation from this wider perspective, it should make more sense to you. As a result, your taking of direction should become more palatable, your execution more effective, and your progress toward your taking over your boss's job more rapid because you understand the bigger picture.

While bosses differ in style, what you have to insist on from any boss is that you be given the opportunity to learn and expand your competence. Get away as quickly as possible from the situation in which you are strictly a gofer. Actively seek to work for those who have the reputation for developing their subordinates. Don't be afraid to speak up in this regard. You are the first and most effective advocate for your career goals. No one else will take such good care of your future. Make sure you make your views known in a positive and constructive way. If the organization doesn't tolerate your taking an active role in your own career path, then maybe you should steer your career path elsewhere. Of course, the more effective you are in what you do and the more potential others see in you, the easier it is to make good things happen for yourself.

The finding of a "mentor" has been cited as a necessary ingredient for career advancement. Certainly this helps, but it doesn't normally come unmerited. Having a mentor means you have someone of influence higher up in the organization who is looking out for your career and advancement. While the selected person merited such treatment by working effectively, he or she must keep producing. It is not a situation you can force or fake your way into. It starts with finding the right kind of stimulating boss who will give you the opportunity to produce meaningful results and then it means going to work.

Peripheral Aspects

In the final analysis, only one person makes chief, every one else plays the role of Indian. For most of us our choice is relegated to what type of Indian we want to be. Ninety-nine percent of those who at the start say that their career goal is to run the company never make it. In many cases, those who never had it in mind as a goal make it instead. The point is that if you never get to whatever level you may have set as a goal for yourself, you are not a failure. It is important to put your career goals and accomplishments in perspective for your own peace of mind.

Too often overlooked are the positive peripheral aspects of a career in business. The deep and lasting associations established provide added dimensions to one's life. The constant challenge to one's wit and intelligence provides stimulation as well as opportunity for personal growth. The opportunity to make a positive contribution to the organization provides a source of great personal satisfaction.

THE JOB MARKET TODAY

Over the last five years, two workplace trends have significantly affected the working environment in which college graduates find themselves. The first is the ubiquitous penetration of the computer into every facet of American business operations. The second trend, which is partly driven by the first, is the increasing instability of work life in an American business landscape today where layoffs have become a permanent part of business tactics. Both of these trends place further emphasis on the need for new, college-educated workers to choose jobs where they will learn transportable skills.

The Personal Computer Revolution

The personal computer revolution has made it possible to bring the productivity and quality-enhancing power of the computer to the administrative and managerial parts of a business. A study performed by economist Alan Krueger has found that just over two thirds of workers with college or higher education used computers in their work in 1993. That is up from 42 percent in 1984, and the percentage of people using computers as an integral part of their jobs will continue to rise. Also, those with a college degree were twice as likely to use computers at work as those with only high school diplomas. So the odds are high that you will encounter computers soon after you arrive at your first job.

This inevitable emergence of computing power has two implications for the new college graduate. The first is that the graduate who has a more than passing experience in the use of computers has a very desirable qualification that can yield an advantage in his or her job search. This does not mean that you must be able to program the computer or make the physical connections to the peripherals. It does mean that you ought to have an understanding of the computer as a work tool, including an appreciation for how spreadsheet, word processing, database, graphics, and other programs can be utilized to produce a more effective work result.

After you are employed, it means that you should place a premium on gaining an ability to use the large amounts of information and computing power available as a means to do a better job for yourself and your organization. This ability will come from mastering the basics through working with the computer and then applying the thinking processes and imagination gained from your educational experiences to get the most out of these basic computer skills in terms of output. Making the computer "sing songs" (i.e., do analyses that truly inform) that no one else can make it "sing" is one of the surest roads to advancement in large business organizations today. However, if you are not a maestro at the computer keyboard, you will still need to master its more mundane uses. These skills, whether highly creative or boringly routine, are necessary and will be transportable.

Rising Job Instability

As I was growing up in the 1950s, I can remember the strident battles between the American car makers and the United Auto Workers or the steel manufacturers and their unionized workers over job security. In those days, the risk of losing one's job from the vagaries of an employer or the economy were almost universally a blue-collar concern. The vast majority of white-collar workers normally went to a job that was implicitly considered as lifetime employment. There seemed to be an unspoken social contract in effect. If the white-collar worker satisfactorily performed his job functions, the company would continue to employ him, barring some economic disaster. Conversely, if the company paid a fair wage and provided at least some minimum benefits, the worker would continue to provide his labor.

In the 1970s, that contract changed from the employee's viewpoint. With the vogue of career planning and the rise of headhunters to facilitate movement, white-collar workers began to look in an orchestrated way for career advancing opportunities beyond their current employers. In the 1980s, employers turned the tables and began to lay off millions of "staff" workers who were considered not profit producing. Further along in the Eighties, technological changes and regulatory changes produced employee terminations of earthquake proportions at formerly rock-solid employers like AT&T and IBM, as well as at many other U.S. companies. And, as the decade closed, foreign competition was placing increasing pressure on U.S. companies to become ever more productive. In response to all these changes and pressures, some perceptive people developed in the 1990s a solution that harnessed the growing power and decreasing costs of computing with a rethinking of the way the basic processes of a business are done to improve business productivity and profitability—an approach dubbed "reengineering." Under the banner of reengineering, American businesses today are continuing to lay off workers throughout their organizations in astoundingly high numbers.

At this point, the implicit expectations of lifetime employment have become moot. This places an even higher premium on using a criteria of "What will I learn that I can take with me?" as one of your highest criteria for targeting and choosing a first job opportunity. Remember that you will be employed at the discretion of your employer and, while you should avoid being paranoid, you are probably two or three times more likely to have that employment terminated involuntarily on short notice than you would have been in 1980.

Gaining intangible job rewards—such as industry knowledge and contacts or learning the basic skills of a fundamental process like sales—becomes even more important in today's workplace. For example, if a sales job is your target, you should find out who has the best training program within your chosen industry and focus on that company as your first choice. Once you are in that first job, you should dedicate yourself to learning everything that would be of value no matter where you are working. You will most likely also find that by learning and practicing these key skills, you will also be enhancing your chances for long-term advancement where you are currently working.

Some Final Advice

While the job selection process can be systematized to some degree, a good deal of intuition is also involved. When judging a company, trust the way you feel about its people and your chemistry with them. If you find the interviewer and the managers you subsequently meet attractive, compatible, and stimulating, trust the feeling. The odds are that you can prosper working in their environment.

The people for and with whom you work on your first job, as well as the potential for your career growth, are much more important than the salary, the title, or even the company. Your growth and success are primarily dependent on how well you exploit the potential and how effectively you work with those people.

In starting out you will probably be better served joining a large, well-established company. You will get better basic training and have more opportunity to grow at this stage.

Be sure to get the information you feel you need to make a good decision before accepting any offer. Always ask to talk to people of your own age group who have come into the company in the past few years. This is the best way to get a realistic look at what it's like to work there and how you career might progress. And remember: Make the best decision you can, but don't agonize over making the perfect decision. This is only your first job, not a lifetime choice.

Finally you may wonder if trotting off to graduate business school immediately after graduation might make sense. In general, you will get far more out of business school by going after two or three years of work experience. This will allow you to assimilate the knowledge against a real world background. Furthermore, you will know better whether you need this education after you've been out working.

THE NEW M.B.A.

Until the late 1970s, a master's degree in business administration provided the ticket to the fast track at many companies. But, as that degree has become more and more common in the 1980s, it became more of a necessity just to gain high visibility jobs in middle management. By 1990, there was such a glut of M.B.A.s that one in four business school graduates were without a job at graduation. Things began improving in 1992, and now in 1995, another bull market for M.B.A. graduates is in full swing. Continued strong demand for M.B.A. graduates is expected.

This strong uptick in the M.B.A. market is attributable to several emerging changes in the U.S. economy of the mid-1990s. First, the investment banks are seeing a resurgence in deal opportunities as the economy has improved. This has brought a strong source of M.B.A. jobs back into the market. Also, the cuts in corporate staff and middle management as well as the unending list of companies being reengineered have created a major growth market in consulting firms' recruiting. Finally, as companies reorganize responsibilities in flatter, more horizontal organizational structures, broader, more flexible managers are being sought to replace the old corporate managers who have been retired early or let go. In the words of one corporate recruiting executive, "Hiring an M.B.A. is the least costly way we have to fill newly defined management positions after our organizational restructuring. We don't have to pay a recruiter and we don't have to pay for relocation. And we get a more innovative and motivated employee as a result."

In the new corporate would, those who seem to get the best job offers are those whose undergraduate education and job experience encompass technical disciplines such as engineering and computers. Potential employers are prizing such cross-disciplinary managers more and more. With so much of current and future profit-performance-improvement programs dependent upon applying computer technology to work process and service enhancement, such managers are seen as better able to smooth transitions and accomplish the changes needed. However, signing up these new managers is not quite as inexpensive as the recruiter above may lead one to believe.

For the graduates of America's best business schools a down market may still mean a starting salary in the high five figures. As the tables below show, in a good year a starting salary in the low six figures can be easily achievable for those in the top of their class. Of the 4,608 M.B.A.s in the class of 1994 who responded to a *Business Week* survey, almost 13 percent (594 graduates) said they would earn six figures in salary, signing bonus, and other compensation in their first year. The M.B.A. who landed such a job is likely to be male (81 percent), 28 years old, a graduate of the Stanford Business School, and a recruit of the consulting firm of McKinsey & Co. The following statistics are taken from the *Business Week* survey.

LEADING BUSINESS SCHOOLS WITH HIGHEST PERCENTAGE OF GRADUATES RECEIVING SIX-FIGURE FIRST-YEAR COMPENSATION:

Stanford	53.7
Harvard	52.1
Dartmouth	39.2
Wharton	33.3
Northwestern	30.8

Applications to the 450 business schools in the United States remain strong. About 84,600 masters degrees in business were granted in 1994, up from about 77,000 in 1990, as compared with 22,000 in 1970 and 4,600 in 1960. Applications to Stanford rose 38 percent in 1994. A look at the median compensation offers being made by companies to graduates of the top schools indicates why. *Business Week* reported in 1994 that the median offer to graduates of the business schools at Harvard and Stanford exceeded $100,000. Signing bonuses of up to $30,000 were handed out, plus interest-free loans, stock options, tuition reimbursements of up to $40,000, free cars, and relocation allowances.

Other top schools with very high *average* starting salaries included:

MIT	$75,000
Dartmouth	71,400
Columbia	67,447
Carnegie Mellon	66,447
University of Virginia	64,748
Duke	63,940

STARTING SALARIES OF M.B.A. GRADUATES, BY INSTITUTION

Rank/School	1994 Median Starting Salary
1. Massachusetts Institute of Technology (Sloan)	$68,000
2. University of Pennsylvania (Wharton)	68,000[1]
3. Stanford University	70,000
4. Harvard University	68,000[1]
5. Northwestern University (Kellogg)	62,000[1]

STARTING SALARIES OF M.B.A. GRADUATES, BY INSTITUTION

Rank/School	1994 Median Starting Salary
6. Dartmouth College (Tuck)	$65,000
7. University of Chicago	60,000
8. Duke University (Fuqua)	61,800
9. University of Virginia (Darden)	58,000
10. University of California at Berkeley (Haas)	60,000
11. Columbia University	61,000
11. University of Michigan	65,080
13. University of California at Los Angeles (Anderson)	58,500
14. Carnegie Mellon University	56,400
14. Cornell University (Johnson)	58,500
14. Yale University	55,000
17. New York University (Stern)	57,200
18. University of North Carolina, Chapel Hill (Kenan/Flagler)	56,000
19. University of Texas at Austin	54,000
20. Purdue University (Krannert)	50,000
21. Indiana University at Bloomington	54,000
22. Georgetown University	55,000
23. Emory University (Goizueta)	53,500
24. University of Rochester (Simon)	50,000
25. Ohio State University (Fisher)	43,500

[1] Estimate.

SOURCE: Association of MBA Executives, Inc. Reprinted by permission.

AVERAGE SALARIES OF M.B.A. GRADUATES BY INDUSTRY, 1989–92

Industry	Average Salary 1989	Average Salary 1992	Industry	Average Salary 1989	Average Salary 1992
Accounting, Corporate	$49,620	$48,243	Electronics	$52,122	$52,397
Accounting, Public	50,055	50,502	Financial Services	63,503	63,015
Aerospace	47,899	50,765	Food and Beverage	56,520	61,440
Automobiles	54,051	55,368	Government/ Nonprofit	42,767	44,266
Banking, Commerical	47,482	50,763	Health Care	47,002	50,465
Banking, Investment	74,895	77,264	Insurance	46,980	51,023
Chemicals	56,815	59,738	Management Consulting	58,903	63,213
Computers/Office Equipment	53,297	55,017	Oil	52,124	53,290
			Telecommunications	54,261	59,089

SOURCE: Association of M.B.A. Executives, Inc. Reprinted by permission.

AVERAGE SALARIES OF M.B.A. GRADUATES BY FUNCTION, 1989–92

Industry	Average Salary 1989	Average Salary 1992	Industry	Average Salary 1989	Average Salary 1992
Accounting/Audit	$43,946	$45,260	Marketing	$51,848	$52,012
Consulting	61,504	61,777	Operations/ Production Management	46,304	49,546
Engineering	45,826	47,952	Project Management	52,753	54,679
Finance	55,464	58,486	Planning/Corporate Staff	51,361	52,023
General Management	67,309	71,511	Sales	52,862	52,501
Human Resources	51,389	53,965			
Information Systems	45,046	47,659			

SOURCE: Association of M.B.A. Executives, Inc. Reprinted by permission.

AVERAGE SALARIES OF MBA GRADUATES BY REGION, 1989–92

Region	Average Salary 1989	Average Salary 1992	Metropolitan Areas	Average Salary 1989	Average Salary 1992
New England	$54,585	$55,124	Atlanta	$57,513	$61,171
Northeast	52,066	55,616	Boston	56,197	58,581
Mid-Atlantic	52,786	55,989	Chicago	47,064	50,162
Southeast	48,347	48,635	Cincinnati	46,908	50,171
South	41,446	45,104	Dallas/Fort Worth	47,550	49,010
Central South	44,719	51,364	Houston	58,176	60,978
Central North	51,525	50,270	Los Angeles	56,703	56,129
Southwest	45,496	46,584	New York	55,419	55,521
West	48,088	48,897	Philadelphia	45,902	46,100
Pacific	52,841	51,315	Pittsburgh	57,719	57,503
Midwest	51,434	53,089	St. Louis	49,856	58,664
			San Francisco	54,099	56,284
			Washington, D.C.	50,652	55,360

SOURCE: Association of M.B.A. Executives, Inc. Reprinted by permission.

WORKING OVERSEAS

In addition to the tens of thousands of military personnel still stationed outside the United States and the 50,000 students studying abroad, more than two *million* Americans live and work overseas. More and more Americans are discovering that by combining the good salaries paid in many foreign countries with the tax advantages of living outside the United States, it is possible to save and return home with a substantial nest egg.

The kind of jobs available to Americans overseas usually require particular skills or training not available locally. This rules out such jobs as truck drivers and laborers but often includes specialized equipment operators and journeymen. There are jobs overseas for just about any profession, discipline, or craft and in almost any field including construction, engineering, health care, education, and training.

Education, training, and experience are the keys to getting a job overseas, just as in the United States. Most jobs tend to be for management and supervisory personnel or the highly technically trained and experienced professional. In the construction field, for example, there are jobs for managers and engineers, of course, but there are also jobs for superintendents and foremen, estimators and office managers, equipment operators and surveyors. Most of the craft jobs will be filled by locals or third country nationals, e.g., Filipinos or Indians. But often these workers are supervised by experienced American craftsmen.

The same is true in most other fields. There is a strong demand for doctors, nurses, and technicians, but jobs for practical nurses, aides, orderlies, etc., are usually filled by locals or third country nationals. American teachers can find jobs overseas teaching American children or teaching English as a second language. There are also opportunities for experienced American servicemen and women in training foreign military forces. And the list goes on and on.

Jobs are available in almost every region of the world as the following description makes clear.

Middle East—Saudi Arabia, Kuwait, United Arab Emirates, Bahrain, Qatar, and Yemen all have large populations of Americans living and working there. Jobs then tend to be the highest paying and most plentiful of current job opportunities for Americans abroad. David Lay, author and veteran expatriate, reports, "If you're willing to go where the work is, the Middle East has by far the most lucrative employment opportunities in the world for Americans overseas!" Lay further states that not only do salaries often range up to 50 percent higher than in the United States, but Americans who are out of the United States for 330 days of 12 consecutive months are eligible for a tax exemption of $70,000 per year. He cautions, however, that Americans are often subject to the income tax of the host country. But, fortunately, most Middle East countries do not tax foreigners, or their own citizens in most cases. Lay's current book, *Getting Your Job in the Middle East,* is available through DCL Publishing Company (P.O. Box 16347, Tampa, FL 33687-6347 or by calling toll free 1-800-835-2246, ext. 73).

Far East—Indonesia, China, and even Hong Kong and Singapore offer many opportunities for Americans. *The Wall Street Journal* prints an edition covering just this part of the world and many jobs are advertised there each week.

Africa—Most of the African nations are still in a developing state and offer many jobs to Americans. There are also many nonprofit organizations that send Americans to Africa, such as the World Health Organization. Many of these jobs are available through the United Nations and information may be obtained through its various organizations, most of which are in New York City.

Central and South America—Although fewer jobs exist here than in other regions, in the mining and petroleum producing countries such as Venezuela, Chile, and Peru, many American companies hire U.S. citizens. Most large U.S. companies that export products or services overseas have representatives and sometimes even manufacturing plants in Central and South America.

Europe—Countries in Western Europe have people well qualified for most jobs, but there are opportunities for Americans to work with American companies. (Language capability obviously becomes more important in European countries other than the United Kingdom.) Jobs for computer specialists and systems analysts are usually available; so too are marketing and sales positions either for U.S. companies or foreign companies representing or utilizing American products and services. Jobs for teachers of English as a second language as well as many higher education openings for engineers and scientists are usually plentiful, but competition can be keen.

Most European countries have the same difficulties as the United States in filling highly technical or professional positions and often make exceptions to immigration policies to facilitate recruiting of foreign nationals.

Many jobs in Eastern Europe should become available to Americans once the national economies rebound and especially after U.S. companies begin operations there.

SALARIES OF EXECUTIVES AT CHARITABLE ORGANIZATIONS

Public scrutiny of executive salaries at charities dates back to the 1992 ouster of United Way of America president William F. Aramony, who was earning $463,000 a year in salary and benefits. The attention to the finances also revealed that United Way directors in at least 16 major cities earned over $100,000 a year. Executives at other charitable organizations found themselves defending their compensation to donors, the press, and even Congress, which debated legislation to limit the salaries of executives. But while the number of inquiries about the executives' pay has gone down since then, the pay levels have not. In fact, salaries have actually increased on the average, as boards of directors of charities with lower-paid executives have felt a need to increase salaries to keep them on a par with other organizations.

According to a 1994 survey of 210 major charities by *The Chronicle of Philanthropy,* 61 charities paid their presidents at least $200,000 (the salary earned by the president of the United States), and three—all of them hospitals—paid their presidents more than a half million dollars. The highest paid executive was Paul A. Marks, president of Memorial Sloan-Kettering Cancer Center in New York, who earned $1.15 million in salary and benefits; the median salary was $190,022. The following tables list the most recent compensation totals (including salary and quantifiable benefits) for leaders of some well-known charitable organizations. These figures are now a matter of public record since all groups seeking non-profit status must report the salaries of their hightest-paid employees to the federal government.

TOTAL COMPENSATION FOR LEADERS OF SELECTED NON-PROFIT ORGANIZATIONS, 1994

Organization (Location)	Chief Executives	Total Compensation[1]
	Arts and Culture	
John F. Kennedy Center for the Performing Arts (Washington, D.C.)	Lawrence J. Wilker, Managing Director	$248,299
	Mstislav Rostropovich, Music Director	355,365
Lincoln Center for the Performing Arts (New York City)	Nathan Leventhal, President	355,533
	James Norton, Stagehand	201,994
Metropolitan Opera Association (New York)	Joseph Volpe, General Manager	389,000
	Marilyn Shapiro, Executive Director, External Affairs	304,000
Music Center of Los Angeles County	Esther Wachtell, President[2]	200,000
	Susan Pearce, VP	107,109
New York City Ballet	Arnold Goldberg, Orchestra Manager	156,000
	Gordon D. Boelzner, Music Director	122,000
	Christian Groups	
American Bible Society (New York City)	Eugene B. Habecker, President	$211,755
	Maria I. Martinez, VP for National Programs	128,863
Christian Broadcasting Network (Virginia Beach, VA)	M. G. Robertson, Chief Executive Officer	6,372
	Sheila D. Walsh, Co-host	154,339

TOTAL COMPENSATION FOR LEADERS OF SELECTED NON-PROFIT ORGANIZATIONS, 1994

Organization (Location)	Chief Executives	Total Compensation[1]
Christian and Missionary Alliance (Colorado Springs)	David L. Rambo, President	$80,404
	Duane A. Wheeland, VP	70,090
Focus on the Family (Colorado Springs)	Paul Nelson, Executive VP[9]	105,361
	Mike Trout, Senior VP[9]	117,917
Billy Graham Evangelistic Association (Minneapolis)	Billy Graham, Chief Executive Officer	95,746
	John R. Corts, Chief Operating Officer	124,108
Colleges and Universities		
Brigham Young University (Provo, Utah)	Rex E. Lee, President	$138,386
	Reed M. Izatt, Professor of Chemistry	133,335
University of Southern California (Los Angeles)	Steven B. Sample, President	263,656
	Larry Dean Smith, Head Football Coach	726,448
Case Western Reserve University (Cleveland)	Agnar Pytte, President	268,631
	J. Blumer, Professor	288,076
University of Chicago	Hannah H. Gray, President[2]	303,000
	Samuel Hellman, Dean of Medical School	597,717
Columbia University (New York)	Michael Sovern, President[2,3]	439,559
	Eric Allen Rose, Assistant Professor of Surgery	1,386,873
Cornell University (Ithaca, NY)	Frank H. T. Rhodes, President	274,929
	Wayne Isom, Professor	1,780,013
Dartmouth College (Hanover, NH)	James O. Freedman, President	303,673
	Andrew G. Wallace, Medical School Dean	259,740
Duke University (Durham, NC)	H. Keith H. Brodie, President[2]	386,190
	Ralph Snyderman, Dean of Medical School	444,360

TOTAL COMPENSATION FOR LEADERS OF SELECTED NON-PROFIT ORGANIZATIONS, 1994

Organization (Location)	Chief Executives	Total Compensation[1]
Georgetown University (Washington, D.C.)	Leo J. O'Donovan, President	$220,807
	Robert B. Wallace, Professor and Chairman, Department of Surgery	700,498
Harvard University (Cambridge, MA.)	Neil L. Rudenstine, President	241,645
	Daniel Tosteson, Dean of Medical School	312,934
John Hopkins University (Baltimore)	William C. Richardson, President[4]	368,725
	John L. Cameron, Professor	555,299
Massachusetts Institute of Technology (Cambridge, MA)	Charles M. Vest, President	318,652
	R. J. Thome, Department Head	266,433
University of Miami (Coral Gables, FL)	Edward T. Foote, President	310,981
	John Uribe, Associate Professor	536,866
New York University (New York City)	L. Jay Oliva, President	332,377
	Saul Farber, Provost, Medical Center	346,345
Northwestern University (Evanston, IL)	Arnold R. Weber, President	354,928
	Artur Raviv, Professor of Finance	337,300
University of Pennsylvania (Philadelphia)	Sheldon Hackney, President[2]	310,923
	Alan Wein, Professor, Urology	1,104,000
Princeton University (Princeton, NJ)	Harold T. Shapiro, President	295,494
	Randall A. Hack, President of Princeton University Investment Company	243,900
Stanford University (Palo Alto, CA)	Gerhard Casper, President	225,286
	John Niederhuber, Professor of Surgery	1,288,542
Washington University (St. Louis)	William H. Danforth, Chancellor	144,896
	James L. Cox, Professor of Surgery	589,034

TOTAL COMPENSATION FOR LEADERS OF SELECTED NON-PROFIT ORGANIZATIONS, 1994

Organization (Location)	Chief Executives	Total Compensation[1]
Yale University (New Haven, CT)	Benno C. Schmidt Jr., President[2]	$314,349
	John C. Baldwin, Professor of Cardiothoracic Surgery	502,996
Education Groups (Miscellaneous)		
National Merit Scholarship Corp. (Evanston, Il)	M. Elizabeth Jacka, President	$170,625
	Marianne C. Roderick, Executive VP	109,669
Phillips Academy (Andover, MA)	Donald W. McNemar, Headmaster	167,001
	Neil Cullen, Chief Financial Officer	118,181
United Negro College Fund (New York City)	William H. Gray, III, President	175,000
	Virgil E. Ecton, Senior Executive VP	126,000
Environmental and Animal Defense Groups		
Ducks Unlimited (Memphis)	Matthew B. Connolly, Executive VP	$215,174
	Ed Puls, Former Chief Financial Officer	146,606
Environmental Defense Fund (New York City)	Frederic Krupp, Executive Director	234,573
	Marcia Aronoff, Director of Programs	133,031
Greenpeace Fund (Washington, D.C.)	Steve D'Esposito, Executive Director[2]	49,281
	Venola Johnson, Treasurer	38,697
Humane Society of the United States (Washington, D.C.)	John A. Hoyt, Chief Executive Officer	172,442
	Paul G. Irwin, President	156,556
National Audubon Society (New York City)	Peter A. A. Berle, President	197,137
	Susan Martin, Senior VP	135,178

TOTAL COMPENSATION FOR LEADERS OF SELECTED NON-PROFIT ORGANIZATIONS, 1994

Organization (Location)	Chief Executives	Total Compensation[1]
National Wildlife Federation (Washington, D.C.)	Jay D. Hair, President	$275,329
	William H. Howard, Executive VP	156,922
National Resources Defense Council (New York City)	John H. Adams, Executive Director	159,740
	Tom Cochran, Senior Scientist	112,440
Nature Conservancy (Arlington, VA)	John C. Sawhill, President	202,118
	W. William Weeks, Chief Operating Officer	142,372
North Shore Animal League (Port Washington, NY)	David J. Ganz, President	211,153
	Edward Hamilton, Veterinarian	108,595
Wilderness Society (Washington, D.C.)	Karin Sheldon, Acting President[2]	113,620
	Grant P. Thompson, Executive VP	111,625
World Wildlife Fund (Washington, D.C.)	Kathryn Fuller, President	201,650
	Paige MacDonald, Executive VP	174,400
Health Charities		
American Cancer Society (Atlanta)	John R. Seffrin, Executive VP	$253,537
	Gerald P. Murphy, VP	205,220
American Heart Association (Dallas)	Dudley H. Hafner, Executive VP	311,064
	Rodman Starke, Senior VP	213,610
American Lung Association (New York City)	John R. Garrison, Managing Director	225,898
	Allen B. Rubin, Chief Operating Officer	138,260
Arthritis Foundation (Atlanta)	Don L. Riggin, President	190,022
	Arthur I. Grayzel, Senior VP	174,016

TOTAL COMPENSATION FOR LEADERS OF SELECTED NON-PROFIT ORGANIZATIONS, 1994

Organization (Location)	Chief Executives	Total Compensation[1]
Cystic Fibrosis Foundation (Bethesda, MD)	Robert K. Dresing, President[2]	$322,351
	Robert J. Beall, Executive Medical VP	259,434
March of Dimes Birth Defects Foundation (White Plains, NY)	Jennifer Howse, President	161,443
	Vince A. Coughlin, VP	141,403
Muscular Dystrophy Association (Tucson, AZ)	Robert Ross, Executive Director	302,341
	Gerald Weinberg, Director, Field Organization	223,529
National Easter Seal Society (Chicago)	James E. Williams, Jr., President	195,000
	Donald E. Jackson, Executive VP	143,104
National Multiple Sclerosis Society (New York City)	Michael Dugan, President	183,592
	Thor Hanson, Senior Development Officer	248,454
Planned Parenthood Federation of America (New York City)	David J. Andrews, Acting President[2]	212,756
	Michael Policar, VP, Medical	171,557
Hospitals		
ALSAC/St. Jude's Research Hospital (Memphis)	Arthur W. Nienhuis, Director	$359,658
	Salwa Moustafa, Anesthesiologist	312,442
Baylor College of Medicine (Houston, TX)	William T. Butler, President	451,052
	Bobby R. Alford, Executive VP	398,387
City of Hope (Los Angeles)	Sanford M. Shapero, President	374,639
	Karen M. Warren, Executive VP	279,513
Massachusetts General Hospital (Boston)	J. Robert Buchanan, Executive VP	572,251
	Robert Crowell, Surgeon	451,484

TOTAL COMPENSATION FOR LEADERS OF SELECTED NON-PROFIT ORGANIZATIONS, 1994

Organization (Location)	Chief Executives	Total Compensation[1]
Mayo Foundation for Medical Education and Research (Rochester, MN)	Robert R. Waller, President	$454,905
	C.G.A. McGregor, Surgeon	449,448
Memorial Sloan-Kettering Cancer Center (New York City)	Paul A. Marks, President	1,145,000
	David A. Hidalgo, Chief Attending Surgeon	899,683
Mount Sinai Medical Center (New York City)	John W. Rowe, President	994,725
	Joel Kaplan, Senior VP, Clinical Affairs	1,205,689
Rush-Presbyterian-St. Luke's Medical Center (Chicago)	Leo M. Henikoff, President	441,757
	James W. Williams, Director of the University Transplant Program	692,650
Scripps Clinic and Research Foundation (La Jolla, CA)	Charles C. Edwards, President	457,987
	Lauren W. Blagg, President, Scripps Memorial Hospitals	372,049
Shriner's Hospital for Crippled Children (Tampa)	Newton McCullough, Director of Medicine	271,449
	Colin Moseley, Chief of Staff	267,006
Human Service Groups		
American Red Cross (Alexandria, VA)	Elizabeth H. Dole, President	$201,650
	J. Daniel Connor, Principal Officer, Southern California Region	342,901
Catholic Charities (Alexandria, VA)	Thomas J. Harvey, President	61,995
	Joe A. Heiney-Gonzalez, Deputy to President	58,360
Covenant House (New York City)	Sister Mary Rose McGeady, President	125,469
	James Harnett, Secretary[5]	133,281
Disabled American Veterans (Cincinnati)	Charles E. Joeckel, Jr., National Adjutant[2]	169,639
	Jesse Brown, Executive Director, Washington	113,796

TOTAL COMPENSATION FOR LEADERS OF SELECTED NON-PROFIT ORGANIZATIONS, 1994

Organization (Location)	Chief Executives	Total Compensation[1]
Goodwill Industries International (Bethesda, MD)	David M. Cooney, President	$198,153
	Stephen L. Snyderman, MIS Director	104,382
Habitat for Humanity (Americus, GA)	Millard Fuller, President	41,534
	David Rowe, Director, Int'l Severance Pay	48,692
Hadassah, the Women's Zionist Organization of America (New York City)	Beth Wohlgelernter, Executive Director	106,000
	Alan Tigay, Executive Director, Magazine	86,806
Lions International Foundation (Oak Brook, IL)	Patricia F. O'Kelley, Division Manager	80,629
	Edward A. Lester, Manager, Donor Services	61,332
Rotary International (Evanston, IL)	Spencer Robinson, Jr., General Secretary	184,274
	James R. Fallen, Finance Officer	104,520
Salvation Army (Alexandria, VA)	Kenneth L. Hodder, National Commander	48,233
	Jeffrey S. McDonald, Publications Manager	63,854
Second Harvest (Chicago)	Christine Vladimiroff, President	101,220
	Hilary Freeman, VP, Planning	77,582
Volunteers of America (Metairie, LA)	J. Clint Cheveallier, President	254,078
	Thomas J. Clark, VP	190,055
YMCA of the USA (Chicago)	David R. Mercer, Executive Director	230,630
	John E. Danielson, Associate Executive Director	176,913
YWCA of the USA (New York City)	Gwendolyn C. Baker, Executive Director	137,156
	Jane Towater, Associate Executive Director	108,513

TOTAL COMPENSATION FOR LEADERS OF SELECTED NON-PROFIT ORGANIZATIONS, 1994

Organization (Location)	Chief Executives	Total Compensation[1]
International Relief and Development Groups		
AmeriCares Foundation (Pittsburgh)	Robert Macauley, Chief Executive Officer	0
	Stephen M. Johnson, President	$165,076
CARE (Atlanta)	Philip Johnston, President	262,532
	William Novelli, Executive VP[6]	227,565
Catholic Relief Services (Baltimore)	Kenneth F. Hackett, Executive Director	110,000
	John A. Donnelly, Deputy Executive Director	95,000
Christian Children's Fund (Richmond, VA)	Paul F. McCleary, Executive Director	154,615
	Margaret E. McCullough, Deputy Executive Director	105,631
Compassion International (Colorado Springs)	Wallace H. Erickson, Chief Executive Officer	120,129
	Wesley Stafford, Executive VP	91,439
Larry Jones International Ministries/Feed the Children (Oklahoma City)	Larry Jones, President	123,361
	Frances Jones, Executive VP	90,747
MAP International (Brunswick, GA)	Larry E. Dixon, President	89,405
	Richard W. Wagner, Executive VP	100,859
Mennonite Central Committee (Akron, PA)	John A. Lapp, Executive Secretary	51,691
	Lynette Meck, U.S. Executive Secretary	47,743
Project Hope/People-to-People Health Foundation (Millwood, VA)	William B. Walsh, Jr., President	174,901
	Robert Crane, Senior VP, Medical Operations	138,332
Save the Children (Westport, CT)	Charles MacCormack, President	178,586
	James Bausch, Former President	273,025

TOTAL COMPENSATION FOR LEADERS OF SELECTED NON-PROFIT ORGANIZATIONS, 1994

Organization (Location)	Chief Executives	Total Compensation[1]
U.S. Committee for UNICEF (New York City)	Lawrence E. Bruce, Jr., President[2]	$141,000
	Richard Gorman, Senior VP for Development and Public Affairs	165,000
World Vision (Monrovia, CA)	Robert Seiple, President	119,428
	John Jemelian, Senior VP for Finance and Administration	104,637
Jewish Federations		
Greater Miami Jewish Federation	Jacob Solomon, Executive VP	$159,500
	Carol L. Effrat, Assistant Executive VP	115,000
Jewish Federation Council of Greater Los Angeles	Merv Lemmerman, Executive VP[2]	191,615
	Loren Basch, Director of Campaign[2]	148,729
Jewish Federation of Metropolitan Detroit	Robert P. Aronson, Executive VP	206,075
	Joseph Imberman, Endowment Director	104,974
United Jewish Appeal—Federation of Jewish Philanthropies (New York City)	Stephen D. Solender, Executive VP	308,696
	Adam Kahan, Chief Operating Officer	217,861
United Jewish Appeal, National (New York City)	Brian J. Lurie, Executive VP	275,749
	Leon J. Twersky, Assistant Secretary	207,503
Museums and Libraries		
American Museum of Natural History (New York City)	George D. Langdon, Jr., President	$274,335
	Myra Biblowit, Senior VP for Development	182,850

TOTAL COMPENSATION FOR LEADERS OF SELECTED NON-PROFIT ORGANIZATIONS, 1994

Organization (Location)	Chief Executives	Total Compensation[1]
Art Institute of Chicago	James N. Wood, Director of the Museum	$239,033
	Robert E. Mars, VP, Administrative Affairs	215,532
Carnegie Institute (Pittsburgh)	Robert C. Wilburn, President	166,950
	Andrew J. Hungerman, Assistant Treasurer	114,703
Los Angeles County Museum of Art	Michael Shapiro, Director	139,393
	Julie Johnston, Director of Development	96,073
Metropolitan Museum of Art (New York City)	Phillipe de Montebello, Director	204,564
	William H. Luers, President	189,730
Museum of Fine Arts (Boston)	Alan Shestack, Director	205,461
	Morton J. Golden, Deputy Director	186,247
Museum of Modern Art (New York City)	Richard E. Oldenburg, Director	194,064
	Sue B. Dorn, Deputy Director of Development and Public Affairs	161,282
National Gallery of Art (Washington, D.C.)	Earl A. Powell, III, Director	25,000
	E. Roger Mandle, Deputy Director	202,622
New York Public Library	Timothy S. Healy, President	155,470
	John H. Masten, Executive VP	213,837
Smithsonian Institution (Washington, D.C.)	Robert McC. Adams, Secretary[7]	219,313
	Donald Moser, Editor	217,881
United States Holocaust Memorial Museum (Washington, D.C.)	Jeshajahu Weinberg, Museum Director	205,248
	Joseph Brodecki, Campaign Director[1]	174,119

TOTAL COMPENSATION FOR LEADERS OF SELECTED NON-PROFIT ORGANIZATIONS, 1994

Organization (Location)	Chief Executives	Total Compensation[1]
Miscellaneous Philanthropic Organizations		
Independent Charities of America (San Francisco)	Patrick Maguire, President	$175,000
National Academy of Sciences (Washington, D.C.)	Frank Press, President[2]	317,580
	Robert M. White, President, National Academy of Engineering	219,628
Salk Institute for Biological Studies (San Diego)	Renato Dulbecco, President[2]	273,204
	Delbert E. Clanz, Executive VP	335,434
U.S. Olympic Committee (Colorado Springs)	Harvey W. Schiller, Executive Director	376,429
	John Krimsky, Jr., Deputy Secretary	282,977
Public Affairs Groups		
Anti-Defamation League of B'nai B'rith (New York City)	Abraham H. Foxman, National Director	$209,728
	Sheldon Fleigelmann, Development Director	141,149
Carter Center (Atlanta)	John Hardman, Executive Director	118,990
Heritage Foundation (Washington, D.C.)	Edwin J. Feulner, President[8]	377,904
	Edwin Meese, Distinguished Scholar	226,864
Mothers Against Drunk Driving (Irving, TX)	Robert King, Executive Director	142,376
	Joseph King, Director, Marketing and Development	108,223
National Association for the Advancement of Colored People (New York City)	Benjamin L. Hooks, Executive Director[2]	190,285
	Wade Henderson, Washington Bureau Director	72,960
National Urban League (New York City)	John Jacob, President	195,427
	Frank Lomax III, Executive VP	139,135

TOTAL COMPENSATION FOR LEADERS OF SELECTED NON-PROFIT ORGANIZATIONS, 1994

Organization (Location)	Chief Executives	Total Compensation[1]
Public Broadcasting		
KCET Community Television of Southern California (Los Angeles)	William H. Kobin, President	$259,552
	Donald G. Youpa, Executive VP	182,147
KCTS Television (Seattle)	Burnill Clark, President	175,952
	Walter Parsons, Senior VP	107,939
KQED (San Francisco)	Anthony S. Tiano, President	153,889
	Robert Johnston, Jr., Chief Financial Officer	114,972
Public Broadcasting Service (Alexandria, VA)	Bruce Christensen, President[2]	148,402
	Jennifer Lawson, Executive VP	118,400
Thirteen/WNET (New York City)	William F. Baker, President	215,719
	Lester M. Crystal, Executive Producer	358,858
WETA (Arlington, VA)	Sharon Rockefeller, President	175,683
	Neil B. Mahrer, Executive VP	208,789
WGBH Educational Foundation (Boston)	Henry P. Becton, President	185,412
	Norman Abram, Talent	234,250
WTTW/Chicago Educational Television Association	William J. MacCarter, President	168,067
	John Callaway, Senior Correspondent	166,859
United Way		
United Way and Community Chest of Greater Cincinnati	Richard Aft, President	$204,460
	Pradip Patel, VP, Finance & Administration	108,357
United Way/Crusade of Mercy (Chicago)	Jack Prater, President[2]	200,114
	Frank Karr, Senior VP	120,005
United Way for Southeastern Michigan (Detroit)	H. Clay Howell, President[2]	203,262
	Warren T. Burt, Jr., VP, Administration	148,830
United Way of Allegheny County (Pittsburgh)	William J. Meyer, President	103,500
	Robert J. Krasman, Treasurer	81,502

TOTAL COMPENSATION FOR LEADERS OF SELECTED NON-PROFIT ORGANIZATIONS, 1994

Organization (Location)	Chief Executives	Total Compensation[1]
United Way of Central Indiana (Indianapolis)	Irvin S. Katz, President	$103,500
	Dale F. DePoy, VP, Finance and Administration	81,502
United Way of Central Maryland (Baltimore)	Norman O. Taylor, President[10]	195,171
	James W. Brooks, Chief Financial Officer	87,813
United Way of Franklin County (Columbus, OH)	William L. Keller, President	160,248
	Keith Barsuhn, VP, Contributor Services	84,644
United Way of Greater Los Angeles	Herbert L. Carter, President	205,694
	Richard Sykes, Senior VP	135,456
United Way of Greater Rochester (Rochester, NY)	Joseph G. Calabrese, President	146,825
	William G. McCullough, Executive VP	89,603
United Way of Greater St. Louis	Martin B. Covitz, President[2]	206,430
	Stanley Wakeham, Senior VP, Campaign	142,248
United Way of King County (Seattle)	Roberta van der Voort, President[2]	174,617
	Rodney Wheeler, VP Resource Development	94,849
United Way of Massachusetts Bay (Boston)	Marian L. Heard, President	142,826
	Richard A. Millott, Senior VP	110,321
United Way of Metropolitan Atlanta	Mark L. O'Connell, President	180,244
	Brian Gallagher, Group VP	43,083
United Way of Metropolitan Dallas	Edward E. McDunn, President	165,600
	J. J. Guise, Vice Chairman, Board of Directors	130,625
United Way of New York City	Ralph Dickerson, Jr., President	263,663
	Lawrence Mandell, Executive VP	143,156
United Way of Southeastern Pennsylvania (Philadelphia)	Ted L. Moore, President	203,192
	Al J. Sassone, VP	139,301

TOTAL COMPENSATION FOR LEADERS OF SELECTED NON-PROFIT ORGANIZATIONS, 1994

Organization (Location)	Chief Executives	Total Compensation[1]
United Way of the Bay Area (San Francisco)	Thomas Ruppaner, President	$184,981
	Frank Melcher, Executive VP	141,461
United Way of the Minneapolis Area	James C. Colville, President	195,567
	Terri D. Barreiro, Senior Director	99,780
United Way of the National Capital Area (Washington, D.C.)	Oral Suer, Executive VP	217,420
	Kenneth R. Unzicker, Corporate Affairs and Associate Campaign Director	167,665
United Way of the Texas Gulf Coast (Houston)	Judith B. Craven, President	140,000
	Mike Bisesi, Senior VP	83,506
United Way Services (Cleveland)	Jack C. Costello, President	209,560
	Gloria Pace King, Senior VP	123,050
	Youth Groups	
Big Brothers/Big Sisters of America (Philadelphia)	Thomas McKenna, National Executive Director	$108,010
	Dagmar McGill, Deputy National Executive Director	74,647
Boy Scouts of America (Irving, TXS)	Ben H. Love, Chief Scout Executive[2]	287,217
	Joseph L. Anglim, Chief Financial Officer[2,11]	423,746
Boys and Girls Clubs of America (New York City)	Thomas G. Garth, National Director	207,738
	Joseph R. Burkart, Assistant National Director	152,025
Camp Fire Boys and Girls (Kansas City, MO)	K. Russell Weathers, Executive VP	148,179
	Emerson Goodwin, Director of Development and Communications	91,822

TOTAL COMPENSATION FOR LEADERS OF SELECTED NON-PROFIT ORGANIZATIONS, 1994

Organization (Location)	Chief Executives	Total Compensation[1]
Father Flanagan's Boys Home (Boys Town, NB)	Rev. Valentine J. Peter, Executive VP	$20,000
	Patrick Brookhouser, Director, Boys Town National Research Hospital	223,609
Girl Scouts of the U.S.A. (New York City)	Mary Rose Main, National Executive Director	212,088
	Florence Corsello, Controller	144,551
Junior Achievement (Colorado Springs)	Karl Flemke, President	202,146
	Ralph Schulz, Executive VP	148,174
Special Olympics International (Washington, D.C.)	Robert S. Shriver, III, President	150,000

[1]Compensation figures include benefits where applicable, but not expense allowances.
[2]No longer holds position.
[3]Includes $32,615 in supplemental pay in lieu of a waived pension contribution.
[4]Includes $72,357 for housing.
[5]Includes a one-time payment of $16,093.
[6]Includes pay for unused vacation in the amounts of $30,538 for Mr. Johnston and $19,518 for Mr. Novelli.
[7]The institution also provides Mr. Adams with use of a house it purchased in 1984 for $485,000.
[8]Includes bonus of $159,100.
[9]Includes relocation expenses of $10,150 for Mr. Nelson and $25,276 for Mr. Trout.
[10]The institution also provided $70,241 in moving expenses, closing costs on a new house, sales commission on Mr. Taylor's previous house, and temporary housing in Baltimore.
[11]Mr. Anglim, who retired in 1992 after 40 years of employment, received an annual salary of $185,000 and an annuity of $352,502.
SOURCE: *Chronicle of Philanthropy*, May 17, 1994.

Appendix

Where to Seek Further Information

WHERE TO START

Whether you are young and just beginning to look for your first job or a bit older and returning to the workforce after an illness or staying home with the young children, the best way to start your search is with a visit to your local library. The same is true for the 10 million Americans who change occupations each year.

If you are like most people you are puzzled or confused by the incredible assortment of jobs that exist in the United States, and the best way to overcome those feelings is by educating yourself about the job market. What jobs interest you? Are you qualified? What jobs are actually available?

The two most comprehensive books are the 1,000-page *Professional Careers Sourcebook* (Gale Research Publishing) and *The Occupational Outlook Handbook, 1994–95,* produced by the U.S. Department of Labor (this book can also be purchased at any U.S. government bookstore, or by calling the office of the Superintendent of Documents in Washington, 202-783-3238. It costs about $25). Both books contain job descriptions, and the names and addresses of associations that can provide further information on career possibilities.

If You Are Moving

The best place to obtain general information about local job markets is through the labor departments of each state. Every state produces something and some (California, Florida, Arizona, New York, for example) devote a great deal of time and energy to creating large amounts of data. A full listing of state offices with addresses, phone and fax numbers is given below. If you write or call be sure to ask for local area information as well; the larger states have branch offices in major cities too, so ask for those numbers. Of course, you should also contact the local chamber of commerce in the area, and it's always worth calling the mayor's office as well, since the people there will often direct you to the appropriate department.

For up-to-the-minute information about job growth in every metropolitan area, check the monthly *Blue Chip Job Growth Update* published by the Economic Outlook Center at Arizona State University.

STATE LABOR DEPARTMENTS

ALABAMA

Labor Market Information
Department of Industrial Relations
649 Monroe Street, Rm. 422
Montgomery, AL 36131
205-242-8855 (FAX 205-240-3070)

ALASKA

Research & Analysis
Department of Labor
P.O. Box 25501
Juneau, AK 99802-5501
907-465-4518 (FAX 907-465-2101)

ARIZONA

Department of Economic Security
1789 West Jefferson
P.O. Box 6123, Site Code 733A
Phoenix, AZ 85005-6123
602-542-3871 (FAX 602-542-6474)

ARKANSAS

State & Labor Market Information
Employment Security Division
P.O. Box 2981
Little Rock, AR 72203
501-682-3198 (FAX 501-682-3713)

CALIFORNIA

Employment Data & Research Div.
Employment Development Dept.
P.O. Box 942880, MIC 57
Sacramento, CA 94280-0001
916-427-4675 (FAX 916-323-6674)

COLORADO

Labor Market Information
393 So. Harlan, 2nd Floor
Lakewood, CO 80226
303-937-4947 (FAX 303-937-4945)

CONNECTICUT

Research & Information
Employment Security Division
Connecticut Labor Department
200 Folly Brook Boulevard
Wethersfield, CT 06109
203-566-2120 (FAX 203-566-1519)

DELAWARE

Office of Occupational & LMI
Delaware Department of Labor
University Plaza, Building D
P.O. Box 9029
Newark, DE 19702-9029
302-368-6962 (FAX 302-368-6748)

DISTRICT OF COLUMBIA

Chief of Labor Market Information
Dept. of Employment Services
500 C Street, N.W., Rm. 201
Washington, D.C. 20001
202-724-7213 (FAX 202-639-1766)

FLORIDA

Bureau of Labor Market Information
Department of Labor & Employment Security
2012 Capitol Circle, S.E., Rm. 200
Hartman Building
Tallahassee, FL 32399-0673
904-488-1048 (FAX 904-488-2558)

GEORGIA

Labor Information System
Department of Labor
148 International Boulevard NE
Atlanta, GA 30303
404-656-3177 (FAX 404-651-9568)

HAWAII

Research & Statistics Office
Dept. of Labor & Industrial Relations
P.O. Box 3680
Honolulu, HI 96813
808-586-8999 (FAX 808-586-9022)

IDAHO

Research & Analysis
Department of Employment
317 Main Street
Boise, ID 83735
208-334-6169 (FAX 208-334-6427)

ILLINOIS

Economic Information & Analysis
Department of Employment Security
401 South State Street, Rm. 215
Chicago, IL 60605
312-793-2316 (FAX 312-793-6245)

INDIANA

Labor Market Information
Dept. of Employment & Training Services
10 North Senate Avenue
Indianapolis, IN 46204
317-232-7460 (FAX 317-232-6950)

IOWA

Audit & Analysis Department
Department of Employment Services
1000 East Grand Avenue
Des Moines, IA 50319
515-281-8181 (FAX 515-281-8195)

KANSAS

Labor Market Information Services
Department of Human Resources
401 SW Topeka Boulevard
Topeka, KS 66603
913-296-5058 (FAX 913-296-0179)

KENTUCKY

Labor Market Research & Analysis
Department for Employment Services
275 East Main Street
Frankfort, KY 40621
502-564-7976 (FAX 502-564-7452)

LOUISIANA

Research & Statistics Division
Dept. of Employment & Training
P.O. Box 94094
Baton Rouge, LA 70804-9094
504-342-3141 (FAX 504-342-9193)

MAINE

Division of Economic Analysis & Research
ME Department of Labor/BES
20 Union Street
Augusta, ME 04330
207-289-2271 (FAX 207-289-5292)

MARYLAND

Office of Labor Market Analysis & Information
Dept. of Economic & Employment Development
1100 North Eutaw Street, Rm. 601
Baltimore, MD 21201
301-333-5000 (FAX 301-333-7121)

MASSACHUSETTS

Division of Employment Security
19 Staniford Street, 2nd Floor
Boston, MA 02114
617-727-6868 (FAX 617-727-0315)

MICHIGAN

Bureau of Research & Statistics
Employment Security Commission
7310 Woodward Avenue
Detroit, MI 48202
313-876-5904 (FAX 313-876-5244)

MINNESOTA

Research & Statistical Services
Department of Jobs and Training
390 N. Robert St., 5th Floor
St. Paul, MN 55101
612-296-6546 (FAX 612-296-0994)

MISSISSIPPI

Labor Market Information Dept.
Employment Security Commission
P.O. Box 1699
Jackson, MS 39215-1699
601-961-7424 (FAX 601-961-7405)

MISSOURI

Research & Analysis
Division of Employment Security
P.O. Box 59
Jefferson City, MO 65104-0059
314-751-3591 (FAX 314-751-7973)

MONTANA

Research & Analysis
Dept. of Labor and Industry
P.O. Box 1728
Helena, MT 59624
406-444-2430 (FAX 406-444-2638)

NEBRASKA

Labor Market Information
Department of Labor
550 South 16th Street
P.O. Box 94600
Lincoln, NE 68509-4600
402-471-9964 (FAX 402-471-2318)

NEVADA

Employment Security Research
Employment Security Department
500 East Third Street
Carson City, NV 89713
702-687-4550 (FAX 702-687-3424)

NEW HAMPSHIRE

Labor Market Information
Department of Employment Security
32 South Main Street
Concord, NH 03301-4587
603-228-4123 (FAX 603-228-4172)

NEW JERSEY

Policy & Planning
Department of Labor
John Fitch Plaza, Rm. 1010
P.O. Box CN 056
Trenton, NJ 08625-0056
609-292-2643 (FAX 609-292-6692)

NEW MEXICO

NM Department of Labor
401 Broadway Boulevard, NE
P.O. Box 1928
Albuquerque, NM 87103
505-841-8645 (FAX 505-841-8421)

NEW YORK

Div. of Research & Statistics
NY State Department of Labor
State Campus, Bldg. 12, Rm. 400
Albany, NY 12240-0020
518-457-6181 (FAX 518-457-0620)

NORTH CAROLINA

Labor Market Information Division
Employment Security Commission
P.O. Box 25903
Raleigh, NC 27611
919-733-2936 (FAX 919-733-8662)

NORTH DAKOTA

Research & Statistics
Job Service North Dakota
P.O. Box 1537
Bismarck, ND 58502
701-224-2868 (FAX 701-224-4000)

OHIO

Labor Market Information Division
Bureau of Employment Services
P.O. Box 1618
Columbus, OH 43215
614-752-9494
(FAX 614-644-3579)

OKLAHOMA

Research Division
Employment Security Commission
2401 N. Lincoln, Rm. 310
Oklahoma City, OK 73105
405-557-7116 (FAX 405-557-7256)

OREGON

Research & Statistics
Oregon Employment Division
875 Union Street, N.E. Rm 207
Salem, OR 97311
503-378-3220 (FAX 503-373-7515)

PENNSYLVANIA

Research & Statistics Division
Department of Labor & Industry
1213 Labor & Industry Building
Harrisburg, PA 17121
717-787-6466 (FAX 717-772-2168)

PUERTO RICO

Research & Statistics Division
Dept. of Labor & Human Resources
505 Munoz Rivera Ave., 17th Floor
Hato Rey, PR 00918
809-754-5332 (FAX 809-751-7934)

RHODE ISLAND

Labor Market Information & Management Services
Department of Employment & Training
107 Friendship Street
Providence, RI 02903
401-277-3704 (FAX 407-277-2731)

SOUTH CAROLINA

Labor Market Information
Employment Security Commission
P.O. Box 995
Columbia, SC 29202
803-737-2660 (FAX 803-737-2838)

SOUTH DAKOTA

Labor Information Center
Department of Labor
P.O. Box 4730
Aberdeen, SD 57402-4730
605-622-2314 (FAX 605-622-2322)

TENNESSEE

Research & Statistics Division
Department of Employment Security
500 James Robertson Parkway
11th Floor
Nashville, TN 37245-1000
615-741-2284 (FAX 615-741-3203)

TEXAS

Economic Research & Analysis
Texas Employment Commission
1117 Trinity St., Rm. 208-T
Austin, TX 78778
512-463-2616 (FAX 512-475-1241)

UTAH

Labor Market Information & Research
Department of Employment Security
140 East 300 South
P.O. Box 11249
Salt Lake City, UT 84147
801-536-7425 (FAX 801-536-7420)

VERMONT

Policy & Information
Department of Employment & Training
5 Green Mountain Drive
P.O. Box 488
Montpelier, VT 05602
802-229-0311 (FAX 802-223-0750)

VIRGIN ISLANDS

Research & Analysis
Department of Labor
P.O. Box 3359
St. Thomas, VI 00801
809-776-3700 (FAX 809-774-5908)

VIRGINIA

Director
Economic Information Service Division
VA Employment Commission
P.O. Box 1358
Richmond, VA 23211
804-786-7496 (FAX 804-225-3923)

WASHINGTON

Employment Security Department
605 Woodview Drive, S.E.
Lacey, WA 98503
206-438-4800 (FAX 206-753-4851)

WEST VIRGINIA

Assistant Director
Labor & Economic Research
Bureau of Employment Programs
112 California Avenue
Charleston, WV 25305-0112
304-348-2660 (FAX 304-348-0301)

WISCONSIN

Labor Market Information Bureau
Department of Industry, Labor & Human Relations
201 East Washington Ave., Rm. 221
P.O. Box 7944
Madison, WI 53707
608-266-5843 (FAX 608-267-0330)

WYOMING

Research & Planning
Division of Administration
Department of Employment
P.O. Box 2760
Casper, WY 82602
307-265-6715 (FAX 307-235-3293)

Index

A

B

C

D

E

F

G

H

I

J

K

L

M

N

O

P

R

S

T

U

V

W

Z